Principles, Methodologies, and Service–Oriented Approaches for Cloud Computing

Xiaoyu Yang
University of Reading, UK

Lu Liu
University of Derby, UK

Managing Director:	Lindsay Johnston
Editorial Director:	Joel Gamon
Book Production Manager:	Jennifer Yoder
Publishing Systems Analyst:	Adrienne Freeland
Development Editor:	Christine Smith
Assistant Acquisitions Editor:	Kayla Wolfe
Typesetter:	Erin O'Dea
Cover Design:	Jason Mull

Published in the United States of America by
Business Science Reference (an imprint of IGI Global)
701 E. Chocolate Avenue
Hershey PA 17033
Tel: 717-533-8845
Fax: 717-533-8661
E-mail: cust@igi-global.com
Web site: http://www.igi-global.com

Library of Congress Cataloging-in-Publication Data

Principles, methodologies, and service-oriented approaches for cloud computing / Xiaoyu Yang and Lu Liu, editors.
    pages cm
  Summary: "This book investigates the use of service-oriented computing technologies in addressing supporting infrastructure of the cloud, including new challenges in modeling and simulation"-- Provided by publisher.
  Includes bibliographical references and index.
  ISBN 978-1-4666-2854-0 (hardcover) -- ISBN 978-1-4666-2855-7 (ebook) -- ISBN 978-1-4666-2856-4 1. Cloud computing. I. Yang, Xiaoyu, 1968- II. Liu, Lu, 1980-
  QA76.585.P75 2013
  004.67'82--dc23
                                    2012034437

British Cataloguing in Publication Data
A Cataloguing in Publication record for this book is available from the British Library.

Table of Contents

Section 1
Principles and Fundamentals

Chapter 1

N. Krishnadas, Indian Institute of Management, India
R. Radhakrishna Pillai, Indian Institute of Management, India

Chapter 2

John P. Sahlin, The George Washington University, USA

Chapter 3

Adrian Jackson, Edinburgh Parallel Computing Centre, The University of Edinburgh, UK
Michèle Weiland, Edinburgh Parallel Computing Centre, The University of Edinburgh, UK

Chapter 4

Ahmed Shawish, Ain Shams University, Egypt
Maria Salama, British University in Egypt, Egypt

Section 2
Security

Chapter 5

Steven C. White, Missouri University of Science and Technology, USA
Sahra Sedigh, Missouri University of Science and Technology, USA
Ali R. Hurson, Missouri University of Science and Technology, USA

Section 3
Service-Oriented Approaches

Section 4
Methods, Technologies, and Applications

Detailed Table of Contents

Section 1
Principles and Fundamentals

Chapter 1
N Krishnadas, Indian Institute of Management, India
R Radhakrishna Pillai, Indian Institute of Management, India

Cloud Computing is emerging as a promising cost efficient computing paradigm which professionals believe is an absolutely new trend and will represent next level of internet evolution. Though the presence of Cloud computing is ubiquitous, it still lacks consensus on a proper definition and classification of the major Clouds in effect today. It also suffers from major criticism of being a hype/fad and some researchers claim that it is just an extension of already established computing paradigms. This chapter attempts to deal with such criticisms by comprehensively analyzing the Cloud definitions and diagnose the components of the same. It performs a comprehensive study of more than 30 definitions given by Cloud computing professionals and published in research papers. These definitions are then analyzed under more than fifteen components, each of which is discussed in the chapter. This study is backed by empirical work, to understand Cloud computing from different angles and come up with a comprehensive definition. It also analyses the present Cloud service providers and the level of services they provide to bring about a clear picture of Cloud computing. Based on the comparison, the pending issues in Cloud computing are discussed.

Chapter 2
John P. Sahlin, The George Washington University, USA

Defining Cloud Computing can be difficult, as each organization often has its own spin on the definition. Despite being hard to define, Gartner Research named Cloud Computing as one of the top technologies to watch in 2010, 2011, and 2012. At its core, Cloud Computing is a technical architecture that meets a specific business need. This chapter traces the roots of Cloud Computing from its origins in mainframe distributed computing, discusses the basics of the Cloud Computing model today, and offers insights for future directions that are likely to be pursued in the Cloud Computing arena. A number of challenges to Cloud Computing are identified, including concerns of security and how to deal with the rise of mobile computing. The chapter ends with recommendations on how to choose which Cloud model is most appropriate to meet your organization's needs and how to establish a successful Cloud strategy.

Chapter 3

Adrian Jackson, Edinburgh Parallel Computing Centre, The University of Edinburgh, UK
Michèle Weiland, Edinburgh Parallel Computing Centre, The University of Edinburgh, UK

This chapter describes experiences using Cloud infrastructures for scientific computing, both for serial and parallel computing. Amazon's High Performance Computing (HPC) Cloud computing resources were compared to traditional HPC resources to quantify performance as well as assessing the complexity and cost of using the Cloud. Furthermore, a shared Cloud infrastructure is compared to standard desktop resources for scientific simulations. Whilst this is only a small scale evaluation these Cloud offerings, it does allow some conclusions to be drawn, particularly that the Cloud can currently not match the parallel performance of dedicated HPC machines for large scale parallel programs but can match the serial performance of standard computing resources for serial and small scale parallel programs. Also, the shared Cloud infrastructure cannot match dedicated computing resources for low level benchmarks, although for an actual scientific code, performance is comparable.

Chapter 4

Ahmed Shawish, Ain Shams University, Egypt
Maria Salama, British University in Egypt, Egypt

Cloud Computing is gaining a considerable attention in the past few years, where hardware and software are provided on-demand as a service through internet following the simple pay-as-you-go financial model. Using such powerful technology, several projects, in different areas, have been built like supporting academic and scientific researches, providing governmental services, and developing business applications. Unfortunately, the previous works and ongoing researches in these areas are scattered among the literature, on the internet, and from research groups, which makes it hard for researchers to be involved in such vast wave of researches. This chapter carefully reviews the emergence of the Cloud in all of the above mentioned areas through a wide range of well classified researches, projects, and applications that have been either innovated or improved due to the Cloud disclosure. Moreover, the chapter comparatively discusses the previous work done in these fields and explores the opened research points.

Section 2
Security

Chapter 5

Steven C. White, Missouri University of Science and Technology, USA
Sahra Sedigh, Missouri University of Science and Technology, USA
Ali R. Hurson, Missouri University of Science and Technology, USA

Computer security is a complex undertaking within the traditional client-server architecture. As services and data are moved to the Cloud, security requirements change and become even more complex. Existing client-server security practices can be extended to address challenges specific to the Cloud environment. In this chapter, a contrast is made between traditional client-server environment with a Cloud environment - in terms of security challenges and solutions. In addition to enumerating and contrasting traditional challenges and solutions, the authors describe security challenges and solutions particular to the Cloud computing environment. The chapter describes, in terms of the pillars of security, key issues that should be addressed by an organization as it migrates to Cloud environments and propose solutions to these issues.

Chapter 6

Hussain Al-Aqrabi, University of Derby, UK
Lu Liu, University of Derby, UK

The authors present the key security challenges and solutions on the Cloud with the help of literature reviews and an experimental model created on OPNET that is simulated to produce useful statistics to establish the approach that the Cloud computing service providers should take to provide optimal security and compliance. The literature recommends the concept of unified threat management for ensuring secured services on the Cloud. Through the simulation results, the authors demonstrate that UTM may not be a feasible approach to security implementation as it may become a bottleneck for the application Clouds. The fundamental benefits of Cloud computing (resources on demand and high elasticity) may be diluted if UTMs do not scale up effectively as per the traffic loads on the application Clouds. Moreover, it is not feasible for application Clouds to absorb the performance degradation for security and compliance because UTM will not be a total solution for security and compliance. Applications also share the vulnerabilities just like the systems, which will be out of UTM Cloud's control.

Chapter 7

Hassan Takabi, University of Pittsburgh, USA
James B. D. Joshi, University of Pittsburgh, USA
Gail-Joon Ahn, Arizona State University, USA

Cloud computing paradigm has recently gained tremendous momentum. It has been found very promising for significant cost reduction and the increased operating efficiencies in computing. However, security and privacy issues pose as the key roadblock to its rapid adoption. In this chapter, the authors present the security and privacy challenges in Cloud computing environments and discuss how they are related to various delivery and deployment models, and are exacerbated by the unique aspects of Clouds. The authors also propose a comprehensive security framework for Cloud computing environments and discuss various approaches to address the challenges, existing solutions and future work needed to provide a trustworthy Cloud computing environment.

Section 3
Service-Oriented Approaches

This chapter presents some actual results from two big German Cloud projects: the Leading-Edge Cluster project Service Design Studio and the associated Fraunhofer Innovation Cluster Cloud Computing for Logistics. Existing services can be enhanced using the Service Design Studio environment and then be deployed and offered in the Logistics Mall, which may combine them using process models. To reach these objectives, different standards are combined for service description in functional and business view, business object description in domain and technical view, and process model description on different abstraction levels. First results are already in use by the logistics industry. These innovations together have the potential to advance the logistics market towards modern IT strategies. Flexible, individual logistics business process models allow small and medium enterprises a technological catch up with large companies and to focus on their core business.

Chapter 9

Cloud computing is a new paradigm for the intent of distributed resources sharing and coordinated problem solution. Affected by the Cloud trend and Service-Oriented need, many existing software systems will become legacy systems. These legacy software systems will need Cloud Oriented reengineering, which can facilitate the legacy systems reusable in Cloud Oriented architecture and allow the integration of legacy resources with Cloud features. This research focuses on establishing a general framework to assist with the evolution of legacy systems into Cloud environments. The methodology includes various phases, which use reverse engineering techniques to comprehend and decompose legacy systems, represent legacy resources by XML as Cloud component and integrate these Cloud components into Cloud environment. In this research, a legacy banking system has been chosen as a case study to prove the feasibility of the proposed approach. The legacy banking system can be transformed to run as a Service-Oriented Cloud application, which illustrates the proposed approach is powerful for utilising reusable legacy resources into Cloud environment.

    Jianxin Li, Beihang University, China
    Linlin Meng, Beihang University, China
    Zekun Zhu, Beihang University, China
    Xudong Li, Beihang University, China
    Jinpeng Huai, Beihang University, China
    Lu Liu, University of Derby, UK

In this chapter, the authors propose a Cloud service ranking system, named CloudRank, based on both the user feedback and service testing. In CloudRank, we design a new ranking-oriented collaborative filtering (CF) approach named WSRank, in which user preferences are modeled as personal rankings derived from user QoS ratings on services to address service quality predication problem. Different from the existing similar approaches, WSRank firstly presents a QoS model which allows users to express their preferences flexibly while providing combination of multiple QoS properties to give an overall rating to a service. Secondly, it measures the similarity among users based on the correlation of their rankings of services rather than the rating values. Nevertheless, it is neither accurate nor sufficient to rank Cloud services merely based on users' feedbacks, as there are many problems such as cold-start problem, absence of user feedback, even some service faults occurred in a service workflow, so to get an accurate ranking, an active service QoS testing and fault location approach is required together with WSRank. Therefore, in CloudRank, the authors also designed an automated testing prototype named WSTester to collect real QoS information of services. WSTester integrates distributed computers to construct a virtual testing environment for Web service testing and deploys test tasks onto distributed computers efficiently.

    Khandakar Ahmed, RMIT University, Australia
    Altaf Hussain, Shahjalal University of Science and Technology, Bangladesh
    Mark A Gregory, RMIT University, Australia

Implementing Single Sign-On (SSO) in a Cloud space for a spectrum of services and applications is an interesting research avenue for scientific communities in the field of secure identity and access management for Cloud Computing. Using an SSO implementation, in the backend, users can navigate any or all of the supported applications or resources without the need to repeatedly provide credentials. In this chapter, the authors present an efficient and robust Cloud Single Sign-On Architecture (CSSOA) model based on a token security mechanism. Service Oriented Architectures (SOAs) are one of the enabling technologies for solving complex service oriented real world challenges, and hence, CSSOA has been implemented using SOAs. In the authors' CSSOA model, a CSSO SOAP authentication service is distributed among the Cloud servers while the CSSO database service is centralized.

Section 4
Methods, Technologies, and Applications

Chapter 12

Jinlei Jiang, Tsinghua University, China & Research Institute of Tsinghua University in Shenzhen, China
Xiaomeng Huang, Tsinghua University, China
Yongwei Wu, Tsinghua University, China & Research Institute of Tsinghua University in Shenzhen, China
Guangwen Yang, Tsinghua University, China

We are now living in the era of big data. The large volume of data raises a lot of issues related to data storage and management, stimulating the emergence of Cloud storage. Unlike traditional storage systems such as SAN (Storage Area Network) and NAS (Network Attached Storage), Cloud storage is delivered over a network and has such features as easy to scale and easy to manage. With Cloud storage shielding complex technical details such as storage capacity, data location, data availability, reliability and security, users can then concentrate on their business rather than IT (Information Technology) system maintenance. However, it is not an easy task to develop a Cloud storage system because multiple factors are involved. In this chapter, the authors show their experience in the design and implementation of a Cloud storage system. They detail its key components, namely the distributed file system Carrier and the data sharing service Corsair. A case study is also given on its application at Tsinghua University.

Chapter 13

Weijia Song, Peking University, China
Zhen Xiao, Peking University, China

Cloud computing allows business customers to elastically scale up and down their resource usage based on needs. This feature eliminates the dilemma of planning IT infrastructures for Cloud users, where under-provisioning compromises service quality while over-provisioning wastes investment as well as electricity. It offers virtually infinite resource. It also made the desirable "pay as you go" accounting model possible. The above touted gains in the Cloud model come from on-demand resource provisioning technology. In this chapter, the authors elaborate on such technologies incorporated in a real IaaS system to exemplify how Cloud elasticity is implemented. It involves the resource provisioning technologies in hypervisor, Virtual Machine (VM) migration scheduler and VM replication. The authors also investigate the load prediction algorithm for its significant impacts on resource allocation.

Chapter 14

Vishal Anand, The College at Brockport, USA

The virtualization of both servers and substrate networks will enable the future Internet architecture to support a variety of Cloud computing services and architectures, and prevent its ossification. Since multiple virtual networks (VN) or virtual infrastructure (VI) and services now share the resources of the same underlying network in a network virtualization environment, it is important that efficient techniques are developed for the mapping of the VNs onto the substrate network. Furthermore, due to the sharing of resources, the survivable design of VNs is also very important, since now even small failures in the substrate network will cause the disruption of a large number of VNs that may be mapped on to the substrate network. In this work, the author studies the problem of survivable virtual network mapping (SVNM) and first formulates the problem using mixed integer linear programming (MILP). The author then devises two kinds of algorithms for solving the SVNM problem efficiently: (1) Lagrangian relaxation-based algorithms including LR-SVNM-M and LR-SVNM-D and (2) Heuristic algorithms including H-SVNM-D and H-SVNM-M. The author then compares the performance of the algorithms with other VI mapping algorithms under various performance metrics using simulation. The simulation results and analysis show that the algorithms can be used to balance the tradeoff between time efficiency and mapping cost.

Chapter 15

Pan He, Chongqing University, China
Qi Xie, Chongqing University, China

The reliability of applications in Cloud will be highly affected by the reliability of underlying service component. Service pools with redundant services are mainly used to improve the reliability of service composition. This chapter proposes an optimal service pool size configuration method aiming at minimizing the overall cost or response time of service composition while meeting certain reliability constraints. The reliability, cost, and response time analysis of service composition with multiple service pools is first analyzed using probability analysis method and architecture-based approach. After that, the optimization problem is presented and classified into three categories. For single-objective problems, a dynamic programming algorithm is presented to get near-optimal solutions. For multi-objective problems, a hybrid genetic algorithm is proposed to search nondominated sets of solutions. This hybrid genetic algorithm employs a sensitivity-based local search operator. Empirical studies results showed that the algorithms could find optimal solutions for the three kinds of problems and they outperformed the exiting approaches including greedy selection method and traditional genetic algorithms.

Chapter 16

James Hardy, University of Derby, UK
Lu Liu, University of Derby, UK
Cui Lei, Beihang University, China
Jianxin Li, Beihang University, China

Virtualisation is massively important in computing and continues to develop. This chapter discusses and evaluates the virtualisation technologies and in particular, a state-of-art system called iVIC (the Internet-based Virtual Computing) developed by Beihang University, China as it provides an all-in-one example of many of the major headline Cloud Computing titles of SaaS, IaaS, and HaaS. The chapter considers several virtualization packages which are either commercial, community, or experimental, before focusing on iVIC, a virtual machine cloning system that may be beneficial in a learning or office environment. The chapter introduces a test environment which is used to assess the performance of the iVIC process and the virtual machines created. Power requirements of virtual, as opposed to physical machines, are compared and evaluated. The chapter closes with conclusions regarding virtualisation and iVIC.

Foreword

The Cloud computing paradigm has emerged as an efficient approach which enables ubiquitous, on-demand access to a shared pool of flexibly reconfigurable computing resources including networks, servers, storage, applications, and services that can be rapidly deployed with minimal management effort or service provider interactions. As a logical extension of Grid-computing, Cloud computing has attracted attention worldwide, ranging from casual Internet users to IT giants (e.g. Microsoft, Google, Amazon, HP). There is no doubt that the innovations of Clouds have offered many interesting research avenues in scientific communities.

Although recent advances in Cloud computing, including computation, storage, networking, and associated infrastructure innovations, are providing exciting opportunities to make significant progress in the implementation and realisation of Cloud-based systems, there are still considerable technical, legal, governance, and trust issues to be overcome. Issues such as low bandwidth to access the Cloud (e.g. uploading large datasets), fear of loss of data, potential breach of confidentiality / service level agreements for data and service, and lack of clear understanding of Cloud principles, methods, and technologies are recurring themes.

Given this context, this edited book brings together a collection of chapters written by professionals worldwide that elaborate on the Cloud principles, discuss innovative methods and technologies, and examine Cloud practice and applications. The book categorizes the topic of Cloud computing into 4 major themes, namely, (i) principles and fundamentals, (ii) security, (iii) service-oriented approaches, and (iv) methods, technologies, and applications. It presents novel insights regarding the principles, methodologies and service-oriented computing approaches required to address the supporting infrastructure of the Cloud.

The book is a timely contribution to the community. The researchers, engineers, and IT professionals who work in the field such as Cloud computing and distributed computing will find this book useful. The book could also be employed as a reference book for under- and post-graduate students who study computer science and information technologies.

It is my pleasure to recommend this book to you!

Peter M. A. Sloot
University of Amsterdam, The Netherlands

Peter Sloot *is a Professor of Computational Sciences at the University of Amsterdam, The Netherlands. He is also an endowed Professor of Complex Systems, NTU, Singapore, and endowed Professor of Advanced Computing, St. Petersburg State University, Russia. He studied natural information processing in complex systems by computational modeling and simulation as well as through formal methods. His work is applied to a large variety of disciplines with a focus on -but not limited to- biomedicine. Recent work is on modeling the virology and epidemiology of infectious diseases, notably HIV, through complex networks, cellular automata, and multi-agents. Recently in his work he tries to build bridges to socio-dynamics. Currently he leads two large EU projects: ViroLab1 and DynaNets2 and supervises research from various NIH, NSF, NWO, and Royal Academy projects. He published over 470 papers, books, chapters, and edited volumes. He has given over 20 radio and TV interviews on various scientific topics, including two documentaries of his work.*

Preface

Cloud computing as a new computing paradigm has attracted considerable attentions worldwide. It can provide scalable IT infrastructure, QoS-assured services and customizable computing environment, where a pool of virtualized, scalable, and manageable computing power, storage, platforms and services can be provisioned on-demand to customers over the Internet.

Although Cloud computing features such as SPI model (i.e. "Software As a Service," "Platform As a Service," "Infrastructure As a Service"), "Pay-as-you-go computing," virtualization, scalability and elasticity, and data centers are now getting widely recognized and there are many public and community Clouds that are available, how to use appropriate methodologies and technologies to facilitate implementing Cloud-based systems, bringing Cloud into scientific research, governmental service provision, and business, adapting existing IT systems to Clouds, tackling associated pressing issues (e.g. security, elasticity), et cetera still present challenges. One of reasons is that we still lack clear understanding in Cloud computing principles, further investigation into the enabling methods and technologies, and application practices.

The purpose of this book is to present a deep insight into the Cloud computing principles, examine the associated methods, technologies, and service-oriented approaches that can be employed to the development of successful Cloud. Hence this book is structured into the following four themes:

- **Section 1:** Principles and Fundamentals
- **Section 2:** Security
- **Section 3:** Service-Oriented Approaches
- **Section 4:** Methods, Technologies and Applications

Section 1: Principles and Fundamentals

Understanding the principles and fundamentals of Cloud computing is vital in Cloud implementation and associated research. This theme contains 4 book chapters.

Though the Cloud computing attracts more attentions and being widely used, it still lacks an agreement on a proper definition and classifications. It suffers from criticism as a hype and being claimed to be just an extension of already established computing paradigms. Chapter 1 gives a comprehensive definition of Cloud computing and comparison analysis of three major Cloud providers and open source technology solutions. This chapter investigates 31 Cloud computing definitions, each of which is analyzed under 16 construct components (a weight is given to each component) from different perspectives. It is identified that key features of Cloud computing include: Internet/Web based service model, SPI model, on-demand utility computing, virtualization, and scalability/elasticity. Followed by a comprehensive definition of Cloud computing presented, the identified issues are discussed based on the comparison analysis of three

Cloud service providers (e.g. Azure, Amazon Web Service, Google Application Engine) and two open source Cloud computing technologies and solutions (i.e. Eucalyptus, OpenNebula).

Chapter 2 traces the roots of Cloud computing, discusses the principles of the Cloud computing model today, and gives insights for future directions of Cloud computing. This chapter identifies a number of challenges that Cloud computing is currently facing, make recommendations on how to choose most appropriate Cloud computing model, and establish a successful Cloud Strategy to meet organizations' needs.

Can Cloud computing now technically be used to replace a local computing with better performance? High Performance Computing (HPC) is getting more widely used in scientific research, and can Cloud computing deliver on-demand HPC as it claims?

In order to investigate these interesting issues, Chapter 3 undertook some benchmarking analysis to compare the performance between NGS Cloud and local laptop, and Amazon EC2 and a super computer (e.g. HECToR XT4) from perspectives of low-level benchmark, I/O benchmark and application benchmark. Some interesting discoveries have been found from this benchmarking analysis (i) The low-level benchmark analysis between NGS Cloud and local computing resource (i.e. MacBook Pro), shows that local computing resources performs better than NGS cloud, while application-level benchmark shows that performance (e.g. runtime) are comparable between NGS Cloud and local computing resource. (ii) It is identified that generally if the high-performance computing involves inter-core communication, the supercomputer usually performs better than Amazon EC2 (due to fast networking facilities), while if the computing involves intra-core communication (less than 8 cores) that involves less/no cross-node communication, Amazon EC2 performs better. From usability perspective, using supercomputer and EC2 have its own advantages and disadvantages.

Cloud computing has been used in academic scientific research, governmental services provision, and business applications. But most of the associated work are loosely scattered in the literatures. Chapter 4 presents a survey on the use of Cloud computing in academia, government, and business via some typically research projects and applications. Some issues identified from the survey are also discussed.

Section 2: Security

As data and services are moved to the Cloud, security requirements become even more complex. How to ensure the security of services and data in the Cloud has been increasingly become a concern. This part presents 3 chapters in relation to Cloud security.

Chapter 5 claims that the existing client-server security practices can be adapted to address the challenges specific to the Cloud environment. This chapter conducts a comparison analysis of security challenges and solutions between traditional client-service environment and Cloud environment from the perspectives of five identified security pillars: confidentiality, integrity, availability, non-repudiation, and authenticity. Security challenges, solutions, and associated issues to Cloud computing are particularly discussed.

Chapter 6 gives a thorough literature review covering the key issues in relation to Cloud security, and conducts an interesting experiment in relation to Cloud security. It is identified from the literature that the concept of Unified Threat Management can be used to ensure the secured services on the Cloud. Followed by the literature review, a simulation model was created. The simulation results show that the Unified Trust Management Cloud can create the bottleneck and may not be effective in Cloud security management.

In addition to giving an overview of security and privacy challenges in Cloud computing, and how these challenges are associated with various delivery and deployment models, Chapter 7 proposes a security framework for Cloud computing where a *Services Integrator* is used to facilitate collaboration among different service providers by composing new services. The service integrator comprises components that are responsible for the establishment and maintenance of trust among the local provider domains, and between the providers and the users. Possible approaches to deal with different security issues in Cloud are also discussed.

Section 3: Service-Oriented Approaches

The computing stack, from applications we write, to the platforms we built upon, to the operating systems we use, are now moving from product- to a service-based economy. Cloud computing can be represented as a stack of service offering categories. From the foundational services to more complex services, this stack of services includes Internet-based services, infrastructure as services, platform as services, and software as services. Service-oriented approach can provide a standard-based approach to define service interfaces and predictable service operations, and can bring the benefits of language-neutral integration, components reuse, development agility and leveraging existing systems. Hence service-oriented approach can be used in the Cloud implementation, deployment or adapting existing system to the Cloud. In this theme, the editors include 4 chapters about the employment of service-oriented approach in Cloud computing.

Chapter 8 gives a case of using Cloud computing in business, i.e. use Cloud computing in a small and medium enterprise. This case involves a service design and process design of a Logistics Mall Cloud in Germany. Logistics is a cost factor and a competitive factor in shopping market. As most logistics companies are small and medium companies, they lack efficient IT solutions hence result in obsolete technologies, high costs of IT operations, poor documentation, security deficits, expensive licensing models, high maintenance efforts, etc. For example, BPM (business process management) software and associated maintenance are often expensive. Cloud computing (especially the SaaS model) provides a potential to these small and medium companies to use BPM software at a lower cost without worrying about infrastructure and software maintenance issues. This chapter presents how Cloud computing and service-oriented approach (i.e. BPM software in the Cloud) can advance the logistics market towards modern IT strategies by using the Cloud computing.

As Cloud computing is emerged as new computing paradigm, many existing software systems that are still being used now become legacy systems in some sense. This imposes a requirement that these legacy software systems need certain Cloud-oriented reengineering work so that they can be reused in Cloud computing environment and be equipped with Cloud-specific features. In Chapter 9, a general framework to assist with the evolution of legacy systems into the Cloud environments is developed. This methodology consists of several phases, which include using reverse engineering techniques to comprehend and decompose legacy systems, representing legacy resources as Cloud component using XML, and integrating these components into Cloud environment. In the case study, a legacy banking system is transformed to run as a Service-Oriented Cloud application.

As Cloud computing and service computing are now getting converged, in particular, the software is deployed as service over the Internet, how to select a qualified service that can also meet users' QoS requirements has become an interesting topic. In Chapter 10, a Cloud service ranking system is proposed based on both user feedback and service testing (i.e. CloudRank). A ranking-oriented collaborative filtering approach, and an active service QoS testing and fault location approach are employed in the ranking system.

Chapter 11 uses a service-oriented approach to provide a Cloud security solution. Single Sign On (SSO) provides a research direction in secure identity and access management for Cloud computing. Using SSO, users can navigate the supported applications or resources without the need to repeatedly provide credentials. This chapter discusses a Cloud Single Sign-On Architecture (CSSOA) model based on a token security mechanism. The service-oriented approach has been employed in implementing the CSSOA, where a Cloud Single Sign-On SOAP authentication service is distributed among the Cloud servers sharing a centralized CSSO database service.

Section 4: Methods, Technologies, and Applications

Knowing more appropriate techniques, methods, and best practices that can be used to implement the Cloud-based system or to tackle the challenging issues in relation to Cloud is no doubt necessary. This section contains 5 chapters that identify and highlight the innovative methods, enabling technologies, and applications for Cloud computing.

Cloud storage and preservation can provide a virtualized on-demand storage service over the Internet. With Cloud storage service, users can concentrate on their business or research without worrying about underlying technical details such as storage capacity, data location, data availability, reliability and confidentiality, and system maintenance. Developing an appropriate Cloud-based storage service is not trivial. Chapter 12 details an analysis, design and implementation of campus Cloud storage and preservation service, which contains a distributed file system (i.e. Carrier) and the data sharing service (i.e. Corsair). How to address some challenges issues in relation to Cloud storage is also described (e.g. file virtualization). A case study of using this Cloud storage service at Tsinghua University in Beijing is discussed.

Cloud scalability/elasticity is a significant feature in Cloud computing, and identified as one of critical challenges for Cloud computing. Chapter 13 implements an Infrastructure-as-a-Service Cloud model for on-demand resource provisioning, which involves the resource provisioning technologies in hypervisor, Virtual Machine (VM) migration scheduler and VM replication. The chapter also investigates the load prediction algorithm for its significant impacts on resource allocation.

As currently multiple virtual networks, virtual infrastructures or services share the resources of the same underlying network in a network virtualization environment, it is necessary to develop useful techniques that can help mapping the virtual network onto the substrate network. Chapter 14 investigates the problem of Survivable Virtual Network Mapping (SVNM) and devises two kinds of algorithms to solve the SVNM problem. The simulation results and analysis show that the algorithms can be used to balance the tradeoff between time efficiency and mapping cost.

The reliability of applications in Cloud will be highly affected by the reliability of underlying service component. Service pools with redundant services can be used to improve the reliability of service composition. Chapter 15 proposes an optimal service pool size configuration method aiming at minimizing the overall cost or response time of service composition while meeting certain reliability constraints.

Virtualization is one of key enabling technologies for Cloud computing. Chapter 16 reviews several virtualization technologies, and gives an evaluation and performance comparison to the "Internet-based Virtual Computing" (iVIC) system.

Xiaoyu Yang (Kevin X. Yang)
University of Reading, UK & Senior Member, Wolfson College, University of Cambridge, UK

Acknowledgment

We would like to thank authors for their contributions, including those whose chapters are not included in this book.

We also would like to express our gratitude to Editorial Advisory Board members, for their support and contributions to this book.

We would like to acknowledge thoughtful work from many reviewers who provided valuable evaluations and recommendations, including those whose names are not listed.

Section 1
Principles and Fundamentals

Chapter 1
Cloud Computing Diagnosis:
A Comprehensive Study

N. Krishnadas
Indian Institute of Management, India

R. Radhakrishna Pillai
Indian Institute of Management, India

ABSTRACT

Cloud Computing is emerging as a promising cost efficient computing paradigm which professionals believe is an absolutely new trend and will represent next level of internet evolution. Though the presence of Cloud computing is ubiquitous, it still lacks consensus on a proper definition and classification of the major Clouds in effect today. It also suffers from major criticism of being a hype/fad and some researchers claim that it is just an extension of already established computing paradigms. This chapter attempts to deal with such criticisms by comprehensively analyzing the Cloud definitions and diagnose the components of the same. It performs a comprehensive study of more than 30 definitions given by Cloud computing professionals and published in research papers. These definitions are then analyzed under more than fifteen components, each of which is discussed in the chapter. This study is backed by empirical work, to understand Cloud computing from different angles and come up with a comprehensive definition. It also analyses the present Cloud service providers and the level of services they provide to bring about a clear picture of Cloud computing. Based on the comparison, the pending issues in Cloud computing are discussed.

INTRODUCTION

With Gartner predicting the Cloud computing market to reach $150.1 billion in 2013, the entire IT industry is looking upon Cloud computing as the most powerful computing paradigm of the future. The growing complexity of the computational world in terms of processing large volumetric data resulted in a need of a cost-efficient model that could support the processing using clusters of commodity computers. Cloud computing has evolved as a computing paradigm to support such data processing. According to Dean and Ghemawat (2008), Google maintains more than 20 terabytes

DOI: 10.4018/978-1-4666-2854-0.ch001

of raw web data which is quite tough to process using distributed computing. Cloud computing can handle massive data at this level and render services on the demand using pay-for-use models.

Put in simple terms, the concept of Cloud computing is that computing resources will reside somewhere other than the computer room and that the users will connect to it using the resources as and when required. In effect, it displaces the infrastructure to the network so that the overall cost with respect to the management of hardware/software resources is reduced (Hayes, 2008). It appears to be highly disruptive technology (Bhaskar et al., 2009) hinting to the future where computation moves from local computers to centralized facilities operated by third party compute and storage utilities (Foster et al., 2008).

Many argue that Cloud computing is not a new paradigm and that its concept is based upon some already known and established computing paradigms. It is argued that way back in 1961, it was predicted by John McCarthy that "computation may someday be organized as public utility". It is said also that Cloud computing draws on basic concepts of virtualization, utility computing or distributed computing (Aaron, 2007; Kai, 2008; Dejan, 2008). This chapter tries to understand all aspects related to Cloud computing and understand how it is different from the existing paradigms.

Variety of technologies related to Cloud computing makes the overall concept a very confusing one (Kai, 2008). There is a little consensus on the definition of Cloud computing (Foster et al., 2008) and the confusion about the term makes it a general term for any solution that allows outsourcing concerning the infrastructure and all kinds of hosting (Luis et al., 2009). Also, it is well known fact that Cloud computing is not the first technology that has come under criticism of being a buzzword/hype. According to Gartner's Hype Cycle (Gartner, 2008) technology evolves from over-enthusiasm through a period of disillusionment to a gradual understanding of technology relevance and the role in a market/domain. It can be clearly seen that Cloud Computing falls in the first stage of

the hype cycle which is termed as positive hype. To avoid confusion resulting from this stage, this study attempts to diagnose Cloud computing and to bring out all possible associated aspects.

A clear analogy of Cloud computing can be drawn with Grid computing which faced the same issue of lack of a crisp definition. There were some accepted definitions like Foster (Foster et al., 2001; Foster et al., 2002), according to which the aim of Grid computing was to enable resource sharing and coordinated problem solving in dynamic, multi-institutional virtual organizations. However, there was no consensus on the same. Grid computing as a paradigm can also be observed under Gartner's Hype cycle. Figure 1 reveals the popularity of Cloud and Grid computing in terms of the number of searches being made worldwide.

From Figure 1, it is clear that Grid computing has lost its popularity and no major activity/event has taken place in the recent years (The letters A to G indicate some big events related to the search topic). However, the graph gives a totally different scenario of Cloud computing which has gained immense popularity in the recent years and there are many major events clustered in short period of time. These events are- A: Google looks to be 'Cloud-computing' rainmaker for other online business services, B: Microsoft's Top Software Architect, a Cloud Computing Advocate, Quits, C: Cloud computing 'could give EU 763bn-euro boost, D: Technology expo in Germany harnesses 'Cloud computing', E: Local IT firm unveils Cloud computing services, F: Cloud Domestic Cloud computing estimated to grow at 53 Study.

For Cloud computing to sustain this peak, its definition needs to be more transparent and thus requires good empirical study for the same. Therefore, this study attempts to comprehensively study the components of Cloud computing and diagnose it to come up with an exhaustive explanation of the concept. Though providing a concise definition is one of the targets of this chapter, the main aim is to understand different components of Cloud computing from the lens of multiple definitions. This chapter proceeds as follows. First, in Section

Figure 1. Google search trends for grid computing and cloud computing

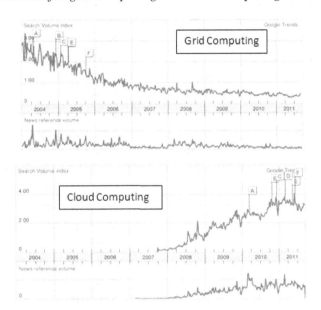

2, light is thrown on previous research attempts on similar lines explaining the gap in literature. Section 3 takes up all components of Cloud computing (using which the definitions are analyzed) and is explained in detail. Section 4 describes the data collection (definitions) methods and explanation of the empirical study. In Section 5, an attempt has been made to analyze the results of the study to come up with a comprehensive definition of Cloud computing. Last section (Section 6) deals with comparison of the various Cloud computing services being offered till date and analysis of these services under the umbrella of components of Cloud computing discussed in previous sections.

RELATED WORK

Several taxonomies have been developed for Cloud computing blueprint in the past. However, majority of them suffer from the major disadvantage of being created from the perspective of vendors that are part of the Cloud computing activity. The perspective of developing taxonomy and reviewing the definitions from the enterprise IT point of view is missing. Bhaskar et al (2009). attempts to

diagnose the Cloud computing architecture and come up with taxonomy. However, it lacks the review of well known Cloud computing definitions and is limited only to the architecture of Cloud computing. Though, it covers the concept of XAAS (Everything is a service) comprehensively, but it misses out on the exhaustive coverage of other aspects of Cloud computing like scalability (infrastructure), elasticity etc. Moreover, the focus was more on applying the taxonomy to Cloud Service Providers (CSP) than developing the taxonomy per se. A more accepted definition of Cloud computing is given by US National Institute of Standards and Technology (NIST) and it acts a working definition (Mell and Grance, 2009). However, this definition is not backed by empirical research and a general listing of components is provided.

Luis et al. (2009) attempts to review the Cloud computing definitions but uses a common source of Cloud computing Journal for all the definitions covered. Also, the no. of components under which the definitions are analyzed is not comprehensive. The final definition proposed based on the review has no empirical justification and offers just a collection of concepts discussed in the definitions reviewed. Hence, this study analyzes more than thirty definitions from multiple sources, resulting in more than fifteen components under which analysis is performed. Also, weights are assigned to the components to give multiple views of analysis in the final diagnosis of Cloud computing. In terms of Cloud service providers, some studies have revealed the differences in terms of the architecture but misses on the in-depth analysis which includes the cost of subscription. This chapter tabulates the cost comparison of two service providers on the same parameters adding to the analysis of competition on price.

COMPONENTS OF CLOUD COMPUTING

Analysis of large number of definitions has resulted in inclusion of diverse aspects related to Cloud computing. These aspects forms the base of analysis for the Cloud Services Providers discussed in upcoming sections. The list of components is explained below:

- **Utility Computing:** This aspect of Cloud computing is one of the most important aspects as it was ranked as top priority in two of the four types of analysis conducted (described in coming sections). Some definitions (Ben Kepes, Kevin Hartig) mentioned the overlap of Cloud computing with utility computing, where as some quoted it as an updated version of utility computing. In a utility computing model, customers are charged according to the transfer of content and the utilization of storage (Broberg et al., 2008). The most common aspect of utility computing that is often confused with Cloud computing is the business model of collaboration and pay-as-you-go service. Utility computing is not a new paradigm of computer infrastructure, rather it is a model which pack-

ages the computing resources and distributes it (Foster et al., 2008).

- **Saas, Paas and Iaas:** They stand for Software as a Service, Platform as a Service and Infrastructure as a Service respectively. These are different categories of Cloud services that are delivered and consumed in real time over internet. Though there are other forms of services like HaaS (Hardware as a service), FaaS (Framework as a service), DaaS (Development, Database, Desktop as a service) clubbed under XaaS (Everything as a service) (Baran, 2008); Software, Platform and infrastructure appeared most commonly in the definitions reviewed so far.

- **Software as a Service (Saas):** These services are of great interest to large number of users as they deliver single application through the browser using a multi-tenant platform. Alexander et al. (2009) differentiates basic application services and composite application services. Composite applications use mash-up support systems allowing the social networks to be used as basic services. This service of Cloud computing alleviates the customers from the trouble of software licensing and upfront investment in the servers. Salesforce.com is an excellent example among enterprise applications (Adamov and Erguvan, 2009; Salesforce, 2008).

- **Platform as a Service (Paas):** These services are appreciated by the developers where they get a platform including systems and environments. Developers can use this platform to build their own applications that run on service provider's infrastructure and it comprises of developing, testing, deploying and hosting life cycles. Microsoft Azure is a well known example of this (Microsoft, 2009).

- **Infrastructure as a Service (Iaas):** Iaas offers delivery of computer infrastructure that provides the benefit of usage based schemes and higher flexibility. Many organizations manage large set of computing resources which they can organize (splitting, assigning and resizing) to build on demand ad-hoc systems with of the help of virtualization.

- **Software Service Model & Outsourcing:** This aspect of Cloud computing is seen as another most important factor of Cloud computing which is evident from the analysis of the results. The users of Cloud computing are the customers in the service model and they pay for service based upon the service level agreements (SLA) (Yang X. 2011). SLA is a contract that is agreed upon between a customer and a service provider (Kaiqi and Harry, 2009). The usage of services by the customers is without the knowledge of the underlying architecture of the service providers.

In this model, service provider uses service center as a collection of resources to host the service applications for customers. Customer sends a service request that is transmitted to the Web Server and service center that are owned by service provider over the network (Martin and Nilsson, 2002). One important aspect of this kind of a service model is Quality of Service (QoS) which in turn affects the customer satisfaction (Van et al., 2003; Schneider and White, 2004) It deals with the problem of computer service performance modeling subjected to different metrics like network utilization, response time, throughput etc. All these have been studied in literature (Yang et al. 2012; Mei et al., 2006; Lu and Wang, 2005; Karlapudi and Martin, 2004), however there is still an acute need for proper evaluation parameters and standardization of the service level agreements. The standardization should ensure that the traditional system centric resource management would not act as an incentive

in Cloud Service model. Instead, market oriented resource management (Buyya et al., 2005; Stuer et al., 2007) is required to regulate the demand and supply and also to provide lucrative offers to both customer and service provider.

Outsourcing from the customers end is often associated with the service model. Vogels (2008) describes the elimination of an upfront commitment by Cloud users allowing startups to start small and scale hardware resources when needed. This essentially means shifting of the computational resources or outsourcing to the vendor/Cloud service provider.

- **Virtualization:** Virtualization has been mentioned as the most prominent technology underlying Cloud computing from service provider's point of view. This technology enables the abstraction of computing resources such that single physical machine is able to function as set of various logical virtual machines (Barham et al., 2003). This can result in multiple benefits of agility, flexibility, cost reduction etc and in turn will enhance the overall business value. The central highlight of this technology is to host multiple isolated operating system environments on a single physical machine. Also it caters to both data (files, database etc) and computing resources (EGEE, 2008).

This technology has become inevitable component of Cloud computing due its practical and direct significance in the computing business model. Virtualization enables application/server consolidation by increasing the efficiency of multiple applications running on the same server. It supports configurability and quick recovery from unplanned outrages (Foster et al., 2008). The post-service aspects of Cloud computing like monitoring and maintenance can also be automated via virtualization.

- **On Demand Computing (Pay as you Go):** This feature of Cloud computing has received considerable importance in the definitions reviewed by this study. Consumers should be able to access the computing resources from the Cloud anywhere in the world on demand. Also, the customer will pay for the computing resources on a consumption basis. This is unlike the traditional software business model for software that opts for onetime payment for unlimited use per system. Hence, the name 'Pay as you go'. Customers pay for the computing resources by means of customized service level agreement hiding the underlying technological infrastructure (Kaiqi and Harry, 2009).

- **Scaling:** According to Gartner, a computing service like Cloud computing should be massively scalable for it to be credited true Cloud computing facility. Immediate scalability and resource usage optimization has been mentioned as the key elements of Cloud computing by many authors (Jeremy, 2008). Cloud computing frees programmers of dealing with scalability issues (Kemal and Martin, 2008). Bhaskar et al. (2009) describes the scalability of Cloud computing as horizontal scalability through load balancing and application delivery solutions.

- **Elasticity:** In economic terms, Cloud computing aims at converting capital expenses to operating expense (Michael et al., 2009). The analysis of definitions makes it very clear that Cloud computing is driven by economies of scale (Silvestre, 1987). Its ability to add or remove resources conveniently with a very short lead time provides Cloud computing with an edge over other computing paradigms. Server utilization in data centers generally range from 5 to 20% (Rangan, 2008; Siegele, 2008). Users generally provision their servers for the peak load and hence there is a terrible loss of computational abilities during the non-peak hours. Further insight to this aspect is brought about in the underutilization and over-utilization concept covered in the coming parts.

- **Hardware/software Investment:** Cloud computing lessens the burden of hardware and software investment of the customers. It mainly targets the reduction in capital expenditure and this aspect is explored in various studies (Roy, 2008; Paul, 2008). This reduction is achieved via utilizing the vast computational resources of the vendor which by using effective technology is delivered as a service to the customers.

- **Internet/Web Service:** This component is covered in almost all the definitions reviewed so far. There is a consensus on Cloud computing being an internet /web service and that the different services (infrastructure, software, and platform) are delivered to customers using web interface and internet.

- **Automation of resource provisioning:** Cloud computing aims at a future where customers need not care about the scaling of web applications because the entire process is automated. This is possible with monitoring and increasing automation of resource provisioning. This aspect is important to shape the future of Cloud Computing, as what customers look for is convenient availability of computational resources with automated provisioning of resource.

- **Under-Utilization and Over-Utilization:** Though these two aspects received low rankings in the final analysis of definitions, it demonstrates one important feature of Cloud computing. The computing resources can be dynamically re-configured to manage a variable load that allows for optimal resource utilization (Luis et al., 2009). Under-utilization basically refers to the idle servers while over utilization can be attributed to blue screen due to more than estimated load. When users provide provision for peak load it leads to under-utilization, whereas provisioning for average load leads to disadvantage of turning away excess users thus loosing customer loyalty and decreasing the probability of repeat customers.

- **Reduced Time:** This aspect of Cloud computing focus on three aspects of time a) Time to complete the service request from customers point of view b) Time to dynamically change the computing requirements (lead time) and c) Time to process the computations on the "Cloud". All three conditions are necessary for customer satisfaction and to claim that Cloud computing leads to time savings.
- **Extension of Client/Server Model:** Very few definitions have quoted Cloud computing as an extension of client/server model (Alok, 1992). Though Cloud computing is a service model based on Internet/Web, it deviates from typical client/server model in many ways. The world is realizing the potential of Cloud computing and it is estimated that there will be a $160 billion addressable market opportunity (Hamilton, 2008). Morgan Stanley research study (Morgan, 2008) has also identified Cloud computing as one of the prominent technology trends. Hence, there is an immense potential in Cloud computing and excellent features that differentiates it from traditional client/server model.

ANALYSIS OF DEFINITIONS: METHOD DESCRIPTION

For analysis purpose, thirty-one definitions were reviewed. These included the definitions given by Cloud computing experts (Jeremy, 2008), published in the Cloud Computing Journal (seventeen definitions). The remaining definitions were taken up from published papers on Cloud computing. No component of definition was missed, though the similar sounding components were clubbed under the same category. A review of all these components resulted in sixteen components, most of which has been described in the previous section.

This study differs from other reviews (Bhaskar et al., 2009; Luis et al., 2009) of Cloud computing in terms of the comprehensiveness and the assignment of weights for each component. If one definition covers say 'n' components. Then all n components are assigned weights W1, W2,... ...,Wn respectively in such a way that:

$$W1 + W2 + W3 + \dots Wn = 1 \tag{1}$$

$$0 < Wi \leq 1, \text{ Where } 1 \leq i \leq n \tag{2}$$

These weights are assigned on the following criteria:

1. The components that are over emphasized/repeated/projected exclusively are given the highest weightage. The number of repetitions of a component in a definition/paper adds to the weight assigned.
2. In case components 'n' components are equally projected or mentioned only once, then the weights are assigned equally.
3. The components which are not explicitly stated in the definition but are derived to have almost similar meaning are given less weightage.
4. The components that have minor contribution to the overall definition receive less weightage.

Assignment of weights: Based on the four guidelines above, five Cloud computing experts were asked to assign the weights for the definitions in the sample set across sixteen components. An individual assignment of weights by the five experts was followed by a group rating to reach the consensus. The second round of rating (group) involved calculation of average weights for the components where consensus could not be reached. The results of second round were compared with the individual ratings and the final weights were fairly consistent with the individual assessment.

This method results in a table of dimension: 31*16 (See Appendix-A), where all the individual weights can be denoted by Wij.

Wij: i represents the definition number and j represents the component number

$1 \leq i \leq 31$: 31 definitions are reviewed AND $1 \leq j \leq 16$: Resulting components are 16

$0 < Wij \leq 1$ and For all i between 1 and 31 (both inclusive) $\sum j = 1$ to $16 Wij = 1$

Apart from the weightage, count of different components was also recorded. For each weight Wij>0, the count was recorded as 1 so that the sum count of all the components can be obtained. Thus for each component 'j' a sum count Sumj was obtained which demonstrated the total number of times component j has appeared in all the definitions reviewed so far. Post count calculation, total weights were obtained for all individual components 'j'. Weightj represents the sum of weights which component j has received spread over all the definitions. For the purpose of analysis from multiple angles, rankings were developed for the different components using four methods described below:

1. **Rankings based on Total Weights and Numbers:** For all components 'j' the product of total occurrences and total weight was calculated and they were subsequently sorted in descending order. This analysis reveals the overall popularity of the components in the definitions reviewed so far.
   a. **Formula:** Total Scorej= Sumj * Weightj (For all components j)
2. **Rankings based on only Average Weights:** For standardization, total score does not reveal fair figures for analysis of definitions. Hence, this method takes up the average weight instead of total weight for a particular component j.
   a. **Formula:** Average_weightj= Weightj/ Sumj (For all components j)
3. **Rankings based on only Numbers (Sum):** This method provides an angle of analysis which is independent of the weight allocation. It is purely on the basis of sum of total counts for each component 'j' which demonstrates the popularity of the component in the definitions reviewed.
   a. **Formula:** Sumj (For all components j)
4. **Rankings Based on only Total Weight:** This method provides an angle of analysis which is independent of the number of times a component has featured in a definition.
   a. **Formula:** Weightj (For all components j)

The results of all these methods are discussed in the next section.

ANALYSIS OF RESULTS

The snapshot of top five components in terms of the rankings generated by the method discussed above is presented in Table 1.

The results reveal that Cloud computing is essentially an Internet/Web Based Service. However absence of this component in the top five rankings indicate that it is very obvious component of Cloud computing and hence is not projected exclusively in the definitions. Other component that is inevitable part of Cloud computing is "software service model" and that the customers are outsourcing their computing infrastructure to the Cloud service providers. Virtualization features in top list using all the angles of analysis; which indicates the central underlying technology of Cloud computing (Kim, et al., 2009). Another feature that appears in all the top lists is the scalability. Cloud computing differentiates

Table 1. Snapshot of top five components using different methods

Rankings Based on Total Weights			Rankings Based on only Average Weights		
Rank	Component	Total_avg	Rank	Component	Average Weight
1	Utlity Computing & SAAS, PAAS	4.9	1	Utlity Computing & SAAS, PAAS	0.54
2	Scaling	4.5	2	Virtualization	0.34
3	Software/Service Model/Outsourcing	4.4	3	On Demand Computing/ Pay as You Go	0.31
4	Internet/Web Service	4.2	4	Scaling	0.30
5	Virtualization	3.7	5	Multi-Platform	0.30
Rankings Based on Total Weights and Numbers			Rankings Based on only Numbers (Sum)		
Rank	Component	Total_No_Avg	Rank	Component	Numbers
1	Internet/Web Service	75.6	1	Internet/Web Service	18
2	Scaling	67.5	2	Scaling	15
3	Software/Service Model/Outsourcing	66	3	Software/Service Model/Outsourcing	15
4	Utlity Computing & SAAS, PAAS	44.1	4	Virtualization	11
5	Virtualization	40.7	5	On Demand Computing/ Pay as You Go	11

from other computing paradigms with some key advantages of scalability and elasticity. The way in which services are delivered to the customer uses the one demand computing where the users pay for the exact usage of computational resources. This is the reason why on demand computing (Pay as You Go) has also featured in both the numbers and weight analysis.

If virtualization is the underlying technology behind Cloud computing, it is evident from the results that the architecture is layered one, with multiple layers being SaaS, PaaS and IaaS. Together, it has been termed as XaaS (Everything as a service) (Baran, 2008) in literature. Hence, it is a form of utility computing offering multiple services as a web service. In order to provide platform as a service, it is important to provide multi-platform computing services which form an essential component.

Under utilization and over utilization avoidance received low priority in different methods because they do not form a part of definitions. They are certain characteristics of Cloud computing which

will support the computing paradigm trend. Other components that receive low scores might show their importance as characteristics of Cloud computing rather than being a part of definition. Other such components are reduced time and automation of resource provisioning. The component that received least scores using all the methods of analysis is that Cloud computing is similar to/ extension of client-server model. This is very clear from explanation of various components of Cloud computing discussed in previous sections. Based on the four angles of analysis, this study attempts to come up with a comprehensive definition of Cloud computing. This definition highlights the core concepts (top ranking components) of Cloud computing and describes the characteristics of the computing paradigm (low ranking components).

Cloud computing is an Internet/Web based service model that delivers computing resources (software, platform and infrastructure) on demand with the help of underlying technologies like virtualization. The customers pay according to the exact usage

9

of services and gain the advantage of automated resource provision, scalability and elasticity. This computing paradigm frees the users from the burden of under-utilization and over –utilization of resources and thus outsources the risk to the service providers.

COMPARISON OF VARIOUS CLOUD COMPUTING SERVICES

With the attractive predictions about Cloud computing market, many IT giants have already come up with Cloud services. Owing to the lucrative benefits, many clients have already subscribed to Cloud computing services (More than 200 organizations already subscribed to salesforce.com). The development of Cloud computing infrastructure has been taking place from both academic and industrial fronts. The former includes initiatives like Virtual Workspaces (Keahey et al., 2005), Open Nebula (OpenNebula, 2010) and Reservoir. The latter includes service like Amazon Elastic Compute Cloud (EC2) (Amazon, 2009), Google App Engine (Google_app, 2009) and Microsoft Azure (Microsoft_azure, 2010). These three services will be the focus of comparison in this study. All the three services combined can explain the entire spectrum in which the entire Cloud computing services can be placed and explained.

There are certain open source initiatives like Eucalyptus (Daniel et al., 2009) which implements infrastructure as a service designed to be conve-

nient, easily modifiable and extendable. Most of the services allow uploading XEN (Barham et al., 2003) virtual machine images to vendor's infrastructure and gives client APIs to manage them. Open source Cloud computing offers building block required for controllable identity verification and contributes in mechanisms around digital identity management (Cavoukian, 2008). This study includes a comparison of two well known open source initiatives Eucalyptus and OpenNebula.

Moving from open source Cloud service providers to the proprietary ones, three major services have been taken up in this study. This includes Amazon EC2, Google App Engine and Microsoft Azure. The spectrum of Cloud computing services denotes the level of control on the software stack. At one end lies the Cloud computing service like Amazon EC2 that provides control to nearly the entire stack, right from the kernel upwards. At the other end, lie application domain specific platforms like Google App Engine and Sales-Force.com (Salesforce, 2009). They provide less control on the software stack and can be termed as software development platform. Between the extremes, lie the Cloud services of Microsoft Azure which provides computing resources that stands between flexibility and programmer convenience. The spectrum is shown in Figure 2.

Amazon EC2 Service instance almost looks like physical hardware. It charges the user for the time when the instance is alive. However, there are services (Amazon S3) in which user is charged based on data transfer including both uploads and

Figure 2. Cloud computing service spectrum

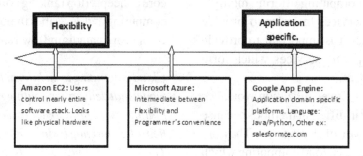

downloads (Amazon S3, 2009). There is almost no restriction on the kind of applications that can be hosted. This adds on to the low level of virtualization that gives freedom for the developers to code whatever they want.

Google App Engine is targeted at web applications using Python and Java language. It provides a web based admin console for the user to manage the web applications. There is clear separation between a stateless computation and a stateful storage tier (Michael et al., 2009). The process of availing services is based on request-reply and is rationed in terms of the CPU time used by App Engine in servicing a particular request.

Microsoft Azure acts as an intermediate between the two Cloud services mentioned above. It provides an integrated development, controlled Cloud environment and hosting facilities. From developers point of view, they gain advantage of managing all operations (create, host, manage and scale) at one place using Microsoft Data Centers. Azure applications use .NET libraries and compiled to the Common Language Runtime (language independent environment). Thus, though there is a choice of language, user cannot control the underlying operating system or routine.

Therefore, five service providers have been discussed in this section which includes two open source projects. These services are compares on common features and some components indicating key highlights of the five services are briefed in Table 2. The cost comparison of the major Cloud computing services (excluding open source) is also presented in Table 3.

Future Directions: Based on the comparison of existing Cloud computing services, it is clear that there are certain issues which remain unresolved with the service providers. One major issue

Table 2. Comparison of Azure, App Engine, and Amazon Service

	Amazon Web Services	Azure	Google App Engine	Eucalyptus	Open Nebula
Offering (Service Model)	Iaas and Xen Images	PaaS	Saas (To some extent PaaS)	IaaS	IaaS
Control Interface	API, Command Line	API, Command Line	API	Web Based Application or Control Panel	Web Based Application or Control Panel
Autoscaling and Load Balancing	Yes (charged)	Yes (charged)	Yes (Free)	Yes (Free)	No
Technological Model	X86 ISA with the help of Zen VM	Common Language Runtime	Application structure/ framework, Java and Python handlers	Hibernate, Axis 2, Java	Java, Ruby
Virtualization	OS level running on Xen hypervisor	Hypervisor	Multitenant Architecture	Xen hypervisor	KVM & on demand access to EC2
Storage	Simple DB; Simple Storage Service (S3)	SQL Data Services, Azure Storage Service	MegaStore/Big Table	Walrus	SQLLite3
Security	Type II (SAAS 70 Type II) certification	Token Service (STS)	Google Secure Data Connector	WS Security	Firewall, VPN Tunnel
Outage Recorded	S3 Outage (Allen, 2008)	Malfunctioning (Nicholas, 2009)	Partial Outage (Stephen, 2008)	NA	NA
Guaranteed Network Availability	99.95%	99.9%	99.9%	99.9%	

Table 3. Cost comparison: Google App Engine (GAE), Microsoft Azure, and Amazon EC2

Category	Amazon EC2	Microsoft Windows Azure	Google App Engine
Subscription Type	Use Based and Subscription Plans	Use Based and Subscription Plans	Use Based
Source	aws.amazon.com	microsoft.com	code.google.com
Inbound Bandwidth Price	0¢ per GB	10¢ per GB	10¢ per GB
Outbound Band-width Price	12¢ per GB	15¢ per GB	12¢ per GB
Base Plan Cost	8.50¢ per hour	12¢ per hour	0¢ per hour
Base Plan Details (Findthebest, 2011)	1.7GB RAM, 160GB local storage, 1 EC2 Compute Unit	1.6 GHz CPU, 1.75 GB RAM, 225 GB Instance Storage, Moderate I/O Performance.	The first 500 MB of persistent storage are free and comes with enough CPU and bandwidth for about 5 million page views a month.

is the security of data on Cloud and the service providers should collaborate to come up with strong service level agreements with high security. Further, clients have no option to monitor the data and know what kind of mechanisms are going on to process the data. Service providers should be more transparent with their technology and offer transparent monitoring tools to the user to ensure trust levels. It is noted that most of the service providers fail to guarantee the trust levels. Further, the comparison of outrage recorded across the service providers urge the need of ensuring proper backup mechanisms. Failure of service, even for an hour will collapse the scope of wide implementation of Cloud computing in future. Therefore, service providers need to ensure that all the pending issues like portability, security, privacy, standards, Cloud computing economics, multi-supplier sourcing etc are taken care of. This will increase the implementation level of Cloud computing and would make it a promising technology than just a hype.

Further, with the rise of mobile applications and browser applications, internet based on-demand services of Cloud computing should be competitively priced. It is important for the client to think about only what they want rather than how they want making the entire process of dealing with the demand online. This has a promising future

as many organizations seek to focus on their core competencies and outsource the applications/software development. With the presence of strong Cloud computing platform offering services on demand, there is a lot of demand to be catered for. It could make the business world more organized, efficient and specialized. However, with the rise of Cloud computing platforms the future also hints at strict maintenance procedures that could provide high reliability and increased uptime performance. To upgrade the underlying hosts, Cloud servers migrate and might require sever reboot. A set of protocols for the maintenance procedure will ensure smooth transitions and better cloud computing experience.

CONCLUSION

Cloud computing is coming up as a promising paradigm to serve as computing utility. The market predictions are attractive and many organizations have already started moving to the "cloud". There is an acute need of certain standards that can prevail in Cloud computing environment. However, to set up such standards it is important to understand Cloud computing and all its aspects, as ambiguity in definition still prevails about this computing paradigm. Hence, this study has attempted to highlight the essential components of Cloud computing and compare the existing popular Cloud computing services. This comparison led to development of future objectives for service providers that would ensure greater implementation of Cloud computing. It provided an approximate view of issues that were still pending to be resolved in context of Cloud computing as a business opportunity. This chapter would provide as a base for further research on wide aspects of Cloud computing. The importance of inter disciplinary research in Cloud computing is relevant and much needed to shape up the trends of Cloud computing in future.

REFERENCES

Aaron, W. (2007). Computing in the clouds. *netWorker*, *4*, 16–25.

Adamov, A., & Erguvan, M. (2009). The truth about Cloud computing as new paradigm in IT. In The 3rd International Conference on Application of Information and Communication Technologies – AICT2009, Azerbaijan-Baku, (pp.1-3)

Alexander, L., Markus, K., Jens, N., Stefan, T., & Thomas, S. (2009). What's inside the Cloud? An architectural map of the Cloud landscape. Proceedings of the 2009 ICSE Workshop on Software Engineering Challenges of Cloud Computing, (pp. 23-31).

Allen, S. (2008). Update from Amazon regarding Friday's S3 downtime. Retrieved February 3, 2008, from http://www.centernetworks.com/amazon-s3-downtime-update

Alok, S. (1992). Client-server computing. *Communications of the ACM*, *35*(7), 77–98. doi:10.1145/129902.129908

Amazon. (2009). Amazon elastic compute cloud (EC2). Retrieved March 10, 2010, from http://www.amazon.com/ec2/

Amazon S3. (2009). Amazon S3: Simple storage service. Retrieved March 10, 2010, from http://www.amazon.com/s3/

Baran, D. (2008). Cloud computing basics. Retrieved November 10, 2008, from http://www.webguild.org/2008/07/cloud-computing-basics.php

Barham, P., Dragovic, B., Fraser, K., Hand, S., Harris, T., & Ho, A. … Warfield, A. (2003). Xen and the art of virtualization. In Proceedings of the 19th ACM Symposium on Operating Systems Principles, SOSP 2003, Bolton Landing, USA.

Bhaskar, P. Rimal, Eunmi, C., & Ian, L. (2009). A taxonomy and survey of cloud computing systems. In Fifth International Joint Conference on INC, IMS and IDC, (pp. 44-51).

Brian de. H. (2008). Cloud computing - The jargon is back! Cloud Computing Journal, online. Retrieved from http://cloudcomputing.sys-con.com/node/613070

Broberg, J., Venugopal, S., & Buyya, S. (2008). Market-oriented grids and utility computing: The state-of-the-art and future directions. *Journal of Grid Computing*, *6*(3), 255–276. doi:10.1007/s10723-007-9095-3

Buyya, R., Abramson, D., & Venugopal, S. (2005). The grid economy. Proceedings of the IEEE, 93(3), 698_714.

Cavoukian, A. (2008). *Privacy in the clouds: Privacy and digital identity - Implications for the Internet*. Information and Privacy Commissioner of Ontario.

Daniel, N., Rich, W., Chris, G., Graziano, O., Sunil, S., Lamia, Y., & Dmitrii, Z. (2009). Eucalyptus: An open-source Cloud computing infrastructure. Journal of Physics: Conference Series, 180.

Dean, J., & Ghemawat, S. (2008). MapReduce: Simplified data processing on large clusters. *Communications of the ACM*, *51*(1), 107–113. doi:10.1145/1327452.1327492

Dejan, M. (2008). Cloud computing: Interview with Russ Daniels and Franco Travostino. *IEEE Internet Computing, 5,* 7–9.

Derrick, K., Bahman, J., Paul, M., Franck, C., & David, P. A. (2009). Cost-benefit analysis of Cloud Computing versus desktop grids. Proceedings of the 2009 IEEE International Symposium on Parallel&Distributed Processing, (pp. 1-12).

EGEE-II Members. (2008). An EGEE comparative study: Grids and clouds - Evolution or revolution. Technical report, Enabling Grids for E-sciencE Project. Electronic version. Retrieved from https://edms.cern.ch/document/925013/

Findthebest. (2011). Retrieved December 10, 2011, from http://cloud-computing.findthebest.com

Foster, I., Kesselman, C., Nick, J., & Tuecke, S. (2002). *The physiology of the grid: An open grid services architecture for distributed systems integration.* Globus Projet.

Foster, I., Kesselman, C., & Tuecke, S. (2001). The anatomy of the Grid: Enabling scalable virtual organization. *International Journal of High Performance Computing Applications, 15*(3), 200–222. doi:10.1177/109434200101500302

Foster, I., Zhao, Y., Raicu, I., & Lu, S. (2008). Cloud computing and grid computing 360-degree compared. Proceedings of the IEEE Grid Computing Environments Workshop, (pp. 1-10).

Galen, G., & Eric, K. (2008). What Cloud computing really means. InfoWorld. Retrieved from http://www.infoworld.com/article/08/04/07/15FE-cloud-computing-reality_1.html

Gartner Group. (2008). Gartner's hype cycle report, 2008. Technical report, Gartner Group. Available at http://www.gartner.com/

Google. _app engine. (2010). Retrieved from http://appengine.google.com

Hamilton, D. (2008). Cloud computing seen as next wave for technology investors. Financial Post. Retrieved from http://www.financialpost.com/money/story.html?id=562877

Hayes, B. (2008). Cloud computing. *Communications of the ACM, 51*(7), 9–11. doi:10.1145/1364782.1364786

Jeremy, G. (2008). Twenty one experts define Cloud computing. Virtualization. Retrieved from http://virtualization.sys-con.com/node/612375

Kai, H. (2008). Massively distributed systems: From grids and p2p to clouds. In The 3rd International Conference on Grid and Pervasive Computing - GPC-Workshops.

Kaiqi, X., & Harry, P. (2009). *Service performance and analysis in cloud computing* (pp. 693–700). Congress on Services.

Karlapudi, H., & Martin, J. (2004). Web application performance prediction. In Proceedings of the IASTED International Conference on Communication and Computer Networks, (pp. 281- 286).

Keahey, K., Foster, I., Freeman, T., & Zhang, X. (2005). Virtual workspaces: Achieving quality of service and quality of life in the grid. *Science Progress, 13*(4), 265–275.

Kemal, A. D., & Martin, A. W. (2008). *Emergence of the academic computing clouds.* ACM Ubiquity.

Kim, K. H., Beloglazov, A., & Buyya, R. (2009). Power-aware provisioning of Cloud resources for real-time services. In Proceedings of the 7th international Workshop on Middleware for Grids, Clouds and E-Science, (pp. 1-6). New York, NY: ACM.

Lu, J., & Wang, J. (2005). Performance modeling and analysis of Web Switch. In Proceedings of the 31st Annual International Conference on Computer Measurement (CMG05), Orlando, FL, Dec 2005.

Luis, M. V., Luis, R. M., Juan, C., & Maik, L. (2009). A break in the clouds: towards a cloud definition. ACM SIGCOMM Computer Communication Review, 39(1).

Martin, J., & Nilsson, A. (2002). On service level agreements for IP networks. In Proceedings of the IEEE INFOCOM.

Mei, R. D., Meeuwissen, H. B., & Phillipson, F. (2006). User perceived quality-of-service for voice-over-IP in a heterogeneous multi-domain network environment. In Proceedings of ICWS.

Mell, P., & Grance, T. (2009). *The NIST definition of cloud computing*. National Institute of Standards and Technology.

Michael, A., Armando, F., Rean, G., Anthony, D. J., Randy, K., & Andy, K. … Matei, Z. (2009). Above the clouds: A Berkeley view of cloud computing. UC Berkeley Reliable Adaptive Distributed Systems Laboratory. Retrieved from http://www.eecs.berkeley.edu/Pubs/TechRpts/2009/EECS-2009-28.pdf

Microsoft. (2009). Azure services platform. Retrieved March 10, 2009, from http://www.microsoft.com/azure

Microsoft Azure. (2010). Retrieved March 12, 2010 from http://www.microsoft.com/azure/

Morgan Stanley. (2008) Technology trends. Retrieved Feb 10, 2008 from http://www.morganstanley.com/institutional/techresearch/pdfs/TechTrends062008.pdf

Nicholas, K. (2009). Microsoft's cloud Azure service suffers outage. Retrieved from http://www.eweekeurope.co.uk/news/microsofts-cloud-azure-service-suffers-outage-396

OpenNebula. (2010). Project. http://www.opennebula.org/.

Paul, F. (2008). The cloud is the computer. IEEE Spectrum Online. Retrieved from http://www.spectrum.ieee.org/aug08/6490

Rajkumar, B., Chee, S. Y., Srikumar, V., James, B., & Ivona, B. (2009). Cloud computing and emerging IT platforms: Vision, hype, and reality for delivering computing as the 5th utility. *Future Generation Computer Systems, 25*(6), 599–616. doi:10.1016/j.future.2008.12.001

Rangan, K. (2008). *The cloud wars: $100+ billion at stake. Tech. rep*. Merrill Lynch.

Robert, F. (2009). Digital libraries: The systems analysis perspective: library in the clouds. OCLC Systems & Services. *International Digital Library Perspectives, 25*(3), 156–161.

Roy, B. (2008). Cloud computing: When computers really rule. Tech News World. Retrieved from http://www.technewsworld.com/story/63954.html

Salesforce. (2008). Salesforce.com for Google App engine: Connecting the clouds. Retrieved from http://developer.force.com/appengine

Salesforce. (2009). Salesforce customer relationships management (CRM) system. Retrieved from http://www.salesforce.com/

Schneider, B., & White, S. S. (2004). *Service quality: Research perspectives*. Thousand Oaks, CA: Sage Publications.

Siegele, L. (2008). Let it rise: A special report on corporate IT. The Economist.

Silvestre, J. (1987). Economies and diseconomies of scale. The New Palgrave: A Dictionary of Economics, Vol. 2, (pp. 80–84).

Soumya, B., Indrajit, M., & Mahanti, P. K. (2009). Cloud computing initiative using modified ant colony framework. World Academy of Science. *Engineering and Technology, 56*, 221.

Stephen, S. (2008). Google App Engine suffers outages. Retrieved from http://news.cnet.com/8301-10784_3-9971025-7.html

Stuer, G., Vanmechelena, K., & Broeckhovea, J. (2007). A commodity market algorithm for pricing substitutable grid resources. *Future Generation Computer Systems, 23*(5), 688–701. doi:10.1016/j.future.2006.11.004

Van, L. B., Gemmel, P., & Van, D. R. (Eds.). (2003). Services management: An integrated approach. Financial Times. Harlow, UK: Prentice Hall.

Varia, J. (2008). Amazon white paper on Cloud architectures. Retrieved from http://aws.typepad.com/aws/2008/07/white-paper-on.html

Vogels, W. (2008). A head in the clouds—The power of infrastructure as a service. In First Workshop on Cloud Computing and in Applications (CCA '08).

Yang, X. (2011). QoS-oriented service computing: Bring SOA into cloud environment. In Liu, X. (Ed.), *Advanced design approaches to emerging software systems: Principles, methodology and tools.* Hershey, PA: IGI Global. doi:10.4018/978-1-60960-735-7.ch013

Yang, X., Nasser, B., Surrige, M., & Middleton, S. (2012). A business-oriented cloud federation model for real time applications. In *Future generation computer systems.* Elsevier. doi:10.1016/j.future.2012.02.005

APPENDIX: WEIGHT ALLOCATION IN THE COMPONENT-DEFINITION TABLE

The expansion of the components is given below.

Definition Source	c1	c2	c3	c4	c5	c6	c7	c8	c9	c10	c11	c12	c13	c14	c15	c16	Total
Markus Klems	0.4	0.2		0.1	0.1	0.1	0.1										1
Reuven Cohen		0.4				0.1		0.3	0.2								1
Jeff Kaplan						0.2				0.4	0.4						1
Douglas Gourlay						0.4						0.4	0.2				1
Praising Gaw		0.6				0.4											1
Damon Edwards		0.5				0.2								0.3			1
Brian de Haaff											1						1
Ben Kepes										0.2	0.8						1
Kirill Sheynkman		0.3										0.4		0.3			1
Kevin Hartig												0.4	0.3	0.3			1
Jan Pritzker							0.1					0.2	0.3	0.3	0.1		1
Trevor Doerksen	0.2											0.8					1
Thorsten von Eicken						0.3							0.4	0.3			1
Don Dodge		0.3				0.4				0.3							1
Irving Wladawsky Berger												0.8	0.2				1
Ben Kepes						0.2				0.3				0.5			1
Bill Martin	0.2	0.2				0.2				0.1				0.3			1
Cloud computing and Grid computing 360 compared (Paper) [4]		0.4										0.1	0.3	0.2			1
Library in the clouds: (Paper) [49]						0.3							0.3	0.3		0.1	1
Cloud computing: ACM Communications (Article) [2]												0.7		0.3			1
Eucalyptus: an open-source cloud computing infrastructure (Paper)[47]		0.2				0.2						0.4		0.2			1
Cloud computing and emerging IT platforms: Vision, hype, and reality for delivering computing as the 5th utility (Paper) [50]						0.2							0.4	0.4			1
A Break in the Clouds: Towards a Cloud Definition (Paper) [8]		0.3								0.1		0.2		0.4			1
What Cloud Computing Really Means (InfoWorld Article) [51]	0.1	0.1				0.1						0.2	0.2	0.3			1
Cloud computing - the jargon is back! (Article) [52]			0.1			0.2	0.4						0.3				1
The Cloud Is The Computer (IEEE Article) [37]						0.2					0.4			0.4			1
Above the Clouds: A Berkeley View of Cloud Computing (Paper) [32]	0.1	0.2				0.1				0.2	0.2		0.2				1
A Taxonomy and Survey of Cloud Computing Systems (Paper) [53]		0.3											0.4	0.3			1
Cost-benefit analysis of cloud computing versus desktop grids (Paper) [53]				0.1	0.1		0.5			0.3							1
Cloud Computing Initiative using Modified Ant Colony Framework (Paper) (Soumya, Indrajit and Mahanti, 2009)		0.2				0.2			0.3					0.3			1
Service Performance and Analysis in Cloud Computing (Paper) [18]		0.3				0.2							0.3	0.2			1
Total	1	4.5	0.1	0.2	0.2	4.2	1.1	0.3	0.5	2.3	4.9	3.7	4.4	3.4	0.1	0.1	
Maximum	0.4	0.6	0.1	0.1	0.1	0.4	0.5	0.3	0.3	0.4	1	0.8	0.4	0.5	0.1	0.1	

Number	Component
c1	Elasticity/User Friendliness
c2	Scaling
c3	Reduced Time
c4	Under-Utilization
c5	Over-Utilization
c6	Internet/Web Service
c7	Automation of Resource provisioning
c8	Multi-Platform
c9	Data-Centric
c10	Hardware/Software Investment
c11	Utility Computing & SAAS, PAAS
c12	Virtualization
c13	Software/Service Model
c14	On Demand Computing
c15	Public facing API
c16	Extension of Client/Server

Chapter 2
Cloud Computing:
Past, Present, and Future

John P. Sahlin
The George Washington University, USA

ABSTRACT

Defining Cloud Computing can be difficult, as each organization often has its own spin on the definition. Despite being hard to define, Gartner Research named Cloud Computing as one of the top technologies to watch in 2010, 2011, and 2012. At its core, Cloud Computing is a technical architecture that meets a specific business need. This chapter traces the roots of Cloud Computing from its origins in mainframe distributed computing, discusses the basics of the Cloud Computing model today, and offers insights for future directions that are likely to be pursued in the Cloud Computing arena. A number of challenges to Cloud Computing are identified, including concerns of security and how to deal with the rise of mobile computing. The chapter ends with recommendations on how to choose which Cloud model is most appropriate to meet your organization's needs and how to establish a successful Cloud strategy.

INTRODUCTION: DEFINING THE CLOUD

I shall not today attempt further to define the kinds of material I understand to be embraced within that shorthand description; and perhaps I could never succeed in intelligibly doing so. But I know it when I see it. ~ Hon. Potter Stewart (U.S. Supreme Court Justice)

Why did Gartner Research place Cloud Computing at the top of the list of most important technology focus areas for the past three years straight

(Avram, 2011; Gartner, 2010; McDonald, 2010)? In today's world of tight budgets and even tighter profit margins, speed to capability is paramount; Cloud Computing has proven effective in enterprise class business environments (Zhang, Zhang, Chen, & Huo, 2010). As Golden (2010) identifies in the Harvard Business Review, Cloud Computing is a key enabler for the business agility so desperately sought since the advent of business operating on Internet time. Cloud Computing is frequently discussed in technology and business trade literature, but general consensus on the definition of Cloud is as nebulous as the image its name conjures.

DOI: 10.4018/978-1-4666-2854-0.ch002

The University of California, Berkeley describes Cloud Computing as providing the illusion of infinite computing resources to end users on demand while eliminating the upfront investment necessary to implement such services (Armbrust et al., 2009). Buyya, et. al. define Cloud Computing as separate from Grid or Cluster computing environments from a market perspective, identifying Cloud Computing as a function of participating communities entering into a contractual service agreement governed by Service Level Agreements (SLAs) (2009). Neither of these definitions is sufficiently broad to cover the various permutations of Cloud Computing industry today.

Perhaps the most comprehensive definition of Cloud Computing comes from the U.S. National Institute of Standards and technology NIST. According to Mell and Grance (2011), NIST defines Cloud Computing as having five separate characteristics and three basic models as shown in Table 1 and Figure 1.

The NIST definition of Cloud Computing provides a sufficiently broad definition to cover all types of Cloud models including public, private, and hybrid Cloud approaches and Cloud Computing efforts to improve the efficiency of an organization rather than to drive top line revenue growth. The primary failure of many Cloud Computing definitions (Armbrust et al., 2009) is that they are overly restrictive and focus solely on Cloud Computing as an Internet-based approach toward providing services to other clients and/or end users. While this approach is certainly valid, it ignores the very important use cases of Cloud Computing in the public sector to consolidate costs and save money or of private or public-private hybrid Clouds to enhance security and other services within an organization.

A careful review of the NIST definition of Cloud Computing shows that Cloud Computing is not really a new way of doing business, but a logical extension of computing models established during the 1960s with mainframe computing. Figure 1 traces the technology enablers that are necessary to effect Cloud Computing as defined by NIST. Most of these technology enablers have been in use by industry long before people started talking about the "Cloud." As anything other than an abstracted infrastructure that performs "stuff" (sometimes referred to as a "Magic Cloud"). Cloud Computing is not magic. It is the logical extension of a business model that has proven useful to businesses since the 1960s; the only real difference is that the technology has improved.

Table 1. NIST definition of cloud computing

Essential Characteristics of Cloud Computing	
On-demand service	Consumer can unilaterally (and automatically) provision computing capabilities such as server time and storage
Broad network access	Capabilities are available over a network and accessed by heterogeneous client base
Resource pooling	Computer resources are abstracted and pooled to serve multiple consumers
Rapid elasticity	Capabilities can be rapidly provisioned to scale up, out, or down quickly to meet changing business needs
Measured Service	Metering service to monitored and control resources automatically for optimized resource allocation
Cloud Computing Service Models	
Software as a Service (SaaS)	Consumer accesses a service provider's applications through a network infrastructure with no underlying control of the infrastructure or application capabilities/baseline or need for application maintenance
Platform as a Service (PaaS)	Consumer deploys and maintains applications in a pre-defined development of production environment (environment includes predefined set of tools and programming languages)
Infrastructure as a Service (IaaS)	Consumer deploys and maintains applications (including operating system) on automatically provisioned computing capabilities (e.g., server time, storage, network, etc.)

Figure 1. Cloud computing models and technology enablers

Cloud Computing Models: A Stairway to the Clouds			Cloud Computing Technology Enablers			
IaaS	PaaS	SaaS	IaaS	PaaS	SaaS	Service Management
		End User Application	• Server Virtualization • Virtual Networking • Data Encryption • Storage Area Networking (SAN) • Network Attached Storage (NAS) • Community of Interest (COI) Segregation	• Application Virtualization • Desktop Virtualization • Virtual Desktop Interface (VDI) • Containerized Applications • Automated Provisioning • Map/Reduce	• Service Oriented Architecture (SOA) • Enterprise Service Bus (ESB) • Data Service Bus • Data Distribution Service (DDS) • Standardized Data Dictionary / Ontology	• Network Monitoring • Application Platform Interface (API) • Quality of Service (QoS) Management
	Core Applications, Development Environment					
Virtualization, Operating System, Patch Management,						
Hardware, Network, Facilities						
Service Management						

ORIGIN OF A MODEL: A HISTORY OF CLOUD COMPUTING

One's past is what one is. It is the only way by which people should be judged. ~ Oscar Wilde

Clearly, Cloud Computing represents a new way of doing business, but is it really new? Is Cloud Computing just hype, or is there substance behind the punditry? Before any realistic discourse regarding the benefits of Cloud Computing can begin, it is critical to understand the origins of Cloud Computing in other Distributed Variable Rate Computing Models.

As Lenk, Klems, Nimis, Tai, and Sandholm argue, the Cloud Computing model is characterized by virtualization of physical infrastructure resources, middleware applications, business applications, and network services (2009). The underlying technology to virtualize these services and resources was not developed specifically for Cloud Computing, but helped establish the rise of Cloud Computing as the model for enabling flexibility and growth in business enterprise (Golden, 2010; Zhang et al., 2010). Table 2 describes the basic evolution of computing models and technology advancements that ultimately led to the Cloud Computing model's evolution as well as a list of the key references used to draw the links from one model/technology to the next.

As is true with any technology advancement, the linkages from the mainframe computing model to Cloud Computing is not a dialectic model with strong one-to-one relationships; it more resembles a family tree structure, where a single model influenced a number of technology advancements, which enabled new models of computing. Figure 2 describes the basic "genealogy" of Cloud Computing (categorized by the three Cloud service models as defined by NIST) as it evolved from mainframe computing through Electronic Data Information (EDI) Value Added Networks (VAN) and Application Service Providers (ASPs), ultimately leading to what is known as Cloud Computing today. Figure 2 indicates not only the links in the evolutionary chain, but also identifies the literature reflected in this paper that helps establish those links.

After a review of the available literature, it is clear that while technology advancements have driven an evolving face of distributed computing, the nature of distributed computing has not changed in the past 50 years. Clear linkages exist from the mainframe distributed computing model of the 1960s to today's Cloud Computing model.

Mainframe Timeplexing and EDI VANs

In the 1960s, the value of computers had moved beyond scientific research and into the business world. The unique ability of mainframe computers to allocate processing capacity in discrete sections to process diverse functions simultaneously made it highly useful to large corporations needing flexible solutions to process massive amounts of data in multiple ways. Originally, the mainframe computer was able to provide processing capability to remote users to conduct limited tasks, but in the late 1960s and early 1970s, the business world's need for flexibility drove explosive growth in innovation and new capabilities were delivered with an almost frantic pace (Greenstein & Wade, 1998). In the early 1970s, the research to leverage the resource allocation architecture of mainframes resulted in the same server virtualization models that are in use today (Ueno & Hasegawa, 2009). Because of their flexibility and capacity for rapid scaling to multiple simultaneous functions, mainframe computing systems became commonplace (if not a standard of excellence) in the business world. In the 1970s, this distributed computing model was applied to large corporations with a need to maintain and manage data that was housed at different offices or subsidiary organizations (Kossmann, 2000). The object of this model was to leverage the capabilities of mainframe servers to process multiple tasks at the same time to provide computing resources from a shared infrastructure throughout a distributed complex of offices within a large corporation.

The EDI VAN concept expanded the mainframe distributed computing model of distributing server resources by extending computing resources to outside partner organizations. Procurement, invoicing, shipping, and warehousing data were transferred across a network of computers from one company to another. This approach was originally intended to replace paper communications with electronic communication to increase the speed of communications and reduce the need for paper invoicing (Bailey, & Bakos, 1997). The true value of EDI VANs soon came to light as their use was shown to improve efficiency and reduce costs of doing business (Smith & Kumar, 2004).

What is common to both models is the need to abstract the computing system from the business users. Key to this abstraction is the ability to establish a virtual infrastructure that is available to external users and/or subscribers. As discussed by Peterson, Shenker, and Turner (2005), the need to provide a common infrastructure that was available to many users in various abstracted forms eventually led to the development of virtualization technology. The collaborative nature of EDI VANs drove a requirement to establish virtual networks within a physical network infrastructure to ensure that sharing financial EDI with a partner did not result in accidental data spillage to other partners within the EDI VAN (Peterson, Shenker, & Turner, 2005). One significant challenge to general adoption of the mainframe computing model of abstracting hardware was the fact that the x86 server architecture did not support true virtualization (Adams & Agesen, 2005), resulting in significant performance loss when virtualizing servers. Intel and AMD soon overcame this hurdle and server virtualization model gained rapid acceptance in the mid- and small-business companies that could not normally afford expensive mainframe and EDI infrastructures.

Table 2. Brief history of cloud computing literature

Timeline	Approach / Technology	General Aspects of Approach	References
1960s	Mainframe / Timeplexing	Sharing of distributed resources	Bailey & Bakos
1980s	EDI VAN	Extension of distributed resources across multiple partners to enable efficient financial transactions	Bailey & Bakos; Peterson, Shenker, & Turner
1985	Virtualization	Abstraction of hardware platforms from software applications	Barham, et al.; Soletsz, et al.; Peterson, Shenker, Turner
1993	Application/ Network/ Website Monitoring	Provide condition and performance assessment of infrastructure	Mell & Grance; Peterson, Shenker, &Turner; Seltsikas & Currie
1998	B2B E-Commerce	Extend EDI VAN model to allow dynamic addition of business partners and include more transaction types	Bailey & Bakos
1999	Application Service Provider	Provide outsourced utility computing model for infrastructure and applications; abstract the data center from the organization	Barham, et al.; Soletsz, et al.; Peterson, Shenker, Turner; Seltsikas & Currie; Smith & Kumar; Soletsz, et al.
2005	Service Oriented Architecture	Abstract the application form the end user; provide all data as tagged service to which people/systems could subscribe	Chang, He, & Castro-Leon
2008	Cloud Computing	Provide everything as a service (i.e. applications, data, infrastructure), enable automatic provisioning and metered services	Chang, He, & Castro-Leon; Chouhan; Lenk, et al.; Mell & Grance; Motahari-Nezhad, Stephenson & Singhal

B2B E-Commerce and the Application Service Provider

In the late 1990s, experiments with electronic commerce became common. Despite spectacular failures, it was generally accepted that an e-commerce presence on the Internet was necessary for a retail company to survive. The advent of e-commerce resulted in a resurgence of interest in the success of EDI VANs to improve efficiency of transactions between businesses (Bailey & Bakos, 1997). Two critical technologies converged to enable this new Business to Business Electronic Commerce (B2B E-Commerce) model: increased security and adoption of the Internet, and adoption of standards for transactions and interfaces between companies (Albrecht, Dean, & Hansen, 2005). The EDI VANs established a set of standards for business to business interaction, and allowed to flexibility and scalability to add new organizations into the B2B partnership rapidly. These standards evolved from proprietary agreements among large organizations; their eventual adoption as industry-wide standards resulted in significant reductions in cost, delays, and errors associated with manual processing (Albrecht et al., 2005).

As B2B E-Commerce was evolving, the ASP model of delivering applications to clients using the Internet as a transport mechanism was also developing. The ASP delivered software to companies as a service and often provided per seat or per office licensing fees over a period of time (Seltsikas & Currie, 2002). This model was especially attractive to mid-sized companies needing to support their growing businesses, but lacking the capital (or will to absorb the risk) necessary to build enterprise-class infrastructures. According to Smith and Kumar (2004), the rapid adoption of the ASP model was heavily influenced by the desire to have information systems that support an increasingly distributed workforce.

The ASP model drew from the virtualization technologies used in EDI VANs and applied emerging technology that provided pools of data storage and applications in a packaged mechanism, further abstracting the software from the hardware layers of infrastructure. As Barham et al. noted the increase in server storage requirements for distributed data systems drove a need to pool units of storage to enable flexible scaling of the data storage (2003). The virtualization of data storage units was delivered first by Storage Area Networks (SANs) and later by Network Attached Storage (NAS) devices. Both enabled organizations to allocate storage dynamically to a system, even at times with no disruption of service. Another adaptation of the server virtualization technology allowed a company to establish virtual platforms that were fully supported and maintained; ASP clients no longer needed to worry about losing application function due to server maintenance because the application "container" could be shifted to alternate computing and network resources (Soletz, Potzl, Fiuczynski, Bavier, & Peterson, 2007).

Virtualization was not the only technology that the EDI VANs contributed to the advent of the ASP. The methods used by EDI VANs for monitoring networks and the development of application programming interfaces (APIs) to ensure the interfaces were functioning properly were key technology enablers for the ASP market. A critical component of providing software as a service was the ability to monitor and manage the network's performance as well as that of the service provided (Mell & Grance, 2011). Smith and Kumar (2004) indicate that one of the most attractive benefits of the ASP model to industry was that it replaced the best effort model support provided by corporate Information Technology (IT) organizations with a contractually obligated Service Level Agreement (SLA) to maintain a certain amount of responsiveness, server availability, etc. In order to ensure performance (and prevent loss of revenue), an ASP needed to be able to monitor the services they provided; ideally, an ASP would know of a problem and have resolved it long before the client noticed the issue. Because the ASP provided more than simple network

Figure 2. Genealogy of cloud computing

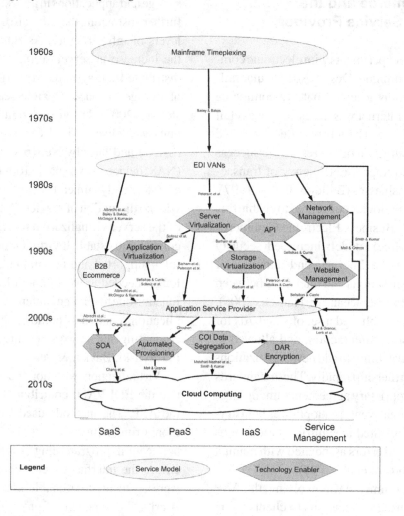

transport and EDI interfaces, reliable methods of monitoring application and website performance was necessary (Seltsikas & Currie, 2002).

SOA and Cloud Computing

The ASP model spawned a new wave of technology providers that offered applications as a service rather than as a permanent asset. The concept of delivering IT infrastructure as a service eventually evolved into designing systems with service orientation in mind. In 2006, Chang, He, and Castro-Leon argue that service-orientation of infrastructure would have dramatic impacts on how IT infrastructure is managed. This prediction

came true and was realized in what is now known as Cloud Computing.

ASPs were the first organizations to implement business models and pricing structures to offer acquisition of software as a monthly service fee (Weinhardt, Anandasivam, Blau, & Stößer, 2009). This emerging market drove significant changes in the way applications were developed. Software developers realized that designing applications to operate as services would simplify management of the application and underlying infrastructure and help reduce overall operating costs for the service provider (Chang, He, & Castro-Leon, 2006). This Service Oriented Architecture (SOA) for application development enabled providers to provide an abstraction layer among the external functionality or software, the data being exposed to other systems, and the underlying architecture. Albrecht, Dean, and Hansen argue that SOA is actually an extension of the requirements for service discovery and transactions that were first seen in EDI Vans and eventually in B2B E-Commerce (2005). SOA development relies on new technologies such as standardized Extensible Markup Language (XML) messaging, publication of services using the Web Services Definition Language (WSDL), and discovery of available services using the Universal Description Discovery and Integration (UDDI) registry (McGregor & Kumaran, 2002).

In order to keep sustainment costs low, ASPs needed to find a way to provide applications in a predictable and automated manner. As Chouhan argued, automatic provisioning technology helped ASPs reduce maintenance costs and provide a stable baseline across a heterogeneous client enterprise, increasing the overall effectiveness of the client support organization (2006). Smith and Kumar (2004) noted that security of data was of paramount concern for ASPs as they hosted business-critical (and often proprietary) data for a variety of clients; this issue became even more critical for the Cloud Computing model, as platforms and infrastructure are virtualized into an often single pool of resources to be shared across the entire enterprise. As technology for data segregation improved, the ASP models for separating customer data using physical separation of data stores (e.g., separate spindles within a SAN, physically separate NAS devices, etc.) evolved to Community of Interest (COI) Segregation with encryption (Motahari-Nezhad, Stephenson, & Singhal, 2009).

As defined by NIST, the ability to monitor services provided is critical to a successful Cloud Computing environment (Mell & Grance, 2011). ASPs struggled with these same issues of monitoring and Service Level Agreement; the technologies developed for ASPs combined with the ability to provision services and applications automatically greatly enhanced the ability for organizations to meter those services (Chouhan, 2006; Smith & Kumar, 2004). Jiang and Xu offered an interesting model for ASPs based on automatic provisioning of services on a hosting utility platform; the Service on Demand Architecture (SODA) model of metering services dynamically based not only on subscription but also usage demand (2003).

The SODA model is exactly the type of metering services NIST describes as necessary for a successful Cloud Computing environment (Mell & Grance, 2011). Lenk, Klems, Nimis, and Tai argue that the increasingly available batch of new technologies and interfaces associated with SOA development in a Web 2.0 environment greatly improves the nature of the services available in the ASP model and transforms many ASPs to computing Clouds (2009). Because most Cloud services are provisioned via the Internet as web services and because of general adoption of standards such as UDDI and WSDL for development and declaration of web services, the SOA framework is a natural fit for managing the orchestration, discovery, publication, subscription, and visualization of Cloud services (Wang, Tao, Kunze, & Rattu, 2008).

The dynamic nature of the Cloud Computing paradigm sets it apart from other models discussed. The NIST definition of Cloud Computing identifies "on-demand self-service" as the first essential characteristic of Cloud Computing (Mell & Grance, 2011). As Chouhan argue, the use of automated provisioning services would greatly extend the ASP model to allow more dynamic provisioning of services and enable the Cloud (2009). Buyya, Yeo, Venugopal, Broberg, and Brandic (2008) identify dynamism as the key identifying characteristic of Cloud Computing, but also note that the Cloud model highly leveraged the successes of past distributed computing models such as ASP, B2B E-Commerce, and others by relying on virtualization (server, network, and storage), Service Level Agreements and advanced systems monitoring, and integrated web services.

The Cumulus project by the Rochester Institute of Technology to integrate a series of scientific grid computing infrastructures into a single Cloud identifies the primary difference between the grid infrastructures and the Cloud design as its dynamic quality for users to customize their interface to the system and demand resources in terms of performance requirements (i.e. SLAs) rather than in discrete units of capacity (e.g., n number of servers, y amount of network bandwidth, etc.) (Wang, & von Laszewski, 2008).

CLOUD COMPUTING IN THE PRESENT

He who controls the present, controls the past. He who controls the past, controls the future.
~ George Orwell

While the distributed model is not necessarily a new model, the technologies associated with modern Clouds have certainly advanced in the past 50 years. These technological advances have made possible such evolutionary changes in the way technology is used by consumers that it warranted a new name: Cloud Computing. What has characterized this modern instantiation of distributed variable rate computing is its adaptability to customer demand. Users can request new applications and infrastructure on demand, even requesting elastic services that expand and contract with traffic usage. The modern Cloud Computing environment is like a highway that adds lanes during rush hour, but shrinks to a single lane road at 2 AM to conserve resources.

When people are asked to give examples of Cloud Computing, most would make references to Amazon's or Microsoft's services, or one of a few e-book systems. While these models do indeed qualify as Clouds, Cloud Computing is so much more than accessing applications using the pay per view on demand model. Today, Cloud Computing models for business take one of three general approaches, which coincide with the three implementation models identified in the NIST definition of Cloud Computing: Application Stores (SaaS), Storage Clouds (IaaS), and Application Development Platforms (PaaS). After discussing these three models, this chapter will explore the primary differences among Cloud Implementation Models, and finally discuss the many challenges associated with Service Level Agreements (SLAs) in Cloud Computing.

Application Stores: Software for Sale

As mentioned previously, this model for Cloud Computing is probably the best understood by the general population. At its most basic, a service provider allows on demand access to software applications that can be downloaded instantly to a user device (often a smart phone or other portable device). The application may be available for a limited time (following the pay per view model of cable service providers) or as a permanent installation. Since the early evolution of this model by ASPs, several industry leaders have adopted this model for deploying applications, most notably, Microsoft and Oracle. Even federal agencies are adopting this Cloud Computing model: the U.S. Defense Information Systems Agency (DISA) now provides applications on demand for users.

In 1998, USinternetworking was founded by executives from Digex, Sun Microsystems, and SGI to evolve the hosting market into a new model of providing both infrastructure and applications as a managed service to clients. USi provided a new model for enterprise applications such as e-mail, Enterprise Resource Planning (ERP), and Customer Relationship Management (CRM) delivered over the Internet with a fixed monthly cost and little capital investment. The intent was to revolutionize the industry and make high end applications available to small and mid-size organizations. The result was an explosion of providers offering managed application services in remote data centers and the birth of the ASP industry. Major players in the ERP and CRM markets took advantage of this model and offered their enterprise applications as services including Oracle's Business On Line (BOL) and Siebel's SalesForce.com, both leaders in the Cloud Computing industry today.

Microsoft also offers its Office productivity suite as an on demand subscription service with the Office 365 offering with price points and services intended for business professionals, or small to mid-sized companies. The value of this offering extends beyond simple access to the applications; these services can include 24x7 technical support and guaranteed availability of up to 99.9% (Microsoft, 2012). Microsoft's partner organizations specializing in Cloud Computing have extended the Office 365 suite to provide even more services to client organizations. CenterBeam, Inc. began as a managed desktop service organization and has since expanded its offerings to extend its service offerings to include a Cloud-based service, which is based on the Microsoft Office Desktop Productivity Suite, but provides additional capabilities for administration and detailed security options not available in Office 365 and traditionally associated with on-premise application deployment (CenterBeam, 2012). Founded in 2002, Managed Solution, Inc. started as a technical consulting firm helping companies implement and manage networking solutions, but quickly evolved into a service-based organization. Managed Solution extends the capabilities of the Microsoft Business Productivity Online Suite by providing active monitoring and management of the Cloud-based solution, as well as adding Cloud based unified communications and managed infrastructure services to provide a full complement of business productivity services that integrate with remote and on-premise technical support personnel for its clients (Managed Solution, 2012).

Despite what many have argued, Cloud Computing is not restricted to the private sector, focused on selling services for a fee. The United States Defense Information Systems Agency (DISA) is one of many federal government agencies that established an enterprise Cloud infrastructure to capitalize on the successes of private companies to provide scalable, on demand computing resources to make capabilities available to the government agency enterprise (Lentz, 2009). The DISA Rapid Access Computing Environment (RACE) was designed to allow Department of Defense (DoD) activities on demand access to applications and other enterprise data resources in both the classified and unclassified environments (Defense Information Systems Agency, 2009). With RACE, an end user can purchase, and download applications within 24 hours of initial request, far less than the typical DoD acquisition cycle which often takes as long as two years to field a new system to an operational fleet (Defense Information Systems Agency, 2010). The largest challenge to Cloud Computing in the public sector is establishing business value for the investments required to develop a private Cloud when security concerns prevent the use of a public Cloud model, as the public sector operates on a cost basis rather than a profit basis (Sahlin, 2011).

Storage Clouds

As the need for data grows, IT professionals are faced with a quandary: where will all of this data (files, emails, documents, archives, copies of copies, etc.) be stored? Virtualizing the storage containers is a cost-effective method for providing an enterprise storage solution. The advent of the Infrastructure as a Service (IaaS) model of Cloud Computing offers a slight twist on the enterprise storage model. Unlike the enterprise virtual storage approach that large scale companies have been pursuing more than 20 years, Storage Clouds democratize the offering, allowing small businesses and even private individuals access to this otherwise enterprise storage solution with high reliability and a relatively low usage cost.

Sometimes referred to as storage as a service, Storage Clouds differ from most virtualized storage solutions in that the data is stored across multiple servers within a large scale infrastructure rather than on dedicated servers normally associated with traditional network storage solutions (Wu, Ping, Ge, Wang, & Fu, 2010). Dispersion of storage resources claims a number of benefits to the end user, including reliability, elasticity, and cost effectiveness. The reliability benefit of this approach is clear: storage Clouds would be architected with sufficient redundancy to ensure that a loss of one node would not result in a system outage (Wu, Ping, Ge, Wang, & Fu, 2010); building redundancy into the system architecture allows providers to offer storage services with availability guarantees of up to 99.999% (Henderson & Allen, 2010). Elasticity benefits the end user by providing virtually limitless storage. As a user's storage needs increase, the service provider simply increases the service level (at an additional fee). The service provider is responsible for managing the size of the infrastructure and will provide system upgrades as necessary to ensure sufficient capacity.

The appeal of reduced costs is a strong one for both large enterprises seeking to cut operating costs and small businesses who lack the capital for major infrastructure investment. Storage Clouds are very attractive in this regard as they generally offer very low usage rates in comparison to the investment required for a high availability enterprise storage solution. It is important, however, for each enterprise to conduct a cost benefit analysis of entering into a long term lease arrangement with a Storage Cloud provider. In a recent study, Walker, Brisken, and Romney determined that depending on the duration of the arrangement and amount of storage required over time, leasing storage from a Cloud service provider may prove to be far more expensive from a net present value perspective in the long run (2010).

Amazon led the charge among Storage Cloud service providers, offering the Simple Storage Service (S3) and the Elastic Compute Cloud (EC2) as storage offerings (Wang, Wang, Ren, & Lou,

2009). With service offerings priced low enough for an individual to purchase storage with a credit card, all users had access to elastic, high availability storage. Other service providers followed, including Rackspace, Nirvanix, and Egnyte. Each provider offers different levels of service and the restrictions vary. Rackspace and Amazon limit storage objects to 5 GB; Nirvanix does not provide a Service Level Agreement with its standard offering (SLAs are available at a premium price); and each provider offers different levels of storage security. In a study of Storage Cloud providers, Henderson and Allen found that while Amazon provided the poorest speeds for downloads, it also provided the most flexible platform (2010).

Two significant issues with Storage Clouds include latency associated with remote storage and security of storing critical data in the Clouds. The issue of security will be discussed later in this chapter. While providing a great deal of flexibility and reliability, Storage Clouds often have issues of system latency. Latency of virtualized storage is not limited to Storage Clouds, and has resulted in a variety of tiered storage models in large scale enterprises to optimize the performance of high value/often used data in a virtualized infrastructure (Coughlin, 2010). What is unique to the public Storage Cloud model is the reliance on the Internet for access to the remote storage. Latency associated with Internet transport can be driven by a variety of causes including issues with the local Internet Service Provider (ISP), congestion during recurring peak traffic times, and the occasional special event such as the Victoria's Secret Lingerie Show.

Application Development Platforms: Hadoop and the Rise of Platform Clouds

The various Cloud Computing offerings available today are focused on providing distributed computing resources to the small enterprises and even private individuals. Storage Clouds (IaaS) provide space for data storage either for online access or offline archiving, and Application Hosting services (SaaS) provide software to end users on a service fee model (similar to Pay Per View cable programming). The final model of Cloud Computing (PaaS) is geared less to the end user and more toward the application developer. By providing a set of standardized and powerful APIs, the PaaS providers have enabled software developers to focus solely on the main processes and presentation of information, rather than attempt to code to a complex distributed infrastructure. It also allows the developer to take advantage of massive parallelism, which greatly enhances performance of complex operations across a broad infrastructure. The argument supporting Cloud Computing was the exact slogan used by many Application Service Providers: let the service provider worry about IT infrastructure (bottom line savings) while the service consumer worries about serving its clients and increasing sales (top line growth). The overall business model is to allow software vendors to provide their software to clients on a monthly service fee vice a capital investment for infrastructure, software licensing, and installation/configuration (Chappell, 2009a).

Some industry players presume to redefine the term "platform" and suggest that by offering a prebuilt Operating System and application base for use by clients constitutes a platform service model; this in fact is tantamount to relabeling a hosted application. According to NIST, the PaaS model must include not only the prepackaged environment and suite of applications, but also a set of tools to modify the environment (Mell & Grance, 2011). The core value of a PaaS offering (and what sets it apart from the other models) is the ability to develop new applications that would be made available in the Cloud. PaaS is about jumpstarting the application development process and providing a distributed development environment across a virtualized infrastructure (Kambatla, Pathak, & Pucha, 2009).

Not surprisingly to many, leaders in the Software as a Service model such as Microsoft and SalesForce.com have entered into the Platform as a Service market, offering a distributed computing model for its applications. Microsoft's Azure platform makes available office applications, while allowing companies to "focus on solving business problems and addressing customer needs" (O'Neill, 2009; Windows Azure Platform, 2012). The Windows Azure service provides an environment for developing and running Windows-based applications in Microsoft Data Centers for use by remote site clients (Chappell, 2009).

Perhaps the most challenging aspect of establishing a platform for developing applications is providing a method for applications developers to write code to a completely abstracted hardware and software environment. The increasing ubiquity and power of threaded architecture servers brought a new challenge to distributed computing applications: how does one distribute threaded processes across multiple servers to take advantage of parallelism without redeveloping the application? The developers at Google found an answer by developing a feature called Map/Reduce, which allows them to process petabytes of data each day across a heterogeneous environment (Dean & Ghemawat, 2008). The Map/Reduce function analyses an inherently threaded process, breaks it into a series of subprocesses that can be run across thousands of dissimilar computing nodes, and recompiles the final solution (Sandholm & Lai, 2009).

This is a critical technology advancement for Cloud service providers because Map/Reduce and other Data-Intensive Scalable Computing (DISC) based solutions eliminate the problem of queue backlogs that are often caused in local clusters of threaded processors attempting to conduct multiple processes at once (Sandholm and Lai, 2009; Wang, Que, Yu, Goldenberg, & Sehgal, 2011). Even small clusters of high performance servers can seem slow because they attempt to force all processes through a single process queue, which becomes backlogged, resulting in performance congestion. Similar to a two lane highway, the system is able to operate at high speeds during off peak times, but queue backlogs result in traffic congestion during the rush hour commute. In contrast, the Map/Reduce function sends the threads to multiple queues in shorter bursts (alternate routes via surface streets). This separation of process queues results in fewer queue backlogs, and significantly performance advantages over traditional High Performance Computing architectures (Hill & Humphrey, 2009).

The Google Application Engine leverages the Map/Reduce function as well as other rich APIs to establish a DISC-based development environment on a massively scalable infrastructure (Sledziewski, Bordbar, & Anane, 2010). The GAE Software Developer's Kit runs on local machines to simulate the Cloud environment, but takes advantage of the Cloud infrastructure by passing mapped subprocesses to the back-end infrastructure in a massively parallel fashion, and then compiling the final solution prior to presentation. By abstracting the underlying infrastructure to the application developer, the Map/Reduce API simplifies the application development process, and allows the developer to focus on the functionality of the application while relying on the Map/Reduce API to determine how best to leverage the underlying infrastructure.

Google's sole ownership of the Map/Reduce function was short-lived. Soon enough, the open source community solved the distributed computing problem with Hadoop, an open architecture development platform including a Map/Reduce feature. Hadoop revolutionized the PaaS market, enabling several organizations to make distributed computing infrastructures to the Cloud application development community, leveraging an open source development environment that is designed to scale from a single node to thousands of nodes in a heterogeneous computing environment (Apache Hadoop, 2012). Quick adoption of Hadoop's open architecture led to an explosion of PaaS offerings in the commercial market, including the Amazon Elastic Compute Cloud (EC2), Eucalyptus (Elastic Utility Computing Architecture for Linking Your Programs To Useful Systems), Facebook, and IBM's Blue Cloud (Borthakur, et al. 2011; Kambalta, Pathak, & Pucha, 2009; Sandholm and Lai, 2009).

One further benefit of DISC architectures such as Hadoop is that this massive parallelism across a heterogeneous environment enables a true utility computing model for Cloud service providers. By making the Map/Reduce function available to the OA development community, the Hadoop user community helped ushered in a revolution in the application development market and transformed Cloud Computing. By leveraging an abstracted heterogeneous environment, a Cloud service provider can increase or decrease system performance based on usage simply by adding more map functions (Borthakar, et al., 2011; Kambalta, Pathak, & Pucha, 2009). Before this technology, service providers were forced to provide oversized infrastructure to ensure adequate performance during peak usage, clearly an inefficient and complex method of doing business.

Hadoop's famous ease of use makes platform Clouds accessible to developers who are not accustomed to distributed environments. However, Hadoop and other DISC solutions have a few areas for improvement. Hadoop's underlying structure of serialized recompiling has been criticized as a source of performance backlog (Wang, et al. 2011). Further, while Hadoop is well regarded as easy to set up, it has hundreds of individual configuration settings; optimizing Hadoop can be a challenge for even the most advanced user (Kambalta, Pathak, & Pucha, 2009).

Cloud Implementation Models

Despite early arguments that Cloud services must be provided over the Internet, a variety of implementation models have evolved in the Cloud Computing industry. Today, most industry analysts recognize three separate implementation models for Cloud Computing: public Clouds, private

Clouds, and hybrid Clouds. The following definitions are provided from the NIST definition of Cloud Computing (Mell & Grance, 2011).

- **Private Cloud:** The Cloud infrastructure is provisioned for exclusive use by a single organization comprising multiple consumers (e.g., business units). It may be owned, managed, and operated by the organization, a third party, or some combination of them, and it may exist on or off premises.
- **Public Cloud:** The Cloud infrastructure is provisioned for open use by the general public. It may be owned, managed, and operated by a business, academic, or government organization, or some combination of them. It exists on the premises of the Cloud provider.
- **Hybrid Cloud:** The Cloud infrastructure is a composition of two or more distinct Cloud infrastructures (private, community, or public) that remain unique entities, but are bound together by standardized or proprietary technology that enables data and application portability (e.g., Cloud bursting for load balancing between Clouds).

Each implementation model has its benefits and challenges; a public Cloud offers a maximum accessibility for end users and requires the lowest initial capital investment requirement. In addition, public Clouds could be considered more "green" as they consolidate computing resources and ultimately save energy; in a recent white paper by SalesForce.com, the public Cloud model can effect up to a 95% reduction in infrastructure and energy costs compared to an on-premise infrastructure (2011). The main drawback many identify with the public Cloud is in the realm of security. Many are concerned about access of private information via the Internet due to poor security practices; other security concerns focus on the notion that all of one's data eggs are in one public basket – if the public Cloud fails, all

access to data and applications are interrupted (Intel IT Center, 2011; Sahlin, 2011). The private Cloud model is the contrapositive to the public Cloud model: where the public Cloud exists in a remote outsourced datacenter, the private Cloud is insourced in a corporate datacenter and may be accessed via the Internet but may also be limited to a corporate intranet or Virtual Private Network (VPN) connection. While the private Cloud may require more capital investment to establish an environment, there are significant arguments favoring a private Cloud over a public Cloud. The main strength of the private Cloud approach is the direct control an organization has over the infrastructure and services offered (Ideas International, 2011; Intel IT Center, 2011). An organization offering a private Cloud can tailor exactly which services are provided and what QoS is provided; a public Cloud environment must cater to the majority of client organizations in order to maintain profitability. Further, a technically savvy organization can actually save money by implementing a private Cloud because it can focus only on the services it needs and not pay for superfluous services that do not directly add business value; an Oracle white paper details an organization that achieved a 90% Total Ownership Cost (TOC) savings by implementing a streamlined private Cloud (Bain, Merchant, Minns, & Thomas, 2010)

Service Level Agreements (SLAs): Monitoring Cloud Performance

One of the primary characteristics of Cloud Computing models that set it apart from other clustered system architectures (e.g., corporate mainframe systems, extranets, etc.,) is that the performance of a Cloud Computing is based on expectations set by Service Level Agreements (SLAs) (Buyya, et. al., 2009). These SLAs establish the degree of service that will be provided and may include metrics for Quality of Service (QoS), overall availability (A_o), and customer service ticket performance (Sahlin, Sarkani, and Mazzuchi, 2011; Sahlin,

Sarkani, and Mazzuchi, 2012). These SLAs developed primarily from the ASP market as ASPs began to provide hosted applications with some guarantee of service and performance. An SLA is a contractual commitment between the Cloud Service Provider (CSP) and the Cloud service consumer stating that the service will be available for a given percentage of time (usually 99% or higher) and may include performance metrics such as customer service ticket resolution (e.g., first call resolution percentage, average time to resolve, etc.) or QoS. The penalty for failing to meet these SLAs is usually a payment by the CSP to the client and usually takes the form of a refund against the next monthly service fee. SLAs may include the right for a consumer to end the service agreement if the CSP fails to meet its SLA obligations for a number of performance periods.

SLAs are critical in order for the Cloud Computing service model to function in a public environment. The issue of SLAs becomes more complex in a private Cloud environment. Can an organization fire itself for failure to meet its SLA obligations? Perhaps not. Even if internal "customers" cannot terminate a service agreement with an internal CSP, these metrics can serve as decision support tools to justify alternate sourcing decisions for the service that may include transitioning to an external CSP if the internal team continues to fail meeting its obligations.

One challenge of developing useful SLAs in a Cloud Computing environment is the dependence on the Internet and/or other extended networks (e.g., corporate Extranet) for a significant portion of the end to end transport of data and services. How can an organization commit to a level of service when a significant portion is dependent on a system under which the organization has no control? Generally, SLAs are restricted to availability of service as measured from the external edge of the CSP's architecture (usually a border gateway router or some other externally facing device). In this way, the CSP can avoid making

SLA payments to its clients because of a large scale service interruption of major Internet Service Providers or large scale power outages.

A second major challenge of developing meaningful SLAs is in defining what one means by availability and QoS. As mentioned previously, overall availability (A_O) can take many forms and is generally advertised as inclusive of the entire system; after careful inspection of the terms and conditions of the service agreement, it becomes clear that the "system" ends with the CSP's edge router. QoS is even more difficult to measure. Many CSPs provide QoS guarantees in terms of the IEEE Standard 802.16 for Local and Metropolitan Area Networks thresholds for acceptable signal loss and jitter, or guaranteed performance by citing benchmarks for Commercial Off the Shelf (COTS) equipment such as provided by the Standard Performance Evaluation Cooperative (SPEC.org) (2011). An alternative to providing performance benchmarks is for the CSP to ensure dedicated access to a subset of the Cloud Computing infrastructure in terms of lease agreements (Buyya, et. al. 2009). Sahlin, Sarkani, and Mazzuchi propose an alternate QoS metric based on the overall end to end System Goodput (G_S) of a distributed computing architecture (2012). This G_S metric combines a variety of end to end service performance metrics and should be adopted by CSPs in order to provide meaningful SLAs.

THE FUTURE OF CLOUD COMPUTING

Science fiction writers foresee the inevitable, and although problems and catastrophes may be inevitable, solutions are not. ~ Isaac Asimov

Predicting the future of trends in technology is tricky business. How can we with any confidence take a stand regarding how technology will evolve? Edward Cornish, co-founder of the World Future

Society and editor of The Futurist magazine, argues that while we cannot accurately predict specific futures, we can depend on a certain continuity between past and present to predict where technology may evolve. Cornish identified six "Supertrends" that shape the future: Technological Progress, Economic Growth, Improving Health, Increasing Mobility, Environmental Decline, and Increasing Deculturalization (2004). Cloud Computing trends are shaped heavily by four of these six Supertrends (Technological Progress, Economic Growth, Increasing Mobility, and Increasing Deculturalization). By identifying how these Supertrends affect the path technology evolution can take, one can predict how Cloud Computing will be shaped by those forces to increase mobility and force technology to mature in order to support economic growth in various places.

When discussing the future of technology one must evaluate current trends in comparison to the technology's history. This chapter has traced the beginnings of Cloud Computing, linking it to early distributed computing architectures such as Time Sharing and Multiplexing, and following the technology evolution through EDI VANs, e-commerce, and the ASP market. The current Cloud Computing models and trends toward open source development and massive parallelism (as evidenced by the strong popularity of frameworks such as Hadoop) point to four specific future areas for evolution in the Cloud Computing arena:

- Computing Climates
- Microclimates
- Swarm Computing
- Cloud Services as a Service (CSaaS)

Computing Climates: Self-Organizing Cloud Communities

When thinking about the future for Cloud Computing, the 2002 movie Minority Report comes to mind. In one scene in this movie the main character

Chief John Anderton (played by Tom Cruise) stood in the middle of a holographic computer interface, dragging and dropping screens using thin air as a virtual touch screen. Many thought the concept of this virtual touch screen was a great idea; today, touch screen technology is commonplace. What was far more interesting from an adaptive technology perspective was the idea that one could connect information from disparate sources (and having very different characteristics) on the fly to produce a union that was much more than the sum of its common elements.

Whether this holographic "Minority Report interface" will ever be realized is uncertain. What is certain and inevitable is that end users will reach the limits of current data schemes rapidly as they attempt to coalesce more and more data into meaningful information. End users will slam against these barriers like brick walls. They will become frustrated with the simplistic overlays of information that currently serve as operational pictures: they are little more than clusters of data stacked upon each other with no real transformation of data.

Dynamically adaptive systems are those that monitor the current operating environment and modify themselves at runtime either to respond to a security threat, tune performance, or increase overall stability (Cheng, Sawyer, Bencomo, & Whittle, 2009). While current research in adaptive systems is focused on large scale enterprises or power grid systems, these models can easily be applied to smaller scale Clouds to ensure high performance given a broad range of network access (Polze & Tröger, 2011).

The pinnacle of the adaptive system is one that acts like a human being – it would act and react intelligently without human interaction. Unfortunately, many adaptive systems are hampered by the way they are taught to think. Systems that approach autonomicity from a purely rules-based approach will never reach this aim. Without proper context, some rules will not yield the optimal result or simply fail to make sense at all. The reason rules-based systems will never quite reach their goal of approximating intelligent interaction is because human intelligence is only partially based on rules. The concept of associative memory is simple to describe, yet difficult to replicate in computer systems: human memory is based on a combination of logical and associative relationships. Associative memory is what causes some people to feel danger when they see red, but others feel joy.

The core problem with rules-based systems is that the system models must be extremely complex in order to account for all environmental variables. Most computer models simply ignore significant portions of data, yielding inappropriate results. As a system model approaches a complete description of its respective environment, it becomes extremely fragile, unable to deal with the dynamic nature of data over time; the model's validity expires shortly after the point in time for which it was developed (Saffron Technology, 2005). Research into solving this problem has been focused primarily in the neural networks space. System designers are looking increasingly at biological models for insight into better models.

Fuzzy logic research focuses on improving the nature of rules-based engines so they can be dynamically tuned. Most fuzzy-logic engines either lack a rule pruning capability, resulting in a series of rules that are no longer applicable to the environment, or the rule set that governs the nature by which the rules change is often a static external source (Tung & Quek, 2010). A far more elegant approach would be one where the system adapts its rules based on incremental learning. Tung and Quek (2010) propose an evolving neural fuzzy semantic memory (eFSM) model system that begins to categorize sample data using fuzzy "IF-THEN" statements and then builds upon the model with incrementally more complex (and real) data.

Rules and relational databases are limited in that the questions to be answered by the relation-

ships must be known while the system is being designed. However, an associative memory system would learn to establish relationships on the fly as connections are being made at run time. In a very real and natural sense, the system would have the capacity to learn by asking new questions (Aparicio, 2010).

As the models for Dynamically Adaptive/ Autonomic Systems evolve using Associative Memory and other constructs that mimic biological or meteorological system behavior, Cloud Computing environments will take advantage of ever-improving rules-based engines. Eventually, these engines designed to provide dynamic scaling and performance tuning of a given system will evolve into a series of self-organizing Cloud environments. These dynamic Clouds will adapt to the needs and constraints of their external environments and rearrange system resources and call upon outside Clouds to lend resources to solve the problem at hand, deconstructing the ad-hoc environment when the additional resources or tasks are no longer necessary. Effectively, the Cloud Computing model will evolve into a true climate arrangement where various Cloud Computing environments collaborate in an automated and interdependent fashion to provide the most efficient method to provide resources to the end user.

Microclimates: A New Model for Cloud Computing

One undeniable truth about data is that we have a lot of it. Decision makers often find themselves crippled by the sea of data before them; they simply don't know where to start. If Cloud Computing is going to provide a resolution to this problem, system designers must change the way they think about the Cloud. The goal of Cloud Computing must shift from being the conduit to a ubiquitous enterprise data store to providing a localized view of data that is relevant to the user's perspective and adaptive to his or her specific needs.

To borrow from former U.S. House Speaker Thomas "Tip" O'Neal, all data and apps are local. The idea that a Cloud can and must only be a ubiquitous enterprise resource is overly restrictive and will eventually doom the Cloud to oblivion.

In order to survive in the future business market, the Cloud must adapt and become more local, more personal, offering Microclimates of capability that operate locally, but participate globally. Figure 4 depicts a possible model for Microclimate Cloud Computing.

Significant advances in current technology are making microclimates possible, including adaptive systems, associative memory, and mobile computing. Advanced technologies such as Hadoop make such regionalization possible, as it allows enterprise activities to be split into multiple parallel activities and then reconstructed at the enterprise level. Further, advances in personal mobile computing and the ubiquity of tablets and smart phones that can generate and process a large volume of data mandates that a regionalized version of a Cloud be executed. It is not feasible to send all the data from a mobile device to an enterprise resource, especially given the Quality of Service (QoS) that most technology users have come to expect. Rather, it is more useful to process as much data as possible in situ and sending a limited data set heavily tagged. By splitting the computation into multiple subtasks

and transferring the metadata, mobile devices are able to handle complex functions while maintaining an acceptable level of QoS (Borthakur, et al., 2011, Wang, et al., 2011).

The U.S. Military has adopted this approach of processing data in theatre and sending only the metadata unless specifically requested for use by unmanned systems with a data model called Tasking, Collection, Processing, Exploitation, and Disseminate (TCPED) (U.S. Navy, 2011). The TCPED model considers the significant limitations of satellite communications (Cook, 2009) by driving independent operations as far as possible into the field, both collecting and processing data locally, and sending metadata to the home command. The field commander or intelligence analyst then reviews the metadata and chooses which specific data sets to review in detail. The TCPED model is viewed as being the key to agility in a rapidly changing world with limited bandwidth and an unlimited thirst for information (Corrin, 2011).

Mobile computing and other models (e.g., military tactical environments) involving the need for time sensitive access to information in bandwidth constrained (or partially available) scenarios will develop a subculture of Cloud Climates described above. In this model, the Cloud Communities will be limited in scope and only interoperate with each other, isolated by physical, geographical, or even governance issues (e.g., security classifications).

Figure 3. The ubiquitous (enterprise) cloud model

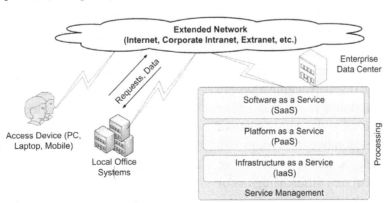

Figure 4. Microclimates - regionalizing the cloud

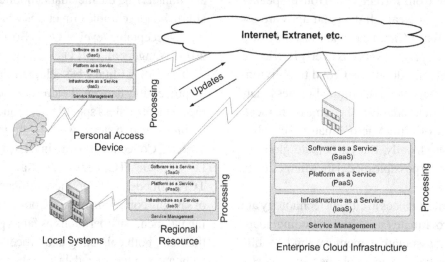

End user devices accessing these Clouds will have subsets of the Cloud logic locally in order to provide in situ processing of data and streamline the amount of metadata that is transferred to the primary Cloud. This "Microclimate" model for Cloud Computing will likely evolve more in the private space than in the public Cloud Computing model, but may also apply to certain public Cloud Computing constructs such as scientific and research Clouds.

Swarm Computing

Taking a cue from nature, the third future trend expected in Cloud Computing is in the realm of swarm tactics. Just as insects and small animals exhibit emergent system behavior as a large group, Cloud Computing will eventually take advantage of the concepts of swarming to solve increasingly difficult problems of resource availability and complex data analysis. Swarm algorithms operate on the premise that diversity within a system (or system of systems) results in new thinking or behavior. The more diverse the components of a system, the more explorative the system will behave to solve problems, taking advantage of logic and functions from very different regions or industry verticals to solve the increasingly com-

plex challenge of big data analytics and predictive reasoning (Yin, Glover, Lguna, & Zhu, 2011). By evaluating the applicability of elite solutions originally focused on specific problem sets, a swarm environment can adopt the elite solution logic and apply the algorithms to a broader spectrum of concerns. In the same method as worm-based malware searches available networks for new platforms to infect, the swarm computing concept searches the enterprise (i.e., Internet, Extranet, etc.) for available logic patterns and algorithms to exploit for expanded purposes.

A swarm computing methodology could also take advantage of massive abstraction of infrastructure. Virtualization and service abstraction technology such as Map-Reduce and Hadoop seek to "hide" the underlying infrastructure from the code, allowing portability and rapid expansion of function logic across multiple infrastructure nodes to even out the peaks and valleys of infrastructure utilization. Swarm computing would adopt this process and take advantage of advances in grid computing and service abstraction to allow every computing node (i.e. booth centralized and end-user devices) to lend processing power to the overall Cloud enterprise to increase ad-hoc resource pooling. Effectively, swarm computing is the logical next step from Cloud federation to allow for interoperability and seamless resource sharing in a QoS guaranteed environment (Yang, Nasser, Surridge, & Middleton, 2012). Similar to The Borg of Star Trek fame, all devices will become part of a universal Cloud environment of decentralized processing in support of the common good.

Cloud Services as a Service (CSaaS)

As the models of Cloud Computing evolves, so too will the services provided to customer organizations. The core assumption of moving to an external Cloud service provider (CSP) is that a CSP is more adept at providing said service in a manageable and affordable manner than developing the technology and personnel to maintain it in house. As Cloud Computing models become more complex and evolve into interdependent climates, monitoring Cloud Computing performance becomes extremely difficult. How can an end user measure compliance with SLAs for overall availability (AO) when the underlying Cloud Computing infrastructure is based on an ad-hoc combination of self-organizing environments?

Out of this complexity will rise the need to provide Cloud Services as a Service. These services will generally focus on management and monitoring tasks such as Security, Performance Monitoring, and Compliance Reporting. CSPs will adopt automated testing techniques to provide services to monitor and test Cloud Computing service levels by performing automated functions that mimic selected end user use cases. By acting as a corporate watch dog, CSaaS offerings will provide monitoring of another CSP's offering or even a private Cloud Computing infrastructure and would act as an independent agent to ensure compliance with statutory and corporate policy guidelines.

Another side of the CSaaS coin would be providing Security as a Service. This service offering could take many forms and include monitoring for events, intrusion detection and prevention,

configuration management and security patch compliance, and even simulated attacks to test the mettle of the CSP's own security team (e.g., White Hat/Red Team events). The degree that Security as a Service will be adopted by the general public will focus on two main questions:

1. Can an active security monitoring service be provided without impacting my system's performance?
2. How can I ensure that the results of my security scans will not be released publicly?

The answer to these questions may vary among organizations. Certainly, a military organization is not likely to outsource security monitoring to an external commercial CSP, nor would many commercial organizations feel comfortable with another company having the "keys to their kingdom" but this and other Cloud Service as a Service offerings could evolve as private Cloud services as well. Providing CSaaS within a private Cloud could be an approach developed by organizations as a safeguard to outsourcing its business functions to a public CSP.

SOLUTIONS AND RECOMMENDATIONS

Before opting to delve into the Cloud Computing industry, one must consider a few questions. Which Cloud Computing model is right for my organization? Should my organization adopt Cloud Computing now or wait for some future generation of the Cloud model to evolve? Is my data appropriate for a Cloud-based infrastructure?

These and other questions are critical to answer prior to deciding whether and how to execute a Cloud Computing approach for your organization. Perhaps most important of all is to answer the question of whether Cloud Computing is secure enough to expose your organization's data (or a portion thereof) to the external world. The following section offers some thoughts on determining how to execute a Cloud Computing strategy that balances the need to expose data with the need to protect that data using a Defense in Depth technique. After deciding that a portion of your data can be placed on the Cloud in a (reasonably) secure manner, it is important to determine whether the Cloud Computing model is appropriate for your organization and its business model; perhaps only some of your data should be placed on the Cloud, maybe your organization's people and processes are not ready for operating in the Cloud. Finally, once deciding that a Cloud Computing strategy makes sense for you, it is important to choose which model and CSP is right for your organization. This section ends with a recommended framework using a Balanced Scorecard approach as a decision support tool to evaluate multiple Cloud Computing options.

Defense in Depth: A Model for Cloud Security

A final area of research into the future of Cloud Computing is in security. Gartner Research predicts that by the end of 2016, 50% of Fortune 1000 companies will have customer related (and potentially sensitive data) stored in public Clouds (Avram, 2011). As distributed computing approaches the utility resource model, questions of privacy abound: Can I be sure that my data is secure? How can my service provider ensure that my trade secrets are not available to my competitors? Is storage over the Internet capable of providing the availability I need for my data?

These concerns are not entirely unfounded; in a recent study, the United States Government Accountability Office (U.S. GAO) identified that the Cloud Computing model introduces a number of security issues including reliance on a vendor to implement security controls, dependence on a vendor (to remain in business), insecure/ineffective identity management, and unclear respon-

sibilities for incident response (2010). Security issues have been identified as a critical concern that has hampered adoption of the public Cloud model by certain industries that consider their data mission critical (Asprey, 2012; Intel, 2011).

Typical security measures to ensure the confidentiality, integrity, and availability of data do not always translate in Cloud Computing architectures. For example, encryption is a common method for protecting data that is problematic in the Cloud. Downloading and decrypting data for local use has proven inefficient in a massively distributed environment with dynamically allocated resources. While some promising research has been conducted in the field of homomorphic encryption (i.e. processing operations on encrypted data in kind without first downloading and decrypting), the experiments have proven cumbersome and expensive; practical applications for general use are not expected for several years (Anthes, 2010).

Cloud Computing focuses on outsourcing infrastructure to a service provider, often driving issues with regulatory compliance (e.g., HIPAA, Sarbanes-Oxley, PCI). Regardless of whether the service provider implements the proper data segregation and security controls to ensure compliance, it can be difficult to prove compliance as the details of the service provider's infrastructure is often considered proprietary. This concern of compliance reporting and governance has slowed the overall adoption by U.S. Federal Government agencies of Cloud Computing models (United States Government Accountability Office, 2010). Cloud Computing service providers must be able to provide assurance of implementation of not only adequate security controls but also of proper segregation of data and architectures to protect the confidentiality and integrity of data.

In addition to data confidentiality (i.e. privacy), enterprises considering data storage in a Cloud environment must consider issues of data integrity. In a traditional remote storage enterprise, integrity is generally not an issue, because data are stored in dedicated storage nodes. In a Cloud model, the data is stored across an abstracted infrastructure with multiple, physically redundant nodes. The Cloud Computing model of dynamic resource allocation and access to data complicates the problem of data integrity, as multiple users/servers could be accessing data simultaneously from different nodes. Research in homomorphic processes has shown promise in dynamic data operations to prevent data inconsistencies from unauthorized or simultaneous access ensuring data correctness in a Cloud Computing data scheme (Owens, 2010).

Storing applications and data in an abstracted infrastructure drives clear security risks of data privacy and integrity; however there is another security challenge that is not often discussed: how to keep the Cloud from going rogue. The virtualization technology used to effect elasticity in the Cloud infrastructure introduces a unique security threat: replication of viruses across the Cloud (Owens, 2010). In 2010, NIST identified a vulnerability associated with virtualization engines in which a cyber-attack could traverse across multiple virtual machines managed by the same hypervisor (National Vulnerability Database, 2010). The elasticity and automated provisioning that make the Cloud Computing model beneficial to end users could result in a massive self-replicating virus storm. Future efforts in securing the Cloud must focus on securing the elastic nature of Cloud Computing. This challenge to secure the elasticity of the Cloud can prove extremely complex, as the business model for Cloud Computing drives a need for a common management platform (Owens, 2010).

Of course, this dark Cloud has a silver lining: Cloud Computing can actually enhance some aspects of security. Abstraction of the Cloud infrastructure can improve protection against cyber-attacks by obscuring the lower levels of the infrastructure form the attacker. Further, the general use of virtualization of operating systems can improve the overall security posture by easing the deployment of security patches and provides a cost effective disaster recovery solution (United States Government Accountability Office, 2010).

Most security experts recommend a Defense in Depth approach toward security, whereby the data and applications in the Cloud are assigned various levels of criticality and protected accordingly, just as one may leave his or her wallet lying on the dresser, but keep more valuable items in a safe (or a bank). Data should be treated the same way: leaving less critical data on the outskirts of the security perimeter, while the most critical data is maintained under much tighter security. The value of this approach is that it allows users access to the data they need daily, while maintaining a modicum of security and monitoring. As the less critical data become targets for hackers, intrusion detection and response mechanisms are used to prevent hackers from accessing the vital data (Intel IT Center, 2011, Pirooz, 2011).

In addition, choosing a public-private hybrid Cloud implementation has distinct security advantages as it provides fault tolerance against the inherently brittle nature of a public Cloud model, where all the eggs of data reside in a single virtual basket (Sahlin, 2011). This is an extension of the Defense in Depth concept of maintaining only a certain amount (and type) of data in the public aspect of the Cloud.

To Cloud or Not to Cloud? That is the Question

More important than which Cloud model or provider is the right solution for an organization is whether an organization should execute a Cloud strategy. Not all data is appropriate for a Cloud based solution. Some data (e.g., corporate proprietary information, design specifics, trade secrets) may be too valuable to transfer to the Cloud, especially if an organization is considering a public Cloud approach. Similar to a Defense in depth security approach, an organization should determine which applications and data should be transferred to the Cloud. Like all technical solutions, Cloud Computing does not have to be an all or nothing approach, and a company can make a very expensive mistake by transferring too much to the Cloud without a reason to do so.

Once an organization has decided whether to move to the Cloud, an organization must consider the following questions:

Does this Cloud strategy make business sense? As mentioned previously, Cloud Computing is fundamentally a business strategy; if it does not provide an organization with a solid business case within an acceptable risk threshold, it is not an appropriate solution. It may be that the business case will have to be developed with a measure of creativity. This is especially true when considering Cloud Computing for the public sector which doesn't operate on a profit basis, because financial Return on Investment is not a valid criterion as it is in commercial environments.

Which service model is most appropriate for my organization? Based on the needs of a given organization, some service models may be more appropriate than others. An organization with a strong application development team may want tighter control over the services offered; perhaps a private or hybrid IaaS Cloud is more appropriate than a public SaaS model. In comparison, a small business with limited access to technology professionals and a small capital expenditure budget may prefer a public SaaS model in order to capture speed to market.

Do I understand the cost benefit profile? Cloud Computing is first and foremost a business strategy; often, a Cloud approach is recommended based on a specific Return of Investment calculation over time. With cost/benefit projections, the Devil can be in the details (or in this case, the assumptions). Before entering into a Cloud service provider agreement or investing in a private Cloud infrastructure, be sure to understand the assumptions that went into the cost model. How well-defined are the requirements for the

service? Can the scope of the implementation be controlled in order to control implementation costs? Are hardware/software quotes validated and guaranteed? If using a public or hybrid Cloud approach, is the pricing model from the service provider clear? Be careful of hidden costs associated with utility-based pricing (e.g., $X per hour of server usage, or per Y,000 user sessions per day), as these variable costs can increase rapidly and often without being noticed.

How can I protect my data in the Cloud? An organization should never cede its responsibility to protect its vital data and trade secrets. Outsourcing to a Cloud service provider does not mean absolution of responsibility for security. Before agreeing to a Cloud service contract, an organization should carefully negotiate the roles and responsibilities for security. An organization should visit the datacenters of potential service provider to determine how they ensure services, how fault tolerant the facilities are, whether they maintain backup power generation capabilities, etc. Finally, do not sacrifice security for convenience: do allow access to your core applications via the Internet, never administer your applications over a public unencrypted circuit, and never deploy a Cloud based solution without boundary protection (e.g. firewalls).

What is my contingency plan? Some consider contingency planning having a plan to fail. Unfortunately, far too many good ideas fail during execution because Systems Engineers and Project Managers did not consider the risks of a project. Before executing a Cloud strategy, an organization should consider at least one backup plan to provide services in case of unforeseen events that prevent the launch of a Cloud-based system within an acceptable timeframe. This type of planning may include maintaining a private network capability in parallel to the Cloud-based service for a period of time to ensure service (even if performance degraded) if the Cloud-based service fails to meet expectations. This private capability could be used to enable temporary operations while the performance issues with the Cloud service are resolved, or it could be used as a permanent off-ramp.

Choosing the Right Cloud Provider: A Balanced Scorecard Approach

Congratulations! You have weighed the options, considered security issues, and decided that at least some of your data should be in a Cloud based environment. So which one is right for you?

Just as not all Cloud models are the same, Cloud service providers can vary greatly in the service models provided, limitations, and costs. Navigating the morass of hype and data sheets to determine which Cloud service provider is right to meet a given organization's needs can be challenging. Menzel and Ranjan (2011) offer a very useful decision support tool that compares service providers using a set of criteria based on capabilities, QoS guarantees, network bandwidth, and cost. Cloud Genius allows a user to cut through the marketing and providing a real head to head comparison using discrete criteria using a balanced scorecard type approach.

As is the case with any decision support tool, Cloud Genius must be used with a solid understanding of the core assumptions involved. One of the baseline assumptions used by Mezel and Ranjan (2011) is that QoS output is directly related to server and network perfomance characteristics. It is a commonly held misconception in the Informaiton Technology industry to assume that the overall system performance can be increased by merely using faster servers or increased network bandwidth. What this assumption ignores is the nature of the system queue and backlog that can impede performance dramatically; this is especially true for complex systems such as Cloud Computing infrastructures that leverage Hadoop (Borthakur, et al., 2011, Wang, et al., 2011). The issue of system queueing and backlog has been shown to be so critical to overall system performance, that even using servers that are one or two

generations old can have no aprpeciable difference in overall system performance (Sahlin, Sarkani, & Mazzuchi, 2011).

The best approach for choosing a Cloud service provider is to develop a balanced scorecard, using discrete criteria such as proposed by Menzel and Ranjan (2011), but modified to meet a specific organziaiton's unique needs. For example, if service availabiliity is more critical than guaranteed system performance, perhaps a hyrbid Cloud approach is the best solution, ensuring fault tolerance. If initial cost is more imporant than Total Ownership Cost, then a public Cloud model leveraging an existing infrastructrue is more appropriate. The training of the personnel required to manage the Cloud Computing environment cannot be ignored. Outsourcing the infrastructrue to a CSP does not absolve an organization from the decidedly non-trivial responsibility to maintain the lifecycle service oriented processes and content of a Cloud environment. Simply managing the actvie workflow queues can be daunting for an organization and requires dedicate staff within the organization; this fucntion of workflow management cannot be outsourced to a CSP (Yang, Bruin, & Dove, 2010). Ultimately, the optimal approach is to identify which criteria matter most to the organizaiton's specific needs, apply criteria weighting (if applicable), and then begin a head to head comparison.

In order to choose a Cloud service provider, one must consdier a variety of questions relevant to one's organizational needs. This author recommends a Balanced Scorecard Approach toward comparing multiple Cloud service providers. This author has had a great deal of success using a modified version of the Kaplan-Norton Balanced Scorecard as a Decision Support tool, as it provides an easily discernable comparison of multiple Courses of Action (COAs) across a series of criteria (1996). In the case of deciding among CSPs (including the option of insourcing with a private Cloud COA), the following crieria are proposed:

- **Investment Cost (IC):** The amount of startup capital required to implement this COA. Startup capital involves procurement of equipment and software, but also includes the development cost of the COA.
- **Profit Margin (PM):** The percentage of profit projected compared to all costs over time (IC, operating costs, development costs, personnel costs, and system upgrades). For non commercial ventures (e.g., government Clouds, private Clouds, etc.), recommedn PM be replaced by Total Ownerhsip Cost (TOC).
- **Configuration Management (CM):** The degree of flexibility/ownership the organization has in making changes to the Cloud Computing infrastrucutrue and capabilities.
- **Personnel (P):** The degree to which the COA alters the organizaiton's personnel profile. Will the COA require hiring new employees, and/or redoployment/layoff of current staff?
- **Training (T):** The degree to whicch new training of current staff is required to support the COA.
- **Facilities (F):** The degree to which the organization must invest in new facilities (e.g., data center space, power, Heating/Ventillation/Air Conditioning, etc.) to support the COA.
- **COA Risk (R_{COA}):** Overall Risk score of the COA. Risk is calculated by identifying risk statements relevant to the COA, and assessing their Likelihood (L) and Impact (I). The formula proposed below assumes that risks are assessed against a 5 x 5 scale based on the ANSI Standrards for

Project Management defined by the Project Management Institute (). Using this formula, the total risk value of a given risk statement Ri is:

$$R_i = L_i * I_i$$

The total COA Risk Score of the COA is an average of the indvidual COA risk scores:

$$R_{COA} = \frac{\sum_1^i R_n}{i}$$

This Balanced Scorecard approach is particularly useful with Executive Management; the author recommends combining the Kaplan-Norton Balanced Scorecard with a Stoplight Framework using a traditional Red/Yellow/Green designation to provide a visual image of the relative strength/weakness of a particular Cloud Computing COA. By assiging a numerical value to each evaluation color, one can translate this qualitiative assessment to a quantitative approach. It is critical in developing the Balanced Scorecard to define what one means by and evaluation of Red/Yellow/Green for each criterion. Table 3 provides a useful approach toward quantifying the essentially qualitative measures on the Balanced Scorecard.

A sample Balanced Scorecard is provided as Figure 5.

Note that in this case, all criteria are weighted equally, therefore the overall COA Evaluation (E_{COA}) is calculated as a staright average (see Box 1).

This equal weighting may or may not be appropriate for a given organizaiton. Some organizaitons may consider protection of its current workforce as more improtant than investment

Box 1.

$$E_{COA} = \langle IC_{COA} \mid PM_{COA} \mid CM_{COA} \mid P_{COA} \mid T_{COA} \mid F_{COA} \mid R_{COA} \rangle$$

Table 3. Sample balanced scorecard criteria

Criterion	Red (1)	Yellow (2)	Green (3)
Investment Cost (IC)	High	Medium	Low
Profit Margin (PM) / Total Ownership Cost (TOC)	Low PM High TOC	Medium PM Medium TOC	High PM Low TOC
Configuration Management (CM)	Organization has no control over Infrastructure and Services offered. Structured change windows only.	Organization can have dedicated Infrastructure, Services Offered as optional (additional fees). Structured change windows only.	Organization maintins full control over Infrastructure, Services Offered, and Change Windows
Personnel (P)	COA requires hiring entirely team of personnel, possible layoff of existing personnel.	Current personnel can be trained to support Cloud environment. May require staff augmentmentation for specialized functions.	Current staff is adequate to manage Cloud infrastructure/ services.
Training (T)	Significant technology and operations concepts training requried to maintain Cloud environment.	Subsection of staff requires training in techncial aspects of maintaining Cloud environment.	Current staff is fully trained to support organizaiton's techncial requirements to maintain Cloud environment. End user process training may be required.
Facilities (F)	COA requires signficant investment in new facilities and/or complete disposal of current facilities and infrastructure investments.	COA requires some investment in facilities or invovles invovles disposal of some current infrastructure.	COA requires minor investment in existing facilities investments and/or can resue existing facilities.
Risk (R)	$R_{COA} > 17$	$17 > R_{COA} \geq 9$	$R_{COA} < 9$

costs. A startup may feel it is acceptable to pay more in the long run (TOC) if it ensures a low initial investment. Each organzaiton should modify this Balanced Scorecard and the relatvie weighting of the criteria to meet its needs.

SUMMARY

Any sufficiently advanced technology is indistinguishable from magic. ~ Arthur C. Clarke

Cloud Computing is a hot topic in the technology industry today; however the myriad of definitions of the model mystifies more often than illuminates. Few people can adequately define Cloud Computing beyond the phrase "Magic happens here." NIST offers the most complete and concrete definition for Cloud Computing, offering not only a list of essential characteristics for the Cloud (i.e. on-demand service, broad network access, resource pooling, rapid elasticity, and measured service), but also classifies Cloud Computing into a variety of service models: Software as a Service (SaaS), Platform as a Service (PaaS), and Infrastructure as a Service (IaaS) (Mell & Grance, 2011). Cloud Computing and SOA development have proven effective in enterprise class business environments, and while those same benefits are available to small businesses, significant barriers

Figure 5. Sample balanced scorecard (in this case, recommending a private cloud)

COA	IC	PM	CM	P	T	F	R	E_{COA}
CSP A	3	1	1	3	1	1	3	1.85714
CSP B	2	2	2	1	3	2	1	1.85714
CSP C	2	3	2	2	2	3	1	2.14286
Private	2	3	3	2	2	2	2	2.28571

to entry (especially dependence on low bandwidth) exist and current Cloud architectures leave room for significant performance improvement (Khalid, 2010; Wang, et al. 2011, Zhang et al., 2010).

Wang, Tao, Kunze, and Rattu (2008) argue that Cloud Computing is vastly different from prior models, but concede that the need for distributed computing and flexibility of infrastructure to respond to a rapidly changing business environment is the same challenge that the IT industry has been facing for the past 50 years with the mainframe distributed computing model. At its core, the Cloud Computing paradigm delivers computing resources to external users as a utility and Cloud service providers are compensated on a per use basis (Buyya et al., 2008; Mell & Grance, 2011). The parallels among the nature of Cloud Computing and previous models intended to meet this business need are clear. While the progression from mainframe distributed computing to EDI VANs to ASPs and SOA and eventually to Cloud Computing is less of a deterministic march through history and more of a casual stroll through time, the path is clearly marked by literature. Technology advancements such as virtualization, system monitoring and management, and automated provisioning provided the catalysts to evolve the face of computing models to what is now known as Cloud Computing, but the soul of Cloud Computing is the same as the distributed computing models from 50 years ago; it seems that Cloud Computing is the new black.

What is the future for Cloud Computing? A cynic might say that after a series of mediocre successes in the business world, the term Cloud Computing will go the way of SOA, ASP, and the dodo: killed off by predatory marketeers searching for the next new thing. A more introspective look at Cloud Computing and the trends that shape its future reveals a bright future for the model. Cloud Computing will take advantage of advances in mobile computing, associative memory, and dynamically adaptive systems and evolve into four new models: Computing Climates, Microclimates,

Swarm Computing, and Services as a Service, resulting in flexible and highly personalized experiences for users, systems, and services as they act as consumers of the Cloud. Even if it loses the Cloud Computing moniker in time, distributed variable rate computing is here to stay.

Like any technical solution, Cloud Computing is not a panacea; it is a tool that can effect a business solution. And like all tools, it is only effective if it is appropriate to the problem at hand. Not all data and applications are appropriate for a Cloud-based solution. Perhaps the most critical key to a successful implementation of Cloud Computing is choosing which data and applications should (and more importantly, what should not) migrate to the Cloud. Cloud Computing only makes business sense when it makes business sense. This chapter offers a Balanced Scorecard approach toward choosing among the various Cloud Computing service models and providers.

REFERENCES

Adams, K., & Agesen, O. (2006). A comparison of software and hardware techniques for x86 virtualization. Proceedings of the 12th International Conference on Architectural Support for Programming Languages and Operating Systems (pp. 2-13). doi:10.1145/1168857.1168860

Albrecht, C. C., Dean, D. L., & Hansen, J. V. (2005). Marketplace and technology standards for B2B e-commerce: Progress, challenges, and the state of the art. *Information & Management, 42*, 865–875. doi:10.1016/j.im.2004.09.003

Anthes, G. (2010). Security in the cloud. *Communications of the ACM, 53*(11), 16–18. doi:10.1145/1839676.1839683

Apache Hadoop. (2012). Welcome to Apache Hadoop. Retrieved January 12, 2012, from http://hadoop.apache.org/

Aparicio, M. IV. (2009). *Making memories: Applying neuron-inspired associative memories to national, business, and consumer intelligence.* Cary, NC: Saffron Technology, Inc.

Armbrust, M., Fox, A., Griffith, R., Joseph, A. D., Katz, R., & Konwinski, A. … Zaharia, M. (2009). Above the clouds: A Berkeley view of cloud computing. Berkeley, CA: University of California Berkeley. doi:10.1.1.150.628

Asprey, D. (2012, January 06). The cloud ate my homework. Retrieved from http://Cloudsecurity.trendmicro.com/the-Cloud-ate-my-homework/

Avram, A. (2011). Gartner's predictions for the next 5 years. Retrieved January 15, 2012, from http://www.infoq.com/news/2011/12/Gartner-Predictions-Next-5-Years

Bailey, J. P., & Bakos, Y. (1997). An exploratory study of the emerging role of electronic intermediaries. *International Journal of Electronic Commerce, 1*(3), 7–20.

Bain, S. A., Merchant, F., Minns, B., & Thomas, J. (2010, March). Building a dynamic infrastructure with IBM power systems: A closer look at private cloud TCO. Retrieved December 22, 2011, from http://public.dhe.ibm.com/common/ssi/ecm/en/pow03043usen/POW03043USEN.PDF

Barham, P., Dragovic, B., Fraser, K., Hand, S., Harris, T., & Ho, A. … Warfield, A. (2003). Xen and the art of virtualization. Proceedings of the 19th ACM Symposium on Operating Systems Principles (pp. 164-177). doi:10.1145/945445.945462

Borthakur, D., et al. (2011, June). Apache Hadoop goes realtime at Facebook. SIGMOD '11: Proceedings of the 2011 International Conference on Management of Dat (pp. 1071–1080). doi: 10.1145/1989323.1989438

Buyya, R., Yeo, C. S., Venugopal, S., Broberg, J., & Brandic, I. (2008). Market-oriented cloud computing: Vision, hype, and reality for delivering computing as the 5th utility. Paper presented at the 2009 9th IEEE/ACM International Symposium on Cluster Computing and the Grid, Shanghai, China. doi:10.1016/j.future.2008.12.001

Buyya, R., Yeo, C. S., Venugopal, S., Broberg, J., & Brandic, I. (2009). Cloud computing and emerging IT platforms: Vision, hype, and reality for delivering computing as the 5th utility. *Future Generation Computer Systems, 2009.* doi:doi:10.1016/j.future.2008.12.001

CenterBeam. (2012). CenterBeam 365+ enterprise-class cloud solution. Retrieved January 12, 2012, from http://www.centerbeam.com/managed-it-services/CenterBeam365/

Chang, M., He, J., & Castro-Leon, E. (2006). Service-orientation in the computing infrastructure. Proceedings of the 2nd IEEE International Symposium on Service-Oriented System Engineering (SOSE'06) (pp. 27-33). doi:10.1109/SOSE.2006.35

Cheng, B. H. C., Sawyer, P., Bencomo, N., & Whittle, J. (2009). A goal-based modeling approach to develop requirements of an adaptive system with environmental uncertainty. *Lecture Notes in Computer Science, 5795,* 468–483. doi:10.1007/978-3-642-04425-0_36

Chouhan, P. K. (2006). Automatic deployment for application service provider environments. Doctoral Dissertation.

Cloud Security Alliance. (2009). Security guidance for critical areas of focus in cloud computing v2.1. http://www.cloudsecurityalliance.org

Cook, K. (2009). Current wideband MILSAT-COM infrastructure and the future of bandwidth availability. Paper presented to the 2009 IEEE Annual Conference, Big Sky, MT. doi: 10.1109/AERO.2009.4839401

Cornish, E. (2004). *Futuring: The exploitation of the future*. Bethesda, MD: World Future Society.

Corrin, A. (2011, June 9). Navy needs a way to handle UAV, sensor data. Defense Systems. Retrieved December 29, 2011, from http://defensesystems.com/articles/ 2011/06/09/naval-it-day-afcea-tcped-intelligence-data-challenge.aspx

Coughlin, T. M. (2009). Virtualization of consumer storage. Paper presented to the 2010 IEEE 14th International Symposium on Consumer Electronics, Braunschweig, Germany. doi: 10.1109/ISCE.2010.5523736

Defense Information Systems Agency. (2009). DISA offers cloud computing with RACE. Retrieved October 15, 2010, from http://www.disa.mil/news/pressreleases/ 2009/race_100509.html

Defense Information Systems Agency. (2009). Rapid access computing environment (RACE). Retrieved October 15, 2010, from http://www.disa.mil/race/

Ganek, A. G., & Corbi, T. A. (2003). The dawning of the autonomic computing era. *IBM Systems Journal*, *42*(1), 5–18. doi:10.1147/sj.421.0005

Gartner. (2010). Gartner identifies the top 10 strategic technologies for 2011. Retrieved January 18, 2012, from http://www.gartner.com/it/page.jsp?id=1454221

Golden, B. (2009). How cloud computing can transform business. Retrieved August 15, 2011, from http://blogs.hbr.org/cs/2010/06/business_agility_how_Cloud_com.html

Greenstein, S. M., & Wade, J. B. (1998). The product life cycle in the commercial mainframe computer market, 1968-1982. *The Rand Journal of Economics*, *29*(4), 772–789. doi:10.2307/2556093

Henderson, T., & Allen, B. (2010). Cloud storage goes first class. Network World, August, 25-28.

Hill, Z., & Humphrey, M. (2009). A quantitative analysis of high performance computing with Amazon's EC2 infrastructure: The death of the local cluster? Proceedings of the 10th IEEE/ACM International Conference on Grid Computing (pp. 26-33).

Ideas International. (2011, February). Private clouds float with IBM systems and software. Retrieved December 28, 2011, from http://public.dhe.ibm.com/common/ssi/ecm/en/xbl03006usen/XBL03006USEN.PDF

IEEE Standard 802.16 Working Group. (2004). IEEE standard for local and metropolitan area networks part 16: Air interface for fixed broadband wireless access systems (revision of IEEE standard 802.16-2001).

Intel, I. T. Center. (2011, September). Planning guide; Cloud security. Retrieved December 15, 2011, from http://www.intel.com/content/www/us/en/Cloud-computing/Cloud-computing-security-planning-guide.html

Jacobellis v. Ohio. (1964). Retrieved October 10, 2010, from http://caselaw.lp.findlaw.com/cgi-bin/getcase.pl?navby=case&court=us&vol=378&invol=184#197

Jiang, X., & Xu, D. (2003). SODA: A service-on-demand architecture for application service hosting utility platforms. Proceedings of the 12th IEEE International Symposium on High Performance Distributed Computing (pp. 174-183).

Khalid, A. (2009). Cloud computing: Applying issues in small business. 2010 International Conference on Signal Acquisition and Processing (pp. 278-281). doi:10.1109/ICSAP.2010.78

Kim, W. (2009). Cloud computing: Today and tomorrow. *Journal of Object Technology*, *8*(1), 65–72. doi:10.5381/jot.2009.8.1.c4

Kossman, D. (2000). The state of the art in distributed query processing. *ACM Computing Surveys*, *32*(4), 422–469. doi:10.1145/371578.371598

Kplan, R. S., & Norton, D. P. (1996, January-February). Using the balanced scorecard as a strategic management system. *Harvard Business Review*, 3–13.

Lenk, A., Klems, M., Nimis, J., Tai, S., & Sandholm, T. (2009). What's inside the cloud? An architectural map of the cloud landscape. Proceedings of the ICSE Cloud '09 Workshop (pp. 23-31).

Lentz, R. F. (2009). *Statement by Mr. Robert F. Lentz Deputy Assistant Secretary of Defense, for Cyber, Identify, and Information Assurance before the U.S. House of Representatives Armed Services Committee Subcommittee on Terrorism, Unconventional Threats, & Capabilities*. Washington, DC: United States House of Representative.

Managed Solution. (2012). Managed Solution. Retrieved December 28, 2011, from http://www.managedsolution.com/index.html

McDonald, M. P. (2009). Leading times of transition: The 2010 CIO agenda. Retrieved July 13, 2010, from http://blogs.gartner.com/mark_mcdonald/2010/01/19/leading-in-times-of-transition-the-2010-cio-agenda/

McGregor, C., & Kumaran, S. (2002). Business processing monitoring using web services in B2B E-commerce. Proceedings of the International Parallel and Distributed Processing Symposium.

Mell, P., & Grance, T. (2011). *Special publication 800-145: The NIST definition of cloud computing*. Washington, DC: National Institute of Standards and Technology.

Menzel, M., & Ranjan, R. (2011). CloudGenius: Automated decision support for migrating multi-component enterprise applications to clouds. Technical Report, Retrieved January 6, 2012 from http://arxiv.org/abs/1112.3880v1.

Microsoft. (2012). Microsoft Office 365. Retrieved January 10, 2012, from http://www.microsoft.com/en-us/office365/what-is-office365.aspx#fbid=ruAfeIsNEjx

Microsoft. (2012). Windows Azure. Retrieved January 10, 2012, from http://www.windowsazure.com/en-us/pricing/free-trial/?WT.mc_id= MSCOM_EN_US_SEARCH_EDITORSCHOICE_123LMUS014358

Morgan Stanley Research. (2009). The mobile internet report: Ramping faster than desktop internet, the mobile internet will be bigger than most people think. Retrieved from http://www.morganstanley.com/institutional/techresearch/pdfs/mobile_internet_report.pdf

Motahari-Nezhad, H. R., Stephenson, B., & Singhal, S. (2009). *Outsourcing business to cloud computing services: Opportunities and challenges*. IEEE Special Issue on Cloud Computing.

National Vulnerability Database. (2009). Vulnerability summary for CVE-2009-3733. Retrieved November 13, 2010, from http://web.nvd.nist.gov/view/vuln/detail?vulnId=CVE-2009-3733

O'Neill, M. (2009, April 29). Connecting to the cloud, part 1: Leverage the cloud in applications. Retrieved January 5, 2012, from http://www.ibm.com/developerworks/library/x-Cloudpt1/

Owens, D. (2010). Securing elasticity in the cloud. *Communications of the ACM*, *53*(6), 46–51. doi:10.1145/1743546.1743565

Peng, J., Zhang, X., Lei, Z., Zhang, B., Zhang, W., & Li, Q. (2009). Comparison of several cloud computing platforms. Proceedings of the Second International Symposium on Information Science and Engineering (pp. 23-27). doi: 10.1109/ISISE.2009.94

Peterson, L., Shenker, S., & Turner, J. (2005). Overcoming the Internet impasse through virtualization. *Computer*, *38*(4), 34–41. doi:10.1109/MC.2005.136

Pirooz, S. (2011). Cloud security: The best defense is a good offense. Retrieved January 12, 2012, from http://www.centerbeam.com/business-advantages-of-outsourcing-IT/Cloud-security/key-considerations-when-moving-to-the-Cloud/

Polze, A., & Tröger, P. (2011). Trends and challenges in operating systems—From parallel computing to cloud computing. *Concurrency and Computation*. doi:doi:10.1002/cpe

Russell, L. W., Morgan, S. P., & Chron, E. G. (2003). Clockwork: A new movement in autonomic systems. *IBM Systems Journal, 42*(1), 77–84. doi:10.1147/sj.421.0077

Saffron Technology. (2005). Saffron Technology: Technical white paper. Morrisville, NC: Author.

Sahlin, J. (2011). Workshop: Cloud architectures for government. Paper presented at the NDIA Cloud Computing Symposium, San Diego, CA. Retrieved December 22, 2011, from http://www.ndia-sd.org/attachments/article/76/Sahlin_Cloud%20for%20Government %20Workshop.final.pdf

Sahlin, J., Sarkani, S., & Mazzuchi, T. (2011). Enterprise consolidation for DoD using AdvancedTCA. Proceedings of the 7th Annual AdvancedTCA Summit & Exposition. Retrieved January 12, 2012, from http://www.advancedtcasummit.com/English/ Collaterals/Proceedings/2011/20111101_S2-101_Sahlin.pdf

Sahlin, J., Sarkani, S., & Mazzuchi, T. (2012). Optimizing QoS in distributed systems/cloud computing architectures. *International Journal of Computers and Applications, 42*(18), 14–20. doi:10.5120/5791-8097

SalesForce.com. (2011). SalesForce.com and the environment: Reducing carbon emissions in the cloud. Retrieved October 25, 2011, from http://www.sfdcstatic.com/assets/pdf/misc/WP_WSP_Salesforce_Environment.pdf

Seltsikas, P., & Currie, W. (2002). Evaluating the application service provider (ASP) business model: The challenge of integration. Paper presented at the 35th Hawaii International Conference on System Sciences, Big Island, HI.

Sheu, P. C.-Y., Wang, S., Wang, Q., Hao, K., & Paul, R. (2009). Semantic computing, cloud computing, and semantic search engine. Proceedings of the 2009 IEEE International Conference on Semantic Computing (pp. 654-657). doi: 10.1109/ICSC.2009.51

Sledziewski, K., Bordbar, B., & Anane, R. (2009). A DSL-based approach toward software development and deployment on cloud. Proceedings of the 2010 24th IEEE International Conference on Advanced Information Networking and Applications (pp. 414-421). doi: 10.1109/AINA.2010.81

Smith, M. A., & Kumar, R. L. (2004). A theory of application service provider (ASP) use from a client perspective. *Information & Management, 4*, 977–1002. doi:10.1016/j.im.2003.08.019

Soltesz, S., Potzl, H., Fiuczynski, M. E., Bavier, A., & Peterson, L. (2007). Container-based operating system virtualization: A scalable, high performance alternative to hypervisors. Paper presented at EuroSys' 07, Lisboa, Portugal. doi:10.1.1.88.8563

Standard Performance Evaluation Corporation. (2011). The SPEC organization. Retrieved from http://www.spec.org/spec/

Tung, W. L., & Quek, C. (2010). eFSM - A novel online neural-fuzzy semantic memory model. *IEEE Transactions on Neural Networks, 21*(1), 136–157. doi:10.1109/TNN.2009.2035116

Ueno, H., & Hasegawa, S. (2009). Vintage: Hitachi's virtualization technology. Paper presented at the 4th International Conference on Grid and Pervasive Computing, Geneva.

United States Government Accountability Office. (2010). *GAO report to congressional requesters: Information security federal guidance needed to address control issues with implementing cloud computing*. Washington, DC: U.S. GAO.

United States Navy. (2011, February 25). Information dominance, agile acquisition and intelligence integration: Q&A with Terry Simpson, PEO C4I's Principal Deputy for Intelligence. Retrieved December 30, 2011, from http://www.public.navy.mil/spawar/Press/Documents/Publications/2.23.11_TerrySimpson.pdf

Walker, E., Brisken, W., & Romney, J. (2010). To lease or not to lease from storage clouds. *Computer, 43*, 44–50. doi:10.1109/MC.2010.115

Wang, C., Wang, Q., Ren, K., & Lou, W. (2009). Ensuring data storage security in cloud computing. Paper presented to the 2009 17th International Workshop on Quality of Service, Charleston, SC. doi: 10.1109/IWQoS.2009.5201385

Wang, L., Tao, J., Kunze, M., & Rattu, D. (2008). The Cumulus Project: Build a scientific cloud for a data center. Paper presented at Cloud Computing and its Applications, Chicago, IL. http://cca08.org/papers/Paper29-Lizhe-Wang.pdf

Wang, L., & von Laszewski, G. (2008). Scientific cloud computing: Early definition and experience. Proceedings of the 10th IEEE International Conference on High Performance Computing (pp. 825-830). doi:10.1109/HPCC.2008.38

Wang, Y., Que, X., Yu, W., Godenberg, D., & Sehgal, D. (2011, November). Hadoop acceleration through network levitated merge. Proceedings of the 2011 International Conference for High Performance Computing, Networking, Storage and Analysis (SC) (pp. 1–10). E-ISBN: 978-1-4503-0771-0

Weinhardt, C., Anandasivam, A., Blau, B., & Stößer, J. (2009). Business models in the service world. IT Pro, March/April, 36-41

Wu, J., Ping, L., Ge, X., Wang, Y., & Fu, J. (2009). Cloud storage as the infrastructure of cloud computing. Proceedings of the 2010 International Conference on Intelligent Computing and Cognitive Informatics (pp. 380-383). doi: 10.1109/ICICCI.2010.119

Yang, X., Bruin, R. P., & Dove, M. (2010). Developing an end-to-end scientific workflow: A case study of using a reliable, lightweight, and comprehensive workflow platform in e-Science. *IEEE Computational Science & Engineering*. doi:10.1109/MCSE.2009.211

Yang, X., Nasser, B., Surrige, M., & Middleton, S. (2012, March 10). A business-oriented cloud federation model for real time applications. *Future Generation Computer Systems*. doi:10.1016/j.future.2012.02.005

Yin, P.-Y., Glover, F., Laguna, M., & Zhu, J.-X. (2011, April-June). A complementary cyber swarm algorithm. *International Journal of Swarm Intelligence Research, 2*(2), 22–41. doi:10.4018/jsir.2011040102

Zaharia, M., Konwinski, A., Joseph, A. D., Katz, R., & Stoica, I. (2011). Improving MapReduce performance in heterogeneous environments. Proceedings of the 8th USENIX Conference on Operating Systems Design and Implementation.

Zhang, S., Zhang, S., Chen, X., & Huo, X. (2009). Cloud computing research and development trend. Proceedings of the 2010 IEEE 2nd International Conference on Future Networks (pp. 93-97). doi: 10.1109/ICFN.2010.58

KEY TERMS AND DEFINITIONS

Cloud Computing: A model for enabling ubiquitous, convenient, on-demand network access to a shared pool of configurable computing resources (e.g., networks, servers, storage, applications, and services) that can be rapidly provisioned and released with minimal management effort or service provider interaction.

Infrastructure As A Service (IaaS): The capability provided to the consumer is to provision processing, storage, networks, and other fundamental computing resources where the consumer is able to deploy and run arbitrary software, which can include operating systems and applications. The consumer does not manage or control the underlying cloud infrastructure but has control over operating systems, storage, and deployed applications; and possibly limited control of select networking components (e.g., host firewalls).

Platform As A Service (PaaS): The capability provided to the consumer is to deploy onto the cloud infrastructure consumer-created or acquired applications created using programming languages, libraries, services, and tools supported by the provider. The consumer does not manage or control the underlying cloud infrastructure (e.g., network, servers, operating systems, or storage), but has control over the deployed applications and possibly configuration settings for the application-hosting environment.

Quality Of Service (QoS): Any metric used to describe the overall user experience or to guarantee a subset of a system for use in a Cloud Computing environments. QoS can be used to manage service queues, prioritize traffic, or describe the end to end performance of a system (as in the System Goodput G_s metric proposed in this chapter).

Service Level Agreement (SLA): An agreement between two parties regarding the management of a distributed computing environment. SLAs establish the degree of service that will be provided and may include metrics for Quality of Service (QoS), overall availability (A_o), and customer service ticket performance. SLAs are traditionally associated with contractual obligations and include a penalty provision for failing to meet SLA targets within a given performance period.

Software As A Service (SaaS): The capability provided to the consumer is to use the provider's applications running on a cloud infrastructure. Applications are accessible from various client devices through either a thin client interface, such as a web browser (e.g., web-based email), or a program interface. The consumer does not manage or control the underlying cloud infrastructure (e.g., network, servers, operating systems, storage, or individual application capabilities), with the possible exception of limited user-specific application configuration settings.

Virtualization: A form of service abstraction allowing portions of the infrastructure to be "hidden" from the application logic, increasing portability and flexibility of the environment.

Chapter 3
Cloud Computing for Scientific Simulation and High Performance Computing

Adrian Jackson
Edinburgh Parallel Computing Centre, The University of Edinburgh, UK

Michèle Weiland
Edinburgh Parallel Computing Centre, The University of Edinburgh, UK

ABSTRACT

This chapter describes experiences using Cloud infrastructures for scientific computing, both for serial and parallel computing. Amazon's High Performance Computing (HPC) Cloud computing resources were compared to traditional HPC resources to quantify performance as well as assessing the complexity and cost of using the Cloud. Furthermore, a shared Cloud infrastructure is compared to standard desktop resources for scientific simulations. Whilst this is only a small scale evaluation these Cloud offerings, it does allow some conclusions to be drawn, particularly that the Cloud can currently not match the parallel performance of dedicated HPC machines for large scale parallel programs but can match the serial performance of standard computing resources for serial and small scale parallel programs. Also, the shared Cloud infrastructure cannot match dedicated computing resources for low level benchmarks, although for an actual scientific code, performance is comparable.

1. INTRODUCTION

Service-oriented computing, with its focus on coupling distributed components through well-defined interfaces and protocols, can be seen as an extension to concepts such as distributed computing and even grid computing. Likewise,

Clouds can very much be seen as an evolution from Grid computing, with the addition of virtualisation and sharing of resources. Distributed and Grid computing have long been exploited for high performance computing and scientific simulation and as such Cloud computing, and service-oriented architectures, are an interesting

DOI: 10.4018/978-1-4666-2854-0.ch003

and exciting potential platform for scientific users and their computing simulation needs.

In general the virtualisation overheads of the technology used to build modern Clouds are accepted to add little in the way of computational overheads (Huber 2011, Barham 2003), so the experience a user should obtain on a standard Cloud infrastructure should vary little from that of their own desktop or server environments, with the exception of the specifics of the hardware underlying the Cloud and the knowledge the user has of that hardware. However, there are a number of areas of Clouds that are potentially interesting for a user interested in using Clouds for high performance computing (HPC) or scientific simulation, particularly the specifics of the HPC hardware used in the Cloud and how it compares with current HPC machines, and also those Clouds that provide non-exclusive access to hardware resources.

To obtain a fuller understanding of these aspects of modern Cloud technologies, and build a clearer picture of the functionality that a typical scientific user could experience using such technology, we undertook some benchmarking of different Clouds to attempt to evaluate performance and draw some parallels with existing hardware or usage scenarios, included both low-level and applications based benchmarks.

2. EVALUATION OF CLOUD INFRASTRUCTURES

For our investigations we used two different Cloud infrastructures; the Amazon Web Services Elastic Compute Cloud (Amazon EC2) and an academic Cloud infrastructure provided by the UK National Grid Service (NGS)[1]. We chose Amazon because, at this point in time, it is one of the largest commercial Cloud resource providers. It is also easy to gain access to; all a prospective user requires is a credit card and an Amazon account, and im-

mediate access can be obtained. Amazon offer access to a range of resources (different sizes, operating systems, exclusive or non-exclusive use and so on) for different prices.

The NGS experimental Cloud service was the second infrastructure we used. Unlike Amazon, it can only provide non-exclusive access, thus allowing us to evaluate the impact that sharing the computational resources can have for the user. It also enabled us to directly compare an academic Cloud infrastructure to a commercial Cloud.

2.1. Benchmarks

The massive computational resources offered by (chiefly commercial) Cloud providers now offer a potential alternative to the specialist High Performance Computing (HPC) machines used for scientific simulation codes by academia and industry worldwide. Amazon, for instance, target this market explicitly by including HPC-specific images in their range of products. However, it is not immediately clear what performance these Cloud resources really offer, or what costs are associated with them, what functionalities they provide or how good their usability is, and how they compare with current HPC technologies in general.

Clouds for HPC or heavily computational loads offer exclusive access to computing hardware (i.e. only one virtual machine will be running on a processor or node). However, there are a range of Clouds that do not guarantee exclusive access to computational resources. In this situation, low-level benchmarks that evaluate the performance impact of this sharing of resources are essential to enable users to make an informed choice over the computing resources to use for their particular requirements.

Therefore, as previously mentioned, both the Amazon EC2 and the NGS Cloud were used for the performance benchmarks. The Amazon Cloud was used to evaluate the parallel functionality currently being offered (i.e. the performance going beyond a single image) and the NGS Cloud was used for the low-level benchmarks of shared Cloud resources.

2.2. NGS Cloud

The NGS Cloud pilot comprised hardware from two institutions that host the Cloud services: The University of Edinburgh (as part of their ECDF[2] system), and the University of Oxford (whose facilities are used in this study). The Cloud was set up as a pilot prototype service for interested users to access in order to enable them to evaluate Cloud computing and its potential for use with their applications or use cases. The hardware used to host the Cloud services in Oxford consists of five nodes, with the following specification:

- 2 x AMD dual-core Opteron, 2.6Ghz with 8GB ram (4 nodes)
- 4 x AMD dual-core Opteron, 2.6Ghz with 32GB ram (1 node)

All our tests were run on the four thin nodes. It should be noted that this hardware is approximately 4-5 years old.

The NGS Cloud offers four different generic Linux images – we chose the CentOS 5.3 and Ubuntu 9.04 images, allowing us to directly compare any overheads introduced by the operating system. The images are very basic and do not come with compilers, editors, or build tools; all these need to be installed by the user.

As mentioned earlier, it is important to note that access to the hardware that runs this Cloud is not exclusive: the hardware can host multiple instances of images and the resources are shared between users, thus exclusive access is possible, but cannot be guaranteed. Any benchmarking results therefore not only reflect the performance of the underlying system, but will also be dependent on the usage of the hardware by other users.

2.3. Amazon EC2

Amazon's Cloud infrastructure, the Elastic Compute Cloud (EC2), offers customers the opportunity to buy compute time on virtualised resources. Amazon offers a wide range of different types of compute images at different prices, from basic, low-memory images at $0.16 an hour, to specialized high-performance images at $1.60 per hour[3].

For the work undertaken in this study, which aims at testing the suitability of EC2 for parallel computation, the high-performance Cluster Compute images were used. Each node consists of two 2.3GHz quad-core Intel Nehalem processors (i.e. 8 compute cores in total) and has 23 GB of memory shared between those cores. The nodes are connected with 10 Gigabit Ethernet, which gives a theoretical data rate of ten gigabits per second.

2.4. Comparison HPC Platform: HECToR XT4

In order to be able to get a picture of the Amazon EC2 HPC performance as opposed to a dedicated HPC system, we used a traditional supercomputer as a comparison platform. For this study we used HECToR, the UK's national high-performance computing service. It is used by scientists from across the UK and Europe for a wide range of scientific application areas.

At the time the benchmarks presented here were run, HECToR was a Cray XT4 with two dual-core AMD Opteron 2.3 GHz nodes (i.e. 4 compute cores per node) with 8GB RAM and Cray's SeaStar2 3D torus network. Whilst the processors are commodity components that can be found in many compute infrastructures, the strength of the system lies in its proprietary high-speed network, which has reduced communication latency and high bandwidth. The communication network makes the XT4 architecture highly suitable for tightly coupled, communication intensive applications.

The Cray's SeaStar2 network had 6 links which are used to implement a 3D-torus of processors. The point-to-point bandwidth between nodes was 2.17 GB/s, and the minimum bi-section bandwidth was 4.1 TB/s. The latency between two nodes was around 6μs.

As with the Amazon resources, HECToR has also been upgrade since this study was carried out and in its current incarnation is now a Cray XE6 with a new high performance network between nodes and two 16-core AMD Interlagos processors per node.

3. SHARED CLOUD PERFORMANCE

We undertook a number of low-level performance benchmarks (aimed at testing the underlying hardware performance) and serial application benchmarks to evaluate the Eucalyptus Clouds provided by the NGS. They are detailed in the following subsections.

3.1. STREAM

STREAM[4] is a synthetic benchmark of a system's sustainable memory bandwidth using four simple computational kernels. Memory bandwidth is an important performance factor in all scientific applications: the performance of an application is often no longer limited by the clock speed of the CPU, but on the rate at which data can be read from and written to memory. The four tests in the STREAM benchmark are:

- COPY: $a(i) = b(i)$
- SCALE: $a(i) = q*b(i)$
- SUM: $a(i) = b(i) + c(i)$
- TRIAD: $a(i) = b(i) + q*c(i)$

The length of the vector that is used by the benchmark should be sufficiently large so as to avoid seeing the benefits of cache effects in the results. Here, we chose a vector of length N=5,000,000, which is an equivalent of 114.4MB of memory being used. Each test is repeated 10 times and only the best results are used to calculate the bandwidth.

Table 1 shows the results for all four tests on an Ubuntu instance and a CentOS instance. Their performance is compared to a MacBook Pro laptop with a dual-core Intel Core i5 CPU (2.4GHz) and 8GB of memory. The tests are repeated three times on each platform to quantify performance consistency. It is immediately obvious from the numbers in the table below that consistency is indeed a problem for both Cloud instances. The memory bandwidth can vary more than a factor of two between runs. On the MacBook Pro laptop however, the performance is very consistent.

The CentOS instance appears to slightly outperform the Ubuntu instance, yet both their performances are at a minimum 60 times worse than the laptop. The reasons for this poor performance is probably twofold: firstly, the resources are virtualised, and thus access to the hardware needs to be managed through the Xen hypervisor; secondly, access to the resources is not exclusive, so it is entirely possible that the activity of other users affected the outcome of this benchmark. As a user, it is not possible though to find out what these activities are or how many other users are on the same hardware. The tests have been repeated at different times of day however the performance picture was consistently poor for memory bandwidth.

Figure 1 shows a similar performance picture, using the runtimes for the Triad benchmark. It is again clear from this representation that the performance varies greatly between different runs, though the average runtime clusters around the 8 to 10 seconds margin for both types of instances.

3.2. IOZone

The IOZone[5] benchmark tests a system's file IO performance. Reading from and writing to files can be a significant bottleneck for IO intensive

Table 1. Memory bandwidth achieved using the STREAM benchmark on an Ubuntu instance, a CentOS instance, and a MacBook Pro laptop. The table shows the results for 3 runs, plus the average.

N=5,000,000		Rate (MB/S)			
	Benchmark	Run #1	Run #2	Run #3	Average
Ubuntu	Copy	90.30	64.49	158.54	104.45
	Scale	34.43	33.86	23.70	30.66
	Add	85.33	61.34	104.60	83.76
	Triad	16.21	36.87	26.91	26.66
CentOS	Copy	41.00	106.13	72.31	73.15
	Scale	35.25	24.14	30.38	29.92
	Add	75.83	75.24	77.88	76.32
	Triad	15.06	17.82	18.88	17.25
MacOSX	Copy	6345.15	6339.16	6360.79	6348.37
	Scale	6337.60	6365.37	6290.32	6331.10
	Add	6837.24	6819.73	6826.30	6827.75
	Triad	6837.98	6827.04	6807.00	6824.01

applications, so it is important to understand the performance implications. IOZone measures a range of file operations, such as read/write, random read/write, strided read and so on. In our tests, we ran the benchmark in fully automated mode, i.e. testing all the file operations for record sizes from 4KB to 16MB and for file sizes from 64KB up to 512MB. However on the Cloud instance, the maximum file size to complete successfully was 256MB.

Figure 2 shows the throughput of a "random write" operation: this test measures the performance of writing a file with access to random locations in a file. The throughput for file sizes

Figure 1. Variation in runtimes for the STREAM Triad benchmark on the two cloud instances

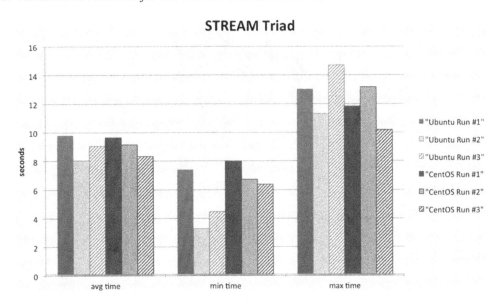

up to 1MB is in the region of 2000MB/s for record sizes of 256KB. This rate starts dropping significantly for larger files and is reduced to less than 50MB/s for the largest files. Table 2 shows a brief performance comparison between the Cloud instance and the MacBook Pro for these large files: the numbers highlight that the Cloud struggles with the larger files, especially with the smaller record lengths. It needs to be noted however that this comparison is not entirely fair, as the MacBook Pro has a considerable performance advantage due to the use of a solid state, rather than spinning, disk.

The "random read" operation is the counterpart to the previous benchmark – it measures the performance of reading a file while access is made to random locations in this file. The throughput performance is plotted in Figure 3. The performance behaviour can be separated into three distinct sections: files up to 512KB; files from 1MB up to 32 MB; and finally the largest files

from 64MB up to 256MB. The performance reflected by these sections is probably closely tied to cache effects (especially the small files with larger record lengths). Similarly to the "random write" test, it can again be seen that the Cloud instance struggles with the large files, with a significant drop in performance.

3.3. OCCAM1DCSEM

The OCCAM1DCSEM is an open-sourced code used to generate 1D models of control-source electromagnetic (CSEM) data. It is used in this study as an example of a typical serial scientific application and the performance is tested on the two Cloud instances as well as the MacBook Pro laptop (i.e. the type of hardware which may be used by a scientist). The OCCAM1DCSEM code comes with a number of real data and synthetic data example test cases, which we used to illustrate performance:

Figure 2. Throughput performance of the Random Write operation on a CentOS instance for various record and file sizes

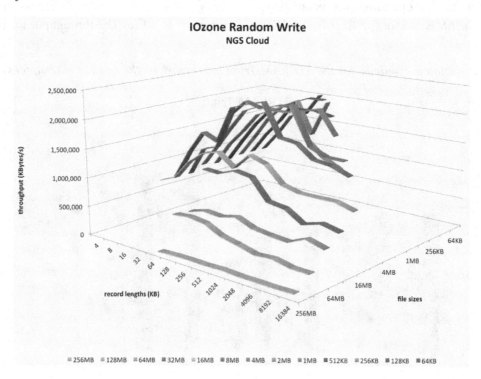

- Synthetic data
  - DeepOcean
  - CanonicalSolve3DRotation
- Real data
  - San Diego Trough South
  - San Diego Trough North

All four test cases are distributed as part of the OCCAM1DCSEM package.

Unlike the previous tests, which are benchmarks stressing very specific components of a system, the performance between the three platforms that are being tested does not differ significantly at all. In addition, multiple runs of the same test on one platform do not exhibit any performance variability. Figure 4 is a graph of the overall runtimes of the four example data sets mentioned earlier. The runtimes are clearly pretty uniform across the systems.

The Cloud shows much better performance than expected (based on previous benchmark results). Part of the explanation for this is that the performance-limiting factors (such as IO and memory) do not play a defining role in this application (it is primarily dependent on compute performance). Another possibility would be that the Cloud instances had exclusive access to the hardware while running the OCCAM1DCSEM tests. In order to be able to draw any conclusions on the real performance, it would be necessary to profile the application while at the same time monitoring the usage of the Cloud and its underlying resources.

4. HPC CLOUD PERFORMANCE

Application codes that are used for scientific simulation are often parallelised. The reason is that the problems being addressed are often to large or compute intensive to be solved in serial, or that they would simply take too much time to

Figure 3. Throughput performance of the Random Read operation on a CentOS instance for various records and file sizes

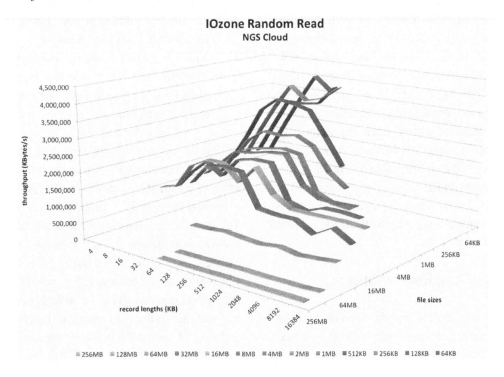

Table 2. File IO performance (random write on 256 MB file) comparison between the CentOS instance and MacBook Pro, using different record lengths

RandomWrite 256MB throughput (MB/s)	64KB	128KB	256KB	512KB	1MB	2MB	4MB	8MB	16MB
CentOS	28	41	47	43	55	39	39	38	44
MacOSX	2445	2527	2518	2598	2586	1835	1799	221	151

reach a solution. A key performance factor for such codes is therefore the speed at which physically distributed computational resources (be they processing units, nodes or images) can communicate with each other. In a parallel environment, the overall time to completion is dictated by the slowest component.

A second important element is data: scientific applications can generate vast amounts of data that needs to be available for processing beyond the application's runtime. The performance of the Input/Output (I/O) system is therefore also of significance.

4.1. Low Level Benchmarks

We chose the Intel MPI Benchmarks (IMB), because they offer both parallel communication performance and parallel I/O system benchmarks. In fact, the IMB suite consists of three parts: IMB-MPI1, which addresses the classical message-passing functionalities; IMB-EXT, which focuses on single-sided communication (a functionality that allows a process to directly access the memory of another process); and IMB-I/O, which looks at the performance of parallel reads/writes. In this study, we concentrate on the standard message-passing performance (as single-sided communication is much less widely used), as well as some basic MPI-I/O results.

4.1.1. PingPong Benchmarks

The most basic test that can be used to measure any communication overheads as well as a net-

work's throughput capabilities is the PingPong benchmark: a single message of a given size is passed from process A to process B (*ping*) and then passed back to process A (*pong*). The benchmark is implemented using the basic MPI_Send and MPI_Receive functions. Communicating values between single processes is a very common operation in parallel codes and understanding its performance is therefore vital.

Figure 5 shows the timings of the PingPong benchmark on both EC2 and XT4. The graph shows three different types of runs:

- **Intra-node measurements:** Performance of the benchmark between processes which are on the same node;
- **Inter-node measurements:** Two processes placed on different nodes, requiring the benchmark to use the network;
- **Multi inter-node measurements:** Multiple sets of PingPong benchmarks, each pair placed on different nodes using an 8x2 mapping.

For the intra-node test, i.e. when running the PingPong benchmark with both processes being placed on the same node, the performance exhibited by both EC2 and XT4 is comparable. The communications network is not being used and the benchmark in fact measures the speed of accessing the memory using MPI functions. For messages larger than 128 Bytes, EC2 shows better performance. This is, in fact, not surprising and due to the difference in the architecture and size of the nodes between the two systems.

Figure 4. Performance of OCCAM1DCSEM using two synthetic and two real data sets, comparing the performance on two cloud instances and a MacBook Pro laptop

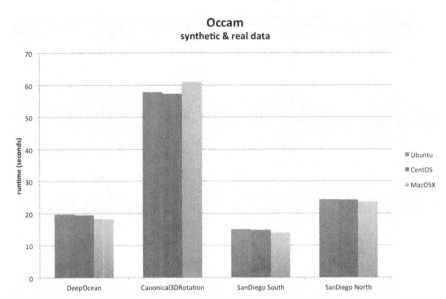

Remember that a single node on the XT4 consists of a quad-core AMD Opteron processor with 8GB of main memory, whereas an EC2 node consists of two quad-core Intel Nehalem processors with a total of 23GB of memory. Even though only two processes are involved in the benchmark, for large messages the access to the extra memory resources gives EC2 the edge.

This picture changes in favour of the XT4 however once the benchmark is forced to run across two nodes and use the communications network: the Cray is faster by an order of magnitude and the benefits of a high-performance interconnect become clear. With its inferior network, the EC2 Cloud struggles for performance.

The "multi" benchmarks are used to simulate a system under a full workload and all resources are used, so any artificial performance benefits that are the result from access to large amounts of main memory disappear. As the MPI communication is again forced to used the interconnect network, the XT4 again outperforms the Cloud.

Figure 6 shows the message throughput levels (in Mbytes per second) for the PingPong benchmark. The graph confirms the performance picture given by the timings and shows, perhaps more clearly, how a simulated full workload affects the performance. Throughput tops out at 85MBytes/s on EC2, whereas 475MBytes/s are achieved on the XT4.

4.1.2. Alltoall Benchmarks

While the PingPong benchmark is an example of point-to-point communication, the Alltoall benchmark tests collective communication where every process sends N bytes to all other processes and receives N bytes from those processes in return (i.e. a total of N bytes * #processes). The benchmark uses the MPI_Alltoall function. Similarly to the PingPong benchmark, collective communications are very common in parallel scientific codes and can often be bottlenecks as they can only complete if all participating processes execute them at the same time.

Figure 7 shows the timings of the Alltoall benchmark from 2 to 16 cores, comparing EC2 and XT4. For 2 and 4 cores, the performance dif-

Figure 5. Timings for the PingPong benchmark on EC2 and XT4

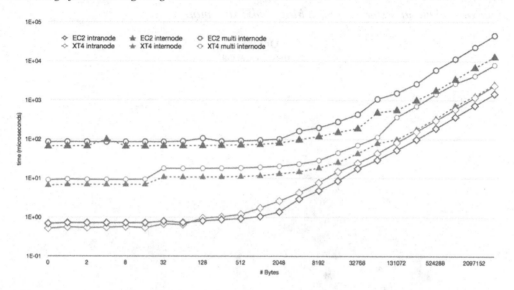

ference is relatively small, and for small message sizes, EC2 outperforms the XT4 – again, this is not surprising as the benchmarks run internal to the nodes and the more powerful Intel CPU and memory system will give EC2 the better performance. On 8 cores (which fit inside a node on EC2, but across two nodes on the XT4), the performance benefit of the intra-node communication on the Cloud becomes even clearer for messages up to 16KB where the timing difference is nearly an order of magnitude. Essentially, the EC2 can copy data to and from shared memory, where the XT4 needs to explicitly send data via the interconnect. However, for larger messages this benefit, which stems from the intra-node cache efficiency, mostly disappears as messages become too large to fit into the cache.

On 16 cores, both systems are forced to use the interconnect – here, the superior network on the XT4 makes a significant difference (up to an order of magnitude) for all message sizes.

4.1.3. Barrier Benchmark

Synchronisation of the concurrent processes is a vital part of parallel computing. It is needed to ensure that at points of communication, processes

have reached a given point in the program execution and will communicate the correct values to each other. In MPI, a common way of achieving synchronisation between processes is to call an MPI_Barrier, which will pause the execution of the program. The barrier is be activated by the first process to reach that part of the program, and it is released once all processes have reached it.

However, even if a program does not call MPI_Barrier explicitly, it may still have global synchronisation. MPI collective communication functions need to be executed by all processes at the same time and therefore contain an implicit global barrier. The collective communication routines implement functionality such as calculating a global sum or average of a particular value, or copying some data from one process to every process in the simulation. One of the reasons that collective communications are often a performance bottleneck is that global synchronisation can be very computationally expensive when using large numbers of processes and as such can have a significant impact on the overall performance of a parallel program.

Figure 8 shows the timings for the Barrier benchmark on 2 to 16 cores, using three different mappings: the "auto" distribution places

Figure 6. Throughput for the PingPong benchmark on EC2 and XT4

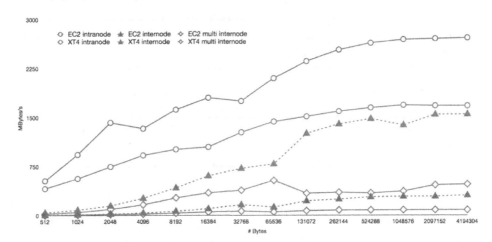

processes in an ideal fashion, i.e. if they fit onto a single node they will be mapped accordingly; the "8x2" distribution forces the barrier to be run across nodes; and the "8x2 multi" distribution uses all cores for multiple barrier across nodes, e.g. if 16 cores are available, this distribution will run 2-core barriers simultaneously.

Again, it is easy to spot the performance benefits of intra-node communication: for 2 and 4 cores, there is not much difference in performance between EC2 and the XT4, and on 8 cores, EC2 is slightly faster. However, as with the previous benchmarks, the big performance difference is exhibited by those benchmarks that force the use of the interconnect. The time to call a barrier jumps from 6μs on 8 cores to 170μs on 16 cores on EC2, whereas on the XT4 the differences is 11μs on 8 cores versus 19μs on 16 cores.

Figure 7. All-to-all performance comparison between EC2 and XT4

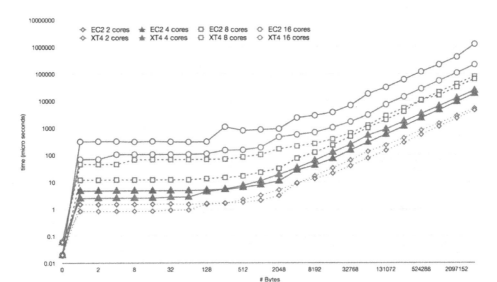

4.2. I/O Benchmarks

The IMB IO benchmarks measure the MPI IO performance, both in serial and in parallel. A wide range of tests are available, but we chose three representative cases that are common in parallel applications to study in more detail.

4.2.1. Master I/O

"Master IO" is a widely used read/write pattern in parallel computing, where a single process is performing all of the application's input and output. Two different types of write operations can be performed: blocking and non-blocking. In the non-blocking case, the CPU is artificially stressed immediately after initiating a transfer to simulate an asynchronous program flow. Figure 9 shows the time (in microseconds) taken by the benchmark to write files with varying sizes from 1 Byte up to 16MB on both EC2 and XT4. The difference between the *_indv and *_expl tests is a slightly different method of accessing the files: the *_indv tests are based on MPI_File_write, a blocking, non-collective operation with an

individual file pointer; and the *_expl test are based on MPI_File_write_at, also a blocking, non-collective operation but which is passed a file position directly as an argument.

The Amazon Cloud outperforms the XT4 all the way up to the largest files for all write methods, except the for the MPI_File_write test. For small file sizes, the XT4 appears to incur a significant amount of overhead penalties, which starts to be masked for larger files, at which point the performance catches up with EC2. Both systems are affected by OS jitter and cache effects, OS jitter referring to the effect on the performance of the operating system performing system operations whilst the benchmark is running (this is non-deterministic, so may impact the benchmark or may not, and can partially account for the variability in the benchmark results). IO functionality can also benefit from buffering of the IO by the system (this is the aforementioned "cache effects") but again this is dependent on what other operations and IO are occurring in the system at the time of the benchmark. Both these effects can be responsible for the variability in the performance obtained from the IO system on the resources we

Figure 8. Performance comparison of the MPI_Barrier benchmark using three different process mappings, both inside and across nodes, on EC2 and XT4

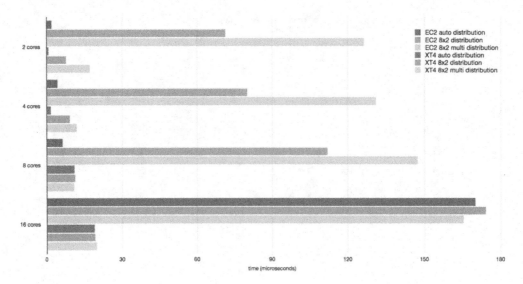

Figure 9. "Master Write" performance on EC2 and XT4

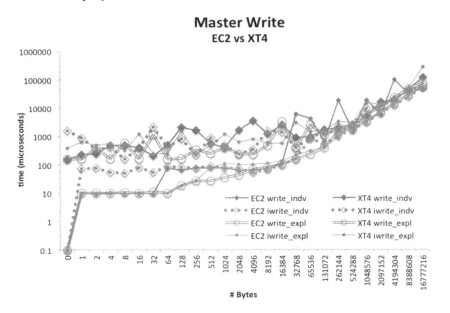

are using. The XT4 appears more prone to this for small files, whereas EC2 shows spikes in the timing curve for larger files. In addition, the XT4 uses a shared filesystem, with the I/O nodes connected to the compute nodes via the same network that is used for MPI communications; its performance can therefore depend on the load it is under. The XT4 filesystem is particularly optimised for writing of large amounts of data (GBs and above) so it is in fact not that surprising that the EC2 performance is better than the XT4 for the file sizes we tested here, especially if the EC2 virtual machines are writing to hard disks attached locally to the compute nodes.

4.2.2. Parallel I/O

Another important IO pattern in parallel computing is simultaneous access to N private files. An application may, for instance, write the state of each process at a certain point in the execution to file in order to be able to restart the calculation from there. The graph in Figure 10 shows the throughput (in MBytes/s) for a parallel write operation on EC2 and XT4 running from 2 up to 16 cores, accessing 1 file per process. Again,

EC2 outperforms the XT4, especially on the small files. This is probably due to the reasons already outlined in the previous paragraph.

Correspondingly, another common parallel read pattern involves N processes all reading information from the same file. Figure 11 shows the throughput performance exhibited by both systems. The file that is being read may be remote to some processes (i.e. does not reside on the process's node) and thus the performance of the network will become apparent. Therefore it is not surprising that the XT4's throughput for files above 512KB is far superior to that of EC2. In fact, for the 16MB files, the XT4 is faster by a factor of ~25.

4.3. Application Benchmark: GENE

While low-level benchmarks give a good insight to the performance of the basic components that make up a parallel scientific application, the information provided by them needs to be complemented by real applications benchmarks. We chose GENE, a gyrokinectic code used to simulate turbulence in plasma, as our representative parallel HPC application. GENE is a widely used and well-engineered

Figure 10. "Parallel Write" of N private files on EC2 and XT4

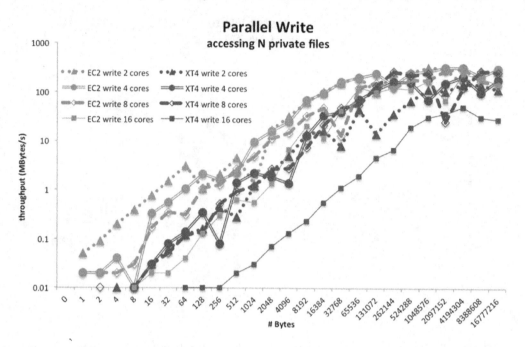

code, which is both compute- and communication-intensive and uses MPI to distribute computation across many processors. The requirements for GENE are: a compiler that supports Fortan95 and the MPI, FFTW 3, LAPACK and BLAS libraries. We built the most recent versions of these libraries for optimal performance.

GENE uses a five-dimensional parallelisation scheme – it is possible to run the application in auto-parallelisation mode, in which the code chooses its own distribution based on the number of cores and the hardware it is running on. Alternatively, the user can specify the distribution by hand. The overall runtime for the auto-parallelisation case is much longer, as the application needs to test all possible combinations before choosing the "optimal" distribution. The dataset used in our study in the standard "Cyclone" base test, which is included in the GENE distribution. Figures 12 and 13 show the times per time step on both EC2 and XT4 from 4 up to 32 cores, using the auto-parallelisation and the manual parallelisa-

tion methods. The speed-up going from 4 cores to 8 cores is a factor of 1.6 (compared to an ideal speed-up of 2) on EC2. We can see that whilst the EC2 gives slightly better compute performance on 4 and 8 cores (1 node on EC2, 2 nodes on XT4), the performance on 16 and 32 cores is far better on HECToR than on the EC2 instances. As soon as the computation involves more than one node on both systems (i.e. form 16 cores onwards), requiring the interconnect to be used for communication, the performance on the EC2 degrades rapidly. The auto-parallel version shows (relatively) better performance overall, yet there is a significant slowdown on 32 cores. Based on the results from the IMB benchmarks, this performance picture is no surprise. While EC2 can hold its own in terms of straight computing power inside a single node (i.e. up to 8 cores), the lack of a low-latency, high-bandwidth network will result in very poor scalability for tightly coupled HPC applications, which rely on fast communication more than on fast computing.

Figure 11. "Parallel Read" of a single common file on EC2 and XT4

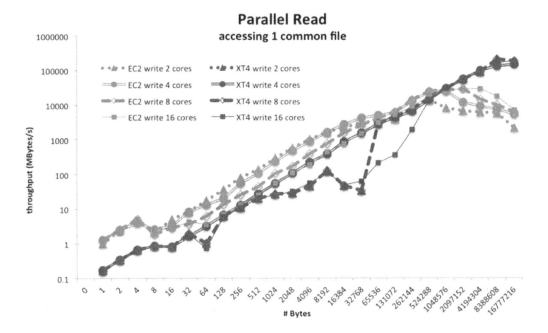

5. USABILITY

One of the selling points of Cloud resources such as those offered by Amazon is their quick access, easy-to-use, nature. A key objective of our study was the evaluation of this claim for HPC, where specialist environments are often a requirement. Dedicated HPC resources are set up with these requirements in mind, whereas Cloud resources need to cater for a much wider user base and thus may not immediately meet the needs of an HPC user.

In terms of access, Cloud and HPC resources vary quite significantly. Once resources have been allocated and an account has been granted, HECToR is simply accessed through an SSH connection. Amazon compute resources can be bought by anyone who can create an Amazon account and has a valid credit card. The instances are managed and set up via a web interface and then, like HECToR, accessed through SSH once they are up and running. For the NGS Cloud we had two options: we could either use the Eucalyptus com-

mand line tools, euca2ools, or a Firefox browser plugin called Hybridfox[6]. We chose the latter, mainly because the command line tools require a long list of dependencies to be installed on an up-to-date Linux system, which was not possible in the time available. The Hybridfox follows the same principles as the Amazon web interface as it is mainly used to manage and launch instances.

Once access has been gained, one of the foremost needs of a HPC user is of course to be able to run parallel jobs. At the time of these benchmarks a single Amazon Cluster Compute virtual machine instance offered access to 8 compute cores (all attached to the same shared memory). Therefore, in order to run larger parallel jobs, with more than 8 processes, it was necessary to start multiple node instances and enable communication between them. One of these instances acts as the master; the remaining ones are treated as compute instances. The setup requires a reasonable amount of user knowledge and effort, although an alternative to this "manual" setup of a cluster environment is the use a cluster setup utility, such as StarCluster[7].

Figure 12. Running GENE on EC2: time per timestep

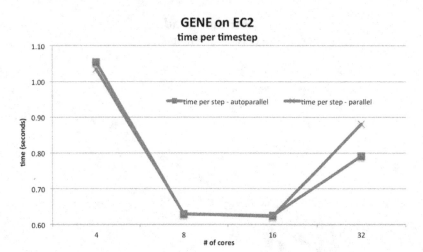

This tool was developed to simplify and automate the configuration of compute clusters hosted on Amazon's EC2; StarCluster includes shared storage across instances with NFS, a batch submission system and tools to manage images and data. In our case, the low-level benchmarks were run on manually configured clusters, whereas the application benchmark GENE was executed in a StarCluster environment.

On a dedicated supercomputer, a user does not need worry about enabling the hardware for parallel jobs, as it was built and configured with that type of utilisation in mind. Batch and queue systems, for instance, are a standard part of HPC services.

In addition to the hardware setup, HPC users require specialist software to build their applications and analyse results; compilers and scientific libraries fall into this category. The steps for setting

Figure 13. Running GENE on HECToR: time per timestep

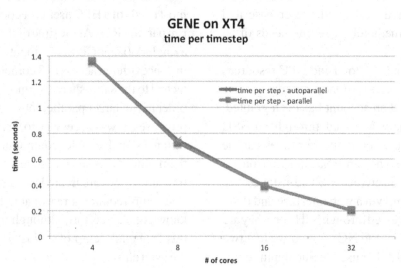

up the software environment are independent from the setup of the clusters themselves. For some of the instance types, Amazon offers a vast range of image configurations, which can be used directly or as starting points for specialised setups. A the time of this study however, the Amazon Cluster Compute images only ran the CentOS4.5 operating system and offered a basic environment, which needed to be updated in order to be suitable for our parallel benchmarks. CentOS4.5 uses GCC4.1.2 – this version of the compiler suite dates from early 2007. It was decided to upgrade the compilers to version 4.4, which is also supported by the OS. We then built the most recent release of the OpenMPI communications library, using this newer version of the compiler. A lot of dependencies in the environment relied on the older compiler and thus had to be reinstalled. The StarCluster tool offers a slightly more sophisticated environment, thus reducing the amount of user effort that is needed to configure the image instances.

Similarly to the hardware setup, a supercomputer will offer an environment that is tailored to large parallel scientific applications. Often several different versions of compilers and libraries are available to users and software is kept up-to-date as part of the service. HECToR for example runs a specialised version of Linux, Compute Node Linux (CNL), provided and customised by Cray. There are five different C, C++, and Fortran compiler suites available on HECToR, along with numerous scientific libraries for architecture-optimised mathematical and computational routines (such as FFT routines, matrix and vector operations, and many other functions commonly used in scientific simulation codes).

In terms of the software environment, the Cloud brings one clear advantage for advanced users: on a HPC service, access privileges are limited and changes to the configuration can only be made by systems support staff. On a Cloud instance however, a user has full access privileges and can configure the environment exactly as they see fit

– there is no danger of "breaking" the system, as it is only a virtual machine image, which can be shut down and restarted at will.

Long job turnaround times on busy supercomputers mean that the Cloud, for some users, potentially has a second advantage over a traditional HPC system. If users create and launch a Cloud image, that image will be available for use immediately (taking into account a short start-up delay). A HPC system is shared among many users and access to the resources is regulated using a scheduling system. The busier the system, the longer a job has to wait in the queue before being allowed to run.

Furthermore, traditional HPC systems generally have restrictive policies governing resource usage in place. Given the nature of these resources, shared between many different users all competing for a finite set of computing resources, access to resources is controlled through a scheduling system. The resources a user can utilise are controlled by the scheduling system, and the policies implemented through the scheduling system by the owners/operators of the resource. In the case of HECToR these policies mainly focus on how many jobs an individual user can run at any given time, and how long an individual job can run for. Currently, the longest run time for a computational program on HECToR is 12 hours, after this the job is terminated. Many computational simulations take far in excess of 12 hours, even when using large numbers of processes to process the work, therefore users have to adapt their programs to cope with a maximum runtime of 12 hours, generally by regularly writing data to disk to enable restart if the program is terminated. This has a cost, both in terms of the computational resources used (writing out data can be expensive from a performance point of view) and in the development effort required to modify programs to undertake this functionality.

HECToR also restricts users to only have 4 running jobs in a job scheduler queue at any given time. This policy is designed to ensure that all users get fair access to the machine, but can restrict a user who has a large amount of simulations to complete quickly.

Cloud resources, on the other hand, generally have no such restrictions. You purchase computing resources and providing you can pay for them you can run them for as long as you require. You can also purchase as many resources as you need, dependent only upon the available resources in the Clouds you have access to, and the associated cost.

While setup and usage of Cloud resources can initially be difficult, especially for less experienced users, the greater level of control over the environment may offer some advantages, for instance if users require non-traditional tools and increased access privileges. In addition, if the turnaround time of a job is more important that the actual performance, an instant access Cloud service can be a viable alternative to an HPC service. However, responsibility for ensuring that software is up-to-date and optimally configured is with the user in the Cloud whereas HPC services generally provide some optimised software and configured environment to ensure users get the best possible performance from the HPC machine.

6. COST

While performance and usability are both important factors when deciding whether to use traditional HPC or commercial Cloud resources, cost is of course another factor that cannot be ignored.

The HECToR HPC service is funded by the UK Research Councils[8] and scientists from UK academia make up the largest part of the user base. In order to get access to the system, the scientists apply for a grant from one of the Research Councils and ask for time of the HPC service as part of that grant. Academic users do not "pay" for the use of HECToR as such, however putting together a grant proposal can be time consuming and success is not guaranteed.

As mentioned earlier, Amazon's business model means that anyone who has a credit card can buy compute time. Users pay for resources and they can typically access these resources immediately. At the time this study was undertaken, one Cluster Compute instance (8 cores) cost $1.60 per hour. The cost of 8 cores per hour on HECToR (as met by the Research Councils) around that same time was approximately £0.80[9].

Since then Amazon have widened their line of products: in addition to the more expensive "on demand" instances (which is what we used), it is now possible to buy compute time in advance. Users can choose to reserve compute time (for light, medium or heavy use) and pay for it in advance, thus decreasing the cost of access. Amazon also offers the opportunity to bid for unused resources: if turnaround time is not vital, users can potentially get cheap access to the Amazon EC2 infrastructure.

There are a couple of pitfalls with the commercial model that users need to be aware of: unlike service such as HECToR, where an access grant includes all costs from compute to network and storage, these costs are extras in an environment such as the EC2. Storage, data transfer and network costs are all accounted and need to be paid for separately. Also, instances are billed for by the minimum unit of 1 hour – even if an instance is only active for a few seconds. Therefore, when using large numbers of instances on a Cloud like Amazon there can be significant extra costs for a computational job depending on the actual time it takes to complete. Consider a simulation that requires 4096 processes. If using 8-core nodes from the Cloud, this would require 512 Cloud instances. If the simulation runs for 4 hrs 59 minutes then the user will be charged for 2560 instance hours. However, if the simulation runs for 5 hrs 1 minute then the user is charged 3072 instance hours. With a cost of $1.60 per hour this is a difference of approximately $820 for two minutes of actual computing resources, whereas traditional HPC resources tend to charge for the actual time used (to the nearest second generally).

However, there are different charging models used in traditional HPC machines. The HECToR service uses the idea of a project with a specific lifetime (generally one to three years) and an allocation of computing time for that project. Then the project members can use the computing time as they like throughout the course of the project, with the understanding that any resources not used by the end of the project are lost. Other HPC services allocate resources for a project on a per month basis, with each project allocated a fixed amount of resources per month for the lifetime on the project. In this model users not utilising computing time in one month lose that computing resource. This model is designed to encourage users to consume their resources consistently throughout the lifetime of their project rather than in a number of large bursts. When facing a charging model like HECToR's the current charging models in the Cloud will not generally provide good value for money for users. However, compared to a model where resources are lost if not used the current Cloud charging models can be beneficial as resources are only charged when actually used.

A commercial Cloud can be expensive to use (and mistakes such as not shutting down instances cleanly or storing unnecessary data cost real money), especially if what users want is on demand access to a compute resource. For academic users, using a service like HECToR is likely to be cheaper than buying cycles from a commercial provider (provided the service is run efficiently and fully utilised), however gaining access to a larger HPC service may not always be straightforward and includes cost in both staff effort and time.

Ultimately, the argument for cost depends on the performance characteristics of the application that is being run, the impact of the absolute time to solution, as well as the availability of access to supercomputers. The choice of Cloud versus HPC needs to be based on all those factors.

CONCLUSION

From the benchmarks we have run we can see that whilst the Amazon compute Cloud does provide resources for large scale parallel programs they do not match the current performance available from existing HPC machines. The cost is comparable between Amazon and the XT4 for compute resources (Amazon is $1.60 per node per hour and the XT4 would be approximately $1.70 per node per hour). However, the cost associated with the XT4 covers all aspects of the service (compute, storage, network data transfer, etc...) whereas Amazon has extra costs for data storage and data transfers across the network.

We can see that for Clouds like the NGS Cloud (an academic, Eucalyptus based Cloud) with shared resources performance can be impaired for serial applications when compared with what can be obtained using local compute servers or resources, however the overall impact is very dependent on the specific hardware requirements of the program are, and of the usage of the shared resources by the other programs using those resources. This makes it very hard to predict the performance that a code will experience prior to runtime. It is also unlikely that any program/simulation code that undertakes significant computation (such as is usually undertaken by programs that use HPC resources) will obtain good performance from such shared resources given the shared nature of the Cloud. However, for programs that undertake pre- or post-processing of data from simulations, offline visualisation, or other functions that do not require exclusive CPU access this type of Cloud could provide a good type of resources (as the cost is likely to be lower than more traditional types of Cloud resources).

Another aspect that should be considered is the effort currently required by users to access and run on the Cloud. The parallel nodes on Amazon required extra setup to enable large (more than 8 core) parallel jobs to be run. Furthermore both Clouds required significant work on the virtual images before they could be used for the application or low-level benchmarks. The Amazon Clouds were reasonably straightforward but still required libraries to be compiled and installed on them. The NGS Cloud virtual images required much more work to configure and setup the disk space and other aspects of the operating system. Once this work has been done it can be re-used but it is not work that can be expected of general computational simulation scientists.

ACKNOWLEDGMENT

We would like to thank the NGS for providing. access to the NGS Cloud resources and support in our use of them.

REFERENCES

Barham, P., Dragovic, B., Fraser, K., Hand, S., Harris, T., & Ho, A. ... Warfield, A. (2003). *Xen and the art of virtualization*. In Symposium on Operating Systems Principles.

Huber, N., Quast, M. V., Hauck, M., & Kounev, S. (2011). Evaluating and modeling virtualization performance overhead for cloud environments. *Proceedings of the 1st International Conference on Cloud Computing.*

ENDNOTES

1. http://www.ngs.ac.uk
2. ECDF – Edinburgh Compute and Data Facility
3. This was true at the time our benchmarks were undertaken. Since then, Amazon have changed their product range and pricing. See http://aws.amazon.com/ec2 for details.
4. http://www.cs.virginia.edu/stream
5. http://www.iozone.org/
6. http://code.google.com/p/hybridfox
7. http://web.mit.edu/stardev/cluster/
8. http://www.hector.ac.uk/abouthector/partners/
9. At today's exchange rate (23rd January 2012), £0.80 = $1.25

Chapter 4
Cloud Computing in Academia, Governments, and Industry

Ahmed Shawish
Ain Shams University, Egypt

Maria Salama
British University in Egypt, Egypt

ABSTRACT

Cloud Computing is gaining a considerable attention in the past few years, where hardware and software are provided on-demand as a service through internet following the simple pay-as-you-go financial model. Using such powerful technology, several projects, in different areas, have been built like supporting academic and scientific researches, providing governmental services, and developing business applications. Unfortunately, the previous works and ongoing researches in these areas are scattered among the literature, on the internet, and from research groups, which makes it hard for researchers to be involved in such vast wave of researches. This chapter carefully reviews the emergence of the Cloud in all of the above mentioned areas through a wide range of well classified researches, projects, and applications that have been either innovated or improved due to the Cloud disclosure. Moreover, the chapter comparatively discusses the previous work done in these fields and explores the opened research points.

INTRODUCTION

Cloud Computing is gaining a considerable attention in the past few years, where hardware and software as a service are delivered on-demand through internet following the simple pay-as-you-go financial model. The source of the Cloud power is its ability to stand at different levels of service: (i) Infrastructure-as-a-Service (IaaS), where Cloud enables access to hardware resources such as servers and storage devices, (ii) Platform-as-a-

Service (PaaS), where Cloud allows the access to software resources such as operating systems and software development environment, and (iii) a Software-as-a-Service (SaaS), where Cloud is an alternative to classical software applications running locally on personal computers which are, instead, provided remotely by the Cloud. Such service-oriented diversity makes the Cloud Computing a very powerful technology and it becomes crucial to understand and explore its methodologies.

DOI: 10.4018/978-1-4666-2854-0.ch004

Cloud Computing has emerged in several spectrums of our life. It invigorates the academic field, the scientific research conduction, the governmental services provisioning, and business applications development, by methods that have been either innovated or improved by the emergence of such promising technology. Each spectrum has taken advantage from the Cloud by its own means. For example, the academic and scientific researches benefit from the Cloud's high performance computation capabilities. Governments gain from the Cloud's availability, infrastructure, and software services offered on demand, while cost minimization and globalism were the main benefit for the business domain.

In the academic field, the emergence of the Cloud is invigorating all of the educational activities and scientific research. For example, the UK government funded MaterialsGrid project inherently encompasses many concepts of the Cloud computing before the term "Cloud " emerged (Yang X. et al. 2010a, Yang X. et al. 2010b, Yang X. et al. 2012b). Various educational platforms have been innovated based on Clouds (Burd, Seazzu, & Conway, 2009), (Erkoç & Kert, 2011), (Tao & Long, 2011) (Cappos, Beschastnikh, Krishnamurthy, & Anderson, 2009), as well as research platforms (IBM/Google Academic Cloud Computing Initiative (ACCI)). Also, academic libraries started moving their systems to the Clouds (OCLC WorldShare), (DuraSpcace), cutting down their costs. Multiple research projects in several areas; such as image processing (Alonso-Calvo, Crespo, Garc´ıa-Remesal, Anguita, & Maojo, 2010), data mining (Grossman & Gu, 2008); are now using the required computational resources from the Clouds, instead of building complex computing infrastructures.

The Governmental services are strongly interested in using Cloud Computing to reduce IT costs and increase capabilities. A growing number of government entities are immigrating to Cloud in order to acquire the infrastructure and software they need while making operations faster,

cheaper and more sustainable. Experts predict that government IT shops can save on equipments, licensing, staffing resources, office space, storage and more. Now, there are Governments that provide IT Cloud service platforms (Catteddu & Hogben, 2009) for governmental use, for offering either IT end-solutions services (Public Works and Government Services Canada (PWGSC)) or public service portals in health (State Legislatures, 2010), business, and schools directories. In addition, governments work on providing Cloud platforms and products for research projects purposes (Seventh Framework Programme).

In the businesses domain, many companies, not only the IT specialized ones, use Cloud-based services such as infrastructure and platform. Such technology helps them to pay as they go without the need of hiring in-house IT services or spending money for hardware. Besides, services are automatically scaled whenever the requirements or utilization are increased or decreased. The advent of Cloud Computing has driven euphoria of what IT and business can do with the access to applications and services across the Internet. Many companies providing web operations; e.g. web hosting (Liu & Wee, 2009), deployment and monitoring (Sedayao, 2008); such as Microsoft, Google and Amazon, took the lead to move to Cloud platforms. Pharmacy management (Lamont, 2010), real-time financial systems (Aymerich, Fenu, & Surcis, 2009) and enterprise fraud management (Unal & Yates, 2010) are examples of the enterprise services that took the lead to employ the Cloud services. The benefits will be tangible and will fundamentally transform enterprises of all sizes around the globe access information, share content and communicate.

Though the heavy rely on Clouds, yet Cloud failures are as complex as the underlying software that powers them. During the past two years, Cloud services have reported a minimal rate of outages in a subset of the entire network. Very few Cloud outages have caused massive data losses, and after reviewing most of these outages, it is clear that

Cloud service providers are still uncertain about how they do upgrades or estimate loads to the network when doing maintenance.

This chapter provides a survey on the Cloud Computing projects in the academic field, governmental services, and business applications, as illustrated in Figure 1. In addition, it also provides a detailed background of the previous work done in each field using classical technologies such as Grid or distributed systems. Open research issues and comparative discussions are appended at the end of each field.

The rest of this chapter is organized as follows: Section 1 presents the academic education and research platforms, along with scientific computing. In Section 2, the governments' work is presented. Enterprise and business solutions are presented in Section 3. The whole chapter is finally concluded.

1. ACADEMIC EDUCATION, RESEARCH PLATFORMS, AND SCIENTIFIC COMPUTING

Cloud Computing has emerged in the academic activities; where each activity has taken advantage from the new technology in its own way. Various

educational services, such as libraries and labs, succeed to reduce their IT costs when moving to Clouds. Also, the research gets benefit from the Clouds in terms of the offered high performance computing and storage capabilities offered.

The first distributed environments were established in academic environments during the previous decade. Recently, Cloud Computing has been emerged as a new potential super structure for academic activities like education, libraries, and scientific computing researches. It also has a strong potential to generate innovative collaboration methods and new behaviors. Various educational platforms have been innovated based on Clouds in order to replace the on campus computers and software by computing resources and applications delivered via the internet to reduce the burden of IT complexity and maintenance. Academic libraries started moving their systems to the Clouds, cutting down their costs and increasing capabilities. From the scientific computing perspective, multiple researches projects in several areas; such as image processing, data mining and others; are now using their required extensive computational resources from the Clouds, instead of building complex computing infrastructures. Educational and research platforms, as well as library and scientific computing are the main topics to be covered for

Figure 1. Cloud computing life spectrums

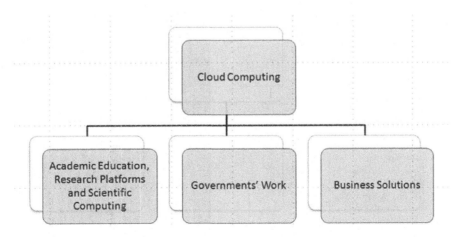

the academia, as demonstrated in Figure 2. These topics will be covered in the following sections, each along with the Cloud-based projects.

1.1 Academic Educational Platforms

The Cloud Computing trend of replacing software traditionally installed on campus computers (and the computers themselves) with applications delivered via the internet is driven by the aims of reducing universities' IT complexity and cost (Sasikala & Prema, 2010). Cloud Computing could be a technological innovation that both reduces IT costs for the college and eliminates many of the time-related constraints for students, making learning tools accessible for a larger number of students (Behrend, Wiebe, London, & Johnson, 2011).

There are many benefits of Cloud Computing for educational institutes:

- With Cloud Computing, universities can open their technology infrastructures to businesses and industries for research advancements.

- The efficiencies of Cloud Computing can help universities to keep pace with ever-growing resource requirements and energy costs.

- The extended reach of Cloud Computing enables institutions to teach students in new, different ways and help them manage projects and massive workloads.

- When students enter the global workforce, they will better understand the value of new technologies (Cloud Computing: Delivering Internet-based information and technology services in real time).

- Cloud Computing allows students and teachers to use applications without installing them on their computers, and also allows access to saved files from any computer with an Internet connection (Siegle, 2010).

1.1.1 Educational Cloud-Based Platforms

To get an idea of this new type of educational platforms, one should look into the following projects: Virtual Computing Lab (VCL) (Burd, Seazzu, & Conway, 2009), Distributed University

Figure 2. Cloud computing in academia

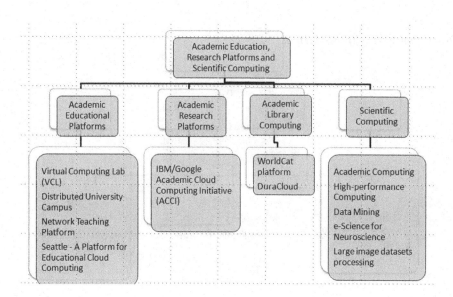

Campus (Erkoç & Kert, 2011), Network Teaching Platform (Tao & Long, 2011), Industry Training Platforms (CloudRooms virtual classrooms), (Junosphere) and Seattle (Cappos, Beschastnikh, Krishnamurthy, & Anderson, 2009) which is a platform for educational Cloud Computing.

1.1.1.1 Virtual Computing Lab (VCL)

The Virtual Computing Lab (VCL) is a Cloud Computing solution that is designed to address the unique needs of academic institutions. Computational resources for teaching staff, students, and researchers require flexibility in order to be effective in diverse environments. The VCL enables this in an unprecedentedly affordable manner (Burd, Seazzu, & Conway, 2009).

Students use computers extensively, both within and outside of the classroom, to conduct research, complete assignments, and interact with instructors and other students. Many colleges and universities provide computing laboratories for students' use, typically distributed across campus locations, containing dozens to hundreds of computers, and providing both general and special-purpose software applications. Campus computing labs (Physical Lab) provide many benefits to students; including enabling them to avoid hardware and software purchase, maintenance, and administration. Conversely, campus computing labs are a considerable expense to educational institutions, as well as their operation, maintenance, and administration is complex. Figure 3 illustrates an interaction scenario with a VLab (Burd, Seazzu, & Conway, 2009).

From a college student satisfaction point of view, students are satisfied with the VLab primarily due to its convenience and accessibility; especially by solving the queuing problem near the end of semesters when students become frustrated by the lack of a line for the next available workstation.

Comparing physical and virtual labs, students must be physically present at a PLab location during hours when the facility is open. In contrast, a VLab is accessible 24:7 from any Internet-connected computing device with sufficient bandwidth and appropriate access software. Both lab types provide access to specialized software applications not installed on student computers, though the VLab extends access to these resources. Access and availability are especially important to the students population since few of them live on or near their university campus and the majority of them work part- or fulltime.

Figure 3. User interaction with a VLab containing multiple workstations

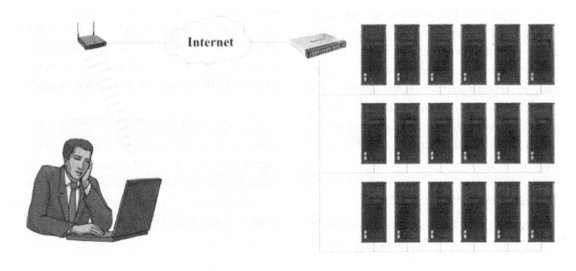

Costs for workstation base units, software, and networking are essentially the same for both lab types, though cabling costs are slightly lower for a VLab due to shorter cable runs. PLabs incur costs for workstation peripherals and furnishings that aren't required for a VLab. The lack of furnishings, lighting, and other "human-oriented" features makes the VLab approximately 25 times more space-efficient than the existing PLab of the same capacity. Quantifying the resulting economic savings is inexact since it depends on actual space costs, opportunity costs for the space savings, and whether alternative student work or meeting space is required when a PLab is converted to a VLab.

1.1.1.2 Distributed University Campus

Cloud Computing is presenting an infrastructure scenario to be used by the universities that have distributed campus. As shown in Figure 4, a community Cloud Computing and storage infrastructure, development platform, and software delivering is presented (Erkoç & Kert, 2011).

The new IT approaches for managing effectively the technological needs of universities; such as delivery of software, providing development platform, data storage and computing; is based on Cloud Computing. Students will have access to all software anytime, anywhere and any technological devices connected internet by suggested Cloud structure. Also, students will have access to development platform, and develop their applications, and store on university infrastructure. In this way, lecturers will focus their basic teaching tasks without disturbance to their workforce. With suggested Cloud structure, universities can open their technology infrastructures to businesses and industries for research advancements and develop university-industry collaboration (Erkoç & Kert, 2011).

1.1.1.3 Network Teaching Platform

Network Teaching Platform became an important modern education method. Network teaching is developed from the computer aided teaching and distance learning. It is a new teaching mode relying on computer network to realize. Students can watch instructional video; download learning materials or online communication with teachers and other operations, which break through the traditional teaching models that suffer from limited time and space. In the network teaching process, students can learn anytime, anywhere to break through the traditional teaching using a simple way to acquire knowledge, to better train students in the initiative, highlighting the individual student learning (Tao & Long, 2011).

With the popularity of network teaching, network teaching platform cannot meet the existing high-performance, low cost, scalability and other needs. The emergence of Cloud Computing provides a new network teaching solutions, to establish a unified, open and flexible network teaching platform and reduce the hardware input. Heilongjiang University has constructed a set of building network teaching with Cloud Computing. As reported, the system has achieved good results, which for the future construction of the network teaching platform provides a new solution.

A framework of the modern distance education platform has been designed based on Cloud service models according to the actual needs to ensure scalability. Figure 5 shows the overall chart of Cloud-based modern distance education platform (Tao & Long, 2011), which mainly consists of Cloud Server, Load Balance Device and Database. At present, the application of Cloud Computing platform of modern distance education is at the primary stage; as few universities pioneered the concept of the Cloud and put it into practice.

1.1.1.4 Industry Training Platforms

Many industry training platforms are leading the way in this field, such as Junosphere, a Cloud-based network labs from Cisco and Juniper (Junosphere), as well as CloudRooms, the virtual classrooms solution from REDTRAY (CloudRooms virtual classrooms).

Figure 4. Cloud computing structure diagram for Distributed University Campus

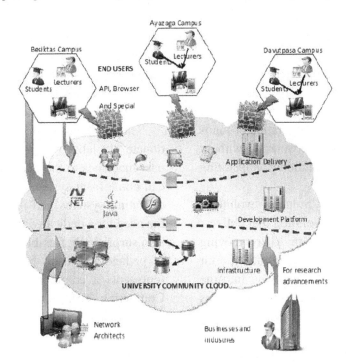

Junosphere gives customers cloud-based network lab access to virtual instances of Junos, allowing engineers to build whatever topologies they need for testing and learning. It is a virtual environment that enables the creation and operation of elements and networks using the Juniper Networks Junos operating system. Offered in the form of software-based services, Junosphere enables customers, partners, and educational institutions to easily experiment, model, and educate by leveraging the flexibility, cost efficiency, and simplicity of a cloud-based delivery model.

Figure 5. Cloud-based network teaching platform framework structure

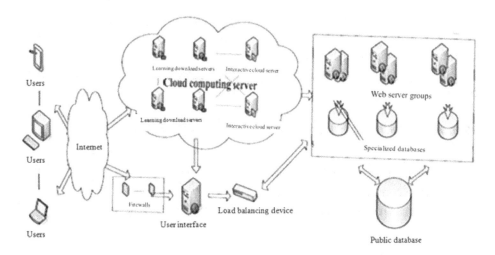

Junosphere Lab enables to create and run exact replicas of physical networks within the virtual Junos environment. Users can model, test and experiment with new features, topologies or services with no risk and dramatically reduced costs. Junosphere Classroom also enables to cost effectively educate students, employees, or partners on the principles and operation of Junos OS, routing protocols, and networking, without the expense of building, maintaining or operating a physical lab (Junosphere).

CloudRooms is a Redtray Solution revolutionary new virtual classroom solution that delivers live online learning anytime, anywhere, moving learning into the future. The bricks and mortar training centers of today are evolving into the virtual training centers of tomorrow. It enables organizations to develop the skills, knowledge and certifications of its people without days out of the office at training courses. CloudRooms is an online, live training centre that allows learning to take place over the internet. The instructor and students communicate using the telephone or Voice over IP (VoIP), and online chat. This allows interaction without compromising either delivery or delegate support. A virtual classroom is a virtual copy of a normal classroom setting. This means there are the usual components of learners attending the training, a live instructor presenting the materials, course notes and joining instructions. The difference is that there is no physical meeting space and everything happens online. By that, CloudRooms ensures that learners still experience the same levels of interactivity as they do in a traditional classroom (CloudRooms virtual classrooms).

1.1.1.5 Seattle: A Platform for Educational Cloud Computing

Seattle is a free educational research platform that is community-driven; a common denominator for diverse platform types; it has been broadly deployed. Companies such as RedHat, Microsoft, Amazon, Google, and IBM are increasingly funding Cloud Computing infrastructure and research, making it important for students to gain the necessary skills to work with Cloud-based resources (Cappos, Beschastnikh, Krishnamurthy, & Anderson, 2009).

Seattle is community-driven; universities donate available compute resources on multi-user machines to the platform. These donations can come from systems with a wide variety of operating systems and architectures, removing the need for a dedicated infrastructure. Seattle is also surprisingly flexible and supports a variety of pedagogical uses, because as a platform it represents a common denominator for Cloud Computing, Grid computing, peer-to-peer networking, distributed systems, and networking. Seattle programs are portable. Students' code can run across different operating systems and architectures without change, while the Seattle programming language is expressive enough for experimentation at a fine-grained level. The current deployment of Seattle consists of about one thousand computers that are distributed around the world. Seattle's is a simple to learn programming language, a subset of the Python language, is expressive enough to allow students to build algorithms for inter-machine interaction. As a result, Seattle is useful in many pedagogical contexts ranging from courses in Cloud Computing, networking, and distributed systems, to parallel programming, Grid computing, and peer-to-peer computing. Seattle is a community-driven effort that depends on resources donated by users of the software (and as such is free to use). A user can install Seattle onto their personal computer to enable Seattle programs to run using a portion of the computer's resources.

Limited compute resources have been a key constraint in teaching distributed systems. Seattle is architected to do this safely and efficiently.

Seattle is lighter-weight software that exposes locality and is therefore suited for students in distributed systems courses. Seattle also comes with a widely accessible ready-to-use platform of thousands of machines. Seattle is simple to use, but target teaching of distributed systems issues that arise at Internet scales. Lastly, because Seattle runs on a variety of embedded platforms with limited resources; such as cellular phones and PDAs; the platform complements prior work on platforms for teaching ubiquitous computing.

1.1.2 Comparing Academic Educational Platforms

The use of Cloud Computing on universities has reported many benefits; such as accessing the file storages, e-mails, databases, educational resources, research applications and tools anywhere for faculty, administrators, staff, students and other users in university, on demand. Furthermore, Cloud Computing reduces universities' IT complexity and cost, by its paradigms and characteristic, service and deployment models. The application program of Cloud is able to save hardware resources, software and services to provide effective protection of the overall security of teaching platform. Cloud Computing provides a new concept for the development of modern education. The application of this concept will extend learning platforms, as well as admit more students into learning.

1.2 Academic Research Platforms

Recently, many research institutes are struggling to adapt Cloud Computing for solving problems that need high computing and storage capabilities. In general, there are three main attractive factors in Cloud Computing with respect to the academic researches:

- The provision of concurrent increase of computing power and storage capacity.
- The ability to accommodate and manipulate the exponentially growing scientific data, which result in delivering more accurate simulation results.

It is worth to mention that IBM and Google were among the first ones to initiate the emergence of Cloud Computing in the academic research under the name of "IBM/Google Academic Cloud Computing Initiative" (ACCI) (IBM/Google Academic Cloud Computing Initiative (ACCI)). This program funds various university research projects, addressed in the Cloud-based platforms section. On the other hand, there are a variety of research platforms implemented based on Grid and volunteer computing, like Globus, BOINC, SETI@Home and Folding@Home. These researches are addressed in the background section.

1.2.1 Background: Distributed Research Platforms

There is a variety of Grid computing and volunteer computing platforms, such as Globus Toolkit and Berkeley Open Infrastructure for Network Computing (BOINC). Both target distributed computation and strive to hide locality and similar information from the programmer.

Globus Toolkit (Foster I. T., 2005) is a popular Grid toolkit, which has been used to build a variety of service-oriented applications. The open source Globus toolkit is a fundamental enabling technology for the Grid; letting people share computing power, databases, and other tools securely online across corporate, institutional, and geographic boundaries without sacrificing local autonomy. The toolkit includes software services and libraries for resource monitoring, discovery, and management, plus security and file management (Globus Toolkit). However, the Globus Toolkit has been widely used as middle-ware in Grid computing environments; it does not support interactive jobs submission, nor is there an interactive extension for Grid computing portals. Only high-level client side tools were provided that encapsulates a variety of distributed Grid operations; such as transferring data, executing jobs, and visualization of its final result across heterogeneous resources. Client tools are capable of providing the most direct and specialized access to Grid resources, but the main limitation of this form is its complication and inconveniency because the end users are required to deploy and conFigure the specialized client applications, libraries and packages.

BOIN is a volunteer computing platform supporting several powered science projects. BOINC leverages donated CPU cycles for computation, particularly spare resources on home machines (BOINC project). SETI@Home (SETI@Home) and Folding@Home (Folding@Home) projects are powered by BOINC. SETI@home is an Internet-based public volunteer computing project employing the BOINC software platform, hosted by the Space Sciences Laboratory, at the University of California, Berkeley, in the United States. Its purpose is to analyze radio signals, searching for signs of extra-terrestrial intelligence, and is one of many activities undertaken as part of SETI (Search for Extra-Terrestrial Intelligence). Folding@home is a distributed computing project designed to use spare processing power on personal computers to perform simulations of disease-relevant protein folding and other molecular dynamics, as well as to improve on the methods of doing so.

Generally, dependability represents a major issue in volunteer computing. Like any project based on volunteer computing, there are factors that may threats the regular running of Globus and BOINC.

1.2.2 Cloud-Based Research Platforms

1.2.2.1 IBM/Google Academic Cloud Computing Initiative (ACCI)

The IBM/Google Academic Cloud Computing Initiative (ACCI) is a joint university initiative to help computer science students gain the skills they need to build Cloud infrastructures and applications (IBM/Google Academic Cloud Computing Initiative (ACCI)).

The IBM/Google initiative aims to provide computer science students with a complete suite of open source based development tools so they can gain the advanced programming skills necessary to innovate and address the challenges of the Cloud Computing model - which uses many computers networked together through open standards - and thereby drive the Internet's next phase of growth. The companies will provide hardware, software and services to augment university curricula and expand research horizons while lowering the financial and logistical barriers for the academic community to explore Internet-scale computing. The following resources are available from IBM and Google to Universities to leverage for their respective projects:

- A cluster of processors running an open source implementation of Google's published computing infrastructure (MapReduce and GFS from Apache's Hadoop project).
- A Creative Commons licensed university curriculum developed by Google and the University of Washington focusing on massively parallel computing techniques.
- Open source software designed by IBM to help students develop programs for clusters running Hadoop. The software works with Eclipse, an open source development platform.
- Management, monitoring and dynamic resource provisioning by IBM using IBM Tivoli systems management software.

Using this virtual IT lab, students will learn how to develop systems and write massively parallel applications that take full advantage of the distributed computing paradigm rather than the conventional one-server, one-application model. Google and IBM's first pilot phase of the ACCI, granted several prominent US universities access to this large infrastructure. The University of Washington was the first to join the initiative, and a short list of other universities was added to pilot the program.

In 2008, the ACCI partnered with the National Science Foundation to provide grant funding to academic researchers interested in exploring large-data applications that could take advantage of this infrastructure. This resulted in the creation of the Cluster Exploratory (CLuE) program, which currently funds 14 university research projects.

1.2.3 Comparing Academic Research Platforms

In the current financial crisis and being challenged by growing needs, universities are facing problems in providing necessary information technology (IT) support for research and development activities. Due to this aspect, universities are confronting with a dramatic increase of costs in higher education, more than the inflation rate and a decrease of budgets, which leads to the pressure of finding some alternative means of reaching their purpose; i.e. the education of students and accomplishing the research. Performing research based the concept of volunteer computing might not accomplish the expected efficiency and effectiveness of all research operations and might not fit all kinds of research projects. Thus, the potential and efficiency of using Cloud Computing in research has been recognized by many universities and research projects, as it is offering them the possibility of concentrating more on teaching and research activities rather than on complex IT configuration and software systems through a fast IT implementation.

1.3 Academic Library Computing

Cloud Computing offers for libraries many interesting possibilities that may help reduce technology costs and increase capacity, reliability, and performance for some types of automation activities.

In libraries, the energy costs associated with servers are not tended to think much about. It is tended to have few servers so that energy costs do not amount to a very large portion of the library's overall expenses. But for those libraries that operate large data centers, power is a huge concern. It takes a lot of energy to run the equipment and almost as much to keep it cool. Avoiding those power costs is no small consideration and can represent a benefit for pushing as much of the computing infrastructure to the Cloud as possible. SaaS and Cloud Computing can reduce energy consumption for a library (Breeding, 2009).

1.3.1 Cloud-Based Library Solutions

While the various models of platform hosting and software-as-a-service have become firmly established in the library automation arena, there are a couple of high-profile examples. OCLC probably ranks as the most prominent example of Cloud Computing in the library arena, producing and maintaining WorldCat platform (OCLC WorldShare), the largest online public access catalog (OPAC) in the world. In the institutional repository arena, DuraCloud (DuraSpcace) has been launched as an interesting example of Cloud Computing.

1.3.1.1 WorldCat Platform

The WorldCat platform involves a globally distributed infrastructure that involves the largest scale library-specific implementation. Its recent plan to offer library automation functions such as circulation, licensing, and acquisitions to complement existing cataloging, resource sharing, and end-user search capabilities will be a major test of its ability to deliver core business services to libraries through a Cloud-computing model (OCLC WorldShare).

1.3.1.2 DuraCloud

DuraCloud is a Cloud-based service developed and hosted by the nonprofit organization DuraSpace. DuraCloud is an open source platform and managed service that provides on-demand storage and services for digital content in the Cloud. This service makes the preservation of the content simple and cost effective. DuraCloud makes it easy to move copies of library content into the Cloud and store them with several different providers, eliminating the risk of storing content with a single Cloud provider (DuraSpcace).

Library of Congress and DuraCloud launched pilot program using Cloud technologies to test perpetual access to digital content, where Dura-Cloud will let an institution provide data storage and access without having to maintain its own dedicated technical infrastructure. DuraCloud will provide both storage and access services, including content replication and monitoring services that span multiple Cloud-storage providers.

1.3.2 Comparing Library Platforms

As Cloud infrastructure becomes more of a standard approach for building applications, many other projects can be expected, both by commercial organizations and in individual libraries, to follow this approach. It becomes more important to take advantage of the most efficient technology models available, especially in these times where libraries must work with constrained financial resources. While the most abstract approach of Cloud Computing may not fit all library technology scenarios, some level of hardware consolidation or abstraction will help to gain efficiencies and performance while reducing costs. The days of each library operating its own local servers have largely passed. This approach rarely represents the best use of library space and personnel. As libraries develop the next phase of their technology strategies, it's important to think beyond the locally maintained computer infrastructure that increasingly represents an outdated and inefficient model. Cloud Computing offers opportunities for libraries to expend fewer resources on maintaining infrastructure and to focus more on activities with direct benefit on library services.

1.3.3 TurnItIn Plagiarism Detection Service

Turnitin is an Internet-based plagiarism-prevention service created by iParadigms, LLC. Typically, universities and high schools buy licenses to submit essays to the Turnitin website, which checks the documents for unoriginal content. The results can be used to identify similarities to existing sources or can be used in formative assessment to help students learn how to avoid plagiarism and improve their writing (turnitin).

1.4 Scientific Computing

The long history of science can be divided into three significant periods: empirical, theoretical and experimental/simulation – The first one was mainly experiential, without facilities to abstract, capture and share scientific knowledge. The second period of the great discoveries was followed by the formulation of the key scientific theories. They have been captured, shared and reused widely. Currently passing the period of the great experimental sciences, torrents of data used for simulation and an unprecedented level of sharing and collaboration among scientists are created.

High-performance scientific computation using Cloud Computing resources became an alternative to traditional resources. The availability of large, virtualized pools of computational resources raises the possibility of a new, advantageous compute paradigm for scientific research. Scientists who do not need advanced network performance,

Cloud Computing can provide convenient access to reliable, high-performance clusters, without the need to purchase and maintain or even understand sophisticated hardware and high-performance computational methods. For developers, Cloud virtualization allows scientific codes to be optimized and pre-installed, facilitating control over the computational environment.

In the following sections, important scientific computing areas are explored; Academic Computing, High-performance Computing (Hazelhurst, 2008), Data Mining (Grossman & Gu, 2008), e-Science initiative (Yang X. et al. 2009), especially for Neuroscience (Watson, Lord, Gibson, Periorellis, & Pitsili, 2008), and Large image datasets processing (Alonso-Calvo, Crespo, Garc´ıa-Remesal, Anguita, & Maojo, 2010). For each scientific area, classical projects are first discussed as background, then projects that have been based on Clouds are explored, and finally a comparison between both is presented.

1.4.1 Academic Computing

Computational Grids are very large-scale aggregates of communication and computation resources enabling new types of applications and bringing several benefits of economy-of-scale. They cover multiple administrative domains and enable virtual organizations. The key characteristic of Grids is their ability to upscale and downscale rapidly and gracefully. So, they provide utility type of computing which enables another type of business model and spawns start-up businesses. The first computational Grids were established in academic environments during the previous decade, and today are making inroads into the realm of corporate and enterprise computing. Recently, Cloud Computing has been emerged as a new potential super structure for academic computing.

Architecturally speaking, Grids represent collections of data centers that are globally, regionally or locally placed and exhibit resilience and high availability (Strong, 2005). Highly abstracted, the Grid can be perceived as a large-scale application execution platform in which aggregation, virtualization and scheduling are the key abstractions enabling Grid operations.

Grids originated in the academic domain which was not so concerned about security and dependability (Delic, On Dependability of Corporate Grids, 2005). While targeting a global interconnected Grid where applications can run flexibly over the entire Grid as needed, some arguments have appeared about the type of Grid applications which will lead to wider usage of Grids with the important observation that the typical workloads for academic/scientific applications are very different from commercial workloads.

The emergence of Cloud fabrics enables new insights into challenging engineering, medical and social problems. Previously, there was no easy means to tackle peta-scale type of problems, nor carry out mega-scale simulation, which Cloud Computing enables. One interesting thread will be to revisit 50 year old problems in Artificial Intelligence or explore further the "Science of Services", both being under the auspices of Complex Systems research. Academic activities are well under way as the scientists have struggled for a long time with vast amounts of data coming not only from the web but also from a rising number of instruments and sensors (Hand, 2007). In several ways the emergence of the computing Cloud is invigorating academic research and having strong potential to spawn innovative collaboration methods and new behaviors (Delic & Walke, Emergence of The Academic Computing Clouds, 2008).

Computational Grids were originated in academic circles, but it looks as if computing Clouds may have a different growth path. Computing Clouds are huge aggregates of various Grids, computing clusters and supercomputers, used by a huge number of people either as users or developers. Thus, Computing Clouds denotes massive participation, collaboration and content creation by millions of users on an omnipresent, always available mega-structure. This poses big challenges, but offers some unprecedented opportunities.

Generally, Cloud Computing has particular strength as it draws on many existing technologies and architecture and integrates centralized, distributed and 'software as service' computing paradigms into an orchestrated whole. For now, Cloud Computing is a very promising computing technology paradigm, especially for the emergence of Academic Cloud Computing.

1.4.2 High-Performance Computing

High-performance computing (HPC) is the use of parallel processing for running advanced application programs efficiently, reliably and quickly. High-performance computing systems are important in scientific computing. The most common users of HPC systems are scientific researchers, engineers and academic institutions. Some government agencies, particularly the military, also rely on HPC for complex applications. High Performance Computing (HPC) allows scientists and engineers to solve complex science, engineering and business problems using applications that require high bandwidth, low latency networking, and very high compute capabilities. Typically, scientists and engineers must wait in long queues to access shared clusters or acquire expensive hardware systems (Hazelhurst, 2008).

Clusters of computer systems, which range greatly in size, are a common architecture for high performance computing. Small, dedicated clusters are affordable and cost-effective, but may not be powerful enough for real applications. Larger dedicated systems are expensive in absolute terms and may be inefficient because many individual groups may not be able to provide sustained workload for the cluster. Shared systems are cost-effective, but then availability and access become a problem.

An alternative model is that of a virtual cluster, as exemplified by Amazon's Elastic Computing Cloud (EC2) that provides a feasible, cost-effective model in many application areas. It provides customers with storage and CPU power on an on-demand basis, and allows a researcher to dynamically build their own, dedicated cluster of computers when they need it. Used by commercial web services deployers, this technology can be used in scientific computing applications. Using Amazon EC2 Cluster instances, customers can expedite their HPC workloads on elastic resources as needed and save money by choosing from low-cost pricing models that match utilization needs. Customers can choose from Cluster Compute or Cluster GPU instances within a full-bisection high bandwidth network for tightly-coupled and IO-intensive workloads or scale out across thousands of cores for throughput-oriented applications. Today, AWS customers run a variety of HPC applications on these instances including Computer Aided Engineering, molecular modeling, genome analysis, and numerical modeling across many industries including Biopharma, Oil and Gas, Financial Services and Manufacturing. In addition, academic researchers are leveraging Amazon EC2 Cluster instances to perform research in physics, chemistry, biology, computer science, and materials science.

Many scientific and other applications require high-performance computing, a catch-all phrase to describe applications characterized by large data sets requiring significant computing resources. Such applications may require hundreds to hundreds of thousands of CPU-hours, and so to be practical, they have to be parallelized. The launch of Amazon's Web Services, in particular the Simple Storage Service (S3) and Elastic Computing Cloud (EC2), provides the scientific community with another possible platform for high-performance computing needs.

There is still the opportunity – indeed need – for sharing. For example, for bioinformatics research, EC2 offers the potential for doing many searches in parallel. However, this requires large amounts of data to be stored in S3. For instance, storing the major bioinformatics databases would be ideally if shared between many users.

Compared to smaller, dedicated clusters, the main disadvantages are communication delays in transferring data and lack of GUI tools. Whether EC2 is cost-effective compared to a dedicated cluster depends on the utilization levels of the machines in the cluster. Where clusters are idle for the majority of the time, the EC2 is an attractive solution. Yet, for many scientific research applications, EC2/S3 will provide a much more cost-effective path that leads to solutions in faster time.

1.4.3 Data Mining

Generally, data mining, the extraction of hidden predictive information from large databases, is a powerful new technology with great potential to help institutes focus on the most important information in their data warehouses. Data mining tools predict future trends and behaviors, allow making proactive, knowledge-driven decisions. The automated, prospective analyses offered by data mining move beyond the analyses of past events provided by retrospective tools typical of decision support systems. Data mining tools can answer business questions that traditionally were time-consuming to resolve. They scour databases for hidden patterns, finding predictive information that experts may miss because it lies outside their expectations.

Historically, high performance data mining systems have been designed to take advantage of powerful, but shared pools of processors. Generally, data is scattered to the processors, the computation is performed using a message passing or Grid services library, the results are gathered, and the process is repeated by moving new data to the processors.

A Cloud-based infrastructure called Sector/Sphere was designed for data mining large distributed data sets over clusters connected with high performance wide area networks. Sector/Sphere is open source and have been used it as a basis for several distributed data mining applications. The infrastructure consists of the Sector storage Cloud and the Sphere compute Cloud. Sector/Sphere supports distributed data storage, distribution, and processing over large clusters of commodity computers, either within a data center or across multiple data centers. Sector is a high performance, scalable, and secure distributed file system. Sphere is a high performance parallel data processing engine that can process Sector data files on the storage nodes with very simple programming interfaces (Grossman & Gu, 2008).

Sector was designed to provide long term persistent storage to large datasets that are managed as distributed indexed files. Different segments of the file are scattered throughout the distributed storage managed by Sector. Sector generally replicates the data to ensure its longevity, to decrease the latency when retrieving it, and to provide opportunities for parallelism. Sector was designed to take advantage of wide area high performance networks when available.

Sphere was designed to execute user defined functions in parallel using a stream processing pattern for data managed by Sector. From functionalities point of view, Sector manages data using distributed, indexed files; while Sphere processes data with user-defined functions that operate in a uniform manner on streams of data managed by Sector. Sector/Sphere scale to wide area high performance networks using specialized network protocols designed for this purpose.

Several applications were built with Sector and Sphere. Angle is a Sphere application that identifies anomalous or suspicious behavior in TCP packet data that is collected from multiple, geographically distributed sites. Angle contains Sensor Nodes that are attached to the commodity Internet and collect IP data. Connected to each Sensor Node on the commodity network is a Sector node on a wide area high performance network. Angle Sensor nodes collects IP data, anonymizes the IP data, and produces "pcap" files that are then managed by Sector. Sphere aggregates the pcap files by source IP and computes files containing features. Briefly, Sector services are used to manage the data collected by Angle and Sphere services are used to identify anomalous or suspicious behavior.

1.4.4 E-Science for Neuroscience

The CARMEN e-science project is a generic e-science platform, designed system to allow neuroscientists to share, integrate and analyze data. An expandable range of services are provided to extract added value from the data. CARMEN is accessed over the web by neuro-informaticians, who are populating it with content in the form of both data and services. CARMEN project is using Cloud Computing to address challenging requirements from the key scientific domain of neuroscience. Its aim is to enable the sharing and collaborative exploitation of both data and analysis code so that neuroscience can get much more value from the collected data. The overall result of this situation is that there are only limited interactions between research centers with complementary expertise, and a severe shortage of analysis tools that can be applied across neuronal systems (Watson, Lord, Gibson, Periorellis, & Pitsili, 2008).

Cloud Computing approach was attractive for meeting the CARMEN requirements largely because of the significant amount of data that will be stored and analyzed by scientists. Estimates put this in excess of 100TB by 2010 for the 20 neuroscientists involved in the project, though if video capture of neuronal activity continues to supersede electrode-based recording this may be a serious underestimate. Where there are huge amounts of data to be processed, it is more efficient to move the computation to the data rather than the other way around. This requires having computational resources closely coupled to the servers holding the data. Cloud Computing offers the chance to do this if the Cloud is internally engineered with fast networking between the storage and computing servers.

The basic aim of CARMEN is therefore to provide a Cloud, named CAIRN, which neuroscientists interact with through a web-based portal. The main abilities required by the neuroscientists are:

- To upload experimental data to the CAIRN.
- To search for data that meets some criteria; e.g. all data captured under particular experimental conditions.
- To share data in a controlled user-defined way with collaborators.
- To analyze data. Meanwhile, it is not possible to define a closed set of services that will meet all the analysis needs of all scientists. But, new algorithms are being investigated all the time, consequently, there needs to be a way for scientists to add new services.

Existing Cloud Computing offerings focus on providing low-level compute and data storage services (e.g. Amazon S3 and EC2). Build applications to support the neuroscience requirements directly on this low-level platform was not the perfect solution, instead to deploy a set of generic e-science services was deployed, and then build domain specific neuro-informatics services and content on top of these, as shown in Figure 6 (Watson, Lord, Gibson, Periorellis, & Pitsili, 2008).

1.4.5 Large Image Datasets Processing

A large number of gigabytes of multimedia information are being generated every day over the world. Institutions, hospitals, companies, and governments are producing large image and video collections. Methods for image storing and processing are needed for managing these multimedia collections. Particularly, the data volumes and processing difficulty associated to very-large images pose a challenging problem.

Nowadays there exist some types of images in certain application areas with very-large sizes due to the progressive increase of resolution and quality in capturing instruments. For example, the Blue Marble project of NASA (National Aeronau-

Figure 6. E-science cloud

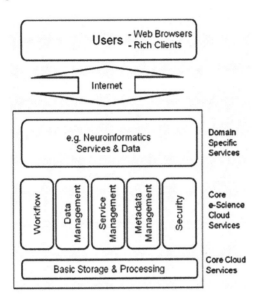

tics and Space Administration) obtains images whose sizes can be over 1 GB (PNG file). Another example can be certain high resolution medical images, such as ultra-high optical coherence tomography images. Working with these images implies large memory and processor resources. These datasets are difficult to manage, and their sizes continue to increase.

Managing large image collections has become an important issue for information companies and institutions. A Cloud Computing service and its application for the storage and analysis of very-large images has been developed. This service has been implemented using multiple distributed and collaborative agents. For image storage and analysis, a region-oriented data structure is utilized, which allows storing and describing image regions using low-level descriptors. Different types of structural relationships between regions are also taken into account. The final purpose is to create a Cloud Computing service capable of storing and analyzing very-large image datasets. This way, the service allows users to access additional virtualized computing and storage resources. Particularly, the service enables to analyze very-

large images by providing both computational and physical resources.

A distinctive goal of this application is that data operations are adapted for working in a distributed mode. This allows that an input image can be divided into different sub-images that can be stored and processed separately by different agents in the system, facilitating processing very-large images in a parallel manner. A key aspect to decrease processing time for parallelized tasks is the use of an appropriate load balancer to distribute and assign tasks to agents with less workload (Alonso-Calvo, Crespo, Garc´ıa-Remesal, Anguita, & Maojo, 2010).

A Cloud Computing service prototype for storing and analyzing images has been developed. The service stores an image and its associated information. Regions, and their relationships, are used as the basic entities for both representing and processing an image. Therefore, the system must be able (i) to extract the image regions (and their relevant relationships), (ii) to process, and (iii) to store them. A problem is that the amount of regions in an image is usually very-large, and the relationships between them can be relatively complex.

The Cloud Computing service has been implemented as a multi-agent system. A schema of the system is depicted in Figure 7 (Alonso-Calvo, Crespo, Garc´ıa-Remesal, Anguita, & Maojo, 2010).

1.4.6 Comparing Cloud-Based Scientific Computing

Scientific Cloud Computing is generally feasible and has advantages for many scientists; e.g. those who moderate computational requirements that cannot be satisfied with a simple workstation, but who lack access to large super computer and storage facilities. Scientific users of computation appreciate the ownership of virtual resources, since this reduces the uncertainly concerning access when needed. This difference between batch

Figure 7. Cloud computing service schema for large images processing

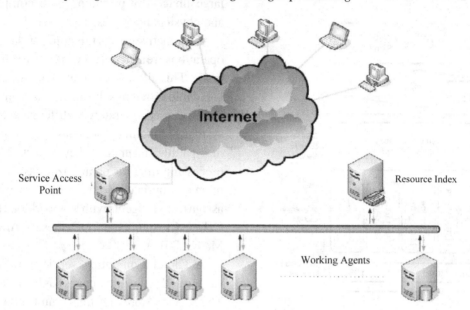

job queues and allocation of virtual resources is a fundamental difference between the Grid and Cloud experiences for the user. Likewise, virtual machines can simplify application deployment by reducing the possible compatibility issues between the application and the hosting environment. This is another fundamental difference and is particularly important for scientific users where numerical accuracy and stability may be an issue. Scientific computing will demand closer coupling of servers, access to data, and the ability to manage performance through proper abstractions exposed through service level agreements. This argues for the separate deployment of science Clouds that have these properties. Hence, even science Clouds may follow the deployment trajectory from private, to federated, hybrid, and finally public Clouds. By that, as soon as Clouds federate, many of the necessary capabilities that have been fundamental to the Grid concept, such as identity management and virtual organizations, will become directly relevant to Cloud environments.

1.5 Summary

In several ways, the emergence of the computing Cloud invigorated academic research and had strong potential to spawn innovative collaboration methods and new behaviors. The academic world got benefits and practical scientific uses, enabling new insights into challenging engineering, medical and social problems. Academic activities are well under way as the scientists have struggled for a long time with vast amounts of data coming not only from the web but also from a rising number of instruments and sensors. Academic computing Clouds appeared, supporting the emergence of Science 2.0 activities. From the Scientific Computing perspective, Cloud Computing is generally feasible and has advantages for many scientists; e.g. those who moderate computational requirements that cannot be satisfied with a simple workstation, but who lack access to large super computer and storage facilities.

As a conclusion of the strong and weak aspects of Cloud Computing in the academic world, the payment per use model and the management policies of risks and security represent positive factors in taking the decision of using Cloud Computing. Concerning the pay-as-you-go model, universities are paying cloud providers only when they access computing services; reducing the costs of under-utilization, and with no longer need to invest heavily or encounter difficulties in building and maintaining complex IT infrastructure. Moreover, Cloud Computing adds value with small capital expenses, assuring at the same time the protection of the environment. At the end, universities and research centers may value the opportunities offered by Cloud Computing through researchers and students and thus leading to innovation.

While several kinds of Cloud Computing platforms exist, the various Cloud implementations share two main features: they abstract the underlying compute components, and operational cost based on actual usage. The pay-as-you-go billing strategy is not new, and has many potential advantages, especially for scientists who do not require 24/7 accessibility. Many computational scientists have used shared compute facilities for decades and are accustomed to being billed per CPU-hour. Yet, what makes Cloud architectures a compelling new product for scientific computing, and what differentiates them from existing supercomputing facilities, is the abstraction of the underlying compute components. These components range from hardware infrastructure to operating systems to software packages for various scientific areas.

2. GOVERNMENTS' WORK

Cloud Computing has also emerged in the governments' services provisioning, where the last has gained from the Cloud's infrastructure and software services offered on demand. Moving to the Clouds, governments succeeded to reduce their IT costs; as well as increasing their services capabilities and availability for their citizens.

A growing number of government entities are examining the benefits of immigrating to Cloud to acquire the infrastructure and software they need

while making operations faster, cheaper and more sustainable. Experts predict that government IT shops can save on equipment, licensing, staffing resources, office space, storage and more. And, if state and local governments combine their purchasing power to acquire computer resources via the Cloud, they can achieve even greater savings. Governments work using Cloud Computing can be categorized mainly in three different areas. Governments provide IT Cloud service platforms for governmental use, for offering either IT end-solutions services or public service portals. Public service portals might be in health, business, and schools directories. Some governments also focus on providing Cloud platforms and products for research projects purposes. The different three areas of governmental work are discussed along with their projects in the following sections, as listed in Figure 8.

2.1 Government Service Platforms

Governments got use to build their own IT infrastructures to offer electronic services to the public. Lately, national governments started to provide Cloud service platforms for government services as a whole. Such kind of Cloud service platforms are used only by government organizations that have administrative access for providing public services; e.g., public administration, internal affairs and healthcare.

In the next sub-sections, an overview about classical technology and telecommunications services that usually governments offer is presented, and then several Cloud IT services offered different governments are discussed.

2.1.1 Background: Governments Technology Infrastructures

Governments were offering a wide range of services to the public in different public sectors, such as health, and internal affairs. Meanwhile, such services were built on classical IT infrastructures,

Figure 8. Cloud computing in governments

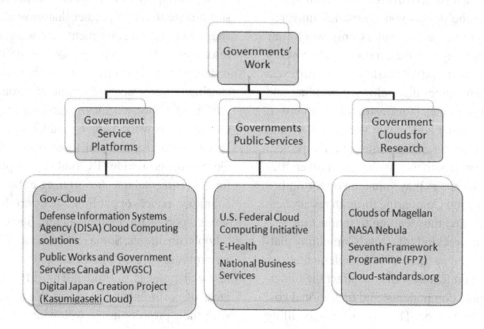

where the governments had to purchase their own servers and software. Building complete IT infrastructures for a service increased the total IT costs for hardware, software, maintenance, updates and administration.

2.1.2 Cloud-Based Infrastructures

2.1.2.1 Gov-Cloud

Gov-Cloud is a Cloud service platform provided by national governments for government services as a whole. This is a hybrid private-partner Cloud since it is used by trusted partners only and only government organizations have administrative access (e.g., public administration, healthcare). Examples include eHealth portal delivered by EuropeanHealth. Gov-Cloud uses a dedicated network infrastructure, which is physically independent of the public Internet. The Gov-Cloud is hosted in multiple geographical locations but virtual machines can be migrated from one site to another (Catteddu & Hogben, 2009).

2.1.2.2 Defense Information Systems Agency (DISA) Cloud Computing Solutions

The DISA is developing a number of Cloud Computing solutions available to US military, DoD government civilians and DoD contractors for Government authorized use (Defense Information Systems Agency (DISA)). They include:

- Forge.mil is a family of services provided to support the DoD's technology development community. The system currently enables the collaborative development and use of open source and DoD community source software. These initial software development capabilities are growing to support the full system life-cycle and enable continuous collaboration among all stakeholders including developers, testers, certifiers, operators, and users.
- GIG Content Delivery Service (GCDS) provides a reliable and secure content and application distribution services solution

that accounts for information assurance and secure delivery of application data to geographically dispersed user communities. GCDS also demonstrates the ability to efficiently obtain and distribute applications and content to end users regardless of the network conditions.

- Rapid Access Computing Environment (RACE) is a quick-turn computing solution that uses the revolutionary technology of Cloud Computing to give the needed platform quickly, inexpensively and securely. RACE is available to US military, DoD government civilians and DoD contractors for Government authorized use.

2.1.2.3 Public Works and Government Services Canada (PWGSC)

The Canadian Government's CTO of Public Works Government Services presented a paper on Cloud Computing and the Canadian Environment. Essentially, the paper outlines the Canadian Government's intention to pursue Cloud Computing. It discusses the advantages of their vast landscape and cold climate as prime reasons for the construction of large energy efficient Cloud Computing data centers (Public Works and Government Services Canada (PWGSC)).

2.1.2.4 Digital Japan Creation Project (Kasumigaseki Cloud)

Japan's Ministry of Internal Affairs and Communications (MIC) released a report outlining the Digital Japan Creation Project (ICT Hatoyama Plan) which seeks to create new Information and Communications Technology (ICT) markets to help boost Japan's economy. Within this plan is an outline to create a nationwide Cloud Computing infrastructure tentatively called the Kasumigaseki Cloud (Ministry of Internal Affairs and Communications Japan (MIC)).

2.1.3 Comparing Classic and Cloud Service Platforms

Building complete IT infrastructures for a governmental service increased the total IT costs for hardware, software, maintenance, updates and administration. But, recently governments started exploring the benefits of Cloud Computing to acquire the infrastructure and software they need while making operations faster, cheaper and more sustainable.

2.2 Governments Public Services

Governments offered a wide range of electronic services; either IT services (mail, cyber-security, web hosting), or web portals for public service, built on top of classical IT infrastructures. Getting use of Cloud Computing features, national governments started to provide Cloud solutions to the public, as well as electronic services built on top of Cloud platforms.

In the next sub-sections, an overview about classical technology and telecommunications services that usually governments offer is presented, and then several Cloud IT services offered different governments are discussed.

2.2.1 Background: Governments Technology and Telecommunications Services

Governments offer a wide range of classical IT and telecommunications services and solutions, ranging from one-off purchases or as part of a total IT solution. Such services might include data center services, cyber-security, hardware and software products and services, serving a wide range of citizens, consumers and businesses. A clear example of governments presenting IT services is U.S. General Services Administration (GSA) (U.S. General Services Administration (GSA)). From another side, governments offered electronic services to the public, in different sectors such as health and internal affairs.

The cost for providing IT services based on classical IT technology is, in fact, high; since it requires software maintenance, administration and updates from one side, and hardware issues from the other side.

2.2.2 Cloud-Based Services

2.2.2.1 U.S. Federal Cloud Computing Initiative

Cloud Computing plays a key role in the President's initiative to modernize Information Technology (IT) by identifying enterprise-wide common services and solutions and adopting a new Cloud Computing business model. The Federal Cloud Computing initiative is a services-oriented approach, whereby common infrastructure, information, and solutions can be shared and reused across the Government. The overall objective is to create a more agile Federal enterprise, where services can be reused and provisioned on demand to meet business needs.

The General Services Administration (GSA) is participating in the Federal Cloud Computing Initiative and is responsible for the coordination of GSA's activities with respect to the Initiative via its Program Management Office (CC PMO). GSA and the CC PMO are focusing on implementing projects for planning, acquiring, deploying and utilizing Cloud Computing solutions for the Federal Government that increase operational efficiencies, optimize common services and solutions across organizational boundaries and enable transparent, collaborative and participatory government. The Federal CIO Council under the guidance of the Office of Management and Budget (OMB) and the Federal Chief Information Officer (CIO), established the Cloud Computing Initiative to fulfill the President's objectives for Cloud Computing.

Projects of the U.S Federal Cloud Computing Initiative include:

- **Apps.gov:** Apps.gov is the official Cloud Computing Storefront for the Federal Government. The site features a complete listing of all General Services Administration (GSA) approved Cloud services available to federal agencies. It was launched in September 2009, as a web-based storefront for federal agencies that makes it easy for them to get Cloud services such as hosted e-mail, word processing, collaboration, website creation and more (State Legislatures, 2010).

- **Data.gov:** As a priority of the Open Government Initiative for U.S. President's administration, Data.gov increases the ability of the public to easily find, download, and use datasets that are generated and held by the Federal Government. Data.gov provides descriptions of the Federal datasets (metadata), information about how to access the datasets, and tools that leverage government datasets. The data catalogs will continue to grow as datasets are added. Federal, Executive Branch data are included in the first version of Data.gov (Data.gov).

- **IT Dashboard:** The IT Dashboard provides the public with an online window into the details of Federal information technology investments and provides users with the ability to track the progress of investments over time. The IT Dashboard displays data received from agency reports to the Office of Management and Budget (OMB), including general information on over 7,000 Federal IT investments and detailed data for nearly 800 of those investments that agencies classify as major (IT Dashboard).

2.2.2.2 E-Health

EuropeanHealth represents a large government health service in Europe but does not describe any specific national health service. EuropeanHealth is composed of public organizations and private suppliers providing eHealth services. It is a very large organization spread across several sites and it caters to 60 million citizens. Prior to using any kind of Cloud infrastructure, it has over 20 IT service providers and more than 50 data centers (Catteddu & Hogben, 2009).

The specific scenario involves an eHealth platform that provides care and monitoring of patients with chronic illnesses in their homes. This general process is described in more detail as follows:

1. A monitoring centre uses an independent Internet-based platform deploying in-home sensors to monitor and interact with elderly patients at home.
2. The monitored variables are analyzed for anomalies based on a profile. A monitoring centre decides when more specialized services are needed (doctors, nurses, etc).
3. Patients may also choose to make information available to external eHealth service providers. Such private information is provided via a centralized database.
4. Services are provided to elderly patients at home using a multimodal interface that adapts to the abilities of the elderly. Avatars and speech synthesis can be used.

The monitored data is available to doctors and hospitals through the unique patient medical record service. Patient information can be accessed through the unique patient identifier. This service provides documentation of a patient's medical history and care. Meanwhile, the project should take into consideration the privacy concerns regarding in-home sensors delivered over the internet; i.e. how to protect the public from personally identifiable information from being made available to the hackers.

2.2.2.3 National Business Services

The Department of the Interior's National Business Center (NBC) is bringing the benefits of Cloud Computing to both NBC's business services clients and data center hosting clients alike through advancements to the highly efficient NBC shared infrastructure. The governments' products and programs include:

- NBC's Hybrid Cloud capability allows customers to combine NBCGrid and NBCFiles with their existing infrastructure - creating front ends to complex web applications and burstable storage and server capacity in concert with existing NBC or client physical infrastructure.
- NBCApps is NBC's Cloud-based application marketplace. A variety of applications are available, including general knowledge worker tools, as well as more highly specialized applications.
- NBCAuth is NBC's SaaS directory service, authentication & SSO product. It allows authentication between the different applications in NBC's Cloud product suite to occur seamlessly, and links back to an agency's internal directory services infrastructure, such as Active Directory.
- NBCFiles is NBC's Cloud storage offering. It allows burstable storage capacity on a metered, pay-per-gigabyte price model. NBCFiles usage and status can be monitored via the unified Cloud.nbc.gov customer portal. NBCFiles' capabilities can be leveraged for application storage and content delivery, or as a backup platform. Multiple security tiers drive pricing, similar to NBC's other offerings. NBCFiles also offers the ability to integrate directly with on-site government networks.
- NBCGrid is NBC's IaaS offering. This service allows the end-user provisioning of a variety of types of servers and operating

systems through a single customer portal at Cloud.nbc.gov. NBCGrid provides technology-agnostic server hosting, with a variety of pricing models, including metered and pre-paid, based on the customer's usage of RAM or CPU per hour.

- NBCStage is NBC's PaaS platform. It allows software developers to build applications with highly scalable capacity, while staying within the bounds of the federal Government's IT regulations and standards. NBCStage has language specific APIs for many common programming languages. NBCStage works in concert with the Federal Government's community of software developers to help make the product reflect their needs. Usage and application monitoring is available from within the Cloud.nbc.gov portal.

2.2.3 Comparing Classic and Cloud Governments' Public Services

Governments, offering a wide range of electronic services for institutions or small businesses built on top of Cloud Computing infrastructures, are cutting down their IT cost compared with building complete IT infrastructures. For instance, hardware purchase and maintenance cost is greatly minimized, as well as infrastructure administration and software maintenance and updates. From another side, governments are also getting use of Cloud platforms to provide public service portals in several areas such as health and internal affairs, still reducing their IT cost to a great extent. Back to the classical way of handling IT services, the cost for providing IT services based on classical IT technology is, in fact, high; for this requires software maintenance, administration and updates from one side, and hardware issues from the other side.

2.3 Government Clouds for Research

As the emergence of Cloud Computing opened a new era for the research, governments started to explore using Cloud Computing for serving research. Cloud projects for the research include projects for testing Cloud Computing capabilities for scientific computing, Clouds for bundling all research-related initiatives together under a common roof and Cloud standardization projects.

In fact, such kind of research projects was not previously present before the emergence of Cloud Computing concept, especially when it comes for bundling all research-related initiatives together under a common roof, playing a crucial role in reaching the goals of growth, competitiveness and employment in various fields. To get an idea of this new type of projects, one should look into Clouds of Magellan (Magellan), NASA Nebula (NASA), Seventh Framework Programme (Seventh Framework Programme) and Cloud-standards.org (Cloud Standards Coordination) examples.

In the following sub-sections governmental Clouds for research are presented with the research projects that were built on top of them.

2.3.1 Clouds of Magellan

A New program funded by the American Recovery and Reinvestment Act through the US Department of Energy (DOE) will examine Cloud Computing as a cost-effective and energy-efficient computing paradigm for scientists to accelerate discoveries in a variety of disciplines, including analysis of scientific data sets in biology, climate change and physics. The DOE is exploring the Cloud concept with its federal partners to identify opportunities to provide better service at lower cost through Cloud services. The DOE National Laboratories are exploring the use of Cloud services for scientific computing. To test Cloud Computing for scientific capability, DOE centers at the Argonne Leadership Computing Facility (ALCF) and the National Energy Research Scientific Computing

Center (NERSC) will install similar mid-range computing hardware, but will offer different computing environments. The combined set of systems will create a Cloud testbed that scientists can use for their computations while also testing the effectiveness of Cloud Computing for their particular research problems. Since the project is exploratory, it's been named Magellan in honor of the Portuguese explorer who led the first effort to sail around the globe and for whom the Clouds of Magellan were named (Magellan).

2.3.2 NASA Nebula

Nebula is a Cloud Computing pilot under development at NASA Ames Research Center. It integrates a set of open-source components into a seamless, self-service platform, providing high-capacity computing, storage and network connectivity using a virtualized, scalable approach to achieve cost and energy efficiencies. The fully-integrated nature of the Nebula components provide for extremely rapid development of policy-compliant and secure web applications, fosters and encourages code reuse, and improves the coherence and cohesiveness of NASA's collaborative web applications. When completed, Nebula will offer cost-effective Infrastructure-as-a-Service (IaaS), Platform-as-a-Service (PaaS) and Software-as-a-Service (SaaS). As a hybrid Cloud, Nebula enhances NASA's ability to collaborate with external researchers by providing consistent tool sets and high-speed data connections (NASA).

2.3.3 Seventh Framework Programme (FP7)

The Seventh Framework Programme (FP7) bundles all research-related EU initiatives together under a common roof, playing a crucial role in reaching the goals of growth, competitiveness and employment; along with a new Competitiveness and Innovation Framework Programme (CIP),

Education and Training Programmes, and Structural and Cohesion Funds for regional convergence and competitiveness. It is also a key pillar for the European Research Area (ERA) (Seventh Framework Programme).

The broad objectives of the FP7 have been grouped into four categories: Cooperation, Ideas, People and Capacities. For each type of objective, there is a specific program corresponding to the main areas of EU research policy. All specific programs work together to promote and encourage the creation of European poles of scientific excellence.

The areas of research include; Health; Food, agriculture and fisheries, and biotechnology; Information and communication technologies; Nanosciences, nanotechnologies, materials and new production technologies; Energy; Environment (including climate change); Transporatation (including aeronautics); Socio-economic sciences and the humanities; Security; and Space.

Research projects led under FP7 are:

- OPTIMIS (Optimized Infrastructure Services) project takes a holistic approach to management of compute Clouds. With the challenges of service and infrastructure providers as the point of departure, OPTIMIS focuses on open, scalable and dependable service platforms and architectures that allow flexible and dynamic provision of advanced services.
- RESERVOIR project is intended to increase the competitiveness of the EU economy by introducing a powerful ICT infrastructure for the reliable and effective delivery of services as utilities. This infrastructure will support the set-up and deployment of services on demand, and competitive costs, across disparate administrative domains, while assuring quality of service.

2.3.4 Cloud-standards.org

Cloud-standards.org is a Wiki site for Cloud Standards Coordination launched by National Institute of Standards & Technology Laboratory (NIST). The goal of the wiki is to document the activities of the various SDOs working on Cloud Standards. Cloud-standards.org is an initiative for editing and sharing a general Cloud Computing standardization positioning; in which more relevant Cloud standardization initiatives can be seen and related. The first informal proposal of the positioning can be seen at Cloud standards positioning (Cloud Standards Coordination).

NIST is positioning its working definition of Cloud Computing that serves as a foundation for its upcoming publication on the topic. Computer scientists at NIST developed this draft definition in collaboration with industry and government. It was developed as the foundation for a NIST special publication that will cover Cloud architectures, security, and deployment strategies for the federal government. NIST's role in Cloud Computing is to promote the effective and secure use of the technology within government and industry by providing technical guidance and promoting standards.

2.4 Summary

Throughout the previously presented projects in various public services and research areas, it becomes a fact that governments started exploring the Cloud concept with its federal partners to identify opportunities for providing better service at lower cost through Cloud services.

Although Cloud Computing is presenting an efficient solution for governments' duties, yet two main concerns arise; cost and security. Projected cost savings have been the main driving point of the Cloud initiative. However, many believe that the cost of transitioning from the current IT infrastructure to the Cloud will entail costs that would far outweigh any savings that may result

in the future. Security is another major concern for Cloud Computing, and multiple incidents in the recent past haven't improved the situation. A list of recent Cloud Computing security breaches has been recorded. For instance, the Pentagon suffered its largest breach, in which hackers obtained 24,000 confidential files, an operation suspected to be carried out by foreign intelligence. In this regard, several government departments, especially those like Defense, State and Homeland Security that deal with confidential information, have found themselves hesitant to place their faith in Cloud Computing. Governments still have serious hurdles to overcome; in terms of public perception of the secure processing of citizens' personal information in Cloud Computing infrastructures. On top of this, there are also legal and regulatory obstacles which prevent many e-Government applications from moving to Cloud. Generally, for Cloud Computing to reach the full potential promised by the technology, it must offer solid information security.

3. BUSINESS SOLUTIONS

Cloud Computing has emerged in various types of business enterprise; where cost minimization was the driving factor of such emergence. Pay-as-you-go financial model offers the enterprises the chance to reduce their cost to the real usage of computational and storage resources. It also takes over the burden of acquiring a complex in-house IT infrastructure with its consequent maintenance and upgrading cost.

In the businesses domain, many companies, not only the IT specialized ones, use Cloud-based services such as infrastructure and platform. Such technology helps them to pay as they go without the need of hiring in-house IT services or spending money on hardware. Besides, services are automatically scaled whenever the requirement or utilization is increased or decreased, where the Cloud adds or remove servers based on the real-time requirement (Yang X., 2012a). The advent of Cloud Computing has driven euphoria of what IT and business can do with the access to applications and services across the Internet. Many companies providing web operations; e.g. web hosting, deployment and monitoring; such as Microsoft, Google and Amazon, took the decision to move to Cloud platforms. Pharmacy management, real-time financial systems and enterprise fraud management are examples of the enterprise services that took the decision to employ the Cloud services. The benefits will be tangible and will fundamentally transform enterprises of all sizes around the globe access information, share content and communicate. Different areas and projects are listed in Figure 9. In the following sections, the emergence of Cloud Computing in the web operations, content delivery networks and enterprise solutions are reviewed and discussed in details.

3.1 Web Operations

Web operations are a domain of expertise within IT systems management that involves the deployment, maintenance, tuning, monitoring and repair

of web-based applications. In fact, web operations were the first to benefit from Cloud Computing platforms. Building a web deployment environment (Liu & Wee, 2009; Yang X. et al. 2012a) and monitoring web traffic (Sedayao, 2008) are moving to built on top of Clouds platforms. Also, social networking web applications (Buyya & Calheiros, 2010), such as Facebook, are deploying on Clouds; for their dynamic content and great traffic. These operations are addressed in the following sub-sections compared with the classical solutions.

3.1.1 Cloud-Based Web Server Farm

Web applications' traffic demand fluctuates widely and unpredictably. The common practice of provisioning a fixed capacity would either result in unsatisfied customers (under provision) or waste valuable capital investment (over-provision). By leveraging an infrastructure Cloud's on-demand, pay-per-use capabilities, the capacity can be matched with the demand in real time.

When architecting a web server farm, how much capacity to provision is one of the hardest

Figure 9. Cloud computing in business

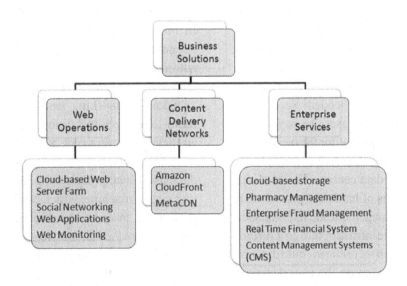

questions to answer because of the dynamic and uncertain nature of web traffic. Many new web applications start with very little traffic since they are hardly known. One day, they may become famous when they hit media (e.g., the slash-dot effect), and visitors flock to the web site, greatly driving up the traffic. Few days later, as the media effect wears off, traffic goes back to normal. Such dramatic change in traffic is often hard, if not impossible, to forecast correctly, both in terms of the timing and the peak capacity required. Thus, it is difficult to determine when and how much capacity to provision. Even if an amount can be determined, provisioning a fixed set of capacity is not a satisfactory solution. Unfortunately, this is still a common practice today due to the difficulties in forecasting and the long lead time to procure hardware. If the capacity provisioned is less than the peak demand, some requests cannot be served during the peak, resulting in unsatisfied customers. On the other hand, if the capacity provisioned is more than the peak demand, large capacity is wasted idling during non-peak time, especially when the peak never materializes.

An infrastructure Cloud, such as Amazon's EC2/S3 services, is a promising technology that can address the inherent difficulty in matching the capacity with the demand. First, it provides practically an unlimited infrastructure capacity (e.g., computing servers, storage) on demand. Instead of grossly over-provisioning upfront due to uncertain demands, users can elastically provision their infrastructure resources from the provider's pool only when needed. Second, the pay-per-use model allows users to pay for the actual consumption instead of for the peak capacity. Third, a Cloud infrastructure is much larger than most enterprise data centers. The economy of scale, both in terms of hardware procurement and infrastructure management and maintenance, helps to drive down the infrastructure cost further.

A Cloud-based web server farm could dynamically adjust its size based on the user demands.

It starts with as little as one web server. During traffic peak, the server farm automatically and instantaneously spawns up more web servers to serve the demand. In comparison, in a traditional enterprise infrastructure, such a scale up both takes a long time (months) and requires manual intervention. Similarly, as traffic goes away, the server farm can automatically shrink down its capacity. Again, scaling down (and stop paying for it) is very hard to achieve in a traditional enterprise infrastructure (Liu & Wee, 2009).

3.1.2 Social Networking Web Applications

Social networks, such as Facebook and MySpace, are popular Web 2.0 based applications. They serve dynamic content to millions of users, whose access and interaction patterns are hard to predict. In addition, their features are very dynamic in the sense that new plug-ins can be created by independent developers, added to the main system and used by other users. In several situations load spikes can take place, for instance, whenever new system features become popular or a new plug-in application is deployed. As these social networks are organized in communities of highly interacting users distributed all over the world, load spikes can take place at different locations at any time. In order to handle unpredictable seasonal and geographical changes in system workload, an automatic scaling scheme is paramount to keep QoS and resource consumption at suitable levels.

Social networking websites are built using multi-tiered web technologies, which consist of application servers such as IBM WebSphere and persistency layers such as the MySQL relational database. Usually, each component runs in a separate virtual machine, which can be hosted in data centers that are owned by different Cloud Computing providers. Additionally, each plug-in developer has the freedom to choose which Cloud Computing provider offers the services that are more suitable to run his/her plug-in. As a consequence, a typical social networking web application is formed by hundreds of different services, which may be hosted by dozens of Cloud data centers around the world. Whenever there is a variation in temporal and spatial locality of workload, each application component must dynamically scale to offer good quality of experience to users.

In order to support a large number of application service consumers from around the world, Cloud infrastructure providers (i.e., IaaS providers) have established data centers in multiple geographical locations to provide redundancy and ensure reliability in case of site failures. For example, Amazon has data centers in the US (e.g., one in the East Coast and another in the West Coast) and Europe. However, currently they (1) expect their Cloud customers (i.e., SaaS providers) to express a preference about the location where they want their application services to be hosted and (2) don't provide seamless/automatic mechanisms for scaling their hosted services across multiple, geographically distributed data centers. This approach has many shortcomings, which include (1) it is difficult for Cloud customers to determine in advance the best location for hosting their services as they may not know origin of consumers of their services and (2) Cloud SaaS providers may not be able to meet QoS expectations of their service consumers originating from multiple geographical locations. This necessitates building mechanisms for seamless federation of data centers of a Cloud provider or providers supporting dynamic scaling of applications across multiple domains in order to meet QoS targets of Cloud customers (Buyya & Calheiros, 2010). A potential solution for meeting the QoS requirements for worldwide customer bases, the MMORPG shared architecture for distributed networks (Lee & Chen, 2010).

3.1.3 Web Monitoring

Intel needed a service that could give an idea of end users' experiences with Intel Corporation's website from different regions of the globe contrast that experience to other comparable websites. A person from China might call Intel and say that performance to Intel's web site is poor. Intel Information Technology (IT) department would have little visibility into the problem. Also, it was needed to compare the end-user experiences using different services for providing web content from a global perspective, i.e. how different providers perform in different regions.

While there are monitoring services that we could have purchased to do this function, Intel is a member of the PlanetLab consortium and has access to over 900 systems at more than 460 sites across the globe. Moreover, we had already developed software to measure the aspects of web performance of interest as well as software to gather the performance data and graph it. Geographics of interest, manually found PlanetLab nodes, were picked and then using PlanetLab's web site, created virtual machines (VMs) on those nodes. Once the VMs were instantiated, the software was installed on the VMs and ran our monitoring application. The display application pulled in data through Intel's firewalls and displayed it on an internal web page (Sedayao, 2008). Figure 10 has a diagram of how this first implementation functioned (Sedayao, 2008).

Using PlanetLab's Service Oriented Architecture (SOA)-like features and Cloud-like infrastructure, it was relatively easy to construct a robust, highly and globally distributed application composed of services available on a Cloud Computing infrastructure.

3.2 Content Delivery Networks

Content Delivery Networks (CDNs) provide improved Web access performance to Internet end-users through multiple, geographically distributed replica servers. A commercial CDN lock-in a customer, i.e. content provider, for a particular period of time under specific Service

Figure 10. Web monitoring cloud implementation

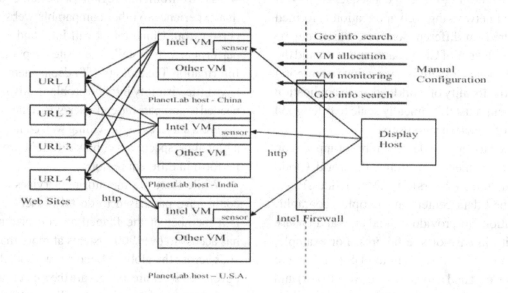

Level Agreements (SLAs) (Yang X., 2011) with a high monthly/yearly fees and excess data charges.

Nowadays, content providers view CDN services as a way to use a shared network infrastructure with improved utility to handle their peak capacity requirements, thus allowing reduced investments in their own Web site infrastructure. Utility refers to the quantification of a CDN's traffic activities and represents the usefulness of its replicas in terms of data circulation in its distributed network. It is vital as system wellness greatly affects the content delivery performance to end-users.

One approach to address these issues is to build a content delivery Cloud, on top of existing Cloud services, e.g. Amazon Simple Storage Service (S3), Nirvanix Storage Delivery Network (SDN), and Mosso Cloud Files. Examples of CDNs built on top of Clouds are Amazon CloudFront (Dignan, 2008), MetaCDN (Kho, 2009).

3.2.1 Amazon CloudFront

Amazon's announcement of the launch of its CloudFront content delivery service alongside its traditional infrastructure services is clear evidence

that Cloud Computing for the content world is only becoming more entrenched.

Amazon CloudFront is a content delivery network (CDN) offered by Amazon Web Services. CloudFront operates on a pay-as-you-go basis. CloudFront has servers located in Europe (United Kingdom, Ireland, The Netherlands, and Germany), Asia (Hong Kong, Singapore and Japan) as well as in several major cities in the United States. CloudFront competes with larger content delivery networks such as Akamai and Limelight Networks. Upon launch, Larry Dignan of ZDNet News stated that CloudFront could cause price and margin reductions from competing CDNs (Dignan, 2008).

3.2.2 MetaCDN

A content delivery Cloud, such as MetaCDN, is an integrated overlay that utilizes Cloud Computing to provide content delivery services to Internet end-users. While it ensures satisfactory user perceived performance, it also aims to improve the traffic activities in its world-wide distributed network and uplift the usefulness of its replicas.

MetaCDN realizes a content delivery Cloud, providing the required features for high performance content delivery. It is an integrated overlay service, which leverages existing storage Clouds. It allows content providers to revel advanced content delivery services without having to build a dedicated infrastructure. When a user requests content, MetaCDN chooses an optimal replica for content delivery, thereby ensuring satisfactory user perceived experience (Kho, 2009).

Figure 11 provides an illustration of MetaCDN (Kho, 2009). It is coupled with each storage Cloud via connectors that provide an abstraction to hide the complexity associated with different access methodologies of heterogeneous providers. End-users can access the MetaCDN overlay either through a Web portal. In this case, the Web portal acts as an entry point to the system and performs application level load balancing for end-users who intend to download content that has been deployed through MetaCDN.

3.2.3 Comparing Content Delivery Networks

The use of Clouds for content delivery is highly appealing as they charge customers for their utilization of storage and transfer of content, typically in order of cents per gigabyte. They offer SLA-backed performance and uptime guarantees for their services. Moreover, they can rapidly and cheaply scale-out during flash crowds and anticipated increases in demand. However, unlike a fully-featured CDN, they do not provide capabilities for automatic replication, fail-over, geographical load redirection and load balancing.

3.3 Enterprise Services

Normally, enterprise services were built on applications that are running within the enterprises to fulfill the business demands. In the recent past, the concept of service in a Cloud environment gained significance with services being hosted in a common Cloud environment within the enterprise or outside the enterprise. Cloud services have the

Figure 11. An abstract view of MetaCDN

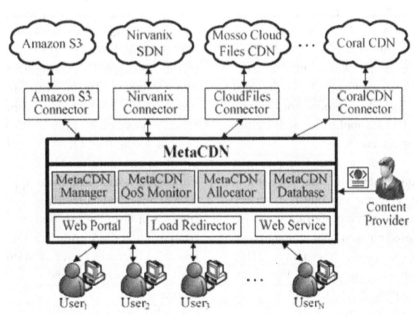

potential to deliver important business benefits to the enterprise, including cost savings, flexibility, resiliency, agility, quicker time to market, better customer service and the ability to handle unexpected spikes in demand.

Traditionally an organization's Enterprise Services Architectures are considered in terms of Business Architecture, Information Systems Architecture (Data and Application Architecture) and Technology Architecture. A variety of enterprise services architectures such as core services, infrastructure services, and technology services are supported by these levels of architecture. Core services are those services that will fulfill the business functionality of the application or of an organization whereas infrastructure services are those services that fulfill support infrastructure such as security. The third type of services, technology services, will satisfy the technical, i.e., nonfunctional services such as scalability and interoperability. Recently Cloud Services started playing a significant role in enterprise services to fulfill the alignment of IT with business.

Enterprise Cloud services provide different types of services, for example, Business Process, Application, Platform, Infrastructure, Security and, of course, Integration as a Service. Some of the common attributes of Cloud services are on-demand self-service, broad network access, resource pooling, rapid elasticity, measured services, and multiple tenants. Among the four areas of enterprise services architecture, Cloud services can play a significant role in information systems architecture, i.e., data and application architecture and technology architecture.

Enterprises are adopting Cloud Computing at a quicker-than-anticipated rate, that situation is attributed to the economic downturn. A variety of applications started moving from an enterprise level to Cloud-based environment, among those we are citing: Cloud-based storage (Rash, 2010) (Saugatuck Technology Inc., 2008), Pharmacy Management (Lamont, 2010), Enterprise Fraud Management (Unal & Yates, 2010) and Real Time Financial Systems (Aymerich, Fenu, & Surcis, 2009). Special interest is paid to Content Management Systems (Kho, 2009).

3.3.1 Cloud-Based Storage

With a Cloud storage solution, user's data is sent to a storage provider and the provider is left to manage it. It sounds simple, and, in concept, it is. On your end, Cloud storage means that you determine what needs to be stored, encrypt that data, and then transmit it across the Internet (or another network) to the provider's site, where there is a repository that's shared among many companies. The provider keeps track of where your data is and makes it available to you when you need it.

Enterprise-class storage providers, such as Iron Mountain, provide very high performance, significant scalability and high levels of security. Northwestern Medical Center in St. Albans, Vt., uses Iron Mountain to store medical images older than five years. As of April 2010, the hospital is still migrating X-ray, MRI and other images, but is already pulling down some images from the Cloud.

Moreover, Cloud Storage can be used from an On-Premise Application. An on-premise storage center which works for data backups for an enterprise system can be replaced with Windows Azure storage blobs. This improves the reliability of the backup, as it gets replicated three times like everything else in Azure. It might also be economically more feasible, given the economies of scale provided by Microsoft's very large data centers. Using the SQL Azure Database, the application can store relational data in the Cloud. For example, it is easier for an application sharing a set of relational tables across multiple instances running in different locations to access the data from a single place. Administration of the database also becomes easier as Microsoft does it at their end. Availability and security of data also increases with 3 backup copies and this storage option becomes comparatively cheaper compared to on-premises storage, thus making it feasible for small companies. Cloud Computing can also be combined with On Premise Application. If the data for an application can be stored in a Cloud, it is not surprising to know that the application's codes can also be run from a Cloud. For example, an on-premises application could sometimes be more efficient in its operation with more processor cores for running CPU-intensive loads. This can be facilitated by creation of more Windows Azure Worker role instances by the application to do this work and shut them down when not needed. As the normal procedure, the charge will be only on the resources used i.e. the number of hours the VMs were running (Rash, 2010).

3.3.2 Pharmacy Management

AWPRx (awprx.com) provides pharmacy benefits management services for workers' compensation organizations. Through its Direct Access software and aided by its Client Protocol Guide, AWPRx validates prescriptions and notifies its clients when medications are filled or need an approval. AWPRx has contracts with more than 60,000 pharmacies that reduce prescription costs for their clients, and an automated prescription process that reduces workers' comp fraud. Poised for significant growth, AWPRx was hampered by management and maintenance of its current IT environment. The company took some interim steps, such as moving to a storage area network environment. However, to eliminate the complex IT infrastructure required for its databases and transaction processing, AWPRx decided to move all of its IT functions to the Cloud. The Direct Access application has been relocated to force. com, a Cloud Computing platform-as-a-service (PaaS) offered by Salesforce (salesforce.com). Additionally, AWPRx opted to store its data in EC2, the elastic Cloud solution provided by Amazon (amazon.com) (Lamont, 2010).

3.3.3 Enterprise Fraud Management

Whether it is check fraud, embezzlement or credit card fraud, enterprise fraud is a serious problem costing hundreds of million dollars every year. Financial institutions and high-net-worth individuals are subject to fraud generated by insiders, customers, and third parties. Enterprise fraud brings many issues with it: fraudulent activity itself costs financial institutions millions of dollars in lost revenue annually; fraudulent activity damages the reputation of banks and causes stocks to plummet; witnessing fraud leads honest employees to seek employment elsewhere, resulting in increased costs of attracting and retaining talent.

One way to do mitigate fraud is by using enterprise fraud management solutions (software) that analyzes the transactions taking place within the financial system. Transaction data that banks are comfortable with sharing are made available to the product multiple times a day. The product then analyzes the data to see if it matches any previously agreed upon patterns. Based on these patterns, if the solution detects fraudulent activity, then an alert is raised and an investigator is assigned to the alert.

Cloud Computing is an up-and-coming architecture with strengths and room for improvement. Cloud vendors use a large number of identically conFigured, low-end servers to scale the computing supply. Cloud relieves the user from the burden of building a high-performing-server architecture, or purchasing licenses to run software, or building them in house. The Cloud also offers little compliance, recovery procedures, or transparency. There are no penalty clauses or SLAs that regulate the Cloud. Financial institutions have strong financial incentives to pursue Cloud investments, and are awaiting the Cloud to improve its legal and operational accountability.

In the age of Cloud, it is an outdated approach to consider software as a physical good or as a mere product. EFM solutions, except those by a handful of vendors e.g. Early Warning, are sold as a software product with fixed-term license. The product gets installed on the computers of financial institutions, behind their security defenses. When there is a problem with the software or the vendor wants to perform upgrades, the vendor has to access the installation behind the bank's security defenses via secure means. However, the end goal for financial institutions is fraud mitigation and management services, rather than purchasing and maintaining fraud solutions as a product. The purchase, implementation, testing, maintenance, and recovery steps inherent to the traditional software-as-a-product model are all hindrances to catching fraud. Given that any two banks have similar enough transaction and reference data, all banks could pour their data into the fraud solution's funnel under a Cloud architecture deemed secure enough by all regulators and related parties (Unal & Yates, 2010).

3.3.4 Real Time Financial System

Financial studies have shown that forecasts can be performed using collected data and information as well as specialized graphs. These similar and mechanical methods can be computerized to create financial models that work on the existing or purposely created real time financial systems.

Real Time Financial System based on Cloud is designed to work both as an internal Grid service (more specifically as a collection of Cloud services) and as a generic web-based application. The system will comprise an intermediate system that acts as gateway between a financial data center and the main part of the Grid managed by the Grid middleware. This intermediate system is called the Financial Primary Server (FPS). The FPS has been designed to enable interoperability with other Grid middleware without too many changes. Clients are managed by the FPS, so no client communicates directly with the Grid. Almost all analyzed data and processed forecasts will be produced internally to the Grid and returned to the clients, through the FPS. The only information

flow that the client receives directly, through the FPS and without other Jumps, concerns the real time quotes (Aymerich, Fenu, & Surcis, 2009).

The system has been designed to operate both in the stand-alone mode and as a computational Grid interface. This particular feature allows to take full advantage of parallel computing and to achieve different levels of scalability:

- **Scalability of the number of clients:** The larger the number of clients, the larger the number of specific analysis and forecast requests. A medium sized computational Grid is able to handle hundreds of thousands of requests in acceptable times.
- **Scalability of quality of the results:** If the system together with the Grids, it is possible to use a larger number of financial models over a greater number of CPUs. Since in this case every financial model will be different, even with minor parameter variations, the results obtained should be more accurate and more reliable.
- **Scalability of real time forecasts:** If the computing is performed inside the Grid, the results will be returned more quickly.

The system is well-adapted for the emerging theories on Cloud Computing and the described services are delivered as Cloud services.

3.3.5 Content Management Systems (CMS)

A content management system (CMS) is a system providing a collection of procedures used to manage work flow in a collaborative environment. These procedures can be manual or computer-based. The procedures are designed to do the following:

- Allow for a large number of people to contribute to and share stored data.

- Control access to data, based on user roles (defining which information users or user groups can view, edit, or publish).
- Aid in easy storage and retrieval of data.
- Control of data validity and compliance.
- Reduce repetitive duplicate input.
- Improve the ease of report writing.
- Improve communication between users.

The role that Cloud Computing played over the past few years is bound to change dramatically, particularly for creators and consumers of content. One of the key benefits to publishers, media companies and content aggregators of Cloud Computing is its massive scalability. With capacity that scales up and down on a real-time basis, services such as Amazon's S3 make it feasible even for new companies to offer sophisticated solutions and for established companies to crunch terabytes of data more economically. The New York Times is gradually converting its internal API to externally facing APIs on Amazon Web Services so that customers can, for instance, license a feed of recipe files or campaign contributions from the newspaper and mix it with their own content (Kho, 2009).

Vendors of textual data would do well to consider how they can use their APIs to package their content with analytical applications, integrate video and audio capabilities, and build in connectors to Web 2.0 technologies to more seamlessly move their content into everyday workflows.

But the main problem that established vendors of content and content services are facing is how to take advantage of the technology. It is by staying flexible and leveraging the web to capitalize on their brand value. Reed Elsevier as an example of a company that is using the enhanced flexibility provided by content Clouds to its advantage.

3.4 Summary

Cloud Computing has moved from a cottage industry to one of the bigger growth areas in the computing business. The tremendous impact of Cloud Computing on business has prompted the United States federal government to look to the Cloud as a means to reorganize its IT infrastructure and to decrease its IT budgets. With the advent of the top government officially mandating Cloud adoption, many government agencies already have at least one or more Cloud systems online.

In fact, due the various and divert needs of any enterprise, a single Cloud cannot fulfill such needs. Thus, businesses moving to the Cloud will not only require the services of many providers, but also need to integrate its applications and data between these different providers. Such integration is a challenge by itself. In addition, service outages also present a risk that should be managed. A number of outage incidents has been recorded among Google, Amazon, Microsoft and Salesforce.com. Those failures have called into question about the reliability of this emergent technology.

CONCLUSION

In this chapter, we have presented a wide range of research projects and business solutions, as well as the applications that have been either innovated or improved by the emergence of Cloud Computing. The chapter illustrates how different fields are leveraging from the Cloud Computing benefits in its different service models and overcoming the drawbacks of the classical IT solutions.

In the academic field, projects like Virtual Computing Lab, Distributed University Campus and Seattle have been built for the purpose of educational platforms. Also, research platforms, such as IBM/Google Academic Cloud Computing Initiative started with the emergence of Cloud Computing. In Library Computing, which is one of the most important academic activities, DuraCloud and WorldCat Cloud-based projects have started cutting down the library computing costs. In the Scientific Computing research field, sophisticated projects like High-Performance Computing, Large images processing, e-Science for Neuroscience are now moving to a better transition since the emergence of Cloud Computing.

As same as the academic field, governments find Clouds a suitable infrastructure for their work; for their IT infrastructures, public services and research platforms. Different governments in USA, Canada and Japan have built their IT infrastructures using Cloud Computing. U.S. Federal Cloud Computing Initiative, e-Health and National Business Services are examples of governmental IT services offered to public. Also, governments started to explore using Cloud Computing for serving research, by building research Clouds such as Clouds of Magellan, NASA Netbula and Seventh Framework Programme.

Similarly in the business and enterprise domain, several applications and enterprise solutions are immigrating to Cloud Computing. Companies offering different web operations started building their solutions on top of Clouds, such as web hosting, social networks applications and web monitoring. Various Content Delivery Networks moved their projects to Clouds, like Amazon CloudFront and MetaCDN. In the same manner, enterprise solutions include Data Storage, Pharmacy management, fraud management, financial systems and Cloud management systems.

From all the previously cited projects, it is notable that the Cloud Computing model introduces several benefits for end users, enterprises, service providers, and scientific institutions. The advantage of dynamically scaling the IT infrastructure on a pay per use basis and according to the real needs of applications, definitely constitute one of the major gains brought by Cloud Computing. Moreover, by moving the IT infrastructure into the Cloud it is not necessary: (i) to bear costs derived from capacity planning for peak loads; (ii) to statically acquire infrastructure due to the sporadic need of large computation power; and (iii) to incur expensive administrative and maintenance costs. These issues are likely to be more important for enterprises and service providers

that can maximize their revenue and cut costs. For what concerns end users, the most interesting aspect of Cloud Computing resides in taking advantage of the multitude of applications already available and having their personal data and documents accessible from anywhere at any time. On the other hand, scientific institutions can be more interested in PaaS and IaaS offerings that allow having complete control over the infrastructure used for scientific research and finely customizing their software systems according to the specific needs of the experiments to be performed. Cloud Computing also ensures the desired Quality of Service, which is established by means of Service Level Agreements. This aspect can constitute an additional value, which could make scientists prefer computing Clouds to traditional Grids for experiments with additional constraints.

Due to its particular nature, Cloud Computing introduces new challenges and new problems yet to be faced, especially from a legal and a security point of view. In the case of public Clouds, systems, applications, and even personal data are hosted into datacenters owned by third parties. These datacenters are often placed into the more convenient geographic location for reducing maintenance and consumption costs. Such places could even be in a different country where different laws on the digital content apply. Similarly, the application can then be considered legal or illegal according to where it is hosted. In addition, privacy and confidentiality of data depends on the location of its storage. In order to address this issue some Cloud Computing vendors have included the geographic location of the hosting as a parameter of the service level agreement made with the customer. Users can have access to different availability zones and decide where to host their applications. Security is another important issue; at the moment it is not clear which kind of measures, apart from the standard security tools, are taken to guarantee the security of the data. While this issue is more compelling for enterprises and end users, there could be relevant implications even in the case of scientific computing: many scientific projects are often funded by federal bodies or directly by the government that often puts severe restrictions in the use and the management of such sensible data.

As Cloud Computing continues to revolutionize applications in academia, government and industry, the transition to this efficient and flexible platform presents serious challenges at both theoretical and practical levels; ones that will often require new approaches and practices in all areas.

REFERENCES

Alonso-Calvo, R., Crespo, J., Garc'ıa-Remesal, M., Anguita, A., & Maojo, V. (2010). On distributing load in Cloud Computing: A real application for very-large image datasets. *Procedia Computer Science*, *1*(1), 2663 2671. doi:10.1016/j.procs.2010.04.300

Aymerich, F., Fenu, G., & Surcis, S. (2009). A real time financial system based on grid and cloud computing. 2009 ACM symposium on Applied Computing, (pp. 1219–1220). Honolulu, Hawaii, USA.

Behrend, T. S., Wiebe, E. N., London, J. E., & Johnson, E. C. (2011). Cloud computing adoption and usage in community colleges. *Behaviour & Information Technology*, *30*(2), 231–240. doi:10.1080/0144929X.2010.489118

BOINC Project. (n.d.). Retrieved January 2012, from http://boinc.berkeley.edu/

Breeding, M. (2009, November). The advance of computing from the ground to the cloud. *Computers in Libraries*.

Burd, S. D., Seazzu, A. F., & Conway, C. (2009). Virtual computing laboratories: A case study with comparisons to physical computing laboratories. Journal of Information Technology Education: Innovations in Practice, 8.

Buyya, R. R., & Calheiros, R. (2010). InterCloud: Utility-oriented federation of cloud computing environments for scaling of application services. 10th International Conference on Algorithms and Architectures for Parallel Processing (ICA3PP 2010), (pp. 13–31). Busan, Korea.

Cappos, J., Beschastnikh, I., Krishnamurthy, A., & Anderson, T. (2009). Seattle: A platform for educational cloud computing. 40th ACM technical Symposium on Computer Science Education (SIGCSE 09), (pp. 111–115). Chattanooga, USA.

Catteddu, D., & Hogben, G. (2009). *Cloud computing security risk assessment. European Network and Information Security Agency*. ENISA.

Cloud Standards Coordination. (n.d.). Retrieved January 2012, from http://www.Cloudbook.net/directories/Cloud-groups/Cloud-standards-coordination

CloudRooms virtual classrooms. (n.d.). Retrieved July 2012, from http://www.redtray.co.uk/cloud-rooms/

Computing, C. Delivering Internet-based information and technology services in real time. (n.d.). Retrieved March 20, 2011, from https://www.ibm.com/developerworks/university/Cloud/

Dashboard, I. T. (n.d.). Retrieved January 2012, from http://www.Cloudbook.net/directories/gov-Clouds/gov-program.php?id=100006

Data.gov. (n.d.). Retrieved January 2012, from http://www.Cloudbook.net/directories/gov-Clouds/gov-program.php?id=100005

Defense Information Systems Agency (DISA). (n.d.). Retrieved January 1, 2012, from http://www.Cloudbook.net/directories/gov-Clouds/disa-defense-information-systems-agency

Delic, K. (2005, December 7-13). On dependability of corporate grids. ACM Ubiquity, 6(45).

Delic, K., & Walke, M. (2008). Emergence of the academic computing clouds. ACM Ubiquity Magazine, 9(31).

Dignan, L. (2008, November). Amazon launches CloudFront; Content delivery network margins go kaboom. Between the Lines. ZDNet.

DuraSpcace. (n.d.). Retrieved January 2012, from http://www.duraspace.org

Erkoç, M. F., & Kert, S. B. (2011). Cloud computing for distributed university campus: A prototype suggestion. International Conference of the Future Education, Florence, Italy. Folding@Home. (n.d.). Retrieved January 2012, from http://folding.stanford.edu/

Foster, I., & Kesselman, C. (2004). *The Grid 2: Blueprint for a new computing infrastructure*. San Francisco, CA: Morgan Kaufmann.

Foster, I. T. (2005). Globus toolkit version 4: Software for service-oriented systems. In Jin, H., Reed, D. A., & Jiang, W. (Eds.), *NPC (Vol. 3779, pp. 2–13)*. Lecture Notes in Computer Science Springer.

Grossman, R., & Gu, Y. (2008). Data mining using high performance data clouds: Experimental studies using sector and sphere. 14th ACM SIG-KDD International Conference on Knowledge Discovery and Data Mining (KDD 08), (pp. 920 – 927). Las Vegas.

Hand, E. (2007). Head in the clouds. *Nature, 449*, 963. doi:10.1038/449963a

Hazelhurst, S. (2008). Scientific computing using virtual high-performance computing: A case study using the Amazon Elastic Computing Cloud. Annual Research Conference of the South African Institute of Computer Scientists and Information Technologists on IT research in developing countries (SAICSIT 08), (pp. 94 – 103). Wilderness, South Africa.

IBM/Google Academic Cloud Computing Initiative (ACCI). (n.d.). Retrieved January 2, 2012, from http://www.Cloudbook.net/directories/research-Clouds/ibm-google-academic-Cloud-computing-initiative

Junosphere. (n.d.). Retrieved July 2012, from https://www.juniper.net/as/en/products-services/software/junos-platform/junosphere/

Kho, N. (2009, March). Content in the cloud. EContent Magazine.

Lamont, J. (2010, January). SaaS: Integration in the clouds. KM World.

Lee, Y., & Chen, K. (2010). Is server consolidation beneficial to MMORPG? A case study of World of Warcraft. Proceedings of the IEEE 3rd International Conference on Cloud Computing, (pp. 435 - 442).

Legislatures, S. (2010). Governments work in the clouds. *Journal of State Legislatures, 36*(4), 10.

Liu, H., & Wee, S. (2009). Web server farm in the cloud: Performance evaluation and dynamic architecture. 1st International Conference on Cloud Computing (CloudCom 09), (pp. 369–380). Beijing, China.

Magellan. (n.d.). Retrieved January 3, 2012, from http://www.Cloudbook.net/directories/research-Clouds/research-project.php?id=100047

Ministry of Internal Affairs and Communications Japan (MIC). (n.d.). Retrieved January 4, 2012, from http://www.Cloudbook.net/directories/gov-Clouds/ministry-of-internal-affairs-and-communications-japan--mic

NASA. (n.d.). Retrieved January 5, 2012, from http://www.Cloudbook.net/directories/gov-Clouds/nasa-national-aeronautics-and-space-administration

OCLC WorldShare. (n.d.). Retrieved January 2012, from http://www.oclc.org

Public Works and Government Services Canada (PWGSC). (n.d.). Retrieved January 6, 2012, from http://www.Cloudbook.net/directories/gov-Clouds/public-works-and-government-services-canada--pwgsc

Rash, W. (2010, February). Cloud-based storage done right. eWeek.com.

Sasikala, S., & Prema, S. (2010). Massive centralized cloud computing (MCCC) exploration in higher education. *Advances in Computational Sciences and Technology*, *3*(2), 111–118.

Saugatuck Technology Inc. (2008). *Meeting the challenges of cloud solutions billing: Outsourcing to a cloud services hub*. IP Applications.

Sedayao, J. (2008). Implementing and operating an internet scale distributed application using service oriented architecture principles and Cloud Computing infrastructure. 10th International Conference on Information Integration and Web-based Applications & Services (iiWAS 08), (pp. 417–421). Linz. SETI@Home. (n.d.). Retrieved January 2012, from http://setiathome.berkeley.edu/

Seventh Framework Programme. (n.d.). Retrieved January 2012, from http://www.Cloudbook.net/directories/gov-Clouds/seventh-framework-programme

Siegle, D. (2010). Cloud computing: A free technology option to promote collaborative learning. *Gifted Child Today*, *33*(4), 41–45.

Strong, P. (2005, July/August). Enterprise grid computing. ACM Queue Magazine.

Tao, Z., & Long, J. (2011). The research and application of network teaching platform based on cloud computing. *International Journal of Information and Education Technology*, *1*(3).

Toolkit, G. (n.d.). Retrieved January 2012, from http://www.globus.org/toolkit/

Turnitin. (n.d.). Retrieved July 2012, from http://www.turnitin.com/

Unal, E., & Yates, D. (2010). Enterprise fraud management using cloud computing: A cost-benefit analysis framework. 18th European Conference on Information Systems (ECIS), Pretoria, South Africa.

U.S. General Services Administration (GSA). (n.d.). Retrieved January 2012, from http://www.gsa.gov

Watson, P., Lord, P., Gibson, F., Periorellis, P., & Pitsili, G. (2008). Cloud computing for e-science with CARMEN. 2nd Iberian Grid Infrastructure Conference, (pp. 3-14). Portugal.

Yang, X. (2011). QoS-oriented service computing: Bring SOA into cloud environment. In Liu, X., & Li, Y. (Eds.), *Advanced design approaches to emerging software systems: Principles, methodology and tools*. Hershey, PA: IGI Global. doi:10.4018/978-1-60960-735-7.ch013

Yang, X., Bruin, R., & Dove, M. (2010a). Developing an end-to-end scientific workflow: A case study of using a reliable, lightweight, and comprehensive workflow platform in e-science. *IEEE Computational Science & Engineering*, *99*, 1.

Yang, X., Bruin, R., & Dove, M. et al. (2010b) A service-oriented framework for running quantum mechanical simulation for material properties over Grids. IEEE Transactions on System, Man, and Cybernetic, Part C: Application and Reviews, 40(4).

Yang, X., Dove, M., & Bruin, R. (2012b). (in press). An e-science data infrastructure for simulations within grid computing environment: Methods, approaches, and practices. *Concurrency and Computation*. doi:10.1002/cpe.2849

Yang, X., Nasser, B., Surrige, M., & Middleton, S. (2012a). A business-oriented cloud federation model for real time applications. *Future Generation Computer Systems*. doi:10.1016/j. future.2012.02.005

Yang, X., Wang, L., & von Laszewski, G. (2009). Recent research advances in e-science. *Cluster Computing Journal Special Issue*, *12*(4), 353–356. doi:10.1007/s10586-009-0104-0

ADDITIONAL READING

Armbrust, M., Fox, A., Griffith, R., Joseph, A., Katz, R., & Konwinski, A. (2009). *Above the clouds: A Berkeley view of cloud computing*. Berkeley, CA: University of California at Berkley.

AWS Case Study: Cloudberry Lab. (n.d.). Retrieved January 2012, from http://aws.amazon. com/solutions/case-studies/Cloudberry-lab/

AWS Case Study: Educations.com. (2011, March 17). Retrieved January 2012, from http://aws.amazon.com/solutions/case-studies/educations-com/

AWS Case Study: European Space Agency. (2011, April 5). Retrieved January 2012, from http://aws.amazon.com/solutions/case-studies/european-space-agency/

AWS Case Study: Guardian Goes to the Cloud. (n.d.). Retrieved January 2012, from http://aws.amazon.com/solutions/case-studies/guardian/

AWS Case Study: JoomlArt. (n.d.). Retrieved January 2012, from http://aws.amazon.com/solutions/case-studies/joomlart/

AWS Case Study: National Renewable Energy Laboratory's OpenEI.org. (n.d.). Retrieved January 2012, from http://aws.amazon.com/solutions/case-studies/openei/

AWS Case Study: National Taiwan University. (2011, May 18). Retrieved January 2012, from http://aws.amazon.com/solutions/case-studies/national-taiwan-university/

AWS Case Study: The Server Labs. (n.d.). Retrieved January 2012, from http://aws.amazon.com/solutions/case-studies/the-server-labs/

AWS Case Study: University of Melbourne/University of Barcelona. (n.d.). Retrieved January 2012, from http://aws.amazon.com/solutions/case-studies/university-melbourne-barcelona/

AWS Case Study: USDA Food and Nutrition Service. (2011, December 7). Retrieved January 2012, from http://aws.amazon.com/solutions/case-studies/usda-fns/

AWS Case Study: Washington Post. (n.d.). Retrieved January 2012, from http://aws.amazon.com/solutions/case-studies/washington-post/

Boch-Andersen, L. (2011, September 15). Enhancing the academic experience at Middlesex University with Cloud. Retrieved January 2012, from http://www.microsoft.eu/Cloud-computing/case-studies/enhancing-the-academic-experience-at-middlesex-university-with-Cloud-c19ml.aspx

Boch-Andersen, L. (2011, September 2011). Finland moving towards online education and collaboration with Cloud Computing. Retrieved January 2012, from http://www.microsoft.eu/Cloud-computing/case-studies/finland-moving-towards-online-education-and-collaboration-with-Cloud-computing-c19ml

Boch-Andersen, L. (2011, April 15). Hospital uses Cloud Computing to improve patient care and reduce costs. Retrieved January 2012, from http://www.microsoft.eu/Cloud-computing/case-studies/hospital-uses-Cloud-computing-to-improve-patient-care-and-reduce-costs-c19ml.aspx

Boch-Andersen, L. (2011, April 11). Private Cloud services for the Government of Catalonia. Retrieved January 2012, from http://www.microsoft.eu/Cloud-computing/case-studies/private-Cloud-services-for-the-government-of-catalonia-c19ml.aspx

Building a dynamic infrastructure with IBM Power Systems: A closer look at private cloud TCO. (2010, March). Retrieved July 2012, from http://www-03.ibm.com/systems/power/solutions/cloud/whitepapers/dyninfrastructure.html

Buyya, R., Broberg, J., & Goscinski, A. (Eds.). (2011). *Cloud computing: Principles and paradigms*. New York, NY: Wiley Press. doi:10.1002/9780470940105

Buyya, R., Broberg, J., & Goscinski, A. (Eds.). (2011). *Cloud computing: Principles and paradigms*. New York, NY: Wiley Press. doi:10.1002/9780470940105

Buyya, R., Pandey, S., & Vecchiola, C. (2009). Cloudbus toolkit for market-oriented cloud computing. 1st International Conference on Cloud Computing (CloudCom 09), (pp. 24 – 44). Beijing, China.

Buyya, R., & Sukumar, K. (2011). Platforms for building and deploying applications for cloud computing. *CSI Communications*, 35(1), 6–11.

Buyya, R., Yeo, C., & Venugopal, S. (2008). Market-oriented Cloud Computing: Vision, hype, and reality for delivering it services as computing utilities. 10th IEEE International Conference on High Performance Computing and Communications (HPCC 08).

Buyya, R., Yeo, C., Venugopal, V., Broberg, J., & Brandic, I. (2009). Cloud computing and emerging IT platforms: Vision, hype, and reality for delivering computing as the 5th utility. *Future Generation Computer Systems*, 25, 599–616. doi:10.1016/j.future.2008.12.001

Buyya, R. R., & Calheiros, R. (2010). InterCloud: Utility-oriented federation of cloud computing environments for scaling of application services. 10th International Conference on Algorithms and Architectures for Parallel Processing (ICA3PP 2010), (pp. 13–31). Busan, Korea.

Case Study: A Chinese municipal government delivers service in the Cloud. (2011, December 28). Retrieved January 2012, from http://www-01.ibm.com/software/success/cssdb.nsf/CS/KJON-8PRULC?OpenDocument&Site=default&cty=en_us

Case Study: EnterpriseDB Finds Significant Savings with AWS. (n.d.). Retrieved January 2012, from http://aws.amazon.com/solutions/case-studies/enterprisedb/

Case Study: Managing Oracle Applications in Cloud. (2012, January 12). Retrieved January 2012, from http://whitepapers.businessweek.com/detail/RES/1325889985_4.html

Case Study: TU München creates a state-of-the-art research environment with a smart Cloud-enabled infrastructure based on IBM Power Systems. (2011, October 10). Retrieved January 2012, from http://www-01.ibm.com/software/success/cssdb.nsf/CS/STRD-8MBGQJ?OpenDocument&Site=default&cty=en_us

Case Study: UWM builds private Cloud-based e-learning facilities with IBM and SAP. (2011, November 2011). Retrieved January 2012, from http://www-01.ibm.com/software/success/cssdb.nsf/CS/STRD-8NNKUK?OpenDocument&Site=default&cty=en_us

Cloud Computing's impact on the network: How to prepare. (2012, January 13). Retrieved January 2012, from http://whitepapers.businessweek.com/detail/RES/1326472732_632.html

Dastjerdi, A. V., & Buyya, R. (2011). A taxonomy of QoS management and service selection methodologies for cloud computing. In Wang, L., Ranjan, R., Chen, J., & Benatallah, B. (Eds.), *Cloud computing: Methodology, systems, and applications*. Boca Raton, FL: CRC Press. doi:10.1201/b11149-8

Eerola, T. European researchers switch from super computers to Cloud Computing. (2011, October 24). Retrieved January 2012, from http://www.microsoft.eu/Cloud-computing/case-studies/european-researchers-switch-from-super-computers-to-Cloud-computing-c19ml.aspx

Heart, T., Tsur, N. S., & Pliskin, N. (2010). Software-as-a-service vendors: Are they ready to successfully deliver? In Oshri, I., & Kotlarsky, J. (Eds.), *Global sourcing of information technology and business processes* (Vol. 55, pp. 151–184). Heidelberg, Germany: Springer. doi:10.1007/978-3-642-15417-1_9

Hilkert, D., Wolf, C. M., Benlian, A., & Hess, T. (2010). The "as-a-service"-paradigm and its implications for the software industry – Insights from a comparative case study in CRM software ecosystems. In Tyrväinen, P., Jansen, S., & Cusumano, M. A. (Eds.), *Software business* (Vol. 51, pp. 125–137). Heidelberg, Germany: Springer Berlin. doi:10.1007/978-3-642-13633-7_11

Hwang, K., & Buyya, R. (2011). Cloud programming and software environments. In Hwang, K., Dongarra, J., & Fox, G. (Eds.), *Distributed and cloud computing: From parallel processing to the internet of things*. San Francisco, CA: Morgan Kaufmann.

Hwang, K., & Buyya, R. (2011). Design of cloud computing platforms. In Hwang, K., Dongarra, J., & Fox, G. (Eds.), *Distributed and cloud computing: From parallel processing to the internet of things*. San Francisco, CA: Morgan Kaufmann.

Kadam, K., Gajre, S., & Paikrao, R. (2012). Security issues in cloud computing. IJCA Proceedings on National Conference on Innovative Paradigms in Engineering and Technology (NCIPET 2012) (pp. 22-26). New York, NY: Foundation of Computer Science.

Keahey, K., Figueiredo, R., Fortes, J., Freeman, T., & Tsugawa, M. (2008). Science clouds: Early experiences in cloud computing for scientific applications. Cloud Computing and its Applications Workshop 2008 (CCA-08), Chicago.

Khajeh-Hosseini, A., Sommerville, I., & Sriram, I. (2010). Research challenges for enterprise cloud computing. 1st ACM Symposium on Cloud Computing (SOCC 2010). Indianapolis, IN.

Klems, M., Nimis, J., & Tai, S. (2009). Do clouds compute? A framework for estimating the value of cloud computing. In Weinhardt, C., Luckner, S., & Stober, J. (Eds.), *Designing e-business systems: Markets, services, and networks* (Vol. 22, pp. 110–123). Heidelberg, Germany: Springer-Verlag. doi:10.1007/978-3-642-01256-3_10

Kondo, D., Javadi, B., Malecot, P., Cappello, F., & Anderson, D. (2009). Cost-benefit analysis of cloud computing versus desktop grids. Proceedings IEEE International Symposium on Parallel & Distributed Processing (IPDPS 09) (pp. 1 - 12). Washington, DC: IEEE Computer Society.

Kundra, V. (2011, August 30). Tight budget? Look to the cloud. New York Times. Retrieved from http://www.nytimes.com/2011/08/31/opinion/tight-budget-look-to-the-cloud.html?_r=3&hp

Kuyoro, S. O., Ibikunle, F., & Awodele, O. (2011). Cloud Computing Security Issues and Challenges. *International Journal of Computer Networks, 3*(5).

La, H. J., & Kim, S. D. (2009). A systematic process for developing high quality SaaS cloud services. 1st International Conference on Cloud Computing (CloudCom 2009), (pp. 278 – 289). Beijing.

Mancini, E. P., Rak, M., & Villano, U. (2009). PerfCloud: GRID Services for performance-oriented development of cloud computing applications. *18th IEEE International Workshops on Enabling Technologies: Infrastructures for Collaborative Enterprises (WETICE 09)*, (pp. 201 – 206). Groningen, The Netherlands.

Mechanical Turk Case Study: Stanford AI Lab. (n.d.). Retrieved January 2012, from http://aws.amazon.com/solutions/case-studies/stanford-ai-lab-interview/

Metri, P., & Sarote, G. (2011). Privacy issues and challenges in cloud. *International Journal of Advanced Engineering Sciences and Technologies*, *5*(1).

Oracle. (2009, October). Oracle white paper—Platform-as-a-service private cloud with Oracle fusion middleware. Retrieved from http://www.oracle.com/us/technologies/cloud/036500.pdf

Pathan, M., Broberg, J., & Buyya, R. (2009). Maximizing utility for content delivery clouds. *10th International Conference on Web Information Systems Engineering (WISE 09)* (pp. 13 - 28). Springer-Verlag Berlin.

Pearson Manages Digital Learning in the Cloud with RightScale. (n.d.). Retrieved January 2012, from http://www.rightscale.com/customers/pearson-manages-digital-learning-rightscale.php

Pirooz, S. (2011). Cloud security: The best defense is a good offense. Retrieved January 2012, from http://www.centerbeam.com/business-advantages-of-outsourcing-IT/Cloud-security/key-considerations-when-moving-to-the-Cloud/

Rackspace, I. (2011). Cloudonomics: The economics of cloud computing. Retrieved from http://www.rackspacecloud.com/cloudu

Sahlin, J., Sarkani, S., & Mazzuchi, T. (2012). Optimizing QoS in distributed systems/cloud computing architectures. *International Journal of Computers and Applications*, *42*(18), 14–20. doi:10.5120/5791-8097

Vecchiola, C., Duncan, D., & Buyya, R. (2010). The structure of the new IT frontier: Market oriented computing. *Strategic Facilities Magazine*, *10*, 59–66.

Voorsluys, W., Broberg, J., & Buyya, R. (2011). Introduction to cloud computing. In Buyya, R., Broberg, J., & Goscinski, A. (Eds.), *Cloud computing: Principles and paradigms* (pp. 1–41). New York, NY: Wiley Press. doi:10.1002/9780470940105.ch1

Vouk, M. A. (2008). Cloud computing — Issues, research and implementations. *30th International Conference on Information Technology Interfaces (ITI 2008)*, (pp. 31 – 40). Dubrovnik.

Wang, L., & Laszewski, G. (2008). Scientific cloud computing: Early definition and experience. *10th IEEE International Conference on High Performance Computing and Communications*, (pp. 825 – 830). Dalian, China.

WebFilings. "Dual-Cloud" Solution Banks On RightScale. (n.d.). Retrieved January 2012, from http://www.rightscale.com/customers/webfilings-dual-Cloud-solution-banks-on-rightscale.php

Yang, X., & Wang, L. et al. (2011). *Guide to e-science: Next generation scientific research and discovery*. Springer.

Zhang, S., Chen, X., & Huo, X. (2010). Cloud computing research and development trend. *Second International Conference on Future Networks (ICFN '10)*, (pp. 93-97). Sanya, Hainan.

KEY TERMS AND DEFINITIONS

Cloud: A large pool of easily usable and accessible virtualized resources (such as hardware, development platforms and/or services). These resources can be dynamically reconFigured to optimum resource utilization. This pool of resources is typically exploited by a pay-per-user model in which guarantees are offered by the Infrastructure Provider by means of customized SLA's.

Cloud Computing: A market-oriented distributed computing paradigm consisting of a collection of inter-connected and virtualized computers that are dynamically provisioned and presented as one or more unified computing resources based on service-level agreements established through negotiation between the service provider and consumers.

Cloud Federation: Deployment and management of multiple external and internal Cloud Computing services to match business needs.

Grid Computing: Basically a paradigm that aims at enabling access to high performance distributed resources in a simple and standard way.

Hybrid Cloud: A Cloud Computing environment in which an organization provides and manages some resources in-house and has others provided externally.

Infrastructure-As-A-Service (IaaS): A provision model in which an organization outsources the equipment used to support operations, including storage, hardware, servers and networking components, where the service provider owns the equipment and is responsible for housing, running and maintaining it and the client typically pays on a per-use basis.

Platform-As-A-Service (PaaS): A Cloud service model which offers an environment on which developers create and deploy applications and do not necessarily need to know how many processors or how much memory that applications will be using.

Private Cloud: A marketing term for a proprietary computing architecture that provides hosted services to a limited number of people behind a firewall.

Public Cloud: One based on the standard Cloud Computing model, in which a service provider makes resources, such as applications and storage, available to the general public over the Internet. Public Cloud services may be free or offered on a pay-per-usage model.

Software-As-A-Service (SaaS): A software distribution model in which applications are hosted by a vendor or service provider and made available to customers over a network, typically the Internet.

Section 2
Security

Chapter 5
Security Concepts for Cloud Computing

Steven C. White
Missouri University of Science and Technology, USA

Sahra Sedigh
Missouri University of Science and Technology, USA

Ali R. Hurson
Missouri University of Science and Technology, USA

ABSTRACT

Computer security is a complex undertaking within the traditional client-server architecture. As services and data are moved to the Cloud, security requirements change and become even more complex. Existing client-server security practices can be extended to address challenges specific to the Cloud environment. In this chapter, a contrast is made between traditional client-server environment with a Cloud environment - in terms of security challenges and solutions. In addition to enumerating and contrasting traditional challenges and solutions, the authors describe security challenges and solutions particular to the Cloud computing environment. The chapter describes, in terms of the pillars of security, key issues that should be addressed by an organization as it migrates to Cloud environments and propose solutions to these issues.

INTRODUCTION

Migrating from the traditional information technology (IT) environment to a Cloud- or service-based environment presents many challenges – among the greatest of which is security of services and data. Over the past few decades, computer security has risen to the top of the priority list, not only for IT, but even for upper-management of all but the smallest organizations. Reports on security breaches and information stolen, exposed, or lost; have become a daily occurrence. Exacerbating these security challenges is migration of the IT industry to a Cloud-based environment,

DOI: 10.4018/978-1-4666-2854-0.ch005

which is being carried out in the interest of more efficient use of resources. IT organizations unable to protect their data in the traditional environment are now tasked with moving the data out of their infrastructure and into the hands of third parties. IT is being asked to protect data when they often have very little control or oversight of where the data is located, who has access to it, and how it is being protected by the third party.

Much of the pressure to move to Cloud computing is coming from stakeholders who are more interested in cost savings and may not understand the risks involved in exposing their services or information to outside vendors, or in some cases public infrastructure shared by millions of other users. The pressure to take advantage of Cloud efficiencies is pushing organizations to make decisions before standards are set and technologies have matured. Some Cloud proponents continue to claim that security in the Cloud is mature and the risks are the same as in traditional IT environments. In many cases, the risks are comparable, but solutions in the traditional environment have had years to mature and advance whereas in the Cloud environment, the technologies are just beginning to emerge. Many of the solutions address only specific areas and do not integrate well with other solutions, or are complex and cumbersome to manage and implement.

The main challenges in moving to the Cloud involve data protection, both at rest and in transit, governance and accountability, access control and authentication, and finally availability. These challenges align with the information security pillars of security. As this chapter will show, moving to the Cloud presents many of the same challenges (resolved by the same solutions) as the traditional client-server environment, but it also presents entirely new challenges. A major stumbling block for Cloud computing security is the lack of tools, techniques, and metrics that would equip customers to understand and assess the Cloud. A fundamental question asked when moving to the Cloud is "how is it possible to retain control and maintain security of data and computation, while ceding control to a third party?"

This chapter investigates security for Cloud environments, with focus on the governance and operations of the Cloud. The first part of the chapter will describe the traditional IT environment, introduce the architecture and service levels of Cloud computing, and examine the pillars of security. The second part of the chapter will discuss specific problems and solutions. The chapter will conclude with a discussion of future avenues for research.

BACKGROUND

The client-server architecture has existed since the start of computing. A mainframe and dumb terminal could be considered the first implementation to meet the definition. If we fast forward to today, we normally associate client-server architecture with a desktop or laptop connecting to some type of server. There are many different applications for this type of architecture; e.g., email, file transfer, or web services. The server runs specialized software that offers services to the client. The server may have more storage, processing power, or other advantages. The client-server architecture has evolved over the years and has become fairly stable in design and management.

An example of simple client-server architecture is a file server. A client computer accesses the file server to create, edit or delete files. The file server performs the sole function of storing the files for the client computer. Multiple client computers can access the same file server and files. The file server runs specialized software to make sure the files are managed correctly.

A more complex example could be an environment with email, web, file, and print servers. In a typical (contemporary) scenario, a client may use services from and simultaneously access and manipulate the resources on all servers. Clients are expecting to have almost unlimited access to resources at their fingertips. Furthermore, we are now moving past clients that are traditional desktops and laptops to more mobile devices such as smart phones and tablets. These devices may have fewer capabilities than a traditional desktop or laptop, but they are designed to take advantage of the services offered in the client-server architecture.

Client-server architecture has several limitations, including serious constraints on scalability of resources. A file server is normally built to specifications, with some planned capacity for growth. As the number of clients grows and the tasks become more resource-intensive, additional hardware (storage or processing power) must be added to the server, or it must be replaced altogether - either solution requires downtime. In contrast, the ability to dynamically allocate considerable resources is a considerable advantage of Cloud computing.

1.1 Cloud Computing

According to the National Institute of Standards and Technology (NIST), (Mell, 2011) Cloud computing is a "a model for enabling convenient, on-demand network access to a shared pool of configurable computing resources (e.g.; networks, servers, storage, applications, and services) that can be rapidly provisioned and released with minimal management effort or service provider interaction." While this definition is comprehensive, the idea of Cloud computing is to create an environment where computing resources are available as needed, when needed, and can be added with very little effort. The need for scalability and adaptability is one of the fundamental motivators of Cloud computing. But this definition does not take into account the complexity behind the scenes to make this type of environment possible.

An example of the benefits of Cloud computing is moving a company's office applications to a hosted service. Regardless of the deployment strategy, a resulting benefit would be the ability

to use the office applications from any computer, without the need to load the applications locally. Another benefit would be the ability to add document storage as needed, instead of trying to approximate the amount of storage needed. Among the drawbacks of migration to the Cloud could be loss of availability - if network connectivity is lost; documents and applications will become inaccessible. Furthermore, when storing documents in a hosted Cloud, additional provisions are required to ensure their security.

1.2 Cloud Deployment Methods

Cloud computing can be configured and/or deployed in myriad ways, and can offer a multitude of services - including applications, database, storage, or processing power. This flexibility is part of the appeal of Cloud computing. Security for each of deployment and/or configuration should be provided based upon what the consumer wants to protect. Broadly speaking, Cloud deployments can be classified as public, private, community, or hybrid.

1.2.1 Public Clouds

Public Clouds are typically hosted and managed by a third party and have numerous clients. A typical scenario is depicted in Figure 1. The public Cloud architecture typically carries higher security risks than other deployment options, due to having multiple users and configurations.

1.2.2 Private Clouds

Private Clouds, such as the example depicted in Figure 2, fall into one of three types. They can be hosted and run by a third party, they can be hosted at the customer's facilities and managed by a third party, or a company can host and manage the private Cloud on its own. Private Clouds are typically dedicated to a single client, and as such, suffer from fewer security risks.

Figure 1. A typical public cloud

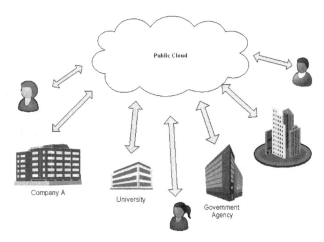

1.2.3 Community Clouds

A community Cloud is a Cloud deployment that is shared among multiple entities for a specific purpose. A good example, depicted in Figure 3, would be a private company, a university, and a government agency that are collaborating on specific research. The Cloud could be used for storage of data that will be shared among the three entities. The benefits of this deployment are a) the ability to share some but not all information, and b) the ability to share with a specific group.

1.2.4 Hybrid Clouds

Hybrid Clouds are a combination of public and private Clouds. A hybrid Cloud tries to take advantage of the security of the private Cloud but utilize the availability and scalability of public Clouds. Hybrid Clouds can be more complex than either private or public Clouds, and can be used to extend an organization's internal infrastructure and expand it by using a public Cloud. An example, depicted in Figure 4, is a web application that runs on a public Cloud infrastructure and uses the public Cloud's middleware to connect back to an internal or private database.

The deployment of the Cloud plays an important role in its security. In the discussion that follows, we introduce the Cloud computing stack and investigate areas where the architecture of the Cloud determines how security should be handled.

1.3 Architectures of the Cloud Computing Stack

1.3.1 Infrastructure as a Service

In the Infrastructure as a Service (IaaS) layer, which is the lowest layer of the Cloud computing stack; the Cloud vendor provides infrastructure such as bandwidth, storage, and processing capability. These services are typically provided through virtualization, but that is not a requirement. At this level, the services provided by the Cloud are the most basic, which necessitates that the organization subscribing to the service take on more of the responsibility of the security. The end user is able to customize the "infrastructure" to their use. This means they may have the ability to manage operating systems, storage, and other components of the system. When allowing access to the virtualized operating system, the organization would be responsible for maintaining the security of the operating system by ensuring

Figure 2. A typical private cloud

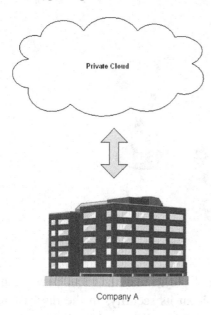

patch management, properly configured services, and account management. A common example of this type of architecture would be Amazon's EC2 or Rackspace.

1.3.2 Platform as a Service

The Platform as a Service (PaaS) layer is normally located in the middle of the Cloud services stack – on top of IaaS. PaaS typically provides application programming interfaces (APIs) or similar services to the organization. At this middle level of the Cloud, the Cloud vendor is usually responsible for the lower level of security - such as operating system and host security. In other words, the vendor provides security at the IaaS level. Related tasks include ensuring that the operating system is patched and up to date or a database is properly secured. The organization using the PaaS is responsible for the middle and upper levels of security. Since this level of the Cloud stack is normally used for developing higher-level applications such as web sites or web applications, the organization utilizing the Cloud is responsible for their security. The organization using the PaaS would also be

responsible for ensuring that connectivity to the APIs or databases is properly maintained. For example, they would be tasked with verifying that a web application built upon Java or Python has been developed correctly and common vulnerabilities have been eliminated. Examples of this type of service would be Microsoft's Azure database or .NET platforms, as well as Google's App Engine. A common method to implement this would be for an organization to purchase the Microsoft Azure service, which would be built upon the Microsoft IaaS model. This allows the purchaser the ability to add capacity as needed without overbuying either the infrastructure or the platform.

1.3.3 Software as a Service

Software as a Service (SaaS) normally provides a user with access to common applications through a web-based interface. Associated services allow a user to access productivity software; such as word processing, spreadsheets, and email; or applications for accounting or customer relationship management. SaaS is normally located at the top tier of the Cloud stack and built upon IaaS and PaaS. The Cloud vendor hosting the SaaS would typically be responsible for security throughout the entire Cloud application. The organization using the SaaS may handle user enrollment security, but the service provider would handle all infrastructure, operating system, application, and database service security. Numerous companies offer SaaS; some well-known examples are Gmail, Hotmail, and Salesforce's customer relationship management (CRM) service. Normally these offerings are built upon the previous two deployments. In terms of Salesforce's CRM, the service is built using IaaS for the storage and server environment; the database, middleware, and software are built at the PaaS layer; and the final product is offered as an SaaS.

As we move forward to investigate at the security of the Cloud, we will refer back to the

Figure 3. A typical community cloud

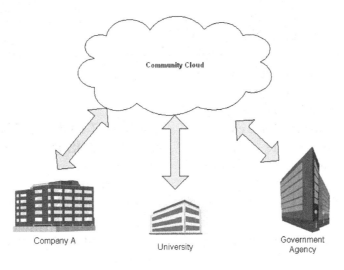

various Cloud architectures and layers of the Cloud stack. As mentioned earlier, security in the Cloud depends on the services purchased and the organizations from which the services are purchased. Certain scenarios are inherently more secure than others.

1.4 Pillars of Security

In the areas of computer and information security, there are normally three, but up to five pillars of security. Each pillar is briefly described below.

1.4.1 Confidentiality

Confidentiality is the concept of preventing the disclosure of information to unauthorized individuals. The basic idea behind this pillar is to keep an organization's information out of the hands of individuals who should not have access to the information.

Several scenarios in the Cloud environment require that confidentiality be maintained. Two major scenarios are the confidentiality of data at rest in the Cloud and the confidentiality of data in transit to or from the Cloud. Once data leaves the internal domain and is transferred outside the traditional perimeter of an organization, the data must be protected from unauthorized access. For

example, an organization that transfers all of its business documents to Google Apps needs assurance that the documents stored are not being accessed by other users or by the organization storing the documents.

1.4.2 Integrity

Integrity requires that undetected modification of data be impossible. The basic concept behind this pillar is the need to ensure that information does not change as it is stored or transmitted. Integrity sometimes presents a challenge in Cloud computing, as it requires that users delegate some level of control to the Cloud administrators.

Integrity is critical for anyone who uses data to make personal or business decisions. If an organization stores its accounting data in a PaaS environment, it must be assured the data has not been modified in storage or in transit, otherwise business partners or shareholders may lose confidence in the organization's ability to operate.

1.4.3 Availability

Information must be available when it is needed. There are many types of availability; such as network availability, application availability, or application response and timeliness. The information must be accessible to the correct individuals, at the time when each individual needs the information. This pillar is often simplistically associated with backups and disaster recovery, but extends beyond simple recovery of data. If a customer service employee is trying to contact a business client, but is forced to wait for an extended period of time due to a problem with the customer relationship management software (CRM), the availability requirement may have been violated.

1.4.4 Non-Repudiation

Non-repudiation is not one of the traditional three pillars of security but it is frequently seen as an important security principle. Non-repudiation implies that one party of a transaction cannot deny having received a transaction, nor can the other party deny having sent a transaction.

1.4.5 Authenticity

Authenticity works hand in hand with non-repudiation. The data owner wants to make sure that the Cloud vendor has received the data that was sent, and the Cloud vendor wants to ensure the data received came from the owner. The data owner also needs to know that any confirmation of receipt actually came from the Cloud vendor.

SECURITY CHALLENGES AND SOLUTIONS IN CLOUD COMPUTING

Security in the Cloud is conceptually similar to security in the traditional client-server environment. The goals are the same, but the solutions implemented are different. In the Cloud computing environment, there is still a need to access data, as well as services such as APIs, web services and interfaces. What is lost by moving to the Cloud is control over the infrastructure and underpinnings of that infrastructure (Damiani, 2007), (Armbrust, 2009), (Samarati, 2010), (Kher, 2005). The organization no longer has direct control over many of the aspects from which information security is internally assessed, such as physical security, personnel security, access security, and operational

Figure 4. A typical hybrid cloud

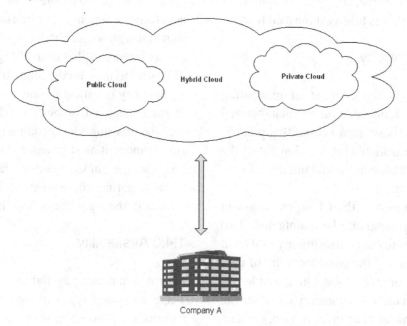

control. The organization is forced to either rely on the vendor to provide these services, or to determine other secure methods to maintain the same levels of security.

For example, when a company hires an IT staff member, the company normally performs a routine background check on the potential employee before he or she is hired. This is part of the personnel security checks carried out before allowing access to company information or infrastructure. In the case of Cloud computing, the consumer must rely on their vendor to perform such checks and ensure that individuals being hired meet the consumer's minimum level of personnel security in order to reduce the risk of a security breach. The goal or metric of personnel security is the same for the consumer, but instead of having direct control over the process, the consumer is forced to delegate the task.

According to a recent publication from the Cloud Computing Alliance (Cloud, 2011), the security of Cloud computing can be assessed from two different perspectives. One is the perspective of the Cloud computing vendor. In order for their operation to be profitable, the vendor must ensure the confidentiality, integrity, and availability of the information it hosts on behalf of another organization. The second perspective is from the viewpoint of the organization seeking a Cloud provider, whose main concern is the confidentiality, integrity and availability of the data and services being hosted by the Cloud vendor.

By looking at the pillars of security, we can loosely group the security challenges for Cloud computing. The groups will overlap, but particular challenges fall under particular pillars. In addition, we can show whether the challenge is unique to the Cloud environment, or if it exists in client-server environments as well. Table 1 summarizes the

Table 1. Classification of security challenges

Primary Pillar Of Security	Security Challenge Category	Security Challenge	Challenge in Cloud Environment	Challenge in Client/Server Environment	Client Issue	Provider Issue
Confidentiality/Integrity /Availability	Governance	Risk to Information	X	X	X	
Confidentiality/Integrity /Availability	Governance	Legal Issues	X		X	
Confidentiality/Integrity	Data Center Operations	Personnel Security	X			X
Confidentiality	Data Protection	Data at Rest	X		X	
Confidentiality	Data Protection	Data in Transit	X		X	X
Confidentiality	Access Control	Authentication of Clients	X	X	X	
Confidentiality	Access Control	Authorization of Clients	X	X	X	
Confidentiality	Access Control	Administration of Clients	X	X	X	
Confidentiality	Access Control	Audit and Compliance	X	X	X	X
Integrity	Integrity	Completeness of Data	X		X	
Integrity	Integrity	Improper/Unauthorized Changes to Data	X		X	
Availability	Data Center Operations	Business Continuity	X	X	X	X
Availability	Availability	Authorization of Clients	X	X	X	
Non-Repudiation	Verification of transactions	Guarantee Delivery of Data to the Sender	X			X
Non-Repudiation	Verification of transactions	Guarantee of the Receiver of Data Receipt	X		X	
Authenticity	Authenticity	Verification of Sender Identity	X			X
Authenticity	Authenticity	Verification of Receiver Identity	X		X	

resulting information. This figure does not address every scenario, and there will be places where the challenges may fall under multiple pillars or could be moved to one environment or the other, but it does capture the loose categorization described earlier in this paragraph.

As we discuss solutions to security challenges in Cloud computing in the remainder of this chapter, we will describe current practices - including academic solutions that hold promise, but have not yet been implemented. The shortcomings of each solution will be identified and mitigation techniques will be proposed.

2.1 Governance in the Cloud

Governance is the first area that should be studied in the analysis of Cloud security – as it is in the traditional IT environment. Governance concerns the development of policies and procedures to manage and maintain control of the information and should be based upon technical, legal, and compliance requirements of the organization.

2.1.1 Risk Management

The first step in examining governance is to identify the information or services that will be migrated to a Cloud services provider. In many cases, best practice would be to take a small amount of data or a small number of services and perform a pilot study to determine how well the process works. This helps to reduce the risk involved with moving major systems to a Cloud environment when an organization has little or no experience in performing associated tasks. Many organizations are concerned with protecting the information that they collect and store. In other cases, no sensitive information is involved, and the infrastructure itself is the entity that needs to be protected. For example, an organization may have a website that performs a function such as calculating currency exchange rates. The organization does not store or collect information, but it is

critical to protect the application itself. The website would not be very popular if it did not calculate the currency exchange rate correctly. Since the organization is using services in the middle of the Cloud stack, some of the security is going to be the organization's responsibility. They will need to ensure that data input fields are properly bound and the application cannot be altered.

Once the information and/or services have been identified, the organization should determine the level of acceptable risk for the information and services, namely:

- Exposed
- Made unavailable
- Modified without knowledge of the organization

After determining the information or services to be moved to a Cloud environment and the risks associated with this migration, the organization can begin to determine the type of Cloud architecture to use, and the level of the Cloud stack from which the services will be used. The latter plays an important role in identifying the entity responsible for security. The lower the level in the stack, the greater the responsibility of the consumer in assuring the security of the Cloud (Cloud, 2011).

Once the Cloud deployment method and Cloud architecture have been determined, the next step in governance is to determine the contractual language in order to acquire the desired configuration from a Cloud provider. This contract must be specific about the responsibility of each party. Relevant issues involve determining who will control access to the data, what method will be used to provide the access, what happens to the data when the contract ends, and what are mechanisms for the consumer to verify that the terms of the contract are being met. In most cases, governance challenges will be of concern to the consumer.

Part of the background work on governance is for an organization to develop a plan to address the risks identified. Again, the same rules apply in the traditional IT environment, but depending on the Cloud environment, there are new and additional challenges that do not exist in the traditional environment. These challenges are due to the lack of control and transparency inherent to most Cloud environments.

2.1.2 Legal Issues

Governance includes an organization's initial efforts to determine how to comply with all federal, state, and local laws and regulations. This process must be well-documented before an organization begins negotiations with Cloud vendors and related responsibilities should be identified and assigned before a contract is signed. Recently, a deal between the city of Los Angeles and Google involving the use of Gmail and Google Applications in an SaaS scenario by city employees had to be scaled back due to the inability of Google to meet some of the federal requirements for criminal justice agencies (Vijayan, 2012). The responsibility for ensuring that the Cloud vendor is meeting requirements ultimately falls on the shoulders of the organization purchasing the services.

Once all legal requirements are identified, an organization should lay out in detail all policies and procedures required to ensure that the Cloud services provider can pass an audit performed by either internal or external auditors. This information should include all technical mechanisms required for carrying out audits for compliance. Lack of transparency of the Cloud provider can pose a significant challenge to this task. Depending upon the architecture, a Cloud provider may or may not be able to provide all the monitoring, log files, or audit trails to prove compliance. In private Clouds where an organization is the only user of the infrastructure, access to those records may be easy to obtain; but in public or hybrid Clouds, access to shared log files or monitoring information may not be possible. One method to meet the compliance requirements is to work with third-party auditing firms that collaborate

with the Cloud provider to perform the audit without providing one organization access to the other organization's information or audits. An organization that is seeking to move to the Cloud cannot rely on the Cloud vendor to handle or be responsible for the security of the information. The responsibility still rests with the organization, which should have a security plan in place before migrating information to the Cloud. A security plan needs to have well-defined policies, procedures, and metrics for security; as well methods for collecting the security metrics.

In addition to identifying audits and the legal requirements, an organization must have a detailed plan on how to handle lawsuits, legal actions, and discovery requirements. The discovery process in legal matters can be complicated in a traditional IT environment; it is even more so in the Cloud environment. Organizations must understand how discovery can impact their data. An organization must determine how legal requests are handled by the Cloud vendor – in particular whether information will be shared by the vendor with legal authorities without consent or knowledge of the organization. In many cases, when legal action is initiated, organizations are required to preserve the information until after the legal action has been settled. Organizations will need to plan for how they will maintain that information. This may require additional storage from the Cloud provider, or the information may have to be moved back into the organization's computing infrastructure. A good example of this type of action was the Yahoo! email discovery court cases (Harley, 2010). A subpoena was presented by law enforcement to Yahoo! to turn over emails. Yahoo! was originally going to comply without notifying the owners of the emails. Yahoo reconsidered and fought the subpoena through the courts.

2.2 Confidentiality

Confidentiality is the concept of preventing the disclosure of information to unauthorized individuals. This concept seems to be fairly simple, but every day brings news of websites that are hacked and information that is stolen. These occurrences happen to all types of organizations – from small businesses to multinational corporations. Even in the traditional system, maintaining confidentiality of information is extremely difficult. In "traditional" client-server systems, numerous techniques are used to prevent unauthorized access to information. Some of these can be extended to the Cloud, but confidentiality in particular poses additional challenges in Cloud environments.

We break down the concept of confidentiality into three major areas – protecting information at rest, protecting information in transit, and access control. While each of these areas is addressed separately, many of the solutions will overlap or can be combined to create a more comprehensive solution.

2.2.1 Confidentiality of Data at Rest

The scale of the Cloud environment eliminates the possibility of using some of the controls that have traditionally been used to prevent the disclosure of information to unauthorized users. For example, in traditional IT, the traffic between users and servers passes over networks controlled by the organization. The traffic and servers are protected because they are behind firewalls and on private networks. This is no longer the case with the Cloud - the traffic and data must pass over public networks and the data is stored on infrastructure that is potentially accessible by any user.

The outsourcing of database services or even file storage (Hacigumus, 2002) have noteworthy implications on confidentiality. The first issue to be addressed is how to store and protect the data that resides in the Cloud. In this situation, the data is moved from an owner-controlled environment to a third-party environment. In the outsourced or Cloud scenario, the data owner cannot guarantee that others will be restricted from viewing, querying, or modify the data.

We enumerate a number of noteworthy methods for achieving confidentiality of data in the remainder of this section. Commercial Cloud deployments have emerged only recently; and as such, the development and implementation of these techniques is still evolving.

2.2.1.1 Fragmentation

Fragmentation can be carried out in multiple levels of the stack. In a file structure (IaaS), the file is split into multiple fragments and stored across multiple servers. Normally the algorithm for splitting the file will make copies of the fragments to store on multiple servers; this will ensure not only fragmentation but also redundancy and availability. The user would need to retrieve the fragments to reconstruct the file. For additional security, the file fragments could be encrypted.

Fragmentation can also be performed at higher levels of the stack, such as the application or database level. At the database level, fragmentation can occur within the database structure. The database can be split in both the horizontal and vertical directions. One possible example of vertical fragmentation is to store high-risk data on systems owned or controlled by the data owner and store non-sensitive data on an outsourced server. This would eliminate the need to encrypt the data on the outsourced server. Drawbacks would include additional overhead in joining the two data sources for queries and other transactions, or making sure that the data stored on the outsourced server cannot be used to infer information about the data stored on the data owner's server. Another drawback to this solution concerns the sharing of data among sites. Part of the benefit of outsourcing database services is the accessibility of data from anywhere. It would also be beneficial for the data to be stored in multiple databases. If sensitive data had to be stored on servers owned by the data owners, this would require either that data be stored in a single centralized location or the data owner have multiple locations under its ownership. Access control could be a potential disadvantage for this solution. Part of the cost savings of outsourcing are achieved through reduction of administrative costs. If the data owner managed the secure data, it would also have to manage access to that data on the internal databases. These requirements would reduce the benefits of using Cloud database services. Availability is also a concern. Latency or loss of service may prevent users from gaining access to the information as needed.

2.2.1.2 Vertical Fragmentation

The typical vertical fragmentation approach makes the assumption that the owner of the data will manage and control sensitive information. Another vertical fragmentation approach changes this concept slightly – storing the data on an outsourced server rather than the systems of the data owner. The advantage to this approach is that the owner no longer has to be directly involved in housing the data, which could be stored in multiple locations to gain the benefits of redundancy and availability. The drawback to this solution is that each of the servers and the individuals querying the data cannot know about the other data locations. So the outsourcing vendor that is used to house the "public" data cannot have access or have knowledge of the confidential data that is stored on another server. If this is compromised, confidentiality of the data will be breached.

Another form of vertical fragmentation involves the use of encryption and fragmentation to protect the data. Some users may not need to know the confidential information. For example, a nurse may not need to know the identities of the patients who are scheduled for surgery but the nurse may need to know what operations are being performed in order to prepare the room or order supplies. The nurse would be able to query the public data without violating the confidentiality of any of the patients. This proposal addresses the issues of data publication and utility. The availability of public or non-identifying data is acceptable, as long as the confidential data cannot be inferred or exposed to non-authorized clients.

2.2.1.3 Horizontal Fragmentation

Horizontal fragmentation is another solution that moves particular rows of data in one database to other databases (Wiese, 2010). This solution has some of the same drawbacks as vertical fragmentation. The data owner needs to make sure that "public" data does not reveal information about the confidential data and that an unauthorized user cannot discover the confidential data through the public data.

2.2.1.4 Association Breaking

Another proposed solution is to break the association of data elements (Damiani, 2005), (Cormode, 2008). This could be done in multiple ways. In many cases, the association of data elements contains the information. For example in a medical database, if the patient's name or identifier can be disassociated from the procedure or medical condition, the confidentiality of the information can be preserved.

2.2.1.5 Encryption

In the traditional environment, data on the file servers or database servers is normally stored in plain text. Users normally do not need to worry about whether a file can be viewed by unauthorized users, because role-based security is applied, and administrators are trusted employees of the organization. In the Cloud, this is not the case. An organization does not know where the data will reside and who will have access to it. Again, we can point to contracts and agreements, but they do not guarantee that the data will not be accessed by Cloud employees or rogue administrators.

Encrypting the data both in transport and in the Cloud is a solution to this problem. All information that is stored in the Cloud will be encrypted (Damiani, 2005), (Miklau, 2003). The challenges associated with this encryption vary from one deployment method to the next. For example, at the IaaS level, a user will normally be storing individual files or documents. At the PaaS level, the user may be saving information directly into a database. When the user needs to access or update the data, they will normally want to work with a subset of the data and efficient retrieval or updating of the data is the challenge. In the case of data in a database, the data will be encrypted, and then sent to the Cloud database to be stored. File storage would be handled in the same manner. The file would be encrypted by the client and then sent to the Cloud for storage. This seems like a simple solution, but its complexity is revealed as use of the information is considered.

Among the questions that arise are the following:

- How do I determine which file contains the information I want, copy the file back to the client, and decrypt it?
- If data is stored in a database and encrypted, how can it be queried or updated?
- Should the data be decrypted prior to being queried? In that case, the data has to be transferred back to the client for decryption. This becomes very inefficient in terms of computational resources and bandwidth.

At the PaaS level, several solutions have been proposed for protecting the data in a database while making it available for queries (Chung, 2005), (Damiani, 2007), (Aggarwal, 2005), (Hacigumus, 2002), (Li, 2011), (Yuping, 2010).

The first part of the problem is how to query (including update queries) the data without requiring that all data in the database be decrypted. If the data needs to be joined with another table or server, this would require both tables to be decrypted and then joined. This solution can very quickly become complex and computationally intensive.

In order to facilitate queries, the encrypted data needs to be identified so that the server does not have to send back all the information to be decrypted for each query. The solution is to create an index for the encrypted data. Several methods for creation of the index are outlined below. Each method has advantages and disadvantages.

One approach is to encrypt the tuple and then add indices for each of the encrypted data elements. The plain text tuple (Lname, Fname, SSN, DOB, Salary, and Project) would be encrypted and stored in the ENC field in the Cloud database. Then indexes would be created for primary keys or data fields of interest. In this example, Lname, SSN, DOB and Project would be key data fields. An index (I1, I2, I3, and I4) would be created for the data elements in those fields (Table 2). If a query was performed to retrieve all records that were associated with the "space" project, the query would search the column I4 and would look for any records that matched "add55". This approach would increase the storage space required on the outsourced server. In addition the client would need to know what the encrypted indexes were before the query could be performed.

Other methods have been proposed for creation of an index for an encrypted data element. One method could be considered a "bucket" technique. This method breaks an attribute into ranges of values. For example, the age attribute could be broken into three buckets – 20 and younger, 21-50, and over 50. The individual tuples would be encrypted and then the index value of the three different groups would be added to the tuple. When the client processed the query, the server would send back the tuples that matched the index and the client would have to discard any decrypted tuples that did not match the exact search criteria.

Using the buckets above, the query could ask for all patients that are under 15. The server would pass all the tuples from bucket 1 to the client (including the tuples for 20 and younger), which would mean that the tuples with ages of 16 to 20 would need to be discarded by the client because the query did not call for them. One benefit of this approach is that the server would not have

Table 2. Plain text data and encrypted data with indices

Plain Text						Encrypted data stored in Cloud				
Lname	Fname	SSN	DOB	Salary	Project	**ENC**	I1	I2	I3	I4
Smith	John	123456789	12/1/1965	50000	space	**aldfjalskd7f**	ald	asdfa	asd12	add55
Smith	Linda	789456123	11/1/1955	55000	water	**aldowiue324**	ald	Oiuo	azc33	bsdf89

to send each tuple back for decryption. It is also harder to gain information about the data, because there is no one-to-one mapping of attribute values to indices. This would help mask the data if someone was watching the transaction with the tuples being passed back to the client. The cost of this approach is additional processing at the client to decrypt all the records and then discard the additional records. In addition, since there are ranges, the "where" clause for a query of all records with age <25 would require the "where" clause to be broken down further; the tuples in both the first and second buckets would need to be returned to the client; who would discard the extra tuples.

A second method for creation of the index is to use a hash function. Hash functions are used to associate a single value - usually a single integer – with one or more data items. Application of the hash function to a specific value of an attribute will always result in the same index. The same hash function can be used in responding to a query - the correct tuples can be returned for decryption at the client. One challenge of hash functions is the possibility of a collision – that two different values of the same attribute may be mapped to the same index value by the hash function. This is beneficial to security and increases the ability to protect the data, since an attacker will not be able to determine a one-to-one relationship between a data value and its index. On the other hand, this could result in unnecessary tuples being retrieved in response to a query of the encrypted data. To improve query performance, the hash function can be adjusted to decrease the collision of data values. The hash function can also be adjusted

to increase the likelihood of collisions, to move towards the bucket approach. Other index methods include B-tree indexes, privacy homomorphism, and splitting and scaling. These approaches are designed for specific data environments. They are designed to provide group by or order by queries over encrypted data. The bucket and hashing methods do not need to retain the ordering of the data to be used, but these other methods do preserve the ordering of the data in the encrypted tables.

The common goal of all of the indexing functions is to create an economical method of querying the data. The common tradeoff is between reducing the encryption overhead (performance) and protecting the data (security). An enhancement to the bucket method would be to create an algorithm that would efficiently balance bucket sizes and performance.

Similar challenges are faced in working with the IaaS architecture; for example, in the file storage scenario. A file cannot simply be named and sent to the Cloud. A file name could be enough to leak information or give an unknown system administrator the idea that a file contains valuable information. Most individuals prefer to name a file something representative of the contents. For example, most users prefer an Excel file with customer account information to be named "Customer_ Accounts.xls," rather than have it encrypted and named "aldk78$.t4s." Encrypting the information before sending it to the Cloud makes it difficult to use or share the information easily. Continuing the filename example, the user would have to remember the encrypted name of each file in order to retrieve it or use it. Sharing files with other users would entail many of the same problems as encountered when working with databases. The user would need to provide other users with the encrypted file name in order to share the file as well as the decryption key for the file. In a traditional IT environment a group of users who access and share common documents would have very little difficulty working with the group's files. It would be easy to understand the naming conventions; i.e. everyone would know the Excel spreadsheet containing the company's accounts receivable would be called "accounts_receivable.xls." An understandable naming convention would not be as easy to implement with the Cloud environment.

There are advantages and disadvantages to each type of encryption. Furthermore, the party responsible for encryption varies based on the level of the Cloud stack. Another factor is the Cloud architecture. In private Clouds, the organization may or may not need to encrypt the data at rest or as it moves within the Cloud.

2.2.2 Confidentiality of Data in Transit

Moving information to Cloud services has become easier for the end-user. With the proliferation of free file sharing, email, and other storage or web services, users are moving information to the Cloud without the knowledge or assistance of an organization's IT staff. This loss of control, especially over sensitive data/information, has become a problem for many organizations. When asked, many end-users state that they move the information because they need remote access to it or need to share it in order to perform their jobs. The end-user is not as concerned about the security of the information, as they are about its functionality. Other employees often feel that the organization's IT staff is not meeting their needs or is too restrictive. Organization need to have policies and procedures in place to inform users how and under what circumstances they can or cannot move information to the Cloud. In addition, organizations need to install monitoring

at the edges of the network to detect movement of information to the Cloud. Some methods for preventing data migration would be the user of web filtering and data loss prevention software. Blocking access to unknown Cloud providers can help, but in some cases, the IT organization is left out of the purchases of Cloud services. Databases and file activity monitoring software can also be used.

In addition to moving information from the organization to the Cloud, other data movements will need to be monitored and performed. Depending on the organization's needs, the information may have to move within the Cloud or between Clouds. Before moving any of the data, the information should be protected by encryption – which can occur at different levels of the Cloud stack (Vimercati, 2007), (Vimercati, 2007). Many Cloud providers tout the availability of information to their customers. This availability comes with challenges. One way to improve the availability of the data is to have multiple copies of the data. When service providers have multiple copies, they will need to ensure the secure transmission of the data between locations.

Continuing the previous example, data should be protected as it is transferred to and from the Cloud. Recall that, in traditional client-server environments, the data owner will most likely control the entire infrastructure and will not be as concerned about transmitting data within the private network. In Cloud environments, that is no longer the case; the data will pass outside the perimeter and go through a public network to the Cloud. Encryption immediately comes to mind as a solution. The information can be encrypted at the client and sent over the public network to be stored in the Cloud, as in Figure 5. This is common practice in many of today's Cloud services. As an example, Hotmail or Gmail can be accessed through a Secure Socket Layer (SSL) connection. The information is encrypted as it passes through the Internet. Other solutions have been touched upon briefly under the confidentiality section of this paper. Instead of encrypting data, it can be tokenized – process similar to fragmentation, but using a public/private Cloud pair. The public data is placed in the public Cloud along with tokens pointing back to a private Cloud that contains the sensitive data. There is no need to encrypt any data before moving it to the public Cloud, but tokens will need to be generated and placed within the data. The tokens take the place of confidential data that an organization does not want to share or make public.

2.2.3 Access Control

Access control is used to protect the data. Users are provided with a user id and password. This allows them to access the information that is intended for them, which may be a subset of the entire system. Among the numerous access control methods available, we will focus on two that are more widely used - role- based and rule-based. Role-based authentication is a common and accepted method for setting up access in traditional systems. Roles, such as support staff or manager, are defined; these roles are then converted to groups or access lists; and a user is defined to have a specific role. The user is then assigned the

role and can be added into the group or given the defined access list.

Rule-based authentication - also a common method for access control, is a granular type of authentication. Rules are based upon objects and specific rules that specify which objects can access other objects. Access control lists (ACLs) are an example of rules-based access. Rule-based access control is used in the traditional client-server environment, and can be used in the Cloud environment as well. Furthermore, the traditional environment employs firewalls and other barriers that prevent unauthorized users from sending or receiving information from the servers and the network. Networks are considered private, and outside entities do not have access to view or use the private resources. Much of the traffic on these private networks is not encrypted or protected, because the connections are on the private network and considered secure. Addressing schemes and network/server segmentation are used to prevent unauthorized access to the private network.

Access control is a fundamental security requirement that impacts all pillars of security; however, we have placed it primarily under the pillar of confidentiality, due to the fact that it is primarily a mechanism to maintain the confidentiality of

Figure 5. Encryption of data in transit

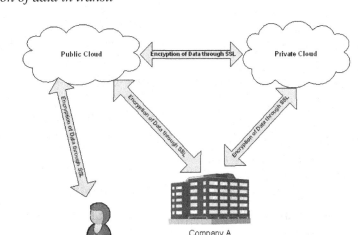

information. Access control prevents unwanted users from accessing confidential information or services– it protects the confidentiality of the information. It also ensures that if a user has access to information or services, he or she is given the correct level of access to carry out the task at hand, while allowing the organization to verify or audit the access. In other words, access control protects the integrity of information. Finally, access control can ensure that a user has the ability to access the information when they need it - it protects the availability of the information (Harney, 2001), (Yu, 2010), (Goyal, 2006).

Access control can be further divided into the following areas:

- Authentication
- Authorization
- Administration
- Audit and compliance

2.2.3.1 Authentication

In the course of authentication, a user is identified and provided with a unique identifier that allows the person to access services and data. Authentication may also be provided to devices, services, or service accounts and administrators. In the traditional client-server environment, an organization would have an internal mechanism to validate a user before giving them access. Moving into the Cloud environment, the ease of sharing information has allowed organizations to distribute their partners and employees throughout the world. This globalization is complicating user validation and authentication. When the IT environment was internal to an organization, it was easier to validate the user - normally through face-to-face contact. Organizations today are now working with thousands of partners and employees that could be located across the globe – significantly complicating the provision of the correct level of access to only those users who should have access to the information, services, or infrastructure in question.

In traditional environments, the user would authenticate with an organization's directory services, such as Microsoft's Active Directory. Directory services can be utilized in the Cloud, but there are challenges to their implementation. In a private Cloud setting, the organization may be able to extend the internal directory services out to the private Cloud through a virtual private network connection. This can also be done in hybrid or public Clouds, but the risk to the internal directory services increases.

Several methods are available for management of user authentication. User identity verification should be pushed down to the lowest level, where authentication can be handled through assertions. In Cloud environments, protocols such as WS-Federation or others based on the Security Assertion Markup Language (SAML) are preferable to directory services for authentication of users (Goodrich, 2008), (XML, 2002). These technologies allow the user management to be carried out at the lowest level and for tokens to be used to present credentials to services for identification of individuals. To improve the authentication process, two-factor (advanced) authentication should be used. Advanced authentication requires two levels of criteria to be met, in contrast to the single level of user id and password. Advanced authentication normally requires a soft or hard token or the use of public-key infrastructure or biometrics to go along with the user id/password combination. Another good solution for Cloud environments is risk-based authentication, which adds another monitoring mechanism to determine whether a user's access pattern is consistent with the normal pattern for the individual. If the usage deviates from the normal pattern, the user is denied access or is required to provide additional evidence.

2.2.3.2 Authorization

User authorization can be managed in a role-based, rule-based, or claims-based fashion – among others. OAuth and User Managed Access (UMA)

(Dannen, 2011) are new standards for user authorization. The traditional IT environment has normally used the role-based model to grant access to data and services. This model works well because it is easy to use, but with Cloud architectures and the concept of access-anywhere, rule-based authorization may be a better solution. Normally, a user using the internal infrastructure would access information and services as needed. In the Cloud environment, the user may be accessing data or services from non-traditional environments, such as airports or restaurants. In those cases, the organization may not want extremely sensitive information to be available to a user, even if he or she is normally authorized for such access. Rule-based authorization allows the organization to grant or deny access based upon the scenario in which it is being requested (Jajodia, 2001).

2.2.3.3 Administration

Administration can be defined in many ways, but in this context, refers to user administration. As organizations take advantage of Cloud environments, the administration or management of the large number of users will become challenging. Users may be located in different geographical areas from the staff that performs the credentialing of users. Many organizations are collaborating with other organizations that have already vetted their employees. If a partner organization has vetted and vouches for an employee, there is no need for another partner organization to duplicate the process. A solution to this challenge takes advantage of authentication mechanisms such as SAML and WS-Federation. A proposed solution is federated identity management, where organizations build a federation that allows member organizations to act as service providers or identity verifiers. The service providers are able to use rule-based or role-based authentication and specify the requirements for a user to gain access to objects or resources. The identity verifiers would vet each user to meet the requirements of the service providers. This would push the administration to the correct level and reduce the redundancy of information collection and administration by the organizations. Some of the disadvantages of this solution is the organizations would need to have the infrastructure in place to join the federation and there would need to be a trust level between the organizations. This type of administration would be available in any level of the architecture and would be used in any of the deployment methods.

Figure 6 shows an example of the process for federated identity management. The user in Organization A attempts to access an application from Organization B. Organization B refers the user to the federated services for identity verification and authorization. Organization A provides the credential information to Organization B and the user is granted access. The administration of the user is left to the Organization A, of which the user is a part, and is not duplicated at Organization B.

2.2.3.4 Auditing and Compliance

Auditing and compliance is an area of Cloud security that is in the very early stages and subject to many changes, due to the deployment and architecture models of the Cloud. Much of the infrastructure that Cloud computing is based upon is not built to support the individualization of log files and audits. For example, at the PaaS level, an organization may share a database platform with multiple organizations. Organization A may have five tables and Organization B may have two tables. With the major database vendors, it may be difficult to separate out the log files for each of the tables. This would prevent the Cloud vendor from providing each organization with a complete log of their table activity.

At the SaaS level, separation of audit logs may be even more difficult. An example may be the use of Google Mail - if an organization shares email services with multiple entities, a request for the audit logs may be something that Google would not be able to provide to one organization without sharing the log entries of other entities' as well.

Many federal laws may require auditing by a third party. In addition, organizations should maintain audit and documentation processes for all IT systems and services, whether they are internal or through the Cloud. This is another instance where security concepts for Cloud services are similar to the traditional IT environment, but the implementation is a little more difficult. Audit requirements should be identified and added into any contract between an organization and Cloud provider. Depending on the Cloud architecture, the metrics required for assessing security may be different. The process to measure and report the metrics in a consistent and timely manner must be prepared before the contract is signed.

Finally, decommissioning or termination of a Cloud contract must ensure the removal of data from the Cloud's infrastructure and control. Depending on the architecture and the type of service contracted, this process will be difficult to verify. This makes the case for always encrypting the data to prevent its compromise. It also eliminates the necessity of verifying the removal of data.

Auditing and compliance challenges will continue to evolve as legal requirements change. In May of 2012, the United States government unveiled a Federal Risk and Authorization Management Program (FedRAMP) (GSA, 2012) which provides a standardized approach for security assessment, authorization and continuous monitoring. This program is designed to provide guidance to service providers and accredit third party assessors in order to provide better accountability for Cloud services.

2.3 Integrity

Integrity requires that it should not be possible to modify data undetectably; i.e. no information can be deleted or modified without the owner's knowledge. For example, in an airline reservation system, the integrity of the seating numbers would need to be maintained; otherwise the reservation system might over or under sell the number of seats, causing financial problems for the airline. In the case of missing information, a client who is querying data hosted on the Cloud must have the ability to guarantee that the data the server sends back is complete and the server did not intention-

Figure 6. Example of federated identity management

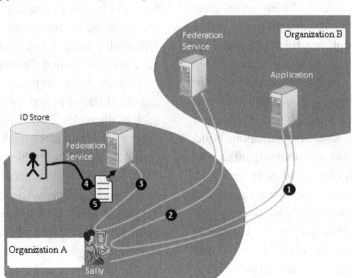

ally send more or less data than was requested. If a professor performs a query to identify all graduate students enrolled in a particular class, he or she would have to feel confident that the Cloud server is sending all records (and only those records) that meet the criteria. The challenge is in detecting modification of the data by the server.

In the traditional client-server environment, all systems are located within the organization's computing environment, managed by the organizational staff, and secured by methods such as firewalls and access control mechanisms. Log files would be used to determine by whom and when a file has been accessed. If data is changed, the log files could be used to determine the user who made the change. In a Cloud environment, this may not be the case. Infrastructure control is up to the Cloud vendor and access to logs and other monitoring functions may be limited.

To address integrity, we must investigate:

- Completeness of the data
- Modification of data at rest or in transit

2.3.1 Completeness/ Correctness of Data

Approaches to determining the correctness of information are usually based on either message authentication codes (MAC) or signatures (Damiani, 2007), (Mykletun, 2004). MACs use a public key shared between the owner and the client. The client uses the key to either verify records or generate MACs for other tuples or data elements. Signatures would use both private and public keys to check integrity. This guarantees that the only entity that could have generated the signature is the data owner. This feature is especially useful when the outsourced database is used or managed by multiple entities. Other data owners would have their own keys and would not be able to change the data and data integrity signature without being detected.

At the PaaS level, an organization may be using a database to store information and can use signatures or MACs to ensure its integrity. Both approaches have disadvantages. For example, the data can be broken down into a variety of groups to verify integrity. The groups could be based upon a table, a tuple, a group of tuples, or individual data elements. Each of these approaches uses a signature to verify the integrity of the data. The difference is in the practicality of the results. Normally queries will not request entire tables, and even though checking integrity at the table level would reduce the amount of overhead needed, most clients do not desire or require the complete table. The tuple is the second level at which integrity can be checked. This level yields a realistic solution, where a client will be provided with the complete tuple for a query, even if only an element or two of the tuple have been requested. The final choice is to guarantee integrity at the element level. This approach would provide the best results in terms of querying the data, but would be difficult to manage, and the overhead for determining as well as storing the signature would increase the amount of processing and storage.

In order to improve the efficiency of integrity checking, a further step would be to chain together the signatures for a range of records (Narasimha, 2006). Several methods exist for this task, with the common idea being to aggregate or chain together individual signatures. The owner can create the aggregated signature and pass it to the client, who can check the returned data against the aggregated signature to verify that the individual tuples or data elements are present and correct.

Another proposed method of verifying the integrity of queried data is AuthDS, where Merkle hash trees or B-trees are used (Devanbu, 2000). The trees are populated beforehand; the hash keys are the leaves on the trees. Data can be verified by using the leaf nodes to generate the higher levels, until the root is calculated. At that point in time, the value can be compared, and if it matches the owner's value, the data element is deemed correct. The main obstacles to this approach are the requirements of a) building trees to handle every type of relation and b) storing the trees, both of which are costly.

Each approach to verifying integrity has advantages and disadvantages in terms of performance and recoverability. The main differences among the methods are the algorithms used to create and chain the signatures. Factors such as complexity of the computation at both owner and client levels, as well as the bandwidth cost to transfer the data and the signatures, are factors by which these methods can be compared.

2.4 Availability

Information must be available when it is needed. This appear to be one of the greatest advantages of Cloud computing. Information storage and provision is outsourced to a vendor that makes access to the data highly-available. The vendor maintains multiple locations and multiple connections to each location where the data is stored. Server maintenance and scheduling outages are no longer concerns for the owners of the data, because the Cloud vendor seamlessly makes the data available at any time.

2.4.1 Backup

Even in the Cloud, every organization needs to develop risk mitigation and contingency plans, as Cloud services can often become unavailable. In early 2011, the high availability (99.999% or five-nines) claim for Cloud environments was put to the test. Amazon had a serious failure in its Cloud services (Leong, 2011). This disruption of service was not only alarming because it happened to one of the premier Cloud computing companies, but also because it impacted a large number of other companies and websites. Another important factor was the time it took for these companies to recover and bring their services back online. When websites are down, businesses are losing revenue as well as the confidence of customers. Availability should be a critical part of every organization's business plan, but this aspect of security is difficult and costly to achieve, even in a traditional client-server environment. The key question is what to do in case of a system failure, natural disaster, or malicious attack. In the traditional computing environment, most organizations have multiple options – some of which are complex and costly. It is up to the organization to determine the type of recovery plan they can afford. Plans typically range from backing up data to tape/disk up to having a complete backup site that is synchronized with the primary site. In case of a failure, this hot site would instantly come online and the organization would experience very little downtime.

Another solution is backing up key data to a tape or disk that is kept at the organization's computing facilities. This could be considered reverse off-site storage as compared to the traditional computing environment. Another solution is to contract with a separate Cloud vendor to host the data in case the primary vendor becomes unavailable. Backups or replication can be used to maintain copies of the information at backup sites. Many Cloud computing vendors have multiple data centers located throughout the world. In the case of database services, the use of replication can not only improve performance by placing the data closer to the clients, but it can also be used for disaster recovery.

2.4.2 Redundancy

Availability also needs to be investigated in terms of service levels; i.e., survivability. Simple access to services does not suffice, the performance of the services provided should also be considered. In recent months, Cloud services have been the target of denial of service attacks that have severely impacted the ability of users to connect to the resources provided by the Cloud. Redundancy needs to be investigated in order to ensure that if one location becomes unavailable, other locations will have up-to-date information and will be able to handle the requests.

Architecting availability in Cloud environments is a difficult task, but the underlying concepts are not far from those of traditional computing environments. The involvement of outside vendors brings into play the other two pillars of security– confidentiality and integrity. Simply copying or restoring data to a new server does not suffice; the infrastructure to allow access to the information must also be rebuilt or replicated.

2.4.3 Data Center Operations

Data center operations for Cloud computing share some requirements with traditional client-server systems. When comparing Cloud providers, data center security should be evaluated in the same fashion as it would be if the organization was to build its own data center. In order to meet availability requirements, the organization needs to identify how the Cloud vendor handles physical security. The placement of the data center should take into account normal data center rules; such as the geographical and political stability of the physical location, and laws governing the locale.

Physical operation parameters, such as maintenance, electrical, HVAC, and fencing also warrant consideration. These are critical areas of concern, especially if a Cloud vendor maintains only one or two locations. It is critical to ensure that security of physical access to the infrastructure is well-documented and maintained. Personnel security is another important component of Cloud security, as it is critical in order to ensure that anyone with access to the facilities, networks, and infrastructure meets the minimum requirements for any applicable laws, regulations, or policies. Remember that in the Cloud, the consumer loses the ability to control all aspects of security and must rely on the provider.

2.5 Non-Repudiation

Non-repudiation is not one of the three traditional pillars of security; nonetheless, it is seen as an important security principle. Non-repudiation implies that one party cannot deny having received a transaction, nor can the other party deny having sent it.

In terms of Cloud computing, non-repudiation can be considered a successor to integrity. The owner of the data should be able to ensure that all the data they are sending to the Cloud is actually being received. For example, in a Cloud database service, a user who sends data to the Cloud would like to know whether the data made it to the Cloud database and whether it is stored there unaltered and in its entirety.

Since non-repudiation in the current Internet environment carries similar concerns, several existing solutions could be used to solve this problem. Signing the information and attaching a unique identifier could be a potential solution. One of the bigger challenges with Cloud computing is trust of the Cloud vendor. In discussing solutions to security issues, we have demonstrated that encryption and hashing or signing of the information seems to be a consistent solution. Using the same technology would also work in achieving non-repudiation.

As is the case with other aspects of security, non-repudiation becomes more difficult in the Cloud environment than it is in the traditional client-server environment. For example, with file storage in the traditional environment, a user does not think twice about whether the server received the file when it was saved. The same thought process occurs with database services - data is updated or inserted, and it is automatically assumed that the data has been saved to the database. With Cloud services, it would not be prudent to assume that the vendor is going to provide the same level of service. Cloud vendors such as Google or Microsoft offer file storage and tout its ease of use – everything is carried out through a web browser window. Significant questions arise; e.g., when a file is copied to Microsoft's SkyDrive, there should be assurance that the file is actually being sent to Microsoft. Most individuals will assume the file is there, because it always is in a traditional environment. This is a simplified example involving only personal information but it can be extended to the business or commercial world. There needs to be some guarantee that the file just saved by a user actually made it to the Cloud vendor and the Cloud vendor is storing it for the user.

A proposed solution (Birget, 2002), (Li, 2005), (Atallah, 2005), (Atallah, 2009) to this problem is to use public and private keys and to perform a "handshake" to make sure the process completes. The use of a trusted third party is also needed. The process is to send along with the data, a signed evidence file that would contain information about the data or file being saved. The signed evidence file would be encrypted by a person or organization's public key. The vendor would then receive the data and evidence file and verify that the file did indeed come from the organization. The reverse process would be carried out when sending data from the Cloud to the organization. The trusted third party would be used when the Cloud vendor does not respond to the organization's request for verification. At that point in time, the organization would contact the trusted third party to ask for assistance in resolving the repudiation. The repudiation could be due to non-malicious events, in which case the third party can verify sending and receiving the information. If the event is due to malicious activity, the trusted third party can verify a claim by either side that they did not receive the data. The drawback to this solution is the overhead needed for every transaction; a trusted third party would need to be involved with both the organization and the Cloud vendor.

2.6 Authenticity

Finally, authenticity needs to be guaranteed. Authenticity is defined as being of undisputed origin or authorship. Authenticity works hand in hand with non-repudiation. The data owner wants to ensure that the Cloud vendor has received the data that was sent and the Cloud vendor wants to make sure the data received came from the owner. The data owner would also like to know that when the Cloud vendor responds with confirmation; the confirmation is actually coming from the Cloud. Authenticity solutions are based upon identity management. The use of private and public keys or digital signatures is a way to ensure the authenticity of the data stored and transmitted among users and between users and the Cloud infrastructure. In order to uses these techniques, the identity of individuals must be established using the methods described above in the authentication and authorization sections.

FUTURE RESEARCH DIRECTIONS

The area of Cloud security is in its infancy. As this chapter has shown, in this first iteration of its development, traditional IT security concepts are being ported to the Cloud setting. Research has been carried out on new ways to handle the challenges, but most of the solutions propose modifications of existing techniques that only partially solve the issues. Comprehensive solutions to the security challenges of Cloud environments are yet to be proposed. Several existing solutions are available for identity management. The same is true for integrity. Encryption of the data can also be carried out in different ways, but each solution operates independently of others. For example, keys and encryption can be used to prove the integrity of the data; they can also be used to protect the data at rest and in transit, and provide access to the data.

Solutions to identity management, authorization, and authentication are other significant challenges and worthy of additional research. As breach after breach has shown, traditional methods will not be sufficient in the new mobile connect-anywhere environment. Research in these areas should identify a comprehensive solution that is efficient and sufficiently strong and robust.

Governance and compliance are areas that have not seen as much research as other more technical areas. These areas are just as critical in terms of research as developing more efficient methods to encrypt information. As with traditional IT environments, methods for defining and measuring security in Cloud environments are incomplete and lacking. If the metrics are not defined and measurable it is difficult to define compliance in the Cloud environment. There is very little standardization on compliance or identifying which vendors meet the requirements to be considered secure or trustworthy. The IT industry continually develops piecemeal solutions. Users install antivirus to protect desktops, laptops, and other devices; but the efficacy of these solutions is questionable. The same can be said of Cloud solutions. Many solutions have been proposed, but their worthiness is yet to be determined.

CONCLUSION

Organizations are beginning to move their critical business data to Cloud services. Whether the service provides email, file storage, or database management, the benefits to a business can be significant. While these services offer benefits, they carry associated risks. In the traditional computing environment, most organizations control their own network, services, and data. The security of the infrastructure has been built in by the organization. The architecture used to ensure this security is complex; moving to a Cloud computing environment only exacerbates this complexity. Organizations cannot necessarily trust computing platforms or the personnel who operate them. This creates new challenges in terms of security.

As described in this chapter, solutions to these problems exist. However, every solution entails an increase in overhead and complexity. Encryption, hashing, message digests, and other verification methods are solutions to many of these problems. Making everything work together becomes the real challenge. An organization will need to evaluate the benefits against the risks for each of the pillars of security. They will need to determine whether it will beneficial to move all or only less sensitive data to the Cloud. Other questions that need to be answered are how to handle outages or security breaches. Even though moving to the Cloud does offer increased performance and capacity, it does not reduce the level of management and planning required for keeping an organization secure and operational.

REFERENCES

Aggarwal, G., et al. (2005). Two can keep a secret: a distributed architecture for secure database services. In Proceedings of the Conference on Innovative Data Systems Research 2005.

Armbrust, M., Fox, A., Griffith, R., Joseph, A. D., Katz, R. H., & Konwinski, A. … Zaharia, M. (2009). Above the clouds: A Berkeley view of cloud computing. (University of California, Berkeley, Tech. Rep. USB-EECS-2009-28).

Atallah, M., Frikken, K., & Blanton, M. (2005). Dynamic and efficient key management for access hierarchies. In Proceedings of Computer and Communication Security.

Atallah, M. J., Blanton, M., Fazio, N., & Frikken, K. B. (2009). *Dynamic and efficient key management for access hierarchies* (pp. 1–43). ACM TISSEC.

Birget, J., Zou, X., Noubir, G., & Ramamurthy, B. (2002). Hierarchy-based access control in distributed environments. In Proceedings of IEEE International Conference on Communications.

Ceselli, E. D., di Vimercati, S. D. C., Jajodia, S., Paraboschi, S., & Samarati, P. (2005). *Modeling and assessing inference exposure in encrypted databases* (pp. 119–152). ACM TISSEC. doi:10.1145/1053283.1053289

Chung, S. S., & Ozsoyoglu, G. (2005). Processing aggregate queries over encrypted relational databases. Technical Report, Case Western Reserve University. Retrieved from http://art.case.edu/anti-tamper.pdf

Cloud Security Alliance. (2011). Security guidance for critical areas of focus in Cloud computing. Retrieved from http://www.Cloudsecurityalliance.org/

Cormode, G., Srivastava, D., Yu, T., & Zhang, Q. (2008). Anonymizing bipartite graph data using safe groupings. In Proceedings of the 34th International Conference on Very Large Data Bases (VLDB 2008).

Damiani, E., et al. (2007). An experimental evaluation of multi-key strategies for data outsourcing. In Proceedings of the 22nd IFIP TC-11 International Information Security Conference.

Damiani, E., De Capitani di Vimercati, S., Foresti, S., Jajodia, S., Paraboschi, S., & Samarati, P. (2007). Selective data encryption in outsourced dynamic environments. *Electronic Notes in Theoretical Computer Science*. doi:10.1016/j.entcs.2006.11.003

Damiani, E., De Capitani di Vimercati, S., Foresti, S., Jajodia, S., Paraboschi, S., & Samarati, P. (2007). An experimental evaluation of multi-key strategies for data outsourcing. IFIP International Federation for Information Processing: *Vol. 232. New Approaches for Security, Privacy and Trust in Complex Environments* (pp. 385–396). Springer. doi:10.1007/978-0-387-72367-9_33

Damiani, E., di Vimercati, S. D. C., Foresti, S., Jajodia, S., Paraboschi, S., & Samarati, P. (2005). Key management for multi-user encrypted databases. In Proceedings of the ACM Workshop on Storage Security and Survivability, (pp. 74-83).

Dannen, C., & White, C. (2011). *Beginning iOS apps with Facebook and Twitter APIs* (pp. 9–14). Apress. doi:10.1007/978-1-4302-3543-9_2

Devanbu, P., Gertz, M., Martel, C., & Stubblebine, S. G. (2000). Authentic third-party data publication. In 14th IFIP Working Conference in Database Security.

di Vimercati, S. D. C., Foresti, S., Jajodia, S., Paraboschi, S., & Samarati, P. (2007). Over-encryption: Management of access control evolution on outsourced data. In Proceedings of VLDB'07.

di Vimercati, S. D. C., Foresti, S., Jajodia, S., Paraboschi, S., & Samarati, P. (2007). A data outsourcing architecture combining cryptography and access control. In Proceedings of the ACM Workshop on Computer Security Architecture, (pp. 63-69).

Geiger, H. (2010). Government drops warrantless email search case, highlighting need for reform. Center for Democracy and Technology. Retrieved May 22, 2012, from https://www.cdt.org/blogs/harley-geiger/government-drops-warrantless-email-search-case-highlighting-need-reform

Goodrich, M. T., Papamanthou, C., Tamassia, R., & Triandopoulos, N. (2008). Athos: Efficient authentication of outsourced file systems. In Proceedings of the International Conference on Information Security (pp. 80-96).

Goyal, V., Pandey, O., Sahai, A., & Waters, B. (2006). Attribute -based encryption for fine-grained access control of encrypted data. In Proceedings of Conference on Computer and Communications Security.

GSA. (2012). FedRamp: Federal risk and authorization management program. U.S. General Services Administration. Retrieved May 23, 2012, from http://www.gsa.gov/portal/category/102371

Hacigumus, H., Iyer, B., & Mehrotra, S. (2002). Providing database as a service. In Proceedings of 18th International Conference on Data Engineering.·

Hacigumus, H., Iyer, B., Mehrotra, S., & Li, C. (2002). Executing SQL over encrypted data in the database-service-provider model. In Proceedings of the ACM Special Interest Group on Management of Data (SIGMOD).

Harney, H., Colgrove, A., & McDaniel, P. D. (2001). Principles of policy in secure groups. In Proceedings of NDSS01.

Jajodia, S., Samarati, P., Sapino, M., & Subrahmanian, V. (2001). Flexible support for multiple access control policies. [TODS]. *ACM Transactions on Database Systems*, 214–260. doi:10.1145/383891.383894

Kher, V., & Kim, Y. (2005). Securing distributed storage: Challenges, techniques, and systems. In Proceedings of the ACM Workshop on Storage Security and Survivability, (pp. 9-25).

Leong, L. (2011). Amazon outage and the autoimmune vulnerabilities of resiliency. Gartner. Retrieved from http://blogs.gartner.com/lydia_leong/2011/04/21/amazon-outage-and-the-autoimmune-vulnerabilities-of-resiliency/.

Li, J., Li, N., & Winsborough, W. H. (2005). Automated trust negotiation using cryptographic credentials. In Proceedings of Conference on Computer and Communications Security (CCS).

Li, M., Yu, S., Cao, N., & Lou, W. (2011). Authorized private keyword search over encrypted data in Cloud computing. Technical report. Retrieved from http://ece.wpi.edu/mingli/

Mell, P., & Grance, T. (2011). *The NIST definition of cloud computing. Special Publication 800-145*. National Institute of Standards and Technology.

Miklau, G., & Suciu, D. (2003). Controlling access to published data using cryptography. In Proceedings of the 29th VLDB Conference.

Mykletun, E., Narasimha, M., & Tsudik, G. (2004). Authentication and integrity in outsourced database. In Proceedings of the 11th NDSS04.

Narasimha, M., & Tsudik, G. (2006). Authentication of outsourced databases using signature aggregation and chaining. Proceedings of the 11th International Conference on Database Systems for Advanced Applications.

Samarati, P., & De Capitani di Vimercati, S. (2010). Data protection in outsourcing scenarios: Issues and directions. In Proceedings of the 5th ACM Symposium on Information, Computer and Communications Security (ASIACCS '10) (pp. 1-14). New York, NY: ACM.

Vijayan, J. (2012). LAPD drops Google Apps plan. Computerworld. Retrieved from http://www.computerworld.com/s/article/9223227/LAPD_Drops_Google_Apps_Plan.

Wiese, L. (2010). Horizontal fragmentation for data outsourcing with formula-based confidentiality constraints. In Proceedings of the 5th International Conference on Advances in Information and Computer Security (IWSEC'10). (pp. 101-116). Berlin, Germany: Springer-Verlag.

XML Encryption Syntax and Processing. (2002). W3C rec. Retrieved from http://www.w3.org/TR/xmlenc-core/

Yu, S., Wang, C., Ren, K., & Lou, W. (2010). Achieving secure, scalable, and fine-grained data access control in Cloud computing. In Proceedings of IEEE International Conference on Computer Communications 2010 (pp. 15-19).

Yuping, Z., & Xinghui, W. (2010). Research and realization of multi-level encryption method for database. 2010 2nd International Conference on Advanced Computer Control (ICACC), Vol. 3, (pp. 1-4, 27-29).

ADDITIONAL READING

Adya, W. J., Bolosky, M., Castro, G., Cermak, R., Chaiken, J. R., & Douceur, J. ... Wattenhofer, R. P. (2002). Farsite: Federated, available, and reliable storage for an incompletely trusted environment. ACM special interest group on operating systems (pp. 1-14).

Agrawal, R., Kierman, J., Srikant, R., & Xu, Y. (2004). Order preserving encryption for numeric data. In Proceedings of ACM SIGMOD 2004, Paris, France.

Alvarez, G., Borowsky, E., Go, S., Romer, T., Becker-Szendy, R., & Golding, R. ... Wilkes, J. (2001). Minerva: An automated resource provisioning tool for large-scale storage systems. ACM Transactions on Computer Systems, (pp. 483-518).

Ateniese, G., Fu, K., Green, M., & Hohenberger, S. (2005). Improved proxy re-encryption schemes with applications to secure distributed storage. In Proceedings of NDSS05.

Chen, T., Chung, Y., & Tian, C. (2004). A novel key management scheme for dynamic access control in a user hierarchy. In Proceedings of the IEEE Annual International Computer Software and Applications Conference, (pp. 396-401).

Chien, H., & Jan, J. (2003). New hierarchical assignment without public key cryptography. *Computers & Security*, *22*(6), 523–526. doi:10.1016/S0167-4048(03)00613-8

Damgard, I., Meldgaard, S., & Nielsen, J. B. (2010). Perfectly secure oblivious RAM without random oracles. (Cryptology ePrint Archive, Report 2010/108).

Goh, E., Shacham, H., Modadugu, N., & Boneh, D. (2003). Sirius: Securing remote untrusted storage. In Proceedings of the Internet Society (ISOC) Network and Distributed Systems Security (NDSS) Symposium, (pp. 131-145).

Pinkas, B., & Reinman, T. (2010). Oblivious RAM revisited. In T. Rabin (Ed.), Proceedings of the 30th Annual Conference on Advances in Cryptology (CRYPTO'10), (pp. 502-519). Berlin, Germany: Springer-Verlag.

Sun, Y., & Liu, K. (2004). Scalable hierarchical access control in secure group communications. In Proceedings of the International Conference on Computer Communications, Hong Kong, China.

Wang, Q., Wang, C., Li, J., Ren, K., & Lou, W. (2009). Enabling public verifiability and data dynamics for storage security in Cloud computing. In Proceedings of European Symposium on Research in Computer Security '09.

Yu, S., Ren, K., Lou, W., & Li, J. (2009). Defending against key abuse attacks KP-ABE enabled broadcast systems. In Proceedings of SECURE-COMM'09.

Yu, T., & Winslett, M. (2003). A unified scheme for resource protection in automated trust negotiation. In Proceedings of Symposium on Security and Privacy.

Chapter 6
IT Security and Governance Compliant Service Oriented Computing in Cloud Computing Environments

Hussain Al-Aqrabi
University of Derby, UK

Lu Liu
University of Derby, UK

ABSTRACT

The authors present the key security challenges and solutions on the Cloud with the help of literature reviews and an experimental model created on OPNET that is simulated to produce useful statistics to establish the approach that the Cloud computing service providers should take to provide optimal security and compliance. The literature recommends the concept of unified threat management for ensuring secured services on the Cloud. Through the simulation results, the authors demonstrate that UTM may not be a feasible approach to security implementation as it may become a bottleneck for the application Clouds. The fundamental benefits of Cloud computing (resources on demand and high elasticity) may be diluted if UTMs do not scale up effectively as per the traffic loads on the application Clouds. Moreover, it is not feasible for application Clouds to absorb the performance degradation for security and compliance because UTM will not be a total solution for security and compliance. Applications also share the vulnerabilities just like the systems, which will be out of UTM Cloud's control.

INTRODUCTION

The evolution of the concept of Cloud computing has changed the way businesses look at IT for fulfilling their needs. IT is now viewed as a massive implementation of integrated hardware, software, platforms and networking from where the businesses can purchase services as per what they need. A Cloud can be viewed as a hypermarket of IT services available at affordable prices based on needs and demands. Hence, it appears that Cloud computing concept has emerged at the right time

DOI: 10.4018/978-1-4666-2854-0.ch006

when such companies were formulating multi-million dollar budgets to upgrade their hardware and software systems. But is Cloud computing ready to the extent that it can be considered as an alternative to hardware and software upgrades, or as an alternative to deployment of new IT systems? Many scholars argue that Cloud is ready, but the most significant challenge is related to security and compliance.

With the growing popularity of Cloud computing, the concerns about security and compliance are also growing. Al-Aqrabi et al. (2012) describes that Cloud computing is gradually gaining popularity among businesses of all types and sizes due to the numerous advantages over self-hosted IT infrastructures (p.1). Businesses do not want to be deprived of the already established and accepted benefits of Cloud computing and hence they require continuous research towards the path to achieve standardised policies and controls on Cloud computing that shall be acceptable to the regulatory bodies (Carroll, Merve and Kotze, 2011, p. 1). It is important for the management of a business to understand what threats and risks exist on Cloud computing infrastructures and what are the feasible mitigation strategies (Carroll, Merve and Kotze, 2011, p. 2). In a survey conducted by Carroll, Merve and Kotze (2011, p. 4), it was observed that the IT managers stated information security, business continuity and regulatory compliance as the top three concerns in moving their business workflows to the Cloud. Ramgovind, Eloff and Smith (2010, p. 1) argued that the full potential of Cloud computing cannot be used for the benefit of businesses unless the security and compliance issues are sorted out. They further elaborated that secured connectivity to Clouds over Internet, data segregation, data location and multi-tenancy are the key issues that are discussed by Gartner and IDC reports on Cloud computing security that are coming in the way of achieving full compliance to the established regulations and acts (p. 3). The main security issues to be solved in the context of connectivity, data segregation, data location and multi-tenancy are:

identity management, authentication, authorisation, confidentiality, integrity, non-repudiation and availability (Ramgovind, Eloff and Smith, 2010, p. 3). At the technical level, Mukhin and Volokyata (2011, p. 738-739) described that Cloud computing comprises new types of vulnerabilities, like – incorrect provisioning in virtualisation, riding and hijacking of virtual sessions, insecure or obsolete cryptography keys, evasion of billing/metering data, data recovery of one user when the resource gets allocated to another user, insufficient virtual network controls, poor authentication and authorisation in the virtual machines, etc. The author has presented this study with the help of background and contextual reviews of Cloud computing security, and a modelling and simulation based experiment to test the feasibility of using security-as-a-service by a separate Cloud provider using unified threat management solutions. The findings of the experiment have been compared with the literature review outcomes to present the conclusions and recommendations. The chapter has been divided into seven sections: the first four sections dedicated to literature review and critical discussions, the next two sections to present the model and analysing its results and the last section to present the conclusions.

BACKGROUND

Cloud Computing Domains

The architecture, deployment, workflows and service procedures of Cloud computing is yet to be standardised. The academic scholars and professional architects have presented their own architectures of Cloud computing in numerous research papers. (Qian, Luo, Du and Guo, 2009, p. 626). NIST has come forward with a draft paper to standardise Cloud computing, albeit currently at high level only. In the NIST's model, Cloud has been presented as an integrated service oriented architecture comprising three forms of offerings – software-as-a-service (SaaS), platform-as-a-service (PaaS) and infrastructure-as-a-service (IaaS). NIST's model proposes that Clouds can take four types of forms – public Clouds, private Clouds, hybrid Clouds and community Clouds. (Badger et al., 2011, p. 14-18) The NIST's model is redrawn and presented in Figure 1.

The key performance attributes of Cloud computing comprises effective implementation of on demand self-services, broad network access, rapid elasticity, measured service and resource pooling (Badger et al. 2011, p. 11-12). The key benefits from Cloud computing hosting are: low-cost high-performance computing, usage based payments, improved performance of business processes, easier maintenance, world-class software tools at affordable costs, no hassles of up-grading, storage/computing on demand, better compatibility and portability of applications, better group collaboration and universal access (Miller, 2009, p. 12-18). Amburst et al. (2009) presented the formula (see Box 1) for calculating economic feasibility of moving business processes to the Cloud (p. 2).

This formula shows that the expected profit from the Cloud should be greater than the existing profit from the self hosted data centre. The formula reveals that higher is the utilisation of self hosted data centre, lower is the feasibility to move to the Cloud.

However Cloud computing has some disadvantages as well. For example, it is not meant for businesses in remote locations that do not have reliable Internet connectivity (Miller, 2009, p. 20). In addition, businesses under high security and compliance pressures should avoid Cloud computing for time being (although may find it feasible in due course) (Miller, 2009, p. 20). According to Amburst et al. (2010), data lock-in (p. 54), data confidentiality and auditing ability (p. 55) and performance unpredictability (p. 56) are among the top five issues to be considered in the process of deciding on moving a business process and its data to the Cloud. In this chapter, the author has focussed on these three issues of Cloud hosting of business processes. In this context, the author has presented a review of existing solutions and also has recommended solutions based on self interpretation of the challenges evident from the simulation exercise. Before getting into the details of these three issues, the author has presented a quick review of service provisioning on Cloud computing.

A. Software as a Service

The SaaS framework on the Clouds have been built using service oriented software tools that can run on any underlying platform and is mostly model driven. XML has been preferred for traditional

Figure 1. The NIST's model of cloud computing

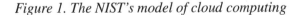
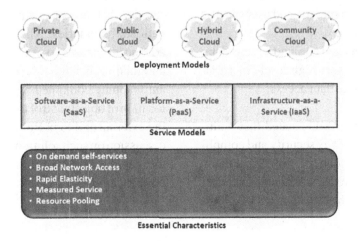

Box 1.

$$UserHours_{cloud} \times (revenue - Cost_{cloud}) \geq UserHours_{datacenter} \times (revenue - \frac{Cost_{datacenter}}{Utilization})$$

computing devices and WML has been preferred for mobile computing devices for hosting application services. This is because the XML and WML formats are self describable, easily discoverable, are not dependent upon a particular programming language or platform, and can work with any database that supports them (Microsoft SQL, IBM DB2, Oracle, My SQL, etc.). (Sharma and Sood, 2011: p. 18-19)

Bolze and Deelman (2011: 183) presented the following characteristics of SaaS:

1. The applications should be designed in such a way that they can effectively utilise large scale computing devices and storages.
2. The applications should be highly sophisticated at the background but very simple at the user interfacing end.
3. The applications and the underlying databases should support multi-tenancy (users and groups of large number of companies can work on the same application).
4. The applications should release processing power and storage on demand rapidly in order to complete heavy duty tasks quickly.
5. The applications should have provisions for universal, domain specific and user specific master data tables.
6. The applications and the underlying databases should support high levels of parallelism and parallel data access.

Ruiter and Warnier (2011) stated that multi-tenancy is viewed as the key security and compliance challenge on the Cloud (p. 356). As per them, many regulations require physical identification of data and its location in the IT systems (358). Some

regulations stated by them are – Sarbanes Oxley Act, Gramm-Leach-Bliley Act, Health Insurance Portability and Accountability Act (HIPAA) and Payment Card Industry Data Security Standard (PCI DSS) (p. 359-360). The SaaS community needs to come forward with solutions to meet the compliance requirements directed by these acts. For example, the author would like to present a noble method of data identification under multi-tenancy. Aulbach, Grust, Jacobs, Kemper and Rittinger (2008) described that multi-tenancy can be implemented on the Cloud by sharing the database schema among multiple tenants (user companies) (p. 1195), which is executed employing database object partitioning (p. 1196) and employing a separate schema object to identify the objects owned by various tenants (p. 1197).

In author's view, this is one of the effective ways of implementing data identification of multi-tenancy setups. The reports generated from the master schema objects can clearly identify which database objects belong to which tenants. In addition, to comply with the "location of data" requirements, the SaaS provider can ensure that the objects belonging to a company under compliance pressure can be distributed to only those servers that are physically located within the national boundaries. All databases have built in advanced features to control object distribution and their replications. A report of schema – tenant mapping combined with a report of physical location of objects and of the servers should satisfy the external auditors. Before we get into detailed discussion on such solutions, let us quickly review the application and infrastructure provisioning on the Clouds.

B. Application Service Provisioning

Application service provisioning on a SaaS Cloud is presented in Figure 2, redrawn based on an illustration by Mietzner and Leymann (2008, p. 6):

La and Kim (2009) discussed that service provisioning on SaaS Clouds differs by users based on their workflows, privileges, logic (p. 282). They further discussed that the resources pooled for service provisioning on SaaS Clouds are hardware and networking, databases, web servers, platform services, specialised software servers (like use case testing tools) and application servers (p. 283). The Cloud resources are pooled and presented to user workflows through composite resource provisioning carried out with the help of service provisioning engines. Some of the provisioning engines used by SaaS providers are Open QRM, Sun N1 provisioning manager and IBM Tivoli provisioning manager. The users connect to their business workflows through web services gateway, and the workflows in turn are served by the resource pool accessible through the service provisioning engine. (Mietzner and Leymann, 2008, p. 4-9) The workflows are created employing standard tools like MPI, Apache Hadoop, Microsoft Dryad and Google Map-Re-duce (Ekanayake, Qiu, Gunarathne, Beason and Fox, 2011, p. 277).

C. Infrastructure Resource Provisioning

Infrastructure resources are provisioned in three ways – server virtualisation (Amazon), technique specific sandbox (Google) and a hybrid of both the techniques (Microsoft). Server virtualisation can be carried out using VMware, Xen virtualisation or Linux virtualisation solutions. (Qian, Luo, Du and Guo, 2009, p. 627-628) However, many academic scholars view virtualisation as the key underlying technology for infrastructure resource provisioning on the Cloud. Wan (2011, p. 305-306) described that Cloud based hypervisors should be deployed on multi-core CPUs on the bare-metal (the underlying real hardware) for optimisation of performance of parallel processing and queuing. In addition, Niyato (2011, p. 100) presented that a virtual machine depository using multiple virtualisation solutions (OS layer virtualisation, Para-virtualisation, application virtualisation and bare metal virtualisation, as described by Wan, 2011, p. 304-305) can be the most effective solution to interface a private Cloud with the public Cloud (i.e., creating a hybrid Cloud). In

Figure 2. Application service provisioning on cloud computing

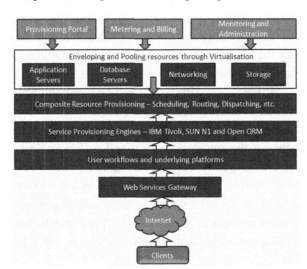

this context, Sotomayor, Montero, Llorente and Foster (2009, 16-18) described that the host based virtualisation deployments need to be managed at the array level (an array comprises a large number of hardware devices) using software based virtual infrastructure management solutions. They demonstrated Open Nebula architecture that can be used for provisioning of hardware resources for the Cloud users using sophisticated virtual machine placement strategies with priority queuing based on immediate (prioritised) provisioning and best-effort (non-prioritised) provisioning (p. 19).

In a virtualisation setup, a server can host multiple virtual machines running their own operating systems. The operating systems of the virtual machines do not communicate directly with the assembly language of the hardware, but communicate with a middleware called "hypervisor." The hypervisor interprets the instructions from multiple operating systems and translates them into consolidated assembly language instructions which are passed on to the CPU. Intel and AMD have developed special CPUs for running hypervisors for virtualisation ready servers. (Phelps and Dawson, 2007, p. 2-7).

D. Configurable Cloud Resource

The Cloud users do not get opportunities to know about the pooled resources made available to them through the provisioning manager. They only have access to the user and development interfaces provided to them by the Cloud service provider. The developers can use standard APIs to add functionalities to the workflows. The APIs do not facilitate development of an entire software product, albeit allow the in-house developers of the user organisation to focus on the business logic and its processes, and create/modify the workflows and the interfaces (forms, reports and documents). (Chorafas, 2011, p. 65-70) Examples of workflows that can be configured on the Cloud are – user and privilege management

workflows, service creation workflows (like, adding mailboxes), software development life cycle (SDLC) workflows, domain specific workflows (HR, Finance, Marketing, etc.) (Litoiu and Litoiu 2010, p. 73-74). Litoiu and Litoiu (2010, p. 75) further emphasised that the resource creation, modification and deletion on Clouds should be managed through an in-house change management system in the user company. All users connect to service oriented virtual machines, and the services provisioning done by the Cloud service provider (using tools like Open Nebula or IBM Tivoli) on such virtual machines are accessed by the end users (Younge, Laszewski, Wang, Lopez-Alarcon, Carithers, 2010, p. 5).

THREATS, VULNERABILITIES, AND RISKS IN CLOUD COMPUTING

Cloud computing platforms may comprise the following threats as described by Bisong and Rahman (2011, p. 36):

1. Unauthorised use of Cloud computing components and resources.
2. Threats and vulnerabilities in the APIs provided to the developers.
3. Malicious insider trading.
4. All possible threats and vulnerabilities associated with shared IT systems and resources.
5. Data manipulation, leakage and loss.
6. Hijacking of accounts or user sessions.
7. Other forms of unknown/emerging threats (Bisong and Rahman, 2011, p. 36).

The users view their virtual machine systems as self sufficient desktops that are isolated from others. However, the virtual machines are hosted on servers on hypervisors. Hence, hypervisors are the targets of the attackers. (Sabahi, 2011, p. 251-254) It may be noted that hypervisors should be viewed as special purpose operating systems that are vulnerable to the traditional exploits that have been troubling operations systems for a long time, like – buffer overflow, DDOS, zero day attacks, viruses, spyware, covert channels, Trojans, etc. It is possible that an attacker can take a valid subscription on the Cloud, take ownership of one or more virtual machines, and begin attacking other virtual machines. It may be noted that there are many exploits that need not be installed on the operating system, albeit they can just be launched from a folder. Hence, traditional security controls are needed on the Cloud as well. (Wen and Xiang, 2011, p. 258-260; Sabahi, 2011, p. 247-248).

Before we study the security threats and controls in detail, let us take a quick look at what are the privacy requirements of users on the Cloud, and where are the challenges.

A. Privacy Requirements

Following are the key privacy requirements on the Cloud, as described by Katzan (2010, p. 5-8):

1. **Identity:** Identity on the Cloud is an entity, which may be a virtual machine or a user or the objects that they are trying to access (an application, a data file, a folder, a document, or a record). For interaction of two entities, it is important that a trust is established between them. For example, a user accessing a folder, a virtual machine connecting to a data file, a user trying to associate a record with a document, etc. In traditional self hosted systems, there are multiple settings possible to establish trust between two identities such that they can interact or a session is denied. (Katzan, 2010, p. 5) The Cloud systems should comprise the proven mechanisms of trust establishment between any two identities, like – identity management tools (LDAP, RADIUS, TACACS, etc.), RSA based public key cryptography issued and managed by a certification authority, secured socket layer,

etc. (Ranganathan, 2010, p. 18-19) NIST recommends Extensible Access Control Mark-up Language (XACML) and Security Assertion Mark-up Language (SAML) as the mechanisms for authentication and authorisation decision making between any two cooperating entities (Jansen and Grace, 2011, p. 22). Both SAML and XACML are emerging as large scale role mining and policy engineering standards for service oriented architecture, and hence are suitable for Cloud computing (Takabi, Joshi and Ahn, 2010, p. 29).

2. **Authentication:** In every IT system, there are multiple levels of authentication depending upon the access rights of the user or the system. Clouds normally have distributed authentication mechanism to distribute load. (Katzan, 2010, p. 5-6) The SaaS provider will be accountable for all authentication levels till the users are allowed to the web apps servers hosting their workflows. The authentication and privileges within the workflows and the backend database objects have to be managed by the user company. The SaaS provider will however be responsible to manage proven mechanisms of trust establishment between any two identities, who ever makes the settings – users or Cloud administrators. For example, if a workflow administrator makes privilege settings, the system supporting these settings is under SaaS provider's ownership. Similarly, if the users make privilege settings for access to database objects, the SaaS provider is responsible to make sure that they work. Overall, the SaaS provider is responsible for effective isolation of two entities, whether users, companies, virtual machines, group of objects in the database, etc. irrespective of who manages the security administration tools – a user or an administrator on the Cloud. The roles should be very clearly

bifurcated between the two parties such that during an incident analysis, it is clear who is accountable (Pearson, 2009, p. 5-8).

3. **Authorisation:** Authorisation is the level of privileges assigned to a requesting entity, depending upon its role defined in the system. It is closely linked with authentication and the details are normally stored on the same systems used to manage authentication. Essentially, authentication and authorisation should be viewed as parts of the same security control because they cannot be delinked. On the Cloud, the roles may be defined by the user company or the SaaS administrator depending upon the object. For example, the SaaS administrator will define roles in the web servers, whereas the user company should have an administrator defining roles in the workflows and backend database objects. (Katzan, 2010, p. 6-7; Jansen and Grace, 2011, p. 24-25) NIST recommends that every user entity and virtual machine entity should have valid authentication and authorisation tagging. Guest accounts or stray accounts (not actively used by any entity) should be strictly prohibited (Jansen and Grace, 2011, p. 23).

4. **Accountability:** This is the most complex challenge on Cloud computing platforms. Given that the underlying systems are owned and managed by the Cloud service providers, technically they are the ones responsible for any breach. However, there can be conflicts. For example, a user company may claim that the security settings in the workflow didn't work, or the Cloud providers may claim that the user company didn't make the settings adequately in the workflow. Hence, essentially it is important that there is a high trust on the capabilities of the underlying platform. The security procedures of the hosting framework should be co-designed by the user company and the Cloud provider. (Pearson and Charlesworth, 2009, p. 6-9) NIST recognises

this aspect and hence has tried to present a method. They have recommended that the Cloud service provider should clearly mention the underlying platforms used for trust management, and the user company should clearly understand the capabilities of the platforms. They should accept the services only when they are satisfied with the platforms, or else use a third party for accessing the Cloud (example, a unified threat management Cloud provider). In general, each migration to the Cloud should be treated as a change management project and an in-depth risk assessment should be carried out by the user companies. The Cloud service providers should fully co-operate by sharing all the information about the platforms and technology (after filtering confidential information as applicable). The agreement between the Cloud service provider and the user company should be based on the risk assessment and impact analysis. NIST recommends a number of best practices that the Cloud provider should adopt (taken from traditional IT risk management practices) to make this process simpler. The accountabilities should be documented very clearly such that there are no conflicts during incident management (Jansen and Grace, 2011, p. 28-29).

B. Component Level Security

There are two key issues in component level security on the Cloud:

1. Trustworthy computing (Katzan, 2010, p. 7; Shen and Tong, 2010, p. 11-15).
2. Auditing and compliance (Gul, Rehman and Islam, 2011, p. 146; Gowrigolla, Sivaji and Masillamani, 2010, p. 294-295; Haan and Xing, 2011, p. 265-266; Wang, Wang, Ren, Lou and Li, 2011, p. 849).

A trustworthy computing should be predictable, reliable and controllable and hence should be secured by design with high level of accuracy (Katzan, 2010, p. 7). At the component level, the trusted computing framework should have a trustworthy hardware, operating system, software tools, applications, maintainability and serviceability (Katzan, 2010, p. 7). As described by Shen and Tong (2010, p. 11-15), the Cloud computing components should benefit from the specifications developed by trusted computing group (TCG) in 2003, which comprises a number of hardware and software vendors. In this model, the hardware, operating system, software systems and applications are viewed as a stack of trustworthy systems certified by the TCG. For example, when Windows operating system is ported on IBM hardware, both vendors ensure complete compatibility and protection. Hence, it is essential that all the components deployed on the Cloud should be the ones certified by TCG (Shen and Tong, 2010, p. 11-15).

However, it is important that the user companies should be confident about the Cloud's trustworthiness. Hence, there should be established mechanisms for auditing the Cloud's trustworthiness. Gul, Rehman and Islam (2011, p. 146), Gowrigolla, Sivaji and Masillamani (2010, p. 294-295), Haan and Xing (2011, p. 265-266), and Wang, Wang, Ren, Lou and Li (2011, p. 849) discussed that the concept of third party auditor and security administration services should be implemented on the Cloud. In this mode, these scholars have recommended different designs and topologies for connecting third party auditors or security administrators with the SaaS or IaaS providers' Clouds. Carvalho (2011, p. 24) recommended that identity management should be provided by separate Cloud service providers called "security-as-a-service," using the traditional concept of "unified threat management" in service oriented mode. As explained by Chao, Bingyao, Jiaying and Wei (2010, 389), unified threat management is a system in which a packet passing through is inspected against all possible

threats before allowing to the destination host. However, the Gartner report recommends that virtualised data centres should have embedded security within the server arrays, by implementing security services on some of the virtualised servers and allowing the incoming user sessions to pass through them to the virtual machines hosting applications. This is because the inter-VM traffic within the same server (virtual networking) cannot be inspected by external network security devices (MacDonald, 2010, p. 11-20).

In this chapter, the author has created an OPNET model comprising a separate security-as-a-service Cloud (designated as UTM Cloud) and tested the simulation of all user traffic passing through the UTM Cloud to the application Clouds. The results of simulation are discussed for analysing the feasibility of this solution vis-à-vis the solution proposed by Gartner report. Al-Aqrabi et al. (2012) stated that the security-as-a-service, or SaaS is good idea for transferring the risks to a service provider specialised in security only, and it can be expected that the service provider has invested in state-of-the-art security products and solutions, rather than transferring the risks to software-as-a-service provider taking security as an embedded responsibility. This may ensure better compliance and better governance of security controls as per the risk assessment models of user companies (p.3). However, the practical feasibility also needs to be ascertained, which is the deliverable of the experiment conducted in this research.

C. Personnel Level Security

As per the above analysis, it is revealed that the personnel level security depends upon the personalisation of each user as an entity on the Cloud. As discussed above, this depends upon the capability of segregating entities on the Cloud, and maintenance of reliable trust management platforms. Trustworthy computing is the answer to this requirement, provided the components used for personalisation and segregation can be identified. In author's view, the Cloud service providers should be able to produce tangible answers to a user's questions, like – how do you ensure my login is protected, how is my login segregated from others, how is my data protected, how is my data segregated from others', etc. The third party auditor should be able to verify the personalisation and segregation effectiveness of the Cloud service providers. Also, Unified threat management (security-as-a-service) may be an effective answer to personalisation and segregation. This is, however, analysed by the author with the help of modelling and simulation of a UTM Cloud serving two application Clouds in this chapter.

SECURITY SOLUTION FOR CLOUD COMPUTING

The steps recommended by NIST for security assessments before moving to the Cloud are worth noting (Jansen and Grace, 2011, p. 30-37):

1. The user company should clearly identify the security and privacy requirements and define the criteria for selecting a SaaS provider.
2. Based on the short listing of SaaS providers (and the related PaaS and IaaS providers), the user company should carry out detailed risk assessment using the information collected from the Cloud providers and mapping with the internal control objectives.
3. The capabilities and commitments of the chosen Cloud provider should be very clearly recorded.
4. All information assets being moved to the Cloud should be listed. An acknowledgement against each asset should be taken from the Cloud provider before moving them. The Cloud provider should tangibly verify if the asset acknowledged by them has been moved to the Cloud.
5. It is advised that a competent legal advisor is involved when the terms of SLA are being drafted. Every line item should have clear accountability description, and no vague

areas should be allowed. The jurisdiction of the conflicts should be clearly agreed, because Clouds are global. All confidentiality and accountability clauses should be in line with legal and regulatory requirements of the jurisdiction.

6. The agreement should clearly mention what and how the reports will be published by the Cloud provider and what and how the user company will audit at the Cloud premises periodically.
7. There should be detailed termination agreement. The roles of both the user company and the Cloud provider should be clearly documented with the help of legal advisor. Issues like data lock-in and other possibilities of hindrances caused by the Cloud provider in withdrawal by the user company should be clearly identified and addressed.
8. There should be special clauses about how the Cloud provider will return the assets to the user company (and vice versa) should be documented. Methods of data destruction and validation should be clearly stated. When the clauses are invoked, it is essential that both parties should follow all separation steps necessary under the regulatory framework to avoid any claims thereafter.

Based on these recommendations by NIST and the literature review in previous sections, let us analyse the three risk mitigation strategies, as recommended by a separate standard by NIST on risk management in special publication 800-30 (Stoneburner, Gougen and Feriga, 2002, p. 27).

A. Transferring the Risks

The process recommended by NIST is essentially a method of transferring risks to the Cloud service provider. The user company may trust its due diligence done in selecting the Cloud service provider and carrying out the risk assessment. In practice, the risk assessment will be based on information shared by the Cloud service provider and its references (other customers). Hence, to a large extent the best that a user company can do is to ensure that the contract comprises all the terms from legal perspective, and the jurisdiction and contract enforcement aspects are carefully documented and agreed. There will be a significant element of risk, which will be out of the control of the user company. Hence, the theories of trustworthy computing and effective trust management, personalisation and segregation practices will enable the user organisation to make a decision. The idea of security-as-a-service appears to be more promising because the risks will be transferred to a service provider specialised in security only, and it can be expected that the service provider has invested in state-of-the-art security products and solutions. However, the idea of all the user traffic passing through the security-as-a-service (UTM) Cloud may not be feasible in practice. The author has tried to present this argument with the help of simulations carried out in this chapter.

B. Absorbing the Risks

As discussed in the literature review, the systems will be owned by the Cloud service provider. However, the security management practices will be shared between the Cloud and the user company. For example, the SaaS provider or UTM service provider will take accountability of the authentication and authorisation services at the virtual machine level, but the user companies will have to take accountability of the security settings of the workflows. Assuming that the SaaS or UTM service provider has taken care of trustworthy computing effectively, all other risks pertaining to workflow security will be the accountability of the user company. Hence, a significant element of risks will have to be absorbed by the user companies as well. There should be effective security administration practices in the user companies as well, which should effectively interface with the service provider's security administration team.

C. Avoiding the Risks

As per NIST's recommendations, risks can be avoided by implementing effective security controls. In the recommendations pertaining to Cloud privacy controls, NIST has mentioned about internal control objectives of a user organisation. As recommended, these objectives should be effectively mapped with the capabilities of the Cloud service providers before selecting the preferred one. If the Cloud service provider is able to publish internal audit reports periodically that tangibly demonstrate the effectiveness of the controls, the user companies can treat the risks as avoided rather than transferred. This is because in a partnership mode, the internal auditors of the Cloud service provider can be treated as internal auditors of the user organisations as well. Both the parties will be under compliance pressure within a jurisdiction and hence mutual partnership to avoid risks is a better arrangement than considering the risks to transferred from one party to another. This arrangement will reduce the chances of conflicts and will increase the longevity of the service oriented IT deployment for the businesses.

MEASURING COMPLIANCE

Ruiter and Warnier (2011, p. 360) stated that the only way to measure compliance is to allow third party auditing of Cloud services by certified bodies or regulatory authorities. The Cloud service providers will be under compliance pressure as much as the user organisations. Hence, they will definitely support third party auditing. However, as argued by Ruan, Carthy, Kechadi and Crosbie (2011, p. 5-6, p. 10-12), the third party auditors are currently not ready with tools, techniques and procedures to audit virtualised computing environments. In the current scenario, compliance can only be measured at the level of a user organisation, whereby the Cloud provider will be required to demonstrate their capabilities related to trust management, authentication and authorisation, segregation, and personalisation. However, a complete auditing of the Cloud providers will not be possible using traditional auditing tools used by third party auditors. Ruan, Carthy, Kechadi and Crosbie (2011, p. 11) further stated that the auditors are not ready with tools for carrying out forensic analysis on the Cloud. Hence, the compliance measurement aspect of Cloud computing is still inadequate and requires significant amount of development and testing.

MODEL DESCRIPTION

In this chapter, the author has presented brief description of the multi-Cloud model created on OPNET academic edition. The model screen shots are presented and explained as in Figure 3.

This screen shows the main interface to the model. The Clouds shown in this interface are created using the IP network Cloud objects in OPNET. An IP network Cloud object can be expanded to enter another palette for carrying out detailed model comprising nodes and links. In the main screen, there are the following components:

1. **The Internet domain:** This is an IP network in which the backbone switches of an ISP (Internet Service Provider) have been modelled. The switches have been used to connect 1500 concurrent users of Cloud hosted applications.
2. **The UTM Cloud:** This is another IP network Cloud object used to model a Cloud infrastructure with security components only. In this model, the UTM (Unified Threat Management) Cloud service provider is the primary interface between the Cloud users (corporates) and the application Clouds.

The UTM Cloud comprises all the security components required to protect the user networks and the application Clouds from Internet based threats. The UTM Cloud is explained in more detail later in this section, immediately after introducing its screenshot.

3. **The Application Clouds (1 and 2):** The application Clouds are IP network Cloud objects comprising application server arrays and database server arrays, connected to a Cloud network. The Application Clouds are explained in more detail later in this section, immediately after introducing their screenshots.
4. All the Clouds are inter-networked using high end enterprise class switches with ATM OC-48 links. The servers are connected to the switches through 1000BaseX links. Hence, all switches possess ATM LAN Emulation enabled.
5. **Application object:** There are seven applications configured with built in load parameters as per default values in OPNET:
    a. **Cloud application:** A HTTP browser based application with light browsing load.
    b. **RDBMS Services:** A high load database service.
    c. **Antivirus and Antispyware application:** A medium load database service.
    d. **Anti-spam application:** A medium load database service.
    e. **Web services firewall application:** A high load database service.
    f. **LDAP services:** A low load database service.
    g. **Overheads:** Encryption overheads configured as a custom application.
6. **Task object:** The custom application for the encryption overheads has been created with the help of the task object. The task attributes configured are presented in the figures below. The encryption overheads have been

Figure 3. The architecture of the model

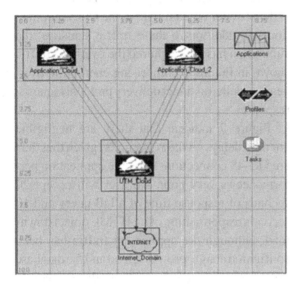

configured as mild background traffic (1 KB to 4 KB per second) with fifteen to twenty packets delivered in one second between source to destination using DDP (direct data placement – RFC 4296) protocol. The sources are the three corporate LANs and the destination is the UTM firewall object. This is an arbitrary choice made to generate a finite encryption overhead traffic on the network. The author has configured six phases in the task object to create application instances. The phases have been triggered at regular intervals at every five seconds after the start of the first phase. The protocol selected is DDP, and hence the overhead will not generate any TCP traffic or sessions, but will throw packets to and fro between the sources and the destinations defined in the phases of the task. In real network as well, the encryption overheads are additional streams of packets that do not contribute to any useful TCP or UDP session. This is the reason for the choice of DDP in the tasks object.

7. **Profile object:** The profile object has been included to configure the behaviour of applications configured on the network. The

applications have been configured to run concurrently with uniform distribution of packets. An exponential, normal or log-normal distribution has been avoided to keep the model behaviour simple. The start time of the applications are within 5 to 10 seconds from the start time of the profile. The start time of the profile is within 50 to 55 seconds from the start time of simulation. A sufficient time gap is needed to allow the network build completely by building of the routing tables at all network devices.

Figure 4 presents the application Cloud object. The servers configured in this object are the LAN objects with multiple server nodes attached to a central backplane chassis. This type of server configuration is similar to a blade server having a centralised chassis and multiple processor cards serving as individual servers. Normally, the processor cards share the storage attached to the entire chassis (not modelled in this project because OPNET academic edition doesn't support advanced server modelling).

The modelling of the LAN Object as a server array is presented in Figure 5. The number of processors is 32, shared among 25 workstations added in the LAN object. Given the huge backplane processing power configured in this object (attributes under red coloured rectangle), the LAN object serves as a LAN of servers and not workstations. Clouds comprise server arrays, and the chassis based servers (commercially known as blade servers) are best components to implement such arrays. The blades also comply with green computing requirement of Clouds as they occupy very small rack space, consume very less power, and dissipate very less heat, when compared with a similar array of standalone servers.

Figure 6 presents the Unified Threat Management (UTM) Cloud. This is the interfacing Cloud between the application Clouds and the Cloud users, with the UTM zone based firewall being the primary interface. The UTM firewall is an advanced stateful inspection firewall with multiple interfaces. In this model, three interfaces have been configured – users' interface, application Clouds' interface and the De-Militarised Zone (DMZ) connected to multiple security servers, viz., UTM LDAP server for authentication and authorisation, UTM spam filter, UTM antivirus cum antispyware server, and UTM web services firewall comprising built in intrusion prevention capabilities (like Checkpoint). Ideally, the author wanted to create server arrays for all these services, but the model was getting too heavy to generate useful results within the maximum cap of 50 million events. Hence, their poor response times in the results will have to be ignored. Each server has been tied with its own application by configuring its "application supported profiles" and "application supported services." The UTM firewall is configured to support "overheads" to simulate the encryption overhead traffic. IT forwards all the traffic to the security servers, and the security servers in turn forwards the traffic to the application Cloud servers. This has been configured by defining the "application source and destination preferences" in the attributes of the servers. As reviewed in the literatures, each security services server works like a database server. For example, the UTM web services firewall comprises a database of exploit signatures and blacklisted/malicious URLs, whereas the anti-virus/anti-spyware server comprises a database of virus and spyware signatures.

The Cloud users are configured as LAN objects comprising 500 workstations each. Overall, 1500 workstations have been configured in the LAN objects. To generate the encryption overhead as the task phases based on direct delivery protocol, the user LANs and the firewalls have been configured as sources and destination, respectively.

ANALYSIS OF RESULTS

Figure 7 shows the application response times:

The database traffic comprises of the security server services as well as the database services

for the Cloud based applications. The http traffic is the browser based traffic of the Cloud applications. In addition to these traffic statistics, the simulation has also captured the overhead traffic shown in Figure 8, comprising encryption overhead modelled as direct delivery protocol requests/responses.

Figure 9 indicate that there are negligible queuing delays on the ATM links (given that they are OC-48 connections), but the application performance is very poor. No user will accept 20 seconds of response time of a DB query and 10 seconds response time of an HTML object download, although the application traffic has been configured at light browsing load and the database traffic has been configured mostly at medium load. This is because the UTM Cloud is the bottleneck. The response times are low in this model because all the traffic is first forwarded to the security services servers (for necessary inspection and clearances) and then delivered to the application servers. The author has configured standalone servers for security services in the UTM Cloud and hence there is a congestion. However, will the situation be different in real world Clouds when the security servers are implemented as large scale arrays? How many firewalls (serving as VPN concentrators) will be required? Will the UTM providers implement large scale firewall arrays as well? A user company will hire the services of only one UTM provider to connect to the application Clouds. This means that there will be fewer UTM Cloud service providers than application Cloud service providers. The cost of implementing large arrays of security servers and firewalls will be very high. Hence, at some stage, the resources on demand (elasticity) of the application Clouds will suffer due to bottlenecks at the UTM Clouds. The users may have to maintain two SLAs – one with the UTM provider and other with the application services provider. Hence, when the response times degrade, the user organisations will have to negotiate with two different parties, and it will be very difficult to ascertain where is the problem. But in such a sce-

Figure 4. The application cloud object

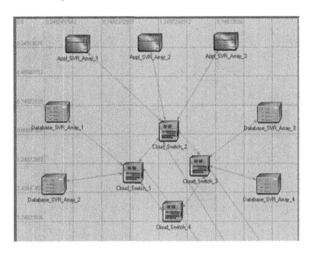

Figure 5. The modelling of the LAN object as the server object

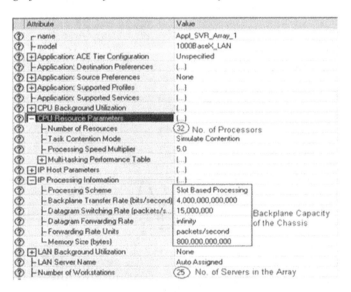

nario, it may be very difficult for the user company to maintain appropriate security and governance of the resources maintained by them on the Cloud. The UTM provider may take accountability of external security threats, but once the traffic has reached the application Cloud, they will be out of this obligation. In such an arrangement, if there is a security incident at the application Cloud, the user company will find it difficult to identify who is accountable – the UTM provider or the Cloud application service provider.

Hence, based on the results of the simulation and the problems evident thereof, the dual party model comprising unified threat management Clouds separated from application Clouds may not be effective in Cloud computing threat management, and resulting risk mitigation. The application Cloud providers will have to launch their own UTM services, or else change the architecture to distributed threat management, like – security services embedded within the application and database servers deployed in the arrays, and the

Figure 6. UTM cloud components

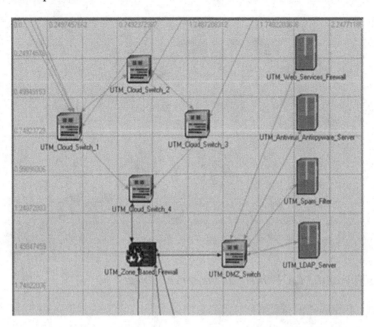

Figure 7. Application response times

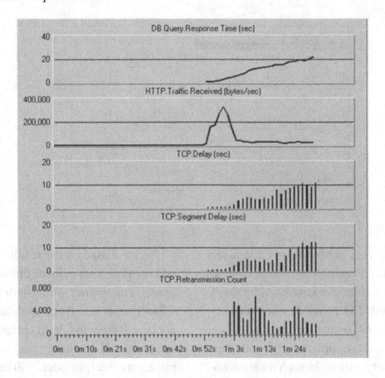

Cloud switches acting as firewalls and intrusion prevention devices. For example, it is possible to configure a Cisco router as a firewall and intrusion prevention device. The mechanism of distributed network admission controls, and authentication/authorisation will have to be implemented. The author would like to present another example. There should be some mechanism to build the

Figure 8. A sample of overhead requests count from one of the user LANs indicating the encryption overhead using direct data placement (DDP) protocol

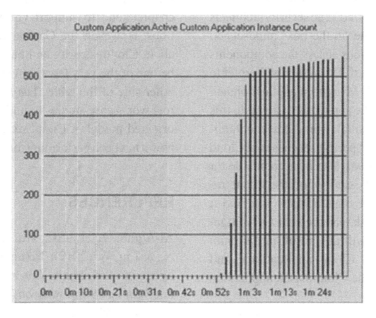

Figure 9. A sample of queuing delays between two inter-cloud links

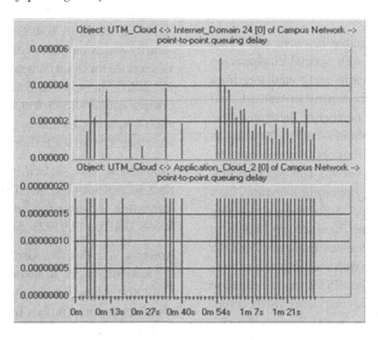

LDAP services within the core database server array in some kind of multi-tenancy configuration. In this configuration, the database objects (tables) defining the multi-tenancy attributes should also comprise the parameters configured in an LDAP server. In this way, the LDAP services will be built within the database servers meant for Cloud applications, and separate LDAP arrays will not be required. Similar mechanisms need to be invented for anti-spam, anti-virus/antispyware, web-services firewalls, etc. The security architects should come out of the "in-the-box" mindset and spread security solutions across the components of an application Cloud. The author will prefer to call it "embedded UTM" within application and database servers of the application Cloud. In this model, there will be single point of accountability from the users' perspective, because the Cloud application provider will also be accountable for data protection and security of the client resources, and the user organisations will find it easier to carry out risk management and mitigation practices. This will also result in optimum performance of the Cloud applications, and added revenues for the Cloud based application service providers.

CONCLUSION

In this chapter, the author has reviewed Cloud computing security with special emphasis on governance of the security and compliance from the perspective of user companies as well as Cloud service providers. A number of literatures have been reviewed to present what can be done to make the Cloud hosted businesses secure, reliable, compliant and long lasting. The NIST recommendations and the supporting literatures have been taken into account. Some literatures highly recommended that the Cloud security should be hosted as a service oriented framework and the accountability should with a separate security-as-a-service provider. The NIST's recommendation on risk assessment and compliance also becomes quite effective in this model because the risk transfer and risk avoidance can be carried out effectively by handshaking with a specialist Cloud service company rather than application Cloud providers that may undertake security as an additional responsibility. However, a report by Gartner recommends that virtualisation security cannot

be implemented in centralised manner following the UTM approach. The simulation results in this chapter tend to support Gartner recommendations. However, the Gartner report doesn't talk about Cloud security and hence this report may be one of the very few that views UTM from the other side of the table. The author recommends real world case studies to understand the service oriented model of Cloud security, and to verify how it has been performing for the user companies.

REFERENCES

Al-Aqrabi, H., Liu, L., Hill, R., Antonopoulos, N., & Liu, W. (2012). Taking the business intelligence to the clouds. *Proceedings of 3th IEEE International Symposium on Dependable Service-Oriented and Cloud Computing* (DSOC2012), (p. 1). Liverpool, UK: IEEE Computer Society Press.

Al-Aqrabi, H., Liu, L., Xu, J., Hill, R., Antonopoulos, N., & Zhan, Y. (2012). Investigation of IT security and compliance challenges in security-as-a service for cloud computing. *Proceedings of 15th IEEE International Symposium on Object/Component/Service-Oriented Real-Time Distributed Computing Workshops* (ISORC2012), (p. 3). Shenzhen, China: IEEE Computer Society Press.

Amburst, M., Fox, A., Griffith, R., Joseph, A. D., Katz, R., & Konwinski, A. (2010). A view of cloud computing. *Communications of the ACM, 53*(4), 50–58. doi:10.1145/1721654.1721672

Amburst, M., Fox, A., Griffith, R., Joseph, A. D., Katz, R. H., & Konwinski, A. … Zaharia, M. (2009). *Above the clouds: A Berkeley view of cloud computing*, (p. 2). (Technical Report No. UCB/EECS-2009-28). Electrical Engineering and Computer Sciences, University of California at Berkeley. Retrieved January 24, 2012, from http://www.eecs.berkeley.edu/Pubs/TechRpts/2009/EECS-2009-28.pdf

Aulbach, S., Grust, T., Jacobs, D., Kemper, A., & Rittinger, J. (2008). Multi-tenant databases for software as a service: Schema mapping techniques. *Proceedings of the 2008 SIGMOD International Conference on Management of Data*, (pp. 1195-1206).

Badger, L., Bohn, R., Chu, S., Hogan, M., Liu, F., & Kaufmann, V. … Leaf, D. (2011). *U.S. government cloud computing technology roadmap – Volume II*, (pp. 10-15). (Special Publication 500-293, NIST). U.S. Department of Commerce.

Bisong, A., & Rahman, S. M. (2011). An overview of the security concerns in enterprise cloud computing. *International Journal of Network Security and its Applications, 3*(1), 30-45.

Bolze, R., & Deelman, E. (2011). Exploiting the cloud of computing environments: An application's perspective. In S. A. Ahson & M. Ilyas (Eds.), *Cloud computing and software services: Theory and techniques* (pp. 173-196). CRC Press, Taylor and Francis Group.

Carroll, M., Merwe, A., & Kotze, P. (2011). Secure cloud computing: Benefits, risks and controls. *Information Security South Africa Conference*, (pp. 1-9).

Carvalho, M. (2011). SECaaS–Security as a service. *ISSA Journal, 20-24.*

Chao, Y., Bingyao, C., Jiaying, D., & Wei, G. (2010). The research and implementation of UTM. *IET International Communication Conference on Wireless Mobile and Computing,* (pp. 389-392).

Chorafas, D. N. (2011). *Cloud computing strategies* (pp. 65–70). London, UK: CRC Press, Taylor & Francis Group.

Ekanayake, J. Qiu, X. Gunarathne, T, Beason, S., & Fox, G. (2011). High-performance parallel computing with cloud and cloud technologies. In S. A. Ahson & M. Ilyas (Eds.), *Cloud computing and software services: Theory and techniques,* (pp. 276-307). CRC Press, Taylor and Francis Group.

Gowrigolla, B., Sivaji, S., & Masillamani, M. R. (2010). Design and auditing of cloud computing security. *5th International Conference on Information and Automation for Sustainability*, (pp. 292-297).

Gul, I., Rehman, A. U., & Islam, M. H. (2011). Cloud computing security auditing. *International Conference on Next Generation Information Technology* (pp. 143-148).

Han, S., & Xing, J. (2011). Ensuring data storage security through a novel third party auditor scheme in Cloud Computing. IEEE International Conference on Cloud Computing and Intelligence Systems, (pp. 264-268).

Jansen, W., & Grance, T. (2011). *Guidelines on security and privacy in public cloud computing,* (pp. 4-60). Special Publication 800-144. National Institute of Standards and Technology (NIST), U.S. Department of Commerce.

Katzan, H. Jr. (2010). On the privacy of cloud computing. *International Journal of Management and Information Systems, 14*(2), 5–12.

La, H. J., & Kim, S. D. (2009). In Jaatun, M. G., Zhao, G., & Rong, C. (Eds.), *A systematic process for developing high quality SaaS cloud services* (*Vol. 5931*, pp. 3–8). Lecture Notes in Computer Science Berlin, Germany: Springer-Verlag. doi:10.1007/978-3-642-10665-1_25

Litoiu, M., & Litoiu, M. (2010). *Optimizing resources in cloud, a SOA governance view. Proceedings of Governance of Technology, Information and Policies: Addressing the Challenges of Worldwide Interconnectivity, 7 December 2010* (pp. 73–74). Austin, Texas: ACM.

MacDonald, N. (2010). *Securing the next-generation virtualized data center*, (pp. 2-50). (Gartner Report no. G00173434).

Mietzner, R., & Leymann, F. (2008). *Towards provisioning the cloud: On the usage of multi-granularity flows and services to realize a unified provisioning infrastructure for SaaS applications* (pp. 1–8). IEEE Computer Society Congress on Services. doi:10.1109/SERVICES-1.2008.36

Miller, M. (2009). *Cloud computing: Web based applications that change the way you work and collaborate online* (pp. 24-30). Que Publishing, Pearson.

Mukhin, V., & Volokyata, A. (2011). Security risk analysis for cloud computing systems. *The 6th IEEE International Conference on Intelligent Data Acquisition and Advanced Computing Systems: Technology and Applications*, September 15-17 2011, Prague, Czech Republic, (pp. 737-742).

Niyato, D. (2011). Optimization-based virtual machine manager for private cloud computing. *IEEE Third International Conference on Cloud Computing Technology and Science*, (pp. 99-106).

Pearson, S. (2009). *Taking account of privacy when designing cloud computing services*, (pp. 2-10). Produced by HP laboratories for IEEE.

Pearson, S., & Charlesworth, A. (2009). *Accountability as a way forward for privacy protection in the cloud. Proceedings of CloudCom 2009, December 2009* (pp. 3–15). Beijing: Springer.

Phelps, J. R., & Dawson, P. (2007). *Demystifying server virtualization taxonomy and terminology*, (pp. 1-9). Report ID Number: G00148373. Gartner Research.

Qian, L., Luo, Z., Du, Y., & Guo, L. (2009). In Jaatun, M. G., Zhao, G., & Rong, C. (Eds.), *Cloud computing: An overview (Vol. 5931*, pp. 626–631). Lecture Notes in Computer Science Berlin, Germany: Springer-Verlag. doi:10.1007/978-3-642-10665-1_63

Ramgovind, S., Eloff, M. M., & Smith, E. (2010). *The management of security in cloud computing* (pp. 1–7). IEEE Information Security for South Africa. doi:10.1109/ISSA.2010.5588290

Ranganathan, V. (2010). Privacy issues with cloud applications. *iS Channel, 5*(1), 16-20. London School of Economics and Political Science.

Ruan, K., Carthy, J., Kechadi, T., & Crosbie, M. (2011). *Cloud forensics: An overview*, (pp. 1-16). Centre for Cybercrime Investigation, University College Dublin.

Ruiter, J., & Warnier, M. (2011). Privacy regulations for cloud computing: Compliance and implementation in theory and practice. In Gutwirth, S., Poullet, Y., De Hert, P., & Leenes, R. (Eds.), *Computers, privacy and data protection: An element of choice* (1st ed., pp. 355–389). Springer. doi:10.1007/978-94-007-0641-5_17

Sabahi, F. (2011). Virtualization-level security in cloud computing. *IEEE Computer Society 3rd International Conference on Communication Software and Networks*, (pp. 250-255).

Sharma, R., & Sood, M. (2011). *Cloud SaaS and model driven architecture* (pp. 16–23). New Delhi, India: RG Education Society, IETE.

Shen, Z., & Tong, Q. (2010). The security of cloud computing system enabled by trusted computing technology. *IEEE 2nd International Conference on Signal Processing Systems*, (pp. 11-15).

Sotomayor, B., Montero, R. S., Llorente, I. M., & Foster, I. (2009). Virtual infrastructure management in private and hybrid clouds. *IEEE Internet Computing, 13*(5), 14–22. doi:10.1109/MIC.2009.119

Stoneburner, G., Gouguen, A., & Feringa, A. (2002). *Risk management guide for information technology systems*, (pp. 3-55). Special Publication 800-30, National Institute of Standards and Technology (NIST), U.S. Department of Commerce.

Takabi, H., Joshi, J. B. D., & Ahn, G. (2010). Security and privacy challenges in cloud computing environments. *IEEE Security and Privacy*, *8*(6), 24–31. doi:10.1109/MSP.2010.186

Wan, Z. (2011). A network virtualization approach in many-core processor based cloud computing environment. *Third International Conference on Computational Intelligence, Communication Systems and Networks*, (pp. 304-307).

Wang, Q., Wang, C., Ren, K., Lou, W., & Li, J. (2011). Enabling public auditability and data dynamics for storage security in cloud computing. *IEEE Transactions on Parallel and Distributed Systems*, *22*(5), 847–859. doi:10.1109/TPDS.2010.183

Wen, F., & Xiang, L. (2011). The study on data security in cloud computing based on virtualization. *International Symposium on IT in Medicine and Education* (pp. 257-261).

Younge, A. J., Laszewski, G. V., Wang, L., Lopez-Alarcon, S., & Carithers, W. (2010). Efficient resource management for cloud computing environments. *Proceedings of the International Conference on Green Computing,* (p. 5).

Chapter 7
Security and Privacy in Cloud Computing:
Towards a Comprehensive Framework

Hassan Takabi
University of Pittsburgh, USA

James B. D. Joshi
University of Pittsburgh, USA

Gail-Joon Ahn
Arizona State University, USA

ABSTRACT

Cloud computing paradigm has recently gained tremendous momentum. It has been found very promising for significant cost reduction and the increased operating efficiencies in computing. However, security and privacy issues pose as the key roadblock to its rapid adoption. In this chapter, the authors present the security and privacy challenges in Cloud computing environments and discuss how they are related to various delivery and deployment models, and are exacerbated by the unique aspects of Clouds. The authors also propose a comprehensive security framework for Cloud computing environments and discuss various approaches to address the challenges, existing solutions and future work needed to provide a trustworthy Cloud computing environment.

INTRODUCTION

Cloud computing has recently generated huge interest within computing research communities. It separates information resources from the underlying infrastructure and the approaches used to deliver them. Cloud computing tries to consolidate the economic utility model with the advances in many existing approaches and computing technologies including distributed services, applications, as well as large information infrastructures that are built on top of huge pools of computers,

DOI: 10.4018/978-1-4666-2854-0.ch007

networks, and storage resources. It has been found to offer tremendous promise to enhance collaboration, agility, scale and availability. Its definitions, attributes, characteristics, underlying technologies and risks have been evolving and will change over time. From an architectural perspective, confusion and disagreements exist in IT communities about how a Cloud is different from existing models and how these differences might affect its deployment and widespread adoption. Some see a Cloud as a novel technical revolution while others consider it a natural evolution of technology, economy and culture (Cloud Security Alliance 2011). Nevertheless Cloud computing is a very important paradigm that promises to provide significant cost reduction through optimization and the increased operating and economic efficiencies in computing (Cloud Security Alliance 2011; Catteddu & Hogben 2009) Furthermore, Cloud computing has the potential to significantly enhance collaboration, agility, and scale, and, thus, to enable a truly global computing model over the Internet infrastructure.

While several researchers have tried to define Cloud computing, currently, there is no single agreed upon definition. The US National Institute of Standards and Technology defines it as follows: "Cloud computing is a model for enabling ubiquitous, convenient, on-demand network access to a shared pool of configurable computing resources (e.g., networks, servers, storage, applications, and services) that can be rapidly provisioned and released with minimal management effort or service provider interaction. This Cloud model is composed of five essential characteristics, three service models, and four deployment models" (Mell & Grance 2011). In order to understand the importance of Cloud computing and its adoption, one needs to understand its principal characteristics, its delivery and deployment models, how the customers would use or benefit from these services and how these services need to be safeguarded. The five key characteristics of Cloud computing include on-demand self-service,

ubiquitous network access, location independent resource pooling, rapid elasticity, and measured service; these are all geared towards allowing the seamless and transparent use of Clouds (Mell & Grance 2011). Rapid elasticity allows resources provisioned to be quickly scaled up or down. Measured services are primarily derived from properties of the business model and indicate that Cloud service provider controls and optimizes the use of computing resources through automated resource allocation, load balancing and metering tools (Cloud Security Alliance 2011; Catteddu & Hogben 2009; Yang X. et al. 2012).

Despite the enormous opportunity and value that the Cloud presents for organizations, without appropriate security and privacy solutions designed for Clouds this potentially revolutionizing computing paradigm could become a huge failure (Takabi, Joshi & Ahn 2010b). Customers are concerned about the security and privacy risks of Cloud computing and the fact that they lose direct control over the security of their systems when they migrate to the Cloud. Several surveys of potential Cloud adopters indicate that security and privacy are the number one concern delaying its adoption and it will likely continue to keep some companies out of Cloud computing (Bruening & Treacy 2009). Hence, understanding the security and privacy risks in Cloud computing and developing efficient and effective solutions are critical to the success of this new computing paradigm. When we move our information into the Cloud, we may lose control over it. The Cloud gives us access to the data, but the challenge is to ensure that only authorized entities have access to that data. It is crucial to understand how we can protect our data and resources from a security breach in the Cloud that provides shared platforms and services. It is critical to have appropriate mechanisms to prevent Cloud providers from using customers' data in a way that has not been agreed upon in the past.

The three key Cloud delivery models are Software as a Service (SaaS), Platform as a Service

(PaaS), and Infrastructure as a Service (IaaS). In IaaS, the Cloud provider provides a set of infrastructural components that are virtualized, such as, virtual machines, networks and storage, on which the customers can build and run applications. The most basic component is a virtual machine (VM) and the virtual operating system (OS) where the application will reside. Issues such as trusting the virtual machine image, hardening hosts, and securing inter-host communication pose significant challenge in IaaS. PaaS enables the programming environments to access and utilize the additional application building blocks. Such programming environments have a visible impact on the application architecture. One such impact would be that of the constraints on what services the application can request from an OS. For example, a PaaS environment may limit access to well-defined parts of the file system, thus requiring a fine-grained authorization service. In SaaS, the Cloud providers enable and provide application software enabled as on-demand-services. As clients acquire and use software components from different providers, securely composing them and ensuring that information handled by these composed services are well protected become crucial issues.

The Cloud deployment models include public Cloud, private Cloud, community Cloud, and hybrid Cloud. Public Cloud refers to an external or publicly available Cloud environment that is accessible to multiple tenants, while private Cloud is typically a tailored environment with dedicated virtualized resources for a particular organization. Similarly, community Cloud is tailored for a particular group of customers. Hybrid Cloud is combination of two or more of the previous Cloud deployment models.

In this chapter, we present unique issues of Cloud computing that exacerbate security and privacy challenges in Clouds, discuss these challenges, some possible approaches and research directions to address them. We also propose a comprehensive security framework for Cloud computing environments. We present the security framework and discuss key existing solutions, and some approaches to deal with security challenges. The framework consists of different modules to handle security, and trust issues of the key components of Cloud computing environments. These modules deal with issues such as identity management, access control, policy integration among multiple Clouds, trust management between different Clouds and between a Cloud and its users, secure service composition and integration, and semantic heterogeneity among policies from different Clouds.

RELATED WORK

The recent efforts from National Institute of Standards and Technologies (NIST) have attempted to promote the effective and secure use of the technology within government and industry by providing technical guidance and promoting standards. The NIST has released an early definition of Cloud computing and also documents on how to effectively and securely use the Cloud computing paradigm (Mell & Grance 2011). The Cloud Security Alliance is an effort to facilitate the mission to create and apply best practices to secure Cloud computing [Cloud Security Alliance 2011]. Its initial report, "Security Guidance for Critical Areas of Focus in Cloud Computing", outlines areas of concern and guidance for organizations adopting Cloud computing. The intention is to provide security practitioners with a comprehensive roadmap for being proactive in developing positive and secure relationships with Cloud providers (Chen, Paxson & Katz 2010). Takabi et al. (2010b) discuss security and privacy challenges in a Cloud computing environment (Takabi, Joshi & Ahn 2010b). They present unique issues of Cloud computing that exacerbate security and privacy challenges in Clouds, discuss these challenges, some possible approaches and research directions to address them. They have also proposed SecureCloud, a comprehensive security framework for Cloud computing environments (Takabi, Joshi & Ahn 2010a). The framework consists of different modules to handle security, and trust issues of key components of Cloud computing environments. These modules deal with issues such as identity management, access control, policy integration among multiple Clouds, trust management between different Clouds and between a Cloud and its users, secure service composition and integration, and semantic heterogeneity among policies from different Clouds.

Jaeger et al. discuss security challenges in the Cloud, a foundation of future systems' security and key areas for Cloud system improvement (Jaeger & Schiffman 2011). Kandukuri et al. present security issues that have to be included in service layer agreement (SLA) in Cloud computing environment (Kandukuri, Paturi, & Rakshit 2009, Yang X. 2011).

Jensen et al. provide an overview on technical security issues of the Cloud (Jensen et al. 2009). They start with real-world examples of attacks performed on the Amazon EC2 service, and then give an overview of existing and upcoming threats to the Cloud. They also briefly discuss appropriate countermeasures to these threats, and further elaborate on issues to be considered in future research. Gruschka et al. present taxonomies and classification criteria for attacks on Cloud computing based on the notion of attack surfaces and try to anticipate the classes of vulnerabilities that will arise from the Cloud computing paradigm (Gruschka & Jensen 2010). Tian et al. (2009) present a new database service provider (DSP) re-encryption mechanism to implement flexible access control enforcement in the database as a service (DaaS) paradigm (Tian, Wang & Zhou 2009). The basic idea of the approach is that the DSP uses different re-encryption keys for users of the system. Their approach can relieve the users from the complex key derivation procedure while implementing the selective access control of the encrypted data by the DSP.

SECURITY AND PRIVACY IN CLOUD

Cloud computing environments can be deemed as an instance of the multi-domain environment where each domain employs different security, privacy and trust requirements and potentially employ various mechanisms, interfaces, and semantics. Such domains could represent individually enabled services or other infrastructural or application components. Service-oriented architecture (SOA) is naturally relevant technology to facilitate such multi-domain formation through service composition and orchestration (Catteddu & Hogben 2009). We articulate the key security and privacy challenges that Cloud computing raises (Takabi, Joshi & Ahn 2010a).

Identity and Access Management (IAM)

By using Cloud services users can easily access their personal information and it is also available to various services across the Internet. We need to have an identity management mechanism for authenticating users and services based on credentials and characteristics (Bertino, Paci & Ferrini 2009). The concepts behind IAM used in traditional computing are fundamentally different from those of a Cloud environment. One key issue in Cloud concerning IAM is the interoperability issues that could result from using different identity tokens and different identity negotiation protocols. Existing password based authentication has an inherent limitation and poses significant risks. An IAM system should be able to accommodate protection of private and sensitive information related to users and processes. How the multitenant Cloud environments could affect the privacy of identity information has not been yet well understood. In addition, the multi-jurisdiction issue can complicate protection measures (Bruening & Treacy 2009). While users interact with a front end service, this service may need to ensure that his/her identity is protected from other services that it interacts with (Bertino, Paci & Ferrini

2009; Ko, Ahn & Shehab 2009). Segregation of customer's identity and authentication information is a crucial component, especially in multitenant Cloud environments. It is also important that the IAM components can be easily integrated with the other security components.

Heterogeneity and diversity of services, and the multiple domains' diverse access requirements in Cloud computing environments would require fine-grained access control policies. In particular, access control services should be flexible enough to capture dynamic, context or attribute/credential based access requirements, and facilitate enforcement of the principle of least privilege. Such access control services may need to integrate privacy protection requirements expressed through complex rules. It is important that the access control system employed in Clouds is easily managed and its privilege distribution is administered efficiently. It is also important to ensure that the Cloud delivery models provide generic access control interfaces for proper interoperability, which demands a policy neutral access control specification and enforcement framework that can be used to address cross-domain access issues (Joshi et al. 2004). Also, the access control models should be able to capture relevant aspects of SLA agreements. The utility models of Clouds demand proper accounting of activities of users and services which raises significant privacy issues, as the customer may not want to let a provider maintain such detailed accounting records other than for billing purposes. The outsourcing and multi-tenancy aspects of Clouds could exacerbate customers fears about accounting logs. Hence, privacy aware framework for access control and accounting services is very crucial. Such a framework should be easily amenable to compliance checking.

Trust Management and Policy Integration

In a Cloud, multiple service providers can co-exist and collaborate to provide various services to customers. There are some questions that need to be answered with regards to their collaboration and their interactions with customers. Does the customer trust the Cloud service providers? Do various Cloud service providers trust each other? How can they negotiate the trust? Is the trust static/dynamic? What are the requirements to manage trust? In Cloud computing environments, the interactions between different service domains driven by service requirements can be expected to be very dynamic/transient and intensive in nature. Furthermore, the customers' behavior can evolve rapidly, thereby affecting established trust values. Efficient techniques are needed to manage evolving trust. This suggests a need for an effective trust management solution to efficiently capture a generic set of parameters required for establishing trust and to manage evolving trust and interaction/sharing requirements.

The Cloud service providers may need to compose multiple services to enable bigger application services which are presented to customers. They may have different approaches to provide security and privacy mechanisms. Hence, it is necessary to address heterogeneity among their policies and ensure that the dynamic collaboration is handled in a secure manner. Existing literature has shown that even though individual domain policies are verified to be correct, security violation can easily occur when they are integrated (Zhang & Joshi 2009). Hence, access control policies need to be carefully managed to ensure that the integration of multiple policies does not lead to any security breaches. The policy integration component in the Cloud should be able to address challenges such as semantic heterogeneity, secure interoperability, and policy evolution management. It is important to have secure interoperation mechanisms to ensure that no security breaches are created during the interoperation. In addition, policy engineering mechanisms are needed to integrate access policies of different Cloud service providers and define global access policies to accommodate all collaborators' requirements. Furthermore, semantic heterogeneity exists among policies from different service providers that may cause semantic conflicts and/or inconsistencies among their policies. Semantic heterogeneity needs to be taken into account and there is a need to automatically detect these possible conflicts and resolve them.

Secure Service Management

A considerable number of services are expected to be available in the Cloud, which could be used by customers for their needs or in combination with other services. In the Cloud computing environments, Cloud service providers collaborate to provide newly composed services that meet customers' needs. A service integrator provides a platform that enables independent service providers to orchestrate and interconnect services, and cooperatively provide services that meet customers' protection requirements. Although many Cloud service providers provide their services with Web Services description language (WSDL), the traditional WSDL cannot fully meet the requirements of Cloud computing services description (Takabi, Joshi & Ahn 2010b). In Clouds, issues like QoS, service price, and SLAs are critical for service search and service composition. These issues need to be addressed to describe services and introduce their features, to find best interoperable services, to integrate them without violating the service owner's policies, and to ensure that SLAs are satisfied. In essence, an automatic and systematic service provisioning and composition approach that considers security and privacy issues is crucial.

Privacy and Data Protection

Many organizations are not comfortable storing their data and applications on systems that reside outside of their physical on-premise data centers where they do not have control over them (Takabi, Joshi & Ahn 2010b). This may be the single most fear that Cloud clients may have. By migrating workloads to a shared infrastructure,

customers' private information is on increased risk of potential unauthorized access and exposure. In all the challenges above, privacy is a core issue that needs to be addressed, such as the need to ensure privacy of identity information, policy components during integration, transaction histories, etc. Cloud service providers must assure their customers and provide a high degree of transparency into their operations and privacy assurance. Privacy protection mechanisms need to be potentially embedded in all the security solutions. A related issue is data provenance; increasingly, it is becoming important to know who created a piece of data, who modified it and how, etc. Provenance information could be used for various purposes such as traceback, auditing, history based access control, etc. Achieving a good balance between data provenance and privacy is a significant challenge in a Cloud where a strict physical perimeter is abandoned.

Intrusion Detection and Prevention

Intrusion Detection and Prevention Systems (IDPSs) are one of the most popular tools to defend the computation and communication infrastructures. While some of the current host based IDPSs (HIDPSs) or network based IDPSs (NIDPSs) have been developed for the Cloud computing environment and been used in practice, they do not fulfill the requirements for an extremely challenging collaborative environment such as Cloud environment (Taghavi, Takabi & Joshi 2011). Reactive IDPSs that support real-time responses to the attacks are not practical in dynamically changing Cloud environments and can cause huge overheads whereas passive approaches are not efficient in terms of response time and may lead to serious performance issues and hamper collaboration among different Cloud service providers. Considering dynamicity of the Cloud environment, filtering rules and access lists should dynamically evolve to be able to deal with attacks in diverse Cloud environments. Moreover, in a Cloud environment attacks may be directed against resources located within the Cloud infrastructure or may be originated through one of the virtual machines within a physical host. We need a proper defense mechanism to effectively detect and react to the attacks in a distributed manner. Further, a homogeneous IDPS infrastructure is needed for heterogeneous Cloud environments to facilitate defense management.

Encryption and Key Management

One of the core mechanisms that Cloud should use for data protection is strong encryption supported by an efficient key management solution. If a Cloud service provider is not able to encrypt a file, store it securely and transfer it to another location, it will be very difficult to secure the Cloud environment. The resources are protected using encryption while access to protected resources is enabled by key management. Issues like encrypting data in transit over networks, encrypting data at rest and encrypting data on backup media should be taken into account. Also, the possibility of exotic attacks in Cloud makes more crucial that the Cloud providers develop solutions for encrypting dynamic data, including data residing in memory. More work is needed to overcome barriers to adoption of robust key management schemes. There are several key management challenges within Cloud such as secure key stores, access to key stores, key backup and recoverability that should be handled in an appropriate way.

Data encryption in storage, in transit, and in backup must be applied to key stores themselves too. Only entities that specifically need the individual keys should have access to key stores. Moreover, there should be policies to better protect the key stores using control access; for example, an entity that uses a given key should not be the entity that stores that key. Secure backup and recovery solutions also must be implemented to protect mission-critical data in case of accidental loss of keys.

Portability and Interoperability

When moving to the Cloud, organizations must understand that they may have to change Cloud providers in the future and should consider portability and interoperability up front as part of security assurance of any Cloud. Since there is no interoperability standards, transitioning between Cloud providers may be a painful process. However, some simple architectural considerations can help minimize the damage but the means to address these issues depend on the type of the Cloud service sought. From a security perspective, the primary concern is how to maintain consistency of security controls while changing environments.

Risk Management

Risk management, in general includes the methods and processes used to evaluate risks and opportunities related to the achievement of the stated objectives. In a Cloud environment, there are many variables, values and risks that may affect the decision whether an organization should adopt a Cloud service. An organization should weigh those variables to decide whether the Cloud service is an appropriate solution for achieving its goals. Basically, Cloud services and security should be seen as supply chain security issues meaning that the service provider relationships and dependencies should be examined and assessed to the extent possible.

Organizational Security Management

Adoption of Cloud computing by enterprises significantly changes the existing enterprise security management and information security life cycle models. In particular, the shared governance can become a significant issue if not properly addressed. Despite potential benefits of using Clouds, it may mean less coordination among different communities of interest within the client organization (Takabi, Joshi & Ahn 2010b).

The dependence on the external entities can also raise fears about timely response to security incidents, and for implementing systematic business continuity and disaster recovery plans. Similarly, risk and cost benefit analysis will need to involve external parties. The customers consequently need to consider newer risks introduced by a perimeterless environment, possible data leakage within multi-tenant Clouds, and resiliency issues such as local disasters in and economic instability of the providers. Similarly, the insider attack surface is significantly extended when customers outsource data and processes to a Cloud. Within a multi-tenant environment, one tenant could be a highly targeted attack victim and the other tenants can be significantly affected by attacks on that tenant. Existing life cycle models, risk analysis and management processes, penetration testing and service attestation need to be critically re-evaluated to ensure that the potential benefits of Clouds can be enjoyed by Cloud clients. Information security area has faced significant problems in establishing appropriate security metrics for consistent and realistic measurements that help the crucial risk assessment task. Significant effort is needed to re-evaluate best practices, and develop standards to ensure deployment and adoption of secure Clouds. These issues would necessitate a well-structured cyber-insurance industry; however, the global nature of Cloud computing can make the issue very complex. For example, healthcare providers are willing to move their electronic medical record (EMR) systems to Clouds to remove the barrier of geographical distances among providers and patients. It is critical in this situation to ensure that EMR systems are compliant with government regulations such as the Health Insurance Portability and Accountability Act (HIPAA). A HIPAA compliance management approach is needed to ensure this compliance (Wu, Ahn & Hu 2012). To achieve this goal, first policy patterns from both HIPAA regulations and EMR systems' policies can be extracted, along with a generic policy specification scheme. Then, a transfor-

mation and compliance analysis method can be used to determine whether an EMR system is in compliance with HIPAA regulations by leveraging logic-based reasoning techniques (Wu, Ahn & Hu 2012).

SECURITY FRAMEWORK FOR THE CLOUD

In this section, we propose a security framework for a Cloud computing environment. We can leverage some of the existing research on multi-domain policy integration and the secure service composition to build a comprehensive policy based management framework. First, we provide an overview of the framework and its components. Then, we discuss approaches to address security and privacy requirements of Cloud service providers, service integrators and Cloud environments in general. The overall security framework and key components of the Cloud computing environment are depicted in Figure 1. The Services Integrator facilitates collaboration among different service providers by composing new services. Each service integrator has components that are responsible for the establishment and maintenance of trust among the local provider domains and between the providers and the users, provisioning desirable services and generating global policies. The service integrators discover services from different service providers or other service integrators, carry out negotiations, integrate the services to form groups of collaborating services and provide them to users.

A. Security Management

The security management component provides the security and privacy specification and enforcement functionality. The identity and access management module is responsible for authenticating users and services based on credentials and characteristics as well as employing the access policies while the pri-

Figure 1. The proposed security framework for cloud computing environments

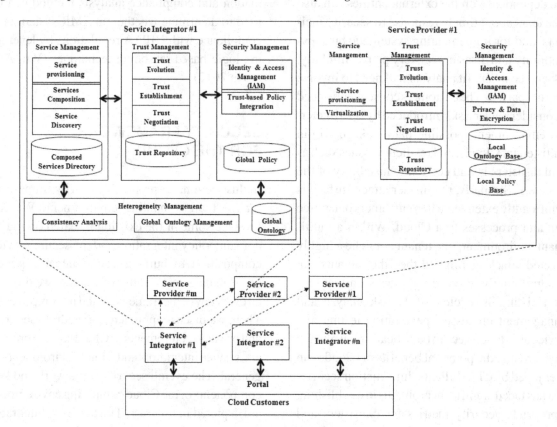

vacy and data protection module is responsible for privacy needs and protection of outsourced data. In the service integrator, the trust-based policy integration (TPI) module administers trust and facilitates trust-based policy integration among different services from different service providers.

Identity and Access Management

In a distributed environment like Cloud, users have control in disclosing their identities via trusted identity providers and are responsible for managing their information across various Cloud service providers. User-centric IAM has recently received significant attention for handling private and critical identity attributes (Ko, Ahn & Shehab 2009). In this approach, an identity will have identifiers or attributes that identify and define a user. A user-centric approach allows users to control

their own digital identities and also takes away the complexity of IAM from the enterprises, thereby, allowing them to focus on their own functions. Normally, users can access the Cloud from various places such as home, office, school or public places. Therefore, it is critical for users to export their digital identities and transfer them to various computers in a secure manner. User centric IAM also implies that the system properly maintains the semantics of the context of identity information for users, and sometimes constrains and relaxes them in order to find the best way to respond to a user request in a given situation. Other federated IAM solutions are currently being pursued that would also benefit Cloud environments (Bertino, Paci & Ferrini 2009; Ko, Ahn & Shehab 2009).

While a user agent negotiates with service providers and identity providers, the IAM component can be extended to inform users about the risk involved in disclosing certain identity information to service providers (Ahn & Sekar 2011). The goal is to provide users with quantifiable risk values and help them to make informed decisions when disclosing identity information. To have a common understanding of identity attributes, OWL can be used to construct an identity attribute ontology (IAO) to capture object-oriented relationship of identity attributes among various Cloud service providers (Ahn & Sekar 2011). Then, an ontology-based user-centric IAM can be developed to perform risk analysis and evaluation for identity attributes which is used by users to make a decision on disclosing these attributes to various Cloud service providers (Ahn & Sekar 2011).

It is important to ensure that where needed the IAM services in the Cloud are integrated with an enterprise's existing IAM framework (Takabi & Joshi 2010; Takabi, Joshi & Ahn 2010). In some cases, it is important to have privacy-preserving protocols to verify various identity attributes. One approach towards this is to use zero-knowledge proof based techniques (Bertino, Paci & Ferrini 2009). Existing techniques for use of pseudonyms and accommodating multiple identities to protect users' privacy can further help build a desired user-centric federated IAM for Clouds.

Several access control models exist in the literature that caters to various types of security requirements. As previously mentioned, there is a crucial need for Cloud providers to provide a generic support for a flexible, policy neutral access control model to accommodate access requirements mentioned earlier. Based on the requirements, various access control models can be used. Role Based Access Control (RBAC) has been widely accepted as the most promising approach because of its simplicity, flexibility in capturing dynamic requirements, and its support for the principle of least privilege and efficient privilege management (Bertino, Paci & Ferrini 2009; Teo & Ahn 2007). Furthermore, RBAC

is policy neutral, can capture a wide variety of policy requirements, and is best suited for policy integration needs discussed earlier. RBAC can also be used for usage control purpose which generalizes access control to integrate obligations and conditions into authorizations. Obligations are defined as requirements that the subjects have to fulfill for access requests. Conditions are environmental requirements independent from subject and object that have to be satisfied for the access request. Due to the highly dynamic nature of the Cloud, obligations and conditions are crucial decision factors for richer and finer controls on usage of resources provided by the Cloud. Recent RBAC extensions such as credential-based RBAC (Bhatti et al. 2003), Generalized Temporal RBAC (GTRBAC) (Joshi et al. 2005; Bhatti et al. 2005), and location based RBAC models provide necessary modeling constructs and capabilities to capture context based fine-grained access control requirements. In Clouds, users are usually not known a priori to the service providers so it is difficult to assign users directly to roles in access control policies - use of credential/attribute based policies may enhance this capability. However, little work exists in employing RBAC and extensions within intensely service oriented environments such as Clouds.

Privacy and Data Protection

Data in the Cloud is typically in a shared environment. Furthermore, a Cloud provider has some control of the Cloud users' data. One approach is to limit providers' control of data and enable clients to fully control their own data. The data owner should have full control on who gets the right to use data and what they are allowed to do with it once they gain access. In order to provide this control on data in the Cloud, a standard-based heterogeneous data-centric security approach that shifts data protection from system and applications is very crucial. In this approach, documents need to be self-describing and defending regardless of their environments. Cryptographic approaches and usage policy rules need to be considered. When someone wants to access data, the system should check its policy rules, and reveal it only if the policies are satisfied. Existing cryptographic techniques can be utilized for data security. However, privacy protection and outsourced computation need significant attention - both of these are relatively new research directions. Data provenance issue has just begun to be addressed in the literature. In some cases, information related to a particular hardware component (storage, processing or communication) needs to be associated with a piece of data.

Another solution to mitigate privacy concerns of Cloud customers is that Cloud service providers offer an efficient audit service to enable users check the integrity of their stored data (Zhu et al. 2012a). It might be expensive and not practical for users to audit the integrity of data stored in Cloud themselves. Thus, Cloud computing environment should offer public auditability where a third party auditor (TPA) performs periodic auditing of the outsourced data on behalf of the users. A dynamic audit service can be developed to support dynamic data operations and timely anomaly detection in an untrusted outsourced storage (Zhu et al. 2012a). The TPA should be able to verify data integrity without being required to retrieve a copy of the whole data, supervise outsourced data and offer efficient evidences for anomalies. The audit mechanism must ensure that the security of verification protocol cannot be compromised using dynamic data operations, detect errors and abnormal behaviors in a timely manner (Zhu et al. 2012a). The audit service should include tag generation, periodic sampling audit, and audit for dynamic operations. The applications should be authorized by data owner to manipulate outsourced data. Therefore, the authorized applications should present authentication information to TPA and unauthorized modifications of data

can be detected in audit or verification processes. The goal here is to enhance credibility of Cloud storage services without increasing data owner's burden (Zhu et al. 2012a).

Provable data possession (PDP) can be used to ensure the integrity of data in storage outsourcing (Zhu et al. 2012b). In a distributed Cloud storage where multiple Cloud service providers store and maintain client's data cooperatively, an efficient PDP scheme is needed to support the scalability of service and data migration. The best approach is to use a cooperative PDP (CPDP) scheme based on homomorphic verifiable response (HVR) and hash index hierarchy (HIH) (Zhu et al. 2012b). In the HIH approach, the responses of the clients' challenges computed from multiple CSPs are combined into a single response as the final result. The HVR technique implements an efficient construction of collision resistant hash function, which can be viewed as a random oracle model in the verification protocol. Based on these two techniques, a cooperative PDP scheme is built to support dynamic scalability on multiple storage servers. The security of CPDP scheme is proven based on multi-prover zero-knowledge proof system, which can satisfy completeness, knowledge soundness, and zero-knowledge properties. CPDP can resist various attacks even if it is deployed as a public audit service in Clouds (Zhu et al. 2012b).

Trust-Based Policy Integration

Several recent works have focused on multi-domain access control policies and policy integration issues, which can be adopted to build a comprehensive policy management framework in Clouds (Catteddu & Hogben 2009; Bertino, Paci & Ferrini 2009). Existing work on multi-domain access control policies have addressed the issue of (i) integrating policies to ensure secure interoperation and (ii) policy engineering mechanisms to integrate access policies of different policy domains and define global access policies

(Takabi et al. 2009; Takabi, Joshi & Ahn 2010a). Some approaches include policy algebra that can facilitate specification of various combinations of policies from different policy domains. Secure interoperation can be achieved in a centralized or decentralized fashion (Takabi et al. 2009). In a centralized approach, a global policy is created that mediates all accesses and is appropriate for a Cloud application that is composed of various services with different requirements and is more or less fixed. In a more dynamic environment, the domains are transient and may need to interact for a very specific purpose; a centralized approach is not appropriate in such cases. More decentralized approaches are needed in such cases. Specification frameworks are needed to ensure that the cross domain accesses are properly specified, verified and enforced. SAML, XACML, and WS standards are viable solutions towards these needs (Takabi et al. 2009). However, support for fine-grained RBAC capabilities may be limited as indicated by RBAC specific multi-domain policy specification and enforcement frameworks in XRBAC (Teo & Ahn 2007).

One issue that needs to be taken into account in policy integration mechanisms is policy analysis. The goal of policy analysis is to detect redundant, overlapping and conflicting policies and resolve anomalies. A solution is needed to facilitate collaborative policy analysis in Cloud computing environment. A generic approach can be developed for ontology-based policy anomaly management (Hu, Ahn, & Kulkarni 2011). It uses the notion of policy ontology to capture common semantics and structure of different types of access control policies. First, information such as policy domain concepts, structure of policy and semantics of policy is used to extract policy ontology. This policy ontology can be extended to capture changes in the access control policy specifications. Then, the policy ontology is instantiated using the structure and semantic information extracted from a particular policy to generate a representation of that particular type of access control policy. These representations are translated to binary decision

diagram (BDD) based policies to be used by the policy based segmentation technique to detect potential anomalies. Finally, a fine-grained policy resolution can be performed to remove the conflicts (Hu, Ahn, & Kulkarni 2011).

Policy engineering mechanisms are crucial to define global policies to accommodate all collaborators' requirements. Emerging role mining techniques can be useful to support this (Ko, Ahn & Shehab 2009). Role mining utilizes the existing system configuration data to define roles. It first considers the existing users' permissions and aggregates them into roles (Joshi et al. 2004). In the Cloud, users acquire different roles from different domains based on services they need. To define global policies, we can utilize these RBAC systems' configurations from different domains to define global roles and policies. Each global role can include roles from different domains that have been assigned to the same groups of users. Several new approaches have been proposed for role engineering that could be adopted in Clouds for policy engineering purposes. Role engineering approaches are also needed to address policy evolution or changing requirements. Changes to the existing role set may cause disruptions to the organization and prevent it from proper functioning. So, role mining should look for a set of roles as close as possible to both the existing set of roles and the optimal set of roles. One possible approach is StateMiner (Takabi & Joshi 2010c) that introduces new measures for optimality and presents a heuristic solution to find an RBAC state with the smallest structural complexity and as similar as possible to both the existing state and the optimal state.

Intrusion Detection and Prevention System

It is necessary to provide a distributed, collaborative, and data-driven intrusion detection and prevention (DCDIDP) that utilizes the resources in the Cloud since suspicious activities can increase and dynamically evolve (Taghavi Zargar, Takabi

& Joshi 2011). The goal would be to provide a homogeneous IDPS for all the Cloud providers that collaborate in a distributed manner. Using the DCDIDP, Cloud providers can collaborate with other peers in a distributed manner and as close as possible to attack sources and at different levels of operations to respond to attacks. We combine the advantages of Cloud computing and the concept of collaboration to make the attack detection and prevention faster and more efficient. The DCDIDP can apply differentiated level of security strength to users based on their degree of abnormality and make it possible to detect and prevent attacks at application, platform, and infrastructure levels considering each level's specifications and vulnerabilities.

B. Trust Management

The trust management component is responsible for negotiation, establishment, and evolution of trust. In the Cloud, there is a challenging need of integrating requirements-driven trust negotiation techniques with fine-grained access control mechanisms. There are some critical questions that need to be answered: how do we establish trust and determine access mapping to satisfy inter-domain access requirements? How do we manage and maintain dynamically changing trust values and adapt the access requirements as trust evolves? Existing trust negotiation mechanisms primarily focus on credential exchange (Blaze et al. 2009; Zhang & Joshi 2009), and do not address a more challenging need of integrating requirements-driven trust negotiation techniques with fine-grained access control mechanisms (Zhang & Joshi 2009; Shin & Ahn 2005). Due service oriented nature of the Clouds, trust levels should also be integrated with the service. The key idea is that the more services a Cloud service provider offers the higher the trust level that needs to be established. Another problem is that we need to establish bi-direction trust in the Cloud. That is, the users should have some level of trust on the providers to choose their services

from, and the providers also need to have some level of trust on the users to release their services to. One possible direction is to develop a trust management approach that includes a generic set of trust negotiation parameters, is integrated with service, and is bi-directional. As the service composition dynamics in the Cloud can be very complex, trust and access control frameworks should include delegation primitives (Shin & Ahn 2005). Existing work related to delegation, including role-based delegation has focused on issues related to delegation of privileges among subjects and various levels of controls with regard to privilege propagation and revocation. Efficient cryptographic mechanisms for trust delegation involve complex trust chain verification and revocation issues raising significant key management issues. These approaches need to be incorporated in service composition frameworks (Blaze et al. 2009).

C. Service Management

In order to optimize resource utilization, Cloud service providers most often, but not always, utilize virtualization technologies that separate application services from infrastructure. In the Cloud, service providers and service integrators need to collaborate to provide newly composed services to customers. The service management component is responsible for secure service discovery, composition and provisioning. A service provider uses virtualization in order to offer services to users more efficiently. The service discovery module is responsible for finding different services that the provider domains or other service integrators offer. After discovering services, the service integrator needs to negotiate with the provider domains and compose new desirable collaborating services for users using the service composition module. The collaborating services come from different domains and the service integrator needs to consider trust between the collaborating provider domains when composing new services. The service provisioning module provides services for users based on bidirectional trust between the service integrator and its users.

An automatic and systematic service provisioning and composition approach that considers security and privacy issues is very important for cloud environments. It would allow describing services with unified standards to introduce their functionalities, discovering existing interoperable services and securely integrating them to provide services. Such approaches need to include a declarative language to describe services, their features, and mechanisms to provision appropriate services and to compose them. The Open Services Gateway Initiative (OSGi) (Ahn, Hu & Jin 2009) service platform is an extensible integration platform that provides an open, common architecture for service providers, developers, software venders, gateway operators and equipment vendors to develop, deploy and manage services in a cooperative way. Researchers have developed ways to configure and map the OSGi authorization mechanism to RBAC (Ahn, Hu & Jin 2009). Declarative OWL-based language can be used to provide a service definition manifest including a list of distinct component types that make up the service, the functional requirements, component grouping and topology instructions, etc. OSGi can be adopted to develop an agent-based collaboration system for automatic service provisioning. One of the crucial challenges of such collaboration systems is that of dynamic access control to resources shared by agents and to control collaborative actions that are geared towards a collaboration goal. Such a model should emphasize capability based agents to facilitate role mapping and group situation driven permission assignment to allow capturing dynamic access policies that evolve continuously.

D. Heterogeneity Management

One key aspect of the complex Cloud computing environments is the semantic heterogeneity among different service providers' policies since they may have different approaches to provide security mechanisms. The global ontology management module is responsible for providing global ontology and supporting semantic heterogeneity concerns related to policies. Little attention has been given to automatic detection of semantic conflicts among different service providers' policies. While XML has been adopted as the preferred language for information sharing it has been found inadequate for describing information semantics (Bertino, Paci & Ferrini 2009). RDF, on the other hand, provides a facility for describing semantics by supporting description of an element's attributes and properties (Zhang & Joshi 2009; Kodali, Farkas & Wijesekera 2004). Although semantics can be captured using RDF, representing relations between the various concepts is essential for facilitating semantic integration of policy information within interacting domains. Ontology-based approach is the most promising method to address the semantic heterogeneity issue (Chakraborty & Ray 2006; Takabi & Joshi 2012a; Takabi & Joshi 2012b]. To support the development of ontologies, both XML-Schema and RDF-Schema can be used to accommodate the domain-specific concepts (Joshi et al. 2004). It is to be noted, however, that although RDF is based on XML syntax and OWL is based on the RDF-S representation of concepts, and either of these technologies is not likely to completely subsume the lower technology in Clouds. An OWL based solution can be developed to support semantic heterogeneity across multiple providers in the Cloud. In developing this solution, we can adopt a system-driven policy framework to facilitate the management of security policies in heterogeneous environments and a policy enforcement architecture (Kim, Joshi & Kim 2008; Chakraborty & Ray 2006). Several inference engines are available that can be used for inferring the semantics of policies. The consistency analysis module is used to check the correctness of the integrated policies.

FUTURE RESEARCH DIRECTIONS

Security applications delivered as Cloud-based services could have a dramatic impact on the industry. Cloud computing will enable security controls and functions to be delivered in new ways and by new types of service providers. It will also enable enterprises to use security technologies and techniques that are not otherwise cost-effective. Security as a Service is being used more and more and experiencing a significant growth. However, lack of common standards is causing it to lose the potential economic and competitive benefits. More research is needed to facilitate worldwide implementation of security as an outsourced commodity.

CONCLUSION

Although security issues are delaying the adoption of Cloud computing, it is increasingly being pursued and hence we need to provide security mechanisms to ensure that its benefits are fully realized. Various issues discussed in this chapter show that existing solutions for security and privacy need to be critically reevaluated with regards to their appropriateness for Clouds. Many enhancements in existing solutions as well as more mature and newer, integrated solutions are urgently needed. We have also presented a comprehensive security framework for Cloud computing environments. We have described its components, discussed existing solutions and identified possible approaches to deal with different security issues related to the Cloud.

ACKNOWLEDGMENT

This research has been supported by the US National Science Foundation award IIS-0545912. We would like to thank the anonymous reviewers for their helpful comments.

REFERENCES

Ahn, G. J., Hu, H., & Jin, J. (2009). Security-enhanced OSGi Service Environments. *IEEE Transactions on Systems, Man and Cybernetics. Part C, Applications and Reviews, 39*(5), 562–571. doi:10.1109/TSMCC.2009.2020437

Ahn, G. J., & Sekar, P. (2011). Ontology-based risk evaluation in user-centric identity management. In K. Hagimoto, H. Ueda, & A. Jamalipour (Eds.), IEEE International Conference on Communications (ICC) (pp. 1-5). Kypto, Japan: IEEE Press.

Bertino, E., Paci, F., & Ferrini, R. (2009). Privacy-preserving digital identity management for cloud computing. *IEEE Computer Society Data Engineering Bulletin, 1*(32), 1–4.

Bhatti, R., Joshi, J. B. D., Bertino, E., & Ghafoor, A. (2003). Access control in dynamic XML-based web-services with X-RBAC. In L. J. Zhang (Ed.), First International Conference in Web Services (pp. 243-249). Las Vegas, USA.

Bhatti, R., Joshi, J. B. D., Bertino, E., & Ghafoor, A. (2005). X-GTRBAC: An XML-based policy specification framework and architecture for enterprise-wide access control. [TISSEC]. *ACM Transactions on Information and System Security, 8*(2), 187–227. doi:10.1145/1065545.1065547

Blaze, M., Kannan, S., Lee, I., Sokolsky, O., Smith, J. M., Keromytis, A. D., & Lee, W. (2009). Dynamic trust management. *IEEE Computer, 42*(2), 44–51. doi:10.1109/MC.2009.51

Bruening, P. J., & Treacy, B. C. (2009). Cloud computing: Privacy, security challenges. Privacy & Security Law Report, the Bureau of National Affairs, Inc.

Catteddu, D., & Hogben, G. (2009). Cloud computing: Benefits, risks and recommendations for information security. European Network and Information Security Agency (ENISA) Report. Retrieved August 10, 2011, from http://www.enisa. europa.eu/act/rm/files/deliverables/Cloud-computing-risk-assessment/at_download/fullReport

Chakraborty, S., & Ray, I. (2006). TrustBAC: Integrating trust relationships into the RBAC model for access control in open systems. In I. Ray (Ed.), 11th ACM Symposium on Access Control Models and Technologies (SACMAT06) (pp. 49-58). Tahoe City, UT: ACM Press.

Chen, Y., Paxson, V., & Katz, R. H. (2010). What's new about cloud computing security? Technical Report No. UCB/EECS-2010-5, EECS Department, University of California at Berkeley. Retrieved August 10, 2011, from http://www.eecs.berkeley.edu/Pubs/TechRpts/2010/EECS-2010-5.html

Cloud Security Alliance. (2011). Security guidance for critical areas of focus in cloud computing V3.0. Retrieved December 10, 2011, from https://cloudsecurityalliance.org/guidance/csaguide.v3.0.pdf

Gruschka, N., & Jensen, M. (2010). Attack surfaces: A taxonomy for attacks on cloud services. 3rd IEEE International Conference on Cloud Computing (CLOUD), (pp. 276-279).

Hu, H., Ahn, G. J., & Kulkarni, K. (2011). Ontology-based policy anomaly management for autonomic computing. In C. Pu & J. Caverlee (Eds.), 7th International Conference on Collaborative Computing: Networking, Applications and Worksharing (CollaborateCom2011), Orlando, FL, USA. Berlin, Germany: Springer.

Jaeger, T., & Schiffman, J. (2011). Outlook: Cloudy with a chance of security challenges and improvements. *Security & Privacy*, *8*(1), 77–80. doi:10.1109/MSP.2010.45

Jensen, M., Schwenk, J., Gruschka, N., & Iacono, L. L. (2009). On technical security issues in cloud computing. 2nd IEEE International Conference on Cloud Computing (Cloud 2009), (pp. 109-116). Bangalore, India.

Joshi, J. B. D., Bertino, E., Latif, U., & Ghafoor, A. (2005). A generalized temporal role-based access control model. *IEEE Transactions on Knowledge and Data Engineering*, *17*(1), 4–23. doi:10.1109/TKDE.2005.1

Joshi, J. B. D., Bhatti, R., & Bertino, E., & Ghafoor. (2004). Access control language for multi domain environments. *IEEE Internet Computing*, *8*(6), 40–50. doi:10.1109/MIC.2004.53

Kandukuri, B. R., Paturi, R., & Rakshit, A. (2009). Cloud security issues. In 6th IEEE International Conference on Services Computing (SCC'09), (pp. 517-520). Bangalore, India.

Kim, M., Joshi, J. B. D., & Kim, M. (2008). Access control for cooperation systems based on group situation. In E. Bertino & J. B. D. Joshi (Ed.), 4th International Conference on Collaborative Computing: Networking, Applications and Worksharing (CollaborateCom2008) (pp. 11-23). Berlin. Germany: Springer.

Ko, M., Ahn, G. J., & Shehab, M. (2009). Privacy enhanced user-centric identity management. In G. Fettweis (Ed.), IEEE International Conference on Communications (pp. 1-5). Dresden, Germany: IEEE Press.

Kodali, N. B., Farkas, C., & Wijesekera, D. (2004). Specifying multimedia access control using RDF. Journal of Computer Systems, Science and Engineering, *19*(3).

Mell, P., & Grance, T. (2011). The NIST definition of cloud computing. (NIST Special Publication 800-145). Retrieved August 10, 2011, from http://csrc.nist.gov/publications/nistpubs/800-145/SP800-145.pdf

Shin, D., & Ahn, G. J. (2005). Role-based privilege and trust management. Computer Systems Science & Engineering Journal, *20*(6).

Subramanyan, R., Wong, E., & Yang, H. I. (Eds.). (2010). 34th Annual IEEE Computer Software and Applications Conference Workshops (COMP-SACW 2010) (pp. 393-398), Seoul, South Korea: IEEE Press.

Taghavi Zargar, S., Takabi, H., & Joshi, J. B. D. (2011). DCDIDP: A distributed, collaborative, and data-driven intrusion detection and prevention framework for cloud computing environments. In C. Pu & J. Caverlee (Eds.), 7th International Conference on Collaborative Computing: Networking, Applications and Worksharing (CollaborateCom2011), Orlando, FL, USA. Berlin, Germany: Springer.

Takabi, H., & Joshi, J. B. D. (2010c). StateMiner: An efficient similarity-based approach for optimal mining of role hierarchy. In B. Carminati (Ed.), 15th ACM Symposium on Access Control Models and Technologies (pp. 55-64). Pittsburgh, PA: ACM Press.

Takabi, H., & Joshi, J. B. D. (2012a). Policy management as a service: An approach to manage policy heterogeneity in cloud computing environment. In R. H. Sprague (Ed.), 45th Hawaii International Conference on System Sciences (HICSS). IEEE Press.

Takabi, H., & Joshi, J. B. D. (2012b). Semantic based policy management for cloud computing environments. *International Journal of Cloud Computing, 1*(2), 119–144. doi:10.1504/IJCC.2012.046717

Takabi, H., Joshi, J. B. D., & Ahn, G. J. (2010a). SecureCloud: Towards a comprehensive security framework for cloud computing environments. Cited in S. I. Ahamed, D. H. Bae, S. Cha, C. K. Chang, H. Takabi, J. B. D. Joshi, & G. J. Ahn (Eds.), Security and privacy challenges in cloud computing environments. IEEE Security and Privacy, 8(6), 24-31.

Takabi, H., Kim, M., Joshi, J. B. D., & Spring, M. B. (2009). An architecture for specification and enforcement of temporal access control constraints using OWL. In E. Damiani, S. Proctor, & A. Singal (Ed.), 2009 ACM Workshop on Secure Web Services (pp. 21-28). Chicago, IL: ACM Press.

Teo, L., & Ahn, G. J. (2007). Managing heterogeneous network environments using an extensible policy framework. In R. Deng & P. Samarati (Eds.), 2nd ACM Symposium on Information, Computer and Communications Security (pp. 362-364). Singapore: ACM Press.

Tian, X., Wang, X., & Zhou, A. (2009). DSP re-encryption: A flexible mechanism for access control enforcement management in DaaS. 2nd IEEE International Conference on Cloud Computing (Cloud 2009), (pp. 25-32). Bangalore, India.

Wu, R., Ahn, G. J., & Hu, H. (2012). Towards HIPAA-compliant healthcare systems in cloud computing. 2nd ACM SIGHIT International Health Informatics Symposium (IHI 2012), Miami, Florida, USA. ACM Press.

Yang, X. (2011). QoS-oriented service computing: Bring SOA into cloud environment. In Liu, X. (Ed.), *Advanced design approaches to emerging software systems: Principles, methodology and tools.* Hershey, PA: IGI Global. doi:10.4018/978-1-60960-735-7.ch013

Yang, X., Nasser, B., Surrige, M., & Middleton, S. (2012). *A business-oriented cloud federation model for real time applications. Future Generation Computer Systems.* Elsevier.

Zhang, Y., & Joshi, J. B. D. (2009). Access control and trust management for emerging multidomain environments. In Upadhyaya, S., & Rao, R. O. (Eds.), *Annals of emerging research in information assurance, security and privacy services.* Emerald Group Publishing Limited.

Zhu, Y., Ahn, G. J., Hu, H., Yau, S. S., An, H. G., & Chen, S. (2012a). Dynamic audit services for outsourced storages in clouds. IEEE Transactions on Services Computing, 1-15.

Zhu, Y., Hu, H., Ahn, G. J., Yu, M., & Chen, S. (2012b). Cooperative provable data possession for integrity verification in multi-cloud storage. *IEEE Transactions on Parallel and Distributed Systems*, *99*, 1–14.

ADDITIONAL READING

Ahmed, M., Xiang, Y., & Ali, S. (2010). Above the trust and security in cloud computing: A notion towards innovation. IEEE/IFIP 8th International Conference on Embedded and Ubiquitous Computing (EUC), (pp. 723-730).

Almorsy, M., Grundy, J., & Amani, S. I. (2011). Collaboration-based cloud computing security management framework. IEEE International Conference on Cloud Computing (CLOUD).

Basescu, C., Amarie, A. C., Leordeanu, C., Costan, A., & Antoniu, G. (2011). Managing data access on clouds: A generic framework for enforcing security policies. IEEE International Conference on Advanced Information Networking and Applications (AINA '11).

Bernstein, D., & Vij, D. (2010). InterCloud security considerations. IEEE Second International conference on Cloud Computing Technology and Science (CloudCom), (pp. 537-544).

Celesti, A., Tusa, F., Villari, M., & Puliafito, A. (2010). Security and cloud computing: InterCloud identity management infrastructure. 19th IEEE International Workshop on Enabling Technologies: Infrastructures for Collaborative Enterprises (WETICE), (pp. 263-265).

Christodorescu, M., Sailer, R., Schales, D. L., Sgandurra, D., & Zamboni, D. (2009). Cloud security is not (just) virtualization security. 2009 ACM Workshop on Cloud Computing Security (CCSW '09).

Deng, M., Milan, P., Marco, N., & Ilaria, B. (2011). A home healthcare system in the cloud--Addressing security and privacy challenges. IEEE International Conference on Cloud Computing (CLOUD), (pp. 549-556).

Di Modica, G., & Tomarchio, O. (2011). Semantic security policy matching in service oriented architectures. In D. S. Milojicic & M. Kirchburg (Eds.), 2011 IEEE World Congress on Services (pp. 399-405). Washington, DC: IEEE Press.

Dowell, S., Barreto, A., Michael, J. B., & Man-Tak, S. (2011). Cloud to cloud interoperability. In I. Ray (Ed.), 6th International Conference On System of Systems Engineering (SoSE) (pp. 49-58). Tahoe City, CA: ACM Press.

Echeverria, V., Liebrock, L. M., & Shin, D. (2010). Permission Management System: Permission as a service in cloud computing. In S. I. Ahamed, D. H. Bae, S. Cha, C. K. Chang, R. Subramanyan, E. Wong & H. I. Yang (Eds.), 34th Annual Computer Software and Applications Conference Workshops (COMPSACW '10) (pp. 371-375). Seoul, Korea: IEEE Press.

Gansen, Z., Chunming, R., Gilje, J. M., & Eika, S. F. (2010). Deployment models: Towards eliminating security concerns from Cloud computing. International Conference on High Performance Computing and Simulation (HPCS), (pp. 189-195).

Grobauer, B., Walloschek, T., & Stocker, E. (2011). Understanding cloud computing vulnerabilities. *IEEE Security & Privacy*, *9*(2), 50–57. doi:10.1109/MSP.2010.115

Haoyong, L., & Yin, H. (2011). Analysis and research about cloud computing security protect policy. International Conference on Intelligence Science and Information Engineering (ISIE), (pp. 214-216).

Hu, Y. J., Wu, W. N., & Yang, J. J. (2011). Semantics-enabled policies for information sharing and protection in the cloud. In A. Datta, R. Rogers, & S. Shulman (Eds.), 3rd International Conference on Social Informatics (SocInfo'11) (pp. 49-58). Singapore.

Itani, W., Kayssi, A., & Chehab, A. (2009). Privacy as a service: Privacy-aware data storage and processing in cloud computing architectures. 8th IEEE International Conference on Dependable, Autonomic and Secure Computing (DASC '09), (pp. 711–716).

Jansen, W. A. (2011). Cloud hooks: Security and privacy issues in cloud computing. 44th Hawaii International Conference on System Sciences (HICSS), (pp. 1-10).

Jasti, A., Shah, P., Nagaraj, R., & Pendse, R. (2010). Security in multi-tenancy cloud. IEEE International Carnahan Conference on Security Technology (ICCST), (pp. 35-41).

Jensen, M., Schäge, S., & Schwenk, J. (2010). Towards an anonymous access control and accountability scheme for cloud computing. In W. Chou & A. M. Goscinski (Eds.), 3rd International Conference on Cloud Computing (Cloud '10) (pp. 540-541), Miami, FL: IEEE Press.

Jia, W., Zhu, H., Cao, Z., Wei, L., & Lin, X. (2011). SDSM: A secure data service mechanism in mobile Cloud computing. IEEE Conference on Computer Communications Workshops (INFOCOM WKSHPS), (pp. 1060-1065).

Jing, X., & Jian-Jun, Z. (2010). A brief survey on the security model of cloud computing. 9th International Symposium on Distributed Computing and Applications to Business, Engineering and Science (DCABES '10).

Jung, Y., & Chung, M. (2010). Adaptive security management model in the cloud computing environment. 12th International Conference on Advanced Communication Technology (ICACT), Vol. 2, (pp. 1664-1669).

Kandukuri, B. R., Paturi, R., & Rakshit, A. (2009). Cloud security issues. 6th IEEE International Conference on Services Computing (SCC'09), (pp. 517-520). Bangalore, India.

Kim, A., McDermott, J., & Myong, K. (2010). Security and architectural issues for national security cloud computing. 30th IEEE International Conference on Distributed Computing Systems Workshops (ICDCSW), (pp. 21-25).

Kretzschmar, M., Mario, G., & Sebastian, H. (2011). Security management areas in the intercloud. IEEE International Conference on Cloud Computing (CLOUD), (pp. 762-763).

Li, J., Zhao, G., Chen, X., Xie, D., Rong, C., Li, W., et al. (2010). Fine-grained data access control systems with user accountability in cloud computing. In G. Zhao & J. Qiu (Ed.), Second International Conference on Cloud Computing Technology and Science (CloudCom '10) (pp. 89-96). Indianapolis, IN: IEEE Press.

Li, Y., Shi, Y., Guo, Y., & Ma, W. (2010). Multi-tenancy based access control in cloud. In Y. He (Ed.), 2010 International Conference on Computational Intelligence and Software Engineering (CiSE) (pp. 1-4). Wuhan, China: IEEE Press.

Liu, J., Wan, Z., & Gu, M. (2011). Hierarchical attribute-set based encryption for scalable, flexible and fine-grained access control in Cloud computing. In F. Bao & J. Weng (Eds.), 7th International Conference on Information Security Practice and Experience (SPEC'11) (pp. 98-107). China: Springer.

Meiko, J., Jorg, S., Jens-Matthias, B., Nils, G., & Luigi Lo, I. (2011). Security prospects through cloud computing by adopting multiple clouds. IEEE International Conference on Cloud Computing (CLOUD), (pp. 565-572).

Na, S. H., Park, J. Y., & Huh, E. N. (2010). Personal cloud computing security framework. IEEE Asia-Pacific Services Computing Conference (APSCC), (pp. 671-675).

Nguyen, T. D., Gondree, M. A., Shifflett, D. J., Khosalim, J., Levin, T. E., & Irvine, C. E. (2010). A cloud-oriented cross-domain security architecture. Military Communications Conference (MILCOM 2010), (pp. 441-447).

Pearson, S., & Benameur, A. (2010). Privacy, security and trust issues arising from cloud computing. IEEE 2nd International Conference on Cloud Computing Technology and Science (CloudCom), (pp. 693-702).

Popa, L., Yu, M., & Ko, S. Y. (2010). CloudPolice: Taking access control out of the network. Hotnets '10.

Prasad, P., Ojha, B., Shahi, R. R., Lal, R., Vaish, A., & Goel, U. (2011). 3 dimensional security in Cloud computing. 3rd International Conference on Computer Research and Development (ICCRD), (pp. 198-201).

Prasadreddy, P. V. G. D., Srinivasa, R. T., & Phani, V. S. (2011). A threat free architecture for privacy assurance in cloud computing. IEEE World Congress on Services (SERVICES), (pp. 564-568).

Preiya, V. S., & Pavithra, R. (2011). Secure role based data access control in cloud computing. *International Journal of Computer Trends and Technology, 1*(2).

Sabahi, F. (2011). Cloud computing security threats and responses. IEEE 3rd International Conference on Communication Software and Networks (ICCSN), (pp. 245-249).

Sandhu, R., Boppana, R., Krishnan, R., Reich, J., Wolff, T., & Zachry, J. (2010). Towards a discipline of mission-aware cloud computing. 2010 ACM Workshop on Cloud Computing Security Workshop (CCSW '10).

Santos, N., Gummadi, K. P., & Rodrigues, R. (2011). Towards trusted cloud computing. Proceedings of the 2009 Conference on Hot Topics in Cloud Computing.

Sasaki, T., Nakae, M., & Ogawa, R. (2010). Content oriented virtual domains for secure information sharing across organizations. 2010 ACM Workshop on Cloud Computing Security Workshop (CCSW '10).

Sengupta, S., Kaulgud, V., & Sharma, V. S. (2011). Cloud computing security--Trends and research directions. In Y. He (Ed.), 2011 IEEE World Congress on Services (pp. 524-531). Washington, DC: IEEE Press.

Srivastava, P., Singh, S., Pinto, A. A., Verma, S., Chaurasiya, V. K., & Gupta, R. (2011). An architecture based on proactive model for security in Cloud computing. 2011 International Conference on Recent Trends in Information Technology (ICRTIT), (pp. 661-666).

Tchifilionova, V. (2010). Security and privacy implications of Cloud computing: Lost in the Cloud. IFIP WG 11.4 International Conference on Open Research Problems in Network Security (iNetSec'10).

Tsai, W., & Shao, Q. (2011). Role-based access-control using reference ontology in clouds. 10th International Symposium on Autonomous Decentralized Systems (ISADS), (pp. 121-128).

Verma, A., & Kaushal, S. (2011). Cloud computing security issues and challenges: A survey. *ACM Transactions on Information and System Security*, *193*(4), 445–454.

Wang, G., Liu, Q., & Wu, J. (2010). Hierarchical attribute-based encryption for fine-grained access control in Cloud storage services. 17th ACM Conference on Computer and Communications Security (CCS '10).

Wu, R., Ahn, G. J., Hu, H., & Singhal, M. (2010). Information flow control in Cloud computing. 6th International Conference on Collaborative Computing: Networking, Applications and Worksharing (CollaborateCom), (pp. 1-7).

Yu, Sh., Wang, C., Ren, K., & Lou, W. (2010). Achieving secure, scalable, and fine-grained data access control in Cloud computing. In M. C. Chuah, R. Cohen, & G. Xue (Eds.), 29th Conference on Information Communications (Infocom'10) (pp. 1-9). San Diego, CA: IEEE Press.

KEY TERMS AND DEFINITIONS

Access Control: Access control systems provide the essential services of authorization that determines what actions a subject is allowed to do on an object. In access control systems, subjects are the entities that perform actions and objects are the entities representing resources on which the action is performed.

Cloud Computing: Cloud computing is a model for enabling ubiquitous, convenient, on-demand network access to a shared pool of configurable computing resources (e.g., networks, servers, storage, applications, and services) that can be rapidly provisioned and released with minimal management effort or service provider interaction.

Cloud Service Provider: A Cloud service provider is an entity that offers one or more Cloud based services that are used by Cloud users.

Interoperability: Interoperability refers to the ability of systems to work together, exchange information, and use the exchanged information without any restricted access or implementation.

Policy Management: The process of defining, modifying and managing access control policies in a system is called policy management.

Semantic Heterogeneity: Semantic heterogeneity means that different entities in a system have differences in interpretation of the meaning of data.

Semantic Interoperability: Semantic interoperability is the ability of computer systems to communicate information in a way that the exchanged information can be automatically and meaningfully interpreted by the receiving system the same as the transmitting system intended. In order to achieve semantic interoperability, both systems should use a common information exchange reference model and they should derive the same inferences from the same information.

Section 3
Service–Oriented Approaches

Chapter 8
Service Design and Process Design for the Logistics Mall Cloud

Sebastian Steinbuß
Fraunhofer ISST, Germany

Norbert Weißenberg
Fraunhofer ISST, Germany

ABSTRACT

This chapter presents some actual results from two big German Cloud projects: the Leading-Edge Cluster project Service Design Studio and the associated Fraunhofer Innovation Cluster Cloud Computing for Logistics. Existing services can be enhanced using the Service Design Studio environment and then be deployed and offered in the Logistics Mall, which may combine them using process models. To reach these objectives, different standards are combined for service description in functional and business view, business object description in domain and technical view, and process model description on different abstraction levels. First results are already in use by the logistics industry. These innovations together have the potential to advance the logistics market towards modern IT strategies. Flexible, individual logistics business process models allow small and medium enterprises a technological catch up with large companies and to focus on their core business.

INTRODUCTION

For many markets, logistics is a cost factor and a competitive factor. In Germany, it has a volume of more than 200 billion €/year. It is Germany's third-largest sector following the automotive industry and mechanical engineering. Most logistics companies (over 90 percent) are SMEs (small and medium enterprises) in Germany.

The flexibility and dynamics of logistics business processes has reached a level which can no longer be handled by conventional forms of organization - efficient IT solutions are mandatory. Most logistics companies, especially SMEs, do not have sufficient IT expertise, capacity or capital required to close the gap between requirements and status quo in logistics IT. SMEs usually have small IT departments with a small number of employees

DOI: 10.4018/978-1-4666-2854-0.ch008

and limited capabilities. Deficits include outdated technologies, high, fixed costs of IT operations, poor documentation, security deficits, expensive licensing models, high maintenance efforts, and many contract partners. A flexible adjustment of business processes and interfaces is complex, lengthy, expensive and risky.

Cloud computing (especially in SaaS models) and BPM (business process management) are able to solve most of these problems, but there are serious barriers to an enterprise-wide use of BPM software: cost, resource availability, feature/function limitations and cultural barriers (Silver, 2009): BPM software (on premise) often is expensive in license and maintenance cost and new IT resources are often needed to cover peak loads. High cost per employee and extensive training is needed and the ROI is initially unproven. As BPM aims at change and optimization of business processes, it provokes resistance about possible risks.

BPM software in the Cloud (BPaaS) reduces these barriers. Its goal is to raise BPM from isolated projects to a broad pragmatic enterprise-wide deployment. BPaaS enables usage-based pricing without initial cost or maintenance cost (which reduces TCO) as well as on demand dynamical scaling of virtualized resources and tools being available over the net.

Especially for SMEs with few staff and limited financial resources it is important to respond quickly and inexpensively to changing circumstances. Their business people should be empowered by simple Web tools to build process models from available domain-specific building blocks, redesign and experiment and iteratively improve and deploy process models easily and quickly with low cost and low risk. This requires BPaaS techniques to be able to bridge the business IT gap, as described in this chapter.

Cloud computing is considered as a megatrend, which will have an impact on the use of information technology in all application domains. In their report on the future of Cloud computing (Jeffrey & Neidecker-Lutz, 2010) a European expert group identifies the provisioning of application-area-specific Cloud services, also called "vertical Clouds", as a significant business opportunity. The Leading-Edge Cluster LogisticsRuhr (http://www.effizienzcluster.de) shares this view and has declared the development of a domain-specific logistics Cloud as a strategic objective. It is Germany's biggest logistics research initiative including 120 enterprises and 11 research institutes. The use of modern information technology for logistics is summarized in its leading topic logistics-as-a-service. With the use of Cloud technologies and service-oriented architecture (SOA) principles, the Service Design Studioi, as one of about thirty projects in the LogisticsRuhr cluster, together with the associated Fraunhofer Innovation Cluster Logistics Mall (http://www.ccl.fraunhofer.de/en.html) are targeting the individualization of logistics business processes and services by standardization of reference services, process model fragments and business objects.

The Logistics Mall (Holtkamp et al., 2010) available today (http://www.logistics-mall.com) is a Cloud-based virtual marketplace for logistics applications and a usage environment for rented logistics applications hosted in a community Cloud (according to the NIST definition of Cloud computing (Mell & Grance, 2009)). It is currently extended towards also selling and using services and process models to orchestrate applications, services and people in the Cloud. By using offers from the Logistics Mall, investment in an own infrastructure and the corresponding know-how can largely be avoided. Demand-driven access to rented customized software and services via standard Web browsers becomes possible. After contract signing, billing is done based on resource usage; the user does not pay for unused features. This contrasts expensive license fees for monolithic, multi-featured logistics applications on premise, like a warehouse management system available today. Such systems are successively replaced by smaller interoperable subsystems, provided as services and combined by customer-individual process models. Additionally, on the provider side, even smaller logistics service providers may quickly realize service offers for the Mall.

The Service Design Studio expects the emergence of Cloud-oriented service marketplaces (Stemmer 2011), like the Logistics Mall, in the next few years. These Cloud-oriented service marketplaces will appear for different domains and in different countries with different laws. The Service Design Studio addresses service providers who want to offer their services on several marketplaces (e.g., the Logistics Mall). While the functional abilities of these services stay the same, the non-functional properties may differ. Non-functional properties can be the pricing, security constraints or offered service level agreements (SLAs). A Cloud-oriented service marketplace may support different payment modalities, security abilities, e.g. encryption or authentication methods, or quality of service (QoS). On the other hand, a service provider has a certain business model for the services offered. The business model must be adapted to the target runtime, i.e. the Cloud-oriented service marketplace. There is no appropriate tool for these tasks available nowadays. The Service Design Studio provides this functionality and demonstrates the technical feasibility of this approach.

The general objective of creating a SOA in combination with Cloud platforms is facing many challenges. By choosing the logistics domain, the Service Design Studio and the Logistics Mall profit from several existing standards, like SCOR, the Supply Chain Operations Reference (Supply Chain Council, 2011) or OAGIS, the Open Applications Group Integration Specification (Open Applications Group, 2011). The results can finally be transferred to other domains. Service design and process model design for traditional SOA is different from SOA in Clouds. Services are traded on Cloud-based marketplaces and need – in addition to a functional service description in e.g. Web Service Description Language (WSDL) – a non-functional service description to offer information

about the costs and price model of a service call, the guaranteed service levels or security constraints. Process model design for Clouds must be flexible and must address the needs of logistics experts, not IT experts. Current approaches like USDL, the Universal Service Description Language (Barros & Oberle, 2012) for service design and BPMN 2.0, the Business Process Model and Notation (OMG, 2011) for process model design do not fit all identified needs. Other approaches target challenges like message routing (Baude et al., 2010) to enable SOA in the Cloud.

This chapter combines these techniques to solve the problems mentioned in the beginning. The rest of this chapter is organized as follows. We give some background on related work, followed by an overview of the Logistics Mall, and a brief overview of existing logistics standards used by the Service Design Studio and the Logistics Mall. Subsequently, service design for Cloud marketplaces and the need for a holistic service description and for interoperation of applications and services in the Cloud are discussed. A flexible way to realize such interoperation requires business process management. We then present an approach closing the gap between business and IT being typical in BPM solutions, which has two fundamental pillars: a standards-based business object model for the logistics domain with coupled business and IT views, and a business process modeling approach using pre-implemented building blocks – the offers from the Logistics Mall. The chapter closes with our future research directions and a summary of the results achieved so far.

BACKGROUND

There are only few research projects and approaches treating process model execution in the Cloud, especially for the logistics domain. None of them achieved the goal of filling the business-IT gap: The InterlogGrid project (http://www.interloggrid. org) uses Grid technology for fragmented logistics applications, which also results in scalable systems. It concentrates on CPU-intensive functions and there is no shop. The Logistic Service Bus project (http://www.lsb-plattform.de) supported by German BMBF performs general research on IT systems for logistics. The service-oriented application platform for Logistics (SOA4LOG, http://v02.viom-system.de/soa4log) develops a modular online platform with domain-specific components, but uses a platform-internal data model, no standard. ADiWa (Alliance Digital Product Flow, http://www.adiwa.net) analyses intelligent business process models based on the Internet of Things and RFID-tagged products. It focusses on orchestration networks of transport using real-time information from the Internet of Things and has no Cloud aspect. ADEPT2 (Göser et al., 2006) focusses on dynamic change of running processes and migration of running processes to new process models, and also supports a plug-and-play mechanism for application integration by selecting operations of orchestrated components from a repository and use them as activities in a process model. However, it has no Cloud focus and is not based on a domain business object model but complex types are simply of type Object. The Cloud development platform RunMyProcess (http://www.runmyprocess.com) available in the Google Apps marketplace provides multi-tenant drag-and-drop design of workflows for orchestration of Google Apps. However, it does not address the business IT gap.

Concerning service Cloud and service marketplaces, the following approaches are noteworthy: InDiNet (http://www.software-cluster.org/en/projects/joint-projects/indinet-en) as part of the Leading-Edge Software Cluster focusses on innovative services for the future Internet, which can be distributed on marketplaces with new business models. The target is the development of a generic platform based on proven practice. The main research areas are quality management and generic interoperability. The TEXO project being part of the THESEUS program (http://www.theseus-programm.de/en) of the German Federal Ministry of Economics and Technology develops an infrastructure for the Internet of services (http://www.internet-of-services.com). It focusses on USDL and the corresponding tools. Main results from TEXO are the USDL specification, the USDL editor and a Service Delivery Platform (SDF). The USDL editor is an eclipse-based tool which is compliant to the USDL specification. As a target platform for USDL, the SDF contains an execution environment and a marketplace for USDL-based services. Other European projects like RESERVOIR (http://62.149.240.97), SLA@SOI (http://sla-at-soi.eu), SOA4ALL (http://www.soa4all.eu) and others were involved in the emergence of USDL.

For more background information see the Additional Reading section.

SERVICE DESIGN AND PROCESS DESIGN FOR THE LOGISTICS MALL CLOUD

Overview of the Logistics Mall

The Fraunhofer Innovation Cluster "Logistics Mall – Cloud Computing for Logistics", founded by Fraunhofer Institute for Material Flow and Logistics (IML) and Fraunhofer Institute for Software and Systems Engineering (ISST) in cooperation with TU Dortmund, supports logistics companies to meet the requirements sketched in the introduction.

The basic idea is "logistics on demand". Customers benefit from cost and performance transparency by the pay-per-use and SaaS principle of the Cloud. This creates the opportunity to acquire a wide range of services from one source - the Logistics Mall. Providers benefit from an IaaS/PaaS infrastructure (Mell & Grance, 2009), in which a multitude of Cloud-based logistics-related services and software can be offered and even orchestrated using business process models.

In market studies (Fraunhofer IML, 2010) it was found that such a solution is appreciated by both logistics users and logistics application providers.

The Mall is both a virtual market place for logistics IT applications, services, and processes and a customizable platform for using ordered products in the Cloud. This is supported by its main components:

- The Mall Market Place (MMP), being the shop for the logistics industry
- The Customized Access Framework (CAF), being the product access and operation platform of a customer

Already today (http://www.logistics-mall.com), existing applications are made available in the Mall. These applications may communicate through customer-driven data and interface converters.

This chapter is about the current extensions of the Mall. Logistics modules can be combined via standardized business objects and standards-based message exchange. The Mall will offer the possibility to acquire and run individual services and individual logistics process chains in the Cloud. It then provides an infrastructure to design individual customer process models via a graphical modeling tool. IT suppliers offer their software and services in the Mall and logistics process designers may combine these building blocks using process models.

To be able to sell and use applications via the Mall (Logistics-as-a-Product), they initially have to be adapted to the Mall's Cloud infrastructure. Migrating applications into the Mall may also involve steps for:

- Interoperation with other applications (Logistics-as-a-Service, combinable with other services)
- Process-based coordination of applications (Logistics-by-Design of process models)

As shown in Figure 1, there are two kinds of interfaces an application (or service) has to support: a Cloud interface to integrate with the Mall Cloud (supporting e.g. SSO and portlet integration), and an orthogonal interoperation interface to integrate with other applications, being inside or outside the Cloud, which can be used by individual process models. These interfaces use defined Mall interoperation standards based on established business standards and an interoperation infrastructure. Gsell and Nagel (2012) provide a detailed overview of the technical aspects of the Logistics Mall.

We currently use a cluster of virtual machines hosted by the Mall operator, using VMware vSphere 4.1 ESX for server virtualization. This

Figure 1. Application migration interface

is the basis for gaining Cloud characteristics such as defined in (Mell & Grance, 2009) and also for portability to public Cloud platforms. We successfully ported the Mall for example to Amazon EC2.

Standardization of Services, Business Process Models, and Business Objects

There are several existing reference process models, services and business objects for the logistics domain: e.g. the SCOR reference model (Supply Chain Council, 2011) describes typical logistics supply chain process patterns. It is an abstract process definition adaptable to the needs of a company. SCOR process models consist of sets of reference activities on different abstraction levels which can finally be refined for a specific company and which can be implemented using services and manual tasks.

OAGIS (Open Applications Group, 2011) is an eBusiness transaction standard including a detailed technical business object model, which covers many typical business objects from logistics and many related domains like finance and manufacturing. It is a Web EDI format and also defines interface services to be implemented by applications (Holby & Trieneckens, 2010). Like SCOR, OAGIS leaves the details of these implementations to the application. Hence, it is necessary to refine these abstract definitions to achieve an executable set of interoperable services. Since OAGIS is very complex, we add a logistics domain model as an abstract view.

The SCOR process reference model together with its BPMN 2.0 refinements (OMG, 2011) as well as the logistics domain model together with its mapped detailed OAGIS business object model is good scaffolding for modeling logistics processes to be executed within the Logistics Mall.

Beneath the definition of a process reference model, SCOR provides a standard alignment to software features and functionality (Huan, 2004). Thus there are standardized services defined in the SCOR model for distinct SCOR processes. Although these services are not necessarily mapped to a technical representation, e.g. WSDL, a clear mapping to an implementation can be found (Huan, 2005). For services beyond the SCOR model a standardized representation can be achieved by the requesting community, like the customers and user group of the Logistics Mall.

Service Design for Cloud Marketplaces

A Cloud-oriented service-marketplace like the Logistics Mall supports three central features. The underlying foundation is a Cloud infrastructure, as described above. Based on the Cloud infrastructure, there is an execution environment for applications, services and processes, which hereby have access to value-added or reusable services of the marketplace, like user management or a billing infrastructure (Zhang & Zhou, 2009). This is the platform for the marketplace. The platforms may differ in the amount and in the abilities of the provided value-added services or in the type and the abilities of the underlying execution environment and infrastructure. On top of such a marketplace, there is a trading service or a shop frontend, which extends the functionality of a service registry. While a service registry can find a service provider by the functional abilities, a trading service offers searching by non-functional properties. A human or a machine can make a lookup for a service and the registry then returns a set of services implementing appropriate methods.

With a trading service the search can be refined by non-functional aspects like the costs of a service call, service level agreements and security aspects like ciphering or authentication. These aspects must be attached to the WSDL functional service description, e.g. by using USDL (Barros & Oberle, 2012; see also W3C, 2005) from the Theseus TEXO project (Theseus, 2011; see also SAP AG, 2011). The description of these aspects must be interpretable by the trading service to support semantic search and must be executable by the execution environment provided by the marketplace. Security constraints must be enforced and the service calls can be charged. Nowadays, it is usual to create the functional part of a service description, done by a developer. The non-functional part of a service description should be created by a service designer, which needs other skills than a developer. The service designer knows about the business model for a service, the contracts with the specific marketplace provider and the expectations of his customers, which must be mapped to the SLAs. These essential non-functional properties may be complemented by special non-functional properties like the carbon footprint of the service, e.g. for a package delivery service, or the availability of a certificate, e.g. the International Food Logistics Standard. Therefore, the service designer needs a tool to create a holistic service description with a functional and a non-functional part, which can be exported to different service-marketplaces and execution environments.

The Service Design Studio focusses on a holistic modeling of services, the export of services to trading services as core components of a Cloud-oriented service-marketplace and the enforcement of non-functional aspects in SOA and Cloud execution environments. Non-functional aspects are arranged as a set of envelopes around the service description in the core (see Figure 2). The functional description of the service contains a domain part in natural language, displayed in a shopping frontend for a human reader, and a technical part, e.g. a WSDL description.

For the creation of a holistic service description it is necessary to develop a tool which supports the design steps as described above. The tool Service Design Studio (SDS) is a Java-based Web application. The core functionality is implemented by an integrated editor. In addition, it offers repositories to store service descriptions, aspects, aspect templates, target platforms and user-related data. Furthermore, a basic support for collaborative work is planned.

The tool SDS imports aspects, aspect templates and supported target platforms. An aspect is the

design-time representation of the non-functional aspect envelope. While an aspect is not configured, an aspect template is pre-configured in a reusable way, e.g. a pricing aspect with monthly base fee, where the service designer only needs to configure the fee amount. A configured aspect bound to a service is named aspect instance.

To attach non-functional aspect envelopes to a service description, the service designer imports a WSDL into the SDS. In the SDS editor the envelopes can be attached by drag and drop and the service description part in natural language can be edited. When binding the service to a certain target platform the SDS checks if all configured aspects can be executed by the selected platform. If the holistic service description is valid, the service can be exported to the marketplace and to the execution environment of the target platform (see Figure 3). In addition to this core functionality, the SDS has management functions for integrated repositories, a basic user and rights management and an integrated help system.

The SDS converts the imported WSDL to an internal format, the semantic service description, which can store the information on aspects, their configuration and the target platforms. It is used internally and can be converted to the requested format of a target platform. It is compatible to USDL (Barros & Oberle, 2012) to support a ge-

Figure 2. Service encapsulated with non-functional aspects as envelopes

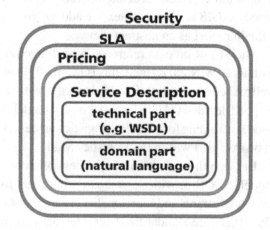

Figure 3. Overview service design studio (tool)

neric, vendor-neutral format. In contrast to USDL, it can assign an aspect to the methods of a service, not only to the whole service. This facilitates the reuse of aspect templates. Aspects are assignable to methods, to a whole service or both, e.g. the pricing aspect is assignable to the whole service, while the security aspect can be assigned to both. Furthermore, aspects can be differentiated by feasibility. An aspect like pricing or security is displayed in the marketplace and must be executed by the execution environment in conjunction with a value-added service like a billing service or a security token service. Another type of aspect does only have a representation in the marketplace, similar to a marking interface in a programming language. An aspect which indicates the availability of a certain certificate, e.g. about the carbon footprint of the service, should be displayed in a shopping frontend or must be readable by a service consumer from the trading service. These kinds of aspects have no impact on the execution of the service.

The core concept of the SDS is proven in a prototype implementation which includes the SDS tool, the semantic service description and the aspects billing and security. A reference implementation of a target platform includes a simple marketplace (SDS-Mall) instead of trading service and an execution environment. The trading service will be added in a next step. The execution environment is based on existing implementations of the WS*-specifications, like WS-Trust and WS-Policies. The compatibility to these standards enables existing SOA platforms to act as underlying platforms for a Cloud-oriented service marketplace. Subsidiarily to the compatibility to USDL, a service can be deployed to USDL-compliant target platforms.

A Cloud-oriented service marketplace will succeed if it provides support for basic services, which are the scaffolding for higher-level services. One important class of services are application interface services or application adapters, which can be interpreted as services being implemented by an application. OAGIS includes sample Web services for all defined business objects, which can be implemented as adapter services. These services are the basis for a flexible application interoperation controlled by process models. Another class of services important for logistics is periphery services. Logistics systems are often directly connected to the real world, e.g. reading and printing barcodes or accessing RFID tags (Holtkamp et al., 2010). These devices are located on premise and are addressable by periphery services in the Cloud. The Logistics Mall supports the asynchronous communication with some basic periphery devices, like (handheld) scanners and printers. While scanners act like sensors which collect data, printers act like actors. These principles can also be used with other devices which communicate asynchronously. Value-added services offered on a marketplace, e.g. data converters or monitoring services, enrich the use of these devices and make the marketplace more attractive to end-users and service providers.

The Leading-Edge Cluster LogisticsRuhr consists of 30 projects. More than the half of these projects is developing Web-based software. The Service Design Studio is developing technologies and a tool which enables these applications to become distributable on the Logistics Mall or similar Cloud-oriented service marketplaces. In conjunction with other services or applications offered in the Logistics Mall, customers cannot only choose the services used in their business processes by functional abilities, but also by non-functional aspects. The semantic service description of the SDS contains information about a service, its aspects and target platforms. With an export to a certain platform the tethered value-added service gets configured. In fact the security provider and the billing service of the Logistics Mall get configured when deploying to the Logistics Mall. A deployment on another platform like the SDS-Mall analogously configures the value-added services of this platform. The Service Design Studio simplifies the deployment to a Cloud-oriented service marketplace like the Logistics Mall.

In the logistics-specific subprojects of the Leading-Edge Cluster LogisticsRuhr, many logistics services will be developed (based on a commonly developed logistics business objects model), which can finally be offered in the Logistics Mall and used in business process models.

Iscan and Flake (2012) discuss the technical details of the execution environment of the Service Design Studio and the mapping of aspects to WS*.

Cloud-Based Interoperation of Applications and Services

Logistics services or applications like a warehouse management system, a transport management system or ERP (enterprise resource planning) systems and even smaller logistics modules and services, which we call apps are seldom used stand-alone – they have to interoperate, e.g. by exchanging messages. Interoperation is needed for different applications of a customer all available via the Mall (i.e., in the Cloud), but also between applications in the Cloud and applications the customer already uses on premise. Both scenarios are already shown in Figure 1.

Widely accepted e-business standards are central for interoperation of applications – they are used on top of technical interoperation standards. Not only the business objects exchanged need to be standardized to ease communication with different kinds and instances of other applications, the protocol steps also have to be considered.

Today, many e-business standards exist. We compared and evaluated transaction standards and selected OAGIS (OAGi, 2011), the Open Application Group Integration Specification. The reasons are:

- It is a powerful, adaptable and extensible horizontal standard, based on Core Component Technical Specification CCTS (UN/CEFACT, 2009) and many other standards.
- It is mature (first version in 1996, now version 9.5) and in real use (broad industrial support in many countries).

- A logistics module and many logistics-related definitions already exist (e.g. container, shipment, item, pick list), only few extensions are needed.
- It is technology-neutral, but includes Web service definitions, and there is a Cloud initiative.
- EDIFACT formats (in widespread use) are convertible to OAGIS.

The benefit of using such a widely accepted standard is that the format of most messages ever needed is already defined based on the long experience of a large expert group. Only few definitions have to be added, based on the standard's extension mechanism. These definitions are in turn based on CCTS and its Core Component Library CCL, a mature reservoir of components used as semantically described building blocks in OAGIS and several other standards. Thanks to its many optional attributes, even simple messages can be exchanged conformant to the standard. However, if special information is needed, its position and format is already defined, thus minimizing data mapping needs.

This enables a stable, standards-based interoperation interface of applications or services, initially implemented as needed (filling only needed data elements) and subsequently completed as needed. The same standardized interface can be used for many different partners, and additional EDI converters can be provided due to the widespread use of this format in the logistics domain.

OAGIS defines several BODs (business object documents) exchanged between applications. Each BOD is composed of an ApplicationArea (the document header) and a DataArea, consisting of a verb and a noun. The verbs define actions to be performed on the nouns, which represent the main business objects, visible in the application or service interface.

For each noun, there is a Web service having methods representing all meaningful verbs of that noun. BODs are used as message formats for these methods. OAGIS comes with sample WSDL definitions (the OAGIS services).

For each application or service running in or outside the Mall, its required OAGIS services can be implemented e.g. towards the enterprise service bus (ESB) used in the Mall, or simply by using message exchange. It can communicate with other application also implementing such standard interfaces (or via an EDI converter).

Closing the Gap between Business and IT in Business Process Management

Most BPM toolsets have different tools for process modeling by domain experts (phase 1 in Figure 4, modeling a business process using activities A1, A2, etc.) and for the later implementation of these process models by IT personal (phase 2, implementing each Ai by some implementation Ii, e.g. by a service call). But for the Logistics Mall our vision is to deploy and execute modeled business processes by a click of a button, not involving IT knowledge or IT personal. This is only possible, if we model with already implemented building blocks with standard interfaces using standardized data formats. In this case we have a phase inversion, also depicted by Figure 4: the application or service provider (i.e. the provider of I1, I2, etc.) not only provides normal metadata, but also process model-related metadata for his offer (phase 1). This serves as an implementation of a process model fragment. Process modeling and modifications of process models are then the following steps. The modeled process is always directly executable, since it uses implemented building blocks using standardized data models in its interfaces.

BPMN 2.0 optimally supports this idea, since it uses the same notation for process modeling and for process model deployment and execution. The latter has additional attributes set in its standardized exchange format BPMN 2.0 XML. Here, the task description with all implementation-relevant attributes of the process-relevant service metadata is inserted for the modeled tasks.

Moreover, the idea is also practical in the context of the Logistics Mall, since the scope of its process models is limited to the logistics domain, limited in complexity (if complex logic is seen in the applications) and even stronger limited to only orchestrate concrete applications and services offered via the Logistics Mall. Basic services (such as a mail service) will be offered for free, to get a critical mass of building blocks.

Nicholas Carr (2003) wrote: "IT Doesn't Matter": companies cannot achieve competitive advantage only through the use of IT, since IT is no limited resource and other companies may use similar IT (but perhaps not SMEs due to the cost factor of IT). Such benefits only arise because a company does something better than others, concerning their business strategies. The approach presented here refutes this argument, since companies may flexibly and quickly map their respective business peculiarities of various departments directly to IT. Any IT which flexibly allows realizing and changing core business strategies does matter.

There is a second building block to close the gap: the logistics business object model (BO model). It follows the same principle in its two views. There is an abstract domain view defined by UML diagrams, which hides the complex details of the underlying OAGIS Logistics Overlay. The abstract model was constructed based on the technical standard (again some kind of phase inversion) by several logistics experts of Fraunhofer IML and in conjunction with other Leading-Edge Cluster logistics projects, to assert both the refinement relation of the two models and at the same time the understandability by domain experts. While the technical model is in English only, both the domain model and the application or service metadata and process metadata are multilingual

and commented (descriptions can be displayed in the process modeler in a selected language). The domain views are only used during process modeling. When the model is stored, the mapping is executed as needed (setting values of some attributes in the standard BPMN 2.0 XML exchange format) and no more necessary at runtime.

We call this the double barbell principle, since for both, behavior (the process model) as well as data structure (the business objects), the corresponding domain view and technical view are closely related in advance like a barbell (compare Figure 5). The technical views cannot be constructed as a later refinement (of arbitrary BOs or activities), since no IT personal should be involved. Instead, the barbells are constructed only once by the providers of applications and then reused in any process models. The standard BO model is important to avoid complex data mappings, as the standard activity model is to avoid complex implementation. Both are done only once, not for any new process model or model changes. This is especially important in a Cloud environment, since Web interfaces for the implementation tasks are difficult to develop.

Business Object Design for the Logistics Domain

Business Objects (BOs) characterize relevant objects in a given domain by structured sets of attributes. They are used for the orchestration of applications and services and for the communication between them (Böhmer et al., 2012). There may optionally be a physical counterpart (a real object) which is characterized. A business object has an abstract functional view and a detailed technical view, both may have different forms of representation.

A BO model in functional view is a domain model, represented e.g. as an ontology or as an UML class diagram, as sketched in Figure 6 (the complete model cannot be shown here). It

Figure 4. Process model implementation: conventional approach vs. logistics mall approach

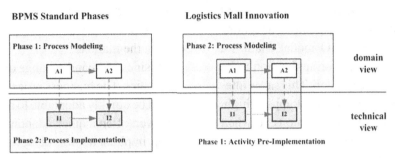

Figure 5. Two barbells pre-connecting domain view and technical view of data and activity

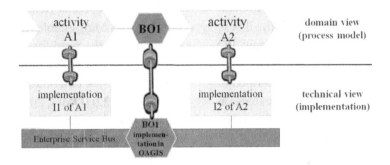

abstracts from all technical details not needed by business users or domain experts. In a business process model usually only the names and states of BOs and a few control flow-relevant attributes will appear, as explained below.

A BO in technical view is a software artifact that describes an object in all relevant detail and serves for the passive control of all system components (applications, services, infrastructure components, process models) by being the unit of standardized communication between them. It includes a set of attributes, possibly deeply structured, having inner BOs and complex attribute groups as well as relationships to other BOs. BOs (in transfer format) separate state and structure from their behavior, because they are communicated between different systems (and possibly also between different layers and components of one system). This works out because behavior is not transportable and is to be coordinated flexibly by higher-level business process models, and

emergence should be avoided. Therefore, OAGIS is used as a transfer and transaction standard, which adds behavior aspects in form of verbs denoting desired actions of the receiver (intelligent receiver, not intelligent data) and provides a standardized transport header. A BO thus exists in different inter-convertible technical representation formats: the standard transfer format may be parsed into equivalent Java objects (with methods in their types) and may also be persisted in a database (e.g. in form of XML or of table structures using JPA (Java Persistence API)). The persistent representation form is the master copy of the BOs and is hosted in a unique application or service (the object's owner), which is responsible for the BO's life cycle. The object owner can be an instance repository, or a complex application like a warehouse management system. All other types of representation (and even other persistent representations) are object copies related to the object owner.

BOs are used as a standard for the communication between apps, as depicted in Figure 7. Instead of using individual point-to-point connections between apps, a common BO model enables a single integration of an app or application to be interoperable with any other app. This saves integration effort, when the number of apps is high, or even with a few apps after some time when several changes have to be applied.

For the logistics domain we conducted an analysis to construct the domain BO model. OAGIS was selected as a transaction standard (and its nouns and their components are used as standardized technical BO representation). These technical BOs were mapped to the domain BO model. Here some objects and attributes were found missing in OAGIS, which were defined in an OAGIS overlay, being the standard extension mechanism of OAGIS. Moreover, we only use the subset of OAGIS required for logistics.

Business Process Model Design for the Cloud

In times of currency turmoil, international competition and tight profit margins, efficient internal process management including partner interactions are essential for logistics companies, especially for SMEs. Since prices are dictated by the market, only the internal optimization of process models can help. Only individual process models, not the standard ones, can make a difference in the market.

Business demands change quickly, especially in logistics. The business processes of a company should be quickly adaptable to new requirements. However, often a quick adaptation is not feasible as the implementation of new logistics process models, designed by logistics experts, also requires additional IT support that takes time to be brought in place. To speed up implementation, the Logistics Process Designer LPD, as part of the Logistics Mall, enables quick process adaptations without the need for in-depth IT expertise and enables deployment of these process models merely by a click of a button. It is based on standard BPMN 2.0 (OMG, 2011), generated from a simpler domain-oriented process model and used for process execution.

Different scenarios and protocols can be realized based on the asynchronous exchange of BODs, as depicted in Figure 8, an UML sequence diagram. Here, some customer orders goods from a supplier, and for the shipment a logistics carrier is used. The process starts by sending a Process-PurchaseOrder BOD message from customer IT to supplier IT, and the latter acknowledges the order using a BOD. Communication proceeds

Figure 6. Logistics domain model

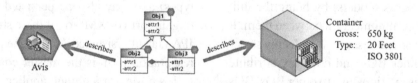

Figure 7. Benefits of a standard business object model

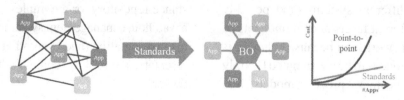

as needed, until finally the invoice is sent to the customer IT and acknowledged.

As stated above, these BODs are message formats in OAGIS Web services. A flexible orchestration of services, some of which constituting the OAGIS application interface services of involved parties, can be defined using business process models. A reusable top-level structure of logistics process models is defined in the SCOR model. But since the details of SCOR are not freely available, it is seldom used by SMEs – therefore its use is optional in process model design.

Process models designed with the LPD focus on the refinement of activities of one partner (the process owner), and this refined process model may communicate with cooperation partners via send/receive tasks as depicted in Figure 8.

The lowest level of a process model consists of atomic activities (i.e. tasks) that map directly to methods of services provided by the Mall, e.g. OAGIS interface services of the different applications to be orchestrated. From these building blocks, a process designer can assemble or modify process models without detailed IT knowledge: for each task all relevant (interface) services of currently integrated systems are shown as apps, to be used for drag & drop implementation of tasks. There even may be more than one predefined IT mapping for a task (which can then be selected and exchanged), but each task has at least one implementation.

But this does not require a bottom-up approach of modeling: In a top-down approach, a process modeler will use empty sub-processes as main modeling elements, which can be refined later into tasks and/or further empty sub-processes. When all sub-processes at all levels only contain sets of tasks (linked by control flow), these tasks can be "operationalized" by one of their predefined implementations. This is shown in Figure 9, a screen design of the Logistics Process Modeler (LPD), where a first sub-process has been refined into two activities.

Figure 9 also depicts the basic modeling principles of the LPD, supporting domain experts

Figure 8. OAGIS logistics scenario no 59, extract (OAGi, 2011)

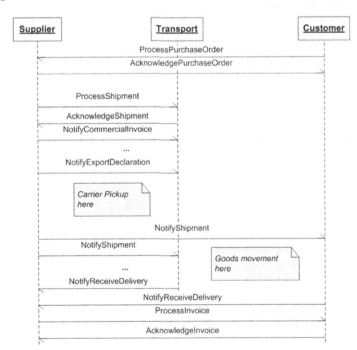

with a simplified view of BPMN 2.0 process models composed of predefined building blocks: on the left side there is a categorized palette of pre-implemented activities ordered by logistics categories, from which concrete activities can be selected by drag and drop. In contrast to normal BPMN editors, activities or tasks cannot be dragged and then named arbitrarily, but only predefined named tasks can be used as building blocks.

For each of the predefined tasks their input BOs and output BOs are defined (although not shown in Figure 9 to keep the model display simple, but displayable). This information is used for guiding the process modeler: firstly, when two tasks are connected, the connection can be verified based on the types and states of all BOs on both ends. Secondly, for a given task, all possible successors can be searched. Here it is important to distinguish control flow (the arrows denoting time sequence) from data flow (available BOs): a successor task can also make use of BOs which have been produced in the process before, not only those from its direct predecessor. We do not support detailed pre and post conditions on the activities. However, BOs can have state annotations (as in BPMN 2.0),

and the state is additionally used to validate the process models.

Additionally, arbitrary named elements from the top right palette can be used to compose process models, i.e. control flow arrows, gateways (for conditional and parallel flow), exceptions (i.e. boundary events of different kinds, like timer, error), and sub-processes (for grouping and top-down modeling), as well as message events (for connecting remote process partners by sending and receiving messages, as depicted in Figure 9). This defines the BPMN 2.0 subset used in the LPD. We even omitted pools and lanes. The models always have one white box pool (for the process owner) and any number of black box pools (for cooperation partners, not shown in the model). The roles for the tasks are inherited from their implementations.

Process Execution in the Cloud

When a process is modeled or has be changed, it can be deployed by a click to a test environment of virtual machines in the Cloud, and tested with app stubs or apps in test modus, which then mainly consume input and return some results. For a

Figure 9. A logistics process modeler screen design

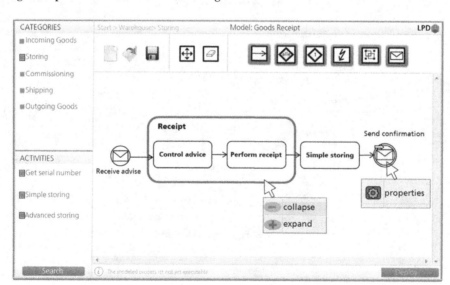

subsequent integration test, a deployment to an integration environment with apps working on test data is needed and cooperation partner input data will be generated. Hereafter, a deployment to the production environment can be done. Old process instances will continue with the old model, but newly started processes will follow the new orchestration pattern. If any test fails, currently an IT expert is still needed.

For process execution a business process engine is needed. Thanks to the use of the BPMN 2.0 standard, the engine is in principle exchangeable (with some differences in linking the implementations). The engine can be selected depending on the needs of the Mall operating company.

FUTURE RESEARCH DIRECTIONS

Mashups are (Web) applications, which create new content through a flexible combination of existing sources using open APIs (e.g. Web Services). Prefabricated components (with GUI) can be combined into new applications by users. Business mashups or composite applications are controlled mashups, which can be handled by business users (taking into account semantic conditions). Business process mashups are business mashups of process models, composed of components over the dimensions of control flow, data flow and multi-user support (Daniel et al., 2010).

The presented approach tries to achieve the latter. However, our business process mashups of pre-implemented activities are not yet quite controlled. Improved pre and post conditions beyond our business object taxonomy and state matching approach are needed to better assert a correct control and data flow and thereby a technically correct orchestration of components and business partners. Here semantic business process management may help, which applies Semantic Web concepts (ontologies with rules and inference engines) to all BPM phases, as done in the EU-funded project SUPER (http://www.

ip-super.org), also aiming at filling the semantic gap between business and IT, but with different and additional means.

Many aspects of our work could not be discussed in this chapter or are still open research: e.g. what are the best reusable components/apps for the logistics domain and how can they be customized, how to use shared multi-tenant business object repositories, how are process models tested (e.g. simulation and debugging modes and environments), who is allowed to deploy new or changed process models, what kind of collaborations of people or groups and between business and IT departments are meaningful, legal impacts, security aspects, what price models and SLA models will be supported, can process models become an easily customizable products to rent in the Mall? This has to be discussed in further publications due to lack of space. In this chapter we had to focus on initial technical problems and solutions in the Mall Cloud context.

One of the main targets of the Service Design Studio is to prove if the USDL is applicable to the logistics domain. The generic approach of the USDL does not inhibit the adoption of USDL, but coincidentally this approach leads to a complex mode of operation. It is still necessary to develop process models which ease the general adoption of USDL. The development of business models is incumbent to service designers without technical skills. These people must be enabled to handle the service description beyond the functional description. Furthermore the USDL lacks the ability to map a specific property to a service method. An extension to USDL which enables this mapping would be feasible like shown by the Service Design Studio and should be integrated to upcoming USDL standard (W3C, 2005).

Beneath the non-functional aspect of a service description and the technical representation of the functional part it is necessary to standardize the domain part of the service description. In conjunction with a meta model for the technical representation which can be transformed to a

SOAP-based service interface or a RESTful service interface would lead to more exchangeability of service providers and the underlying platforms.

The presented results enable new business opportunities in the logistics domain, like delivery fulfillment for eCommerce. The operator of a Web shop can simply attach the necessary process of consignment and delivery of goods. On the other hand the discussed methodology is also applicable to different domains. The differentiation to approaches like those from Yang and Bruin (2010) or Yang and Nasser (2012) is still open work.

CONCLUSION

According to Mummigatti (2010) the advantages of BPM in the Cloud or BPaaS are in three areas: economic (initial capital investment, pay per use, short contract times, and resources on demand), architectural (common Web accessible environment, resources for development and provisioning) and strategic (outsourced ownership, focus on core business, collaboration across and within enterprise, agility). These properties of Cloud computing are ideal for SMEs to solve their IT problems. These arguments especially apply to business process management software offered as a Cloud service, which reduces risks and resistance to using BPM in a company but preserves its advantages: to respond quickly to changing circumstances. On the other hand, with the rising of Cloud-oriented service marketplaces the use and offering of services will be easier, especially for SMEs. Current Cloud computing technologies are good scaffolding for the development of distributable services. In conjunction with the growing interest in Cloud-based services and processes, service marketplaces and execution environments for processes and workflows will appear. While the execution technology for services in a Cloud environment exists, there is still the necessity for adequate tools for service design and process model design. The Service Design Studio investigates these needs and creates a tool which is aligned to the logistics domain. Opposite to this, the generic USDL with the generic USDL3-Editor shows the ability to be a core technology for this evolution. But there is still the requirement for process models to simplify the use of USDL. Finally, Cloud computing offers high potential to SMEs (Dillion, Wu & Chang, 2010); hence technologies and tools need a high level of maturity to succeed.

We presented our approaches: the Logistics Mall – a flexible cost-saving solution for SMEs to cope with today's quickly changing logistics requirements, as well as the Service Design Studio supporting services in the Cloud with a focus on their non-functional properties, and the relationships of both. Both are results of big German Cloud projects. These innovations have the potential to advance the logistics market towards modern IT strategies. By use of Cloud technology and BPM technology in combination, customers benefit from smaller operating costs and investments needed, and in addition flexible, individual logistics business processes allow SMEs for the first time a technological catch up with large companies. They can thus focus on their core business. This is in particular supported by the presented double barbell approach to close the business IT gap, i.e. by process modeling with pre-implemented building blocks (the offers of the Logistics Mall) having standard logistics business object based interfaces.

REFERENCES

Amazon (2011). Amazon elastic compute cloud. Retrieved from http://aws.amazon.com/ec2

Barros, A., & Oberle, D. (Eds.). (2012). Handbook of service description. Springer. Retrieved from http://www.springer.com/computer/database management & information retrieval/book/978-1-4614-1863-4

Baude, F., Filali, I., Huet, F., Legrand, V., Mathias, E., Merle, P., et al. (2010). ESB federation for large scale SOA. In Proceedings of the 2010 ACM Symposium on Applied Computing (pp. 2459-2466).

Böhmer, M., Daniluk, D., Schmidt, M., & Gsell, H. (2012). Business object model for realization of individual business processes in the logistics domain. In Clausen, U. (Ed.), *Efficiency and logistics*. Berlin, Germany: Springer. doi:10.1007/978-3-642-32838-1_25

Carr, N. G. (2003, May). IT doesn't matter. In Harvard Business Review. Retrieved from http://hbr.org/2003/05/it-doesnt-matter/ar/1

Daniel, F., Koschmider, A., Nestler, T., Roy, M., & Namoun, A. (2010). Toward process mashups: Key ingredients and open research challenges. In Proceedings of the 3rd and 4th International Workshop on Web APIs and Services Mashups.

Dillon, T., Wu, C., & Chang, E. (2010). Cloud computing: Issues and challenges. In 2010 24th IEEE International Conference on Advanced Information Networking and Applications (AINA). DOI: 10.1109/AINA.2010.187

Fraunhofer, I. M. L. (2010). Market study cloud computing for logistics. Retrieved from http://www.ccl.fraunhofer.de/presse-medien/publikationenICS

Göser, K., Jurisch, M., Acker, H., Kreher, U., Lauer, M., Rinderle-Ma, S., et al. (2007). Next-generation process management with ADEPT2. In Proceedings of the BPM 2007 Demonstration Program, CEUR-WS.org Workshop Proceedings, Vol. 272, Brisbane, Australia, Sept. 2007 (pp. 3-6).

Gsell, H., & Nagel, R. (2012, June). Application integration in the logistics mall. Paper presented at the SDPS 2012 - 17th International Conference on Transformative Science, Engineering, and Business Innovation, Berlin, Germany.

Holby, H., & Trienekens, J. (2010). Challenges in business systems integration. *Computers in Industry*, *61*(9), 808–812. doi:10.1016/j.compind.2010.07.006

Holtkamp, B., Steinbuß, S., Gsell, H., Löffeler, T., & Springer, U. (2010). Towards a logistics cloud. In Proceedings of the Sixth International Conference on Semantics Knowledge and Grid, SKG 2010, Ningbo, China.

Huan, S., Sheoran, S., & Wang, G. (2004). A review and analysis of supply chain operations reference (SCOR) model. *Supply Chain Management: An International Journal*, *9*(1), 23–29. doi:10.1108/13598540410517557

Huang, S., Sheoran, S., & Keskara, H. (2005). Computer-assisted supply chain configuration based on supply chain operations reference (SCOR) model. DOI: http://dx.doi.org/10.1016/j.cie.2005.01.001

Iscan, H., Flake, S., Tacken, J., Ley, M., & Schmülling, C. (2012, June). Service design studio (SDS) – The execution environment of the service design studio. Paper presented at the SDPS 2012 - 17th International Conference on Transformative Science, Engineering, and Business Innovation, Berlin, Germany.

Jeffrey, K., & Neidecker-Lutz, B. (Eds.). (2010). The future of cloud computing – Opportunities for european cloud computing beyond 2010. Expert Group Report, European Commission, DG INFSO.

Mell, P., & Grance, T. (2009). The NIST definition of cloud computing. Working Paper, National Institute of Standards and Technology. Retrieved from http://csrc.nist.gov/publications/drafts/800-145/Draft-SP-800-145_cloud-definition.pdf

Mummigatti, V. (2010). The emerging confluence of BPM and cloud computing. White Paper, Virtusa Corporation. Retrieved from http://www.virtusa.com/practices/bpm

OMG. (2011). Business process model and notation (BPMN), version 2.0. Retrieved from http://www.omg.org/spec/BPMN/2.0

Open Applications Group. (2011). OAGIS release 9.5. Retrieved from http://www.oagi.org

SAP AG. (2011). Internet of services. Retrieved from http://www.internet-of-services.com

Saugatuck Technologies. (2008). Understanding the cloud taxonomy. Retrieved from http://www.slideshare.net/Rinky25/understanding-the-cloud-taxonomy

Silver, B. (2009). BPM and cloud computing. BPMS Watch, Industry Trend Reports. Retrieved from http://www.brsilver.com/bpm-and-cloud-computing-white-paper

Stemmer, M., Holtkamp, B., & Königsmann, T. (2011). Cloud-orienterte Service-Marktplätze (Cloud-oriented service marketplaces). White Paper, Fraunhofer ISST. Retrieved from http://www.isst.fraunhofer.de/Images/Fraunhofer-ISST_CSMP-Whitepaper_www_tcm81-98065.pdf

Supply Chain Council. (2011). Supply chain operations reference (SCOR) model, version 10. Retrieved from http://supply-chain.org/scor

Theseus. (2011). TEXO – Infrastructure for Web-based services. Retrieved from http://theseus-programm.de/en/914.php

UN/CEFACT. (2009). Core components technical specification, Version 3.0. Retrieved from www.unece.org/cefact/codesfortrade/CCTS/CCTS-Version3.pdf

VMware, Inc. (2011). VMware and your cloud. Retrieved from http://www.vmware.com/files/pdf/cloud/VMware-and-Cloud-Computing-BR-EN.pdf

W3C. (2005). Unified service description language incubator group. Retrieved from http://www.w3.org/2005/Incubator/usdl

Yang, X., Bruin, R., & Dove, M. (2010). Developing an end-to-end scientific workflow: A case study of using a reliable, lightweight and comprehensive workflow platform in e-science. *IEEE Computational Science & Engineering, 12*(3).

Yang, X., Nasser, B., Surridge, M., & Middleton, S. (2012). A business-oriented cloud federation model for real-time applications. Future Generation Computer Systems, Elsevier. Retrieved from http://dx.doi.org/10.1016/j.future.2012.02.005

Zhang, L.-J., & Zhou, Q. (2009). CCOA: Cloud computing open architecture. In IEEE Conference on Web Services ICWS 2009 (pp. 607-616).

ADDITIONAL READING

Allweyer, T. (2010). Human-readable BPMN diagrams - Refactoring OMG's e-mail voting example. Retrieved from http://www.bpmn-introduction.com/HumanReadableBPMNDiagrams.pdf

Armbrust, M., Fox, A., Griffith, R., Joseph, A., Katz, R., & Konwinski, A. … Zaharia, M. (2009). Above the clouds: A Berkeley view of cloud computing. Technical Report No. UCB/EECS-2009-28. University of California at Berkley, USA.

Buyya, R., Yeo, C., Venugopal, S., Broberg, J., & Bradic, I. (2008). Cloud computing and emerging IT platforms: Vision, hype and reality for delivering computing as 5th utility. 10th IEEE International Conference on High Performance Computing and Communications.

Cardoso, J., Barros, A., May, N., & Kylau, U. (2010). Towards a unified service description language for the internet of services: Requirements and first developments. IEEE International Conference on Services Computing, IEEE Computer Society Press.

Cardoso, J., Winkler, M., & Voigt, K. (2009). A service description language for the internet of services. In Alt, R., Fahnrich, K.-P., & Franczyk, B. (Eds.), First International Symposium on Services Science (ISSS'09). ISBN: 978-3-8325-2169-1

Foster, I., Zhao, Y., Raicu, I., & Lu, S. (2008). Cloud computing and grid computing 360-degree compared. Grid Computing Environments Workshop.

Lamanna, D., Skene, J., & Emmerich, W. (2003). SLAng: A language for defining service level agreements. Proceedings of the Ninth IEEE Workshop on Future Trends of Distributed Computing Systems.

Lenk, A., Klems, M., & Nimis, J. Tai, & S., Sandholm, T. (2009). What's inside the cloud? An architectural map of the cloud landscape. ICSE Workshop on Software Engineering Challenges of Cloud Computing.

Mather, T., & Latif, S. (2009). *Cloud security and privacy*. O'Reilly.

OASIS. (n.d.). Web service security (WSS). Retrieved from http://www.oasis-open.org/committees/tc_home.php?wg_abbrev=wss

OASIS. (n.d.). Web service secure exchange (WS-SX). Retrieved from http://www.oasis-open.org/committees/tc_home.php?wg_abbrev=ws-sx

OASIS. (n.d.). Web services federation (WSFED). Retrieved from http://www.oasis-open.org/committees/tc_home.php?wg_abbrev=wsfed

OASIS. (n.d.). Security assertion markup language (SAML). Retrieved from http://saml.xml.org/saml-specifications

OMG. (2010). BPMN 2.0 by example. Retrieved from http://www.omg.org/spec/BPMN/2.0/examples/PDF/10-06-02.pdf

Sahai, A., Durante, A., & Machiraju, V. (2002). *Towards automated SLA management for Web services. HPL2001310R1*. HP Laboratories.

The Cloud Security Alliance. (2010). Top threats to cloud computing. Retrieved from http://www.cloudsecurityalliance.org

Tosic, V., Patel, K., & Pagurek, B. (2002). WSOL - Web service offerings language. Revised Papers from the International Workshop on Web Services, E-Business, and the Semantic Web, (pp. 57-67).

Vouk, M. (2008). Cloud computing – Issues, research and implementations. 30th International Conference on Information Technology Interfaces.

Wachs, M., Xu, L., Kanevsky, A., & Ganger, G. (2011). Exertion-based billing for cloud storage access. HotCloud11, 3rd USENIX Workshop on Hot Topics in Cloud Computing.

Wang, Y., Huang, C., Li, Y., Choud, P., & Yang, Y. (2011). QoSaaS: Quality of service as a service. Hot-ICE'11 Workshop on Hot Topics in Management of Internet, Cloud and Enterprise Networks and Services.

KEY TERMS AND DEFINITIONS

Business Objects (BOs): Describe relevant (physical) objects in a domain by structured sets of attributes. A business object has an abstract domain view and a detailed technical view, both may have different forms of representation. The former is used in process modeling, the latter in technical communication.

Business Process Management (BPM): A business approach to focus on aligning all aspects of an organization and a technical approach targeting to support the business approach. We bear on the technical approach, which focusses on process definition, simulation, implementation, execution and monitoring.

Business Process Model: Describes a business process of a company in the form of a logical sequence of activities to achieve a business result. It may also be used for the orchestration of services and applications.

Cloud Computing: We refer to the NIST working definition (Mell & Grance, 2011).

Innovation Cluster: A regional, application-oriented Fraunhofer cooperation between industry and research in the context of the German pact for research and innovation of the federal government.

Leading-Edge Cluster: Part of the High-Tech Strategy for Germany of the German Federal Ministry of Education and Research (see http://www.hightech-strategie.de/en).

Service: A standardized functional interface for Software as a Service. It is offered by a service provider and used by a service consumer.

Chapter 9

An Approach to Evolving Legacy Software System into Cloud Computing Environment

Shang Zheng
De Montfort University, UK

Hongji Yang
De Montfort University, UK

Feng Chen
De Montfort University, UK

Jianzhi Li
De Montfort University, UK

ABSTRACT

Cloud computing is a new paradigm for the intent of distributed resources sharing and coordinated problem solution. Affected by the Cloud trend and Service-Oriented need, many existing software systems will become legacy systems. These legacy software systems will need Cloud Oriented reengineering, which can facilitate the legacy systems reusable in Cloud Oriented architecture and allow the integration of legacy resources with Cloud features. This research focuses on establishing a general framework to assist with the evolution of legacy systems into Cloud environments. The methodology includes various phases, which use reverse engineering techniques to comprehend and decompose legacy systems, represent legacy resources by XML as Cloud component and integrate these Cloud components into Cloud environment. In this research, a legacy banking system has been chosen as a case study to prove the feasibility of the proposed approach. The legacy banking system can be transformed to run as a Service-Oriented Cloud application, which illustrates the proposed approach is powerful for utilising reusable legacy resources into Cloud environment.

1. INTRODUCTION

Cloud computing (Armbrust et al. 2009; Zheng et al. 2011b) has emerged as an important trend in information technology in recent years. Cloud computing provides a paradigm for provisioning and releasing computing resources, e.g., software, hardware, infrastructure, platforms, etc., with minimal management efforts, meanwhile enable convenient service, on demand network access to a shared pool of those configurable resources. It is more favourable to purchase or lease those resources with low cost than to build software and underlying infrastructure such as servers,

DOI: 10.4018/978-1-4666-2854-0.ch009

storage, and hardware and so on with higher cost. Hence, Cloud computing is becoming the preferred environment for those applications with large scalability, dynamic collaboration and flexible resource requirements. Running existing applications in Cloud environment will increase resource utilisation and sharing. From economic aspect, the business is always re-organising, changing its boundaries and reconfiguring its activities. From technical aspects, integrating legacy systems towards Cloud environment will become a major trend in Service-Oriented environments.

This research focuses on establishing a general framework to assist with the evolution of legacy systems into Cloud environment. This research proposes a solution for migrating legacy systems using a Cloud interface to enable the dynamic activation and Cloud resources discovery. Reusing the legacy systems in Cloud systems will allow the enterprise to take advantage of the broad commercial support provided by Cloud technology.

In this research, a new approach of Cloud Oriented software system evolution is proposed. First, reverse engineering techniques are used for program comprehension and design recovery. Then the legacy software systems are decomposed into a hierarchy of subsystems by defining relationships among the entities of the underlying paradigm of the legacy system. The decomposition is driven by program slicing and clustering technique. Next, Cloud components are created by wrapping objects and defining the interface. Finally, Cloud components are allocated to Cloud environment by specifying the requirements of the system.

2. RELATED WORK

2.1. Resource Oriented Software Evolution

In (Huang et al. 2003), various issues and challenges in web-based systems development and maintenance are described, especially in the public

domain. Evolvable web-based system architecture is introduced for management systems, and some designs and implementation tradeoffs are discussed as well. (Stroulia et al. 2000) suggest applying conventional reverse engineering techniques, such as code analysis and clone detection, to reduce duplicated content and to maintain web-based systems. The developed system includes the HTML parser and analysers that separate content from layout by integrating into HTML pages scripts for retrieving the dynamic data from special database.

In (Tonella et al. 2003), the researchers propose a cluster method, which is based on the automatic extraction by the keywords in web pages. Lixto (Estievenart et al. 2003) is a wrapper generation tool that is well suitable for building HTML/XML wrappers. (Moreira et al. 2001) propose an approach to integrating WWW information, which is based on the development of a canonical domain model in XML and the wrapping of existing WWW applications with wrappers capable of communicating about entities in this common model with the applications and with an intermediary mediator.

2.2. Service-Oriented Software Evolution

Along with the popularity of the Internet, a great number of attentions have been focused upon Service-Oriented computing (SOC). SOC is the computing paradigm that utilises services as fundamental resources for developing applications. Because services provide a uniform and standard information paradigm for wide range of computing devices, they will be very vital in the next phase of distributed computing development. The developers can compose existing web service components to create new applications and evolve legacy systems to be suitable for complex service requirements. In (Jiang and Stroulia, 2004; Chung et al. 2007), a technique for wrapping existing web applications with WSDL descriptions is built so that providers with a presence on the "browser-accessible web" can easily transfer their functionalities to other applications. The SOSR methodology is focus on service orientation and its specific tasks, using UML modelling technique to support software developers to evolve a legacy software system. In (Chen et al. 2005), the researchers also present an approach to supporting Service-Oriented evolution.

2.3. Cloud Oriented Software Evolution

Although Service-Oriented software evolution has developed well, the new requirements are waiting for the new paradigm that can be suitable for the dynamic environment. Both academy and enterprise have studied and proposed a few architecture frameworks to connect Cloud computing with Service-Oriented methodologies.

With years of efforts, Cloud researchers have successfully developed Cloud computing, including security solutions, resource management methods, information collection, and data management services. Due to the ultimate goal of Cloud computing is to design an infrastructure, which supports dynamic, resource sharing, there, is a need for evolving legacy systems into in the Cloud environment.

Many researchers believe that the legacy software systems can be evolved into Service-Oriented Cloud architecture. Hence, the researchers have made a few progress about the software evolution based on Service-Oriented Cloud architecture.

The Cloud computing architecture (Rochwerger et al. 2009), Reservoir, which is proposed to create an association with multiple Cloud providers. In Reservoir architecture, the computational resources within one site are partitioned by the virtualisation and utilised into virtual environment. A software platform for .NET based Cloud computing named Aneka in (Vecchiola et al. 2008) is introduced. It is an extensible and scalable Service-Oriented environment, which enables developers to operated easily .Net applications

with the supports of multiple programming models and APIs, and it can be considered as a pure PaaS Cloud solution. (Chauhan and Ali Babar, 2011) provides a method to migrate special software system to the SaaS system. As suggested by Yang X. (2011; 2012), the researchers have proposed a Cloud model and discussed the relationship between Service-Oriented Architecture and Cloud environment. However, these researches do not implement the service to run on different environments; Moreover, legacy resources are collected as services that might not be necessary for the entire Cloud computing environment.

To the best of our knowledge, there are not many processes and methodological supports that are specifically developed for migrating existing systems to Cloud computing environment. In order to make the evolution more unified and easily, this research proposes the migration efforts by taking guidance from methodologies reported in (Weiser, 1984; Tip, 1995; Li, 2006; Bianco et al. 2007; Khajeh-Hosseini et al. 2010).

3. PROPOSED FRAMEWORK

This research focuses on establishing a general framework and methodology to support the evolution of legacy systems into Cloud computing environment. A new approach of Cloud Oriented legacy software evolution is described, in which a Service-Oriented solution is applied to enable the Cloud service activation. First, reverse engineering techniques are used for program comprehension and redesign. Then the legacy software systems are decomposed into a set of subsystems. The decomposition is completed by program slicing. Next, Cloud components are created by wrapping techniques with AST analysis and XML. Finally, Cloud components are allocated to Cloud computing environment by identifying the system's requirements and characteristics of the network.

Based on the reverse engineering technology, the proposed approach allows legacy system to be reused as Cloud components. As shown in Figure 1, the framework of the Cloud Oriented software evolution approach may consist of multiple phases as follows:

- Reverse engineering techniques are used for program comprehension and redesign. The legacy software systems are decomposed into a set of subsystems by describing relationships among the entities.
- Legacy components are changed by an extended computational process.
- Cloud services are defined, packed, migrated and deployed into Cloud environment.

In this figure, the resources contain the legacy components and additional software components, the services can be shown and used by the business and end-user.

The detailed process includes components identification, components transformation and Cloud components packing, and these three phases will be discussed in the following sections.

4. COMPONENTS IDENTIFICATION

Component based software engineering is a process that aims to design and construct software systems using reusable software components. The component paradigm starts with the assertion of an assembly-oriented view of software engineering, building software applications by wrapping the ports and connectors of a set of pre-fabricated parts (components) within a component context. Mostly, legacy systems are huge and complex. Using components based development approach to evolving legacy systems is less risky and highly transport and it will bring more flexibility, scalability, reusability and reliability. In addition, this approach is low cost and easy to implement.

In this section, the program slicing technique is used to decompose system, understand program, eliminate dead code and choose selected code segments function. The software cluster-

ing technique is used to group large amounts of entities in a dataset and capture reusable legacy code segments into clusters according to their relationship and similarity from legacy systems, and create a hierarchical structure of these reusable legacy code segments.

4.1. Decomposition Process

Decomposing a program entails the identification and the reorganisation of different program components. These components can be distinguished in interface components, application logic components, and database components. Program slicing is a method for automatically decomposing a program by analysing its control and data flow. The proposed research focused on static slicing. Based on the original definition of program slicing, a static program slice S consists of all statements in program P that may affect the value of variable v at some point p. With the support of slicing technology, legacy systems can be divided into some concerned program parts and remove the useless assets. Program sling is desirable to extract legacy system effectively at high levels of abstraction of the program. Traditional, it is an established technique for reverse engineering. For the proposed approach of Cloud Oriented evolution, program slicing is used to decompose legacy system, understand program, eliminate dead code and remove selected code segments function independently.

Taking the control and data flow of a legacy system as inputs, the sets of statements and predicate nodes in the Graph as well as the sets of program nodes in the Graph can be returned. In this way, the subprograms of all the programs in the legacy system would be analysed, and each program is analysed only after the programs with calls that have been analysed. Similarly, the subprograms of a program are visited according to the partial order induced by the reverse internal call.

Computing a slice from a control flow graph is a two-step process: at the first step, requisite data flow information is computed and then this

Figure 1. Framework of cloud oriented legacy system evolution

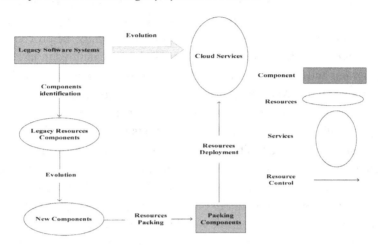

information is used to extract the slice. The data flow information is the set of relevant variables at each node n. For the slice with respect to <s, v>, the relevant set for each node contains the variables whose values affect the computation of v at s. The second step identifies the statements of the slice, which include all nodes (statements) n that assign to a variable relevant at n and the slice taken with respect to any predicate node that directly controls n's execution. In the proposed approach, rules of slicing and chopping are based on dividing the system into independent, stable and high reusable parts. Each part can be evolved and served as Cloud service resources. Meanwhile, these parts could be connected with each other flexibly and effectively. This requirement makes sure that all parts can be integrated as a whole service of the system without slicing.

The program slicing in this research refers to software systems written in procedural languages. The example system is typically composed of a set of programs that is related through external calls, and can be represented by a graph. The call relationship on the subprograms of a program can also be represented by a graph. The slicing algorithm of each subprogram can be expressed:

1. Define control flow graph.

2. Take control graph of a legacy system as inputs.
3. Analyse the subprograms of all the programs.
4. Compute the initial sets of control flow graph.
5. Traverse backward the flow graph.
6. Absorb all nodes in a slice.

In this research, the proposed approach has chosen a bank management system as the case study. This free licence software is offered by MYCPLUS for academic purpose with the source code, which is open to use, to modify and to be changed as requirements. This is an automatic software system for Bank Management, which can handle accounts of customers. This bank management system is chosen as legacy software, which will be prepared to evolve to the Cloud computing environment.

This legacy application is a C program with 22 functions and about 1300 lines of code. It composed of a set of programs related through external calls, it can be characterised by asset of modules and a set of call relationships among modules, where each module is represented by a circle, and a line connecting two modules represents each call relationship. Program or subsystems in this banking system could be constructed to a set of subprograms related through internal calls. The program provides primitives to explicitly define subprograms and to express internal calls. The call relation on the subprograms of a program can be represented by a graph whose nodes correspond to the program subprograms and edges to describe the internal calls. This representation is referred as a program call graph. Since the fully implemented system is quite complex, only parts of the system are presented. Figure 2 describes the part of banking system in System Call Graph. In this figure, the call graph just lists 15 subprograms and each number represents each subprogram. The relationship among them can be seen clearly. The part of banking system call graph will be utilised in the process of cluster analysis of the system structure.

The Figure 3 presents the control flow graph of loan payment subprogram. Node 8 is dependent on node 6 because: (a). node 6 describes variable monthly, (b). node 8 mentions variable monthly, and (c). there exists a path 5->6->8 without intervening definitions of monthly. Node 8 is control dependent because there exists a path 5->6->8, and Node 7 is control dependent because there exists a path 5->6->7. Node 11 and node 7 are post-dominated by node 2, but they are not post-dominated each other.

Figure 4 shows the slice of the payment subprogram with respect to the principle ({payment}). It is sliced from the code in Figure 3, including only those statements that could affect the value of the variable payment at line 14.

Based on the slicing process, finally, the legacy banking system can be easily understood and decomposed into a few legacy code segments. The dead codes can also be removed from the original system and the function of selected code is independent.

4.2. Hierarchical Clustering for Legacy Systems Analysis

Software clustering technique groups large amounts of entities in a dataset into clusters according to their relationship and similarity. It is applied to capture reusable legacy code segments, which

are independent, self-contained, coarse-grained and loose coupling. Current cluster analysis offers a wide range of procedures for identifying underlying structures in large sets of objects and revealing relationships between objects or the classes of objects. From the point of a view of Cloud environment Oriented programming, components are good candidates for modelling units of distribution because they encapsulate attributes and methods to act as independent entities communicating through passing messages.

The proposed approach in this research has preferred hierarchical algorithm (Meng et al. 2005) for component identification in legacy systems over optimising algorithms because they support a manual refinement of the clustering granularity and they are more suitable for further restructuring as Cloud component by their hierarchical structure. After selecting a clustering tree level, the user can move upward or downward in the tree, if the clusters at the selected level are too specific (some codes to be migrated are missing) or too general (migration candidates do not share a recognisable template). Most clustering techniques utilise certain criteria to decompose a system into a set of meaningful modular clusters. Such criteria attempts to achieve a cluster with low coupling, high cohesion, interface minimisation and shar-

Figure 2. Part of banking system call graph

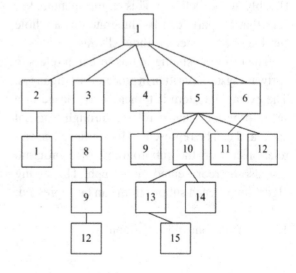

ing of neighbour resources. In the context of the Cloud Oriented migration, this research strives to produce clusters that assemble the maximal size of source code entities that are related to a component candidate.

The hierarchical clustering approach can be expressed as follows.

Given a set of documents:

1. Start with a set of singleton clusters, each containing one document and initially unmarked.
2. Repeat the following steps iteratively until there is only one cluster left unmarked.
   a. Identify the two most similar unmarked clusters, and mark them.
   b. Form a (new, unmarked) parent for these clusters by merging them together into a single cluster.
   c. Update the similarities among the clusters.

Next, an improved hierarchical clustering analysis method is proposed to extract independent services from legacy code. The resulting hierarchical structure may be represented by a binary tree or "dendrogram", from which the desired clusters may be extracted. This clustering method analyses legacy code and expresses the results in a dendrogram, which presents a hierarchic view of the legacy system. This hierarchic view consists of different levels of abstraction from source code to subsystems. This bottom-up clustering method is feasible and efficient for understanding legacy system.

The method includes three rules and they can be described:

- **Obtaining data matrix:** The matrix is symmetrical and 1 entry is used in the main diagonal. The numeric values (1 or 0 entries), which show the number of inter-connections among functions, are obtained from a static analysis of the source code.
- **Computing the resemble coefficients for the matrix:** 1 to 1 match has been utilised according to the two twice weight.
- **Executing cluster algorithm:** The clustering algorithm has been pre-discussed, which is a sequence of operations that incrementally groups similar entities into clusters. The sequence starts with each entity in a separate cluster. At each step, the two clusters that are closest to each other (indicated by smallest Sorenson coefficient) are merged and the number of clus-

Figure 3. Control flow of loan payment subprogram

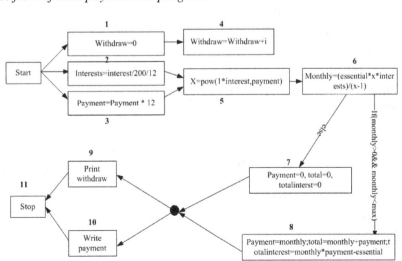

ters is reduced. Once these two clusters have been merged, the resemblance coefficients between the newly formed cluster and the rest of the clusters are updated to reflect their closeness to the new cluster.

In order to extract a functional component from legacy code, a cutting point must be figured out in the dendrogram. This cutting point affects the number and quality of the components derived from the dendrogram. It is an elementary factor for determining the granularity of extracted components. So far, the cutting point is determined with architects' participation and user requirements for the new Cloud components. Other existed and recovered design information facilitates this decision-making process. This clustering method together with human supervision restructures legacy systems into coarse-grained and loose-coupling components.

According to these rules, Figure 5 shows the hierarchical cluster analysis result and Figure 6 shows the dendorgram output. This clustering can provides a powerful analysis on legacy systems, and represents them into the loose-coupling modules.

5. COMPONENT TRANSFORMATION

After the process of component decomposition, the reusable class components can be easy to finding through the cluster analysis graph. Next, it is needed to consider that the quality requirements for Cloud would take effect in service and software model (Zheng et al. 2011a; Jia and Zheng, 2012). Due to the rapid development of computer hardware and software, the different platforms and end users have their own requirements on the service. In order to make the component that can integrate the functional and non-functional requirements to become the Cloud component, this section describes how to transform the requirements to code.

As shown in Figure 7 and Figure 8, the transformation rules and the requirement evolution schema have been described.

With the evolution schema and transformation process, the reusable component can update its content with the requirements including functional and non-functional types. An extended framework for software evolution has been illustrated in Figure 9.

The framework includes three layers, named Cloud Requirements, Non-Functional Requirements (NFR) and Functional Requirements (FR). All these transformation in the framework can be implemented by WSL tool (Yang and Ward, 2003).

The approach can be used as follows: the source code of legacy reusable component is first analysed, and then divided into SOR (Structure-Oriented Requirement) and OOR (Object-Oriented Requirement) in the Functional Requirement layer, where the extraction could be executed by WSL. Second, the effect caused by quality factors (Non-Functional Requirements) needs to take out. Finally, in order to reuse the components in the Cloud environment, the related interfaces should be design in the code. The correctness can be ensured by transformation rules in WSL tool.

Figure 4. Slice of payment subprogram (14, {payment})

```
(1)   float essential;
(2)   float interest;
(3)   float payment;
(4)
(5)   interests = interest /200/12;
(6)   payment = payment *12;
(7)
(8)   x = pow (1* interests, payment);
(9)   monthly = (essential *x* interests ) / (x-1);
(10)
(11)  if ((0<monthly) && (monthly < max))
      { payments = monthly;  total = monthly *
payment;
         totalinterest = (minthly*payment - essential;}
   (12) else { payment = 0, total = 0, totalinterest =
0;}
   (13)
   (14) write (payment)
```

There are three possible paths for the evolution:

- Non-Functional Requirements (NFR) can be added/extended by inserting the required extra qualities. The NFR can be then transformed into an equivalent programming language (through either transformation or straightforward translation). In this path, the procedural nature of the legacy system is kept.
- If OOR (Object Oriented Requirements) is sought, object extraction is performed to obtain an equivalent OOR code. Then the OOR code is extended/improved. Subsequently, this is transformed to an Object Oriented language. SOR is similar with this.
- For reusing the components in Cloud computing environment, following the construction of Functional Requirements and Non-Functional Requirements code, the Cloud Specification can be described with adding Cloud attributes.

According to the Figure 9, the transformation will seek the structural parts and OO parts from the legacy code. Therefore, the complexity of the process will depend on the design goal. In this research, the research focuses on the selected procedure code. For the OO components, the process will also be suitable in theory. This will be proved in the future research; meanwhile, the comparison will also be discussed.

6. CLOUD SERVICE DESCRIPTION, IMPLEMENTATION, AND DEPLOYMENT

This section describes the approach of migration and packs the extracted legacy assets as Cloud components. After the components are transformed to Cloud components, the components need to be migrated into Cloud environment. There are three steps in this section, which include Cloud service description, implementation and deployment. In this research, the Cloud services will be packed by eclipse tool, and deployed the Cloud environment-Google App Engine (2008) The Google Plugin can be added into eclipse tool, and then the eclipse can build the Cloud service easily and upload the service to Cloud environment.

6.1. Cloud Service Description

Once a software component has been extracted from a legacy system, or has been built as a new component, its interface can be extracted and represented by XML. XML is used to describe the structure of the data, XSL language is used to manipulating XML from one structure into another. In addition, Java is used to encapsulate them with a few simple classes and implement the application. For legacy systems, which are not written in Java, wrap technique is applied to supply a Java interface for them.

Web interfaces have been utilised to connect applications that have been thought of previously as traditional, single-user ones. In this research, Extensible Style sheet Language (XSL) is utilised to achieve the web interface transformation and to provide a better control over legacy systems. Extensible Style sheet Language Transformations (XSLT) is an XML-based language that is used for the transformation of XML documents. It can manipulate XML from one structure into another. Therefore, it can be completed through transforming XML into HTML or other XML document structures.

In Cloud Oriented software evolution, the application of XML does not replace HTML documents completely. HTML is created for content presentation on client browser. Its elements and attributes are dedicated to document structuring and user interactive actions such as collecting user input information from the browser and submit-

Figure 5. Cluster analysis result of banking system

	intro()	menu	acc	acc-gui	getacc	savacc	update	process	list	print	list-gui	transca	trans-gui	showtran	modtran	see	report	de-gui	deposit	modcho	withdraw	modmeu
	F1	F2	F3	F4	F5	F6	F7	F8	F9	F10	F11	F12	F13	F14	F15	F16	F17	F18	F19	F20	F21	F22
F1	1	0	0	0	0	0	0	0	0	0	0	0	0	0	0	0	0	0	0	0	0	0
F2	0	1	0	0	0	0	0	0	0	0	0	0	0	0	0	0	0	0	0	0	0	0
F3	0	0	1	1	1	1	0	1	0	0	0	0	0	0	0	0	0	0	0	0	0	0
F4	0	0	0	1	0	0	0	0	0	0	0	0	0	0	0	0	0	0	0	0	0	0
F5	0	0	0	0	1	0	0	0	0	0	0	0	0	0	0	0	0	0	0	0	0	0
F6	0	0	0	0	0	1	1	0	0	0	0	0	0	0	0	0	0	0	0	0	0	0
F7	0	0	0	0	0	0	1	0	0	0	0	0	0	0	0	0	0	0	0	0	0	0
F8	0	0	0	0	0	0	0	1	1	0	0	1	0	0	0	0	0	0	0	0	0	0
F9	0	0	0	0	0	0	0	0	1	1	1	0	0	0	0	0	0	0	0	0	0	0
F10	0	0	0	0	0	0	0	0	0	1	0	0	0	0	0	0	0	0	0	0	0	0
F11	0	0	0	0	0	0	0	0	0	0	1	0	0	0	0	0	0	0	0	0	0	0
F12	0	0	0	0	0	0	0	0	0	0	0	1	1	1	0	1	0	0	0	1	0	0
F13	0	0	0	0	0	0	0	0	0	0	0	0	1	0	0	0	0	0	0	0	0	0
F14	0	0	0	0	0	0	0	0	0	0	0	0	0	1	0	0	0	0	0	0	0	0
F15	0	0	0	0	0	0	0	0	0	0	0	0	0	0	1	0	0	0	0	0	0	0
F16	0	0	0	0	0	0	0	0	0	0	0	0	0	0	0	1	1	0	0	0	0	0
F17	0	0	0	0	0	0	0	0	0	0	0	0	0	0	0	0	1	0	0	0	0	0
F18	0	0	0	0	0	0	0	0	0	0	0	0	0	0	0	0	0	1	0	0	0	0
F19	0	0	0	0	0	0	0	0	0	0	0	0	0	0	0	0	0	1	1	1	1	1
F20	0	0	0	0	0	0	0	0	0	0	0	0	0	0	1	0	0	0	1	0	0	0
F21	0	0	0	0	0	0	0	0	0	0	0	0	0	0	0	0	0	0	0	0	1	0
F22	0	0	0	0	0	0	0	0	0	0	0	0	0	0	0	0	0	0	0	0	0	1

ting it. HTML should be used as a protocol for information representation and collection, but not for information storage management.

Many web-based systems can dynamically produce HTML pages from XML documents via XSLT and is used to format or transform XML content from one style to another. The benefit of the approach is that the developers can save many efforts to duplicate the legacy code, all features from legacy systems are inherited and they can be enriched with Cloud features. Furthermore, they can easily be integrated with each other and perform dynamic services in Cloud computing environment.

XSL can be used not only for formatting an entering document structure but also for formatting the data returned from the legacy system into a usable structure for the function or application using API. XSLT processing often starts with reading a serialised XML input document into the source tree and ends with writing into an output document. The output document may be XML, HTML, plain text or any other format that the XSLT processor is capable of producing. The transformation is achieved by a set of template rules. A template rule associates a pattern, which matches nodes in the source document with a sequence constructor.

While the Cloud components become Cloud services, the Cloud services need to be described first. The first step in writing a Cloud service is to describe the service resources. This step do not concern with the inner workings of that service, it mainly focuses on specifying which service is provided and indicating which operations will be available to the clients. The service interface is called port type (portType). The WSRF in this part is used to keep the state of resources.

The next step is to integrate the relevant information into XML components, which could be easily deployed into Cloud computing environment. In this research, the XML representation is not only used for the component wrapping, but also for the sources code analysis such as the presentation of AST. Specifically, the tree hierarchical structure of the Cloud component is mapped into XML elements and attributes. Each node and edge in the AST is mapped to an XML element tag. AST have been successfully used by the data flow analysis and so on. Meanwhile, it is also utilised for the purpose of analysing and transforming source code entities. In the proposed approach, the AST has been analysed to develop

Figure 6. Clusters' dendogram of banking system

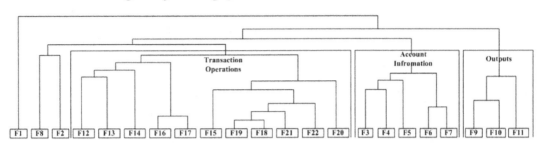

Cloud components. In this banking system, the loan payment subprogram of AST is given as Figure 10. Figure 11 describes the XML description repository according to AST representation and relevant information.

The proposed Cloud service component is called as Sum Service (SumService). It integrates the loan payment components from the legacy banking system, with the additional function components from a legacy calculator system. It may allow users to have the following operations: (a) sum the total payment of all credit cards per month, (b) sum the paying and payout monthly and (c) assist to manage personal financial affairs. Sum Service will have the following resource properties (RP): Loan Payment (string), Interests (string), Payment (string), Value (integer), Last operation performed (string), GetValue (this operation is used to access the Value RP). In this service, once a new resource is created, the "value" RP is initialised to zero, and the "last operation" RP is initialised to "none". The addition and subtraction operations expect only one integer parameter. This parameter is added/subtracted to the "value" RP, and the "last operation" RP is changed to "addition" or "subtraction" accordingly. This service also can be extended by adding more functions. This example is just a proof of concept in this research. Typical services are generally much more complex and could perform more operations than it does in this case study.

The service description is described and executed by WSDL, although it maybe a bit harder to understand than some other interface languages (such as Java interface). The main reason to choose WSDL is that, although Java interfaces are easier to write and understand, they may create more problems than WSDL does. Considering this, the WSDL is used.

The Sum.wsdl file describes the service interface. It should be placed in the examples/SumService folder. The service interface introduces how the external changes can interact with this service, specifically the operations that can be achieved on it. Figure 12 gives the WSDL file of the SumService. The <portType> element defines the operations: add, subtract, and getValueRP, along with all the essential message and types. All operations consist of input and output message, illustrated by the above <message> tags. The wsrp:ResourceProperties attribute of the portType element is used to indicate what the service's resource properties are. The resource properties must be stated in the <types> section of the WSDL file. The resource properties are used to keep all status information. With the help of the wsdlpp:extends attribute of the portType element,

Figure 7. Reusable component evolution schema

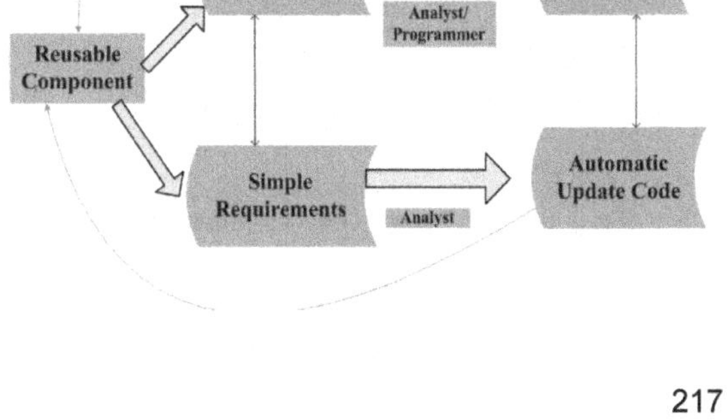

217

Figure 8. Transformation procedure between requirements and code

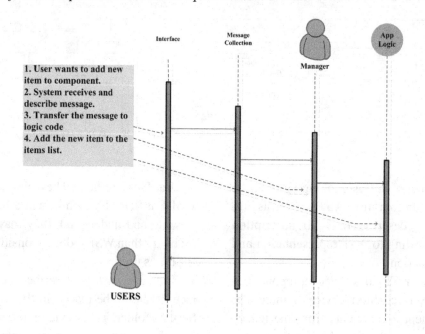

Figure 9. An extended framework for software evolution

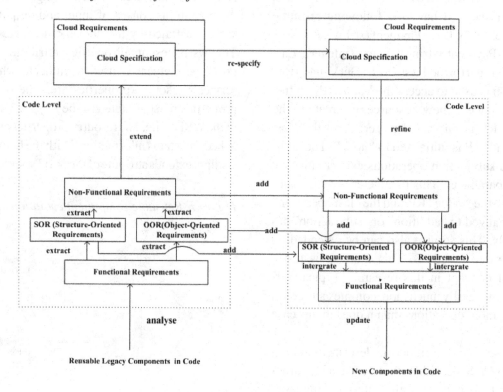

existing WSRF portTypes can be contained in the own portType without having to copy-and-paste from the official WSRF WSDL files. A WSDL Preprocessor will use the value of that attribute to produce correct WSDL code, which includes the own portType definitions and any WSRF portType that may be required in the service.

6.2. Services Implementation

The implementing services step shows how the service performs the operations. The service realisation is completed by Java. Qualified name (QName) contains namespace and local name, which is used to mention the related entity. For example, the QName of the Value RP is:

```
{http://examples.strl.org/sum/sum
service}Value
```

This is a general string description of QName. The namespace is put among curly braces, and the local name will be putt after the namespace. A qualified name is characterised by Java using the QName class. Since the service's qualified names should be referred commonly, it is better to place them all in a separate interface. As Figure 13 shows, the SumQNames.java file is a suitable interface class that includes the QName URI/namespace constants relevant to the Cloud services. It should be put in the org/strl/examples/services/Sum/impl folder. After implementing this interface class, these constants can reproduce themselves in the project.

The request and response message of GetResourceProperty correspond to the QName of resource element. The components of the GetResourceProperty request message that can be further showed in Figure 14 and the response message in Figure 15.

Figure 10. AST representation of loan payment subprogram

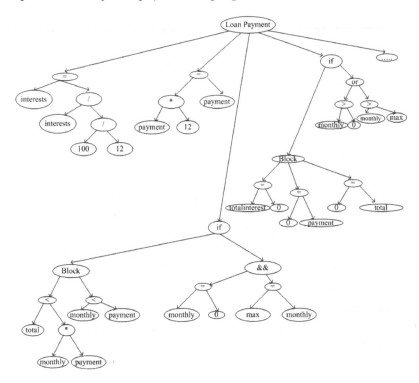

Figure 11. XML representation repository for AST

```
<repository>
<component package="bank.Loan_payments" name="Source">
<propertyDefinition type=" " name=" " value=" "/>
<port objectPackage="bank.payments" objectName="payment"
portName="payment"/>
<implementation language="Cloud" platform="Cloud" url="file:.">
<action portName="payments">
<binding method="getpayments"> ... </binding>
<classPerformanceModel type="initial" url="http:" />
</action>
</implementation>
<implementation language="Cloud" platform="Cloud" url="file:."> ... </
implementation>
</component>
<object package="bank.Loan_payments" name="payment" >
<method name="getpayments" type="action">
<argument typeName="payments" typePackage="bank.Loan_payments" />
</method>
</object>
</repository>
```

The two figures represent a request message that is used to retrieve two resource property elements from the WS-Resource that completes the loan payment portType and the result of response value of the request. As Figure15 shows, this identifier information is carried in the SOAP header element.

In the case study, the service implementation contains a single Java class with the code for the service. It can be divided into two classes: one for the service and the other for the resource. The SumService.java file is the service implementation that provides the core functionality to expose local directory information. It should be put in the org/strl/examples/services/Sum/impl project folder. The source for this Java class can be seen in Figure 16.

6.3. Service Deployment

In this section, it presents the process of building and deploying the Cloud service. A launch configuration is offered by Eclipse for executing one or more Ant buildfile targets. Ant, an Apache Software Foundation project, is a Java build tool. It permits programmers to forget the individual steps involved in acquiring an execution from the source files, which will be completed by Ant. Each project is different, so the individual steps are packed in a buildfile. This buildfile expresses Ant on what it should compile, how it should compile, and when it should compile.

This file should be added to the project's root directory. The document for this file is shown as Figure 17.

Until now, all essential files have been prepared, and the package explorer in eclipse should be seen as Figure 18.

In the eclipse IDE, this step can be executed by clicking on the buildservice.xml and choose "Run as" option. In the run as> external tools setup page, the buildfile is shown as: *${work-space_loc:/SumService/buildservice.xml*, and the base directory is shown as: *${workspace_loc:/ SumService}* in the main option. Moreover, the property file in the properties option is placed as: *${workspace_loc:/SumService/buildservice. properties}*. Then the service building can be completed by performing the buildservice.xml.

Finally, when the buildservice.xml has been successful in eclipse and, the Google Plugin for Eclipse adds several buttons to the eclipse toolbar. Then the service can be uploaded to Cloud environment.

Figure 12. WSDL file of SumService

```
</xsd:element>
<xsd:element name="getValueRPResponse" type="xsd:int"/>
<!== Resources Properties == >
<xsd:element name="LegacyBankSystem" type="xsd:string"/>
<xsd:element name="CreditCardSystem" type="xsd:string"/>
<xsd:element name="LoanPayment" type="xsd:string"/>
<xsd:element name="Interests" type="xsd:string"/>
<xsd:element name="Payment" type="xsd:string"/>
<xsd:element name="Value" type="xsd:int"/>
<xsd:element name="LastOp" type="xsd:string"/>
<xsd:element name="SumResourceProperties">
<xsd:complexType>
<xsd:sequence>
<xsd:element ref="tns:Value" minOccurs="1" maxOccurs="1"/>
<xsd:element ref="tns:LastOp" minOccurs="1" maxOccurs="1"/>
</xsd:sequence>
</xsd:complexType>
</xsd:element>
</xsd:schema>
</types>
<!== Messages == >
<message name="AddInputMessage">
<part name="parameters" element="tns:add"/>
</message>
<message name="AddOutputMessage">
<part name="parameters" element="tns:addResponse"/>
</message>
<message name="SubtractInputMessage">
<part name="parameters" element="tns:subtract"/>
</message>
<message name="SubtractOutputMessage">
<part name="parameters" element="tns:subtractResponse"/>
</message>
<message name="GetValueRPInputMessage">
<part name="parameters" element="tns:getValueRP"/>
</message>
<message name="GetValueRPOutputMessage">
<part name="parameters" element="tns:getValueRPResponse"/>
</message>
<!== Porttype == >
<portType name="SumPortType"
wsdlpp:extends="wsrpw:GetResourceProperty"
wsrp:ResourceProperties="tns:SumResourceProperties">
<operation name="add">
<input message="tns:AddInputMessage"/>
<output message="tns:AddOutputMessage"/>
</operation>
<operation name="subtract">
<input message="tns:SubtractInputMessage"/>
<output message="tns:SubtractOutputMessage"/>
</operation>
<operation name="getValueRP">
<input message="tns:GetValueRPInputMessage"/>
<output message="tns:GetValueRPOutputMessage"/>
</operation>
</portType>
</definitions>
```

7. COMPARISON AND EVALUATION

From software evolution perspective, few of them link legacy system evolution and Cloud computing together. Most of these researches concentrate on the reusable resources recognition from legacy systems, but the components cannot be migrated to the Cloud computing environment directly. Most current research papers of Service-Oriented software evolution still keep on the web services. Even though some researches have studied the Cloud computing oriented evolution area, only focus on parts of reengineering process and do not give a unified approach of the legacy systems evolution towards Cloud environment. Current approaches about reengineering legacy systems with Cloud technique are not matured, and novel approaches are required in this research area.

Different from the related studies, a general approach is described in this research for the Cloud computing oriented legacy software evolution, which includes the components identification used in Cloud computing environment, Cloud components description and Cloud integration. The techniques such as program slicing, the component based development methods and the up to date standards WSRF are used in this approach to

Figure 13. QNames.java file of SumService

```
package org.srtl.examples.services.Sum.impl;
import javax.xml.namespace.QName;
public interface SumQNames
{ public static final String NS = "http://examples.srtl.org/sum/sum service";
        public static final QName RP_VALUE = new QName (NS, "Value");
        public static final QName RP_LASTOP = new QName (NS, "LastOp");
        public static final QName RESOURCE_PROPERTIES = new
        QName (NS,"sumResourceProperties");
                                                }
```

Figure 14. Request message representation

```
<soap:Envelope>
   <soap:Header>
   <tns:resourceID> Loan Payment </tns:resourceID>
   </soap:Header>
   <soap:Body>
     <wsrp:GetMultipleResourceProperty>
      xmlns:tns=  https://... >
      <wsrp:ResourceProperty>
       tns: Interests
      </wsrp:ResourceProperty>
      <wsrp:ResourceProperty>
       tns: Payment
      </wsrp:ResourceProperty>
     </wsrp:GetMultipleResourceProperty>
   </soap:Body>
</soap:Envelope>
```

Figure 15. Response message representation

```
<soap:Envelope>
   <soap:Body>
     <wsrp:GetMultipleResourcePropertyResponse>
     <Interests> "interests"</Interests>
     </wsrp:GetMultipleResourcePropertyResponse>
     <wsrp:GetMultipleResourcePropertyResponse>
     <Payment> "payment"</Payment>
     </wsrp:GetMultipleResourcePropertyResponse>
   </soap:Body>
</soap:Envelope>
```

Figure 16. Service implementation code of SumService

```
package org.strl.examples.services.Sum.impl;
import java.rmi.RemoteException;
import org.globus.wsrf.ResourceContext;
import org.globus.wsrf.Resource;
import org.globus.wsrf.ResourceProperties;
import org.globus.wsrf.ResourceProperty;
import org.globus.wsrf.ResourcePropertySet;
import org.globus.wsrf.impl.ReflectionResourceProperty;
import org.globus.wsrf.impl.SimpleResourcePropertySet;
import org.strl.examples.Sum.SumService.AddResponse;
import org.strl.examples.Sum.SumService.SubtractResponse;
import org.strl.examples.Sum.SumService.GetValueRP;
public class SumService implements Resource, ResourceProperties
{       /* Resource Property set */
        private ResourcePropertySet propSet;
        /* Resource properties */
        private int value;
        private String lastOp;
        /* Constructor. Initialises RPs */
        public SumService() throws RemoteException {
                /* Create RP set */
                this.propSet = new
SimpleResourcePropertySet(SumQNames.RESOURCE_PROPERTIES);
                /* Initialise the RPs */
                try {
                        ResourceProperty valueRP = new
ReflectionResourceProperty(SumQNames.RP_VALUE, "Value", this);
                        this.propSet.add(valueRP);
                        setValue(0);
                        ResourceProperty lastOpRP = new ReflectionResourceProperty(
                        SumQNames.RP_LASTOP, "LastOp", this);
                        this.propSet.add(lastOpRP);
                        setLastOp("NONE");
                } catch (Exception e) {
                                throw new RuntimeException(e.getMessage());} }
        /* Get Setters for the RPs */
        public int getValue() {
                return value;      }
        public void setValue(int value) {
                this.value = value;          }
        public String getLastOp() {
                return lastOp;          }
        public void setLastOp(String lastOp) {
                this.lastOp = lastOp;          }
        /* Remotely-accessible operations */
        public AddResponse add(int a) throws RemoteException {
                value += a;
                lastOp = "ADDITION";
                return new AddResponse(); }
        public SubtractResponse subtract(int a) throws RemoteException {
                value -= a;
                lastOp = "SUBTRACTION";
                return new SubtractResponse(); }
        public int getValueRP(GetValueRP params) throws RemoteException {
        return value; }
        /* Required by interface ResourceProperties */
        public ResourcePropertySet getResourcePropertySet() {
                return this.propSet; }
}
```

Figure 17. Buildfile document of SumService

```
package=com.strl.examples.services.sum
interface.name=Sum
package.dir=org/strl/examples/services/Sum
schema.path=examples/SumService
service.name=SumService
gar.filename=org_strl_examples_calculator

build.packages=/share/globus_wsrf_common/build-packages.xml
build.tomcat=/share/globus_wsrf_common/tomcat/tomcat.xml
gar.name=//eclipse/workspace/ProvisionDirService/org_strl_examples_sum
tomcat.dir=/tomcat5
```

Figure 18. Updated package explorer

analyse legacy systems, define Cloud components and build Cloud applications.

The research results meet these criteria as follows:

Can this approach handle the variety of Cloud computing based systems?

In this research, the proposed framework employs reverse engineering technique to decompose legacy software systems and redesign reusable resources by XML. Then by using WSDL to define the resources properties and interfaces, using Java tool to implement the service, and finally the legacy resources can be successfully transformed into the Cloud services.

Are the legacy system component identification and representation methods effective and feasible for the Cloud computing oriented legacy software system evolution process?

In this research, reverse engineering techniques are employed to help the legacy system component identification for use in Cloud computing environment. The program slicing technique is used to decompose system, understand program, remove dead code and choose useful code segments independently by component interface parameters determination and source code deep understanding.

Then, for the Cloud XML component description and migration, by recursively traversing the hierarchy of the component entities, the tree hierarchical structure of the component is mapped into XML elements and attributes. The proposed approach effectively integrates the software evolution techniques into the Cloud computing development process.

Is the approach feasible for realisation?

Quite a lot attention was paid to the practical part of the approach during development. The processes of legacy component identification, XML representation and Cloud services integration are not only theoretically correct, but also practicable for real legacy systems. The case study describes that the approach is a "workable" one, and it is feasible in practice.

Is the approach capable for business-scaled systems?

The approach can be capable for business-scaled systems. It implements an infrastructure based on latest standard Cloud computing techniques, which are beneficial to large scale system integration to deploy legacy resources into the Cloud computing environment.

CONCLUSION

Cloud computing is a new paradigm and currently few active researches has been conducted to evolve legacy systems into Cloud computing environment. However, most researches are necessary and significant in this area to spread legacy resources used in Cloud computing environment. In this research, a solution for migrating legacy software systems to Cloud computing environment has been proposed.

It is argued that the detailed component mining approach needs to be tailored according to the features of legacy systems. Although the implemented program slicing techniques are not new, the comprehensive analysis ensures the reusable legacy code efficiently.

Through the discussion in this research, it is concluded that the legacy system evolution can assist Cloud application evolution. The proposed evolution approach is powerful for migrating reusable legacy resources into Cloud computing environment, building Cloud applications across distributed environment, and Service-Oriented entities. Based on the process of system decomposition, resources representation and Cloud components integration have been illustrated in this research, the legacy systems can be successfully evolved into the Cloud computing environment. As part of our future work, we plan to integrate software architecture style as additional factor to extend the proposed approach, and more case studies will be chosen to enrich the framework.

REFERENCES

Armbrust, M., Fox, A., Griffith, R., Joseph, A. D., Katz, R. H., & Konwinski, A. ... Zaharia, M. (2009). *Above the clouds: A Berkeley view of cloud computing*. EECS Department, University of California, Berkeley. Tech. Rep. UCB/EECS-2009-28.

Bianco, P., Kotermanski, R., & Merson, P. (2007). *Evaluating a service oriented architecture*. Software Engineering Institute, Carnegie Mellon University. Tech Report ESC-TR-2007-015.

Chauhan, M. A., & Ali Babar, M. (2011). Migrating service-oriented system to cloud computing: An experience report. *CLOUD '11 Proceedings of the 2011 IEEE 4th International Conference on Cloud Computing*, (pp. 404-411). 4-9 July 2011, Washington, DC, USA.

Chen, F., Li, S., & Yang, H. (2005). Feature analysis for service-oriented reengineering. *12th IEEE Asia-Pacific Software Engineering Conference*, (pp. 201-208). 15-17 December 2005, Taipei, Taiwan.

Chung, S., Byang, J., & Davalos, S. (2007). Service-oriented software reengineering: SOSR. *HICSS '07 Proceedings of the 40th Annual Hawaii International Conference on System Sciences*, (pp. 170). 3-6 January 2007, Waikoloa, Big Island, Hawaii, USA.

Estievenart, F., Francois, A., Henrard, J., & Hainaut, J. (2003). A tool-supported method to extract data and schema from web sites. *5th IEEE International Workshop on Web Site Evolution*, (pp. 3-11). 22 September 2003, Amsterdam, Netherlands.

Google App Engine. (2008). Retrieved from https://developers.google.com/appengine/

Huang, Y., Taylor, I., Walker, D., & Davies, R. (2003). Wrapping legacy codes for grid-based applications. *17th International Parallel and Distributed Processing Symposium*, (pp. 139-145). 24-26 April 2003, Nice, France.

Jia, Y., & Zheng, S. (2012). *Software evolution based on service-oriented requirement in internet ware*. 4th International Conference on Computer Research and Development, 21-22 April 2012, Kunming, China.

Jiang, Y., & Stroulia, E. (2004). Towards reengineering web sites to web-services providers. *8th European Conference on Software Maintenance and Reengineering*, (pp. 296-305). 24-26 March 2004, Tampere, Finland.

Khajeh-Hosseini, A., Greenwood, D., & Sommerville, I. (2010). Cloud migration: A case study of migrating an enterprise IT system to IaaS. *IEEE 3rd International Conference on Cloud Computing,* (pp. 450-457). 5-10 July 2010, Miami, USA.

Li, J., & Yang, H. (2006). Reengineering websites into stateful resources for grid service oriented evolution. *International Journal of Multiagent and Grid Systems, 2*(2), 89–100.

Li, J., Zhang, Z., & Yang, H. (2005). A grid oriented approach to reusing legacy code in ICENI framework. *International Journal of Automation and Computing, 3*(1), 47–55. doi:10.1007/s11633-006-0047-3

Meng, F. C., Zhan, D. C., & Xu, X. F. (2005). Business component identification of enterprise information system: A hierarchical clustering method. *Proceedings of the IEEE International Conference on e-Business Engineering*, (pp. 473-480). 18-21 October 2005, Beijing, China.

Moreira, J., Midkiff, S., Gupta, M., Atrigas, P., Wu, P., & Almasi, G. (2001). The NINJA project: Making java work for high performance computing. *Communications of the ACM, 44*(10), 102–109. doi:10.1145/383845.383867

Rochwerger, B., Breitgand, D., Levy, E., Galis, A., Nagin, K., & Llorente, I. M. (2009). The reservoir model and architecture for open federated cloud computing. *IBM Journal of Research and Development, 53*(4), 535–545. doi:10.1147/JRD.2009.5429058

Sneed, H., & Sneed, S. (2003). Creating web services from legacy host programs. *5th IEEE International Workshop on Web Site Evolution*, (pp. 59-69). 22 September 2003, Amsterdam, Netherlands.

Stroulia, E., Thomson, J., & Situ, G. (2000). Constructing xml-speaking wrappers for web applications: Towards an interoperating web. *7th Working Conference on Reverse Engineering*, (pp. 59-68). 23-25 November 2000, Brisbane, Australia.

Tip, F. (1995). A survey of program slicing techniques. *Journal of Programming Languages, 3*(3), 121–189.

Tonella, P., Ricca, F., Pianta, E., & Girardi, C. (2003). Using keyword extraction for web site clustering. *5th IEEE International Workshop on Web Site Evolution*, (pp. 41-48). 22 September 2003, Amsterdam, Netherlands.

Vecchiola, C., Chu, X., & Buyya, R. (2008). Aneka: A software platform for. NET based cloud computing. *High Performance Computing Workshop 2008*, (pp. 267-295). 30 June-4 July 2008, Cetraro, Italy.

Weiser, M. (1984). Program slicing. *IEEE Transactions on Software Engineering, 10*(4), 352–357. doi:10.1109/TSE.1984.5010248

Yang, H., & Ward, M. (2003). *Successful evolution of software systems*. Boston, MA: Artech House.

Yang, X. (2011). QoS-oriented service computing: bring SOA into cloud environment. In Liu, X. (Ed.), *Advanced design approaches to emerging software systems: Principles, methodology and tools*. Hershey, PA: IGI Global. doi:10.4018/978-1-60960-735-7.ch013

Yang, X., Nasser, B., & Surrige, M. (2012). *A business-oriented C federation model for real time applications*. Future Generation Computer Systems, Elsevier. Retrieved from http://www.sciencedirect.com/science/article/pii/S0167739X12000386

Zheng, S., Yang, H., Liu, L., & Wang, J. (2011). *Software evolution in setting internetware*. The 3rd Asia-Pacific Symposium on Internetware. 1-2 December 2011, Nanning, Guangxi, China.

Zheng, S., Yang, H., Ma, Z., & Liu, L. (2011). Understanding software reengineering requirements for cloud computing. *19th IEEE International Requirements Engineering Conference.* 29 August- 2 September 2011, Trento, Italy.

ADDITIONAL READING

Ali Babar, M., & Chauhan, M. A. (2011). A tale of migration to cloud computing for sharing experiences and observations. *Proceedings of the 2nd International Workshop on Software Engineering for Cloud Computing,* (pp. 50-56). 22 May 2011, Hawaii, USA.

Bennett, K. (1995). Legacy systems: Coping with success. *IEEE Software, 12*(1), 19–23. doi:10.1109/52.363157

Bianco, P., Kotermanski, R., & Merson, P. (2007). *Evaluating a service-oriented architecture.* Software Engineering Institute, Carnegie Mellon University. Tech Report ESC-TR-2007-015.

Brereton, O. P., Gold, N. E., Budgen, D., Bennett, K. H., & Mehandjiev. N. D. (2006). *Service-based systems: A systematic literature review of issues.* Keele University.Computer Science Technical Report (TR/06-01).

Butchart, B., Chapman, C., & Emmerich, W. (2003). *OGSA first impression -- A case study reengineering a scientific application with the open grid services architecture* (pp. 810–816). UK e-Science All Hands Meeting.

Buyya, R., Yeo, C., Venugopal, S., Broberg, J., & Brandic, I. (2009). Cloud computing and emerging IT platforms: Vision, hype, and reality for delivering computing as the 5th utility. *Future Generation Computer Systems, 25,* 599–616. doi:10.1016/j.future.2008.12.001

Erl, T. (2004). *Service-oriented architecture - A field guide to integrating XML and Web services.* Upper Saddle River, NJ: Prentice Hall PTR.

Furmento, N., Mayer, A., McGough, S., Newhouse, S., Field, T., & Darlington, J. (2002). ICENI: Optimisation of component applications within a grid environment. *Journal of Parallel Computing, 28*(12), 1753–1772. doi:10.1016/S0167-8191(02)00187-4

Ganesh, J., Moitra, D., & Padmanabhuni, S. (2004). Web services and multi-channel integration: a proposed framework. *Proceedings of the IEEE International Conference on Web Services,* (pp. 70-77). 6-9 June 2004, San Diego, California, USA.

Grossman, R. (2009). The case for cloud computing. *IEEE Computer, 11*(2), 23–27.

Kacsuk, P., Goyeneche, A., Delaitre, T., Kiss, T., Farkas, Z., & Boczko, T. (2004). High-level grid application environment to use legacy codes as OGSA grid services. *5th IEEE/ACM International Workshop on Grid Computing,* (pp. 428-435). 8 November 2004, Washington DC, USA.

Keienburg, F., & Rausch, A. (2001). Using XML/XMI for tool supported evolution of UML models. In the *Proceedings of the 34th Annual Hawaii International Conference on System Sciences,* (pp. 10). 3-6 January 2001, Maui, Hawaii.

Khajeh-Hosseini, A., Greenwood, D., & Sommerville, I. (2010). Cloud migration: A case study of migrating an enterprise IT system to IaaS. *IEEE 3rd International Conference on Cloud Computing,* (pp. 450-457). 5-10 July 2010, Miami, USA.

Kossmann, D., Kraska, T., & Loesing, S. (2010). An evaluation of alternative architectures for transaction processing in the cloud. *Proceedings of the ACM SIGMOD International Conference on Management of Data,* (pp. 579-590). 6-10 June 2010, Indianapolis, Indiana, USA.

Lewis, G., Morris, E., O'Brien, L., Smith, D., & Wrage, L. (2005). *Smart: The service-oriented migration and reuse technique.* Software Engineering Institute, Carnegie Mellon University. Technical Report CMU/SEI-2005-TN-029.

Louridas, P. (2010). Up in the air: Moving your applications to the cloud. *IEEE Software*, *27*(4), 6–11. doi:10.1109/MS.2010.109

Newcomer, E., & Lomow, G. (2005). *Understanding SOA with web services*. Boston, MA: Addison Wesley.

Roure, D., Jennings, N., & Shadbolt, N. (2005). The semantic grid: past, present, and future. *Proceedings of the IEEE*, *93*(3), 669–681. doi:10.1109/JPROC.2004.842781

Sneed, H. (2007). Migrating to web services a research framework. *Proceedings of CSMR 2007 11th European Conference on Software Maintenance and Reengineering: Software Evolution in Complex Software Intensive Systems*, 21-23 March 2007, Amsterdam, the Netherlands.

Stantchev, V. (2009). Performance evaluation of cloud computing offerings. *Advanced Engineering Computing and Applications in Sciences*, (pp. 187-192). 11-16 October 2009, Berlin, Spain.

Strowd, D. H., & Lewis, G. (2009). *T-check in system-of-systems technologies: Cloud computing*. Software Engineering Institute, Carnegie Mellon University. Tech Report CMU/SEI-2010-TN-009.

Vecchiola1, C., Pandey1, S., & Buyya, R. (2008). High-performance cloud computing: A view of scientific applications. *IEEE International Conference on High Performance Computing and Communications*, (pp. 825-830). 25-27 September 2008, Dalian, China.

Wasson, G., & Humphrey, M. (2005). Exploiting WSRF and WSRF.NET for remote job execution in grid environments. *19th IEEE International Parallel and Distributed Processing Symposium*, (p. 12a). 3-8 April 2005, Denver, Colorado.

KEY TERMS AND DEFINITIONS

Abstract Syntax Tree (AST): The data flow analysis and compilers community for the purpose of analysing and transforming source code entities has successfully utilised AST. Such tree-like structures characterise the source program in a top-down process. The internal nodes of the AST represent the non-terminal phrases of the program text, such as statements, operations, and functions. The leaf nodes represent terminal symbols, such as identifiers, and type declarators.

Cloud Computing: There are different views on the emerging paradigm. To our best knowledge, C computing is a model for enabling on-demand network access to a shared pool of computing resources that can be managed with minimal efforts.

Component Based Software Engineering: Component based software engineering is a process that aims to design and construct software systems using reusable software components. The component paradigm begins with the assertion of an assembly-oriented view of software engineering, and builds software applications by wiring together the ports and connectors of a set of pre-fabricated parts (components) within a component context.

Legacy System: This term is currently a well-accepted one with the software community. A legacy software system should be an old technique, application program, computer system or traditional behaviour that continues to be used in the software field.

Service Oriented Computing (SOC): SOC is the computing paradigm that utilises services as fundamental resources for developing applications. Services are self-describing and computational resources that support rapid, automatic, low-cost of distributed systems.

Software Evolution: Due to the rapid development of computer hardware and software, the demands and costs of software changes are increasing continuously. Because changes to software are needed so constantly, the term software maintenance is no longer expressive enough to describe such changes. Software evolution is now becoming the essential technique to control software life-cycle costs. Software evolution is the process of conducting continuous software reengineering. Reengineering implies a single change cycle, but evolution can go on forever.

XML: Extensible Markup Language (XML) has been described a markup language much like HTML. The design goal is for transporting and storing data. XML is about carrying information, while HTML is about playing the information.

Chapter 10

CloudRank:
A Cloud Service Ranking Method Based on Both User Feedback and Service Testing

Jianxin Li
Beihang University, China

Xudong Li
Beihang University, China

Linlin Meng
Beihang University, China

Jinpeng Huai
Beihang University, China

Zekun Zhu
Beihang University, China

Lu Liu
University of Derby, UK

ABSTRACT

In this chapter, the authors propose a Cloud service ranking system, named CloudRank, based on both the user feedback and service testing. In CloudRank, we design a new ranking-oriented collaborative filtering (CF) approach named WSRank, in which user preferences are modeled as personal rankings derived from user QoS ratings on services to address service quality predication problem. Different from the existing similar approaches, WSRank firstly presents a QoS model which allows users to express their preferences flexibly while providing combination of multiple QoS properties to give an overall rating to a service. Secondly, it measures the similarity among users based on the correlation of their rankings of services rather than the rating values. Nevertheless, it is neither accurate nor sufficient to rank Cloud services merely based on users' feedbacks, as there are many problems such as cold-start problem, absence of user feedback, even some service faults occurred in a service workflow, so to get an accurate ranking, an active service QoS testing and fault location approach is required together with WSRank. Therefore, in CloudRank, the authors also designed an automated testing prototype named WSTester to collect real QoS information of services. WSTester integrates distributed computers to construct a virtual testing environment for Web service testing and deploys test tasks onto distributed computers efficiently.

DOI: 10.4018/978-1-4666-2854-0.ch010

1 INTRODUCTION

In recent years, Cloud and service computing paradigms are converging into a powerful platform, and we have witnessed the strong growth of software delivered as service over the Internet where services are offered by leveraging the power of Cloud datacenters. However, how to select qualified services is becoming a key research issue in a large scale Cloud environment. Due to their dynamic nature of the execution environment, Cloud services may encounter various faults, WSTester can find the original failure service although the faults continue to accumulate and spread. Experimental results confirm that CloudRank outperforms the competing approaches significantly, and it benefits from the testing environment and locates the possible faults effectively and efficiently.

In this chapter, our general perspective is to rank the quality of Cloud services by both user feedback and active service testing based on Service-oriented architecture (SOA) technologies (Yang, Nasser, Surrige & Middleton 2012). In recent years, we have witnessed the maturing of SOA technologies and the rising of Cloud services. SOA has been broadly accepted in enterprise computing paradigm because many IT professionals have realized the potential of SOA, especially a Web service based on SOA can dramatically speed up the application development and deployment processes. According to an investigation of Gartner, SOA has been a prevailing software engineering practice, ending the 40-year domination of monolithic software architecture. At the same time, Cloud computing has become an increasingly popular means of delivering valuable, IT-enabled business services. Customers and end users access Cloud services through self-service portals, using and paying for only those services they need, when and where they need them. In a Cloud, the hardware and software infrastructures are provided in a centralized manner, so software as a service (SaaS)

is enabled in a Cloud to provide a new software service mode. All of these technologies show a centralized trend of Web services. Based on the SOA technologies, more and more Web services have been provided in a Cloud.

Due to the dynamic and distributed nature of Internet, services may be artificial and even malicious, which may bring potential security threats to end users. Therefore, it requires an effective method to rank the quality of service (QoS) by the non-functional properties during the process of building critical service-oriented applications. At present, the study of ranking a Web service mainly focuses on two aspects, i.e. services ranking based on predicted QoS values by using collaborative filter algorithms and services ranking based on monitored QoS. In this chapter, we first review existing methods on Web service ranking, and provide a detailed analysis of the collaborative filtering (CF) based Web service ranking. The existing CF approaches have three limitations. Firstly, higher accuracy in rating prediction does not necessarily lead to better ranking effectiveness. Moreover, the ranking accuracy is low because the order in the service ranking list is not sensitive for these approaches. Finally CF-based ranking systems require a large scale of users to provide their QoS records, while in public Internet the number of service users is extremely small, making it hard to be gathered and accurately describe users' preferences.

With the popularity of SOA and many supporting platforms being developed, Web service has become one of the mainstreams to solve the problems of interactions among heterogeneous IT applications in a distributed computational model. The business process driven Web services composition is a popular solution in which process plays a key role in the definition and constraint of IT systems. More and more enterprises have chosen service composition as a way to build and reuse their IT systems aiming to fulfill their core business values efficiently and agilely as well as to provide endurable benefits and flexible strategies to adapt the constantly changing business requirements. Testing of service composition system is essential for verifying and improving the composite service system. However, due to the special characteristics of composite service, compared with the formal verification methods, running tests on virtual computation environment is a relatively practical way to test the composite service. There are many challenges in testing composite service. Due to the distribution and heterogeneity of network environment, traditional manual deployment method is not applicable for dynamic composite service testing, and data input and output among atomic service through SOAP, while faults may be passed on with the process, resulting in fault location being more difficult. The traditional fault detection mechanism may increase the difficulty and workload. Moreover, the description of various test cases, monitoring of distributed testing execution and the analysis of result are also critical issues that need to be resolved.

Based on the above requirements analysis and problem statements, the aims of this chapter are as follows:

First, there will be large amount of services with identical or similar functionalities deployed by different vendors in a Cloud, and users will be overwhelmed by so many candidate services. Therefore, how to evaluate the quality of a Cloud service, and recommend the right service to different users becomes an essential problem. With consideration to the dynamic nature of Cloud services, user preferences and more service non-functional QoS properties should be considered because the similar functional services generally have very different qualities.

Second, many related works based on service feedback have been proposed, and among them, collaborative filtering (CF) is a representative work on Cloud service ranking. The collaborative filtering approach is based on the assumption that a user would usually be interested in those services preferred by other users with similar interests. The CF approach works by collecting QoS ratings of the services from a large number of users and making a ranking of Cloud services for a user based on the preference patterns of other users who have the similar interests with him or her. The CF approach needs huge QoS information provided by users. However, due to Cloud users' inconsistent behavior and the cold-start problems in the CF approach, it is not sufficient to rank Cloud services only based on user feedback. Thus, we have to additionally rank Cloud services through service testing by making use of the distributed Cloud environment.

Third, in order to ensure the quality of services in the Cloud environment, we have to evaluate them through testing beside recommendation. Due to the complexity of execution environment for service composition, how to manage the testing environment is an important problem. To manage testing environment resources more effectively, we regard the testing as a service, and a task manager is used to schedule available testing resources, and assign the test task onto test agents.

Fourth, service composition will invoke a variety of external services with different QoS in the Cloud, some faults may occur in the invoked services. Moreover, the faults often accumulate and disseminate because of the multi-branch characteristics of business process, which makes it difficult to locate the root fault source. But the traditional throw-and-catch mechanism is very preliminary for faults diagnosing, which relies on the developer associating the faults with exceptions at design stage. Therefore, it is important to enable the testing environment to detect the cause of malfunction and then repair it quickly.

Finally, there are many extrinsic factors such as network latency, which may affect the quality of service, so a test probe is used to identify process performance bottlenecks. We design and implement a mechanism for dynamically monitoring of the lifecycle a testing task may have from submission to results display. All of these methods are implemented into a prototype named WSTester.

2 BACKGROUND

Recently, Cloud computing has become a popular computing paradigm with centralized hardware and software infrastructures. Software as a Service (SaaS) is also becoming a new software provision mode. All of these technologies show a centralized trend of Web services. In particular, SOA and related technologies have also been extensively adopted. As an important type of SOA realization technologies, more and more Web services have been provided over the Internet.

2.1 Service Ranking for SOA

In these years, the study of functional properties of Web services is extensive, while the non-functional properties are neglected (ServiceXchange, 2011). However, due to the large amount of services with identical or similar functionalities, users will be overwhelmed by the candidate services. While Web service discovery cannot tackle this problem alone, effective approaches to Web service selection have become more necessary, which is a key research issue in the field of service computing (Papazoglou, Traverso, Dustdar, & Leymann, 2007; Zhang, Zhang, & Cai, 2007). With consideration to the distributed and dynamic nature of Web services, users' preferences and more service properties should be considered because the non-functional properties of services with similar functional properties may vary greatly. These non-functional properties are also known as the Quality of Service (QoS) of a service. The typical QoS properties include response time, price, reputation and correctness etc. Many researchers (Papazoglou, Traverso, Dustdar & Leymann, 2007; Zhang, 2005) believe that QoS

is a key factor in the success of building critical service-oriented applications.

A most straightforward approach of personalized service ranking is to evaluate all the services and then select the services by comparing their QoS values. Such approaches (Al-Masri, & Mahmoud, 2007; Liu, Ngu, & Zeng, 2004) compute service ratings through full service-QoS matrix and then select the service with highest rating. However, it's not practical for a consumer to evaluate the comprehensive QoS information of each candidate service, since it is time-consuming, and some properties are difficult to measure through several Web service invocations, such as reputation and reliability.

In recent years, some research works based on service feedback have been proposed, e.g. rating-oriented CF (Chen, Liu, Huang, & Sun, 2010; Grosclaude, 2004; Sarwar, Karypis, Konstan, & Riedl, 2007; Shao, Zhang, Wei, Zhao, Xie, & Mei, 2007; Zheng, Ma, Lyu, & King, 2009), ranking-oriented CF (Liu, & Yang, 2008), etc. Among them, collaborative filtering (CF) (Goldberg, 1992), firstly proposed by Goldberg et al., in 1992, is a representative technique used by some service ranking systems. Collaborative filtering is the process of filtering for information or patterns, which firstly looks for users who share the same ranking patterns through analyzing user's evaluation on certain properties, and then calculates a predication for them by combining the evaluations of similar users. After more than ten years, CF technology has become more and more mature and been widely used in several famous commercial systems, i.e., GroupLens (Konstan, Miller, Maltz, Herlocker, Gordon, & Riedl, 1997), MovieLens (Miller, Albert, Lam, Konstan, & Riedl, 2003), Amazon.com (Linden, Smith, & York, 2003), Yahoo! Music and Facebook, etc.

There are two types of common approaches in neighborhood-based collaborative filtering: rating-oriented and ranking-oriented. The rating-oriented CF approach first predicts QoS values for an active user based on the QoS records provided by users who have similar historical QoS experiences on commonly invoked Web services and then ranks the services according to the predicted QoS values. The ranking-oriented CF approach proposed by Liu et al. (Liu, & Yang, 2008), uses the Kendall Rank Correlation Coefficient (Kendall, 1938) (or Kendall's τ) to measure the similarity among users by computing the correlation of corresponding personal rankings derived from user ratings. However, users' requirements cannot be fully satisfied by these approaches since they only make value prediction or ranking prediction for single QoS property which is not sufficient to represent the overall quality of Web service.

Assume that for m users and n services, the relationship between users and services is denoted by a $m \times n$ user-service matrix R. Then each entry $r_{i,j}$ in the matrix R represents the QoS ratings of service j observed by user i and $r_{i,j} = \emptyset$ if user i has never invoked service j before. The set of users who have invoked service j is denoted by U_j and the set of services invoked by user i is denoted by S_i.

The rating-oriented approach usually tries to predict the missing values in user-service matrix as accurately as possible. In rating-oriented CF Approach, the Person Correlation Coefficient (PCC) (Robert, & Daniel, 2000) is a popular similarity computation approach, measuring the similarity between users and Web services. The PCC value sim(u, v) of user u and user v can be calculated as follows:

$$Sim(u,v) = \frac{\sum_{i \in S_u \cap S_v} \left(r_{u,i} - \overline{r}_u\right) \cdot \left(r_{v,i} - \overline{r}_v\right)}{\sqrt{\sum_{i \in S_u \cap S_v} \left(r_{u,i} - \overline{r}_u\right)^2 \sum_{i \in S_u \cap S_v} \left(r_{v,i} - \overline{r}_v\right)^2}}$$

(1)

where $\overline{r}_u$ and $\overline{r}_v$ are mean rating values of user u and v, respectively. Similarly, Equation (1) can also

be employed to compute the similarity of two Web services. Three well-known rating-oriented approaches based on PCC are user-based model (Shao, Zhang, Wei, Zhao, Xie, & Mei, 2007) (named UPCC), item-based model (Linden, Smith, & York, 2003) (named IPCC), and the user-based and item-based combined model (Zheng, Ma, Lyu, & King, 2009) (named UIPCC), respectively.

In the ranking-oriented CF approach proposed by (Liu, & Yang, 2008), user preferences are modeled as personal rankings derived from user ratings. The Kendall Rank Correlation Coefficient is used to measure the similarity between users by computing the correlation of corresponding personal rankings. The KRCC value of user u and user v can be calculated by the following formula:

$$Sim(u,v) = 1 - \frac{4 \times \sum_{i,j \in S_u \cap S_v} \tilde{I}\left(\left(r_{u,i} - r_{u,j}\right)\left(r_{v,i} - r_{v,j}\right)\right)}{\left|S_u \cap S_v\right| \times \left(\left|S_u \cap S_v\right| - 1\right)}$$

(2)

where $S_u \cap S_v$ is a subset of services commonly invoked by user u and user v, $r_{u,i}$ is the rating value of service i observed by user u, and $\tilde{I}\left(x\right)$ is an indicator function such that $\tilde{I}\left(x\right) = 1$ $(x < 0)$ and $\tilde{I}\left(x\right) = 0$ $(x \geq 0)$. To predict the full rankings of unrated items, this approach defines a preference function that represents predicted preference relation between items in the form of $\Psi : I \times I \to R$. In the end, a greedy order algorithm is used to compute full rankings.

The problem of rating-oriented CF approaches is that the focus has been placed on approximating the ratings rather than the rankings, which is a more important goal for Web service selection. Moreover, most existing methods predict the ratings for each individual service independently without considering the user's preferences on pairs of services. Suppose we have three services si, sj and sk, for which the true ratings are known to be

2, 4 and 6, respectively and two different methods have predicted the ratings on si, sj and sk to be (3, 9, 14) and (8, 5, 3) respectively. In terms of rating prediction accuracy measured by the absolute deviation (MAE) from the true rating, the second prediction is better than the first one. While using the prediction (8, 5, 3), service si, sj and sk will be incorrectly ordered while the prediction (3, 9, 14) ensures the correct order. The existing CF approaches have two limitations. One is that the order has a high priority rather than its value during a service ranking predication. Moreover, higher accuracy in rating prediction does not lead to better ranking effectiveness.

In the ranking-oriented CF approach proposed by Liu et al., although Kendall's seems to be a reasonable choice for comparing two rankings, there still exist some issues. Let's consider an example with eight different services. We assume their actual ranking order is (8, 7, 6, 5, 4, 3, 2, 1) and two alternate methods have given ranked order (5,6,7,8,4,3,2,1) and (8,7,6,5,1,2,3,4) to them respectively. Compared with the actual ranking order, the former ranking has the first four services in inverse order, while the latter has inverse order for the last four. The Kendall's τ of each ranking with the actual ranking is the same (both equal to 0.6429). Hence, based on the Kendall's τ values, the two methods are equivalent. However, it is much more important to get the "top half" of the list "right" than the "bottom half". The Kendall's τ does not distinguish between the errors that occur towards the top of the ranking list from the errors towards the bottom of the list. While in most cases of Web service selection, we care more about the services that are ranked towards the top of the list because of their higher probability of being selected.

2.2 Service Test and Error Diagnosis

Collaborative service ranking requires a huge number of QoS records. However, the public quality information of Web service is very limited over Internet, which makes it difficult to collect all QoS information from users. In light of this, we design an active detection mechanism to acquire the basic QoS information of services. A prototype named WSTester is implemented and it manages the distributed resources to construct a virtual computing environment for Web services testing, and it is able to decompose the whole testing task into sub-tasks to deploy them onto the distributed nodes in the virtual computing environment.

How to deploy a testing environment quickly for a service is very important, but traditional service testing approaches generally incur high cost to deploy the testing environment. In particular, the emergency of Cloud computing paradigm provides an opportunity for resource integration. Cloud testing is a kind of automated testing mode based on distributed resources, and the centralized Cloud infrastructure can be easily used for service testing to improve the efficiency of automated testing greatly. In a Cloud, service providers can create and manage a distributed test platform, and users can submit test scripts into the Cloud servers. After the server received the scripts, it will analyze and deploy them onto the Cloud platform, and then run the test tasks on the virtual test environment. Besides, Cloud test server provides accurate data analysis and feedback to the user. Currently, there are some well-known Cloud testing provider e.g., Cloud Testing, Keynote and SOASTA CloudTest etc., which mainly support functional and performance testing for Web applications and mobile applications.

At the same time, a complex business process generally integrates a large scale of distributed services, and some errors may occur in the service composition, so it is desirable to present an efficient way to detect and locate possible faults during service execution (Rahmani, & Abolhassani, 2008). Moreover, faults in a composite service often are accumulated and disseminated between services, making it more difficult to locate the original fault. However, traditional throw-and-catch mechanism in Java platform is very preliminary for faults diagnosing, which relies on the developer to anticipate possible faults at the designing stage. Therefore, how to detect such faults during the testing of service composition is also one of the key challenges.

In this chapter, we mainly discuss three types of classic fault (shown in Table1 & Figure 1).

The research on program error trace and diagnosis has become popular in recent years. Wang et al., (Avizienis, Laprie, & Landwehr, 2004) integrates monitoring and diagnostic services into the QoS management framework. The diagnostic service reasons out fault causes using graphical model-based approach and causal networks in networked enterprise system. However, causal network reasoning is not as ideal as QoS diagnosis reasoning engine in the case of uncertain or incomplete information (Ardissono, Console, Goy, Petrone, Picardi, Segnan, & Dupré, 2005; Rahmani, & Abolhassani, 2008). Causal network reasoning may produce ambiguous results when evidence collected is insufficient.

A system monitoring method based on local interaction components model is proposed by Wang, Wang, and Chen (2005), which uses Petri nets to model the external behavior of software components. Associating local controller component with a component to monitor in-out information and compare them with the specific behavior, it can infer the state of the indicated component. Similarly, some researchers (Grosclaude, 2004; Wu, Wei, Ye, Zhong, & Huang, 2010) propose a model based on fault diagnosis method for composite service through adding each service with a local module, and setting a global diagnosis in the whole application context. Local diagnostic modules monitor Web service associated and record interacted information among services. The global diagnosis can infer the root cause of composite service failure with the collaboration of local diagnostic modules. However, this method is debatable in terms of feasibility or costs, if some services are located in remote servers, which makes it impossible to add diagnostic module to every service. Bayesian network is also used in fault diagnostic model (Fu, Zou, Shang, & Jiang, 2008) using Web service reputation quality and historical performance data. By assigning each service with an error probability value in a learning mode, the model diagnosis each Web service in the order of error probability. This method is based on the credibility history of a Web service, but if the historical information of composite service is incomplete or unreliable, a reliable performance is infeasible to be achieved.

3 DESIGNING OF CLOUDRANK

To evaluate the services in a Cloud, we propose a collaborative quality ranking approach named CloudRank for Cloud services (shown in Figure 2), which combines both user feedbacks and service testing. In CloudRank, user preferences are modeled as personal rankings derived from user QoS ratings on services, the major contributions are listed as follows.

First, we design a QoS model which allows users to specify their preferences flexibly while providing combination of multiple QoS properties

Table 1. The types of faults

Fault types	Description
Interrupt Fault	The business process interrupts during the execution, and no response to the next service or client which invokes it.
Loop Fault	The business process continues to execute some sub-processes, but no exit condition for this loop.
Not Excepted Fault	The business process returns an unexpected result to the next service or client which invokes it.

Figure 1. The types of faults

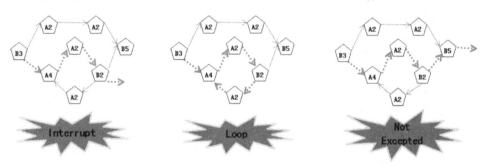

to give an overall rating on services. In this QoS model we describe the quantitative non-functional properties of Web services as quality criteria, including response time (i.e., round-trip time, RTT), price, throughput, security and availability etc. These criteria have different characteristics, for instance, service price is comparatively stable, while RTT and throughput are changing continuously.

Second, we present a similarity measure method that is sensitive to the service position in the ranking list, and it is used to determine a set of users that share similar preferences with the active user. The similarity measure takes into account the positions of concordant pairs appearing in the ranking list, which means that the concordant pairs ranked higher are more important than those ranked lower.

Third, based on the two methods, we use a greedy order algorithm to generate the Cloud ser-

vice ranking for the active user. The greedy order algorithm treats the explicitly rated items and the unrated items respectively, and takes the advantage of user's given QoS ratings to guarantee that the explicitly rated services will be ranked correctly.

Fourth, in order to manage the distributed test environment more effectively, the system collects the available compute nodes to build a virtual testing environment, and all of the nodes register into a server through a default initialization agent. Based on this testing environment, the test requests can be processed with optimal resource consumption.

Finally, in order to handle the possible faults, we build a service composition execution flow model, and the fault transmission flow path can be searched effectively based on this model. Then, the node which causes the process path failure will be identified. In this way, we can find out the source of service fault through default system or user defined checking rules.

Figure 2. Architecture of cloud service ranking based on SOA technologies

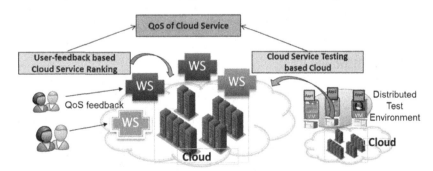

3.1 WSRank: A Ranking-Oriented Collaborative Filtering

3.1.1 Overview of WSRank

In this section, we present the collaborative quality ranking approach (named WSRank) for Web services in CloudRank, which is designed as a four-phase process (depicted in Table 2). The details of each phase will be presented.

The workflow of WSRank is shown in Figure 3, where WSRank takes the candidate service as the input and returns the ranking results.

3.1.2 QoS Model and Ranking Approach

The aim of our approach is to discover Web services with optimal QoS ratings for active users. In CloudRank QoS model, we consider the following QoS properties: response time (i.e., round-trip time, RTT), price, throughput, security and availability. In this chapter, we take RTT and throughput as QoS examples to interpret our approach, and this approach can be easily extended to other properties.

The basic notations used in this chapter are defined as follows:

- **Service Set:** We use $S = \{s1, s2, ...,sn\}$ to denote a set of services with similar functionality, where si $(1 \leq i \leq n)$ is a service, and n is the number of services in S.
- **User Set:** We use $U = \{u1, u2, ..., um\}$ to denote a set of users in the CloudRank system, where uj $(1 \leq j \leq m)$ is a user, and m is the number of users in U, and ua is an active user who has provided some QoS values and now needs to select the best Web service.
- **QoS Vector:** We use $Qu = (qi,1, qi,2, ..., qi,l)$ to denote a QoS vector of service si from the view of user u, where qi,j represents the jth QoS criterion value of service si.

For each user u, we can obtain a following matrix Mu, as shown in Equation (3), by putting all the services' QoS vectors together where each row in Mu represents the QoS vector of some service in S, and each column represents a different QoS criterion value.

Table 2. The four-phase of WSRank

Phase	Description
Phase 1	Based on the QoS model and the utility function, obtain the user-service rating matrix
Phase 2	Calculate the similarity of each user with the active user and identify a set of similar users.
Phase 3	Define a preference function to present the priority of two services.
Phase 4	Use greedy order algorithm to rank the service candidates by making use of the past usage experiences of other similar users.

Figure 3. The workflow of WSRank

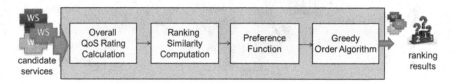

$$M_u = \begin{pmatrix} q_{1,1} & q_{1,2} & \cdots & q_{1,l} \\ q_{2,1} & q_{2,2} & \cdots & q_{2,l} \\ \cdot & \cdot & \cdot \\ \cdot & \cdot & \cdot \\ \cdot & \cdot & \cdot \\ q_{n,1} & q_{n,2} & \cdots & q_{n,l} \end{pmatrix} \qquad (3)$$

There are two steps involved to represent user priorities and preferences. First, as QoS criteria varies in units and magnitude, values of Mu(qi,j) must be normalized to perform QoS-based ranking. Second, the weighted evaluation on criteria needs to be carried out for representing user's constraints, preference and special requirements.

In the normalization step, each criterion value qij is transformed to a real value hij∈ [0, 1] using the Gaussian normalization (Ortega, Rui, Chakrabarti, Mehrotra, & Huang, 1997). This Gaussian normalization will guarantee that 99% of hi,j values are within [0,1]. For hi,j, in [0, 1] after normalization, we give 0 or 1 to them according to their distance from each side. Note that for some criteria, smaller values mean higher service quality. For such criteria, we set hi,j=1/hi,j. Thus, the QoS matrix Mu is transformed into a normalized matrix E'_u.

A weight vector W = (w1, w2, ..., wl) is used to represent user u priorities on preferences given two different criteria with $w_k \in R_0^+$ and $\sum_{k=1}^{l} w_k = 1$. The final QoS ratings vector Ru = (ru,1, ru,2, ..., ru,n) of service u is therefore can be computed with the following formula:

$$r_{u,i} = \sum_{k=1}^{l} w_k h_{i,k}, 1 \leq i \leq n \qquad (4)$$

Finally, we can get a user-service matrix $R_{m \times n}$ where each entry $r_{i,j} \left(1 \leq i \leq m, 1 \leq j \leq n\right)$ represents the QoS ratings of user ui to service sj. But in real-life situations, few users are used to feedback QoS values. Therefore, all the above computation is just for those services which have been fully rated. If any criterion value of a service does not exist, then user's rating on this service is set to ϕ. Table 3 shows an example of user-service matrix.

CloudRank QoS model allows users to characterize their preferences flexibly while providing combination of multiple QoS properties to give an overall rating on services. If users only want to employ a specific QoS property, they just need to set the weight of this property as 1 and otherwise as 0.

The KRCC measure described in section 2 (Equation (2)) does not consider positions of concordant pairs appearing in the ranking list, which means that the concordant pairs ranked higher are as important as those ranked lower. In practice, top concordant pairs of services in the ranking list are more important than the lower ones. Therefore, Yilmaz et al. proposed a new rank correlation coefficient, namely Average Precision Correlation Coefficient (AP) (Yilmaz, Aslam, & Robertson, 2008), by taking the position of concordant pairs in the rank list into account. The AP Correlation Coefficient is an asymmetrical measure, i.e. $\tau_{ap}\left(l_1, l_2\right) \neq \tau_{ap}\left(l_2, l_1\right)$. Given two rank lists l1 and l2, assuming l2 is an actual rank list, and the AP coefficient is generated from the following random method:

1. Picking any service si from the rank list l1 randomly.

Table 3. User-service rating matrix

service user	s1	s2	...	sn
u1	3	2	...	φ
...	...	...	...	...
ua	φ	3	...	φ
...	...	...	...	...
um	5	φ	...	4

2. Picking another service sj from the rank list l1 that is ranked higher than the previous service si randomly.

3. Return 1 if this pair of services are in the same relative order as in rank list l2; otherwise, return 0.

The expected outcome of this random experiment can be written as:

$$p = \frac{1}{N-1} \cdot \sum_{i=2}^{N} \frac{C(i)}{i-1} \tag{5}$$

where C(i) is the number of services ranked higher than si and correctly ranked with respect to the service at rank si in l1. The AP Correlation Coefficient is defined as:

$$\tau_{ap} = p - (1-p) = \frac{2}{N-1} \cdot \sum_{i=2}^{N} \left(\frac{C(i)}{i-1} \right) - 1 \tag{6}$$

In our approach, the similarity of any two users is computed via AP Correlation Coefficient between two different rankings of commonly invoked services given by $Sim(u,v) = \tau_{ap}\left(R_u^{S_u \cap S_v}, R_v^{S_u \cap S_v} \right)$, where $R_u^{S_u \cap S_v}$ is the ranking given by user u over common set of services that user u and v both invoked; similarly for $R_v^{S_u \cap S_v}$.

By calculating the AP similarity values between the active user and other users, the users similar to the active user can be identified. Since employing QoS values of dissimilar users will greatly influence the prediction accuracy for the current user, our approach excludes the users with negative correlations. In our approach, the set of similar users Nu based on AP is identified for the current user u by:

$$N_u = \left\{ v \middle| Sim(u,v) > 0.5, v \neq u \right\}.$$

The value of $Sim(u,v)$ can be calculated by Equation (2).

A user's preference on a pair of services is defined as a mapping of $\Psi : S \times S \rightarrow R$, where $\Psi(i,j) > 0$ means that service si is more preferable to sj for user u and vice versa. The preference function $\Psi(i,j)$ is anti-symmetric, i.e. $\Psi(i,j) = -\Psi(j,i)$. We set $\Psi(i,i) = 0$ for all $i \in S$ and use user-based model to predict the value of preference function $\Psi(i,j)$ of candidate services.

$$\Psi(i,j) = \begin{cases} r_{u,i} - r_{u,j} & i,j \in S_u \\ \dfrac{\sum_{v \in N_u^{i,j}} Sim(u,v) \cdot \left(r_{v,i} - r_{v,j} \right)}{\sum_{v \in N_u^{i,j}} Sim(u,v)} & \text{otherwise} \end{cases} \tag{7}$$

where v is a similar user of the active user u, and $N_u^{i,j}$ is a subset of similar users of u, who have invoked both service si and si.

Given a preference function Ψ, which assigns a score to every pair of services si, sj$\in$S, we choose a quality ranking of services in S that agrees with the pairwise preferences defined by Ψ as much as possible. Let ρ be a ranking of services in S, such that $\rho(i) > \rho(j)$ if and only if si is ranked higher than sj. We then can define a value function $V^{\Psi}(\rho)$ as follows to measure the consistency of the ranking with the preference function.

$$V^{\Psi}(\rho) = \sum_{i,j:\rho(i) > \rho(j)} \Psi(i,j) \tag{8}$$

Therefore, our objective is to produce a ranking ρ^* that maximizes the above objective value function. One possible approach to solve the service ranking problem is to search through all the possible rankings and select the optimal ranking ρ^* that maximizes the value function defined in Equation (10). However, Cohen et al. (Cohen, Schapire, & Singer, 1999) have shown that finding the optimal ranking ρ^* is an NP-Complete problem and proposed a greedy order algorithm (we named such algorithms as GOAP) for finding an approximately optimal ranking. It was also shown that the ranking produced by the greedy order algorithm has a value that is within a factor

2 of the optimal, i.e $V^{\Psi}(\rho) \geq \frac{1}{2} V^{\Psi}(\rho*)$.

However, a GOAP algorithm (Greedy Order Algorithm) treats the explicitly rated items and the unrated items equally, so it does not guarantee that the explicitly rated items will be ranked correctly. In our approach, we take the advantage of user's given ratings to make correction for the initial ranking. Suppose G is a set of services whose ratings have given by a user, the correction procedure is listed as follows:

Step 1: Rank the services in G based on given ratings. $\rho_g(t)$ stores the ranking and t is a service and the function $\rho_g(t)$ returns the corresponding order of this service.

Step 2: For all the services in G, find the service sj with minimum position in $\rho(t)$.

Step 3: Pick the first service si from $\rho g(t)$ and exchange the position of i and j in $\rho(t)$. Then delete i from G and its correspond order $\rho g(t)$. If G is not empty, then go to step 2.

3.1.3 Top-K Service Ranking Algorithm

CF-based rank systems require huge amounts of users to provide their QoS records. However due to the inconsistent behavior of Cloud users and the cold-start problems in the CF approach, it's hard to gather and accurately describe users' preferences. It is not sufficient to rank Cloud services only based on user feedback. Thus, we design a top-K service ranking algorithm through service testing by making use of the distribute Cloud environment. We take RTT, stability, success

rate and availability as an example to describe our top-K ranking approach.

Considering the timeliness of QoS data, the latest QoS data has the most valuable reference. We describe a Markov Chain as a stochastic process K= {st0, st1,…, stn-1} for service availability where state sti with a value 0 or 1 (0 means at time ti service is not available, and 1 represents that at time ti service is available). Then the probability of the service transferring from current state to the available state is calculated as follows:

$$P_{i,j} = \frac{N_{i,j}}{N_i} \qquad (9)$$

where $N_{i,j}$ is the number of the state transitions in the given Markov Chain from state sti to available state st j; N_i is the total number of state transitions in the given Markov Chain from state sti to any arbitrary states.

Suppose we have a Markov Chain of services as follows: K = {1,0,0,1,0,1,1,0,0,1,1,1,0,1,0,1} . The current state is 1, based on Equation 9 we get the availability of s in the following steps: firstly we compute the number of ordered pairs in which the former state is 1 and the second state is also 1 in K as Nt; secondly we computing the number of ordered pairs in which the former state is 1 and the second state is either 1or 0 in K as N; and finally the availability is calculated by the ratio of Nt and N.

To make the top-K service ranking, the Partial Order Relation between services is given below:

Definition1 Partial Order Relation: Suppose Qi and Qj are two QoS vectors of services si and sj respectively. If all QoS criteria values of si are better than sj, we say there exists partial order relation between service si and sj, represented by Dominate (si, sj) =1

Based on Definition 1, the Grade of service si is calculated by Equation 10. We can see that the larger the Grade value is, the better the service is. Finally we give our top-K service ranking algorithm, shown in Algorithm 1.

$$\text{Grade}\left(s_i\right) = \sum_{j=1}^{n} \text{Dominate}\left(s_i, s_j\right), j \neq i \tag{10}$$

The input of Algorithm 1 is the candidate services, the threshold k specifies the maximum number of output, and the output is a ranking service set satisfied with the desired number. Algorithm 1 firstly extracted the QoS vectors for each service, and then sets up the partial order relations between candidate services. Next it calculates the grade value of every service in turn, and finally returns the set of services with top-K grade value.

3.2 WSTester: A Composite Service Testing and Fault Diagnosis

3.2.1 Overview of WSTester

In order to manage a virtual test environment effectively, we design a prototype named WSTester. The whole process of WSTester can be divided into four major steps as shown in Figure 4, where the first step is the test bed management, the second step is test cases management, the third step is the test job execution and faults diagnosis, and the final step the test results generation and analysis.

Previously, a light-weight Test Agent will be installed in every available computer in a Cloud test environment (or a computer resource pool), and WSTester will collect the meta-information of all available computers by their Test Agents. If a tester u wants to test a composite service s, u will firstly submit a request to the Test Server, and the Test Server chooses some Local Test Hosts for this test task based on their workload condition. The workload condition will be monitored by the test probe module of a test agent. Besides, the Test Server can decompose a task into subtasks, and assign them to the selected Test Agent Nodes according to some rules. The Local Test Host will monitor the composite service test execution and locate the fault throughout the process. By the way, the test probe not only can monitor the testing container's status such as task loading, network flow, flow loading and error rating, but also the Local Test Host's information such as usages of CPU, disk, memory and bandwidth etc.

3.2.2 Test Cases and Execution Management

The phase of test case designing is one of most critical technical issues in WSTester. According to statistics, the cost of software test accounts for 30% to 50% of the total cost, of which about 40% is spent on test case designing. Thus, to improve the automation of all stages for testing, efficiency of test case generation is considered to

Algorithm 1. Top-K service ranking algorithm

Input: a service set S; a threshold value of k
Output: the recommended service set S_d
//getting QoS vector for each service
1: **for each** s_i in S
2: get Q_i for s_i *//computing Dominate value for each pair of service*
3: **for each**(s_i, s_j) in S
4: caculate Dominate(s_i, s_j) *//computing grade value for each service*
5: **for each** s_i in S
6: calculate grade(s_i) *//ranking service by their grade values*
10: select service with *top-K* grade value from S into S_d
11: return S_d

Figure 4. The four major steps of WSTester

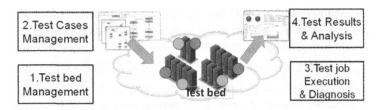

be an important step to reduce test costs, thereby improving the test quality of the overall software development. However, the testers of a service composition now rely mainly on experience to generate test cases manually, which highly reduces the efficiency of service composition development, leads to an inadequate testing of the whole system and the software performance cannot be fully guaranteed.

The test case requires a complete and consistent description, which is important to the comparison of different test results. To achieve this, a test case generally includes two key parts: test process and test assertion information within the specific implementation. The test process is also depicted with a composite service, and the test assertion specifies some statements with expected values to the test cases. After generating test cases, the tester submits them to the Test Server, and the Test Server will deploy them onto the Test Agents which execute the test tasks.

The detailed steps of WSTester are described as Figure 5.

1. All distributed Test Agent Nodes and Local Hosts should register into a centralized information service (implemented as a database).

2. The Service Developer develops a business process expressed as BPMN2.0 [BPMN2.0, 2011] document through service composition.

3. The Service Tester adds some test cases and constraint rules into the BPMN document, and sends a corresponding test request document to the Test Server.

Figure 5. WSTester test procedure

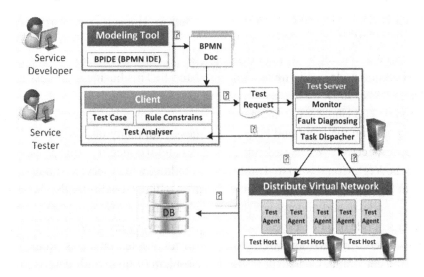

4. The Test Server decomposes the test task into subtasks, and deploys them onto the Test Agent Nodes in available Test Hosts, and the Test Server may collaborate with these Test Hosts to complete the test tasks.

5. All the test cases are monitored in real-time, and the fault sources can be identified where errors occurred during the testing. Finally, the Test Server sends the test results to the client side, and the tester can also give some feedbacks based on the test results to the service developer.

In order to handle the possible faults during the testing, we build a service composition execution flow model based on BPMN, and the fault flow path can be located effectively. Furthermore, the node causing the process path failure can be quickly identified.

In BPMN, there are some element objects and sequence flows on the execution path. We use a 6-tuple, node = (id, type, inDeg, outDeg, inMsg, outMsg), to denote a flow object in BPMN, where id is a unique label of a node, and type is an element of the element node type set {EVENT, ACTIVITY, GATEWAY}. The EVENT can further be represented as START EVENT (the start of a business process), INTERMEDIATE EVENT (...) or END EVENT (the end of a business process). The GATEWAY can be divided into PARALLEL GATEWAY, INCLUSIVE GATEWAY AND EXCLUSIVE GATEWAY. A node∈Node with parameters (inDeg=1 && outDeg>1) is regarded as a branch node (i.e., split node), and a node with parameters (inDeg>1 && OutDeg=1) is a merge node (i.e., join node). The final two parameters inMsg and outMsg contain the input and output data of this activity respectively. We use a 4-tuple SF = (id, nodesrc, nodetgt, CondExpr) to denote a sequence flow in BPMN, where id is a unique label of a flow, and nodesrc and nodetgt are the source node and target node of a FO respectively. CondExpr includes the constraints from nodesrc to nodetgt. If there is no constraint, CondExpr = ∅.

For the purpose of fault location, we propose a directed graph BPMN Execute Flow Model (BEF) by analyzing the control flow in BPMN process. BEF is an execution path model for composite service which will be described later in this section. Based on these definitions, we propose a model, BEF = (Node, Edge, Start, End), to describe a BPMN execution flow, where Node is an element object set, Edge is a directed edge set of sequence flow, Start are the beginning nodes of a BPMN process, and End is final nodes of a BPMN process.

Next we will take an online bookstore process as an example to illustrate the method, more detailed algorithms can be found in our previous work (Zhu, Li, Zhao & Li, 2011). This business process example consists of three service entities: Online Bookstores, Bank and Delivery Company. The procedure is described as follows.

Step 1: A user logins the Online Bookstores, and submits a search request;

Step 2: The server invokes a query service and returns the search results to this user;

Step 3: The user selects the preferred books, and generates the books buying orders;

Step 4: The server confirms the orders and waits for users to pay;

Step 5: The user pays the book through an online banking service;

Step 6: The server confirms user's payment, if success and delivery the books to users;

Step 7: The user acknowledges the received books;

Step 8: This business process is completed.

As shown in Figure 6, this is a complex process with many task nodes and execution paths. A natural concern of this process is that if there is a failure, which service should be responsible for this failure? Traditionally, the tester may have to check all the execution paths and their information of every involved service, but it is inefficient for a complex business process. To address the problem of huge fault detection space caused by multi-branch characteristics in business process execution, we propose a failure path search approach based on the message flow by analyzing the BPMN XML file and the execution results in the log file.

Through throw-and-catch mechanism, we can find any task node λ which suffers failure. In order to find the original failure node within the process, when the task node λ is found FALSE (it is not the fault source), we should search a Path (λ) to locate its source. To find a Path (λ), the corresponding service nodes which ended on the failure service λ should be discovered. We backtrack the execution model from the log files, then find pre-nodes of which the output as the input of λ, and add them into the path until encountered a start event node. Finally, we can get a Path(λ) which contains all related nodes. By this way, we can further find the minimal service nodes which may cause the failure of λ. Instead of checking all the services within the process, we merely need to check and analyze related ones in Path(λ) which reduces the cost while increasing the accuracy.

After that, we will check every service node in Path(λ). We infer the service status from the input and output status. Traditionally, it checks the input/output status by comparing its value with the specific declaration in BPMN file. For example, if it is the expected value, or the dedicated type, it is considered OK; otherwise, it is FALSE

(Wu, Wei, Ye, Zhong, & Huang, 2010). But it is inadequate in some conditions. For example, if an input request of the Find Book Service is book1, but the result is of an unwanted book, which may be also consistent with the constraints. This may lead to a misstated conclusion. In fact, although we do not know the exact result from the input, the output must have some relationship with the input. For example, the result contains information of requested book name or ISBN code and so on. So, we can use the policy file to constrain the input, output value and the possible relationship between them. And we infer the input/output status as follows:

1. If the input satisfies the constraint conditions in the rule policy, it is marked as OK;
2. If the output satisfies the constrain conditions and the rules between input and output, it is marked as OK, otherwise FALSE.

4 IMPLEMENTATION EXPERIENCES

4.2 Implementation of WSRank

Figure 7 shows the system architecture of ServiceXchange designed by BUAA (Beijing University of Aeronautics and Astronautics). ServiceXchange is a Web service repository and search engine providing functions of Web

Figure 6. An online bookstores process

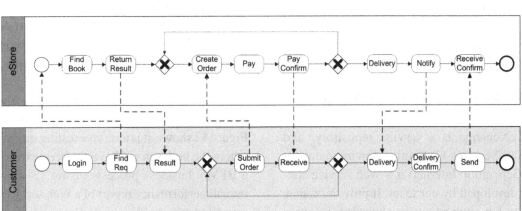

service registering, searching, monitoring etc. Web services are collected into ServiceXchange using a crawler, and a UDDI-like registry is also available for software providers to register their Web service into ServiceXchange. By analyzing the WSDL of Web services, the information such as interface operations and data transmitted is stored in the Raw Info DB. Further knowledge of Web services such as similarity, connectivity, cluster and index are discovered leveraging the data mining technology and stored in Mined Info DB. Users can search Web services by keyword or category.

We design and implement the ranking system WSRank integrated into ServiceXchange, which supports QoS information monitoring and top-K service ranking, and it has become an important component of ServiceXchange. As a Web service repository, there exist a huge number of distributed and reusable services in ServiceXchange. When searching services in ServiceXchange, an active user usually obtains a large set of services with similar functionality, then WSRank can give a personalized optimal service ranking result to the active user.

We briefly show some Web snapshots of our WSRank in Figure 8 and Figure 9. After inputting a keyword, users will get the top-K service list as shown in Figure 8 by selecting expected service number (e.g., top-10, top-20 or all). Through the service name linking, users can view detailed information of each service, including notation, functionality, and non-functionality and reputation etc. The non-functionality of a service is shown via a time-availability curve as shown in Figure 9 and user can choose different service operations and service locations.

4.2 Implementation of WSTester

ServiceXchange is a service repository, and SCENE (Services Computing Environment for Next Generation Internet) is a Web service container developed by our team. It provides a new solution for application development, resource sharing and application integration in a distributed network environment, consisting of Messaging Layer, Public Service Layer, Container Layer, Business Process Engineer Layer and Management Framework Layer.

In SCENE, we design and implement an automated testing tool WSTester, which supports fault diagnosing for Web service composition. The architecture of WSTester is shown in Figure 11, and it is an important component of SCENE. It can assist the test cases generation, test case execution, and faults locating and anlysing within the process with good versatility and high automation.

As shown in Figure 11, the major components of WSTester can be divided into four groups.

1. **Test Case Management:** It includes a BPMN Processor which parses the BPMN document, a Test Case Editor to edit and assign the test cases into BPMN document, and Test Case Optimizer to optimize the test cases.
2. **Runtime Management:** It includes an Environment Monitor to collect the hosts' information, a Runtime Monitor to collect the test agents' information, and a Test Analyzer to analyze the test results.
3. **Test Server:** It includes a Test Environment Manager to manage the test computer pool, a Task Dispatcher to decompose the requested task and deploy the task onto the hosts, and a Fault Detector & Monitor module to backtrack the fault source.
4. **Test Environment:** It includes Test Agent, SCENCE Server, and Execution Engine for service composition and Service Repository.

We also briefly show some Web snapshots of our WSTester in Figure 12 and Figure 13. As Figure 12 shows, it is a service testing monitoring where the nodes in red have not been executed in a BPMN business process. Figure 13 shows an overall performance report of a Web service after several tests.

Figure 7. System architecture of ServiceXchange

Service Xchange
Web Portal
Crawler
WS Registry
Mining Module
Search Module
QoS Monitor
Service Ranking
Persistent Layer
Raw Info DB
Mined Info DB
User DB
QoS DB

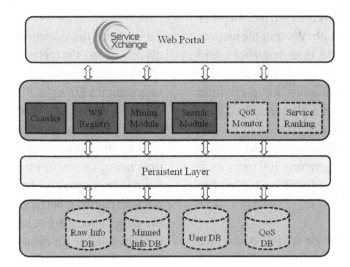

Figure 8. A snapshot of service search result web

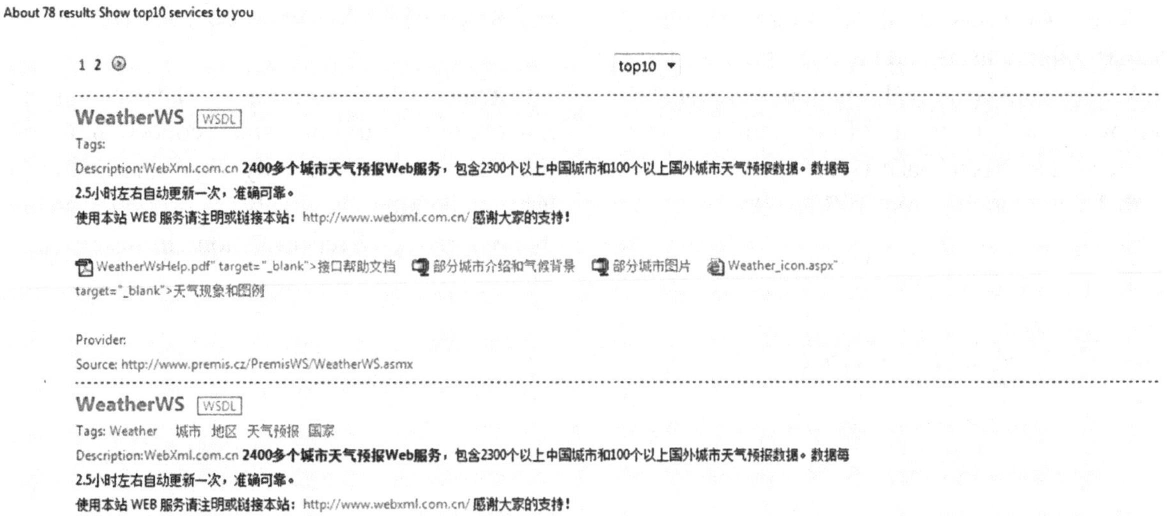

About 78 results Show top10 services to you
1 2
top10
WeatherWS WSDL
Tags:
Description:WebXml.com.cn 2400多个城市天气预报Web服务，包含2300个以上中国城市和100个以上国外城市天气预报数据。数据每
2.5小时左右自动更新一次，准确可靠。
使用本站 WEB 服务请注明或链接本站：http://www.webxml.com.cn/ 感谢大家的支持！
WeatherWsHelp.pdf" target="_blank">接口帮助文档 部分城市介绍和气候背景 部分城市图片 Weather_icon.aspx"
target="_blank">天气现象和图例
Provider:
Source: http://www.premis.cz/PremisWS/WeatherWS.asmx
WeatherWS WSDL
Tags: Weather 城市 地区 天气预报 国家
Description:WebXml.com.cn 2400多个城市天气预报Web服务，包含2300个以上中国城市和100个以上国外城市天气预报数据。数据每
2.5小时左右自动更新一次，准确可靠。
使用本站 WEB 服务请注明或链接本站：http://www.webxml.com.cn/ 感谢大家的支持！

5 SIMULATION RESULTS

We also conducted some simulation to evaluate the effectiveness of CloudRank with some open datasets and environments. The following two datasets are adopted in our simulation:

1. WSRec (Zheng, Ma, Lyu, & King, 2009) dataset, which contains about 1.5 million Web service invocation records of 100 Web services from more than 20 countries. QoS records are collected by 150 computer nodes from Planet-Lab, which are distributed in more than 20 countries as shown in Figure 14. We extract a subset of 300,000 QoS records and 3000 users are generated, each of whom is associated with a QoS profile of all the 100 services.
2. ServiceXchange (ServiceXchange, 2011) dataset, which contains invocation records

of 17000 Web services from 10 countries. QoS records are also collected by computer nodes from Planet-Lab. We spilt the records of each node into 40 time sequences, and get the average RTT, stability, success rate together with availability for each time sequence. Thus each node is attached with 40 QoS records of all 17000 services. We randomly extract 200 services, and for each of the 10 nodes we generate 300 users each of whom is associated with a QoS profile of all 200 services.

As for our QoS model, for WSRec dataset we take two QoS properties, RTT and throughput with equal weight, and for ServiceXchange we take four QoS properties, RTT, stability, success rate and availability with equal weight.

The 3000 users are divided into two parts, one as training users and the rest as active (test) users. To simulate the real situation, we randomly remove some QoS entries of the training matrix and testing matrix to make a set of sparse matrices with density ranging from 10% to 60%.

5.1 Evaluation Metric

To evaluate the effects and efficiency of CloudRank, we use the metric of Mean Absolute Error (MAE), that is one commonly used evaluation metric for traditional collaborative filtering algorithms and it depends on the difference between the truth data and predictions.

As our approach is ranking-oriented rather than rating-oriented, we have to employ metrics for measuring quality of produced rankings. Since AP Correlation Coefficient gives more weight to the errors appearing at high ranking positions, it is more suitable for measuring the services ranking. In our experiments, we also employ the AP Correlation Coefficient (Equation (2)) to evaluate the efficiency of WSRank.

5.2 Impact of Service Numbers

The number of services impacts the personalized ranking of user u. For a small collection, users' preferences were not fully expressed, while a large collection inevitably incorporates many inappropriate preference relations. In these experi-

Figure 9. A snapshot of service QoS web

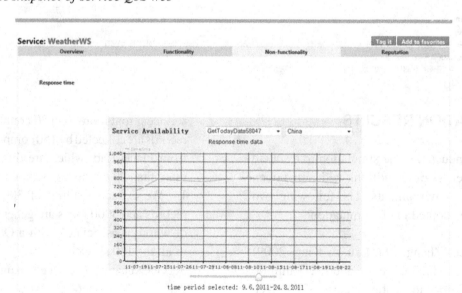

Figure 10. SCENE container

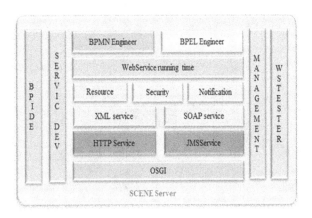

Figure 11. The architecture of WSTester

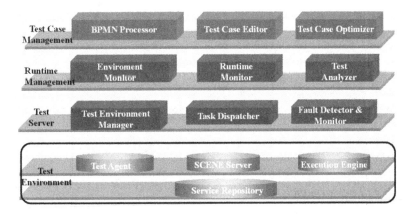

ments, we set different values to |S| and compare two ranking-oriented methods (i.e., GOAP and WSRank) on the experiment data. The density of the training matrix and the testing matrix is 0.6 and 0.3 respectively.

Figure 15 shows changes in performances while the limitation of |S| increases from 10 to 100 by a step of 10 for WSRec dataset and the limitation of |S| increases from 10 to 200 by a step of 10 for ServiceXchange dataset. As can be seen from the figure, the mean AP Correlation Coefficient gradually increases at first, then decreases when the number of services increases and finally reaches a plateau.

Lower mean AP Correlation Coefficient at the beginning is likely due to the incomplete user information, i.e., missing enough preference information to establish similarity relationships among users. The decreasing of mean AP Correlation Coefficient may be caused by inappropriate preference relations. We also observe that along with the continuously increasing of the number of services; the prediction accuracy of our WSRank reaches a plateau in our experiment, which means that WSRank can reach higher prediction accuracy even if the number of services is large.

5.3 Impact of Matrix Density

In this subsection, we study the impact of both training matrix and testing matrix on ranking

Figure 12. A snapshot of test monitoring

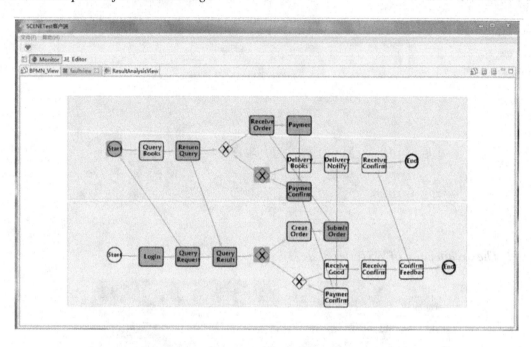

Figure 13. A snapshot of performance report

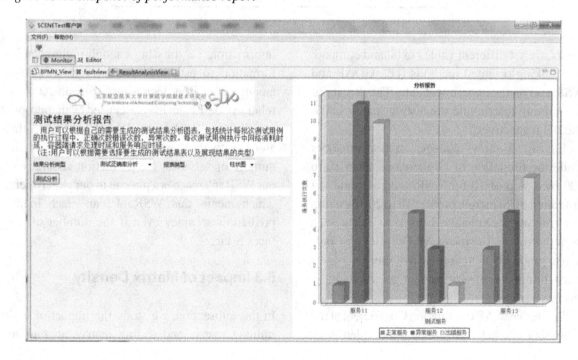

Figure 14. The topology of Planet-Lab

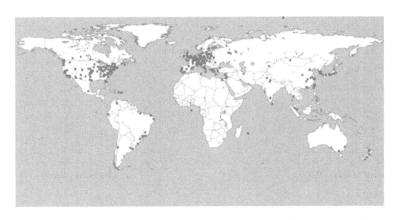

Figure 15. Mean AP correlation coefficient vs. max(|S|) results

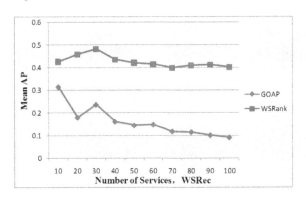 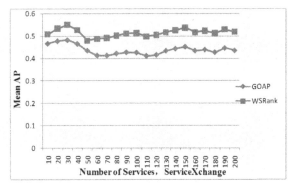

results. In all experiments, we set the number of services as 30, and two ranking-oriented methods (i.e., GOAP and WSRank) are compared.

To study the impact of the testing matrix density on the ranking results, we change the testing matrix density from 10% to 60% with a step value of 10%. In all experiments, we set the training matrix density as 0.3. Figure 17 shows the experiment results. We can see that when the matrix density is increased from 10% to 60%, our WSRank method outperforms the GOAP method consistently. The ranking accuracy of WSRank is significantly enhanced, while the ranking accuracy of the GOAP grows quite slowly. It is mainly because WSRank takes the advantage of user's given ratings to make correction for the initial ranking. This observation indicates that the prediction accuracy of WSRank can be greatly

enhanced by collecting more QoS values to make the testing matrix denser, especially when the training matrix is very sparse.

5.4 Performance Comparison

To study the personalized services ranking performance, we choose four algorithms as the baselines including UPCC, IPCC, UIPCC and the greedy order algorithm using Kendall Rank Correlation Coefficient (GOKRCC) to compare with our ranking approach.

- **UPCC:** This is a classic method (Shao, Zhang, Wei, Zhao, Xie, & Mei, 2007). It employs PCC for computing users' similarities and uses similar users for QoS rating prediction.

Figure 16. Impact of training matrix density

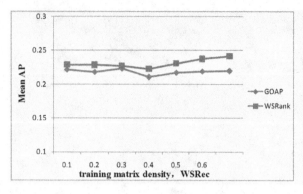
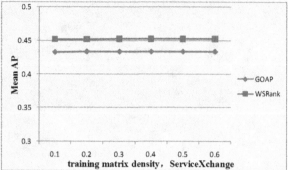

Figure 17. Impact of testing matrix density

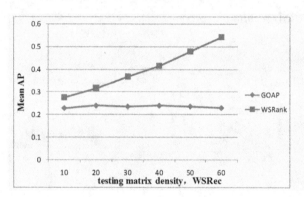
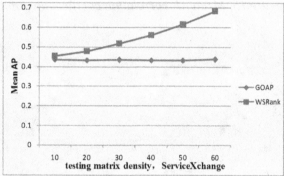

- **IPCC:** This method is item-based (Sarwar, Karypis, Konstan, & Riedl, 2007). It employs PCC for services' similarity computation and predicts QoS ratings by similar services.

- **UIPCC:** This method (Zheng, Ma, Lyu, & King, 2009) combines the user-based and item-based CF approaches and employs PCC for the similarity computation.

- **GOKRCC:** This method (Liu, & Yang, 2008) employs KRCC for the similarity calculation between users and treats the explicitly rated items and the unrated items equally. It does not guarantee that the explicitly rated items will be ranked correctly.

In real-world, the user-service matrices are usually very spare since a user usually only invokes a small number of services. To simulate the real situation, we randomly remove some QoS entries of the training matrix to make a set of sparse matrices with density ranging from 10% to 60%. In terms of the active users, we vary the number of QoS values given by them from 10, 20 to 30, and name them as given 10, Given 20, and Given 30, respectively. The rankings based on the original full matrix are employed as ideal rankings to study the ranking performance. The above four approaches together with GOAP and WSRank method are compared.

In this experiment, we set top-k=10 and λ= 0.8 for UPCC, IPCC and UIPCC. We set number of services with 30 and employ the 0.3 density training matrix. Table 1 shows the ranking prediction accuracy on the AP Correlation Coefficient of different methods. The first three methods in the table are rating-oriented approaches, while the last three are ranking-oriented methods. For each column in Table 4, we highlighted the best performer among all the methods.

Figure 18. Business execution process

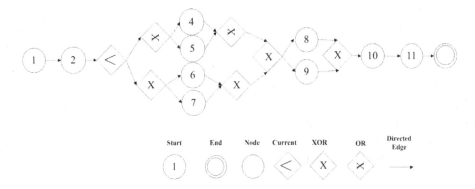

Figure 19. A fault path set

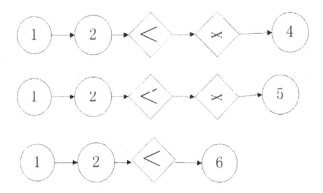

Figure 20. A minimal fault path set

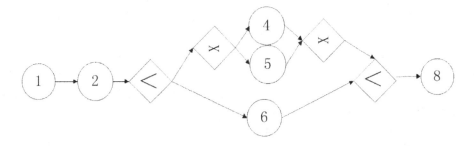

From the results shown in Table 4, we can reach the following conclusions:

- Among all the ranking methods, our WSRank obtains the best prediction accuracy (larger APCC values) under all the experimental settings consistently.

- The ranking-oriented methods (GOKRCC, GOAP and WSRank) consistently outperform rating-oriented approaches (UPCC, IPCC and UIPCC), since ranking-oriented CF methods have taken the user's preferences on service pairs into consideration.

- The fact, GOKRCC, GOAP and WSRank consistently achieve better ranking performance, indicates that the Average Precision Correlation Coefficient is a proper approach for similarity computation in ranking-oriented CF approaches.

- When the density of matrix is increased from 10% to 30%, the ranking accuracy of GOKRCC, GOAP and WSRank is also enhanced, since denser user-item matrix provides more information. However, the ranking accuracy of IPCC, UPCC and UIPCC has no significantly changes, because they mainly focus on accurate prediction on the QoS ratings of a user and make ranking based on these predicted QoS values. In our experiment, these facts are obviously not suitable, since high accuracy in value prediction does not guarantee a high ranking efficiency.

5.5 The Effectiveness of Fault Location in WSTester

We can transform a business execution processes into the BPMN model. As an example shown in Figure 18, this process includes $2\times3\times2=12$ execution paths, and PathSet= {1, 2, PathSet2, PathSet3, PathSet4, 10, 11}, in whichPathSet2= {4, 5}, PathSet3= {6, 7, 6&&7}, and PathSet4= {8, 9}.

If the 11th node has been found be faulty, 12 paths might be traversed in a traditional search method. Based on WSTester, we only need to obtain one fault transition path. FaultPath= {1, 2, FaultPath2, FaultPath3, FaultPath4, 10, 11}, FaultPath2= {4, 5}; FaultPath3= {6}; FaultPath4= {9}. Thus the efficiency has been increased by 90%. In theory, assuming that the process has m possible execution paths, we can obtain an optimization rate of (m-1)/m. In conclusion, the more complex a system is (m value is greater), the higher efficiency can be got. For example, we find three fault paths (shown in Figure 20), if we do not further optimize them, it may bring more overhead. The minimal fault paths algorithm will reduce the redundancy paths, as shown in Figure 21.

To verify the accuracy of the fault location mechanism, we conduct an experiment based on WSTester. In this experiment, we choose four composite services (denoted by service 1, service 2, service 3 and service 4), and we insert errors into every service ten times randomly which makes execution result of the entire service process to be FALSE. The experiment results are shown in Figure 22 for these forty cases, and our mechanism can locate the fault accurately for 8, 8, 9 and 8 times separately, which indicates that the WSTester can precisely locate faults. Such, users can monitor the run-time execution of test and locate the service faults quickly when errors occur. With the fault feedback information, service developers also can modify the service composition and avoid further possible faults.

CONCLUSION

In this chapter, we proposed a Cloud service ranking system, named CloudRank, based on both the user feedback and service testing methods. In CloudRank, we designed a new ranking-oriented collaborative filtering (CF) approach named WSRank, and a QoS model is proposed to allow users to express their preferences flexibly while providing combination of multiple QoS properties to give an overall rating on services. Experimental

Figure 21. Fault location accuracy

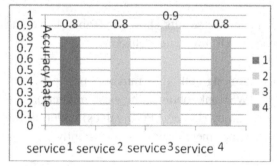

Table 4. Average precision correlation coefficient

Method	Service number = 30				Service number = 40	
	Given 10	Given 20	Given 30	Given 10	Given 20	Given 30
UPCC	-0.6026	-0.5981	-0.6218	-0.4886	-0.5147	-0.5628
IPCC	-0.5419	-0.6029	-0.6248	-0.4725	-0.5146	-0.5602
UIPCC	-0.4245	-0.4747	-0.4913	-0.3744	-0.4126	-0.4554
GOKRCC	0.00069	0.00067	0.00048	-0.0021	-0.0021	-0.0016
GOAP	0.2228	0.2277	0.2389	0.1197	0.1549	0.1558
WSRank	0.2268	0.2753	0.3159	0.1357	0.2082	0.2443
WSRec Dataset Training user = 2700 Density = 0.3						
Method	Service number = 30				Service number = 40	
	Given 10	Given 20	Given 30	Given 10	Given 20	Given 30
UPCC	-0.7421	-0.7826	-0.8235	-0.7539	-0.8025	-0.8174
IPCC	-0.8385	-0.8194	-0.8285	-0.8028	-0.8074	-0.8167
UIPCC	-0.8385	-0.8194	-0.8285	-0.8028	-0.8074	-0.8167
GOKRCC	0.0016	0.0014	0.0014	-0.0029	-0.0029	-0.0028
GOAP	0.4842	0.5088	0.5179	0.4799	0.4948	0.4950
WSRank	0.4938	0.5121	0.5455	0.4892	0.5132	0.5473
ServiceXchange Dataset Training user = 2700 Density = 0.3						

results show that our approach outperforms existing rating-based collaborative filtering approaches and the traditional greedy method. Besides, we designed WSTester which integrates distributed resources to construct a virtual computing environment for Web service testing and to decompose test tasks onto distributed nodes for concurrent test execution. WSTester is able to integrate real QoS information into WSRank, and enhance the accuracy of CloudRank. At the same time, WSTester can track the possible fault source in a service composition. Our research results can be used for the Cloud PaaS (Platform as a Service) providers to rank the deployed services, and help PaaS provider to optimize the quality of services deployed on various datacenters based on analysis.

In a Cloud computing environment, users can get SaaS subscriptions from service vendors instead of traditional perpetual-use license. Besides the service quality ranking information, the security and sharing of service is also an on-going work (Li, Li, Wo, Hu, Huai, Liu, & Lam 2012; Li, Jia, Liu, &Wo 2012) in our team. We are trying to combine a quality ranking approach with the security assurance approach to build a trustworthy Cloud computing and service provision environment.

ACKNOWLEDGMENT

The authors gratefully acknowledge the anonymous reviewers for their helpful suggestions and comments. This work is partially supported by Program for National Nature Science Foundation of China (No. 60903149, 91118008), China 973 Fundamental R&D Program (No. 2011CB302600), China 863 project (No. 2011AA01A202), New Century Excellent Talents in University 2010 and the Fundamental Research Funds for the Central Universities. We would also like to thank RiChong Zhang for his helpful suggestions.

REFERENCES

Al-Masri, E., & Mahmoud, Q. H. (2007). QoS-based discovery and ranking of Web services. Paper presented at the 16th International Conference on Computer Communications and Networks (ICCCN), Honolulu, Hawaii, USA.

Ardissono, L., Console, L., Goy, A., Petrone, G., Picardi, C., Segnan, M., & Dupré, D. T. (2005, May). Towards self-diagnosing Web services. Paper presented at the meeting of the International Workshop on Self-Managed Systems and Services (SELFMAN), Nice, France.

Avizienis, A., Laprie, J., & Landwehr, C. (2004). Basic concepts and taxonomy of dependable and secure computing. *IEEE Transactions on Dependable and Secure Computing*, *1*(1), 11–33. doi:10.1109/TDSC.2004.2

Chen, X., Liu, X., Huang, Z., & Sun, H. (2010, July). RegionKNN: A scalable hybrid collaborative filtering algorithm for personalized Web service recommendation. Paper presented at the International Conference on Web Services (ICWS), Miami, Florida, USA.

Cohen, W. W., Schapire, R. E., & Singer, Y. (1999). Learning to order things. *Journal of Artificial Intelligence Research*, *5*, 243–270.

Fu, X., Zou, P., Shang, Z., & Jiang, Y. (2008). Fault diagnosis for Web service composition based on Bayesian network. *Journal of Computer Applications*, *28*(5), 1095–1097. doi:10.3724/SP.J.1087.2008.01095

Goldberg, D. (1992). Using collaborative filtering to weave an information tapestry. *Communications of the ACM*, *35*(12), 61–70. doi:10.1145/138859.138867

Grosclaude, I. (2004). Model-based monitoring of component-based software systems. Paper presented at the International Workshop on Principles of Diagnosis, Carcassonne, France.

Jin, R., Sun, H., Liu, X., & Li, X. (2010). SOArTester: An automatic composite service testing system based on test case reduction. *Chinese Journal of Electronics*, *38*(2A), 65–70.

Kendall, M. G. (1938). A new measure of rank correlation. *Oxford Journals*, *30*(1/2), 81–93.

Konstan, J. A., Miller, B. N., Maltz, D., Herlocker, J. L., Gordon, L. R., & Riedl, J. (1997). GroupLens: Applying collaborative filtering to usenet news. *Communications of the ACM*, *40*(3), 77–87. doi:10.1145/245108.245126

Li, J., Jia, Y., Liu, L., & Wo, T. (2012). CyberLiveApp: A secure sharing and migration approach for live virtual desktop applications in a Cloud environment. [FGCS]. *Future Generation Computer Systems*, (August): 2011. doi:doi:10.1016/j.future.2011.08.00

Li, J., Li, B., Wo, T., Hu, C., Huai, J., Liu, L., & Lam, K. P. (2012). CyberGuarder: A virtualization security assurance architecture for green Cloud computing. *Future Generation Computer Systems*, *38*(2), 379–390. doi:10.1016/j.future.2011.04.012

Linden, G., Smith, B., & York, J. (2003). Amazon.com recommendations: Item-to-item collaborative filtering. *IEEE Internet Computing*, *7*(1), 263–266. doi:10.1109/MIC.2003.1167344

Liu, L., Antonopoulos, N., Xu, J., Webster, D., & Wu, K. (2011). Distributed service integration for disaster monitoring sensor systems. *IET Communications*, *5*(12), 1777–1784. doi:10.1049/iet-com.2010.0630

Liu, L., Xu, J., Antonopoulos, N., Li, J., & Wu, K. (2012). Adaptive service discovery on service-oriented and spontaneous sensor systems. *Journal of Adhoc & Sensor Wireless Networks*, *14*(1-2), 107–132.

Liu, N., & Yang, Q. (2008). Eigenrank: A ranking-oriented approach to collaborative filtering. Paper presented at the 31st Annual International ACM SIGIR Conference on Research and Development in Information Retrieval (SIGIR), Singapore.

Liu, Y., Ngu, A., & Zeng, L. (2004). Qos computation and policing in dynamic Web service selection. Paper presented at the 13th International World Wide Web conference on Alternate track papers & posters, New York, USA.

Melucci, M. (2007). On rank correlation in information retrieval evaluation. SIGIR Forum, 41(1), 18–33.

Miller, B. N., Albert, L., Lam, S. K., Konstan, J. A., & Riedl, J. (2003). Movielens unplugged: Experiences with an occasionally connected recommender system. Paper presented at the 8th International Conference on Intelligent User Interfaces, Miami, Florida, USA.

OMG. (n.d.). BPMN. Retrieved December 31, 2011, from http://www.omg.org/spec/BPMN/2.0/

Ortega, M., Rui, Y., Chakrabarti, K., Mehrotra, S., & Huang, T. S. (1997). Supporting similarity queries in MARS. Paper presented at the ACM International Multimedia Conference Exhibition, Seattle, USA.

Papazoglou, M. P., Traverso, P., Dustdar, S., & Leymann, F. (2007). Service-oriented computing: State of the art and research challenges. *IEEE Computer*, 40(11), 38–45. doi:10.1109/MC.2007.400

Rahmani, H., & Abolhassani, H. (2008). Composite Web service failure recovery considering user non-functional preferences. In Next Generation Web Services Practices, (pp. 39-45).

Robert, S. P., & Daniel, L. R. (2000). Econometrics models and economic forecasts. McGraw-Hill/Irwin. Retrieved December 31, 2011, from http://www.servicexchange.cn

Sarwar, B., Karypis, G., Konstan, J., & Riedl, J. (2007). Item-based collaborative filtering recommendation algorithms. Paper presented at the 10th International Conference on World Wide Web (WWW), Beijing, China.

Shao, L., Zhang, J., Wei, Y., Zhao, J., Xie, B., & Mei, H. (2007, July). Personalized QoS prediction for Web services via collaborative filtering. Paper presented at the International Conference on Web Services (ICWS), Beijing, China.

Sreenath, R. M., & Singh, M. P. (2003). Agent-based service selection. *Journal of Web Semantics*, 1(3), 261–279. doi:10.1016/j.websem.2003.11.006

Wang, G., Wang, C., & Chen, A. (2005). Service level management using qos monitoring, diagnostics and adaptation for networked enterprise systems. Paper presented at the 9th International Enterprise Computing Conference, Washington DC, USA.

Wu, G., Wei, J., Ye, C., Zhong, H., & Huang, T. (2010, July). Detecting data inconsistency failure of composite Web services through parametric stateful aspect. Paper presented at the International Conference on Web Services (ICWS), Miami, Florida, USA.

Yang, X., Nasser, B., Surrige, M., & Middleton, S. (2012). A business-oriented cloud federation model for real time applications. Future Generation Computer Systems (FGCS), Elsevier. http://www.sciencedirect.com/science/article/pii/S0167739X12000386

Yilmaz, E., Aslam, J. A., & Robertson, S. (2008). A new rank correlation coefficient for information retrieval. Paper presented at the 31st Annual International ACM SIGIR Conference on Research and Development in Information Retrieval (SIGIR), Singapore.

Zhang, J. (2005). Trustworthy Web services: Actions for now. *IEEE IT Professional*, 7(1), 32–36. doi:10.1109/MITP.2005.1407802

Zhang, L., Zhang, J., & Cai, H. (2007). *Service computing*. Beijing, China: Springer and Tsinghua University Press.

Zheng, Z., Ma, H., Lyu, M. R., & King, I. (2009, July). WSRec: A collaborative filtering based Web service recommendation system. Paper presented at the International Conference on Web Services (ICWS), Los Angeles, CA, USA.

Zhu, Z., Li, J., Zhao, Y., & Li, Z. (2011). SCENE-Tester: A testing framework supporting fault diagnosing for web service composition. The 2nd International Workshop on Dependable Service-Oriented and Cloud Computing (DOSC 2011) in conjunction with 2011 IEEE 11th International Conference on Computer and Information Technology (CIT), Paphos, Cyprus, (pp. 109-114).

KEY TERMS AND DEFINITIONS

BPMN: It is short for Business Process Model and Notation, and which is a graphical representation for specifying business processes in a business process model.

Cloud Computing: The delivery of computing as a service rather than a product, whereby shared resources, software, and information are provided to computers and other devices as a utility (like the electricity grid) over a network (typically the Internet).

Collaborative Filtering: A method of making automatic predictions (filtering) about the interests of a user by collecting preferences or taste information from many users (collaborating).

QoS: Short for quality of service, it describes the quantitative nonfunctional properties of Web services as quality criteria, including response time, also called round-trip time (RTT), price, throughput, security, availability etc.

SOA: Short for Service-oriented architecture, a set of principles and methodologies for designing and developing software in the form of interoperable services.

Web Service: A software system designed to support interoperable machine-to-machine interaction over a network. It has an interface described in a specified format (specifically Web Services Description Language, known by the acronym WSDL). Other systems interact with the Web service in a manner prescribed by its description using SOAP messages.

Chapter 11
An Efficient, Robust, and Secure SSO Architecture for Cloud Computing Implemented in a Service Oriented Architecture

Khandakar Ahmed
RMIT University, Australia

Altaf Hussain
Shahjalal University of Science and Technology, Bangladesh

Mark A Gregory
RMIT University, Australia

ABSTRACT

Implementing Single Sign-On (SSO) in a Cloud space for a spectrum of services and applications is an interesting research avenue for scientific communities in the field of secure identity and access management for Cloud Computing. Using an SSO implementation, in the backend, users can navigate any or all of the supported applications or resources without the need to repeatedly provide credentials. In this chapter, the authors present an efficient and robust Cloud Single Sign-On Architecture (CSSOA) model based on a token security mechanism. Service Oriented Architectures (SOAs) are one of the enabling technologies for solving complex service oriented real world challenges, and hence, CSSOA has been implemented using SOAs. In the authors' CSSOA model, a CSSO SOAP authentication service is distributed among the Cloud servers while the CSSO database service is centralized.

1. INTRODUCTION

Cloud Computing enables a method of on-demand convenient network access to a shared pool of configurable computing resources (Jaeger & Schiffman, 2010). According to IBM, it is a new utility computing model based on consumption and delivery, where the user only sees services and has no need to know anything about the underlying technology or implementation (Breiter & Behrendt, 2009). With pools of computation, network, information and storage resources the Cloud offers

DOI: 10.4018/978-1-4666-2854-0.ch011

a collection of services, applications, information and infrastructure. With the promising potential of computing functions as a utility, customers are both excited and nervous. The excitement comes from the chance of disassociating themselves from infrastructure management, and being able to focus on core competencies with an emphasis on the business logic that should be implemented through IT rather than management of IT. On the other hand, customers are nervous with the security risks associated with Cloud Computing which have not been completely addressed yet (Hubbard, et al., 2010, March). However, today's aggressive adoption of immature Cloud Computing services by enterprises creates the need for a strong Cloud-based Identity and Access Management (IAM) system that supports business needs ranging from secure collaboration with global partners to secure access for global employees consuming sensitive information using a range of devices from any location world-wide at any time of day. This strong IAM invariably requires users to enter credentials and login for each application accessed and hence it is quite cumbersome. In order to deliver a unified and seamless migration from one application to another inside a Cloud, an SSO would be a great solution. Implementing SSO in a Cloud environment will require a user to login once to a Cloud and be provided with access to all authorized applications without re-login.

Many enterprises exercise identity management to integrate applications into different domains through an application portal giving users an opportunity to hop among applications without the need for re-authentication. However, this feature cannot be extended to the Cloud Computing architecture. Existing identity management approaches work well for enterprise applications within a corporate data centre or within the same domain while services in Cloud Computing are typically external to the data centre and located within a different domain and hence a new SSO architecture is needed for the Cloud.

For multiple applications, SSO is a centralized authentication mechanism which could be independent and may or may not be interrelated. Here, a user is authenticated once and then all of the user's subsequent service access requests via other applications within the enterprise system are handled seamlessly until the user's login session is terminated. iGoogle login is the best appropriate analogy to visualize this concept where the user once logged in can access multiple applications like Gmail, Google Docs, Google+ accounts etc. without having to re-login to each individual application. SSO provides a few advantages: 1) In SSO users utilise a single username and password which is easier to manage and remember; 2) Additionally, the system administrator can manage user accounts centrally and thus it is easier to provision or de-provision passwords; 3) As SSO users are less likely to lose passwords it reduces the assistance provided to users by the IT helpdesk and hence reduces costs; and 4) The service provider manages a single access mechanism rather than developing and maintaining several identity modules for different applications. However, there are some drawbacks or constraints that need to be traded-off in order to get the benefits. A few of them are: 1) Due to password leaks or misuse, security breaches could affect multiple applications and resources; and 2) Due to the constraint of a single point of failure, there is a need for SSO IAM high availability.

There are various security mechanisms that can be used as part of an SSO mechanism. A few of them are Kerberos TGT (Migeon, 2008; Tagg, 2000; Upadhyay & Marti, 2001), Smart Card (Kao & Milman, 2001; Mauro, Sunyaev, Leimeister, Schweiger, & Krcmar, 2008; Rankl & Effing, 2010), One Time Password Token OTP (Blunk, Vollbrecht, & Aboba, 2002; Tiwari & Joshi, 2009) and Integrated Windows Authentication. Some of the basic implementation considerations include: 1) An ideal SSO should be aware of the applications that it is serving and hence also of encryption or decryption keys for handling the authentication requests; 2) The Authentication Token generated during the first successful login needs to be encrypted or decrypted while it travels among applications; and 3) A central database (can be distributed amongst itself) has to be managed by the SSO service in order to store tokens along with user credentials, public key and access roles.

In this chapter, a secure, efficient and robust CSSOA model is proposed which allows users to use the unique token, a randomly generated 128 bit long Globally Unique Identifier (GUID) (Leach, Mealling, & Salz, 2005; Petrusha, 2011), to access multiple services simultaneously with one single login. The proposed model uses Security Assertion Mark-Up Language (SAML) (Ragouzis, et al., 2008) Authentication Request and Response in order to exchange tokens among applications where applications may be deployed in different servers in the Cloud. In order to ensure confidentiality the token is encrypted using the Cloud public key. During user registration using the CS-SOA model, the user generates an asynchronous public private key pair and sends its public key to the provider which is then stored against the user name. The proposed CSSOA model deals with the implementation considerations mentioned (illustrated in subsequent sections) that an ideal SSO model should be aware of.

The rest of this chapter is organized as follows. Section 2 presents related work with a brief analysis. Section 3 describes the CSSOA model and it's architectural and design view while Section 4 presents the prototype implementation details and performance analysis. Section 5 presents the limitations and challenges while the last section concludes the chapter and highlights the future research direction.

2. RELATED WORK

An approach for the management of SSO authentication, authorization and accounting in Cloud-based services is proposed by Tusa et al. exploiting a DIME Network Architecture (DNA) (Tusa, Celesti, & Mikkilineni, 2011). A DIME (Mikkilineni & Morana, 2010) network is a computing entity which allows fault, configuration,

accounting, performance and security (FCAPS) tasks through five different threads: "F," "C," "A," "P," "S," which are connected on a single channel. A local DIME manager is responsible to manage all DIME components. DIME's core computing element is called the Management Intelligent Computing Element (MICE). For a specific domain, a DIME network is created on IaaS and hence an Identity Provider (IdP) for this specific domain manages all aspects related to user authentication. The aim of this proposed solution is to address the end-user authentication problem within a service provider domain taking advantage of SSO mechanisms with the employment of IdPs. When a user attempts to access a service instance running on a DIME network an IdP, deployed within the virtual infrastructure, first validates the user's identity. The authorization manager then checks whether the user, according to his profile, has access to the requested service or not. Authors in this chapter make reference to the existing SSO solution offering IdP services: Shibboleth, OpenID and SAML; however it is not mentioned which solution is adopted in the proposed solution. It is also not clear whether the existing SSO solutions are adaptable to DIME networks without any modification. The solution is illustrated conceptually and not followed by any model that can be extended to implementation and hence the proposal does not appear to have simulation verification or prototype implementation.

Chord for Cloud (C4C) (Il Kon, Pervez, Khattak, & Sungyoung, 2010) is an SSO identity management scheme, proposed for Cloud applications, built on top of peer-to-peer concepts in order to distribute processing load among nodes within the Cloud. C4C uses a chord algorithm, decreases the number of authentication requests sent to the IdP and disseminates the authentication process within the federated environment of the Cloud. Though SSO methodologies are associated with SOA providing seamless services accessibility, the authors in (Il Kon, et al., 2010) raise concerns about computation service latency and the computation load of asymmetric encryption on the service provider (SP) and IdP when services are hosted in the Cloud. In the proposed scheme, the authors alter the manipulation and storage technique of session information in the Cloud. They curtail the number of interactions required to provide SSO functionality by harnessing implicit benefits of the Cloud – enormous process and storage power. This concept, hence, makes the hosted service more responsive and secure.

In C4C, when a user tries to access a particular service hosted in the Cloud the request first comes to a Cloud Gateway. The Gateway routes the request within the Cloud where the route is selected based on the computing power of the node. The authentication functionality is deployed in a distributed fashion inside the Cloud instead of deploying entirely at a single node. Cloud Intrusion Detection Systems (IDS) and Cloud Firewalls are imposed on every node and hence it enables storage and manipulation of sensitive information with reduced security concerns. Once a user is authenticated by IdP, a third party, the session information is distributed within the Cloud. Thus, in the case of all subsequent requests authenticity can be checked by individual nodes rather than routing the request outside the federated environment of the Cloud. C4C is divided into five different components: Cloud Gateway (CG), Cloud Resource Manager (CRM), Session Manager (SM), Key Manager (KM) and Node Manager (NM). The model is claimed to be simulated using CloudSim after some modification in the Cloudlet package though no result is shown. In the context of the model presented, without simulation verification or prototype implementation it is not clear whether the effectiveness, execution and scalability of the proposed technique are possible or not.

A Kerberos (Migeon, 2008) based authentication for SaaS is proposed by using Secure Enterprise Services Consumption for SaaS Technology Platforms. A number of applications including Microsoft Windows have adopted Kerberos as a methodology for SSO though it is not designed

for the virtualized Cloud environment. The SSO framework proposed in (Bin, Yuan, Xi, & Min, 2009) uses OpenID and OAuth to authenticate and authorize service consumers. However the resource intensive asymmetric encryption required on both sides (Cloud and IdP) is not considered which could lead to a less responsive service.

The SAML 2.0 Web Browser SSO Profile (Hughes & Maler, 2005) is the emerging standard for SSO which defines an XML-based format for encoding security assertions as well as a number of protocols and bindings that prescribe how assertions should be exchanged in a variety of applications and/or deployment scenarios. Several SSO solutions like the Liberty Alliance Project (Framework, 2007) and the Shibboleth Project (Internet2, 2011) implement SAML as the core of their SSO identity management functionality. Google developed SAML-based SSO for its Google Apps Premier Edition (Google, 2008), a service for using custom domain names with several Google web applications.

In (Armando, Carbone, Compagna, Cuellar, & Tobarra, 2008), the authors provide a formal model of the protocol corresponding to one of the most employed use case scenarios of the SAML Web Brower SSO Profile known as the SP-Initiated SSO with Redirect/POST Bindings. SATMC, a state-of-the-art model checker, for security protocols, is used to mechanically analyze the approach. For this analysis, the authors have extended their previous work (Groß, 2003; Hansen, Skriver, & Nielson, 2005) on SAML by: i) considering the latest version of the SAML specifications; ii) relaxing the assumptions on the trustworthiness of the principals; and iii) using a more general model of the transport protocols. A formal model is built in the SAML-based SSO for Google Apps and SATMC is used to analyze it. A severe security flaw, which allows a dishonest service provider to impersonate a user at another service provider, in Google's variant of the protocol has been revealed by SATMC. However, the Google

Computer Emergency Response Team (CERT) released a prompt update to the vulnerability reported describing the problem and Google now offers a new version of SSO which is not vulnerable to this attack.

3. CSSOA DESIGN

3.1 CSSOA Architecture

CSSOA is composed of two core services referred as Cloud Single Sign-On Service (CSSOS) and CSSO Database Service (CSSODS) (see Figure 1(a)). CSSOS is deployed in every Cloud server whereas CSSODS is deployed in a central database server (see Figure 1(b)). CSSOS consists of two services namely CSSO Frontend Service (CSSOFS) and CSSO Backend Service (CSSOBS). CSSOFS provides a web form interface for users to login, access Webservices and send Data Transfer Objects (DTOs) references to the CSSOBS. CSSOBS implements DTOs, Webservice Layer, Business Logic Layer (BLL) and Data Access Layer (DAL) to serve the requests come from the CSSOFS. CSSODS is responsible for storing and modification of user credentials using create, read, update and delete (CRUD) operations according to the CSSOBS logic. CSSOA is unique in its following features and functionalities.

3.1.1 Secure Exchange of Authentication Token

A user needs to provide login credentials to CSSOFS, which is authenticated by the CSSOBS. CSSOBS generates a 128-bit long GUID randomly which is referred to as a token and stored in a central database against the username by the CSSODS. Upon receiving an SAML Authentication Request from an application, the CSSOFS acknowledges by sending a digitally signed (MSDN, 2011; Nebhuth, 2009) SAML response, with accompanying token encrypted by the public key of the Cloud. By using token encryption, the CSSOA disrupts non-authorized access to data, traffic capture and analysis (referred to as confidentiality) and diffuses the chance of modification of the token or introduction of a false token (referred to as integrity). The CSSOA uses a digital signature to protect applications from masquerade attacks by a third party.

3.1.2 Low Communication Overhead and Latency

In order to reduce the response latency from application to user it is necessary to minimize the communication cost. CSSOA deploys an image of a light weight CSSOFS and CSSOBS in every Cloud server whereas the CSSODS is centralized. Hence, a local light weight CSSOFS image promptly takes user login credentials to be hosted in the server where the user initiates interaction with the Cloud application. This distributed deployment scheme is in contrast to centralised IdP and helps to avoid unnecessary redirection from one server to another thereby reducing extra communication and message encryption overhead.

3.1.3 Centralized Seamless Password Provisioning and De-Provisioning Facility

This functionality is very useful for an administrator of an SP enterprise client to manage the enterprise client users by provisioning or de-provisioning authorization to different applications. By utilising this central control it is also possible to define a role which can be applied to a group of users. System administrators can associate or disassociate a user from one or more applications by a single provisioning or de-provisioning action. Since the user credentials are stored centrally in one distributed database it is not unwieldy to upgrade the password on a regular basis.

Figure 1. a) Cloud single sign on architecture, b) schematic interaction among users, cloud servers, and CSSOA

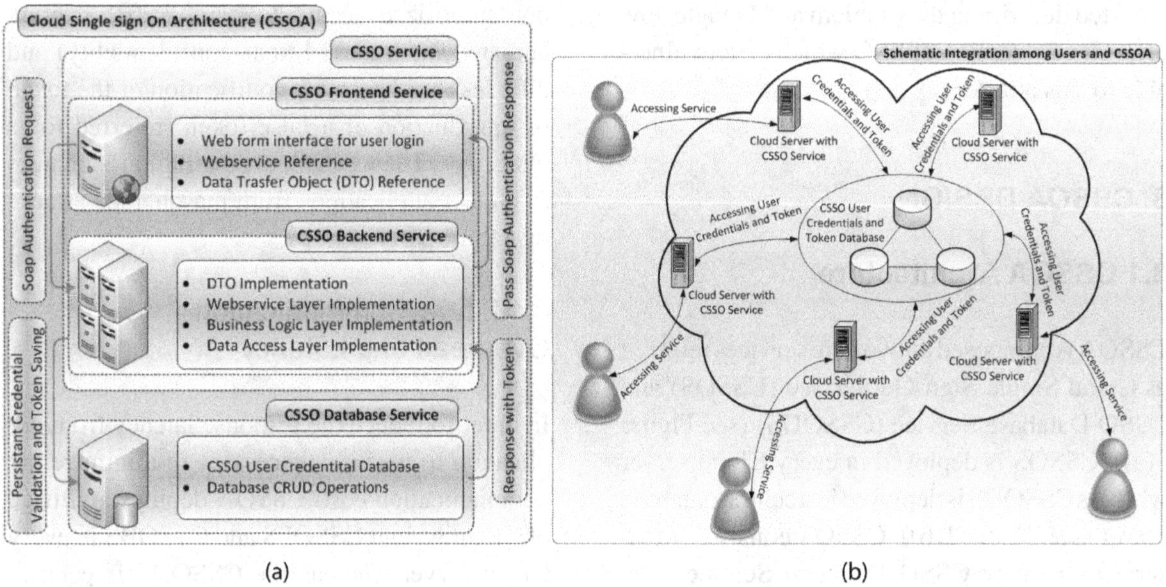

(a)

(b)

3.1.4 Strong Identity Management and User Data Confidentiality

A strong identity management scheme should address four important issues: 1) obvious determination of legitimate users; 2) Authentication of SP; 3) Privacy of legal users; and 4) Establishment of mutual common session key (Huang, Yuan, Chen, Lin, & Teng, 2010; Juang, Chen, & Liaw, 2008; Li, Qiu, Zheng, Chen, & Li, 2010; Saeed & Nammous, 2007). In CSSOA, both entities (user and SP) publish their public key (KP) from the generated public-private key pair (KP and KR) to each other. CSSOA stores the client's public key (KP) against the username in a central database. Each time before transmitting data both the user and the SP send the symmetric session key (K) encrypted by the receiver's public key along with the cipher text encrypted by K. The receiver first retrieves K by decrypting the encrypted key using its own private key (KR) and then deciphers the cipher text using the retrieved K.

3.1.5 Seamless User Migration among Applications

In CSSOA, users can move around among applications seamlessly without the need for further logins. Every time a user moves from one application (ai, where ai is an application and $a_i \in A$, A is the set of all applications) to another application (aj, where $a_j \in A$), the later application sends a digitally signed SAML Authentication Request to the CSSOFS hosted on the same server where aj is also hosted. In this case, the CSSOFS passes the token retrieved from the SAML Authentication Request to the CSSOBS, which checks the validity of the token. The CSSOFS sends an SAML response with the true value of the login flag, if the token is valid, to aj.

3.2 User Registration Phase

In the registration phase, each user registers a unique identity IDi along with providing credentials to the SP via the CSSOFS. After getting an acknowledgement of successful registration, every user device selects two large primes p and q and then computes N=p.q. The user determines the key pair (e, d) in such a way that $e.d \equiv 1 \bmod \phi(N)$, where $\varphi(n) \equiv (p-1)(q-1)$. Finally, the user device protects the secrecy of d and publishes (ei, ni, Ni). The interaction between the user and the CSSO during the registration phase is illustrated in the steps shown in Figure 2.

1. A user sends credentials to the CSSOFS in order to register with the CSSOA architecture of the Cloud.
2. CSSOFS forwards the credentials to CSSOBS for verification.
3. If the registration is successful the CSSOBS forwards credential information to CSSODS for storage.
4. CSSOBS sends ACK/NACK on the basis of the verification status to the user via the CSSOFS.
5. User generates RSA public-private key pair (ei, n) and (di, n).

6. User publishes its public key KP = (ei, n) to the CSSOFS and KP is forwarded to the CSSODS for storing against the user's IDi.
7. CSSOBS publishes the provider's public key referred to as KSPP to the user via the CSSOFS.
8. User sends a nonce (timestamp) encrypted by the provider public key KSPP to the CSSOBS via the CSSOFS.
9. CSSOBS decrypts the nonce using its own private key.
10. CSSOBS sends the nonce (t+1) back via the CSSOFS to the user encrypted by KP.

3.3 User Login Phase

A user can login to an application using one of two ways: i) by accessing the CSSOFS which takes the user credentials and after a successful login the CSSOFS makes the authorized application available to the user; and ii) a user can attempt to access a previously authorized application directly (say ai). In the latter case, ai will redirect the user

Figure 2. User registration phase

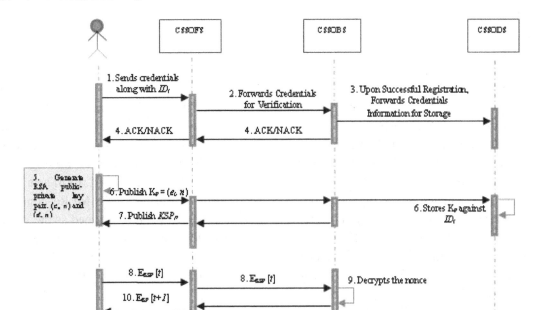

request to the CSSOFS which will be prompted to take user credentials from the user and then redirect the user back to ai.

3.3.1 Case One: Login to the CSSO Service

In this case, a user will first access the CSSOFS, which will take the user's login credentials. The CSSOFS then lists all of the applications to which the user is authorized. When a user selects an application (say ai) from the list, the user will be redirected to the application link which will assert an SAML Authentication Request to the CSSOFS. The CSSOFS will check the user's login status and if the user is logged in then the CSSOFS sends a digitally signed SAML Response along with an encrypted token. Figure 3 is illustrated by the following steps.

1. The user provides valid login credentials along with IDi to the CSSOFS.
2. CSSOFS forwards the user credentials to the CSSOBS for authentication.
3. CSSOBS pulls the user's information from a database via the CSSODS in order to perform authentication matching.
4. CSSOBS generates a 128-bit long GUID as a token and stores it in the database against user id IDi.
5. Upon successful registration ACK is sent otherwise a NACK is sent by the CSSOBS to the user via the CSSOFS.
6. After successful login, the CSSOFS shows the list of authorized applications to the user. The user then selects an application ai from the list and attempts to access the application.
7. The application then sends an HTTP redirect response to the browser i.e. HTTP status 302 or 303. The location HTTP header contains the destination URI of the CSSOFS with an <AuthnRequest> message encoded as a URL query named SAMLRequest. The browser processes the redirect response and issues an HTTP GET request to the CSSOFS

with the SAMLRequest query parameter. The local information is also included in the HTTP response encoded in a RelayState query string parameter. (https://cssofs.cs-soaprototype.com/SAML2/SSO/Redirect? SAMLRequest=request&RelayState=token)

```
<samlp:AuthnRequest
Xmlns:samlp = "urn:oasis:names:tc:SAM
L:2.0:protocol"
Xmlns:saml  = "urn:oasis:names:tc:SAM
L:2.0:assertion"
ID = ID_NUM_1
Version = "2.0"
IssueInstant = "2011-12-25T10:11:43Z"
AssertionConsumerServiceIndex=1>
<saml:Issuer>https://A_NAME[i].cssoa-
prototype.com/SAML2</saml:Issuer>
<samlp: NameIDPolicy
AllowCreate="true"
Format="urn:oasis:names:tc:SAML:2.0:n
ameid-format:transient"/>
</samlp:AuthnRequest>
```

8. The CSSOFS checks whether the user has an existing valid token stored in the database. In this context, the user has a valid token generated in step 4.
9. The CSSOFS builds an SAML assertion representing the user's logon security context. Since a POST binding is being used, the assertion is digitally signed and then embedded within an SAML <Response> message. The <Response> message is then placed within an HTML form as a hidden form control named SAMLResponse. The encrypted token is returned as the value of the hidden parameter named RelayState. The CSSOFS then sends the HTML form back to the browser in the HTTP response.

```
<form method = "post"
action="https://NAME[i].cssoaproto-
type.com /SAML2/SSO/POST.".>
```

Figure 3. User login phase: case one

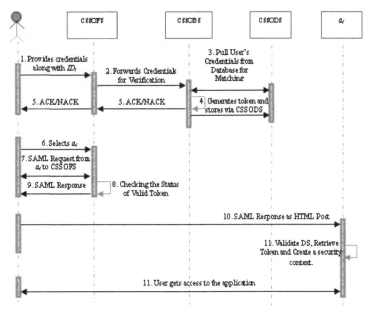

```
<input type="hidden"
name="SAMLResponse" value="response">
<input type="hidden"
name="RelayState" value=EKP[token]>
<input type="submit" value="submit">
......
</form>
```

The value of the SAMLResponse parameter is the base64 encoding of the following <samlp:Response> element:

```
<samlp:Response
        xmlns:samlp = "urn:oasis:nam
es:tc:SAML:2.0:protocol"
        xmlns:samlp = "urn:oasis:nam
es:tc:SAML:2.0:protocol"
        ID = ID_NUM_2
        InResponseTo = ID_NUM_1
        Version = 2.0
        IssueInstant =
"2011-12-25T10:12:38Z">
        Destination = "https:// A_
NAME[i].cssoaprototype.com/SAML2/SSO/
POST">
        <saml:Issuer>https://CS-
SOFSi.cssoaprototype.com/SAML2</
saml:Issuer>
        <samlp:Status>
                <samlp:SatusCode value=
"urn:oasis:names:tc:SAML:2.0:status:S
uccess/>"
        </samlp:Status>
        <saml:Assertion
                xmlns:saml=""urn:oasis:
names:tc:SAML:2.0:assertion"
                Version = "2.0"
                IssueInstant =
"2011-12-25T10:12:38Z"
                <saml:Issuer>https://
CSSOFSi.cssoaprototype.com/SAML2</
saml:Issuer>
                <ds:Signature
                        xmlns:ds=http://
www.w3.org/2000/09/xmld-
sig#> ...... </ds:Signature>
<saml:Subject>
                        <saml:NameID>
                                Format=" ur
n:oasis:names:tc:SAML:2.0:nameid-
```

```
format:transient"
                <token
type=encrypted>EKSP[GUID]</token>
                </saml:NameID>

<saml:SubjectConfirmation
        Method="urn:oasis:na
mes:tc:SAML:2.0:cm:bearer">
                <saml:SubjectConfirm
ationData
                InResponseTo =
ID_NUM_1
                Recipi-
ent = "https://A_NAME[i].cs-
soaprototype.com/SAML2/SSO/
POST"                   Not-
OnOrAfter = "2011-12-25T10:17:38Z">
                </
saml:SubjectConfirmation>
                </saml:Subject>
        </saml:Assertion>
</samlp:Response>
```

10. The browser either by the user's action or execution of an "auto-submit" script, issues an HTTP POST request to send the form to the application ai's assertion consumer service. The value of the SAMLResponse is taken from the HTML form of step 9.

```
POST /SAML2/SSO/POST HTTP/1.1
HOST: A_NAME[i].cssoaprototype.com
Content-Type: application/x-www-form-
urlencoded
Content-Length: ….
SAMLResponse = response
```

11. The application ai receives the <Response> message from the HTML form. ai must first validate the digital signature for authentication by decrypting the token and creating a local security context. The application then provides access to the requested service.

3.3.2 Login Directly to an Application

In this case, a user attempts to access resources directly using an application A_NAME[i].cssoaprototype.com. As the user has no current logon session on this site, the HTTP Redirect binding is used to deliver the SAML <AuthnRequest> message to the CSSOFS and the HTTP Post binding is used to return the SAML <Response> message containing the authentication assertion to the application. Figure 4 illustrates the message flow which includes the following steps:

1. The user attempts to access a resource using the application ai. The user doesn't have a valid logon session.
2. ai sends a HTTP redirect response to the browser. The location HTTP header contains the destination URI of the CSSOFS along with an <AuthnRequest> message encoded as a URL query variable named SAMLRequest.

```
<samlp:AuthnRequest
        Xmlns:samlp = "urn:oasis:nam
es:tc:SAML:2.0:protocol"
        Xmlns:saml  = "urn:oasis:nam
es:tc:SAML:2.0:assertion"
        ID = ID_NUM_1
        Version = "2.0"
        IssueInstant =
"2011-12-25T10:11:43Z"
AssertionConsumerServiceIndex=1>
        <saml:Issuer>https://A_
NAME[i].cssoaprototype.com/SAML2</
saml:Issuer>
        <samlp: NameIDPolicy
                AllowCreate="true"
                Format="urn:o
asis:names:tc:SAML:2.0:nameid-
format:transient"/>
</samlp:AuthnRequest>
```

Figure 4. User login phase: case two

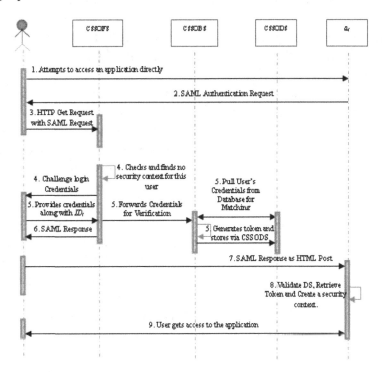

The browser processes the redirect response and issues an HTTP GET request to the CSSOFS with the SAMLRequest query parameter. The local information is also included in the HTTP response encoded in a RelayState query string parameter. (https://cssofs.cssoaprototype.com/SAML2/SSO/Redirect?SAMLRequest=request&RelayState=token)

3. CSSOFS checks and determines that the user has no valid existing security logon context and hence it interacts with the browser to challenge the user to provide valid credentials.
4. The user provides valid credentials which are forwarded to the CSSOBS. The CSSOBS pulls the user's profile to verify. If the verification is successful then the CSSOBS generates a 128-bit long GUID as a token and stores it against user's IDi using the CSSODS.

5. Rest follows steps 9-11 of previous sub-section.

3.4 Migration among Applications

This section illustrates a scenario where a user tries to access resources from an application (say aj) while the user is logged-in and accessing another application (say ai). As the user has no current logon session on the site hosting aj, the HTTP Redirect binding is used to deliver the SAML <AuthnRequest> message to the CSSOFS and the HTTP Post binding is used to return the SAML <Response> message containing the assertion to the application. In this circumstance, the user's credentials are already validated and a valid token has already been generated and stored in the database and hence the CSSOFS will check the validity of the token and sends it along with SAML Response. The scenario is illustrated by the following steps:

1. The user attempts to access a resource from an application aj.

2. aj sends an HTTP redirect response to the browser. The location HTTP header contains the destination URI of the CSSOFS along with an <AuthnRequest> message encoded as a URL query variable named SAMLRequest.

```
<samlp:AuthnRequest
        Xmlns:samlp = "urn:oasis:nam
es:tc:SAML:2.0:protocol"
        Xmlns:saml  = "urn:oasis:nam
es:tc:SAML:2.0:assertion"
        ID = ID_NUM_1
        Version = "2.0"
        IssueInstant =
"2011-12-25T10:11:43Z"
        AssertionConsumerServiceIn-
dex=1>
<saml:Issuer>https://A_NAME[i].cssoa-
prototype.com/SAML2</saml:Issuer>
        <samlp: NameIDPolicy
                AllowCreate="true"
                Format="urn:o
asis:names:tc:SAML:2.0:nameid-
format:transient"/>
</samlp:AuthnRequest>
```

The browser processes the redirect response and issues a HTTP GET request to the CSSOFS with the SAMLRequest query parameter. The local information (encrypted token) is also included in the HTTP response encoded in a RelayState query string parameter. (https://cssofs.cssoaprototype.com/SAML2/SSO/Redirect?SAMLRequest=request&RelayState=token)

3. CSSOFS checks validity of the token which is also stored in the database. In this context, the user has a valid token generated previously before getting access to the first application.

4. Then it follows steps 9-11 of Section 3.3.1

3.5 Single Logout from Multiple Applications

In this scenario, a user visiting the A_NAME[i].cssoaprototype.com Cloud service application Website decides to logout from his web SSO session. The CSSOFS determines whether others Cloud service applications are also participants in the web SSO session, and thus sends a <LogoutRequest> message to open Cloud service application. The application initiating the single logout uses the HTTP Redirect binding with the CSSOFS, while the CSSOFS uses a back-channel SOAP over HTTP binding to communicate with the other Cloud service application, say ai+1. The steps involved in this process are as follows:

1. A user is authenticated by CSSOFS.cssoaprototype.com and is currently consuming services from an application ai by interacting with A_NAME[i].cssoaprototype.com through a web SSO session. The user decides to logout at this stage and selects a link that initiates a single logout.

2. The A_NAME[i].cssoaprototype.com destroys the local authentication session state for the user and then sends an SAML <LogoutRequest> message requesting session logout to CSSOFS.cssoaprototype.com. The request identifies the principal to be logged out using a <NameID> element which contains a token as well as providing a <sessionIndex> element to uniquely identify the session being closed. The <LogoutRequest> message is transmitted using the HTTP Redirect binding and also digitally signed before transmission. By using the digital signature the CSSOFS verifies that the <LogoutRequest> is originated from a known and trusted SP. The CSSOFS pro-

cesses the <LogoutRequest> and destroys the local session information for this user.

3. The CSSOFS determines the other participant Cloud application services in the web SSO session and sends a similar <LogoutRequest> to them. In this scenario, say the other application service is A_NAME[i+1].cssoaprototype.com. The <LogoutRequest> is sent using the SOAP over HTTP binding.

4. The A_NAME[i+1].cssoaprototype.com returns a <LogoutResponse> message containing a status code response to the identity provider. The response is digitally signed and returned using the SOAP over HTTP binding.

5. The CSSOFS returns a <LogoutResponse> message containing a status code response to the original application A_NAME[i].cssoaprototype.com where the global logout has been initiated. The response is again digitally signed and returned using the HTTP Redirect binding.

6. The A_NAME[i].cssoaprototype.com, finally, informs the user that he is logged out of all of the applications.

However, in certain cases a situation might arise where the <LogoutRequest> message can be blocked or interrupted from being sent to other Cloud services due to network problems or DoS attacks. This will drive the interrupted application either into an indefinite waiting state or might result in the application Webservice continuing to identify the user as being authenticated and hence provide a back door for attack. Depending on the application specification policy of the business domain implementation this predicament can be addressed in two ways: (1) either by periodic rechecking of the validity of the token or (2) the token could be validated every time before any data pull request comes from that application. Since, upon recognizing the <LogoutRequest> messages

by the CSSOBS, the token will be deleted from the CSSODS and any further verification request from other applications will be denied.

4. PROTOTYPE IMPLEMENTATION AND EVALUATION

4.1 Prototype Implementation

The proposed CSSOA is designed and implemented on an n-tier based architectural design model. The CSSOA is implemented leveraging the SOAP based Webservice technology in .NET 4. As mentioned earlier, the CSSOA is divided into CSSOS and CSSODS. CSSOS is a light weight service consisting of CSSOFS and CSSOBS. The components of CSSOS were developed in ASP.Net and C#.Net as web applications running on Internet Information Service-7 (IIS-7). The applications or services communicate among themselves using SOAP based Webservices and hence they can be deployed in a distributed fashion into one or more Cloud servers.

CSSOFS provides a basic web interface to the user for login to the Cloud applications portal and facilitates browsing through applications providing the desired services to the user. Apart from acting as the access point to the Cloud it also responsible for providing identity management. It is a two-tier application which includes presentation and helper layers. The presentation layer is responsible for providing the interface to collect credentials from the user while the helper layer provides code to correlate different applications in order to integrate them. The CSSOFS also provides a Webservice reference to the CSSOBS. The CSSOBS authenticates a user by matching the user's login credentials received from the CSSOFS with the credentials stored in the database. The CSSOBS is principally responsible to create a session after login and also to destroy a session to logoff a user. The CSSOFS receives a response from the user and to pass it to the CSSOBS and vice versa. Hence, the CSSOFS acts as middleware between users and the CSSOBS.

The CSSOBS comprises three layers referred to as the Webservice Layer (WSL), Business Logic Layer (BLL) and Data Access Layer (DAL). The WSL facilitates a public Web service implementation, while the BLL contains the logical implementation of the authentication and validation functions. The DAL, finally, implements data access manipulation logic and acts as an interface between CSSODS and CSSOBS.

The CSSOBS pushes CRUD operations via the DAL to the CSSODS which executes the CRUD operations through the MS-SQL database server and thus it acts as the middleware between the CSSOBS and database server. Additionally, the CSSOBS acts as an upper layer on top of MS-SQL. It implements two way data replication (left out of the scope of this chapter due to space constraints) among the distributed database. Before executing any update operation over a data item it imposes a lock message to others databases containing a replica of the data to avoid inconsistency.

Different implemented functioning layers of three services and the interaction between the user and CSSO architecture are depicted in Figure 5. 'Cloud Service Application A' and 'Cloud Service Application B' are two Cloud service applications tested using the prototype implementation. The interaction between a user and the CSSO architecture is illustrated by the following steps considering different possible scenarios:

1. A user can initiate the process using one of two different ways
   a. Direct Service request to 'Cloud Service Application A', or
   b. Direct Service request to 'Cloud Service Application B', and
   c. User first accesses the CSSOFS and then selects an application after successful login.
2. For case 1(a) or 1(b), it was found that the user does not have an active session and hence an SAML authentication request is sent to the CSSOFS hosted in the server where the corresponding application is hosted, referred to by 2(a) and 2(b) to align with the previous sub-steps.
3. CSSOFS checks the security context of the user and login status and finds no active

Figure 5. CSSOA and cloud applications interaction

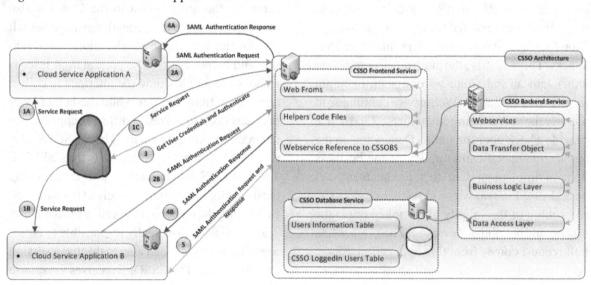

session. Thus, CSSOFS interacts with the user for login credentials.

4. CSSOFS sends a digitally signed SAML Authentication Response with an encrypted token to the corresponding applications. From the SAML Response, the application retrieves the token and gives the user access to the application resources.

5. While using one of the applications a user may also attempt to use another application. In this case an SAML authentication request, containing the user's current session token, is sent to the CSSOFS. If the token is valid then the CSSOFS sends a digitally signed SAML response and returns the token unmodified otherwise repeats from step 3.

6. In the middle of the user's visit, an application may need to validate the token that it has received from the relevant previous SAML response. In this case the application interacts with the CSSOFS in similar fashion explained in step 5.

4.2 Evaluation of the Prototype by Load Test

In order to evaluate the performance of the prototype implementation of a CSSOA, a couple of scenarios were first recorded using the WAPT tool (WAPT, 2003) and saved as profiles. In the first scenario, a user first logs in to the CSSOFS and then accesses Cloud Application A followed by a visit to Cloud Application B. Finally, the user logs out from all applications by clicking logout from either application. In a second scenario, a user first attempts to access Cloud Application A. The application redirects the user's browser to the CSSOFS where the user logs in by providing login credentials. This gives the user access to the application. Then the user accesses Cloud Application B and finally logs out. These two scenarios have been tested in three cases. Firstly, all applications, CSSOFS, CSSOBS and CSSODS

were deployed in one server. Secondly, the applications are distributed across two servers, with each application belonging to one server. The CSSOA consisting of CSSOFS and CSSOBS, in this case, is deployed in both servers. Thirdly, the applications are distributed across five servers, with Cloud Application A belonging to three servers and Cloud Application B belonging to two servers. Cloud Application A, using distributed destinations, is more available than Cloud Application B. Similar to the second case; CSSOA is deployed in each server.

4.2.1 Single Server

4.2.1.1 Performance under No Stress

In order to test this case, the above defined profile with two scenarios was used. The simulation was run for six minutes with 12 virtual users as the maximum using the ramp-up load option. Using the ramp-up load option, the test was configured with one initial user and increased to 12 with one additional user every 30 seconds.

Figure 6(a) shows that the average response time is 0.01 sec irrespective of the number of active users except for a few spikes. The spikes may happen due to network latency or the server's CPU's utilization by another local system program running at that point on the server. Despite having few spikes, not more than 0.14 sec, the average response time was found to be quite reasonable in this case. To find a meaningful correlation certain other parameters have been set for the active user. Figure 6(b) shows the server's CPU utilization against the active user. Where there are a few spikes in the CPU's utilization was found to justify arguing that the cause for spikes in response times could be related to other server applications and latency. In Figure 6(c), the percentage of total errors is shown. In contrast to the response time, it is noticeable that with the increase in the number of users the percentage of errors increases linearly. It was also seen that the average download time (see Figure 6(d)) ranges between 0.01 msec to 0.25 msec except for a couple of variations. In Figure 6(e), the response time, percentage of errors and number of active users are shown together to have a clear analytical view.

4.2.1.2 Performance under Stress

To test this case, the profile with two applications created in the introduction of Section 4.2 was used again. This time the simulation was run for nine minutes with a maximum of 30 virtual users in a ramp-up load. Using the ramp-up load option, the test was configured with two initial users and increased to 30 users in steps of two additional users every 30 seconds. This test scenario was created to see the maximum stress under which the CSSOA can behave normally.

The average response time, as shown in Figure 7(a), is 0.01 sec except for a couple of peaks due to the possible server CPU utilization variations with system load. With more than 17 active users, there was performance degradation and the first average response at this point was 4.0 sec. The next response measured with 27 users was more than 45 sec. Certain other parameters have been set for the active user to find a consequential outcome. Figure 7(b) shows the server's CPU utilization against the active user in order to show the interesting link to the sudden spikes in the response graph. It is noticeable that the CPU utilization also shows a steep fall at the time when the server degradation occurred and the anticipated responses did not occur at the normal frequency. In Figure 7(c), the percentage of total errors shows a similar pattern where the response is a linear upward slope along with the number of active users till six minutes thirty six seconds when the number of virtual user becomes 17. When the number of active users is increased to more than 17 the error rate moves towards zero. The cause behind this sudden steep fall in fact reflects the situation where the CSSOA is unable to cope with the demand. With more than 27 users, none of the users receives any response

i.e. page and hence the percentage error rate is also zero. However, one abnormal spike with more than 25% error rate occurs at 6 min 20 sec, when the response graph shows a spike of 45 sec for 27 active virtual users. The average download time (see Figure 7(d)) shows a similar pattern to the graph (Figure 6(d)) under no stress depicted in the previous sub-section. The download time at the beginning with 2-3 active users show abrupt spikes. This happens because prior to the first request the applications are not being served by the CPU process and hence it takes some time to initialize the application in the server.

4.2.2 Double Server

To test this case, the profile with two scenarios created in Section 4.2 was used. For this test case, both Cloud Application A and Cloud Application B have been deployed across two servers. The CSSOS was deployed in both servers while the CSSODS was hosted in one server. The simulation was run for nine minutes with a maximum of 40 virtual users in a ramp-up load. Using the ramp-up load option, the test was configured with two initial users and increased to 40 users in increments of two users every 30 seconds. This test scenario was created to see the maximum stress and performance of the CSSOA in a distributed scenario.

The average response time, as shown in Figure 8(a), is close to 0.01 sec until the number of active users becomes 15. However, the system behaves normally with an average response of 10 sec with 15 users and after that the system degrades and several spikes occur. The percentage of the server's CPU utilization, percentage of error and average download time (refer Figure 8(b), 8(c) and 8(d) respectively) also correspond to the response time. The interesting thing to note is that the performance has not increased after deploying the applications across two servers. This happens due to the communication overhead which is higher due to the use of distributed servers.

Figure 6. Performance analysis under no stress: a) average response time vs. active users; b) percentage of server's CPU utilization vs. active users; c) percentage of error vs. active users; d) average download time vs. active users; e) response time and percentage of error vs. active users

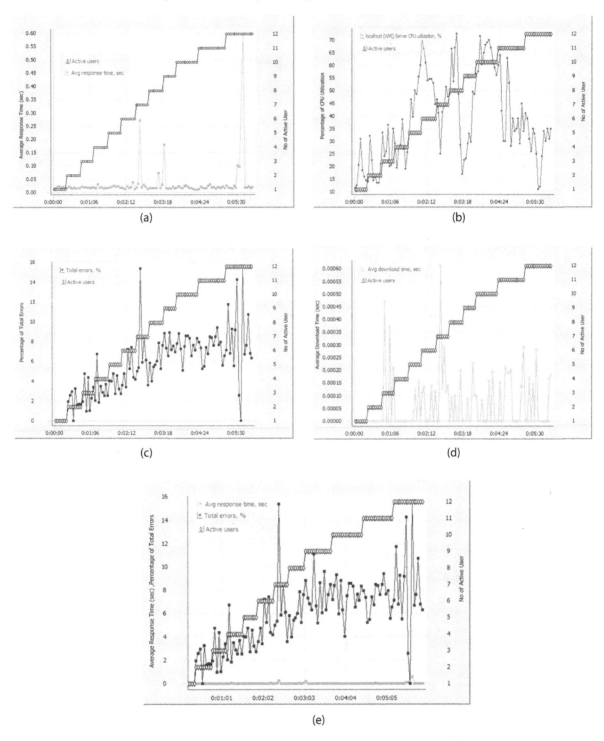

Figure 7. Performance analysis under stress: a) average response time vs. active users; b) percentage of server's CPU utilization vs. active users; c) percentage of error vs. active users; d) average download time vs. active users; e) response time and percentage of error vs. active users

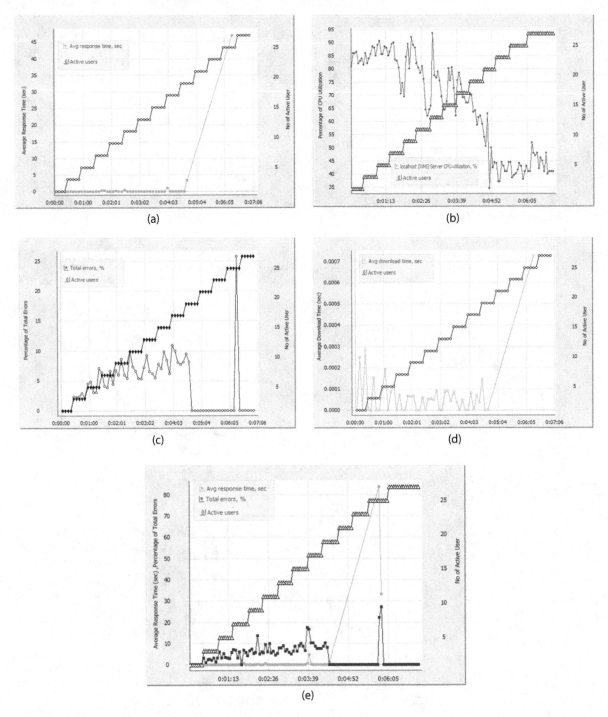

Figure 8. Performance analysis in distributed scenario: a) average response time vs. active users; b) percentage of server's CPU utilization vs. active users; c) percentage of error vs. active users; d) average download time vs. active users; e) response time and percentage of error vs. active users

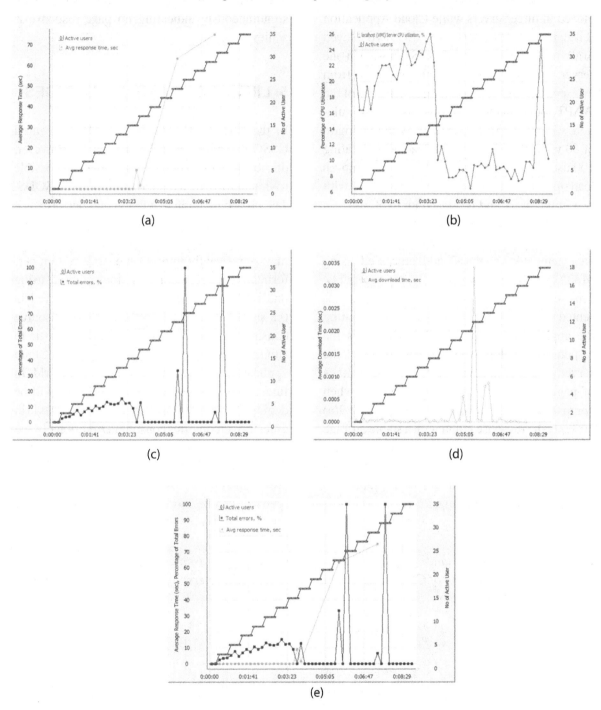

4.2.3 Multiple Server

In this experiment, Cloud Application A is deployed in three servers while Cloud Application B is deployed in two servers. CSSOS is deployed in all five servers while CSSODS is hosted in one server. Two load agents are also executed from two separate machines running two images of the WAPT tool separately. In this case, the simulation was run for fifteen minutes with maximum of 50 virtual users from each load agent totaling 100 users in a ramp-up load. Using the ramp-up load option, each load agent was configured with two initial users and increased up to 50 users in increments of two every 30 seconds. The average of each parameter was calculated from the data generated, analyzed and processed using MATLAB, by the two load agents separately. This setting applies to Figure 9. The graphs presented in Figure 9 show that after distributing the applications across distributed servers the response time along with the percentage of the server's CPU utilization and average percentage of page errors was reasonably improved when compared with the two server setup. Figure 9(a) presents the response graph with a stable average response time of 0.01 seconds until 80 users have been added to the scenario. Figure 9(b) and 9(c) show the correlation to the response graph. The server's CPU utilization ranges between 50%-90%

until the system degrades. The average page error rate increases with the increase in the number of users with a sharp fall to zero once 80 users hit simultaneously indicating no page response is achieved beyond that point.

5. LIMITATIONS AND CHALLENGES

In the core design of the CSSOA, the central CSSO database service is distributed. However, due to a lack of resources it has not been possible to simulate this distributed nature of the CSSODS. The prototype implementation and performance analysis illustrated in Section 4 was based on a central database deployed in one server, which may significantly impact on overall system performance. The model was implemented using one LAN i.e. all the servers were deployed in the same network due to the time and resource constraints though it would be more realistic to simulate the system by distributing the Cloud applications geographically across the world. In future, the extended version of CSSOA will be deployed using Microsoft Azure (Azure, 2011) in order to overcome this constraint. Additionally, the system was tested using the WAPT tool (WAPT, 2003), creating virtual users under a couple of pre-defined scenarios. In a real environment, the scenario can be more dynamic and some more

Figure 9. CSSOA performance graph in distributed environment: a) average response time vs. number of active users; b) avg. (%) of CPU utilization vs. number of active users; c) avg. (%) of page error rate vs. number of active users

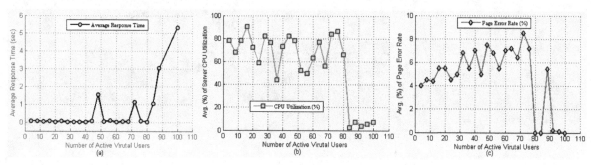

vibrant issues may arise which usually don't turn up in a closed environment. In the proposed CSSOA, service access depends on the service portal though it might be a good option to integrate a service discovery option depending on the SLA and also the authorization policy. In the current version of CSSOA, the CSSOS consisting of CSSOFS and CSSOBS was deployed in every server which might not be a cost effective solution. It is possible to improve outcomes further by focusing on deployment of the CSSOS in fewer servers and to add a dynamic resource discovery module to locate the server providing the CSSOS.

Due to the lack of an adequate Cloud simulator, it was a great challenge to evaluate the proposed SSO architecture. On the other hand, it would be difficult to deploy the system for a large scale evaluation of the prototype implementation, and hence the proposed CSSOA was implemented and deployed with limited functionality in a closed environment. Selecting a suitable load testing tool was an important step. As the CSSOA was deployed as web services and the focus was to perform load and stress testing, a few testing tools, OpenDemand Systems (Open-Demand-System, 2000-2011), NeoLoad (NEOTYS, 2005-2012), Webmetrics (Neustar-Webmetrics, 2012), LoadStorm (LoadStorm, 2008-2011) and WAPT tool (WAPT, 2003), were evaluated, and due to its simplicity, reliability and extended features the WAPT Pro 2.5 tool was selected and used.

FUTURE WORK AND CONCLUSION

The research into an improved SOAP based CSSOA led to a unique model for a secure SSO IAM system. The model was simulated and its performance was rigorously analyzed in order to prove the concept. The SAML used in this model is uniquely modified and the IdP is distributed among servers inside the Cloud. Most of the SSO architecture has one central IdP, creating a

hotspot around it. Moreover, being a single point of failure, this kind of approach is highly prone to failure under stress. The contrasting CSSOA is unique by its distributed CSSOFS nature which reduces stress by leveraging a part of the identity management functionality to each server. The future research steps include extending the model by the inclusion of access management. The Role Based Access Control (RBAC) (Crampton, 2010; Sandhu, Coyne, Feinstein, & Youman, 1996) method can be applied to define the access polices and this policy can be written using extensive access control markup language (XACML) (K. Ahmed, 2011; K. E. U. Ahmed & Alexandrov, 2011; Verma, 2004). An interactive Service Level Agreement (SLA) service will be deployed to set up the SLA with the user during registration. Based on this SLA the RBAC processor will generate access policy files for this user. The access policy files will be written using XACML. Hence, a registered user will get access to the resources based on the decision taken by the RBAC processor after processing the XACML policy sheets. The extended model will be implemented in ASP.Net and C#.Net as web applications running on IIS-7 (Internet Information Service-7). The model will be later deployed using Microsoft Azure (Azure, 2011) and the WAPT tool (WAPT, 2003) will be used to do more rigorous performance and stress tests to verify efficiency, scalability and adaptability of the model.

REFERENCES

Ahmed, K. (2011). *Identity and access management in cloud computing* (1st ed., *Vol. 1*). LAP LAMBERT Academic Publishing. doi:10.1007/978-1-4471-2236-4_6

Ahmed, K. E. U., & Alexandrov, V. (2011). *Identity and access management in cloud computing* (pp. 115–133). Cloud Computing for Enterprise Architectures. doi:10.1007/978-1-4471-2236-4_6

Armando, A., Carbone, R., Compagna, L., Cuellar, J., & Tobarra, L. (2008). Formal analysis of SAML 2.0 web browser single sign-on: breaking the SAML-based single sign-on for google apps.

Azure, M. (2011). Deploying and updating Windows Azure applications. Retrieved from https://www.windowsazure.com/en-us/develop/net/fundamentals/deploying-applications#benefits

Bin, W., Yuan, H. H., Xi, L. X., & Min, X. J. (2009). Open identity management framework for SaaS ecosystem.

Blunk, L., Vollbrecht, J., & Aboba, B. (2002). The one time password (OTP) and generic token card authentication protocols. (IETF Internet Draft, draft-ietf-eap-otp-00.txt).

Breiter, G., & Behrendt, M. (2009). Life cycle and characteristics of services in the world of cloud computing. *IBM Journal of Research and Development*, 53(4), 1–8. doi:10.1147/JRD.2009.5429057

Crampton, J. (2010). XACML and role-based access control. Retrieved from http://dimacs.rutgers.edu/Workshops/Commerce/slides/crampton.pdf

Google. (2008). Web-based reference implementation of SAML-based SSO for Google Apps. Retrieved Novmeber 10, 2011, from http://code.google.com/apis/apps/sso/saml_reference_implmentation_web.html

Groß, T. (2003). Security analysis of the SAML single sign-on browser/artifact profile.

Hansen, S. M., Skriver, J., & Nielson, H. R. (2005). Using static analysis to validate the SAML single sign-on protocol.

Huang, Y. J., Yuan, C. C., Chen, M. K., Lin, W. C., & Teng, H. C. (2010). Hardware implementation of RFID mutual authentication protocol. *IEEE Transactions on Industrial Electronics*, 57(5), 1573–1582. doi:10.1109/TIE.2009.2037098

Hubbard, D., Sutton, M., Deeba, A., Dancer, A., Shea, B., Balding, C., et al. (2010, December 2011). Top threats to cloud computing V1.0. Retrieved December 19, 2011, from https://cloudsecurityalliance.org/topthreats/csathreats.v1.0.pdf

Hughes, J., & Maler, E. (2005). Security assertion markup language (SAML) V2.0: Technical overview. (OASIS SSTC Working Draft sstc-saml-tech-overview-2.0-draft-08). Retrieved December 5, 2011, from http://www.oasis-open.org/committees/download.php/20824/sstc-saml-tech-overview-2%200-draft-11-diff.pdf

Il Kon, K., Pervez, Z., Khattak, A. M., & Sungyoung, L. (2010, 19-23 July 2010). Chord based identity management for e-healthcare cloud applications. Paper presented at the 2010 10th IEEE/IPSJ International Symposium on Applications and the Internet (SAINT).

Internet2. (2011). Shibboleth Project. Retrieved November 10, 2011, from http://shibboleth.internet2.edu/

Jaeger, T., & Schiffman, J. (2010). Outlook: Cloudy with a chance of security challenges and improvements. *Security & Privacy*, 8(1), 77–80. doi:10.1109/MSP.2010.45

Juang, W. S., Chen, S. T., & Liaw, H. T. (2008). Robust and efficient password-authenticated key agreement using smart cards. *IEEE Transactions on Industrial Electronics*, 55(6), 2551–2556. doi:10.1109/TIE.2008.921677

Kao, I. L., & Milman, I. M. (2001). *Method and system for single sign on using configuration directives with respect to target types*. Google Patents.

Leach, P. J., Mealling, M., & Salz, R. (2005). A universally unique identifier (UUID) urn namespace. Retrieved 15 December, 2011, from http://tools.ietf.org/html/rfc4122

Li, X., Qiu, W., Zheng, D., Chen, K., & Li, J. (2010). Anonymity enhancement on robust and efficient password-authenticated key agreement using smart cards. *IEEE Transactions on Industrial Electronics, 57*(2), 793–800. doi:10.1109/TIE.2009.2028351

Liberty Alliance Framework. (2007). Liberty Alliance Project. Retrieved December 10, 2011, from http://www.cs.helsinki.fi/u/chande/courses/cs/MWS/reports/reviews/15_1.pdf

LoadStorm. (2008-2011). Load Storm- Load testing tool. Retrieved October 10, 2011, from http://loadstorm.com/load-testing-tools

Mauro, C., Sunyaev, A., Leimeister, J. M., Schweiger, A., & Krcmar, H. (2008). A proposed solution for managing doctor's smart cards in hospitals using a single sign-on central architecture.

Migeon, J. Y. (2008). The MIT Kerberos administrator's how-to guide. Kerveros Consortium. Retrieved November 30, 2011, from http://docs.huihoo.com/kerberos/adminkerberos.pdf

Mikkilineni, R., & Morana, G. (2010). Is the network-centric computing paradigm for multicore, the next big thing? MSDN. (2011). How to: Sign XML documents with digital signatures. Retrieved December 5, 2011, from http://msdn.microsoft.com/en-us/library/ms229745.aspx

Nebhuth, R. (2009). Daenet's. NET community: Signing a document. Retrieved December 27, 2011, from http://developers.de/blogs/rolf_nebhuth/archive/2009/05/13/signing-xml-documents.aspx

NEOTYS. (2005-2012). Neo Load. Retrieved October 10, 2011, from http://www.neotys.com/

Neustar-Webmetrics. (2012). Webmetrics. Retrieved October 20, 2011, from http://www.webmetrics.com/

Open-Demand-System. (2000-2011). OpenLoad-Load testing software. Retrieved October 5, 2011, from http://www.opendemand.com/openload/

Petrusha, R. (2011). MSDN: GUID structure. Retrieved December 5, 2011, from http://msdn.microsoft.com/en-us/library/cey1zx63.aspx

Ragouzis, N., Hughes, J., Philpott, R., Maler, E., Madsen, P., & Scavo, T. (2008). Security assertion markup language (saml) v2.0 technical overview. *Committee Draft, 2*, 25.

Rankl, W., & Effing, W. (2010). *Smart card handbook* (4th ed.). Wiley. doi:10.1002/9780470660911

Saeed, K., & Nammous, M. K. (2007). A speech-and-speaker identification system: Feature extraction, description, and classification of speech-signal image. *IEEE Transactions on Industrial Electronics, 54*(2), 887–897. doi:10.1109/TIE.2007.891647

Sandhu, R. S., Coyne, E. J., Feinstein, H. L., & Youman, C. E. (1996). Role-based access control models. *Computer, 29*(2), 38–47. doi:10.1109/2.485845

Tagg, G. (2000, 2011, December 15). Implementing a Kerberos single sign-on infrastructure. Information Security Bulletin, Tagg Consulting Ltd [pdf-dokumentti] Marraskuu. Retrieved December 15, 2011, from https://koala.cs.pub.ro/redmine/attachments/download/151/10.1.1.105.9399.pdf

Tiwari, P. B., & Joshi, S. R. (2009). Single sign-on with one time password. Paper presented at the First IEEE Asian Himalayas International Conference on Internet, 2009.

Tusa, F., Celesti, A., & Mikkilineni, R. (2011). AAA in a cloud-based virtual DIME network architecture (DNA).

Upadhyay, M., & Marti, R. (2001). Single sign-on using Kerberos in Java. Sun Microsystems, Inc. Retrieved December 10, 2011, from http://ftp.ssw.uni-linz.ac.at/Services/Docs/JDK1.6.0/technotes/guides/security/jgss/single-signon.html

Verma, M. (2004). XML security: Control information access with XACML. Retrieved from http://www.ibm.com/developerworks/xml/library/x-xacml/

WAPT. (2003). Web application testing (WAPT). Retrieved from http://www.loadtestingtool.com/

Section 4
Methods, Technologies, and Applications

Chapter 12
Campus Cloud Storage and Preservation:
From Distributed File System to Data Sharing Service

Jinlei Jiang
Tsinghua University, China & Research Institute of Tsinghua University in Shenzhen, China

Yongwei Wu
Tsinghua University, China & Research Institute of Tsinghua University in Shenzhen, China

Xiaomeng Huang
Institute for Global Change Studies, China

Guangwen Yang
Institute for Global Change Studies, China & Tsinghua University, China

ABSTRACT

We are now living in the era of big data. The large volume of data raises a lot of issues related to data storage and management, stimulating the emergence of Cloud storage. Unlike traditional storage systems such as SAN (Storage Area Network) and NAS (Network Attached Storage), Cloud storage is delivered over a network and has such features as easy to scale and easy to manage. With Cloud storage shielding complex technical details such as storage capacity, data location, data availability, reliability and security, users can then concentrate on their business rather than IT (Information Technology) system maintenance. However, it is not an easy task to develop a Cloud storage system because multiple factors are involved. In this chapter, the authors show their experience in the design and implementation of a Cloud storage system. They detail its key components, namely the distributed file system Carrier and the data sharing service Corsair. A case study is also given on its application at Tsinghua University.

DOI: 10.4018/978-1-4666-2854-0.ch012

1 INTRODUCTION

It is clear that we are now living in the era of big data. According to IDC (2011), the new digital data has reached 1,200 exabytes in 2010. Still, more and more digital sources are coming. For example, the new generation fine-resolution climate models (Kouzes et al., 2009) will produce 8 petabytes per run for the same simulation, resulting in a 1000-fold increase in data volume. If all the data generated by the ATLAS experiment at the Large Hadron Collider (LHC) at CERN were recorded, they would fill 100,000 CDs (each holding 640 Mbytes) per second. The Large Synoptic Survey Telescope, which will launch to function in 2016, will collect 140 terabytes of information every five days (Cukier, 2010). The large volume of data raises a lot of issues in terms of storage, management and processing. In this chapter, we focus on data storage and management.

SAN (Storage Area Network) and NAS (Network Attached Storage) are two widely used techniques for storage sharing and management. SAN deploys a dedicated network for multiple servers to access storage devices (e.g., disk arrays and tape libraries) and provides no file abstraction, whereas NAS connects to a network and provides file-based data storage services to other devices on that network. Though SAN and NAS have gained wide adoption, they have inherent deficiencies in meeting the new needs. The SAN solution usually uses high-end storage and communication devices and as a result, the one-time cost and total cost of ownership (TCO) are high. As for the NAS solution, since both the data and the control commands flow through the NAS controller, the controller is apt to become a bottleneck of the whole system. In addition, a single NAS appliance has a capacity limit and it is difficult to seamlessly combine the storage space of two different NAS appliances. To deal with the above-stated deficiencies comes into being Cloud storage.

Unlike SAN and NAS, the Cloud storage is delivered over a network, easy to scale and easy to manage. Please note that the network used in Cloud storage is usually the Internet, whereas the network of SAN is a dedicated one and the network used in NAS is a local area network (LAN). With Cloud storage, users need not care about such complex technical details as storage capacity, data location, data availability, reliability and security. The only thing they need to do is to make a contract with a service provider and pay for what they consume. In this way, users can concentrate more on their business rather than IT (Information Technology) system maintenance. It is due to these features that Cloud storage attracts more and more attention. As a result, more and more Cloud storage services are available today, for example, Amazon S3 (Simple Storage Service), Google online storage (GDrive), Microsoft SkyDrive, Dropbox, to name but just a few. In spite of the fact, it is not an easy task to build a Cloud storage system because multiple factors are involved. These factors include but are not limited to: 1) heterogeneity in storage devices, networks and operating systems (OSes), and 2) various workloads to support, and 3) varied requirements on transparency, reliability, scalability, availability, cost and so on. In addition, to the best of our knowledge, the requirement of sharing data among users is not highlighted in current Cloud storage solutions except for GDrive and SkyDrive.

This chapter reports our experience in the design and implementation of a Cloud storage system. It aims to provide an example for people to deliver services of this kind to their users. The rest of the chapter is organized as follows. In the coming section, we give an overview of distributed file system and some related work, and explain the motivation of our work. Then our self-developed distributed file system Carrier and data sharing service Corsair are detailed in Section 3 and Section 4 respectively. Section 5 shows the application of Carrier and Corsair at Tsinghua University. Section 6 highlights our experience. The chapter ends in Section 7 with some conclusions, where some future work is also given.

2 BACKGROUND

2.1 Distributed File System

A file system is an abstraction layer of OSes that is responsible for organizing files and directories. It shields the technical details of the underlying data storage devices (e.g., hard disk drives, floppy disks, optical discs, flash memory devices, and so on) and provides a friendly interface for users to use these devices. Roughly speaking, the functions provided by a file system include device management, space management, file and directory naming, metadata and integrity maintenance, reliability/durability guarantees, and data protection (optional).

A distributed file system (DFS), also known as network file system, is any file system that allows transparent access to files stored on a remote disk via a computer network. From the perspective of software, a distributed file system provides a set of client and server services that allow users to transparently use remote devices in a friendly way. Here the term "server" is an extended concept, covering both the server in the traditional client-server architecture and the server clusters. Please note that the client nodes in a distributed file system have no direct access to the underlying storage devices as does in the local file system. Instead, the access is fulfilled over the network using some protocol. With multiple distributed nodes and network involved, distributed file systems pay much attention to transparent replication and fault tolerance besides the basic functions of a local file system.

From the perspective of users, distributed file systems provide a way for multiple users to share files and storage resources on multiple machines. Such a way not only relieves users of the tedious and headachy work of devices maintenance and management, but also keeps the advantages of file system in using storage devices. With multiple users sharing the same device, the utilization of device is improved. It is in this sense that DFS has become one of the key technologies behind Cloud storage — usually used as a Cloud storage backend.

2.2 Related Work

It is a lasting effort to develop distributed file systems since the first one dawned in 1970s. As a result, many systems are available today. Here we only list a few of them. For more information, please refer to the corresponding pages of Wikipedia.

The Network File System (NFS), which was first released in 1985 by Sun Microsystems and is now in its fourth version (Shepler et al., 2003), is the first and most widely used distributed file system. NFS adopts a traditional client-server architecture where the NFS server maintains a standard view of its local file system and is responsible for handling clients' requests, and the NFS client is in charge of handling access to files stored on the server using the system call supplied by the local operating system. The remote procedure call (RPC) protocol is used for communication between the NFS server and the NFS client. NFS is so successful that it is also adopted by NAS in most cases for file sharing. In spite of the fact, NFS has its shortcomings. The greatest one might be the security problem. RPC, which is the basis of NFS, is inherently insecure and apt to become a common target of exploit attempts, therefore making NFS not usable in a hostile environment like the Internet, especially for sharing sensitive information. The second problem is that the performance of NFS is sensitive to network traffic as well as disk activity on the service side.

The Andrew File System (AFS) (Howard et al., 1988) is a distributed file system developed by Carnegie Mellon University. To guarantee security, AFS provides Kerberos-based user authentication and access control lists on directories for users and groups. To reduce file access time, AFS provides support for file caching in local file system. Though file sharing can be achieved by defining appropriate access control lists on certain directories, this means a lot of administration work.

With the development of Cloud storage, more and more Cloud storage services are available today as aforementioned. Table 1 shows some typical systems and services, where HDFS (Hadoop, 2011), KFS (Kosmosfs, 2011), and Sector (Gu & Grossman, 2009) are all the open-source implementation of GFS (Ghemawat et al., 2003). From the table we can see that it is a consensus to build Cloud storage systems with cheap commodity hardware.

In spite of the fact that GFS and its followers have gained great success in applications, they present some shortcomings in common as stated below.

First, these systems are designed for storing and processing large files. Files of multiple gigabytes are common and therefore, they divided files into fixed-size chunks and chose the chunk size of 64MB (megabyte) as the basic element for storage and processing. Though small files can also be supported, such a scheme is obviously inefficient. Unfortunately, as revealed by some research (Satyanarayanan, 1981; Mullender & Tanenbaum,

1984; Sienknecht et al., 1994; Agrawal et al., 2007), small files dominate our world.

Second, these systems are optimized for specific workloads. Typical workloads supported are large streaming reads, and large, sequential appending writes. Therefore, when applied to other workloads such as random reads and small random writes as in personal data storage, they are inefficient.

Third, interfaces provided by these systems are similar to but not compliant with POSIX (Portable Operating System Interface of Unix) application programming interface (APIs). As a result, traditional applications—applications that are designed and developed on the basis of POSIX-compatible file systems—cannot be deployed and run on the Cloud storage without any modification. The same problem exists with other Cloud storage services.

Fourth and the last, these systems adopt a master-slave architecture, with a single master both to control data replication and garbage collection and to maintain metadata of files. Such a decision simplified system design, but introduced potential problems at the same time. Indeed, in a recent interview (McKusick & Quinlan, 2009),

Table 1. Typical cloud storage systems and services

	Open-source	Storage devices	Adopter/Provider	Main purpose
GFS (Google File System)	No	Cheap commodity hardware	Google	Large-scale data storage and processing
HDFS (Hadoop Distributed File System)	Yes	Cheap commodity hardware	IBM Blue Cloud, Yahoo!, FaceBook	Large-scale data storage and processing
KFS	Yes	Cheap commodity hardware	CloudStore	Large-scale data storage and processing
Sector	Yes	Cheap commodity hardware	Sector-Sphere	Large-scale data storage and processing
S3	No	Cheap commodity hardware	Amazon	Data storage
Cloud Files	Yes	Unknown	Rackspace	Data storage
SkyDrive	No	Unknown	Microsoft	Data storage
CloudComplete	No	Unknown	Nirvanix	Data storage
HybridCloud	No	Unknown	Egnyte	Data storage
Atoms	No	Cheap commodity hardware	EMC	Data storage

Sean Quinlan—the former GFS tech leader— has revealed that a single master soon became a bottleneck of GFS as the size of the underlying storage increased. Therefore, new and scalable schemes are needed for metadata management and system control.

3. DISTRIBUTED FILE SYSTEM: CARRIER

3.1 Assumptions

Carrier does not mean to solve all the problems with existing Cloud storage solutions as mentioned previously. Its purpose is to 1) provide massive yet reliable and scalable storage services through commodity hardware; 2) present a single I/O space for data storing and access; 3) deliver standard data access interfaces for traditional applications; 4) support various workloads that deal with both small and large files. Besides, manageability and fault-tolerance of the whole system are also borne in mind.

The design of Carrier follows the assumptions below.

- The primary application scenario of Carrier is personal data storage and the number of files to be stored would be huge. Therefore, storage capacity of a single I/O space is the first goal. The capacity should be easily enlarged by adding more storage devices as the number of files to be stored increases. Throughput and performance are also critical but considered secondarily.

- The system will run on the non-dedicated cluster of cheap commodity hardware. As a result, besides dealing with component failures on a routine basis as does in GFS, the system should minimize resource (especially bandwidth and memory) consumption. It is generally unacceptable that the performance of the cluster drops great-

ly due to running Carrier services. In other words, Carrier should be light-weighted.

- The size of files stored in the system ranges from several kilobytes to several gigabytes. Though we have to support large files, dealing with millions or even billions of small files (of several kilobytes or less) are more important.

3.2 System Architecture

Borrowing the idea of service-oriented architecture (SOA), Carrier adopts a loosely-coupled architecture consisting of multiple supervisors, multiple clients, multiple metadata servers, and multiple data servers, as shown in Figure 1. As in GFS, each machine in Carrier is running Linux system with commodity hardware. Functions of the machines and modules in Figure 1 are explained below.

The metadata servers maintain all file system metadata. In order to avoid the performance bottleneck of a single master as in GFS as well as a single point of failures, more than one metadata servers are deployed. The data servers provide space to store files. As in GFS, files in Carrier are also split into fixed-size chunks and stored onto several data servers as local files, but the chunk size is smaller (32MB by default) and reconfigurable. The supervisors are designed to handle issues related to system maintenance, including machine failures, replication adjustment, load balancing, data integrity checking, garbage collection, and so on. The clients provide a set of

Figure 1. Carrier architecture

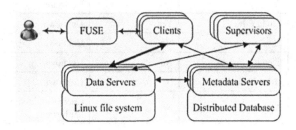

toolkits to access the data and metadata. Besides, a FUSE (Filesystem in Userspace) module is also provided with which users can mount the space in Carrier as a local drive so that traditional applications can be supported.

The principal difference between Carrier and the GFS-like systems in architecture is that the functions of the single master in GFS-like systems are divided and performed by multiple supervisors and multiple metadata servers respectively in Carrier. There is no interaction between clients and supervisors. As in GFS-like systems, there is no file data communication between clients and metadata servers in Carrier.

3.3 Metadata Management

In Carrier, metadata management adopts an out-of-band approach, that is, some dedicated servers are deployed to fulfill the task of metadata management. The metadata servers play a key role in Carrier for they are the "entrance" of the whole system and they determine the scalability of the system to a great extent, especially in terms of capacity and performance.

Since a single metadata server is apt to become a performance bottleneck and cause a single point of failure, multiple metadata servers are deployed in Carrier as shown in Figure 1. These servers are chained together with metadata fully replicated on them. To guarantee the consistency of different metadata servers as well as the performance of metadata operation, pipeline-based mechanism is employed. That is, when a client updates one metadata server, the command will be sent to the next server on the chain at the same time and in turn to other servers until the command is received by all. In such a way, the network load of each server can keep minimum and balanced. Unlike in GFS, metadata in Carrier is stored on disk with only a small portion cached in memory. Such a decision is made for the following reasons.

- Carrier is designed to store huge number of small files and keeping all meta-

data in memory would consume too many resources.

- Metadata servers are served by non-dedicated computers and keeping all metadata in memory would affect their performance.

- Since multiple metadata servers are deployed and the load of each server would not be that heavy. Moreover, metadata cache in client could reduce the load of metadata server further.

- Performance, though considered secondarily, is really a concern. Caching metadata can reduce disk operations and hence improve performance. This is especially beneficial to those "hot" files that are manipulated frequently.

- Users, at a given time, tend to access only part of his/her files rather than all. Therefore, caching the corresponding metadata is enough.

3.4 File Abstraction and Location Transparency

File abstraction and location transparency is a key feature of distributed file systems. Files in Carrier are presented to users in the form of traditional tree structure, or in other words, files in Carrier are organized into directories from the view of end users. At the backend, large files are split into multiple fixed-size chunks and each chunk is stored to one or more data servers as a plain local file. The chunk size is 32MB by default and of course, users can reconfigure it to other values as well. Carrier shields these technical details from users with the metadata maintained by the metadata servers.

In detail, Carrier maintains four major types of metadata using four tables, namely the Filemeta table, the Chunkmapping table, the Hostinf table and the Metalog table. Filemeta records metadata related to the file namespaces, including name, type, time created, last modified time, chunks and other information related to users and privilege. Chunkmapping records the mapping from chunks to data servers, according to which the metadata server can learn the total number of chunks in the system as well as the number of replicas of each chunk. Hostinf is deployed to maintain such information related to data servers as the host name, total space provided, free space available, and the server status. Metalog is an independent table used to record information related to metadata operations, including operation time, name and parameters. This information is useful to file system recovery. Users issue operation requests from the client. Once a request is got, Carrier first finds out all the chunks of the given file by querying the Filemeta table. After that, the Chunkmapping table and the Hostinf table are used to get the real location of each chunk as well as the access point. In the end, operations are done on the desired chunks using machine-specific APIs. In this way, location transparency is achieved.

In order to facilitate running traditional applications over Cloud storage without any modification, Carrier provides support for these POSIX-compliant file operations: *open, creat, close, read, write, lseek, mkdir, rmdir,* and *rename.* Besides these standard APIs, Carrier supplies *list, delete,* and *lookup* operations. List is used to get information about all files and directories within a given directory. Delete is used to delete a given file. To delete a file, Carrier just removes the corresponding metadata records from the metadata servers without reclaiming the physical storage in data servers immediately. Storage reclaim is done by the garbage collection process, which will be detailed later. Lookup is used to get all metadata of a given file. Based on these operations, we synthesize Carrier and FUSE, allowing users to mount the space in Carrier as a local drive and use it in a familiar and friendly way.

3.5 Replication Management

Replication management is supported in Carrier for two purposes: 1) fault tolerance, and 2) performance and throughput.

Since our system is supposed to run on clusters of cheap commodity hardware where component failures are common, chunk replication can avoid data loss due to disk failures as well as guarantee data availability. The philosophy here is that the chance that all machines holding the same chunk crash is much lower than that of a single one. As in GFS, the number of replicas is set to 3 by default and users can adjust this value whenever need. Also, users can specify different replication levels to different files. To save disk space, the replication mechanism is turned off when the system is initialized.

The philosophy of replication-based performance and throughput lies in that replicating one file to different machines can utilize the processing power and the network bandwidth of multiple machines to serve clients. As more power and more bandwidth are utilized, it is a natural result that the performance and throughput improve. In addition, from another point of view, such a way can lower the load of each data server and thus is very suitable for running on non-dedicated clusters as we supposed.

One problem arising with replication supported is how to guarantee the consistency of various replicas. This is an interesting problem with many solutions. Here chain replication (Renesse & Schneider, 2004) is exploited—replicas are created and synchronized along with any modification to files.

3.6 System Management

As the scale of a storage system gets larger and larger, it becomes a more and more complicated and critical task to manage the whole system. To ease the burden of system administration, manageability has become a more and more important concern of modern storage systems. Bearing this in mind, we, as aforementioned, emphasize manageability during Carrier design. Specifically, multiple supervisors are deployed in Carrier to fulfill system management tasks, with a special focus on fault tolerance and garbage collection.

Previously, we have stated that we use multiple servers and data replication to enhance reliability and availability. This forms a good basis but is not enough—we still need to know the status of each server so that some steps can be taken when a server fails. The supervisors exploit some monitor process to achieve the purpose. The monitor process sends heartbeat messages periodically to the metadata servers and the data servers. If there is no response from a certain server after several retries, that server is considered dead and then some steps are taken. The steps are server type dependent and detailed as follows.

When a metadata server is dead, all the subsequent requests are forwarded to other metadata servers. At the same time, the system administrator is informed to restart that server or to replace it with a new one. After the metadata server is restarted or a new one is added, the monitor will synchronize it with existing ones automatically. Once the process is done, the server comes online to handle users' requests.

If a data server fails, access requests to that server are forwarded to other data servers that hold the same chunks. At the same time, the monitor process starts chunk re-replication procedure to generate new replica of the affected chunks on other available data servers. The purpose is to ensure the number of available replicas exceeds the user-specified value. During this procedure, the Chunkmapping table and the Hostinf table are used to locate data servers and to record the new chunk location.

Garbage occurs due to two reasons in Carrier. First, Carrier, like GFS, does not reclaim the physical storage immediately after a file is deleted. Second, since metadata update is done after data operations without atomicity guarantee, chances are that the metadata update fails, making the just created chunk inaccessible by clients.

There are two approaches applicable to garbage collection, namely the metadata server-initiated one and the data server-initiated one. In the metadata server-initiated one, the metadata server will periodically broadcast all its metadata (more precisely, a list of available chunks) to all data servers. With the list got, the data server can then remove those chunks whose identities are not in the list. Given the huge number of files and hence the chunks, such an approach can burden the network. In the data server-initiated one, the data server will periodically send its chunk list to a metadata server. The metadata server, after getting the request, first finds out those unused chunks by some matchmaking algorithm and then sends the result back to the data server. Afterwards, those chunks are removed from the server. Given a large number of data servers available, such an approach imposes heavy load on the metadata server even if we assume multiple servers are deployed. Based on the above analysis, the first approach is selected with some improvements stated below.

The first improvement is that the garbage collection process is initiated by a supervisor rather than by a metadata server. Since supervisors in Carrier hold information about the whole system, the supervisor-initiating approach may make its impact on system as little as possible, for the idlest metadata server and the most right time can be selected to fulfill the task. The second one is that Bloom filter based data compression technique is utilized to ease the burden of network, which will be detailed next.

3.7 Bloom Filter-Based Garbage Collection

Bloom filter, named after Burton Howard Bloom, was first introduced in Bloom (1970). It is a compact probabilistic data structure used to do member query (namely to test whether an element belongs to a set). The key idea of Bloom filter is using a bit array to describe the membership information of a given set. A brief introduction is given below.

To denote the membership information of a set $S=\{s_1, s_2, ..., s_n\}$ of n elements, Bloom filter employs an array A of m bits and defines k different independent hash functions, $h_1, h_2, ..., h_k$ with $1 \leq h_j(s) \leq m$. Initially, all bits of A are set to 0. Then, for each s_i in S, *k* hash functions are calculated with *k* array positions got. Set all the corresponding bits of A to 1 and we then get the final result. To test whether a given element x is in S, the *k* hash functions are calculated again to get *k* array positions. If any of the bits at these positions of A are 1, x is definitely not in S. Otherwise, we think x is a member of S. Since a bit may by chance be set to 1 during member insertion, false positives—an element is incorrectly recognized as a set member—are possible. It is in this sense that Bloom filter is called a probabilistic data structure. In our case, false positives are acceptable.

Let *p* be the desired false positive rate, the relationship between *m*, *n* and *k* can be expressed as follows:

$$\frac{m}{n} = \frac{-k}{\ln(1 - e^{\frac{\ln p}{k}})}$$

The physical meaning of this formula is the minimum number of bits needed per entry to guarantee the desired false positive rate when *k* hash functions are used. In practice, the typical value of *k* ranges from 8 to16. With *k*=8 and *p*=0.001, we get *m*/*n*=14.6, that is, when 8 hash functions are used, to make the desired false positive rate less than 0.001, each entry in the set should be decoded by at least 15 bits. With more bits used, the false positive rate can drop quickly. For example, with *k*=8, when *m*/*n*=20, we get *p*=0.00014, and when *m*/*n*=24, we get *p*=0.000042.

From the above statement, we can see that the size of a Bloom filter, namely the bit array length *m*, is independent of the size of set member.

Therefore, it is more space-efficient than other data structures to represent sets. In our case, the chunk id is of 128 bits, using Bloom filters with *k*=8 and *m*/*n*=16 to decode the chunk list can reduce the traffic to 1/8. In addition, since no member-by-member comparison is needed to do member query, it is also time-efficient. It is on account of these advantages that we employ Bloom filters to do garbage collection. The whole garbage collection procedure is shown in Figure 2. Besides Bloom filters, the idea of chain replication is also deployed to further ease the burden of metadata servers as well as to improve throughput and performance.

3.8 Implementation and Evaluation

Carrier is implemented using Erlang and C where C is used to develop the Fuse module in Figure 1 and Erlang is used to develop other modules. Erlang is selected because it is a general-purpose concurrent programming language with such features required by Carrier as built-in distribution and failure detection, rapid development, low-maintenance and easy upgrade, hot code loading, concurrent processes support, message passing-based interface, reliability-oriented standard library, and so forth. Indeed, owing to these features the core functions of Carrier are implemented with only 6000 lines of Erlang code. In addition, Web services-based interfaces are provided for metadata query, system monitoring, and other interactions related to system management and control. Such a way makes the coupling of different modules loose and thus improves system scalability. In addition, it facilitates new function development as well.

Figure 2. Bloom filter-based garbage collection process

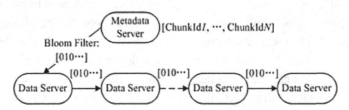

In the end, no Web services-based interfaces are provided for data operations on account of the overhead of Web services and the requirements on performance and throughput.

We evaluated Carrier on a small-scale cluster consisting of 12 nodes where 10 nodes are deployed as data servers, 1 node as metadata server and supervisor, and 1 node as client. Each node is equipped with 1 CPU (Xeon 5110 1.6GHz), 4GB memory, 160GB disk (WDC WD1600AAJS-22PSA0), and Ubuntu 8.04 Server (Linux-2.6.26-2-xen-amd64). These nodes are interconnected via 1Gbps Ethernet. We first tested the performance of metadata operations. The result is shown in Table 2. The create file operation takes more time because data operation is involved—the metadata is not updated until the file is saved to the disks of data servers. As for delete file operation, the performance is high because no data operation is involved as explained before. From the table we can see that the performance of metadata operation is acceptable for the interaction between users and Carrier.

Besides the performance of metadata operations, we also measured the throughput of Carrier and made a comparison with that of HDFS. The result is shown in Figure 3, where the performance ration is defined as the throughput of Carrier divided by the throughput of HDFS. Since HDFS does not support random read and write operation, we only tested the throughput of sequential read and write. Each time, a total of 4GB files are written to and read from Carrier and HDFS respectively. The size of file used for test starts from 128KB and doubles each time. For HDFS, the performance data is got using the self-shipped shell tool. For Carrier, the performance data is got using IOzone, the well-known file system benchmark tool.

From Figure 3 we can see that Carrier excels HDFS in throughput for both read and write operations. As the size of file decreases, the gap between them becomes more and more obvious. Specifically, when the file size is 128KB (small files), the performance of Carrier is about 5 times higher than that of HDFS. When the file size is 16MB (medium files), the performance of Carrier is about 2 times higher than that of HDFS. When the file size reaches 1GB (large files), the gap for write operations only changes slightly, whereas the gap for read operations becomes unobvious and only amount to 1.45 times.

4. DATA SHARING SERVICE: CORSAIR

4.1 An Overview

Corsair aims to 1) provide storage services (more precisely, data upload and download) on top of Carrier as well as other facilities such as NFS, HDFS, and FTP; 2) provide users with a uniform view of the files stored in different facilities; 3) support file sharing among users; 4) supply some advanced services to facilitate file access.

Table 2. Performance of metadata operations in Carrier

Operation	Description	Time/Operation (ms)
Create file	Create 10000 null files	1.955
List file	List a directory of 10000 files	0.015
Delete file	Delete 10000 files	0.0225
Create directory	Create 10000 null directories	0.002
List directory	List a directory of 10000 directories	0.0137
Delete directory	Delete 10000 null directories	0.0215

In functionality, it does have some overlap with Carrier. The reasons why we develop Corsair are as follows.

Firstly, Carrier is a just developed distributed file system and people might not like using it even if it has some good features. For most cases, people prefer to use commercial products or the ones they are familiar with for the concern of reliability and stability.

Secondly, data sharing among users is not well supported by Carrier. Though data sharing could be supported by authorizing the access rights of certain files to a group of users as in Linux and Unix systems, such a way would lay a heavy burden on system administration because a lot of work is needed to manage user groups and to set the corresponding access right. In addition, such a way would leave the system unsecure. Therefore, it is not a good choice.

Thirdly, as the number of files increases, advanced services are needed beyond storage space. File searching and bookmarking are good examples of such services. Unfortunately, neither Carrier nor other distributed file systems provide support for these services.

Fourthly and the last, the Fuse module in Carrier is not supported by the Windows environments. This means Windows users cannot use our service.

Unfortunately, the number of Windows users accounts for nearly 90% of the total targeted users.

Other data platforms such as SRB (2012), iRODS (2012) and gCube (2012) also provide data integration and sharing capability. Corsair is different from them in that these platforms are designed for Grid computing (Foster et al., 2001) with the purpose of resource integration and uniform access and Corsair is designed for personal data storage and sharing. In addition, data sharing in Corsair is fully controlled by users rather than by the system administrators.

4.2 Service Design

The modular architecture of Corsair is shown in Figure 4. It mainly consists of four layers, namely the Storage Facilities layer, the Adaptation layer, the Services layer and the Applications layer. The Storage Facilities layer, just as the name indicated, provides various storage facilities for users to transparently utilize the underlying storage devices. The storage facility can be anything capable of providing storage services. The Adaptation layer provides a set of uniform data access interfaces for the upper services and is in charge of mapping these interfaces to real operations of the underlying storage facilities. In this way, the

Figure 3. Throughput of data operations in Carrier

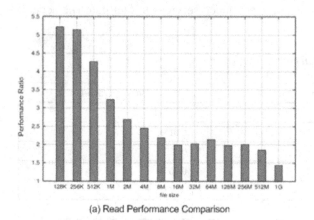

(a) Read Performance Comparison

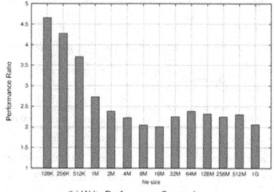

(b) Write Performance Comparison

interface heterogeneity of the underlying storage facilities is shielded. The Services layer provides various functions services needed by the users or by the system itself. Details of these services will be given shortly. The Applications layer provides 3 client tools (i.e., the GUI tool, the Shell tool and the Web Portal) and a set of APIs for end-users or applications to access the services provided.

The services provided by Corsair include bookmark management, naming service, search engine, data transferring, user management, and community management. Details of them are as follows.

Bookmark management and search engine are two services deployed to facilitate system usage. The bookmark management service borrows the idea from current Web 2.0 practice and allows users to create bookmarks of certain files. These bookmarks provide meaningful shortcut to files and can boost the file access process. The search engine is supplied for users to quickly locate the desired files. As the number of files will continue exploding, such a service is just necessary.

The naming service fulfills the task of metadata management. Besides translating logical resource names into physical ones, it maintains a logical view for each user in the form of a mapping file. When users logs into the system, the mapping files will be returned to the client and cached there to boost the following file listing process.

The data transferring service provides various data transport approaches, including resumable transfer, parallel transfer, stripping transfer and 3rd-party transfer. With these approaches, data transfer becomes reliable and efficient. As a result, users can get good experience in using our service.

User management is responsible for user authorization, user authentication and access control. It forms a good basis to guarantee data security. In Corsair, the widely used password-based authentication method is adopted. Community management is used to manage various user communities. A community is a basic unit to control data sharing—files belonging to a community are only visible to those who is a member of that community. We will detail how rapid and flexible data sharing is supported in Corsair shortly.

4.3 Client Tools

As aforementioned, three types of client tools are provided by Corsair, namely the GUI tool, the

Figure 4. The modular architecture of Corsair

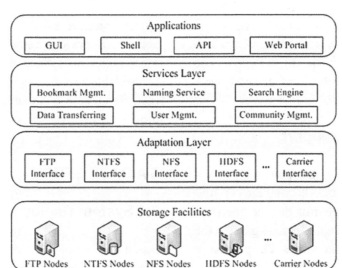

Shell tool and the Web Portal. For the GUI tool, three versions (i.e., Windows version, Linux version and Mac version) are delivered. With more tools and versions available, the diverse taste of users can be met and thus they can get better experience in using the service. This, we think, is beneficial for the service to be subscribed by more. Among these tools, the GUI tool provides richest functions.

The GUI client tool adopts a Windows Explorer-like style design as shown in Figure 5. Such a design is mainly on account of two factors, that is, the number of Windows users accounts for most of the targeted users and providing users with a familiar interface will reduce users' effort in learning a new tool and make the system more attractive.

From Figure 5 we can see that the whole interface of the GUI tool is divided into two columns and five areas. The three areas in the left column, from top to down, are the entrance to local resources, public resources and user-specific network space (login required). This way local and network resources are uniformly integrated. The other two areas in the right column are the file view and the task list. Contents displayed in the user-specific area include user's private storage space, the list of communities that the user joins, and user's bookmarks. The task list shows the files to be uploaded or downloaded as well as the progress of file transfer. From the figure we can also see that a search box is provided, with which users can search certain files by keywords. The searching results will be displayed in the file view area.

4.4 Data Sharing Support

Data sharing is achieved by allocating community-specific storage space and allowing the community administrator to control the membership. In Corsair, each registered users are granted the capability to create communities. The process to create a community is as follows.

Step 1: The user logins to the system via the Corsair Web portal.

Step 2: The user makes an application for creating a community. During the time, the user must specify a name for the community and provide a brief introduction to the community.

Step 3: Administrators of Corsair check the application. Such a step is necessary to prevent users from creating too many communities especially when the storage is provided free of charge.

Step 4: The community is created with its own storage space if the application is approved. By default, the applicant becomes the administrator of the newly created community.

After a community is created, other users can see it in the community list. User can apply for joining any community they are interested in. Once the community administrator approves a user's application, that user gains the right to upload resources to the community space and the right to access the resources within the community space. Since all users of a community can upload resources to or download resources from the space of that community, data sharing is thus achieved.

Compared with other approaches for data sharing, data sharing in Corsair has at least the following two advantages. First, it is more rapid and flexible. The only work needed is to make an application and control the membership. Multiple communities can be created to meet various sharing requirements. Second, the sharing is fully controllable by end users. The community creator (i.e., the default community administrator) has the full control over who can join the community.

5 A CASE STUDY

5.1 System Deployment

Based on Carrier and Corsair, we established a Cloud storage system at Tsinghua University with

Figure 5. Interface of the Corsair GUI client tool

Carrier as a back-end storage facility and Corsair as the front-end service. The configuration of the whole system is illustrated in Figure 6. In our settings, three data centers are used and they are equipped with Carrier, NFS and FTP service respectively. The data center equipped with NFS is a legacy one where a 150TB EMC CX Series storage system is deployed. Since the storage system is mainly used to support the cluster in that center, only 20TB storage is allocated to our system. As for the data center equipped with FTP, it is really a machine that provides FTP service to students on the campus before. The data center equipped with Carrier is a newly-built one, whose details are shown below.

Initially, there are ten machines in the Carrier data center, among which one is used to host the naming service and search engine of Corsair, one runs both as the Web portal of Corsair and as the supervisor of Carrier, and the others are for Carrier—two as metadata servers and six as data

servers. Later, more data servers are added to increase storage capacity. Since the number of users, or more precisely, the load of metadata operations is not too high in our settings, we only deploy two metadata servers for the purpose of reliability and availability. All the machines are commercial off-the-shelf (DELL PowerEdge R710, R510), installed with Linux and ext4 file system. The data center is connected to the campus network (CERNET) via a fiber channel and within the data center, 1Gbps Ethernet is used to connect all the machines. To ensure data reliability, the data replication function is turned on with default settings.

5.2 Usage Statistics

The Cloud storage system was put into operation in December 2008 to provide free storage service for students and teachers on the campus. For each registered user, 2GB private storage space is allocated and for each community, 100GB storage space is allocated. Initially, a total of 40TB storage space is supplied where 20TB is used for public resources and 20TB is used for personal and community resources. The service is so popular that the storage space soon ran out. To meet the need, the storage capacity was first extended to 70TB in July 2009 and then to 100TB in August 2010. Till now, the number of service subscribers has well exceeded 19,000 and more than 500 communities have been created. The daily usage of Corsair service is over 3,000 person-times, with an average throughput of around 1.3TB/day. Totally, the GUI tool (all the three versions) has been downloaded more than 90,000 times.

Based on the running logs about file number, file size, file name extension, capacity usage, directory size, modification and change time, we also gained some insights into Cloud storage usage. The main findings are as follows.

- Currently our Cloud storage system is mainly used for file sharing. According to our statistics, 90% of the storage space is used by communities. While the average number of files per user is 684, the value for community is 7022. Such a finding indicates that users use our service mainly for the sharing purpose and we should pay more attentions to file sharing in Cloud storage systems rather than to personal data backup.
- The 80-20 phenomenon holds in Cloud storage systems. That is, 20% of users contributed more than 80% of the total files. This indicates the benefit of Cloud storage—improved resource usage.
- Small files dominate the system. We found that more than 95% of the files are less than 4MB and they only occupy about 10% of the total space. This verifies our stating point stated in Section 2. As a result, it is necessary to do some optimization for small file read and write.

- The main file size of communities is bigger than that of users. Such a finding implies that users tend to share large files.
- The distribution of file types (indicated by its extension) is not even. Several file types account for about 50% of the total number of files and the JPG and the GIF are the two types of the most files. In addition, nearly 70% of the storage capacity is occupied by 10 file types and the AVI is the most storage-consuming type. With this finding, we can provide some special function or do some specific optimization to give users better experience in using our service.
- There is few file access from 5:00 AM to 7:00 AM. This finding can be used to schedule system-wide management operations such as garbage collection, rebalancing, and components update to make their impact on other tasks as little as possible.

6 DISCUSSION

Previously, we have shown our solution to construct a Cloud storage system. The solution consists of two principal components, namely the distributed file system Carrier and the data sharing service Corsair. As aforementioned, Carrier and Corsair do have some overlap in functionalities—both of them can provide Cloud storage services to users. The main difference is that Carrier highlights data reliability and the performance of operations, whereas Corsair highlights data sharing on the basis of existing storage facilities. In addition, they provide different interfaces to users: the interface of Carrier is compliant with POSIX specification and allows users to mount the remote storage as a local drive via the FUSE module, whereas the interface of Corsair only supports upload and download operations. In the real world, users can deploy only one of them to get less functionality or both of them as we do to get more functions. The decision is based on the factors such as user requirements, storage facilities available and so on.

Figure 6. Topology of the cloud storage system at Tsinghua University

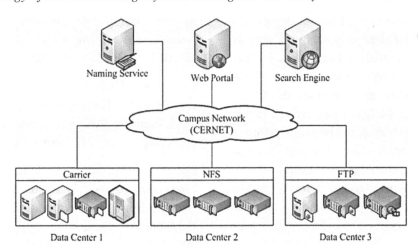

It is not an easy task to build a distributed file system since many factors are involved. The application scenario and users' requirements determine the design choices. For GFS-like systems, they are mainly used for big data processing, where files of several gigabytes are the common case and the main access patterns are sequential reads and data appending. On the contrary, the main application scenario of Carrier is personal data storage, where small files dominate as revealed by the statistical data and where random read and random write are the common case. As a result, both metadata and data operations are more frequent than those of GFS-like systems. This imposes more burdens on the master if only a single master is deployed as in GFS-like systems, making it hard to afford. To deal with the issue, Carrier divides the responsibilities of the master and assigns them to multiple supervisors and metadata servers respectively. Besides, the default chunk size is reduced to 32MB to reduce the waste of storage space; the metadata structure is redesigned to accommodate more files as well as more chunks; the garbage collection process is optimized to ease the burden of metadata servers and the network to meet the requirement of frequent data operations.

In the end, we would like to point out two things. The first one is that using a distributed file system as the backend of Cloud storage is one viable approach, but not the only one. Indeed, there are many other approaches available. For example, Amazon S3 utilizes object store to provide Cloud storage. Compared with these approaches, DFS provides an interface as well as a way of files organization that users are more familiar with. The second one is that data sharing is not a mandatory part of Cloud storage system. However, since the key idea of Cloud computing is to facilitate users and data sharing is really needed by users, we think providing support for data sharing can bring real benefits to users. It is in this sense that we provide this function in our Cloud storage solution. Data sharing in Corsair is different from that of GDrive and SkyDrive in that it is a high-level mechanism and no complex file-level operation controls are involved. In addition, its management cost is much lower.

CONCLUSION

Nowadays Cloud computing has been accepted as an effective way to deliver scalable and on-demand storage and computing services to users via the Internet. However, it is not an easy task to achieve the goal of Cloud computing for many research and engineering challenges are involved. In this chapter, we explained how to design and implement a Cloud storage system with a focus on the back-end distributed file system and the front-end data sharing service. In our experience, to design a more usable and scalable Cloud storage system, a loosely-coupled architecture is necessary and attention should be paid to efficient metadata management, ease of use interface, and the badly-needed functionality of users.

Though our solution has been proved feasible by its application at Tsinghua University, it is far from perfect. For example, the data sharing process still needs some intervention by the service provider (to approve community applications). This would become a burden as the number of applications increases rapidly. To deal with the issue, we plan to replace this by applying some economic-driven policy (e.g., charging more for more communities). In addition, according to users' feedback, allowing users to view some files online is also put into our agenda.

ACKNOWLEDGMENT

The work reported in this chapter is co-sponsored by National Basic Research (973) Program of China (2011CB302505), Natural Science Foundation of China (61073165, 60911130371), and National High-Tech R&D (863) Program of China (2011AA040505). We thank the anonymous reviewers for their valuable comments to improve this chapter.

REFERENCES

Agrawal, N., Bolosky, W. J., Douceur, J. R., & Lorch, J. R. (2007). A five-year study of file-system metadata. In *5th USENIX Conference on File and Storage Technologies* (pp. 31-45). Berkeley, CA: USENIX Association.

Bloom, B. H. (1970). Space/time trade-offs in hash coding with allowable errors. *Communications of the ACM*, *13*(7), 422–426. doi:10.1145/362686.362692

Cukier, K. (2010, February 25). Data, data everywhere. *The Economist*. Retrieved January 10, 2012, from http://www.economist.com/specialreports/displaystory.cfm?story_id=15557443

Foster, I., Kesselman, C., & Tuecke, S. (2001). The anatomy of the grid: Enabling scalable virtual organizations. *International Journal of High Performance Computing Applications*, *15*(3), 200–222. doi:10.1177/109434200101500302

gCube. (2012). *gCube framework*. Retrieved January 10, 2012, from http://www.gcube-system.org/

Ghemawat, S., Gobioff, H., & Leung, S. T. (2003). The Google file system. *ACM SIGOPS Operating Systems Review*, *37*(5), 29–43. doi:10.1145/1165389.945450

Gu, Y., & Grossman R. (2009). Sector and sphere: The design and implementation of à high performance data cloud. *Theme Issue of the Philosophical Transactions of the Royal Society A: Crossing Boundaries: Computational Science, E-Science and Global E-Infrastructure, 367*(1897), 2429-2445.

Hadoop. (2011). *Welcome to Hadoop™ distributed file system!* Retrieved December 10, 2012, from http://hadoop.apache.org/hdfs/

Howard, J., Kazar, M., Menees, S., Nichols, D., Satyanarayanan, M., Sidebotham, R., & West, M. (1988). Scale and performance in a distributed file system. *ACM Transactions on Computer Systems*, *6*(1), 51–81. doi:10.1145/35037.35059

IDC. (2011). *Worldwide enterprise storage systems 2011–2015 forecast: "Emerging" once again is a keyword in the storage market*. IDC #228255, May 2011.

iRODS. (2012). *iRODS: Data grids, digital libraries, persistent archives, and real-time data systems.* Retrieved January 10, 2012, from http://www.irods.org

Kosmosfs. (2011). *Kosmos distributed filesystem.* Retrieved December 10, 2012, from http://code.google.com/p/kosmosfs/

Kouzes, R. T., Anderson, G. A., Elbert, S. T., & Gracio, D. K. (2009). The changing paradigm of data-intensive computing. *IEEE Computer, 42*(1), 26–34. doi:10.1109/MC.2009.26

McKusick, M. K., & Quinlan, S. (2009). GFS: Evolution on fast-forward. *ACM Queue; Tomorrow's Computing Today, 7*(7), 10. doi:10.1145/1594204.1594206

Mullender, S., & Tanenbaum, A. (1984). Immediate files. *Software, Practice & Experience, 14*(4), 365–368. doi:10.1002/spe.4380140407

Renesse, R., & Schneider, F. B. (2004). Chain replication for supporting high throughput and availability. In *6th Symposium on Operation Systems Design and Implementation* (pp. 91-104). Berkeley, CA: USENIX Association.

Satyanarayanan, M. (1981). A study of file sizes and functional lifetimes. *ACM SIGOPS Operating Systems Review, 15*(5), 96–108. doi:10.1145/1067627.806597

Shepler, S., Callaghan, B., Robinson, D., Thurlow, R., Beame, C., Eisler, M., & Noveck, D. (2003). *Network file system (NFS) version 4 protocol.* RFC 3530, Apr. 2003. Retrieved January 10, 2012, from http://datatracker.ietf.org/doc/rfc3530/

Sienknecht, T. F., Friedrich, R. J., Martinka, J. J., & Friedenbach, P. M. (1994). The implications of distributed data in a commercial environment on the design of hierarchical storage management. *Performance Evaluation, 20*(1-3), 3–25. doi:10.1016/0166-5316(94)90003-5

SRB. (2012). *The DICE storage resource broker.* Retrieved January 10, 2012, from http://www.sdsc.edu/srb/index.php

KEY TERMS AND DEFINITIONS

Cloud Computing: A new computing paradigm for service delivery and consumption over the Internet in an on-demand approach.

Cloud Storage: A mode of cloud computing that provides on-demand storage services to users on the charge-per-use basis.

Community: A community is a virtual organization consisting of a group of people who have the demand of sharing data among them.

Distributed File System: Any file system that allows transparent access to files stored on a remote disk via a computer network.

File System: An abstraction layer of operating systems that is responsible for organizing files and directories and that provides a friendly way for users to use storage devices.

Metadata: The data used to describe the characteristics of a resource. To file systems, metadata is deployed to describe file attributes as well as the file system itself.

Scalability: A metric used to measure the ability of a system in dealing with growing amount of work or being enlarged/reduced in terms of capacity, functions, administration and so on.

Service-Oriented Architecture (SOA): A software-developing paradigm that takes services as the basic building blocks and that highlights loose coupling, reusability and autonomy of services.

Chapter 13
An Infrastructure-as-a-Service Cloud:
On-Demand Resource Provisioning

Weijia Song
Peking University, China

Zhen Xiao
Peking University, China

ABSTRACT

Cloud computing allows business customers to elastically scale up and down their resource usage based on needs. This feature eliminates the dilemma of planning IT infrastructures for Cloud users, where under-provisioning compromises service quality while over-provisioning wastes investment as well as electricity. It offers virtually infinite resource. It also made the desirable "pay as you go" accounting model possible. The above touted gains in the Cloud model come from on-demand resource provisioning technology. In this chapter, the authors elaborate on such technologies incorporated in a real IaaS system to exemplify how Cloud elasticity is implemented. It involves the resource provisioning technologies in hypervisor, Virtual Machine (VM) migration scheduler and VM replication. The authors also investigate the load prediction algorithm for its significant impacts on resource allocation.

1. INTRODUCTION

Cloud elasticity refers to the ability of Cloud infrastructure to dynamically make resource provision for Internet applications and services, according to their real time requirements. That feature of Cloud Computing has several appealing implications. It eliminates the dilemma of planning IT infrastructures for Cloud users, where under-

provisioning compromises service quality while over-provisioning wastes investment as well as electricity. It offers virtually infinite resource to Cloud users (Armbrust et al., 2009). It has also made the desirable "pay as you go" accounting model possible.

Planning new IT infrastructure for growing demands of Internet applications is complicated. It calls for successful prediction on how appli-

DOI: 10.4018/978-1-4666-2854-0.ch013

cation loadings would change in the future and is particularly hard for Start-Ups since market response is not clear in advance. When it knocks against flash-crowd, self-maintained servers may fail to satisfy the need of surging requests. On the contrary, over provisioning caused by optimistic prediction leaves the server under-utilized, and consequently causes waste in energy and excess investment in fixed asset. In Cloud environment, however, application maintainers need not worry about such problems since the Cloud resource allocation automatically scales up and down on changing load, and the users are billed accordingly.

Sometimes, particularly in data mining applications, a user may require a large number of servers for a short period. It is hard to satisfy such requirement if it were not for Cloud computing. A successful example is, "The Washington Post uses Amazon EC2 to turn Hillary Clinton's White House schedule—17,481 non-searchable PDF pages—into a searchable database within 24 hours." ("AWS Case Study: Washington Post," n.d.). In colleges, researchers may have similar requirements when processing huge amount of experiment data.

There are different approaches to Cloud elasticity depending on how the Cloud infrastructure is constructed and what types of applications running over it. In the next sections, we are going to introduce some popular technologies adopted nowadays Cloud Services. Then we start from basic components of a Cloud infrastructure to explain our own work that handling Cloud elasticity in a real IaaS service. In the end, we will point out, in our perspective, the trend of Cloud elastic technologies.

2. BACKGROUND

Traditionally, Cloud services are categorized into Infrastructure as a Service (IaaS), Platform as a Service (PaaS) and Software as a Service (SaaS). IaaS provides virtual machines to Cloud users.

IaaS users are responsible for application development, deployment and management. PaaS take the burden of application management by providing development tools and deployment platform. SaaS model is actually "old wine in new bottles" for conventional Internet applications.

In an IaaS system, virtual machines are generally overcommitted to physical servers to maximize profit from hardware investment and cut down power budget. Cloud elasticity in that environment addresses the challenge of resource provisioning for dynamic load of virtual machines. For example, if physical server cannot satisfy the resource requirements of its virtual machines, some of them are going to be migrated to other servers so that application performance is assured.

It is hard for application developers to predict the user load. In PaaS systems, user applications are managed by Cloud infrastructure to relive developers of the difficult of deployment, so that they can concentrate on application function. Generally, the applications deployed in PaaS are developed by designated program language, development tool and libraries and encapsulated in managed execution engines. An execution engine is a sandbox allocated with a share of CPU resource. Execution engines have uniform management interface for life cycle control and performance monitoring. Elasticity mechanism dynamically adjusts the number of execution engines belonging to an application to suit its load.

The situation in SaaS is similar to that in PaaS. A SaaS service could be built upon a PaaS service to indirectly utilize its elasticity mechanism. Some large SaaS services choose to implement dedicated elasticity mechanism for application specific optimizations (Chen et al., 2008) (Chase et al., 2001). Here we just talk about stateless computing resource. The discussion of data storage technologies like Google File System (Ghemawat, Gobioff, and Leung, 2003) and Big Table (Chang et al., 2008) belongs to another dedicated field out of scope of this chapter.

This chapter focuses on the Cloud elasticity technologies adopted in IaaS systems. We are going to illustrate the dynamic resource provisioning mechanisms and policies in the PKU Cloud, a real IaaS system that supporting research in Computer Department of Peking University.

The PKU Cloud adopts typical structure of Cloud infrastructure depicted in Figure 1. Its fundamental part is a virtualized data center hosting several tens of blade servers. The Xen hypervisor virtualize each physical server into several virtual machines. Based on the hypervisors and the virtual machines, the PKU Cloud incorporates peripheral services such as storage, security, and management to provide an integrated solution. Although innovative network structures like FatTree (Al-Fares et al., 2008) and VL2(Greenberg et al., 2009) are emerging, conventional tree structure is the most widely adopted one for data center network. The conventional tree structured data center network is composed of a router, several core switches, and many top of rack switches. In practice, a data center generally has more than one router and core switches for fail-safe or performance purpose. Data center network connect servers to each other and to the outside Internet. Storage Area Network (SAN) connects the servers with back end centralized storage devices.

The PKU Cloud implements elasticity at three levels. Consider a scenario where the load of an application keeps rising. Virtual machines containing the application components begin asking for more CPU and memory from the hypervisor layer. Idle resources of the physical servers are assembled and put into use by the hypervisors. Most of the time, virtual machines are not fully loaded. Physical servers usually have some resource reservation for transient load pulse, even though they are sometimes over-committed. However, the application load keeps going up. Resource reservation in some physical servers is consequently exhausted. In this case, hypervisors has to balance resource allocation among the virtual machines sharing the same physical server to avoid unacceptable degradation of Quality of Service (QoS). In the next section, we are going to discuss in details the resource scheduling technologies at the hypervisor level.

Live migration (Clark et al., 2005) allows a virtual machine to be migrated from one physical server to another, without interrupting the application running in that virtual machine. Ideally, layout of virtual machines on physical servers can be dynamically adjusted with live migration to a state that Service Level Agreement (SLA) is always satisfied as long as there are idle resources available in any physical server in the system. This feature is appealing in case of flash crowd. When application load may get high enough that no matter how the hypervisor allocates the resources to virtual machines, there are always some applications that cannot get enough resource to achieve acceptable performance regarding to SLA. Live migration, however, incurs network overhead because it involves transferring the memory image along with other states of a virtual machine from one server to another. When network resource is busy, using live migration may make the situation worse. In addition, migration may last for an uncertain period of time depending on network traffic; therefore it is unwise to incorporate migration for a transient overload. Due to the limitations of live migration, the aforementioned ideal state is hard to achieve. In the section "elasticity with live migration", we are going to elaborate on how the PKU Cloud uses live migration for resource provisioning.

Performance scalability with service replication has been adopted in web applications (Chase et al., 2001) long before. Stateless tiers of an application, like web front end and thinking logic are replicated in case of flash crowd. An application level switch is responsible for redirecting incoming requests to the right place. In virtualized environment, the mechanism stays the same except that application tiers are encapsulated in virtual machines. But the applications nowadays are growing more and more complicated. On one

Figure 1. Architecture of a virtualized data center

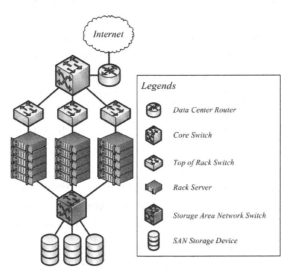

hand, they occupied large amount of memory even in idle. On the other hand, the process of starting or shutting down an application typically lasts too long to react to flash crowd in time. In the section "elasticity in Internet applications", we address those issues with the PKU Cloud approaches to Cloud elasticity at the application level.

The nature of resource scheduling is to provision resources reasonably to applications in the future. If the future load could be known beforehand, an offline algorithm can calculate an ideal resource scheduling solution so that all application requirements are satisfied if possible and that the performance of the Cloud infrastructure is maximized. However, it is usually impossible to know the load in advance. In this case, prediction algorithm, making estimation of a random variable according to its history and other factors, helps understand the trend of how the load would change overtime. Prediction is a well-studied topic in fields such as stock market prediction and weather forecasting. In the field of Cloud computing, many research works and systems have already incorporated that technology. In section "load prediction", we are going to introduce two kinds of load prediction algorithm.

3 RESOURCE SCHEDULING IN HYPERVISOR

Generally, physical servers are overcommitted by virtual machines. For example, a CPU intensive and a memory intensive virtual machine are put together to share a server to improve utilization. Combining virtual machines with alternate peak time takes effect likewise. When load changes, the hypervisor is responsible for adjusting resource allocation among the virtual machines. Three types of resources are usually considered: CPU, memory, and I/O resource. We are going to look into the each kind of resource respectively to understand how elasticity is realized at the hypervisor level. We assume you have basic knowledge of virtualization in this chapter or you can refer to the design of Xen hypervisor (Barham et al., 2003).

3.1 Virtual CPU Scheduler

In Operating System, process scheduling is a well-explored area. OS processes are multiplexed on CPU cores in an elastic time-division manner. Process scheduler incorporates priority and time slice for fair allocation of CPU time as well as maximum utilization. A process can use more CPU time than its share as long as idle CPU times are available. A greedy process, however, is constrained to its fair share so that other processes are not affected negatively. In a virtualized environment, the mapping of OS processes to physical CPU cores is indirect. Firstly, a process is scheduled onto a Virtual CPU (VCPU) of its containing virtual machine by the process scheduler in the guest operating system. When the VCPU acquires CPU time slice, the process is executed. Scheduling VCPUs onto physical CPU cores is performed by VCPU scheduler in the hypervisor. VCPU scheduler and process scheduler have common objectives such as fairness and performance.

All physical servers in the PKU Cloud are configured to use Credit ("Credit Based Scheduler", 2007), the default VCPU scheduler of Xen hypervisor. In Credit, each virtual machine is associated with two properties, a weight and a cap. The weight tells the proportion of CPU time a virtual machine should have relative to each other; while cap tells the upper limit. We use a two-tuple <weight, cap> to represent a virtual machine with its weight and cap. Consider two virtual machines, A <100, 80%> and B <100, 60%>, which share a server. If the CPU load in both of them exceeds 50% of the capacity of the server, they get 50% each. Otherwise, unused CPU time of one virtual machine can be utilized by the other. For example, A can get up to 80% if B uses only 10%, leaving the other 10% CPU time unused. On the contrary, B can get up to 60%.

3.2 Memory Allocation among Virtual Machines

Memory resource is quite different from CPU resource for its usage is almost independent of application load. A sophisticated application may require a large amount of memory even if the load is low (Karve et al., 2006). The hypervisor needs special measurement for memory require-

ment. This is important because allocating and reclaiming memory among virtual machines involves modifying the page table and invalidating the Translation Lookaside Buffer (TLB) which incurs overhead. Sometimes, for security reason, a memory page should be flushed (i.e., zeroed out) before being allocated. Otherwise, data of the virtual machine that page belonged to is leaked to the one getting it.

The PKU Cloud adopts Ballooning (Waldspurger, 2002) technology to share memory between Virtual Machines on the same physical server. When memory is scarce, for example, a new virtual machine being created, unused memory can be squeezed out of other virtual machines and reallocated to the one where it is required. That is achieved by a "balloon" process devised in each guest OS. It is under the control of the hypervisor. When the hypervisor squeezes memory from a virtual machine, it sends a "deflate" request to the balloon process in that virtual machine. Then, the ballooning process requests specified amount of memory from OS. On a successful operation, the balloon process pins the memory it has acquired (so that corresponding pages are never swapped out), picks the corresponding page frames off the page table and hands the frames to the hypervisor. Inversely, when the hypervisor returns memory, the balloon process executes an "inflate" operation. It hooks those page frames to the page table again, unpins the memory and frees it back to OS. The memory is like air that flows from one balloon to another. For this reason, the technology is called "ballooning". Although ballooning provides a mechanism of sharing memory, it is a hard problem to find out how much memory a virtual machine requires. It is similar to the classical problem of determining the size of the process working set. The current solution in the PKU Cloud is Selfballooning (Magenheimer, 2008). It is a daemon residing in Linux guest OS, periodically reading the value of "Commited_AS" item in the "/proc/meminfo" system file as a coarse estimation on future memory usage. According to the estimation, it actively adjusts the memory usage with the balloon driver. That approach can be improved, since we found by experiment that the estimation is too simple to exclude aged page cache. VMware ESX server adopts a random page sampling technique (Waldspurger, 2002) to measure the working set of a virtual machine: during each measurement period, a random subset of pages in the VM's (pseudo) physical memory are invalidated by the hypervisor so that a subsequent access will result in a trap. This allows the hypervisor to collect statistics on how much memory is being actively used by the guest OS. The default sampling rate in ESX is 100 random pages every 30 second. Experiment result in that work showed a smooth and tight track of the actual memory usage. In another work (Wood et al., 2007), swap activities are used as the signal of memory shortage. Once abrupt increase of swap activities of a virtual machine is detected, memory is inflated by a step of 32 megabyte. In practice, that method is so lazy that the application performance is compromised.

Transcendent Memory (TMEM) (Magenheimer, 2009) takes another approach. As we know, page cache used to accelerate the file access tends to eat up memory. While some virtual machine is suffering from the memory shortage, others may occupy a lot in the page cache for infrequently used files. To avoid that unfairness, TMEM maintains a shared memory pool in the hypervisor for centralized management of page cache. The pool is virtualized so that each virtual machine can have one or more virtual pools for convenience. A virtual pool can be ephemeral or persistent. Data put into an ephemeral pool may be forgotten because of memory shortage. But the availability of data put into a persistent pool is guaranteed. To use TMEM, the page cache and swap implementation in guest OS are extended with two operations, precache and preswap, respectively. Before a clean page in the page cache is reclaimed, its data is written to an ephemeral pool. When the page is read next time, the OS

first tries to read it from the ephemeral pool. If the read operation succeeds, which means the data has fortunately survived, a time-consuming disk I/O operation is saved. Since the precache operation works like page cache without using memory dedicated to a virtual machine, a virtual machine only needs to occupy a small amount of memory for OS kernel and application code. Sometimes, a virtual machine needs to swap out some pages. Before the data of a page is eventually swapped out to the disk, the OS tries to put it to a persistent memory pool. If the operation succeeds, data of that page is retrieved from the pool the next time when it is accessed. Again, a disk I/O operation is saved.

TMEM evades the difficulty of working set measurement. But it is more complicated to implement than ballooning. To the time of this writing, TMEM has been implemented in the Xen hypervisor. We plan to update Xen hypervisor in PKU Cloud to support the TMEM.

3.3 Scheduling I/O Resources

Network and disk are two essential I/O resources that are closely related to the application performance. I/O virtualization involves the sharing of a set of network interface cards (NIC) and the disk of a physical server among virtual machines running over it. Hypervisor is responsible for creation of virtual devices exposed to the guest OS and the multiplexing of real I/O devices. In order to understand how I/O resource is scheduled in a virtualized environment, we look into a typical implementation, the split driver model in the Xen hypervisor.

There is a privileged virtual machine, called domain 0, on the Xen hypervisor. It contains all the drivers required to manipulate real devices like gigabyte NICs or IDE disks. Common virtual machines, called domain U, do not have such drivers. They indirectly access the real devices by a mechanism called the split driver model. Each virtual device corresponds to a split driver composed of a front-end and a back-end driver in the domain U and the domain 0, respectively. Both ends are tied together by Xen hypervisor's communication mechanism including shared memory and event channel. The front-end driver accepts requests from the OS in domain U, while the back-end driver handed these requests to a real driver. On receiving data, the back-end driver will notify the front-end driver about new arrivals in the shared memory. I/O resource Schedulers stand between the back-end driver and the real driver. They decide when and in which order the requests are handled.

Although the PKU Cloud follow the traditional I/O scheme and works fine so far, but the intricate characteristics of I/O systems make fairness and isolation quite difficult. Here we name a few to show the tip of the iceberg.

Accessing disk data involves slow mechanical movements. It is hard to determine how long such an operation will take since the associated head position is unknown beforehand. Not to mention Redundant Array of Independent Disks (RAID) or hybrid storage systems composed of Solid-State Drive (SSD) and traditional hard disk. Thereby traditional disk I/O scheduling algorithms like Completely Fair Queuing (CFQ) (Love, 2004) pursuing fairness in request numbers cannot achieve good fairness and isolation. Gulati pointed out that there is a tradeoff between performance and fairness (Gulati et al. 2007). VIOS (Seelam and Teller, 2007) improves by fairly allocating disk time to virtual machines. AutoControl (Padala et al., 2009) extends such fairness to application level.

A virtual disk may be an image file in the file system, a logic unit in the iSCSI storage or a disk partition on a local hard disk. But the I/O scheduler in the guest OS is unaware of that detail. It is generally optimized for a single exclusive hard disk incorporating technics like anticipatory reading and reordering requests for a shorter head movement. At the hypervisor level, however, the I/O requests from different guest OSes are scheduled again. Mutual interference of the two

schedulers may result in an awkward situation. In the XenServer, a commercial version of Xen hypervisor, the noop scheduler using simple FIFO algorithm, is adopted by default at the hypervisor level. Another possibility is to leave that task to the storage system.

Scheduling network resource seems simpler than scheduling disk I/O if only bandwidth of NICs is taken into account. Sometimes, however, the links among switches and routers in data center network may become critical resources due to a hot application or malware. Fairness and isolation at this level is quite difficult. Seawall (Shieh et al., 2011) introduces a sophisticated approach to this problem. It is an end-to-end solution without a central coordinator. Only modification to the hypervisor software is required.

I/O virtualization is a fast changing field. New technologies keep emerging. Our discussion is however limited due to the lack of space.

4 CLOUD ELASTICITY WITH LIVE MIGRATION

Resource scheduling at the hypervisor level realizes limited elasticity owing to the fixed capacity of a physical server. Migration of virtual machines breaks up the limitation by utilizing resources from other servers. Figure 2 sketches how it works. Consider a data center with three physical servers: A, B, and C. At the beginning, as shown in the upper left part of Figure 2, server A and B are running five virtual machines each. They are reasonably loaded (tagged with "WARM"). Server C is standing by to save electricity. When workload grows, server A cannot afford the aggregate resource requirements of its five virtual machines (tagged with "HOT"). We say that server A is a hotspot. A virtual machine scheduler (not shown in Figure 2) detects the hotspot and thereby initiates a migration schedule that migrating two virtual machines from server A to C. After the migration finishes, as shown in the lower right part of Figure 2, the hotspot is resolved. Resource demands of applications are consequently satisfied. Assume that the workload begins to shrink now. Resource utilization of server A and C drops dramatically. The utilization of server A and C (tagged with "COLD") is too low to be power efficiently. The virtual machine scheduler therefore initiates another migration schedule that dynamically consolidates virtual machines on under-utilized servers together. The released server C again enters low power state. Now, the servers return to their original states.

Some important details are left out in the above scenario for abstraction. As we mentioned in the BACKGROUND section, live migration incurs network overhead and takes some time. Only persistent change in resource demands deserves migration. The virtual machine scheduler (VM scheduler) incorporates load prediction techniques, which we will describe later, to differentiate stable workload change from transient fluctuation. Depending on the estimation of future workload, it needs to decide which virtual machine to migrate away and to where. It will be demonstrated later that solving the problem is an NP-hard problem. Only heuristics algorithms are pragmatic. The rest of the section will first illustrate the widely adopted architecture for VM schedulers and then focus on the migration policies. For convenience,

the acronym VM and PM are used in the following text to denote a virtual machine and a physical server/machine respectively.

The VM scheduler of the PKU Cloud is shown in Figure 3. This centralized architecture is also adopted in other VM schedulers such as Sandpiper (Wood et al., 2007), Harmony (Singh, Korupolu, and Mohapatra, 2008) and Usher (McNett et al., 2007). Each PM runs a hypervisor with a Node Manager. The node manager collects from the hypervisor the real-time usage statistics of resources for each virtual machine on that PM. The statistics collected at each PM are forwarded to the VM scheduler. The VM Scheduler is invoked periodically and receives from the Node Manager the resource demand history of VMs, the capacity and the load history of PMs, and the current layout of VMs on PMs.

The VM scheduler has several components. The Load Predictor predicts the future resource demands of VMs and the future load of PMs based on past statistics. The load of a PM is computed by aggregating the resource usage of its VMs. The Node Manager at each node first attempts to satisfy the new demands locally by the resource allocation mechanism in the hypervisor. The Scheduling Algorithm module detects if the resource utilization of any PM is above the hot threshold (i.e., a hot spot). Then it decides on

Figure 2. Elasticity with live migration

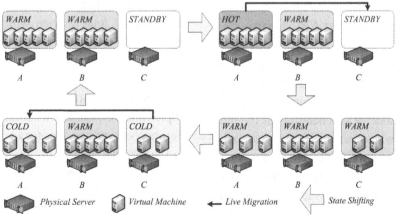

Figure 3. Architecture of a VM Scheduler

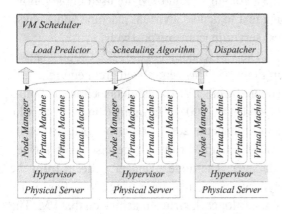

which VMs running on hot spots should be migrated away to reduce their load. It also identifies under-utilized PMs and decides whether they should be released by migrating their VMs away so that they can be turned off to save energy. The Scheduling Algorithm finally compiles a migration list of VMs and passes it to the Dispatcher, who in turn contacts the Node Manager for the execution of the planned migration.

Many algorithms can be incorporated in this framework. One category borrows solutions from well-studied theoretic models (Bobroff, Kochut, and Beaty, 2007) (Xu and Li, 2011). The other use pragmatic heuristics which model expected scheduling objectives (Wood et al., 2007) (Singh, Korupolu, and Mohapatra, 2008). The PKU Cloud incorporated two algorithms. The online bin-packing algorithm belongs to the first category, while the Skewness algorithm belongs to the latter one.

4.1 Online Bin-Packing Algorithm

The classical bin packing problem consists of packing a series of items with sizes in the interval (0, 1] into a minimum number of bins with capacity one. We can model VM scheduling as the bin packing problem where each PM is a bin and each VM is an item to be packed. Resource provision is implicitly assured by the rule that the size of items (resource requirement) is less than the bin

size (resource allocation), while over provisioning is avoid by the objective of using a minimum number of bins. We assume that all PMs are homogeneous with unit capacity. We normalize the resource demands of VMs to be a fraction of that capacity. For example, if a VM requires 20% of the physical memory of the underlying PM, then it corresponds to an item with size 0.2. If other resource types such as CPU and I/O are considered, the size of an item can be represented by a vector whose elements are normalized demands of the VM corresponding to the resource types. That variation is called vector bin-packing.

The bin-packing problem is well-known to be NP-hard. Although it has been studied extensively in the literature, pure theoretic solutions do not work well in data center environments. Offline algorithms can achieve a performance very close to the optimal algorithm, but they assume the entire sequence of items to be packed is known in advance (Garey and Johnson, 1985). More intricately, in data center environment, the size of an item is changing. Rerunning an offline algorithm in each round of scheduling, however, incurs too many migrations to be practical. Online algorithms that pack incoming items incrementally make no attempt to minimize the movements of already packed items because the overhead of migration is hard to model in the framework. When applied to VM scheduling, they need modifications to constrain the frequency of migration.

We have designed a practical online bin-packing algorithm (Xiao et al., 2010) that applied to an IaaS Cloud service which supports over 200 people in a lab of Peking University. We get this core algorithm by extending an existing one-dimensional online bin-packing algorithm (Gambosi, Postiglione, and Talamo, 2000) with the approximation ratio as low as 3/2, which represents a quite good performance for an online algorithm. In the original algorithm, items are categorized into four types: Tiny (T), Small (S), Large (L), Big (B) items. Item size of the four types falls in intervals (0, 1/3], (1/3, 1/2], (1/2, 2/3], (2/3, 1], respectively. There are seven combinations of items in a bin:

- A B-bin has only one B-item.
- An L-bin has only one L item.
- An LT-bin has only one L-item and a certain number of T-items.
- An S-bin has only one S-item.
- An SS-bin has only two S-items.
- An LS-bin has only one S-item and one L-item.
- A T-bin has only a certain number of T-items. It is called unfilled if the available space is no less than 1/3. Otherwise, it is called filled.

On arrival of a new item, an insert operation is executed that keeps the following three rules for bin usage:

- At any time, only six types of bins: B-bin, L-bin, LT-bin, S-bin, SS-bin, T-bin are allowed in the system.
- At any time, if there exists a T-bin, then there is no L-bin, and the available space in any LT-bin is less than 1/3.
- At any time, there are at most one S-bin and at most one unfilled T-bin.

It can be proved that based on the above rules, the approximation ratio of this algorithm is bounded by 3/2. The proof is skipped due to lack of space.

However, the original algorithm cannot handle size changing of an item. We extend it by adding a change operation to handle the situation where item type changes and the above rules are violated. It has been proved that a change operation invokes no more than 7 movements (migrations) and an insert operation no more than 3. This property effectively constrains the number of migrations.

We also extend it to multi-dimensional by breaking down items according to their largest dimensions. The approximation ratio is bounded by 3/2*d, where d is the number of dimension under consideration. The worst case is when each item has a different dominating dimension. For example, when d = 3, the items (1, 0, 0), (0, 1, 0), and (0, 0, 1) can be packed into a single bin under the optimal algorithm, but need three bins in this one. This ratio is rather unimpressive at a first glance. But there are not that many dominating dimensions in practice. Most practical systems consider only one or two types of resources (e.g., CPU and memory) in their allocation decision.

We used several optimizations when applying this algorithm to a real environment. The size of each bin is intentionally shrunk a little compared to the real capacity of the PM. The reserved capacity helps avoid SLA violation in face of transient load fluctuation. Though we assume that PMs are homogeneous, a practical data center generally contains different types of servers. This problem can be solved by grouping identical servers together and running a VM scheduler for each group. Sometimes the whole system under the management of the VM scheduler may be overloaded. In contrast to the assumption of infinite bins, the reality is, bins are used up. To solve this problem, the capacity of bins can be magnified by a certain percentage until a solution is found. That technic makes sure that all PMs are evenly overloaded to avoid any application is unfairly treated.

4.2 The Skewness Algorithm

Bin-packing based algorithms are aggressive in packing VMs. Therefore load change can easily incur migrations. In other words, it trades stability and performance for using a fewer number of active PMs. In practice, however, the loss of QoS is much severer than the waste of electricity to a Cloud provider. The pragmatic algorithms are more conservative. They prefer performance to green computing. Many of them even do not perform green computing (Wood et al., 2007) (Singh, Korupolu, and Mohapatra, 2008).

In favor of performance and stability, we designed a pragmatic algorithm, skewness (Xiao, Song, and Chen, 2011), into the aforementioned Cloud system. It is inspired by the fact that if a PM runs too many memory-intensive VMs with light CPU load, much CPU resources will be wasted because it does not have enough memory for an extra VM. We introduce the concept of skewness to qualify the unevenness in the utilization of multiple resources on a server. Let n be the number of resources and ri be the utilization of the i-th resource. The resource skewness of a server p is defined as

$$skewness(p) = \sqrt{\sum_{i=1}^{n} (\frac{r_i}{\bar{r}} - 1)^2},$$

where $\bar{r}$ is the average utilization of all resources for server p. In practice, not all types of resources are performance critical and hence only bottleneck resources are considered in the above calculation.

We use several adjustable thresholds that control tradeoff between performance and green computing. The "hot threshold" defines the acceptable upper limit of resource utilization. We define a server as a hot spot if the utilization of any of its resources is above the hot threshold. We define the temperature of a hot spot p as the square sum of its resource utilization beyond the hot threshold:

$$temperature(p) = \sum_{r \in R} (r - r_t)^2,$$

where R is the set of overloaded resources in server p and rt is the hot threshold for resource r. (Note that only overloaded resources are considered in the calculation.) The temperature of a hot spot reflects its degree of overload. If a server is not a hot spot, its temperature is zero. The "cold threshold" denotes the acceptable lower limit of resource utilization. A server whose utilization of all resources is under the cold threshold is defined

as a cold spot. The "green computing" threshold defines the utilization level of all active PMs, under which the system is considered power-inefficient therefore green computing operations get involved. Finally, the "warm threshold" defines the ideal level of resource utilization that is sufficiently high to justify having the server running but not so high as to risk becoming a hot spot in the face of temporary fluctuation of application resource demands.

For each scheduling round, the skewness takes two steps, hot spot mitigation and green computing, to calculate a migration list. In hot spot mitigation, we try to solve all hot spots in descending order of temperature. For each hot spot, we try to migrate away the VM that can reduce the server's temperature the most. In those servers that can accommodate the VM without becoming a hot spot, we choose a server with most skewness reduction by accepting this VM as the migration destination. This does not necessarily eliminate the hot spot, but at least reduces its temperature. Hot spot mitigation step is finished after all hot spot are processed. If the overall resource utilization of active servers is lower than the green computing threshold, a green computing step is invoked. In the green computing step, we try to solve cold spots in ascending order of the memory utilization, which representing the efforts taken to solve a cold spot. To resolve a cold spot, all of its VMs need to be migrated away. The destination of a VM is decided in a way similar to that in the hot spot mitigation, but its resource utilization should be below the warm threshold after accepting the VM. We also restrict the number of cold spots that can be eliminated in each run of the algorithm to be no more than a certain percentage, for example 5%, of active servers in the system. Those arrangements are to avoid over consolidation that may incur hot spots later. The movements generated in both steps above are then consolidated so that each VM is moved at most once to its final destination. For example, hot spot mitigation may dictate a VM to move from PM A to PM B, while green computing dictates it to move from PM B to PM C. In the actual execution, the VM is moved from A to C directly.

With lower hot spot threshold, the skewness algorithm reacts earlier to resource shortage by provisioning more resources. Lower cold threshold excludes more servers with relatively low load from being recycled. Lower green computing threshold postpone the green computing operation until the overall load decreases more. Both effects make the skewness algorithm more conservative when performing green computing. It is up to the Cloud provider who decides its tradeoff between performance and green computing. Generally speaking, we recommend low thresholds if applications with unstable workload dominate in the system, because more thrashing workload calls for more conservative resource reservation to absorb transient fluctuation hence SLA is assured.

4.3 Performance of the Two Algorithms

We evaluated both algorithms by simulation to understand their performance. We collected load traces from a wide range of real applications, including Web InfoMall, one of the largest web archive in China, RealCourse, a large scale online learning system that spread over 13 major cities, and Amazing Store, a large P2P storage system. We also collected traces from a DNS server and a mail server for Peking University. Traces are segmented in a per-day granularity. We use random sampling and linear combination to generate workloads at required scales.

Both algorithms are evaluated in four aspects: effect of load balancing, effect of green computing,

stability, and decision time. We use the number of hot spots to quantify the effect of load balancing. Small number of hot spots represents good effect of load balancing. We model the effect of green computing as the number of active physical machines (APM) throughout the evaluation. Less active physical machines mean more efficient usage of power. The stability of an algorithm is represented by the number of live migration. We define decision time as time required for an algorithm to calculate a scheduling plan in each scheduling round. In practice, decision time needs to be short enough that the system load distribution doesn't change significantly when a scheduling plan is calculated.

The numbers in Table 1 are average numbers of hot spots in each round just before scheduling. With bin-packing algorithm, the number of hot spots is almost five times as many as that with Skewness algorithm. The bin-packing algorithm tends to maximize the utilization of resource, therefore it generally pack the APMs tighter than Skewness does. Consequently, with bin-packing algorithm, a hot spot is easy to be triggered due to load fluctuation. Unlike bin-packing, the Skewness maintains each active physical machine reasonably loaded so that transient load fluctuation could be absorbed without cause hot spots. The Skewness algorithm actually trade power consumption for performance. As show in Figure 4, we can see that, Skewness uses 10 - 20% more physical servers than bin-packing algorithm.

Table 2 shows the average numbers of migration in each round issued by both algorithms for the same workload. The migration is much more frequent with bin-packing than with Skewness because bin-packing is more sensitive to load

Table 1. Average number of hot spots

Scale in number of VMs	200	400	600	800	1000	1200	1400
Bin-packing	0.60	1.44	2.39	3.41	4.17	4.91	6.37
Skewness	0.15	0.35	0.48	0.57	0.76	0.98	1.10

variance. In addition, the bin-packing algorithm carefully rules the layout of VMs over PMs; therefore it triggers more movement for adjustment than the Skewness algorithm.

Previous analysis (Xiao et al, 2010) (Xiao, Song, and Chen, 2011) reveals that the time complexity of bin-packing and Skewness algorithm are $O(\log(n))$ and $O(n2)$ respectively, where n is the number of VMs. Experimental results shown in Table 3 perfectly conform to the analysis. The decision time of Skewness is more than one second at a scale of 1400 VMs. In a system with 10,000 VMs it is expected to grow to one minute. The decision time and migration time together would exceed scheduling interval. In practice, however, that is not problematic because the scheduling interval is much longer than one minute for high stability. In addition, Servers in big data centers are generally grouped into smaller resource pool so that the scale is manageable.

5 CLOUD ELASTICITY IN INTERNET APPLICATIONS

Sometimes even if each virtual machine of an application occupied a dedicated physical server, the application load still asks for more resources. In such a situation, resource provisioning with local resource adjustment or migration do not work anymore because those mechanisms are unaware of what applications are running in virtual machines. Many commercial platforms, e.g. Google App Engine, are capable of automatically replicating application instance for surging load. This section focused on the solutions adopted by the PKU Cloud for Web applications.

Figure 5 depicts the common architecture of a web application. The front end switch is typically a Layer 7 switch which parses application level information in Web requests and forwards them to the corresponding applications. The switch sometimes runs in a redundant pair for fault tolerance. In the PKU Cloud, the L7 Switch is running on a dedicated physical server, and application components are encapsulated in virtual machines. It is important that the application components are stateless so that they can be replicated safely. The elasticity of storage system belongs to another research domain out of the scope of this chapter. This section focused on the resource provisioning problem for the application tier.

Generally, a resource scheduler is responsible for the resource allocation. It monitors the load of each application as well as the resource utilization statistics of physical servers. Based on the data it collects and layout of the applications over physical servers, it calculates a new resource al-

Figure 4. Number of active PMs

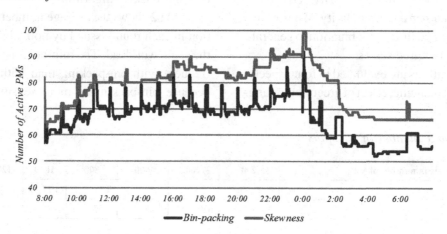

Figure 5. Architecture of a Web application

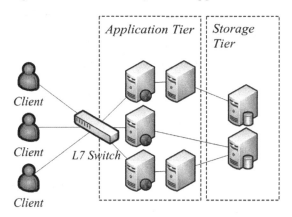

location strategy that is better than the current one. The criteria for a "good" strategy depend on the particular system. The strategy, however, are commonly composed of two parts: the layout of applications' replica on physical servers and the request rates each replica accepts. A minor adjustment involves improving the dispatch policy of L7 switch. A major adjustment asks for starting/stopping a replica or even starting/stopping a physical server.

5.1 Resource Allocation in MUSE

In MUSE (Chase et al., 2001), all applications are replicated on each server. Therefore all servers in the data center form a unified resource pool. Allocating resource to an application means increasing the number of requests processed, while reclaiming resource from an application means reducing the number of requests processed. The convenience of such settings is that once an adjustment is enforced, it takes effect instantly.

The MUSE system allows each application to bid for its requests, for example, one cent for each request below 1,000 per minute and half a cent for each request above 1,000 per minute. Generally, the application would bid lower when its throughput is higher. It models the throughput as a linear function of CPU utilization, whose parameters are calculated from application performance history. Hence the energy cost of processing a request can

be estimated on CPU utilization. By subtract the energy cost from the price an application can afford, the resource scheduler can get the profit by processing each request. The resource scheduler is invoked periodically or by some predefined states such as the occurrence of hot spots. In each round the resources allocations are adjusted in four steps to maximize the total profit. First, the resource with negative return is reclaimed. Then the idle resources, as long as available, are allocated to profitable applications. For each overloaded server, resource allocated to the least profitable applications is reclaimed to bring it back to a normal state. Finally, if there exists any application x whose current bid is higher than application y, then the resource occupied by application y should be reallocated to application x until equilibrium is reached.

This system was designed more than ten years ago when the applications are relatively simple. They do not need much memory so that a server can run a replica of each application. Today, the applications have become much more sophisticated. An application can easily occupy several Gigabytes of memory. Moreover, starting and stopping an application takes a long time. Therefore it is not applicable for the present Cloud environment.

5.2 Starting and Stopping Web Application

Some research works (Karve et al., 2006) (Tang et al., 2007) address resource allocation for sophisticated web applications. They adopt stopping a web application and then starting it on another server as the approach to change the placement of an application. To avoid too much overhead, they manage to minimize the usage of placement. Particularly, the allocation algorithm given by Tang et al. (2007) use network flow programming to maximize the performance of the current placement of web applications. Therefore the placement operation is postponed until the placement cannot satisfy the load anymore.

Table 2. Average number of migration

Scale in number of VMs	200	400	600	800	1000	1200	1400
Bin-packing	4.91	11.66	17.78	23.92	29.95	36.67	43.21
Skewness	0.19	0.36	0.57	0.73	0.90	1.06	1.25

Table 3. Decision time (milliseconds)

Scale in number of VMs	200	400	600	800	1000	1200	1400
Bin-packing	5.9	12.0	19.8	26.0	35.7	39.8	46.4
Skewness	38.8	115.5	233.5	349.9	529.9	674.6	1065.9

The resource allocation can benefit from the VM stop/resume mechanism. VM stop/resume is generally faster than starting/stopping an application directly because they skipped the time-consuming initialization process for large software. The latest stop/resume technology (Zhu, Jiang and Xiao, 2011) can accelerate such an operation to several seconds.

The capacity of data centers in the real world is finite. The illusion of infinite capacity in the Cloud is provided through statistical multiplexing. When a large number of applications experience their peak demand around the same time, the available resources in the Cloud can become constrained and some of the demand may not be satisfied. The amount of computing capacity available to an application is limited by the placement of its running instances on the servers. The more instances an application has and the more powerful the underlying servers are, the higher the potential capacity for satisfying the application demand. On the other hand, when the demand of the applications is low, it is important to conserve energy by reducing the number of servers used.

We develop a system that provides automatic scaling for Internet applications in the PKU Cloud. We model the problem as Class Constrained Bin Packing (CCBP) where each server is a bin and each class represents an application. In the traditional bin packing problem, a series of items of different sizes need to be packed into a minimum number of bins. The class constrained version of this problem divides the items into classes or colors. Each bin has capacity v and can accommodate items from at most c distinct classes. It is "class constrained" because the class diversity of items packed into the same bin is constrained. The goal is to pack the items into a minimum number of bins. The class constraint reflects the practical limit on the number of applications a server can run simultaneously. For J2EE applications, for example, memory is typically the bottleneck resource. The capacity of a bin represents the amount of resources available at a server for all its applications. We develop an innovative auto scaling algorithm that achieves good demand satisfaction ratio and supports green computing.

6 LOAD PREDICTION

Load prediction has significant impacts on resource allocation. With an over-estimated load, a scheduler may allocate more resources than necessary. Therefore some of the resources are wasted. On the contrary, with an under-estimated load, the resource allocation may be insufficient. Consequently, VOD user may complain the video is not fluent and online game players may get angry because they cannot control an avatar.

We found that two categories of load prediction algorithm are widely adopted. One category composed of variations of the Exponentially Weighted Moving Average (EWMA) algorithm. It is designed based on the assumption that the future value of a random variable has strong relation to its recent history. It has been used in TCP for Round Trip Time (RTT) estimation for decades. Algorithms of the other category adopt the auto-regressive (AR) model. It requires more computation than EMWA based algorithms. But it can incorporate periodicity, which is hard to be utilized in EWMA alternatives, for better precision.

6.1 EWMA Variations

With the original EWMA, load at time t is calculated by $E(t) = \alpha * O(t) + (1-\alpha) * E(t-1)$, $0 \leq \alpha \leq 1$, where $E(t)$ and $O(t)$ are the estimated and the observed load at time t, respectively. The parameter alpha reflects a tradeoff between stability and responsiveness. The larger the alpha is, the more agile the estimated load will be (low gain). On the contrary, the smaller the alpha is, the more stable the estimated load will be (high gain).

The load prediction algorithm adopted in MUSE (Chase et al., 2001) is a variation of EWMA. It uses a high gain EWMA and a low gain EWMA. If the latest observed load does not deviate much from recent observations, the low gain EWMA is used. Otherwise the high gain EWMA is used. This eliminates occasionally noisy observations. The output is further processed by a hysteresis filter for stabilization. The working set size estimator (Waldspurger, 2002) in ESX server also incorporates a similar technique. It uses three EWMAs with high, medium and low gain. The highest EWMA is selected as output to avoid under estimation as much as possible.

We designed a "Fast Up and Slow Down" (FUSD) predicting algorithm for the load predictor in the VM Scheduler of the PKU Cloud. It is worth noticing that EWMA does not capture the rising trends of resource usage. For example, when we see a sequence of O(t) = 10; 20; 30;

and 40, it is reasonable to predict the next value to be 50. Unfortunately, when alpha is between 0 and 1, the predicted value is always between the historical value and the observed one. This phenomenon easily cause under provisioning when load is rising. To reflect the "acceleration", we take an innovative approach by setting alpha to a negative value. On the other hand, when the observed resource usage is going down, we want to be conservative in reducing the estimation by using a normal alpha. That's why it is called "Fast Up and Slow Down". It dramatically reduces the number of hot spots and live migration for Skewness and bin-packing VM schedulers.

6.2 The AR Model

In some works, future load is modeled as a linear function of several other factors such as the load history, time, or resource allocation. The parameters can be calculated by training with data in the past. Then the model can predict the future load. This methodology is called Auto-Regression (AR), represented as AR(p), where p is the number of factors considered in this model. AR model works well for periodical load.

The Sandpiper VM scheduler (Wood et al., 2007) adopts AR(1). It models the load at time t as a linear function of the average of n latest observations. It cannot utilize periodicity because it is unaware if the application is periodical. In the research on provisioning servers for connection-intensive services (Chen et al., 2008), AR(n) is used to predict the number and login rate of MSN clients. The load is modeled as a linear function of six independent variables, two of the most recent observations and four of the observations at the same time in last four weeks. The results shows perfect fit between the predicted and the observed load. This is because the load of MSN clients presents perfect periodicity in its weekly pattern. We speculate that most popular Internet applications present such characteristics.

7 FUTURE RESEARCH DIRECTIONS

Cloud ecology involves more than one Cloud vendor. The concept of Cloud federation is proposed to architect software over multiple cloud services (Celesti et al., 2010). Besides vendor lock-in avoidance, applications built on Cloud federation enjoy more options for on-demand resource provisioning. Multiple Cloud services may back up each other for fault-tolerance. Or, with carefully arrangement, it may achieve better performance/price ratio than single-vendor approaches do. In other words, Cloud federation brings new possibilities to Cloud elasticity. However, there are challenges to overcome. It is hard to implementing uniform platform layer incorporating Cloud services with distinct service models and user interfaces. The difference among underlying technologies is obstacle to interoperability. Researchers just begin to tackle those problems. Yang (Yang X. et al., 2012) presented a new Cloud federation model for real time applications capable of on-demand resource provisioning across multiple Cloud vendors.

Live migration of VM plays an important role in Cloud elasticity. Current live migration technology, however, is not fully satisfactory. Remote Direct Memory Access (RDMA) infrastructure was facilitated to speed up live migration (Huang et al., 2007), but it is not always seen in Cloud infrastructure other than those dedicated to scientific computing. MECOM (Jin et al., 2009) adopts compression algorithm to reduce the data transferred during live migration and consequently shorten its total time span. MDD (Zhang et al., 2010) takes data de-duplication to achieve the similar effect. They actually trade CPU cycles and memory space for performance of live migration. Such optimizations are not adequate for migrating VMs away to offload a busy physical server. Post-copy (Hines et al., 2009) approach is capable of migrating CPU load away as soon as possible, but exception of either side of migration could cause crash of the migrating VM. Moreover, applica-

tions in the migrating VM may experience worse performance degradation than that in pre-copy approach. Shrinker (Riteau, Morin, Priol, 2010) has suggested a real-time fingerprint system for memory pages and DHT-based content sharing system to enable live migration over Wide-Area Network. But they didn't solve the hash collision problem. Since there may be no one live migration technology fit for all purpose, we suggest a hybrid solution. Various optimizations for live migration may be combined in a toolkit. It's up to the resource scheduler which optimization(s) to use.

Latest development of virtualization technology arms Cloud infrastructure with new weapons for Cloud elasticity. Snow Flock (Lagar-Cavilla et al., 2009) enables "fork" operation for virtual machines. Fast VM start-up (Zhu, Jiang, and Xiao, 2011) can start up a VM in milliseconds. Both of them can be used to support fast deployment for flash crowd. Partial migration technology (Bila et al, 2012) extends the post-copy approach to temporarily migrate away the active states of an idle virtual machine, so that the physical server has more chances to sleep and therefore save power. New I/O devices are virtualized at hardware level so that each virtual machine could enjoy high performance with pass-through devices. Live migration with pass-through device is not a trifle because of the difficulty of migrating hardware-specific device states. CompSC (Pan et al, 2012), however, has already added support for pass-through NIC to live migration. Incorporating those technologies into existing Cloud is still open to researchers.

CONCLUSION

Cloud elasticity is an appealing characteristic of Cloud infrastructure. It involves scaling up and down resource allocation according to the real time requirements of applications. In face of resource shortage, an elastic system is able to fairly allocate resources. Elasticity is implemented in different levels of the Cloud architecture.

Hypervisor is responsible for allocating local resources to the VMs. CPU scheduling algorithm is similar to the process scheduling in the OS. Proportional application performance can be enforced by adjusting scheduling weights of VMs. Ballooning technology realizes memory allocation by inflating or deflating the balloon process residing in each guest OS, while TMEM maintains a public memory pool for page cache and swap. Scheduling I/O resources is a hot research field, where many problems remain to be solved.

As a global resource scheduling mechanism, live migration has its pros and cons. Its advantage is application neutral, but the overhead of migration should be considered carefully. By modeling the scheduling problem with the bin packing problem, we can exploit the abundant existing algorithms in that well studied field. We introduce a practical, online bin-packing scheduling algorithm. Then we introduced the skewness algorithm that avoids uneven utilization of different kind of resources of a physical server. Both of them are incorporated in a real Cloud system.

With internal information of applications, on-demand resource provision technologies at application level can perform a more precise provision. Taking web application as an example, we introduced several elasticity technologies.

Load prediction has significant impacts on resource allocation. Prediction error may invoke under-provisioning or over-provisioning with unpleasant implications. We introduced two categories of prediction algorithms that widely adopted. EWMA based algorithms are simpler, while AR models are more precise.

We finally pointed out future directions of technologies in this field.

ACKNOWLEDGMENT

This work is supported by National Natural Science Foundation of China Project 61170056.

REFERENCES

Al-Fares, M., Loukissas, A., & Vahdat, A. (2008). A scalable, commodity data center network architecture. Proceedings of the ACM SIGCOMM conference on Data communication, USA, (pp. 63-74). doi: 10.1145/1402958.1402967

Armbrust, M., Fox, A., & Griffith, R. (2009). *Above the clouds: A Berkeley view of cloud computing*. Berkeley: EECS Department, University of California.

AWS Case Study. Washington Post. (n.d.). Retrieved from http://aws.amazon.com/solutions/case-studies/washington-post/

Barham, P., Dragovic, B., Fraser, K., Hand, S., Harris, T., & Ho, A. … Warfield, A. (2003). Xen and the art of virtualization. Proceedings of the Nineteenth ACM Symposium on Operating Systems Principles, USA, (pp. 164-177). doi: 10.1145/945445.945462

Bila, N., Lara, E., Josi, K., Lagar-Cavilla, H., Hiltunen, M., & Satyanarayanan, M. (2012). Jettison: Efficient idle desktop consolidation with partial VM migration. Proceedings of the 7th ACM European Conference on Computer Systems (EuroSys '12), (pp. 1-14). Retrieved from http://lagarcavilla.com/publications/BilaEurosys12.pdf

Bobroff, N., Kochut, A., & Beaty, K. (2007). Dynamic placement of virtual machines for managing SLA violations. International Symposium on Integrated Network Management, Munich, (pp. 119-128). doi: 10.1109/INM.2007.374776

Celesti, A., Tusa, F., Villari, M., & Puliafito, A. (2010). How to enhance cloud architectures to enable cross-federation. Proceedings of the IEEE third International Conference on Cloud Computing (CLOUD), (pp. 337-345).

Chang, F., Dean, J., Ghemawat, S., Hsieh, W. C., Wallach, D. A., & Burrows, M. (2008). Bigtable: A distributed storage system for structured data. *ACM Transactions on Computer Systems, 26(2),* 1–26. doi:10.1145/1365815.1365816

Chase, J. S., Anderson, D. C., Thakar, P. N., Vahdat, A. M., & Doyle, R. P. (2001). Managing energy and server resources in hosting centers. Proceedings of the Eighteenth ACM Symposium on Operating Systems Principles, (pp. 103-116). doi: 10.1145/502034.502045

Chen, G., He, W., Liu, J., Nath, S., Rigas, L., Xiao, L., & Zhao, F. (2008). Energy-aware server provisioning and load dispatching for connection-intensive internet services. Proceedings of the 5th USENIX Symposium on Networked Systems Design and Implementation, (pp. 337-350).

Clark, C., Fraser, K., Hand, S., Hansen, J. G., & Jul, E. Limpach, C., … Warfield., A. (2005). Live migration of virtual machines. Proceedings of the 2nd Conference on Symposium on Networked Systems Design & Implementation, Vol. 2, (pp. 273-286).

Credit Based Scheduler. (2007). Retrieved from http://wiki.xensource.com/xenwiki/CreditScheduler

Gambosi, G., Postiglione, A., & Talamo, M. (2000). Algorithms for the relaxed online bin-packing model. *SIAM Journal on Computing, 5(30),* 1532–1551. doi:10.1137/S0097539799180408

Garey, M. R., & Johnson, D. S. (1985). A 71/60 theorem for bin packing. *Journal of Complexity, 1(1),* 65–106. doi:10.1016/0885-064X(85)90022-6

Ghemawat, S., Gobioff, H., & Leung, S. (2003). The Google file system. Proceedings of the Nineteenth ACM Symposium on Operating Systems Principles, (pp. 29-43). doi: 10.1145/945445.945450

Greenberg, A., Hamilton, J. R., Jain, N., Kandula, S., Kim, C., & Lahiri, P. … Sengupta, S. (2009). VL2: A scalable and flexible data center network. Proceedings of the ACM SIGCOMM Conference on Data Communication, (pp. 51-62). doi: 10.1145/1592568.1592576

Gulati, A., Merchant, A., Uysal, M., Padala, P., & Varman, P. (2009). Efficient and adaptive proportional share I/O scheduling. *ACM SIGMETRICS Performance Evaluation Review, 37(2),* 79–80. doi:10.1145/1639562.1639595

Hines, M., & Gopalan, K. (2009). Post-copy based live virtual machine migration using adaptive pre-paging and dynamic self-ballooning. Proceedings of the 2009 ACM SIGPLAN/SIGOPS International Conference on Virtual Execution Environments (VEE '09), (pp. 51-60). doi: 10.1145/1508293.1508301

Huang, W., Gao, Q., Liu, J., & Panda, D. (2009). High performance of virtual machine migration with RDMA over modern interconnects. Proceedings of the 2007 IEEE International Conference on Cluster Computing, (pp. 11-20). doi: 10.1109/CLUSTR.2007.4629212

Jin, H., Deng, L., Wu, S., Shi, X., & Pan, X. (2009). Live virtual machine migration with adaptive, memory compression. Proceedings of the 2009 IEEE International Conference on Cluster Computing, (pp. 11-20). doi: 10.1109/CLUSTR.2009.5289170

Karve, A., Kimbrel, T., Pacifici, G., Spreitzer, M., Steinder, M., Sviridenko, M., & Tantawi, A. (2006). Dynamic placement for clustered web applications. Proceedings of the 15th International Conference on World Wide Web, (pp. 595-604). doi: 10.1145/1135777.1135865

Lagar-Cavilla, H., Whitney, J., Scannell, A., Patchin, P., Rumble, S., Lara, E., et al. (2009). SnowFlock: Rapid virtual machine cloning for cloud computing. Proceedings of the 4th ACM European Conference on Computer Systems (EuroSys '09), (pp. 1-12). doi: 10.1145/1519065.1519067

Love, R. (2004). Kernel korner: I/O schedulers. Linux Journal. Retrieved from http://www.linux-journal.com/article/6931

Magenheimer, D. (2008, April). Add self-ballooning to balloon driver [Electronic mailing list message]. Retrieved from http://old-list-archives.xen.org/archives/html/xen-devel/2008-04/msg00567.html

Magenheimer, D. (2009). Transcendent memory and Linux. Retrieved from http://oss.oracle.com/projects/tmem/dist/documentation/papers/tmemLS09.pdf

McNett, M., Gupta, D., Vahdat, A., & Voelker, G. M. (2007). Usher: an extensible framework for managing clusters of virtual machines. Proceedings of the 21st Conference on Large Installation System Administration Conference, (pp. 1-15).

Meisner, D., Gold, B. T., & Wenisch, T. F. (2009). PowerNap: Eliminating server idle power. Proceedings of the 14th International Conference on Architectural Support for Programming Languages and Operating Systems, (pp. 205-216). doi: 10.1145/1508244.1508269

Miller, R. (2008). Microsoft: PUE of 1.22 for data center containers. Retrieved from http://www.datacenterknowledge.com/archives/2008/10/20/microsoft-pue-of-122-for-data-center-containers/

Padala, P., Hou, K., Shin, K. G., Zhu, X., Uysal, M., Wang, Z., et al. (2009). Automated control of multiple virtualized resources. Proceedings of the 4th ACM European Conference on Computer Systems, (pp. 13-26). doi: 10.1145/1519065.1519068

Padala, P., Shin, K. G., Zhu, X., Uysal, M., Wang, Z., & Singhal, S. ... Salem, K. (2007). Adaptive control of virtualized resources in utility computing environments. Proceedings of the 2nd ACM SIGOPS/EuroSys European Conference on Computer Systems, (pp. 289-302). doi: 10.1145/1272996.1273026

Pan, Z., Dong, Y., Chen, Y., Zhang, L., & Zhang, Z. (2012).CompSC: Live migration with pass-through devices. Proceedings of the 2012 ACM SIGPLAN/SIGOPS International Conference on Virtual Execution Environments, (pp. 1-12).

Riteau, P., Morin, C., & Priol, T. (2010). Shrinker: Efficient wide-area live virtual machine migration using distributed content-based addressing. Research Report:RR-7198, INRIA. Retrieved from http://hal.inria.fr/docs/00/45/47/27/PDF/RR-7198.pdf

Seelam, S. R., & Teller, P. J. (2007). Virtual I/O scheduler: A scheduler of schedulers for performance virtualization. Proceedings of the 3rd International Conference on Virtual Execution Environments, (pp. 105-115). doi: 10.1145/1254810.1254826

Shieh, A., Kandula, S., Greenberg, A., Kim, C., & Saha, B. (2011). Sharing the data center network. Proceedings of the 8th USENIX Conference on Networked Systems Design and Implementation, (pp. 1-14). Retrieved from http://www.usenix.org/events/nsdi11/tech/full_papers/Shieh.pdf

Singh, A., Korupolu, M., & Mohapatra, D. (2008). Server-storage virtualization: integration and load balancing in data centers. Proceedings of the 2008 ACM/IEEE conference on Supercomputing, USA, 1-12.

Tang, C., Steinder, M., Spreitzer, M., & Pacifici, G. (2007). A scalable application placement controller for enterprise data centers. Proceedings of the 16th International Conference on World Wide Web, (pp. 331-340). doi: 10.1145/1242572.1242618

Waldspurger, C. A. (2002). Memory resource management in VMware ESX server. Proceedings of the 5th Symposium on Operating Systems Design and implementation, (pp. 181-194). doi: 10.1145/844128.844146

Wood, T., Shenoy, P., Venkataramani, A., & Yousif, M. (2007). Black-box and gray-box strategies for virtual machine migration. Proceedings of 4th USENIX Symposium on Networked Systems Design and Implementation, (pp. 229-242). Retrieved from http://www.usenix.org/events/nsdi07/tech/full_papers/wood/wood_html/

Xiao, Z., Song, W., & Chen, Q. (2011). Dynamic resource allocation using virtual machines for cloud computing environment (unpublished paper). Peking University.

Xiao, Z., Song, W., Chen, Q., & Luo, H. (2010). Gone with the cloud: Adaptive resource virtualization for Amazon EC2-like environment (unpublished paper). Peking University.

Xu, H., & Li, B. (2011). Egalitarian stable matching for VM migration in cloud computing. IEEE Conference on Computer Communications Workshops, Shanghai, (pp. 631-636).

Yang, X. (2011). QoS-oriented service computing: Bring SOA into cloud environment. In Liu, X. (Ed.), *Advanced design approaches to emerging software systems: Principles, methodology and tools*. Hershey, PA: IGI Global. doi:10.4018/978-1-60960-735-7.ch013

Yang, X., Nasser, B., Surrige, M., & Middleton, S. (2012). A business-oriented cloud federation model for real time applications. Future Generation Computer Systems, Elsevier. Retrieved from http://www.sciencedirect.com/science/article/pii/S0167739X12000386

Zhang, X., Huo, Z., Ma, J., & Meng, D. (2010). Exploiting data deduplication to accelerate live virtual machine migration. Proceedings of the 2010 IEEE International Conference on Cluster Computing, (pp. 11-20). doi: 10.1109/CLUSTER.2010.17

Zhu, J., Jiang, Z., & Xiao, Z. (2011). Twinkle: A fast resource provisioning mechanism for internet services. 2011 Proceedings INFOCOM, Shanghai, (pp. 802-810).

ADDITIONAL READING

Armbrust, M., Fox, A., & Griffith, R. (2009). *Above the clouds: A Berkeley view of cloud computing*. Berkeley: EECS Department, University of California.

Barham, P., Dragovic, B., Fraser, K., Hand, S., Harris, T., & Ho, A. ... Warfield, A. (2003). Xen and the art of virtualization. Proceedings of the Nineteenth ACM Symposium on Operating Systems Principles, (pp. 164-177). doi: 10.1145/945445.945462

Bobroff, N., Kochut, A., & Beaty, K. (2007). Dynamic placement of virtual machines for managing SLA violations. International Symposium on Integrated Network Management, Munich, (pp. 119-128). doi: 10.1109/INM.2007.374776

Buyya, R., Ranjan, R., & Calheiros, R. N. (2009). Modeling and simulation of scalable Cloud computing environments and the CloudSim toolkit: Challenges and opportunities. International Conference on High Performance Computing & Simulation, Leipzig, (pp. 1-11). doi: 10.1109/HPCSIM.2009.5192685

Chase, J. S., Anderson, D. C., Thakar, P. N., Vahdat, A. M., & Doyle, R. P. (2001). Managing energy and server resources in hosting centers. Proceedings of the Eighteenth ACM Symposium on Operating Systems Principles, USA, (pp. 103-116). doi: 10.1145/502034.502045

Chen, G., He, W., Liu, J., Nath, S., Rigas, L., Xiao, L., & Zhao, F. (2008). Energy-aware server provisioning and load dispatching for connection-intensive internet services. Proceedings of the 5th USENIX Symposium on Networked Systems Design and Implementation, (pp. 337-350).

Chisnall, D. (2007). The definitive guide to the Xen hypervisor. Upper Saddle River, NJ: Prentice Hall PTR: Prentice Hall.

Gulati, A., Merchant, A., Uysal, M., Padala, P., & Varman, P. (2009). Efficient and adaptive proportional share I/O scheduling. *ACM SIGMETRICS Performance Evaluation Review, 37*(2), 79–80. doi:10.1145/1639562.1639595

Hermenier, F., Lorca, X., Menaud, J., Muller, G., & Lawall, J. (2009). Entropy: A consolidation manager for clusters. Proceedings of the 2009 ACM SIGPLAN/SIGOPS International Conference on Virtual Execution Environments, (pp. 41-50). doi: 10.1145/1508293.1508300

Karve, A., Kimbrel, T., Pacifici, G., Spreitzer, M., Steinder, M., Sviridenko, M., & Tantawi, A. (2006). Dynamic placement for clustered web applications. Proceedings of the 15th international conference on World Wide Web, (pp. 595-604). doi: 10.1145/1135777.1135865

Magenheimer, D. (2009). Transcendent memory and Linux. Retrieved from http://oss.oracle.com/projects/tmem/dist/documentation/papers/tmemLS09.pdf

McNett, M., Gupta, D., Vahdat, A., & Voelker, G. M. (2007). Usher: an extensible framework for managing clusters of virtual machines. Proceedings of the 21st Conference on Large Installation System Administration Conference, (pp. 1-15).

Padala, P., Hou, K., Shin, K. G., Zhu, X., Uysal, M., & Wang, Z. … Merchant, A. (2009). Automated control of multiple virtualized resources. Proceedings of the 4th ACM European Conference on Computer systems, USA, (pp. 13-26). doi: 10.1145/1519065.1519068

Padala, P., Shin, K. G., Zhu, X., Uysal, M., Wang, Z., & Singhal, S. … Salem, K. (2007). Adaptive control of virtualized resources in utility computing environments. Proceedings of the 2nd ACM SIGOPS/EuroSys European Conference on Computer Systems, USA, (pp. 289-302). doi: 10.1145/1272996.1273026

Seelam, S. R., & Teller, P. J. (2007). Virtual I/O scheduler: A scheduler of schedulers for performance virtualization. Proceedings of the 3rd International Conference on Virtual Execution Environments, (pp. 105-115). doi: 10.1145/1254810.1254826

Singh, A., Korupolu, M., & Mohapatra, D. (2008). Server-storage virtualization: Integration and load balancing in data centers. Proceedings of the 2008 ACM/IEEE Conference on Supercomputing, (pp. 1-12).

Tang, C., Steinder, M., Spreitzer, M., & Pacifici, G. (2007). A scalable application placement controller for enterprise data centers. Proceedings of the 16th International Conference on World Wide Web, (pp. 331-340). doi: 10.1145/1242572.1242618

Turner, A., Sangpetch, A., & Kim, H. S. (2010). Empirical virtual machine models for performance guarantees. Proceedings of the Conference on Large Installation System Administration Conference, (pp. 1-11). Retrieved from https://db.usenix.org//events/lisa10/tech/full_papers/Turner.pdf

Wang, Y., Wang, X., Chen, M., & Zhu, X. (2008). Power-efficient response time guarantees for virtualized enterprise servers. Real-Time Systems Symposium, Barcelona, (pp. 303-312). doi: 10.1109/RTSS.2008.20

Wei, G., Vasilakos, A. V., Zheng, Y., & Xiong, N. (2010). A game-theoretic method of fair resource allocation for cloud computing services. *The Journal of Supercomputing, 54*(2), 252–269. doi:10.1007/s11227-009-0318-1

Wood, T., Cherkasova, L., Ozonat, K., & Shenoy, P. (2008). Profiling and modeling resource usage of virtualized applications. Proceedings of the 9th ACM/IFIP/USENIX International Conference on Middleware, (pp. 366-387).

Wood, T., Shenoy, P., Venkataramani, A., & Yousif, M. (2007). Black-box and gray-box strategies for virtual machine migration. Proceedings of 4th USENIX Symposium on Networked Systems Design and Implementation, (pp. 229-242). Retrieved from http://www.usenix.org/events/nsdi07/tech/full_papers/wood/wood_html/

Wood, T., Tarasuk-Levin, G., Shenoy, P., Desnoyers, P., Cecchet, E., & Corner, M. D. (2009). Memory buddies: Exploiting page sharing for smart colocation in virtualized data centers. Proceedings of the 2009 ACM SIGPLAN/SIGOPS International Conference on Virtual Execution Environments, (pp. 31-40). doi: 10.1145/1508293.1508299

Yang, X., Bruin, R., & Dove, M. (2010). Developing an end-to-end scientific workflow: A case study of using a reliable, lightweight, and comprehensive workflow platform in e-science. Retrieved from http://doi.ieeecomputersociety.org/10.1109/MCSE.2009.211

Yang, X., Wang, L., & von Laszewski, G. (2009). Recent research advances in e-science. Cluster Computing Special Issue, 12(4), 353-356. Retrieved from http://springerlink.com/content/f058408qr771348q/

Zhu, J., Jiang, Z., & Xiao, Z. (2011). Twinkle: A fast resource provisioning mechanism for internet services. 2011 IEEE Proceedings of INFOCOM, Shanghai, (pp. 802-810).

KEY TERMS AND DEFINITIONS

Cloud User: A cloud user refers to the person who use the service provided by a cloud system. According to the type of cloud service, it may be an application user, a software developer or a system architect.

Live Migration: A running virtual machine can be migrated from one physical machine to another without its application being interrupted. That technology is called live migration.

Proportional Resource Allocation: With a proportional resource allocation strategy, when contention encountered, each entity should get a share of resource proportional to its presetting weights, no matter how greedy the other entities are.

Resource Provisioning: Resource provisioning refers to the process of assembling computing resources like CPU, memory, disk and network I/O to serve application computation.

Resource Scheduler: A resource scheduler refers to the entity that performs resource scheduling task.

Scheduling Algorithm: Scheduling algorithm refers to the detailed process of the policy for resource scheduling.

Service Level Agreement (SLA): SLA is the quantized specification of the service a cloud provider promises.

Chapter 14
Survivable Mapping of Virtual Networks onto a Shared Substrate Network

Vishal Anand
The College at Brockport, USA

ABSTRACT

The virtualization of both servers and substrate networks will enable the future Internet architecture to support a variety of Cloud computing services and architectures, and prevent its ossification. Since multiple virtual networks (VN) or virtual infrastructure (VI) and services now share the resources of the same underlying network in a network virtualization environment, it is important that efficient techniques are developed for the mapping of the VNs onto the substrate network. Furthermore, due to the sharing of resources, the survivable design of VNs is also very important, since now even small failures in the substrate network will cause the disruption of a large number of VNs that may be mapped on to the substrate network. In this work, the author studies the problem of survivable virtual network mapping (SVNM) and first formulates the problem using mixed integer linear programming (MILP). The author then devises two kinds of algorithms for solving the SVNM problem efficiently: (1) Lagrangian relaxation-based algorithms including LR-SVNM-M and LR-SVNM-D and (2) Heuristic algorithms including H-SVNM-D and H-SVNM-M. The author then compares the performance of the algorithms with other VI mapping algorithms under various performance metrics using simulation. The simulation results and analysis show that the algorithms can be used to balance the tradeoff between time efficiency and mapping cost.

INTRODUCTION

With the maturity of networking and changes in user needs, demands on computer networks are also changing rapidly. Network-wide virtualization (Anderson, Peterson, Shenker, & Turner, 2005) can help diversify the Internet and fend off Internet ossification by providing a flexible environment for new and emerging large scale distributed applications such as Cloud and Grid computing (Foster, Zhao, Raicu, & Lu, 2008; Baranovski, et al., 2007; Chowdhury & Boutaba, 2010). With

DOI: 10.4018/978-1-4666-2854-0.ch014

virtualization multiple heterogeneous network architectures can share the same underlying substrate network, and several overlay networks with diverse topologies, as well as bandwidth and resilience properties can be created using the same physical substrate network. Thus, allowing multiple customizable (e.g., customized for a set of users, application, etc.) network architectures over a common physical infrastructure.

Cloud computing is a new paradigm built upon server virtualization within each datacenter (Foster, Zhao, Raicu, & Lu, 2008; Baranovski, et al., 2007). Cloud computing is a pay-per-use model for enabling convenient, on-demand access to a shared pool of configurable computing resources that can be rapidly provisioned and released with minimal management effort or service provider interaction (Yang, 2012). The Cloud infrastructure typically includes the network, server, storage, software stacks and applications. With Cloud computing the network becomes the most critical asset, thereby increasing the impact on network operators, who now have to build highly resilient, high-performance delivery architectures that can scale on-demand. Dynamic optical transport networks (Mukherjee, 2006) using wavelength division multiplexing (WDM) with on-demand capacity provisioning become key in supporting the elastic nature of Cloud computing applications. Furthermore, optical networks can also provide the scalability, availability, reliability, flexibility and agility required by Cloud computing services cost-effectively. The generalized multiprotocol label switching (GMPLS) that extends the MPLS framework can be used to provide the management and control of the optical network.

Since each one of these virtual infrastructure (VI) or virtual network (VN) topologies uses the resources of the same underlying substrate network, it is essential to use these resources efficiently. We use the terms virtual infrastructure and virtual network interchangeably throughout this work. Making an efficient use of the substrate resources requires intelligent techniques

that map the virtual network on to the substrate network e.g., optical network. In Cloud-based or large networked computing systems hardware and software failures caused by various disruptions such as maintenance, fiber cut, policy change and misconfiguration, are a norm instead of an exception. Due to the shared nature of virtualization, in case of a substrate node/link failure, all the virtual networks using that node/link will be affected. The service providers may incur a penalty due to the breaking of service level agreements (SLAs) with the customers. Thus survivability, i.e., the ability of a network or VNs mapped on to the substrate network to recover from failures is of prime importance.

A network virtualization environment consists of a shared infrastructure and VN requests, which consists of a set of VN nodes, with each node requiring some computing resources (e.g., CPU resource) at a separate computing substrate facility node i.e., no two VN nodes can use the computing resources at the same facility node, even if it has sufficient resources for both VN nodes. In addition a VN node also needs to communicate with another VN node to send intermediate results, file data, or some other information. As a result, a VN request imposes strict connectivity requirements among the VN nodes in terms of topology, bandwidth, and delay guarantees to meet the service level agreements (SLA) (Yang 2011). These communication requirements constitute the edges or virtual links of the VN request. Therefore, another important step in network virtualization is mapping these virtual links onto a set of substrate links that can provide unoccupied resources and meet requirements of these communication demands, such as bandwidth and delay. From the point of view of network provider, an effective VN mapping with minimum cost will increase the utility of substrate network and consequently produce more revenues. Furthermore, customers also expect efficient VN mapping since it translates to reduced costs and higher efficiencies in terms of delays and quality of service (QoS).

In this work we study the survivable virtual network mapping (SVNM) problem and design a framework for solving the SVNM problem with resource constraints imposed by the substrate network. The resource capacity requirement of a VN node and VN link in the framework indicates the amount of computing and bandwidth resources required by the VN request, respectively. Similarly, the capacity of substrate nodes and links indicate the upper bound of computing resources and bandwidth they can provision, respectively. We consider regional failure(s); in general, a region refers to a geographic region of nodes and links that may fail simultaneously due to events such as natural disasters (e.g., earthquakes) or intentional attacks (e.g., bombs). Thus, a regional failure refers to a set of substrate nodes and links which is in the same shared risk group (SRG) (Xu, Xiong, Qiao, & Li, 2003). Thus an active regional failure may affect the existing VN mapping. The VN mapping problem with resource constraints is intractable as it is NP-hard (Mosharaf, Rahman, & Boutaba, 2009); hence most works devise heuristic algorithms for solving this NP-hard problem (Yu, Yi, Rexford, & Chiang, 2008; Yu, Anand, Qiao, Di, & Wang, 2010; Yu, Qiao, Anand, Liu, Di, & Sun, 2010; Zhu & Ammar, 2006). In most of these algorithms, node mapping and link mapping are done separately. In particular, the work in (Mosharaf, Rahman, & Boutaba, 2009) proposes the deterministic VN embedding (D-ViNE) algorithm for solving the non-survivable VN mapping problem.

The framework and solutions proposed in this work address two key issues of SVNM problem, namely reducing the VN mapping cost and reducing the computational complexity of the VN mapping algorithm. It should be noted that these two issues are complementary as solutions that help reduce VN mapping costs typically incur higher computational costs and time. In this work, we first model the SVNM problem with resource constraints using the mixed integer linear programming (MILP) approach for achieving the optimal solution for the SVNM problem. We extend our

work on the basis of the MILP model, and propose two kinds of algorithms for solving SVNM problem: (1) Lagrangian relaxation (Pioro & Medhi, 2004) based algorithms including LR-SVNM-D and LR-SVNM-M and (2) Heuristic algorithms including H-SVNM-D and H-SVNM-M. The main idea of these two algorithms is to decompose the primal NP-hard problem into several sub-problems in order to reduce the computational complexity at the expense of increasing the total VN mapping cost. Simulation results shown that the algorithms proposed in this work can balance the tradeoff between VN mapping cost and computational complexity of VN mapping algorithm.

BACKGROUND

In recent years a number of heuristics have been proposed for solving different variants of the virtual network mapping problem. The work in (Luand & Turner, 2006) focuses on the off-line version where the virtual infrastructure traffic requests are known before hand, whereas the work in (Yu, Yi, Rexford, & Chiang, 2008; Mosharaf, Rahman, & Boutaba, 2009; Butt, Chowdhury, & Boutaba, 2010; Lischka & Karl, 2009) focus on the on-line version where the requests arrive according to a specific distribution. To reduce the problem complexity the work in (Luand & Turner, 2006; Yu, Yi, Rexford, & Chiang, 2008) restricts the search space by separating the node and link mapping stages, e.g., handling the node mapping in the first stage and doing the link mapping in the second stage based on the shortest path, k-shortest paths and multi-commodity flow algorithms. The work in (Luand & Turner, 2006; Yu, Yi, Rexford, & Chiang, 2008) also uses preselected node mappings without considering its relation to the link mapping stage. Although such approaches simplify the mapping problem and make it manageable, they result in poor performance.

The work in (Mosharaf, Rahman, & Boutaba, 2009) developed an MILP formulation that coordinates the node and link mapping phases and presented two algorithms deterministic VN embedding (D-ViNE) and randomized VN embedding (R-ViNE) based on LP relaxation with deterministic rounding and randomized rounding strategies, respectively. In the node mapping stage, the work in (Mosharaf, Rahman, & Boutaba, 2009) relaxed the integer program to obtain a linear programming formulation that can be solved in polynomial time, and then used the deterministic D-ViNE and randomized R-ViNE virtual network embedding algorithms to approximate the values of the binary variables in the original mixed integer program (MIP). Once all the virtual nodes have been mapped, multi-commodity flow algorithms are used to get the link mapping solution.

Based on the work in (Mosharaf, Rahman, & Boutaba, 2009), the authors in (Butt, Chowdhury, & Boutaba, 2010) proposed a mechanism to differentiate among resources based on their importance in the substrate topology and re-optimization. However, the integer linear program (ILP) relaxation weakens the coordination between the node and link mapping stages. The authors of (Lischka & Karl, 2009) proposed to map nodes and links during the same stage, and present a backtracking algorithm based on a subgraph isomorphism. In (Lischka & Karl, 2009) the VI links are mapped onto paths shorter than a predefined distance (or hop) value. The authors propose two algorithms to determine the proper distance value, vnmFlib-simple with a fixed distance value and vnmFlib-advanced with an incremental distance value. The vnmFlib-advanced outperforms the vnmFlib-simple algorithm. However both these approaches do not take the link mapping cost during the mapping of the nodes into account. Moreover this work focuses more on finding an isomorphic subgraph to map the virtual infrastructure request but not on finding a cost-efficient solution.

More recently some of the research has addressed the issue of survivable VN design. The work in (Houidi, Louati, Zeghlache, Papadimitriou, & Mathy, 2010) deals with devising distributed survivable VN mapping algorithms without a centralized controller, and the authors of (Liu, Qiao, & Wang, 2009) addressed survivable VI request provisioning and proposed two failure-independent approaches namely cluster and path protection (CPP) and virtual network protection (VNP). However, these failure-independent approaches generally require more redundant resources. The authors of (Rahman, Aib, & Boutaba, 2010) propose a hybrid policy solution to incorporate single substrate link failure the policy is based on a fast rerouting strategy and utilizes a pre-reserved quota for backup on each physical link. This hybrid policy is essentially a restore approach, and cannot guarantee 100% recovery. In (Yu, Qiao, Anand, Liu, Di, & Sun, 2010) we adopt a failure dependent protection approach whereby there is a backup solution associated with each regional failure scenario with the objective of minimizing the redundant resources/cost. This work proposed an efficient heuristic solution to the non-survivable VI mapping (NSVIM) problem, based on which two survivable VI mapping (SVIM) algorithms called Separate Optimization with Unconstrained Mapping (SOUM) and Incremental Optimization with Constrained Mapping (IOCM).

In (Yu, Anand, Qiao, Di, & Wang, 2010) we extend our above work by first developing an improved non-survivable VI mapping (NSVIM*) heuristic. Based on NSVIM* we then develop efficient SVIM heuristics namely separate optimization with unconstrained mapping and redundancy elimination (SOUM*) and incremental optimization with constrained mapping and failure-avoidance (IOCM*). The work in (Yu, Anand, Qiao, & Sun, 2011) focuses on the failure recovery of the substrate nodes to jointly minimize the total amount of computing and bandwidth resources (or cost). In (Yu, Anand, Qiao, & Sun, 2011) the authors adopt a two-step paradigm to fully restore a VI from any single facility node failure by first enhancing a VI with backup virtual nodes and links requiring spare computing and communications resources, and then mapping the enhanced VI to the substrate network. Thus, in this the work we propose two approaches whereby an N-node VI is first enhanced to a 1-redundant and K-redundant VI with N+1 and N+K nodes, respectively, in addition to an appropriate number of redundant virtual links. In the subsequent mapping of the enhanced VI to the substrate network, maximal amount of sharing of the computing and communication bandwidth among the nodes and links in the enhanced VI is exploited. Accordingly, it is possible that some N+k ($1 \leq k \leq K$) substrate nodes are chosen by the algorithm when mapping the enhanced VI with N+K nodes.

NETWORK MODEL AND PROBLEM STATEMENT

In this section we describe our network model and problem statement. We then present the mixed integer linear programming model for the SVNM problem.

Substrate Network

Due to their advantages such as high speed, high signal to noise ratio (SNR), transparent transmission and abundant bandwidth resources, optical WDM mesh networks are playing a major role as substrate networks. We model the substrate network as an undirected graph GS = (VS, ES),

where VS is the set of substrate nodes, and ES represents the set of bidirectional fiber links. We assume that all the substrate nodes are facility nodes with computing resource, and hence VF = VS.

Each facility node $v_F \in V_F$ that can provide computing resources, and c(vF) represents the available capacity of computing resources at facility node vF. The cost of per unit computing resource on facility node vF is cf(vF). For each link $e_S \in E_S$, the available bandwidth capacity is b(es) and the cost of per unit of bandwidth capacity is cl(es). Figure1 (a) shows a substrate network, where the numbers aside the links represent the available bandwidth and the cost of per unit bandwidth capacity and the numbers in the rectangles represent available computing resources and cost of per unit computing resource.

VN Request

A VN request with QoS requirements is modeled as a weighted undirected graph GL= (VL, EL), where VL indicates to the set of VN nodes, and EL represents the set of bidirectional communication demands among the VN nodes.

Each VN node $v_L \in V_L$ needs a certain amount of computing resources for executing the applications, denoted by $\varepsilon(v_L)$. Similarly, each commu-

Figure 1. Mapping a VN request onto a substrate network

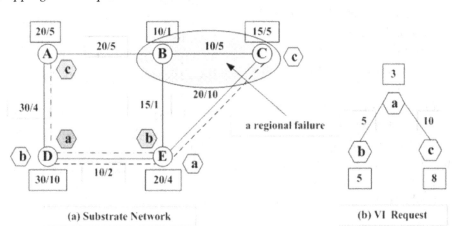

(a) Substrate Network   (b) VI Request

nication demand $e_L \in E_L$ has a bandwidth requirement for information and data exchange, which we denote by b(eL). Figure1 (b) shows a VN request with three VN nodes and two VN links, and associated computing and communication resource requirements.

Regional Failures

The authors in (Murthy & Banerjee, 2009) show that there exist only a finite number of distinct regional failures in a given geographical area. Accordingly, we assume a set of possible regional failures R is given in advance and there is at most one of these regional failures that is active at any time. One or more substrate nodes and relative substrate links will be affected simultaneously while a regional failure $r_i \in R$ $(i = 0, 1, 2 ..... |R| - 1)$ turns from inactive to active state. In fact we can generalize a regional failure to the concept of a shared risk group (SRG) failures. We use r_0 to denote the scenario when no failure occurs.

Survivable VN Mapping Problem

Mapping a VN request GL on to a substrate network GS with survivability against any single regional failure r consists of five parts: initial VN request mapping, redundant facility nodes allocation, redundant link allocation, VN request check-pointing and VN request migration.

Initially, without the consideration of possible failures, we need to allocate a separate facility node and required computing resources for each VN node of the VN request, as well as set up paths and reserve required bandwidth to transmit data or information among the VN nodes. If Num is the number of VN nodes, then exactly Num facility nodes are occupied in this initial request mapping.

In our failure-dependent SVNM approach, we assume that if a facility node initially used by a VN node is within the failed region, we then need

one backup facility node outside the failed region, in order to remap the VN node. Note that the choice of the additional backup facility node(s) depends on the active failure $r_i \in R$, and may differ from one failure to another. To ensure that such a backup facility node can be found in the event of a regional failure occurs, we reserve the backup facility node in advance. Since a regional failure may affect multiple facility nodes allocated for the initial VN request mapping, a sufficient set of redundant facility nodes have to be pre-allocated.

Similarly, for each regional failure $r \in R$, we need to pre-allocate enough redundant bandwidth on the substrate links, which do not belong to regional failure r, to support the communication between the VN nodes under regional failure r. In particularly, if a VN node is to be restored at a pre-allocated backup facility node, we must set up new available paths between that backup facility node and other surviving facility nodes.

To eliminate the need for starting over the job/computation of a VN node when it is disrupted by a failure, we need to check-point the VN node. More specifically, we periodically send the status of the VN node (e.g., virtual machine image) to backup facility node such that the VN request can be restored from a previous saved state when a regional failure occurs. Finally, we need to perform VN request migration, i.e., migrate the failed facility nodes to the backup facility nodes.

In Figure 1, VN nodes a, b and c are initially (before failure) mapped to facility nodes E, D and C using the bandwidth on substrate link E-C and E-D, respectively. The regional failure destroys facility nodes B and C, and the substrate link B-C. The substrate network now remaps the VN request such that the VN node a is now mapped onto facility node D, b is mapped onto facility node E and c is mapped onto facility node A using the bandwidth on substrate links D-A and D-E, and the jobs on these failed facility nodes are migrated to the newly mapped facility nodes.

Problem Description

We assume that the following information is known, based on which we define the problem as follows.

Given: A substrate network GS = (VS, ES), a VN request GL = (VL, EL), a set of possible regional failures R.

Problem: Jointly allocate computing and link capacity resources of substrate network, including the backup resources, such that the total cost of survivable mapping of the VN request, i.e., sum of computation and communication cost is minimized.

Since we assume that no more than one regional failure occurs at any one time, the resources reserved on the facility nodes and fiber links can be shared among the different failure scenarios. Accordingly to ensure survivability under any regional failure, the total computing resources that are allocated on substrate node n, denoted by rnn, is the maximum of all computing resources under any failure. Similarly, the total bandwidth allocated on substrate link e, denoted by rle, is the maximum of all bandwidth resources under any failure.

MILP Formulation for the SVNM Problem

In this work, we use $Sc(e)$ and $Dt(e)$ to denote source and sink node of link e, respectively. To formulate the MILP model for our SVNM problem, we apply the following graph transformation to GS. We add $|V_L|$ virtual nodes into GS; each virtual node corresponds to a VN node in the VN request. Each virtual node is set to have an infinite computing capacity. Each virtual node vL is connected to all the facility nodes $v_F \in V_F$ that has enough available computing resources required by the corresponding VN node vL. We call the links connecting virtual nodes and facility nodes as virtual edges. We assume that the bandwidth resources on each virtual edge are unlimited. Each virtual node vL is unaffected by any regional failure in R. However, for each virtual edge connecting virtual node vL and facility node vF, if vF is within a region $r \in R$, then that virtual edge is also inside the region r. By means of graph transformation, we achieve the following augmented graph G* as $G^* = (V^*, E^*)$, where

$$V^* = V_s \cup V_L,$$

and

$$E^* = E_S \cup \left\{ e \,\middle|\, Sc(e) \in V_F, Dt(e) \in V_L \right\} \cup \left\{ e \,\middle|\, Sc(e) \in V_L, Dt(e) \in V_F \right\}.$$

Based on the above graph transformation, the SVNM problem can be formulated as a mixed integer multi-commodity flow (MCF) problem, in which a communication demand d in GL is considered as a commodity. We present the detailed MILP formulation for SVNM problem as follows. Table 1 lists the key notations used in the MILP model.

Objective function:

$$min \sum_{e \in E_s} fl_e \times cl_e + \sum_{m \in V_s} rn_m \times cn_m \qquad (1)$$

The objective function in (1) minimizes the total mapping cost (cost of CPU and bandwidth resources).

Constraints:

$$\sum_{d \in D} (\chi_e^{d,r} + \chi_e^{d,r}) \leq 2 \times b_e \times \alpha_e^r, \quad \forall e \in E^*, \forall r \in R \qquad (2)$$

$$\alpha_e^r \times \varepsilon(Sc(e)) \leq c(Dt(e)), \forall e \in E_L^*, Sc(e) \in V_L, Dt(e) \in V_S, \forall r \in R \qquad (3)$$

Table 1. Summary of key notations used in the MILP model

Notation	Meaning
$Sc(e)$	The source node of link e.
$Dt(e)$	The destination node of link e.
fl_e	Total bandwidth required on substrate link e.
rn_n	Total computing resources required on facility node n.
$rl_{e,r}$	Total bandwidth required on substrate link e under regional failure r.
$rn_{n,r}$	Total computing resource required on facility node n under regional failure r.
$\chi_e^{d,r}$	The used bandwidth on substrate link e by demand d under regional failure r.
α_e^r	Whether link e is used under regional failure r. 1 if is used, and 0 otherwise.
b_e	Total bandwidth capacity of link e.
cl_e	The cost of per unit bandwidth of substrate link e.
$c(n)$	The computing resources available on facility node n.
cn_n	The cost of per unit computing resource of facility node n.
$\varepsilon(n)$	The computing resources required by virtual node n.
D	The set of communication demands of GL.
b_d	The bandwidth required by communication demand d.
s_d, t_d	The source and sink node of communication demand d.
V^*, E^*	The set of nodes and links of augmented graph G*.
β_e^r	Whether link e is include in regional failure r.
η_m^r	Whether node m is include in regional failure r.
T	Big constant, which equals to 10,000 in this work.

Constraints (2) and (3) are link and node capacity constraints that ensure that the required resources do not exceed the link bandwidth capacity or the node computing resource capacity.

$$\sum_{\substack{e \in E^*, \\ Sc(e)=m}} \chi_e^{d,r} - \sum_{\substack{e \in E^*, \\ Dt(e)=m}} \chi_e^{d,r} = 0, \forall d \in D, \forall m \in$$
$$V^* \setminus \{s_d, t_d\}, \forall r \in R$$
(4)

$$\sum_{e \in E^*, Sc(e)=s_d} \chi_e^{d,r} - \sum_{e \in E^*, Dt(e)=s_d} \chi_e^{d,r} =$$
$$b_d, \forall d \in D, \forall r \in R$$
(5)

$$\sum_{e \in E^*, Dt(e)=t_d} \chi_e^{d,r} - \sum_{e \in E^*, Sc(e)=t_d} \chi_e^{d,r} =$$
$$b_d, \forall d \in D, \forall r \in R$$
(6)

$$\sum_{e \in E^*, Dt(e)=s_d} \chi_e^{d,r} = 0, \quad \forall d \in D, \forall r \in R$$
(7)

$$\sum_{e \in E^*, Sc(e)=t_d} \chi_e^{d,r} = 0, \quad \forall d \in D, \forall r \in R$$
(8)

Equations (4)-(8) are flow conservation constraints. These flow conservations guarantee that a flow on an edge does not exceed the bandwidth capacity of the edge, and the net flow to a node is zero except for the source and destination nodes that produce and consume flows.

$$\alpha_e^r \leq 1 - \beta_e^r, \forall e \in E^*, \forall r \in R$$
(9)

$$\sum_{e \in E^*, Sc(e)=m} \alpha_e^r \leq T \times (1 - \eta_m^r), \forall m \in V_S, \forall r \in R$$
(10)

Constraint (9) and (10) ensure that only when a link or node is available under regional failure r, only then can the link or node be assigned under regional failure r.

$$\sum_{e \in E^*, Sc(e)=m, Dt(e) \in V_S} \alpha_e^r = 1, \quad \forall m \in V_L, \forall r \in R$$
(11)

$$\sum_{e \in E^*, Sc(e) \in V_L, Dt(e)=n} \alpha_e^r \leq 1 - \eta_n^r, \quad \forall n \in V_S, \forall r \in R$$
(12)

Equation (11) ensures that only one substrate node is selected for mapping the virtual node under any regional failure r. Constraint (12) ensures that no more than one virtual node is mapped onto an available substrate node under any failure r; and when the substrate node is unavailable under failure r, there should be no virtual node mapped onto it.

$$\alpha_{e_1}^r = \alpha_{e_2}^r, \forall r \in R, \forall e_1 \in E^*, Sc(e_2) = Dt(e_1), Dt(e_2) = Sc(e_1)$$
(13)

$$rl_{e,r} = \sum_{d \in D} \chi_e^{d,r} \leq 2 \times b_e \times \alpha_e^r, \quad \forall e \in E_s, \forall r \in R$$
(14)

$$rn_{n,r} = \sum_{e \in E^*, Sc(e) \in V_L, Dt(e)=n} \alpha_{mn}^r \times \varepsilon(m), \forall n \in V_s, \forall r \in R$$
(15)

$$rl_{e,r} \leq fl_e, \quad \forall e \in E_s, \forall r \in R$$
(16)

$$rn_{n,r} \leq rn_n, \quad \forall n \in V_s, \forall r \in R$$
(17)

Constraint (13) denotes that the binary variables for the two links in the opposite direction between any node pair have the same value. Constraints (14) and (15) denote the total amount of resources required on each substrate link and node under regional failure r, respectively. Constraints (16) and (17) ensure that the amount of resources required on each substrate link or node under any regional failure r, must not exceed the total amount of resources required on each substrate link or node.

ALGORITHMS FOR THE SVNM PROBLEM

The survivable virtual network mapping problem with link and node capacity constraints can be formulated as an MILP problem as described above. However, this MILP problem is intractable since it is NP-hard. Consequently, we propose Lagrangian relaxation based algorithm (LR-SVNM) and decomposition technique based heuristic algorithm (H-SVNM) in this section, in order to reduce the computational complexity and solve the problem efficiently. The main idea of our algorithms is to decompose the primal problem into |R| sub-problems and solving these sub-problems separately thereby reducing the computational complexity and enhancing the time efficiency.

Heuristic Algorithm for SVNM (H-SVNM)

The work in (Mosharaf, Rahman, & Boutaba, 2009) proposes the D-ViNE algorithm that performs time efficient mapping of non-survivable VNs in various phases. The SOUM* and IOCM* algorithms proposed in (Yu, Anand, Qiao, Di, & Wang, 2010) can recover from failures. In SOUM* algorithm, the SVNM problem can be decomposed into |R| separate non-survivable virtual network mapping (NSVNM) problems for reducing the computational complexity to some extent. However, the performance in terms of mapping cost is not as good, and there is room for improvement.

In this section, we incorporate the advantages of D-ViNE and SOUM* algorithms and propose a heuristic algorithm for SVNM problem, called H-SVNM. In H-SVNM algorithm, the primal problem is also decomposed into |R| sub-problems. We may solve each sub-problem by using the

improved D-ViNE algorithm, called D-ViNE*(as shown in Figure 3), in which we compute p_{z_aver} and Z_{min} for each VN node $v_L \in V_L$ as

$$p_{z\_aver} = average\left\{p_Z \left| \varphi(z) = 0\right.\right\}$$

and

$$Z_{min} = \arg min\{\left|p_z - p_{z\_aver}\right|, \varphi(z) = 0, z \in \Omega(v_L)\}$$

(H-SVNM-D); or each sub-problem will be solved by MILP (H-SVNM-M). Consequently, we achieve the node mapping as $EN\left(v_L\right) \leftarrow Z_{min}$. We can compute the set of mapping solutions for all the sub-problems,

$$E = \{E_i \left| i = 0, 1, 2, \ldots. \left|R\right| - 1\right\}.$$

Since a mapping solution Ei for failure ri, may also be used for recovering from other failures, there may be redundancies in the mapping solution set E. We use the greedy min-cost set cover algorithm (Yu, Qiao, Anand, Liu, Di, & Sun, 2010) to eliminate the redundant mappings in E. The framework of H-SVNM is shown in Figure 2. Details of the H-SVNM algorithm are shown in Figure 4.

Lagrangian Relaxation Based Algorithm for SVNM (LR-SVNM)

Since the original MILP problem is concave, we can use Lagrangian Relaxation approach to solve it by decomposing the NP-hard problem into several sub-problems by relaxing certain constraints. Each sub-problem may also be solved by MILP (LR-SVNM-M), or each sub-problem will be solved by using D-ViNE* (LR-SVNM-D). The framework of LR-SVNM is shown in Figure 3.

In LR-SVNM algorithm, we relax constraints (16) and (17) of the original MILP problem. Here,

Figure 2. The framework of H-SVNM algorithm

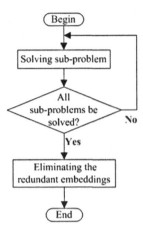

we denote the Lagrange multiplier as λ and θ (where $\lambda \geq 0$, $\theta \geq 0$), then we can write the Lagrangian function by relaxing the coupling constraint (16) and (17) as:

$$L(\lambda,\theta) = \sum_{e\in E_s} fl_e \times cl_e + \sum_{m\in V_s} rn_m \times cn_m$$
$$+\sum_{e\in E_s}\sum_{r\in R}\lambda_{e,r} \times (rl_{e,r} - fl_e) + \sum_{n\in V_s}\sum_{r\in R}\theta_{n,r} \times (rn_{n,r} - rn_n)$$
$$= \sum_{e\in E_s} fl_e \times (cl_e - \sum_{r\in R}\lambda_{e,r}) + \sum_{n\in V_s} rn_n \times (cn_n - \sum_{r\in R}\theta_{n,r})$$
$$+\sum_{r\in R}(\sum_{e\in E_s}\lambda_{e,r} \times rl_{e,r} + \sum_{n\in V_s}\theta_{n,r} \times rn_{n,r})$$

$$(18)$$

In Equation (18), variable fl_e, rn_n, $rl_{e,r}$ and $rn_{n,r}$ are called primal variables and the Lagrange multiplier λ and θ are dual variables. Similarly, the objective function (1) of original MILP problem is primal objective, whereas the minimum value of the Lagrange dual problem (18) is called dual objective and denoted by $\Gamma(\lambda,\theta)$. Then we can formulate $\Gamma(\lambda,\theta)$ as follows:

$$\Gamma(\lambda,\theta) = \inf_{\lambda,\theta} L(\lambda,\theta). \qquad (19)$$

Since the dual function $\Gamma(\lambda,\theta)$ is concave, and can then be maximized to obtain a lower bound on the optimal value of the original MILP problem.

We can formulate the dual problem for the original MILP problem as:

$$\begin{aligned} max \quad & \Gamma(\lambda,\theta) \\ s.t. \quad & \lambda \geq 0, \theta \geq 0. \end{aligned} \qquad (20)$$

The original MILP problem has thus been separated into $|R|$ independent sub-problems to solve it efficiently. Each independent problem can be solved separately by solving the following two sub-problems (21) and (22):

$$min\sum_{e\in E_s} fl_e \times (cl_e - \sum_{r\in R}\lambda_{e,r}) + \sum_{n\in V_s} rn_n \times (cn_n - \sum_{r\in R}\theta_{n,r})$$
$$s.t. \quad fl \geq 0, rn \geq 0.$$
$$(21)$$

$$min\sum_{r\in R}(\sum_{e\in E_s}\lambda_{e,r} \times rl_{e,r} + \sum_{n\in V_s}\theta_{n,r} \times rn_{n,r})$$
$$s.t. \quad constraints(2)\text{-}(15). \qquad (22)$$

The value of λ and θ in problem (21) and (22) are the solutions of dual problem (20). We solve the dual problem (20) by using steepest descent

Figure 3. The framework of LR-SVNM algorithm

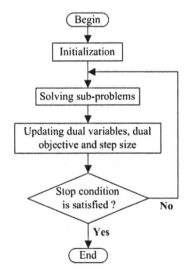

Figure 4. Substrate networks used for simulation experiments: (a) Net-1: a 6-node network, $|R| = 3$, (b) Net-2: CERNET with 10 nodes, $|R| = 4$, (c) Net-3: NSFNET with 14 nodes, $|R| = 4$, and (d) Net-4: USANET with 24 nodes, $|R| = 4$

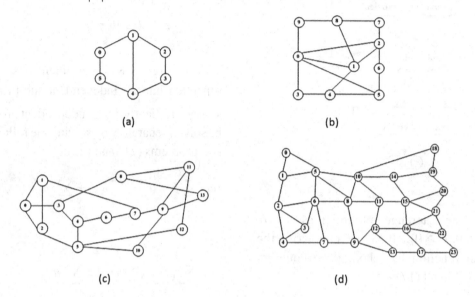

(a)   (b)

(c)   (d)

approach for updating λ and θ after the end of solving problem (21) and (22) as:

$$\lambda_{e,r}(k+1) =$$
$$\left[\lambda_{e,r}(k) + t1_k \times (rl_{e,r}(k) - fl_e(k))\right]^+, \quad (23)$$
$$\forall e \in E_S, r \in R$$

$$\theta_{n,r}(k+1) =$$
$$\left[\theta_{n,r}(k) + t2_k \times (rn_{n,r}(k) - rn_n(k))\right]^+, \quad (24)$$
$$\forall n \in V_S, r \in R$$

where $rl_{e,r}$, fl_e, $rn_{n,r}$ and rn_n are solutions of problem (21) and (22). $t1_k$ and $t2_k$ are step size for the kth iteration that can be computed as follows:

$$t1_k = \tau \times (f^* - \Gamma(\lambda(k), \theta(k))) / \sum_{e \in E_S} \sum_{r \in R} (rl_{e,r}(k) - fl_e(k))^2$$
$$(25)$$

$$t2_k = \tau \times (f^* - \Gamma(\lambda(k), \theta(k))) / \sum_{n \in V_S} \sum_{r \in R} (rn_{n,r}(k) - rn_n(k))^2$$
$$(26)$$

In Equations (25) and (26) f^* denotes the upper bound of dual objective value, and is easy to achieve since any feasible solution for primal problem is an upper bound for dual objective. The iteration for solving the above problems do not stop until a predefined stop condition is satisfied. The dual variable $\lambda(k)$ and $\theta(k)$ will converge to the optimal value λ^* and θ^* while $k \to \infty$ and, the primal variables also converge to optimal values since the duality gap for primal problem is zero and the solution for (21) and (22) are stable. Algorithm 3 displays the detailed LR-SVNM algorithm for the SVNM problem.

RESULTS FROM SIMULATION EXPERIMENTS

We evaluate the performance of our proposed framework and algorithms using detailed simulation experiments. In this section, we give the detailed description for simulation environment and present our main experimental results.

Algorithm 1. D-ViNE* algorithm

1. Initialization. Create augmented substrate graph G*
2. Solve VNE_LP_RELAX

3. for all $v_S \in V_S$ do

4. $\varphi(v_S) \leftarrow 0$
5. end for
6. Initial Connected-Substrate-Node-Set Θ

7. for all $v_L \in V_L$ do

8. if $\Omega(v_L) \cap \left\{ v_S \in V_S \middle| \varphi(v_S) = 1 \right\} = \varnothing$ then

9. VN request cannot be satisfied
10. return
11. end if

12. for all $z \in \Omega(v_L)$ do

13. $p_z \leftarrow \sum_i (f^i_{\mu(v_L)z} + f^i_{z\mu(v_L)})\chi_{\mu(v_L)z}$

14. end for

15. Compute p_{z_aver} as: $p_{z\_aver} = average\left\{ p_z \middle| \varphi(z) = 0, z \in \Theta \right\}$

16. Let $z_{min} = \arg min \left\{ \left| p_z - p_{z\_aver} \right| \middle| \varphi(z) = 0, z \in \Theta, z \in \Omega(v_L) \right\}$

17. Set $M_N(v_L) \leftarrow z_{min}$

18. $\varphi(z_{min}) \leftarrow 1$
19. end for
20. Solve MCF to map virtual edges.

Algorithm 2. H-SVNM algorithm

1. for all $r_i \in R$ $(i = 0....\left| R \right| - 1)$ do

2. $G^* \leftarrow G^* - \left\{ (V_f, E_f) \middle| V_f \in r_i, E_f \in r_i \right\}$

3. Solve each sub-problem by using MILP or D-ViNE* algorithm to get embedding Ei for failure ri
4. end for
5. Call greedy min-cost set cover algorithm to eliminate the redundant embeddings to obtain Ebest.

Simulation Environment

To evaluate the effectiveness of our approaches we conduct simulation studies on four different network topologies as shown in Figure 4. The CERNET, NSFNET and USANET are well-known network topologies that have traditionally been used for conducting network and simulation experiments. The four network topologies chosen vary in terms of the number of nodes, links and connectivity and thus provide a good basis for evaluation of our approaches. In these four substrate networks, all link bandwidth capacities and node resource capacities are assumed to be 50 units. We assume per unit node resource cost and per unit link bandwidth cost to be equal to

Algorithm 3. LR-SVNM algorithm

---

1. Initialization. Set k_{max}, τ_{iter_max} $\lambda(0)$, $\theta(0)$, $k = 0$, $\tau = 1.0$, $\tau_{min} = 0.005$, $\tau_{iter} = 0$, $f_{best} = \infty$.

2. Set $\tau_{iter} = \tau_{iter} + 1$; Solve problem (21) and (22) to achieve solutions $rl_{e,r}(k)$, $rn_{n,r}(k)$, $fl_e^{\wedge}(k)$, $rn_n^{\wedge}(k)$ by using the given value of $\lambda(k)$ and $\theta(k)$.

3. Use solution of problem (21) and (22) to compute:

a. Compute feasible $fl_e(k)$ and $rn_n(k)$ as:

b. $fl_e(k) \leftarrow \underset{r \in R}{Max}\, rl_{e,r}(k)$, $rn_n(k) \leftarrow \underset{r \in R}{Max}\, rn_{n,r}(k)$;

c. Use $fl_e(k)$ and $rn_n(k)$ to compute objective value f of primal problem;

d. If $f < f_{best}$, then: $f_{best} = f$, $fl_e^{best}(k) = fl_e(k)$, $rn_n^{best}(k) = rn_n(k)$, $f^* = f_{best}$;

e. If $\tau_{iter} > \tau_{iter\_max}$, then $\tau = max\left\{\tau \times 0.618, \tau_{min}\right\}$ $\tau_{iter} = 0$.

4. Use solution of problem (21) and (22) to update:

a. Dual objective $\Gamma(\lambda(k), \theta(k))$ (refer to Equations (18)-(19));

b. Dual variables λ and θ (refer to Equations (23)-(24));
   c. Step size t1k and t2k (refer to Equations (25)-(26)).

5. Set k = k+1.

6. Go to Step 2 until $k > k_{max}$.

---

1 unit. In Net-1, Net-2 and Net-3, we randomly choose to fail two substrate nodes when a regional failure occurs; and in Net-4, we randomly fail three substrate nodes when a regional failure occurs. There is at most one active regional failure r at any given time.

The virtual networks or VN requests are generated randomly such that the number of VN nodes is equal to a given number N and the average degree of connectivity of the VN request is about 2.5. We assume that each VN node requires 1 unit computing resource capacity, and 1 unit of bandwidth resources are required by each of the communication demands between the VN nodes. The MILP is solved using the CPLEX solver from ILOG.

In our experiments, we have simulated and compared the performances of following algorithms: IOCM* and SOUM* from (Yu, Anand, Qiao, Di, & Wang, 2010), Lagrangian Relaxation based algorithms for SVNM problem, each sub-problem is solved by D-ViNE* or LR-SVNM-D, Lagrangian Relaxation based algorithms for SVNM problem, each sub-problem is solved by MILP or LR-SVNM-M, Heuristic algorithm for SVNM Problem, each sub-problem is solved by D-ViNE* or H-SVNM-D and Heuristic algorithm for SVNM Problem, each sub-problem is solved by MILP or H-SVNM-M that use different VN mapping strategies. In addition, we also compare the performance of these algorithms with the optimal results obtained from the MILP.

Performance Metrics and Simulation Results

Since the two key issues of SVNM problem algorithm are VN mapping cost and computational complexity. We use the following two metrics to evaluate the performance of the above algorithms.

1. **Total Mapping Cost:** This is the total cost of reserving substrate network resources to tolerate any failure scenario r. The total mapping cost is the sum of the computing cost on all facility nodes and the bandwidth cost on all substrate links.

2. **Time Efficiency:** This is the time consumed by an algorithm for complementing the VN mapping.

We compare the performance of different algorithms in terms of total cost and time efficiency of VN mapping under various substrate network topologies and with different VN requests, i.e., different number of VN nodes and links in the request. We use different notations in our simulation results to indicate the different substrate networks and VN requests that have been used in our experiments. For example, the notation "6-2" denotes "6 substrate nodes and 2 VN nodes". In our simulation studies, we use Net-1, Net-2, Net-3, and Net-4, and the number of VN nodes varies from 2 to 18.

1. **The convergence of LR-SVNM Algorithm:** We set $\lambda(0) = 1$ and $\theta(0) = 3$, in this set of experimental simulations. In Figure 5, the experimental results show that the Lagrangian relaxation based algorithms LR-SVNM can guarantee a solution for primal problem, and furthermore converge to a stable one by solving sub-problems iteratively.

2. **Comparison of total mapping cost:** Figure 6 shows the simulation results that compare the total mapping costs of the various algorithms. We make the following conclusions from simulation results: VN mapping cost of our algorithms is lower than IOCM* and SOUM*. Under small size substrate network (Net-1), heuristic algorithms (H-SVNM and H-SVNM-M) and Lagrangian relaxation based algorithm (LR-SVNM-M and LR-SVNM-D) result in a similar mapping cost, which is similar (or equal) to that of the MILP. However, when the substrate network size is large(Figure 6(b)), H-SVNM-M achieve lower mapping cost than H-SVNM-D, and LR-SVNM-M with better mapping cost than LR-SVNM-D, since the former solve each sub-problem by using the MILP, while the latter employ heuristic based algorithms for solving the sub-problems. H-SVNM-M has a better performance than LR-SVNM-M in terms of mapping cost since Lagrangian Relaxation based algorithm reduce the computational complexity at the cost of losing some feasible solutions to the original problem.

3. **Comparison of time efficiency:** From Table 2 and Table 3 we can see that the time ef-

Table 2. Comparison of time efficiency (1)

Time (Sec.)	Node Number						
	6-2	6-3	6-4	10-3	10-4	10-5	10-6
IOCM*	0.01	0.01	0.04	0.1	0.12	0.35	1.05
SOUM*	0.01	0.01	0.01	0.03	0.1	0.2	0.45
H-SVNM-D	0.4	0.5	0.7	1.1	1.4	1.8	2.6
H-SVNM-M	0.5	0.9	1.9	3.1	23.6	94.5	3126.8
LR-SVNM-M	1.6	3.0	6.4	12.4	83.4	407.3	11345.1
LR-SVNM-D	1.5	1.9	2.0	3.2	4.2	5.3	8.1
MILP	0.3	3.1	6.1	108.1	790514.4	829713.8	875501.5

Table 3. Comparison of time efficiency (2)

Time (Sec.)	Node Number										
	14-6	14-7	14-8	14-9	14-10	24-8	24-10	24-12	24-14	24-16	24-18
IOCM*	1.02	1.2	2.05	2.56	2.67	10	11	11	13	14	12
SOUM*	0.2	0.32	0.38	0.48	0.82	1.14	1.68	2.01	2.23	2.45	2.9
H-SVNM-D	5	6	8	10	13	20	34	50	78	107	155
LR-SVNM-D	65	52	22	30	13	448	107	627	1855	2053	1393

Figure 5. Convergence of the LR-SVNM algorithm

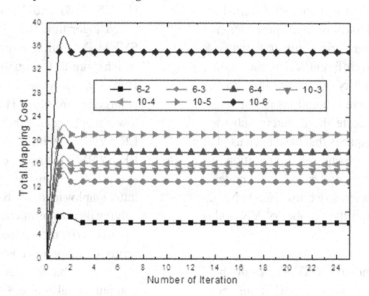

ficiency of our algorithms has been enhanced considerably compared with it of MILP. However, it is not as good as that of IOCM* and SOUM* algorithms. In addition we note that H-SVNM-M has worse performance compared to H-SVNM-D, and the time efficiency of LR-SVNM-M is not as good as it of LR-SVNM-D. The reason for this is that each sub-problem is solved by MILP in H-SVNM-M and LR-SVNM-M, while in H-SVNM-D and LR-SVNM-D all sub-problems are solved by using the heuristic algorithm D-ViNE*. However, we also note that heuristic algorithms H-SVNM-D and H-SVNM-M perform better than Lagrangian relaxation based algorithms LR-SVNM-M and LR-SVNM-D in terms of computational times since the latter have to solve the sub-problems iteratively.

Lagrangian Relaxation based algorithms reduce computational complexity efficiently, enhance time efficiency considerably, and guarantee the solution of original problem to converge to a stable one. However, their performance in terms of mapping cost and time efficiency is inferior to that of the heuristic algorithms, due to their inherent disadvantages such as iterative computation and loss of some feasible solutions. We can achieve a total mapping cost which is similar to the optimal value by using MILP for solving each sub-problem.

Figure 6. Comparison of total mapping cost: (a) simulation results for Net-1, (b) simulation results for Net-2, (c) simulation results for Net-3 and (d) simulation results for Net-4

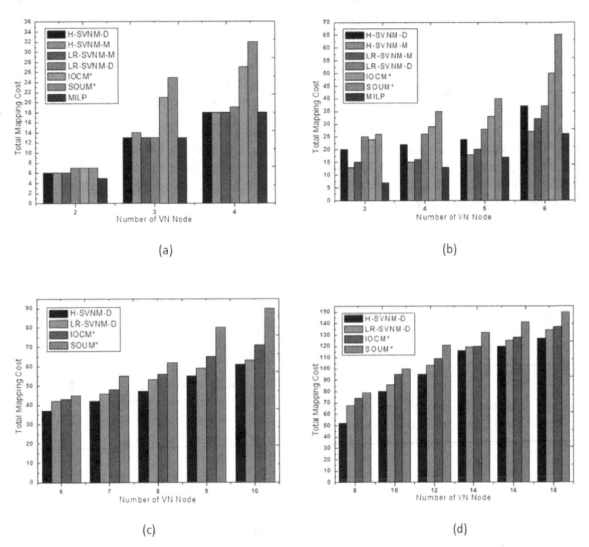

(a)

(b)

(c)

(d)

CONCLUSION

Network virtualization serves as an effective method for providing a flexible and highly adaptable shared substrate network for satisfying a diversity of demands. Thus in such a virtualized environment the problem of efficiently mapping a virtual network onto a shared substrate network becomes important. Since many virtual networks now share the resources of a common substrate network guaranteeing survivability of such a mapping efficiently is increasingly important and challenging. We formulate the survivable virtual network mapping problem with resource constraints as an MILP problem. However, this MILP problem is intractable since it is NP-hard. We propose two kinds of algorithms for solving this problem efficiently: Lagrangian Relaxation based algorithms and heuristic based algorithms. In our algorithms, we decompose primal problem into several sub-problems for reducing the complexity of computation and enhancing time efficiency. We compare the effectiveness of our approaches using detailed simulation under various substrate network and virtual network topologies. Our results show that our algorithms perform well and can provide a balanced tradeoff between time complexity and mapping costs.

In our future research work we propose to design online adaptive algorithms for the mapping of multiple virtual networks simultaneously considering random network failures. In particular, we will consider the case where the VN requests arrive dynamically according to a give distribution; we will explore algorithms that efficiently map the VN request with and without rearranging existing VN request and also consider survivability and bandwidth and resource sharing to minimize VN mapping cost while guaranteeing reliability.

REFERENCES

Anderson, T., Peterson, L., Shenker, S., & Turner, J. (2005). Overcoming the Internet impasse through virtualization. *Computer*, *38*(4), 34–41. doi:10.1109/MC.2005.136

Baranovski, A., Bharathi, S., Bresnahan, J., Chervenak, A., Foster, I., Fraser, D., et al. (2007). Enabling distributed petascale science. Journal of Physics: Conference Series, 78.

Butt, N. F., Chowdhury, M., & Boutaba, R. (2010). Topology-awareness and reoptimization mechanism for virtual network embedding. *Lecture Notes in Computer Science*, 27–39. doi:10.1007/978-3-642-12963-6_3

Chowdhury, N., & Boutaba, R. (2010). A survey of network virtualization. *Computer Networks*, *54*(5), 862–876. doi:10.1016/j.comnet.2009.10.017

Foster, I., Zhao, Y., Raicu, I., & Lu, S. (2008). Cloud computing and grid computing 360-degree compared. Grid Computing Environments Workshop, (pp. 1-10).

Houidi, I., Louati, W., Zeghlache, D., Papadimitriou, P., & Mathy, L. (2010). *Adaptive virtual network provisioning* (pp. 41–48). IEEE SIGCOMM.

Lischka, J., & Karl, H. (2009). A virtual network mapping algorithm based on subgraph isomorphism detection. ACM Workshop on Virtualized Infrastructure Systems and Architectures, (pp. 81-88).

Liu, X., Qiao, C., & Wang, T. (2009). Robust application specific and agile private (ASAP) networks withstanding multi-layer failures. Optical Fiber Conference (OFC), (pp. 1-3).

Luand, J., & Turner, J. (2006). Efficient mapping of virtual networks onto a shared substrate. Washington University Tech. Report, WUCSE 2006-35.

Mosharaf, N. M., Rahman, M. R., & Boutaba, R. (2009). Virtual network embedding with coordinated node and link embedding. IEEE International Conference on Computer Communication (INFOCOM), (pp. 783-791).

Mukherjee, B. (2006). *Optical WDM networks*. New York, NY: Springer.

Murthy, S., & Banerjee, S. (2009). Region-based connectivity - A new paradigm for design of fault-tolerant networks. IEEE Conference on High Performance Switching and Routing (HPSR), (pp. 1-7).

Pioro, M., & Medhi, D. (2004). *Routing, flow, and capacity design in communication and computer networks*. San Fransisco, CA: Elsevier.

Rahman, M. R., Aib, I., & Boutaba, R. (2010). Survivable virtual network embedding. *Lecture Notes in Computer Science*, 40–52. doi:10.1007/978-3-642-12963-6_4

Xu, D., Xiong, Y., Qiao, C., & Li, G. (2003). Trap avoidance and protection schemes in networks with shared risk links groups. *Journal of Lightwave Technology*, *21*(11), 2683–2693. doi:10.1109/JLT.2003.819545

Yang, X. (2011). QoS-oriented service computing: Bring SOA into cloud environment. In Liu, X. (Ed.), *Advanced design approaches to emerging software systems: Principles, methodology and tools*. Hershey, PA: IGI Global. doi:10.4018/978-1-60960-735-7.ch013

Yang, X., Nasser, B., Surrige, M., & Middleton, S. (2012). *A business-oriented cloud federation model for real time applications. Future Generation Computer Systems*. Elsevier.

Yu, H., Anand, V., Qiao, C., Di, H., & Wang, J. (2010). On the survivable virtual infrastructure mapping problem. IEEE International Conference on Computer Communication Networks (ICCCN), (pp. 199-204).

Yu, H., Anand, V., Qiao, C., & Sun, G. (2011). Cost efficient design of survivable virtual infrastructure to recover from facility node failures. IEEE International Conference on Communications (ICC), (pp. 1-6).

Yu, H., Qiao, C., Anand, V., Liu, X., Di, H., & Sun, G. (2010). Survivable infrastructure mapping in a federate computing and networking system under single regional failures. IEEE Global Communications Conference (GLOBECOM), (pp. 1-6).

Yu, M., Yi, Y., Rexford, J., & Chiang, M. (2008). *Rethinking virtual network embedding: Substrate support for path splitting and migration* (pp. 17–29). ACM SIGCOMM Computer Communication Review.

Zhu, Y., & Ammar, M. (2006). Algorithms for assigning substrate network resources to virtual network components. IEEE International Conference on Computer Communications (INFOCOM), (pp. 1-12).

KEY TERMS AND DEFINITIONS

Lagrangian Relaxation: A relaxation which approximates a difficult problem of constrained optimization by a simpler problem. A solution to the relaxed problem is an approximate solution to the original problem.

Mapping: The process of allocating physical network infrastructure including node and bandwidth resources to a virtual network so as to realize the virtual network.

Mixed Integer Linear Programming: A mathematical model for determining the maximization or minimization of a linear program wherein only some of the unknown variables are required to be integers.

Optical Network: A data network built using fiber-optics technology, which transmits information as light, through connected fiber strands. Optical networks offer an enormous increase in both transmission capacity and speed compared to traditional copper-wire based networks.

Regional Failure: Natural or man-made disasters that simultaneously affect a number of nodes and links of the network in the surrounding geographic region.

Resource Sharing: Techniques that exploit the sharing of network resources (usually bandwidth resources) by overlapping the backup bandwidth resources of disjoint failure conditions.

Substrate Network: The actual physical network (e.g. optical network) with bandwidth and node resources.

Survivability: The ability of a network to recover from failures. Requires detection of failure, backup resources and intelligent techniques to use these resources efficiently and reduce network downtime.

Virtual Network (or Virtual Network Request): A network with a logical/virtual topology defining the logical connectivity between virtual nodes and the required nodal and link capacities to which physical infrastructure has to be allocated to realize the virtual network.

Chapter 15
Reliability Analysis of Service Composition with Service Pools and Optimal Configuration of Service Pool Size

Pan He
Chongqing University, China

Qi Xie
Chongqing University, China

ABSTRACT

The reliability of applications in Cloud will be highly affected by the reliability of underlying service component. Service pools with redundant services are mainly used to improve the reliability of service composition. This chapter proposes an optimal service pool size configuration method aiming at minimizing the overall cost or response time of service composition while meeting certain reliability constraints. The reliability, cost, and response time analysis of service composition with multiple service pools is first analyzed using probability analysis method and architecture-based approach. After that, the optimization problem is presented and classified into three categories. For single-objective problems, a dynamic programming algorithm is presented to get near-optimal solutions. For multi-objective problems, a hybrid genetic algorithm is proposed to search nondominated sets of solutions. This hybrid genetic algorithm employs a sensitivity-based local search operator. Empirical studies results showed that the algorithms could find optimal solutions for the three kinds of problems and they outperformed the exiting approaches including greedy selection method and traditional genetic algorithms.

DOI: 10.4018/978-1-4666-2854-0.ch015

1. INTRODUCTION

As the service oriented architecture (SOA) turns out to be a great choice to build business applications(Li et al., 2010), web services and service composition have aroused the attention from both researchers and developers. For example, Google has published a variety of online APIs for users to invoke through standard format as json or xml, including map services(Google, 2012) and so on; there are dozens of services providing weather information throughout the world(WebXml, 2012). While could computing becomes more and more popular (Yang et al., 2012), web service and service compositions also appear to be the fundamental technologies in the Cloud computing environment since they could be invoked through the network (Yang, 2011). For instance, Amazon has delivered a set of services that together form a reliable, scalable, and inexpensive computing platform in the Cloud (Amazon, 2012). To deliver high reliable and sustainable services in Cloud environment, the reliability analysis and optimization of service composition has been a great concern to many researchers. Different from the traditional software components, web service in a composition could be replaced by other services with similar functionality in the runtime. To improve the reliability of web services and the corresponding composition, there are primarily two approaches (Dai et al., 2009). One is to reselect the service to use in the runtime (Zeng et al., 2004), but it is not feasible due to the time complexity of service discovery and selection, which may interrupt the service execution. The other is to rank services in advance and pre-select the service with the highest reliability (Wen et al., 2009). However, the pre-selected service might be unavailable during the runtime, so redundant services should be registered as backups (Zheng & Lyu, 2009). As a result, service pool has become the usual approach to improve the reliability perceived from the user side (Wang et al., 2009). Service pool is a set of redundant services with similar functionality and works like the traditional redundancy mechanism for a single service. Multiple service pools would be registered for different services in a single composition and the services pools are independent from each other.

The size of a service pool refers to the number of redundant services in the pool. Like traditional redundancy mechanism, reliability improvement could be achieved in runtime by increasing the service pool size for each service in a composition. However, increasing service pool size also brings more cost and decreases the overall performance. To achieve a balance between reliability and cost, it is a natural question of how to choose the appropriate size for each service pool in a composition. Existing works on optimal service pool size configuration mainly has three problems: 1) service pool size is determined from experiments without providing an analytical method on the service pool reliability evaluation. 2) Unlike traditional software systems which run on a single machine, response time is also an important measure for service composition or other distributed software systems. However, existing work don't consider the opposite impact of pool size change on service pool reliability and performance. 3) Only the local reliability is taken into consideration when choosing the pool size, while ignoring the whole service composition's reliability.

So this chapter aims to find the optimal service pool size for each service in a service composition aiming to minimize the overall response time and cost used in execution while meeting the reliability constraint. Similar as reliability redundancy allocation problems, cost and response time models are taken as the optimization objective while reliability model is used as the constraint functions. Since the services bind for service composition is available for failover all the time, we consider the active redundancy mechanism and evaluate the reliability, cost and performance model of service pool with different fault tolerant mechanisms. The reliability model of service pool is then combined with architecture-based reliability model to obtain the overall model for service composition with multiple service pools, and so is the case for the response time and cost. Based on the number of the optimization objectives and the different fault tolerant mechanisms, the problems could be categorized into single-objective problems to optimize either cost or time and multi-objective problem to optimize both of them. The cost optimization problem could be presented by a closed-form analytical model, so the Lagrange multiplier method (Bertsekas, 1996) is used to find the optimal solution. A dynamic programming method is used to find optimal solutions for response time optimization problem, which couldn't be presented by a closed-form model. For multi-objective problems, a sensitivity-based hybrid genetic algorithm is used to search the near-optimal solutions. As changes of the size of different service pool would have different impact on the overall reliability or response time, sensitivity analysis is employed to evaluate the impact. The size of service pools with higher impact on overall reliability improvement and lower impact on the performance will have a higher possibility to be increased. Thus, apart from the traditional genetic operators, a sensitivity-based local search operator is employed in this genetic algorithm to improve its effectiveness.

The whole chapter is organized as follows: section 2 provides the background and related work on service pool size choosing methods. Reliability, cost and performance analysis models for service composition with service pools are presented in section 3. Service pool size allocation problem is presented in section 4 with the corresponding algorithms. Empirical studies results and analysis are included in section 5 followed the future research directions in section 6. A brief conclusion of the whole chapter is attached in section 7.

2. BACKGROUND

A service composition is mainly made up of two parts: the workflow of abstract services and the pools of concrete services. Workflow defines the order and pattern of services to be executed, abstract services only define the functions to provide and they will be replaced by the concrete services in the execution time (Ardagna & Pernici, 2007). An example of service composition is given by Figure 1. As shown in Figure 1, S1, S2, ...and S10 are abstract services. Once failure occurs to the in-use service, without any fault tolerant mechanism, the failure will be passed to end users directly. Using service pool with redundant services, the unavailable service could be replaced by others in a single invocation. End users wouldn't perceive the failure until the services in one pool are all down. The concrete services S11, S12 and S13 form up a service pool for S1, S41 and S42 form another service pool and so is the case for S61, S62, S63 and S64. Apart from reliability, response time and cost are also important QoS attributes.

While many researchers have paid attention to fields related to setting up a service pool, only a few attentions are paid on evaluating the reliability of service pool with different pool size and choosing the size of service pool for a web service. Huang et al. (2006) considered the response time increase along with reliability improvement according to the service pool size increase. They proposed an optimal method to select redundant services of the pool aiming at minimizing the average response time. However, their research assumed that the service pool size for each service is certain and emphasized on selecting services with minimal response time according to a certain pool size. It didn't explain how to decide the size in detail. Liu et al. (2009) stated the use of redundant service binding to improve the reliability compared the reliability of capability provision with redundancy n. Experiments were conducted to compare the reliability of capability provision

Figure 1. Example of service composition with service pools

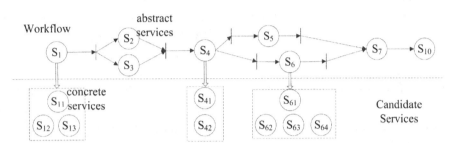

in the networks where one, two and three services providing a required function are bound, respectively. The capability configured with the highest redundancy achieves the highest reliability, so three services could be configured to deliver a critical capability with high assurance requirements. It also suggested that the provision of more services could lead to higher cost and affect affordability. As a result, two services could be considered for the development of non-critical capability, which can achieve a significantly improved reliability (compared with 1 service) with comparable low cost. However, this paper didn't provide a detailed analytical method to choose the pool size achieving the balance between reliability and cost. Meanwhile, it treated the service pool as independent components and didn't consider the change impact on overall reliability or performance of the service composition. Liu et al. (2010) also considered the service pool as a part of service-oriented workflow and presented a dynamic method to change the service pool size according to the workflow changes or reliability requirement changes. However, when choosing the pool size, only the local reliability constraints of the changed part of the workflow were taken into consideration instead of the global constraint. Zheng and Lyu (2008) evaluated several kinds of fault tolerance mechanism using for redundant services in service pool. They assessed the best replica number of redundant services in the service pool to obtain better latency and reliability performance. WS-DREAM used the parallel type of fault tolerance mechanism in the service pool and the experiment data showed that two replicas are

enough to provide high availability in the normal Internet environment, while three replicas are needed to ensure high reliability in the 5% faulty Internet environment. Six replicas obtained the best RTT performance, but not significant. So they finally chose 3 replicas to build a reliable service-oriented web site. Luo et al., (2009) considered redundant resources deployment in SOA and used an optimal method to identify the "weak point" of the framework, on which more redundant resources should be deployed. This chapter aimed at deploying resources for several workflows in the SOA environment and assign backups to those highly-used resources. It emphasized on achieving availability requirements of different workflows and didn't take the cost or performance of those workflows into consideration. Besides, the cost and performance model for resources (hardware, Web Server, OS) was different from that of web services.

3. RELIABILITY ANALYSIS OF SERVICE COMPOSITION WITH SERVICE POOLS

To calculate the service pool size from the point of view of the whole composition, we need to evaluate the reliability, cost and performance of service composition. The reliability evaluation of service composition could be divided into two steps: 1) treat the candidate services for a single abstract service as a whole and evaluate the reliability of the whole service pool with different fault tolerance mechanisms; 2) evaluate the reliability of service composition based on the workflow structure and the reliability of each service pool. And so is the case for performance and cost.

3.1 Reliability, Performance, and Cost Models of Single Service Pool

Two assumptions are made for this section and the following contents in advance.

1. Each service in the pool has the same QoS value, including the reliability, response time and cost. Although there might be some minor differences between the QoS values of these services, they often are selected according to the same QoS constraint. So we omit these differences and use the QoS constraint value to present the mean QoS value.

2. The failure of any in-use service will be successfully captured by monitoring mechanisms.

According to Zheng and Lyu (2008), there are generally two kinds of fault tolerant strategies used in the service pool: sequential-type strategies and parallel-type strategies. Using sequential-type strategy, one service is selected as the primary service in use with the others as the hot-standby backups. Once the primary service is detected to be down, the backup services should be selected to take the work according to specific orders generated in the service selection process (Wen et al., 2009). The kind of mechanism retries services in sequence, so it increases both response time and cost when failure occurs. The reliability of service pool under this scenario is the sum of probabilities of the pool returning successful results to users on different scenarios: Pr {service pool works successfully} = Pr {S1 works successfully} +Pr {S1 fails} * Pr {failure of S1 is captured} * Pr {S2 works successfully} +...According to assumption 2), Pr {failure of S1 is captured}=1. Let Rp denotes the expected reliability of service pool, Ri denotes the reliability of the ith service and n denotes the number of redundant services in the pool. The reliability model is shown as Equation1, where Rm denotes the mean reliability of services in a pool. According to the assumption 1), Equation 1 stands when the number of services in a pool is of high value. When the number of services is low, there might be minor differences between the QoS values of each service and the fluctuation of each service's QoS value can impact the value of Equation 1. However, as we have suggested, concrete services for one abstract service are often selected according to the same QoS constraint, which suggests that the QoS value of each service should be no less than the constraint value. In that case, we will omit these differences and use the reliability constraint value for the mean reliability value Rm.

$$R_p = R_1 + (1 - R_1)R_2 + (1 - R_1)(1 - R_2)R_3 + \ldots$$
$$= \sum_{i=1}^{n} (R_i \prod_{j=1}^{i-1} (1 - R_j)) = \sum_{i=1}^{n} R_m (1 - R_m)^{i-1} =$$
$$1 - (1 - R_m)^n$$

$$(1)$$

Let Tp denotes the expected response time perceived by the end user, Ti denotes the response time of the ith service. The response time of service pool is the sum of response time in different scenarios: Tp=T1*Pr{S1 works successfully}+ (T1+T2) *Pr{S1 fails}* Pr{S2 works successfully}+(T1+T2+T3)*Pr{S1 fails}*Pr{S2 fails}*Pr{S3 works successfully}+...Let Tm and Cm represent the mean response time and cost for services in a pool. Tp could be calculated as Equation 2. Similarly, expected cost of service composition Cp could be calculated by Equation 3

$$T_p = T_m R_m + 2T_m (1 - R_m)R_m + \ldots =$$
$$\sum_{i=1}^{n} i T_m R_m (1 - R_m)^{i-1} =$$
$$\frac{T_m}{R_m} (1 - (1 - R_m)^n (R_m n + 1))$$

$$(2)$$

$$C_p = \sum_{i=1}^{n} i C_m R_m (1 - R_m)^{i-1} =$$
$$\frac{C_m}{R_m}(1 - (1 - R_m)^n (R_m n + 1)) \tag{3}$$

The parallel-type fault tolerant strategy is different from sequential-type strategy in that the backup services are not tried by sequence but in parallel. In other words, any successful service in the pool will return the correct information and only the failure of all the services would cause the failure perceived by the end user. The reliability of service pool under this scenario equals to 1-Pr {all services in the pool fail}, which is the same as Equation 1: 1-(1-Rm)n. This kind of mechanism doesn't provide much difference to the response time of single invocation. However, the cost is highly raised for that every service will be paid for each invocation. The mean response time and mean cost of the service pool is could be represented by Equation 4 and Equation 5. Ni denotes the number of invocations when the ith services' result is taken use of and N denotes the overall number of invocations.

$$T_p = \frac{\sum_{i=1}^{n} N_i T_i}{N} = \frac{\sum_{i=1}^{n} N_i T_m}{N} = T_m \tag{4}$$

$$C_p = \sum_{i=1}^{n} C_i = \sum_{i=1}^{n} C_m = n C_m \tag{5}$$

From the Equation 4 and Equation 5, we could summarize that most of time, the response time is not affected. So we only consider the cost when using parallel type of fault tolerance.

3.2 Reliability, Performance, and Cost Models of Service Composition

Knowing the reliability of each service, the traditional architecture-based reliability model will be used here to evaluate the reliability of service composition. The architecture-based reliability model has been thoroughly researched and applied to component-based software reliability evaluation in decades. In this model, the control flow chart is changed into an absorbing discrete-time Markov chain (DTMC) model, in which each state represents the component and the transition among states denotes the control flow transition (Gokhale & Trivedi, 2006). There are generally six types of patterns in a service composition: sequence, loop, exclusive choice, exclusive join, parallel split, and parallel join (Huang et al., 2009). The first four types of patterns are the same as the control flow transition in traditional software architectures and could obey the feature of Markov chain. The major differences between the structure of service composition and the distributed software are the "parallel split" and "parallel join", which implies that services may be executed in parallel, conflicting with the feature of Markov chains. Let pij denotes the transition possibility of service i to service j in the composition. In the component-based software, the transition probabilities are often calculated from the operational profiles of applications (Gokhale & Trivedi, 2006). If the operational profile of this service composition could be collected, the transition probability pij could be calculated as the probability of service j being invoked on the condition of service i's presence, as shown by Equation 6 (Ren et al., 2009).

$$p_{ij} = \Pr\{S_j \mid S_i\} = \frac{\Pr\{S_j \ \& \ S_i\}}{\Pr\{S_i\}} \tag{6}$$

However, in the service-oriented scenario, it is difficult to get complete operation profiles without monitoring. Therefore, the transition probabilities could only be estimated by the experts or from the number of successive services. In sequence, exclusive join, parallel split, and parallel join patterns, the value of pij equals to 1. In loop and exclusive choice patterns, the value of pij depends on the choice situation. For example, if k services could be transited from Si, the transition probability could be assigned as 1/k.

To transform the service composition into computable DTMC, we will first separate the services with parallel patterns from the whole composition, then calculate the reliability, cost and performance of each sub-composition and at last aggregate these values together.

The separation process mush obeys the following rules: 1) Sub-compositions could be atomic services or a group of composite services. 2) Only three kinds of patterns are allowed between sub-compositions: sequence, parallel join and parallel split. 3) Only four kinds of patterns are allowed inside the sub-compositions: sequence, loop, exclusive choice, and exclusive join. The pseudo code of separation process is given in Box 1.

To illustrate the separation process more clearly, a workflow-based service composition is used as the example (Xia et al., 2006), shown by Figure 2. This composition is used because it has six types of basic workflow patterns.

According to the given selection probability and skipping probability listed in by in Xia et al.' research (2006), we could get the transition probability of the composition above, as shown by Figure 3(a). As parallel split and parallel join exists in the composition, divide the composition into five parts as Figure 3(b) shows, where S-Ci indicates the ith sub-composition. As shown by Figure 3(b), there is no parallel-running relationship between services in each sub-composition. The reliability and quality value for each part are computed and then aggregated together.

After separation, the whole composition is divided into several sub-compositions without parallel processing, so the architecture-based approach could be used. A DTMC model will be built on top of the sub-compositions according to the workflow and the transition probabilities. Each state in the DTMC represents the abstract service in the workflow and the transition between states refers to the transition of control flow between services. Assuming each abstract service is bound with a service pool with at least one concrete service; the atomic service could be viewed as the service pool with only one service. For either type of fault tolerance mechanism, the reliability of a service pool could be evaluated through the same model as Equation 1. The DTMC generated from sub-compositions is an absorbing Markov chain with absorbing states. Using the hierarchy approach (Trivedi, 2001), we could obtain Vj, the mean number of visits to the service pool j which can computed from the transition probability matrix [pij]. The expected reliability of the sub-composition Rs is shown in Equation 7, with mi denoting the number of abstract services in the ith sub-composition, Rpj denotes the reliability of jth service pool.

$$R_s = \prod_{j=1}^{m_i} R_{p_j}^{V_j} \tag{7}$$

Since the sub-compositions are only connected by sequence, parallel-split and parallel-join. The sub-compositions connected by sequence pattern work just like sequential systems, and those between a pair of parallel-split and parallel-join also form up parallel running systems. The reliability of bother two kinds of systems are the product of the reliability of each sub-system. As a result, the reliability of the whole composition Rc is the product of each sub- composition's reliability, as shown by Equation 8. k denotes the number of sub-compositions, m denotes the number of overall services in the composition, nj denotes the size of the jth service pool and Rmj denotes the mean reliability of each service in the jth pool.

$$R_c = \prod_{y=1}^{k} R_{s_y} = \prod_{j=1}^{m} R_{p_j}^{V_j} = \prod_{j=1}^{m} (1-(1-R_{m_j})^{n_j})^{V_j} \tag{8}$$

Similarly, the cost of the overall composition is the sum of the cost of each sub-composition. Using

Box 1.

```
function separate_composition: separating the sub-composition indexing from x1
to x2
input: a matrix representing the transition possibilities between service i
and service j: [pij];
beginning index of the sub-composition: x1; end index of the sub-composition:
x2
output: an array of a pair of indexes representing the sub compositions: sub_
composition_array
if x1= x2, the input sub-composition is a atomic service, put (x1, x2) into
sub_composition_array directly.
else for i= x1 to x2
if   ∑   p  >1, parallel split exists, record i into the list of the begin node
   for all k  ik
of parallel split X1.
for j= x1 to x2
if   ∑   p  >1, parallel join exists, record j into the list of the end node of
   for all k  kj
parallel split X2.
if X1 is not empty, separate_composition ([pij],x1, X1[1]-1);
for k= 1 to sizeof(X1)
        separate_composition([pij], X1[k], X2[k]);
separate_composition ([pij], X2[sizeof(X2)]+1, x2);
else if X1 is empty, put (x1, x2) into sub_composition_array.
```

the hierarchy approach, we can also calculate the cost of sub-composition Cs as the sum of cost of each service pool. The overall cost Cc is shown by Equation 9. Cpj is the mean cost of the jth service pool computed through Equation 3 and Equation 5 depending on different fault tolerance mechanism. Csy is the cost the yth sub-composition.

$$C_c = \sum_{y=1}^{k} C_{s_y} = \sum_{j=1}^{m} V_j C_{p_j} =$$
$$\begin{cases} \sum_{j=1}^{m} V_j \dfrac{C_{m_j}}{R_{m_j}} (1-(1-R_{m_j})^{n_j}(R_{m_j} n_j+1)) & sequential \\ \sum_{j=1}^{m} V_j n_j C_{m_j} & parallel \end{cases}$$

(9)

The response time of sequential systems is the sum of the response time of each part, while the response time of parallel running systems will be the longest time of each part, shown by Equation 10.

$$T_{s_y} =$$
$$\begin{cases} \sum_{j=1}^{m_i} V_j T_{p_j} & sequential\ system \\ \{V_k T_{p_k} \mid for\ each\ j \in [1, m_i],\ V_k T_{p_k} \geq V_j T_{p_j}\} \\ parallel\ system \end{cases}$$

(10)

According to Equation 10, we don't need to consider every service in response time calculation. We suppose Y and Z are the set of indexes of sub-compositions and abstract services used to compute the response time respectively. Since we only consider extra response time using sequential fault tolerance, the overall response time Tc is

Figure 2. Sample service composition

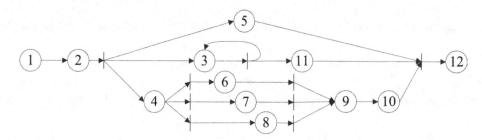

Figure 3. (a) Example DTMC of service composition; (b) separated service composition

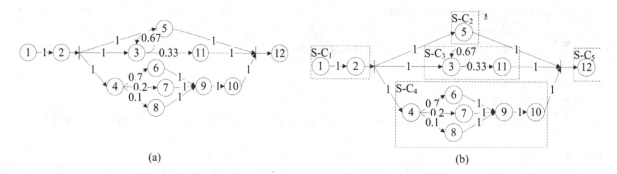

(a)   (b)

shown in Equation 11. The model of response time couldn't be represented in a closed-form analytical model because the value varies according to different sets of Z, which further depends on the structure of the composition, individual service's response time and individual service pool size

$$T_c = \sum_{y \in Y} T_{s_y} = \sum_{j \in Z} V_j T_{p_j} =$$
$$\sum_{j \in Z} V_j \frac{T_{m_j}}{R_{m_j}} (1 - (1 - R_{m_j})^{n_j} (R_{m_j} n_j + 1)) \quad (11)$$

3.3 Sensitivity Analysis

Size change of different pools will have different impact on the value of the overall reliability or overall response time. Sensitivity analysis could help in analyzing the influence of the change in service pool size on the overall performance, cost and reliability metrics. The impact of a change in the size of service pool j on the overall expected reliability can be obtained by differentiating the

expected reliability of the system as given by Equation 8 with respect to nj. From Equation 8, we have the partial differential ∂Rc/∂nj as shown in Equation 12. Since Rc is the same for each nj, the order of values of each partial differentials ∂Rc/∂nj is mainly determined by the value of

$$\frac{V_j(-(1 - R_{m_j})^{n_j}) \ln(1 - R_{m_j})}{1 - (1 - R_{m_j})^{n_j}},$$

defined as dRj. We will take dRj into consideration while evaluating the impact of size change of each service pool on the overall composition reliability.

$$\frac{\partial R_c}{\partial n_j} = \frac{\partial R_c}{\partial R_{p_j}} \cdot \frac{\partial R_{p_j}}{\partial n_j} =$$
$$(V_j R_{p_j}^{V_j - 1} \prod_{k=1 \& k \neq j}^{m} R_{p_k}^{V_k}) \cdot (-(1 - R_{m_j})^{n_j} \ln(1 - R_{m_j})) =$$
$$R_c \cdot \frac{V_j}{1 - (1 - R_{m_j})^{n_j}} \cdot (-(1 - R_m)^{n_j} \cdot \ln(1 - R_m))$$

$$(12)$$

The impact of a change in the size of service pool j on the overall expected cost can be obtained by differentiating the expected cost of the system as given by Equation 9 with respect to nj. The partial differential ∂Cc/∂nj for compositions with sequential and parallel type of fault tolerances is shown in Equation 13. Defining dCj as ∂Cc/∂nj, dCj also will be taken into consideration while choosing the service pool size combination as well as dRj. The impact of a change in the size of service pool j on the overall expected response time can be got by differentiating the expected response time of the system as given by Equation 11 with respect to nj, shown by Equation 14. However, it is also not a closed-form model because of Tc, so the impact of a change in the size of service pool j on the overall expected response time can be calculated as

$$\Delta T_j = T_c\left(n_1, n_2, \ldots n_j + 1, \ldots n_m\right) - T_c\left(n_1, n_2, \ldots n_j, \ldots n_m\right).$$

$$\frac{\partial C_c}{\partial n_j} = \begin{cases} -V_j \dfrac{C_{m_j}}{R_{m_j}}(1 - R_{m_j})^{n_j}(\ln(1 - R_{m_j}) \\ (R_{m_j} n_j + 1) + R_{m_j}) \quad \text{sequential} \\ V_j C_{m_j} \quad\quad\quad \text{parallel} \end{cases}$$

$$(13)$$

$$\frac{\partial T_c}{\partial n_j} = \begin{cases} -V_j \dfrac{T_{m_j}}{R_{m_j}}(1 - R_{m_j})^{n_j}(\ln(1 - R_{m_j}) \\ (R_{m_j} n_j + 1) + R_{m_j}) \\ j \in Z \ sequential \\ V_j \\ j \in Z \ parallel \\ 0 \\ j \notin Z \ sequential \ and \ parallel \end{cases}$$

$$(14)$$

4. OPTIMAL SERVICE POOL SIZE CONFIGURATION

4.1 Problem Formulation

1.   Cost optimization problem (P1)

In cost optimization, we will use the overall cost of the composition as the optimization objective while the reliability of the composition is used as the constraint function. As shown in Equation 15, R0 denotes the reliability constraint for the composition. For cost optimization, both the sequential type of fault tolerance and the parallel type of fault tolerance could both be used.

$$\begin{cases} \text{Min } C_c = C(n_j) \\ \text{s.t. } R_c = R(n_j) \geq R_0 \end{cases} \quad (15)$$

2.   Time optimization problem (P2)

In time optimization, we will use the response time as the optimization objective while the reliability of the composition is used as the constraint function, as shown in Equation 16. For time optimization, only the sequential type of fault tolerance will be taken into consideration.

$$\begin{cases} \text{Min } T_c = T(n_j) \\ \text{s.t. } R_c = R(n_j) \geq R_0 \end{cases} \quad (16)$$

3.   Multi-objective optimization problem (P3)

In multi-objective optimization problem, the response time, the cost and the overall number of redundant services are used as the objectives and the reliability are used as the constraint function, shown by Equation 17. For multi-objective optimization, only sequential type of fault tolerance will be considered.

$$\begin{cases} \text{Min } N = \displaystyle\sum_{j=1}^{m} n_j \\ \text{Min } T_c = T(n_j) \\ \text{Min } C_c = C(n_j) \\ \text{s.t. } R_c = R(n_j) \geq R_0 \end{cases} \tag{17}$$

4.2 Mathematical Solution (for P1)

In P1, since both Rc and Cc could be represented as simple closed-form models, the mathematical method could be used to solve the problem to get the optimal solutions. According to Equation 9, Rc could be converted into a function of nj. To simplify the equations, we define g(n1,n2,…,nm)= Rc-R0 also take the logarithm on it as shown by Equation 18.

$$\ln g(n_1, n_2, \ldots n_m) = \sum_{j=1}^{m} V_j \ln(1 - (1 - R_{m_j})^{n_j}) \geq 0 \tag{18}$$

Let $X_j = 1 - (1 - R_{m_j})^{n_j}$, $\overline{R_{m_j}} = 1 - R_{m_j}$, we can get $n_j = \ln(1 - X_j)\big/\ln \overline{R_{m_j}}$. So g(n1,n2,… nm) could also be converted to g(X1, X2, …Xm), shown by Equation 19. Similarly, Cc could also be converted into a function of Xj and f(X1, X2, …Xm), shown by Equation 20.

$$g(X_1, X_2, \ldots, X_m) = \sum_{j=1}^{m} V_j \ln X_j \tag{19}$$

$$f(X_1, X_2, \ldots, X_m) = \\ \begin{cases} \displaystyle\sum_{j=1}^{m} V_j \frac{C_{m_j}}{R_{m_j}} (1 - R_{m_j}^{\frac{\ln(1-X_j)}{\ln \overline{R_{m_j}}}} (R_{m_j} \frac{\ln(1-X_j)}{\ln \overline{R_{m_j}}} + 1)) \\ \quad sequential \\ \displaystyle\sum_{j=1}^{m} V_j C_{m_j} \frac{\ln(1-X_j)}{\ln \overline{R_{m_j}}} \quad parallel \end{cases} \tag{20}$$

Following the Lagrange multiplier method (Bertsekas, 1996), we construct the auxiliary function F(X1,X2,…,Xm, λ)= f(X1, X2, …Xm)+λg(X1, X2, …Xm), as Equation 21, to calculate the optimal solution, where f(X1, X2, … Xm)denotes the utility function, and g(X1, X2, … Xm) denotes the function for the constraint space.

$$F(X_1, X_2, \ldots, X_m, \lambda) = \\ \begin{cases} \displaystyle\sum_{j=1}^{m} V_j \frac{C_{m_j}}{R_{m_j}} (1 - R_{m_j}^{\frac{\ln(1-X_j)}{\ln \overline{R_{m_j}}}} (R_{m_j} \frac{\ln(1-X_j)}{\ln \overline{R_{m_j}}} + 1)) \\ \quad + \lambda \displaystyle\sum_{j=1}^{m} V_j \ln X_j \quad sequential \\ \displaystyle\sum_{j=1}^{m} V_j C_{m_j} \frac{\ln(1-X_j)}{\ln \overline{R_{m_j}}} + \lambda \displaystyle\sum_{j=1}^{m} V_j \ln X_j \quad parallel \end{cases} \tag{21}$$

The closed lower boundary of the solution to the equation g(X1, X2, …Xm)≥0 will include the optimal solution (Luo et al., 2009). In that case λg(X1, X2, …Xm)≈0 and the value of f(X1, X2, …Xm) will be near equal to the value F(X1,X2,… ,Xm, λ). So the optimal problem is converted to get the minimum value of F(X1,X2,…,Xm,λ). By calculating the following partial derivatives ∂F/∂ni, as Equation 22, we can get the minimum value of F(X1,X2,…,Xm, λ) and meanwhile we can get the corresponding values of Xj and nj, which are the optimal combination of service pool size.

$$\begin{cases} \dfrac{\partial F(X_1, X_2, \ldots, \lambda)}{\partial X_j} = 0 \quad for \ all \ j \in [1, m] \\ \dfrac{\partial F(X_1, X_2, \ldots, \lambda)}{\partial \lambda} = 0 \end{cases} \tag{22}$$

The Lagrange multiplier method could get optimal solutions for the problem P1, but it is quite different to implement in most scenarios because of the complexity of partial derivatives calculation. Meanwhile, sometimes it would be impossible to present a simplified form of the utility function or constraint function. Thus, more general algorithms should be used to solve the problems.

4.3 Dynamic Programming (for P1 and P2)

The traditional exhaustive iteration algorithm could also be employed to find the optimal service pool size combination. Assuming the upper bound of the size to be searched for each service pool is K and the number of abstract services in the composition is m, the time complexity of the traditional method will be O(mK), which might be extremely high for large compositions. To reduce the time complexity of exhaustive iteration algorithm, a greedy selection method based on sensitivity analysis is proposed by He et al. (2011) to get near-optimal solutions in short time. However, this method could not find the real optimal solutions. So, in this subsection, a dynamic programming algorithm (DPA) is proposed to solve more general problems, in which it is difficult to conduct partial derivatives calculation.

Since every abstract service in a service composition has one least one concrete service, we define N as the overall number of extra redundant services in a service composition:

$$N = (\sum_{j=1}^{m} n_j) - m.$$

We can transform the problem into allocating N redundant services among m positions with different reliability and cost (or response time). Number the services from 1 to m, let x(i,j) denotes the best service pool size combination(or best solution) for the optimal problem of allocating j redundant services among first i services,

$$x(i,j) = \left[n_1, n_2, \ldots n_i, \underbrace{1, 1 \ldots, 1}_{m-i} \right], j = (\sum_{k=1}^{i} n_k) - i.$$

We can calculate x(i,j) from the previous solutions as shown by Equation 23, where $\underset{y \in [0,N]}{\prec}$ de-

notes that the selected solution $\prec$ any other solutions in the set.

$$x(i,j) = \begin{cases} \underset{y \in [0,i]}{\prec} \{[x(i-1,j-y),y]\}, & \text{if } i > 1 \,\&\, j > 0 \\ [1,1,\ldots,1]_i, & \text{if } j = 0 \\ [j], & \text{if } i = 1 \end{cases}$$

$$(23)$$

We define a dominate operator $\prec$ as:

x(i,j)1 $\prec$ x(i,j)2, if R(x(i,j)2) < R0 and R(x(i,j)1) > R(x(i,j)2)

or if R(x(i,j)2) ≥ R0 and R(x(i,j)1) ≥ R0 and C(x(i,j)1) < C(x(i,j)2)(or T(x(i,j)1) < T(x(i,j)2)).

The pseudo code of dynamic programming process is given in Box 2.

The DPA could be used for both closed-form models (P1) and other models (P2). Supposing the time complexity of computing the $\prec$ operation is 1, the time complexity of this algorithm is O(m2*N02). Assuming the space complexity for storing the redundancy for each service is 1, the space complexity is O(m2*N0). This algorithm also reduces the time complexity comparing with exhaustive iteration algorithm, the time complexity of which is O(mK). However, this algorithm also has two shortcomings: 1) the overall redundancy N0 could not be determined in advance and lower value N0 still may lead to worse solutions, so we may have to rerun the algorithms for multiple times to achieve the best value of N0; 2) this algorithm could not be used for multi-objective problems like P3.

4.4 Multi-Objective Genetic Algorithm (for P1, P2, and P3)

To solve the multi-objective allocation problems in traditional systems, researchers either transfer the problem into single-objective problem(Sasaki &

Box 2.

```
function dynamic_programming: find optimal solutions for x(m,N0)
input: the mean number of visits to the service pool j: Vj ;
reliability, cost(or response time) of each service Rmj and Cmj(or Tmj);
maximal overall redundancy N0; number of services:m.
output: the best solution for x(m,N0) and the corresponding reliability,
cost(or response time).
for n=m..N0
define X1=an array of size m×(n+1), each node of this array X1(i,j) is a 1×m
vector representing the best redundancy of each service for allocation i-1
redundancy to first j services.
initialize X1(i,1)=[1]m(1≤i≤m), X1(1,j)=[j, (1)m-1](1≤j≤n).
for i=2..m
for j=2..n
for y=0..j, ny=Xi-1(i-1,j-y+1), ny(i)=ny(i)+y
 choose the solution nk ≺other ny (1≤k,y≤j, k≠y)
 record the nk: Xi(i,j+1)=nk
 if R(Xm(m,n+1)) ≥R0, break the outer loop.
end
output Xm(m,n+1), R(Xm(m,n+1)) and C(Xm(m,n+1)) (or T(Xm(m,n+1))).
```

Gen, 2003) or employ evolutionary algorithms to obtain a nondominated set (Busacca, Marseguerra, & Zio, 2001). Among the evolutionary algorithms, NSGA-II (Deb et al., 2002) and the related algorithms are proved to be effective methods to find nondominated solutions. Existing algorithms are too general to be fitted to service-oriented environments because it often take too much time for them to converge to a large set of nondominated solutions while service compositions redundancy allocation calls for real-time processing.

After analyzing the sensitivity of reliability, cost and performance as shown in last section, we can conclude that changing size of different service pool has different impact on the reliability or cost. So the traditional algorithms could be improved on the following two rules.

Rule 1: As we want to get size combination resulting higher reliability and lower cost, we should consider those service pool first, the change of which will have the higher impact on reliability and lower impact on cost (or response time).

Rule 2: With the increase of the service pool size, the reliability of one service will increase, but the increase rate will gradually decrease. That is to say, no matter how large the pool size is, there is a limit for the reliability of one abstract service. So the size searching process for a single service pool could stop when there is only a minor change in the reliability with the increase of size of that pool.

Based on the above considerations, a sensitivity-based hybrid genetic algorithm (HGA) is used to find near-optimal solutions. In the population initialization process of the hybrid genetic algorithm, the sensitivity analysis is employed to assign more redundancy on services having higher impact on reliability improvement and lower impact on cost/time increase. This kind of strategy is used to generate better initial individuals and help the algorithm to converge faster. Since our problem is a discrete optimization problem, the single-point crossover operator and bitwise mutation operator seem to find good solutions in a long time. To decrease the overall computation time, a local search procedure using random walk with direction exploitation method is used to generate new individuals instead of traditional generic operators. To avoid the algorithm to converge to local best solutions to fast, the nondominated sorting method is used to sort and select individuals in the next generation. Similarly, a solution p1 is said to constraint_dominate p2 on the following conditions.

1. In single-objective problems, p1 constraint_ dominate p2 if p1 $\prec$ p2.
2. In multi-objective problems, p1 constraint_ dominate p2 if R(p2) < R0 and R(p1) > R(p2) or if R(p2) ≥ R0 and R(p1) ≥ R0 and none the objective values calculated by p2 is better than that of p1.

The redundancy, cost and response time under two types of fault tolerance mechanism is used as the objective values in nondominated fonts and crowding distance calculation. Nondominated fonts and crowding distance could be calculated using fast_non_dominated_sort() and crowding_distance_assignement() respectively and the details of the two functions could refer to Deb et al.'s research (2002).

The pseudo code of HGA's framework is shown in Box 3.

Two main steps of this algorithm are listed below.

1. Sensitivity-based Population Initialization

The initial population is generated with N individuals P0= {p1,p2,...,pN}. Each individual pi($1 \leq i \leq N$) is an array of integer number range from 1 to a predefined maximal number: pi={n1, n2,..., nm}i. The initial value of nj($1 \leq j \leq m$) will be assigned to 1 by default. Then the sensitivity-based initialization process will be carried to assign a random value from 1 to a predefined maximal value to nj according to the following rules.

Step 1: Calculate a rough sensitivity value for each service j.

From Equation 12, 13, 14, we can observe that the sensitivity of service redundancy change is also related to the value of nj. Generally speaking, with the increase of nj, the sensitivity value will gradually decrease. Besides, the sensitivity of response time change is difficult to be presented in closed form functions. So we define dj($1 \leq j \leq m$) as Equation 24 and take dj into consideration while evaluating the impact of redundancy change of each service.

$$d_j = \frac{\Delta R_j}{\Delta T_j \Delta C_j}$$
$$= \frac{R_c(n_1,...n_j+1,...n_m) - R_c(n_1,...n_j,...n_m)}{(T_c(n_1,...n_j+1,...n_m) - T_c(n_1,...n_j,...n_m))(C_c(n_1,...n_j+1,...n_m) - C_c(n_1,...n_j,...n_m))}$$
(24)

Step 2: For each service j ($1 \leq j \leq m$), a weight value wj, as shown in Equation 25, is assigned according to the value of dj.

$$w_j = \begin{cases} w_{j-1} + \dfrac{d_j}{\sum\limits_{j=1}^{m} d_j} & 1 \leq j \leq m \\ 0 & j = 0 \end{cases}$$
(25)

Step 3: Roulette wheel selection method will be used to randomly select a service k in pi according to the value of wj and assign a random value to nk.

Box 3.

```
Set offspring population Q0=∅, generation counter t=0.
Initialize population P0 with N individuals, P0= {p1,p2,…,pN} based on sensi-
tivity analysis.
While t<tmax(the maximum generation number)
Randomly choose 5% of the individuals from Pt.
For each chosen individual, use random walk-based local search algorithm to
generate new individuals and include the feasible solutions into Qt.
Combine parent and offspring population Rt=Pt ∪Qt.
Calculate objective values and constraints values of individuals in Rt.
Calculate nondominated fonts and crowding distance for elements in Rt.
Sort Rt in descending order using nondominated fonts and crowding distance and
fill Pt+1 with first N individuals.
Set t=t+1.
End
Output Pt
```

2. Random Walk based Local Search Strategy

A local search operator instead of genetic operators will be used to generate new population form the old one. Instead of performing local search on each individual, we will randomly choose about 5% of the solutions to perform local search. To avoid losing generality in local search, the random selection process will be conducted according the following rules.

1. The whole population will be separated into groups according their nondominated fonts. The individual in the same group will have the same font value.

2. The selection will guarantee that each group of solution has a same probability to be selected.

Using this kind of strategy, we can guarantee that solutions with the best or worst font value will all be selected. The local search strategy could be divided into the following steps.

Step 1: Using fast_non_dominated_sort() (Deb et al., 2002) to calculate the fonts of each individual and individual with the font value i will be grouped into Fi.

Step 2: Randomly generate an integer k from 0 to the maximal size of fonts.

Step 3: Choose Fk and randomly select an individual from Fk.

Step 4: After a solution is randomly chosen, the local search strategy iteratively searches its neighbors and includes feasible solutions. In each step of search process, a random cell is chosen from the individual and the value of that cell will be added and subtracted by one. The new generated individuals will be checked whether they are nondominated solutions. If so, they will be included into acceptable solutions and the neighbors of the new individuals will be searched again. The pseudo code of local search method is shown in Box 5.

5. EMPIRICAL STUDIES

In this section, we report our empirical studies results of the above approaches by evaluating a sample service composition. The experimental

Box 4.

```
for i=1..m
randomly generate a value q between 0 and 1.
the first service who meets the following requirement will be selected: wj ≥q
and the index of this service will be recorded as k.
randomly generate nk =a random value between 1 and the maximum redundancy val-
ue.
if the reliability of composition Rc=R(nj) ≥R0, break the loop and start to
generate the next individual pi+1.
end
```

studies were designed to consist of two parts. First, reliability, cost and response time evaluation were carried out using sample data along with sensitivity analysis. Second, the performance of our algorithms was evaluated and the results were compared with sensitivity-based method and some other multi-objective genetic algorithms.

The same example composition shown by Figure 2 is also used in this section. To evaluate the algorithm in this composition, we have simulated 10 groups of reliability, performance and cost data for 12 services in it. These reliability and response time data single service are randomly chosen from the experiment data collected from real services in the network. Two datasets are mainly used to generate the test cases: (1) the QWS Dataset (Al-Masri & Mahmoud, 2007) and (2) dataset collected by WS-DREAM (Zheng & Lyu, 2010). The cost of each service won't change during certain amount of time so we simulate cost data for each service. The selected and simulated data follow the following rules: reliability of single service ≥ 0.85, cost of single service ≤ 100 cents per invocation, mean response time of single service ≤ 500ms. The maximal service pool size is set to 5.

5.1 Reliability Analysis of Service Composition

In this sub-section, a case study is presented to illustrate the reliability, cost and response time analysis process of service composition shown by Figure 2. As we illustrated before, after separation process, the composition in Figure 2 could be transformed to sub-compositions in Figure 3(b). The models will be used in the following experiments. The architecture-based model is used to solve each sub composition to get the Vj for each service in Figure 3(b) as: [Vj]={1, 1,3.03,1,1,0.7,0.2,0.1,1,1,1}. Originally there is no service pool registered for this composition, which means the service pool size is equal to 1 for each service and the reliability of each service is equal to the reliability of the atomic service, so we can achieve Rc=R1R2R33.03R4R5R60.7 R70.2R80.1R9R10R11R12. Similarly, we could get the model for Cc=C1+C2+3.03C3+C4+C5 +0.7C6+0.2C7+0.1C8+C9+C10+C11+C12 and Tc= T1+T2+Max {T5, 3.03T3+ T11, T 4+0.7T 6+0.2T 7+0.1T 8+T 9+T10}+T 12.

Tc= T1+T2+0.7*Max {T5, 3.03T3+ T11, T 4+T 6+T 9+T10}+0.2*Max {T5, 3.03T3+ T11, T 4+T 7+T 9+T10}+0.1*Max{T5, 3.03T3+ T11, T 4+T 8+T 9+T10}+T 12.

A group of sample data randomly chosen from the test cases is taken as the example. The reliability, cost, response time of atomic service is listed in Table 1 along with the overall reliability, cost and response time calculated by our model.

This case study indicates that although each service's reliability is larger than 0.85, the reliability of the whole composition is relatively low

Box 5.

```
function local_search_procedure
input: individual to be searched: xt; the number of times searched: t
output: feasible solutions Q
x=xt, t=t+1, if t > maximal search times, break.
randomly generate index i from 1 to m.
if xt[i] > 1, xt[i]=xt[i]-1, generate neighbors.
if xt constraint_dominate x, include xt into feasible solutions Q and Local_
search_procedure(xt, t).
if xt[i] < predefined max number, xt[i]=xt[i]+1, generate neighbors.
if xt constraint_dominate x, include xt into feasible solutions Q and Local_
search_procedure(xt, t).
end
```

without service pools, so introducing service pool into the composition is necessary. To show the different impact of size change of different service pool, sensitivity analysis was also conducted. First of all, the size of each service pool was increased gradually to show the impact of its change on the service composition reliability. The data in Table 1 was also used as the example to show the result. Figure 4(a) shows the impact of size change of individual service pool. Then, the size of each pool is increased gradually to show the impact of its change on the service composition cost. Two kinds of fault tolerance mechanism bring about different impact. Figure 4(b) shows the impact of size change on cost using the sequential fault tolerance and Figure 4 (c) shows the impact of parallel type. Similarly, the impact of service pool size change on the response time of the service composition is shown in Figure 4(d). For response time increase, only sequential type of fault tolerance mechanism is used.

The results showed that: 1) Size change of different service pool has different impact for the overall reliability, cost or response time. 2) The changing impact gradually decreases with the increase of service pool size, that is to say, changing the pool size of single web service will lead the reliability to reach some limit value. 3) Even the same service also has different impact on

reliability, cost or response time change. 4) Under the two types of circumstance, the size increase of the same service pool will cause different cost to the composition. The overall cost of parallel type is much higher than that of the sequential type as the pool size grows. Besides, the cost of sequential fault tolerance also increases to reach some threshold while the cost of parallel type will continually increase with the pool size. This case study shows the necessity of restrict the size change of service pools in the composition to decrease the cost and response time.

5.2 Single-Objective Optimal Pool Size Configuration

In this sub-section, DPA and HGA are used to solve single-objective optimal pool size configuration problem. The population size of HGA was set to 100 and the number of iteration was set to 200. Two single-objective methods proposed by He et al. (2011): sensitivity-based greedy algorithm (SGA) and general greedy algorithm (GGA) were used to compare with the approaches. To illustrate our methods first, the same group of parameters shown in Table 1 was first used and reliability constraint value was set to 0.95. The original reliability of the composition without service pools is 0.319, so service pool need to

Table 1. Service composition reliability, cost and response time

	S1	S2	S3	S4	S5	S6	S7	S8	S9	S10	S11	S12
R	0.974	0.855	0.880	0.922	0.907	0.892	0.875	0.883	0.894	0.955	0.925	0.941
C(cent)	36.7	60	52.5	10	6.7	70	26.7	13.3	13.3	24.4	5	18
T(ms)	45	71.75	117	105.2	108.2	125.2	110.3	125.2	105.4	129	114	96
Rc	0.319											
Cc(cent)	379.86											
Tc(ms)	681.26											

be deployed for services. Table 2 shows the best solutions obtained by four methods and the result of the exhaustive iteration method (EM). Due to the features of SGA, it is only used for P1. HGA is carried on for only one objective.

Data in Table 2 showed that using both DPA and HGA could find better solutions than other approaches and the solutions found by HGA were quite close to those found by exhaustive iteration method. It suggested that HGA could be used to find optimal solutions for the problem. However, the solutions found by HGA result in a large number of overall redundancy services. Then, the reliability constraint value was set from 0.90 to 0.99 and the same group of parameter was used. For each reliability constraint value, HGA was carried out for 10 times. The best solutions of the four methods were shown in Figure 5 along with the solutions obtained by exhaustive iteration algorithm. The result in Figure 5 showed that HGA outperformed other solutions in both P1 and P2. In few test cases (e.g. R0 =0.99), SGA and CGA seemed to achieve better solutions than HGA, however, the reliability of the corresponding solutions couldn't meet the reliability constraint. DPA could find better solutions than greedy method. However, since the overall number of redundant services is uncertain, DPA couldn't find the best solutions using the minimal overall number of redundancy.

After that, 10 different groups of parameters were used with the same reliability constraint value of 0.95 and the results were plotted in Fig-ure 6. Similar conclusions could be drawn from Figure 6. Experimental results in this section showed that HGA could find the optimal solutions to the single-objective optimization problems. While DPA could only find near-optimal solutions, the performance of DPA is much better.

5.3 Multi-Objective Optimal Pool Size Configuration

In this sub-section, HGA is used to solve multi-objective optimal pool size configuration problem (P3). To compare HGA with other multi-objective algorithms, we choose two types of state-of-art genetic algorithms. One of them is NSGA-II (Deb et al., 2002), which is a most widely used algorithm in multi-objective optimization. The other is MOMA (He et al., in press), which is a multi-objective memetic algorithm used for monitoring resources allocation in service composition. It is built upon NSGA II and the random-walk local search strategy without sensitivity analysis. Besides, the framework of memetic algorithm is quite different from HGA. The population size of the three algorithms was set to 100 and the number of iteration was set to 200. The crossover rate and the mutation rate of NSGA II and MOMA were set to 0.9 and 0.1, respectively. First of all, we used the sample data presented in Table 1 and changed the reliability constraint varies from 0.9 to 0.99. Each experiment was carried out from 10 times and the nondominated solutions obtained by different algorithms were plotted in Figure 7.

Figure 4. Impact of service pool size change on the overall reliability, cost, and response time

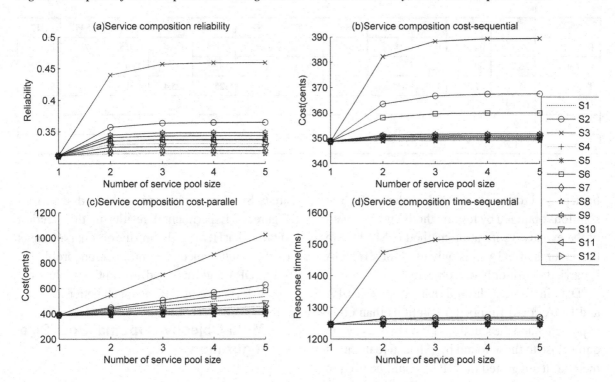

Table 2. Comparison of the best solution obtained by four methods

Service No.		1	2	3	4	5	6	7	8	9	10	11	12	Rc	N	Cc (cents)	Tc(ms)
Sequential type of fault tolerant strategy																	
P1	SGA	2	2	3	3	3	2	3	3	3	2	3	2	0.9566	31	426.8714	749.6068
	GGA	2	3	3	2	2	2	3	3	3	2	2	2	0.9561	29	429.7032	751.6967
	DPA	2	3	3	2	2	2	2	2	3	2	2	2	0.9523	27	429.4359	751.7368
	HGA	2	3	2	4	4	3	2	4	4	2	4	4	0.9500	39	425.8884	741.2334
	EM	2	3	2	4	4	3	3	4	4	2	4	4	0.9500	39	425.8884	741.2334
P2	GGA	2	3	3	2	2	3	3	3	3	2	2	2	0.9632	30	431.2146	751.7368
	DPA	2	3	3	2	2	2	2	2	3	2	2	2	0.9523	27	429.4359	751.7368
	HGA	2	4	2	4	4	4	4	3	4	4	2	4	0.9500	41	426.8274	740.0241
	EM	2	4	2	4	4	4	4	3	4	4	2	4	0.9500	41	426.8274	740.0241
Parallel type of fault tolerant strategy																	
P1	SGA	2	3	3	3	3	2	3	3	3	2	3	2	0.9742	32	1038.5	681.2955
	GGA	2	3	3	2	2	2	3	3	3	2	2	2	0.9561	29	1016.8	681.2955
	DPA	2	3	3	2	2	2	2	2	3	2	2	2	0.9532	27	1010.1	681.2955
	HGA	2	2	3	2	3	2	3	2	3	2	3	2	0.9501	29	967.1527	681.2955
	EM	2	2	3	2	3	2	3	2	3	2	3	2	0.9501	29	967.1527	681.2955

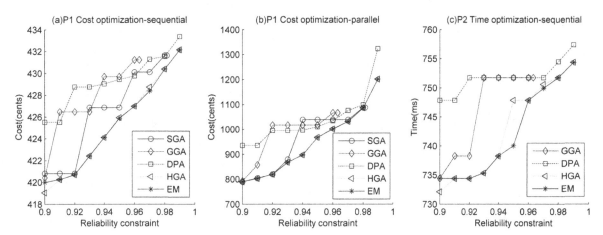

Figure 5. Comparison of algorithms for single-objective problems using different reliability constraint

Figure 6. Comparison of algorithms for single-objective problems using different system parameters

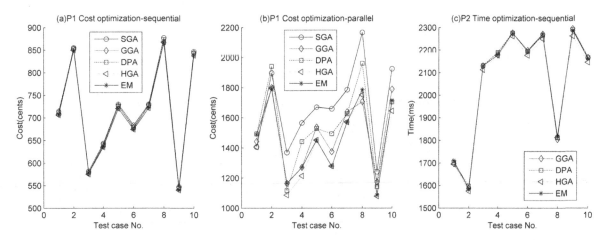

This result in Figure 7 suggested that HGA might be advantageous to other methods. However, the figures are just a simple illustration, and to compare HGA with NSGA-II and MOMA in detail, we use the coverage fraction. The coverage fraction represents the fraction of nondominated solutions obtained by one algorithm, which are covered by the nondominated solutions obtained by another one. It indicates a direct comparison of two set of solutions. The higher coverage fraction indicates that more solutions obtained by one algorithm are covered by that of other algorithms, that is to say, the algorithm is outperformed by the other one. The coverage fraction of the three algorithms was

listed in Table 3. Results in Table 3 showed that except for few test cases, most of the solutions obtained by NSGA II and MOMA were dominated by the solutions obtained by HGA.

Then 10 groups of randomly generated reliability, cost and response time value were used (the reliability constraint value was set to 0.95 in this case). The nondomiated solutions obtained by three algorithms were shown in Figure 8 and the coverage fraction values were listed in Table 4. Figure 8 and Table 4 showed that HGA managed to find better solutions than the other two algorithms.

Figure 7. Comparison of algorithms for multi-objective problems using different reliability constraint

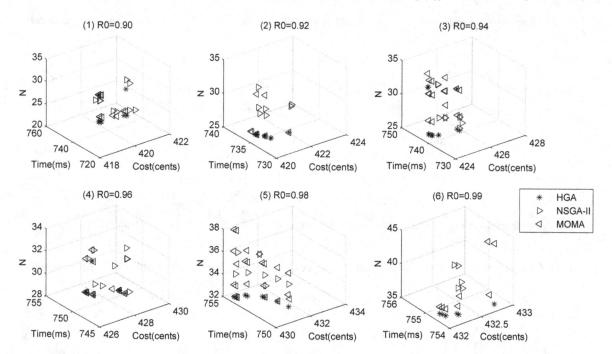

Table 3. Comparison of coverage fraction of three methods using different reliability constraint

Coverage (A cover B)												
Algorithm		**Reliability constraint**										
A	B	0.90	0.91	0.92	0.93	0.94	0.95	0.96	0.97	0.98	0.99	mean
NSGA II	HGA	0.130	0.101	0.075	0.010	0.009	0.078	0.073	0.073	0.007	0.002	0.056
HGA	NSGA II	0.804	1.000	1.000	0.997	0.902	0.904	0.998	0.901	1.000	1.000	0.950
MOMA	HGA	0.418	0.494	0.404	0.261	0.402	0.478	0.441	0.468	0.187	0.311	0.387
HGA	MOMA	0.902	0.995	0.992	0.715	0.705	0.898	0.991	0.798	0.996	0.904	0.890

6. FUTURE RESEARCH DIRECTIONS

The future research on this topic could concentrate on the following three parts. Firstly, the reliability cost and performance model for service composition with multiple service pools should be improved. Currently, only the workflow pattern and service pool reliability was taken into consideration in service composition reliability evaluation. Data transmission reliability and underlying resources reliability should be introduced to the reliability model since the workflow is execute in a decentralized manner and in the network and the reliability of data transmission could not be guaranteed. Secondly, only active redundancy mechanism is considered in the reliability evaluation and the probability model of service pool could be improved using cold redundancy mechanism. Besides, the cold redundancy strategy is often implemented under monitoring mechanism, and we could consider optimizing the resources used for monitoring and the redundant resources together. Thirdly, the multi-objective optimization technique for optimal service pool size configura-

Figure 8. Comparison of algorithms for multi-objective problems using different system parameters

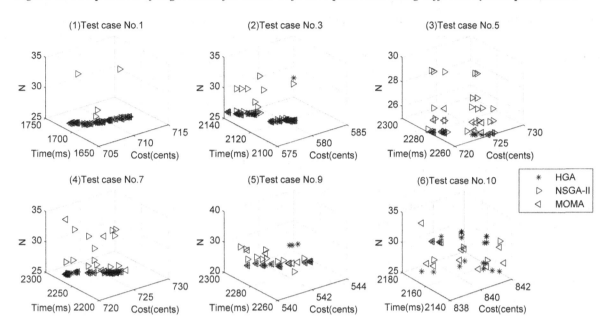

Table 4. Comparison of coverage fraction of three methods using different system parameters

		Coverage (A cover B)										
Algorithm		**Test case No.**										
A	B	1	2	3	4	5	6	7	8	9	10	mean
NSGA II	HGA	0.063	0.252	0.034	0.085	0.043	0.114	0.033	0.057	0.085	0.006	0.077
HGA	NSGA II	0.993	0.988	1.000	0.605	0.812	0.721	0.820	0.991	0.905	0.997	0.883
MOMA	HGA	0.251	0.708	0.459	0.482	0.566	0.600	0.294	0.370	0.543	0.495	0.477
HGA	MOMA	0.977	0.901	0.926	0.865	0.907	0.936	0.670	0.896	0.985	0.804	

tion in service composition could be enhanced. We didn't consider maximizing the reliability in our model. Once the reliability maximization is introduced, the algorithm needs to be modified to solve the new problem.

CONCLUSION

As web service is the key technology in the Cloud environment, the reliability of applications in Cloud will be highly affected by the reliability of underlying service composition. As a result, reliability of service composition has become an essential problem in Cloud computing. In this chapter, we proposed a methodology to choose the optimal service pool size combination for a service composition aiming at minimize the cost or response time of the service composition while meeting certain reliability constraints. This service pool size combination could be used to dynamically configure a service composition. This chapter started with the reliability, cost and performance model for single service pool with redundant services and then combined this model with the architecture-based reliability evaluation model to get the overall reliability, cost and performance for service composition. The sensitivity of size change on each service pool was also analyzed. Then, the optimization problem is presented and classified into three categories. For problems with closed-form models, Lagrange multiplier method is used to calculate the optimal solutions. For more complex problems, dynamic programming method is taken use of to get near-optimal solutions. For multi-objective problems, a hybrid genetic algorithm based on sensitivity analysis is employed to search nondominated sets of solutions. The hybrid genetic algorithm could also be used for single-objective problems. Empirical studies results showed that our algorithms outperformed the greedy selection method and traditional genetic algorithms and the hybrid genetic algorithm managed to find similar solutions as the exhaustive iteration algorithm.

REFERENCES

Al-Masri, E., & Mahmoud, Q. H. (2007). QoS-based discovery and ranking of web services. In *Proceedings 16th International Conference on Computer Communications and Networks* (pp. 529-534). Piscataway, NJ: IEEE Press.

Amazon. (2012). Amazon web services. Retrieved June 1, 2012, from http://aws.amazon.com/

Ardagna, D., & Pernici, B. (2007). Adaptive service composition in flexible processes. *IEEE Transactions on Software Engineering*, *33*(6), 369–384. doi:10.1109/TSE.2007.1011

Bertsekas, D. P. (1996). *Constrained optimization and lagrange multiplier methods*. Belmont, CA: Athena Scientific.

Busacca, P. G., Marseguerra, M., & Zio, E. (2001). Multiobjective optimization by genetic algorithms: Application to safety systems. *Reliability Engineering & System Safety*, *72*(1), 59–74. doi:10.1016/S0951-8320(00)00109-5

Dai, Y., Yang, L., & Zhang, B. (2009). QoS-driven self-healing web service composition based on performance prediction. *Journal of Computer Science and Technology*, *24*(2), 250–261. doi:10.1007/s11390-009-9221-8

Deb, K., Pratap, A., & Agarwal, S. (2002). A fast and elitist multiobjective genetic algorithm: NSGA-II. *IEEE Transactions on Evolutionary Computation*, *6*(2), 182–197. doi:10.1109/4235.996017

Gokhale, S. S., & Trivedi, K. S. (2006). Analytical models for architecture-based software reliability prediction: a unification framework. *IEEE Transactions on Reliability*, *55*(4), 578–590. doi:10.1109/TR.2006.884587

Google. (2012). Google maps API web services. Retrieved June 1, 2012, from https://developers.google.com/maps/documentation/webservices/

He, P., Wen, J. H., & Ren, H. J. (2012). Multi-objective service monitoring rate optimization using memetic algorithm. *Journal of Software*, *7*(5). doi:10.4304/jsw.7.5.990-997

He, P., Wu, K. W., Xie, Q., et al. (2011, August). Near-optimal configuration of service pool size in service composition. Paper presented at the 6th International ICST Conference on Communications and Networking in China (CHINACOM 2011), Harbin, China.

Huang, A. F. M., Lan, C. W., & Yang, S. J. H. (2009). An optimal QoS-based web service selection scheme. *Information Sciences*, *179*(19), 3309–3322. doi:10.1016/j.ins.2009.05.018

Huang, G., Zhou, L., & Liu, X. Z. (2006). Performance aware service pool in dependable service oriented architecture. *Journal of Computer Science and Technology*, *21*(4), 565–573. doi:10.1007/s11390-006-0565-z

Li, G., Muthusamy, V., & Jacobsen, H. A. (2010). A distributed service-oriented architecture for business process execution. ACM Transactions on the Web, 4(1).

Liu, L., Russell, D., Webster, D., et al. (2009). Delivering sustainable capability on evolutionary service-oriented architecture. In Proceedings of the 12th IEEE International Symposium on Object/Component/Service-Oriented Real-Time Distributed Computing (pp.12-19). Los Alamitos, CA: IEEE Computer Society Press.

Liu, L., Webster, D., Xu, J., et al. (2010). Enabling dynamic workflow for disaster monitoring and relief through service-oriented sensor networks. In 2010 5th International ICST Conference on Communications and Networking in China (pp.7). Piscataway, NJ: IEEE Press.

Luo, J., Li, Y., & Pershing, J. A. (2009). A methodology for analyzing availability weak points in SOA deployment frameworks. *IEEE Transactions on Network and Service Management, 6*(1), 31–44. doi:10.1109/TNSM.2009.090303

Ren, Y. X., Gu, Q., Qi, J. X., et al. (2009). Reliability prediction of web service composition based on DTMC. In Proceedings of the 3rd International Conference on Secure Software Integration and Reliability Improvement (pp. 369-375). Piscataway, NJ: IEEE Press.

Sasaki, M., & Gen, M. (2003). A method of fuzzy multi-objective nonlinear programming with GUB structure by hybrid genetic algorithm. *International Journal of Smart Engineering System Design, 5*(4), 281–288. doi:10.1080/10255810390245591

Trivedi, K. S. (2001). *Probability and statistics with reliability, queuing and computer science applications*. New York, NJ: John Wiley & Sons.

Wang, L. J., Bai, X. Y., Zhou, L. Z., et al. (2009). A hierarchical reliability model of service-based software system. In I. Ahamed, E. Bertino, C. K. Chang, et al., (Eds.), 2009 33rd Annual IEEE International Computer Software and Applications Conference (COMPSAC 2009) (pp. 199-208). Piscataway, NJ: IEEE Press.

WebXML. (2012). WeatherWebService. Retrieved June 1, 2012, from http://www.webxml.com.cn/webservices/weatherwebservice.asmx

Wen, J. H., Jiang, Z., & Tu, L. Y. (2009). Task-oriented web service discovery algorithm using semantic similarity for adaptive service composition. *Journal of Southeast University, 25*(4), 468–472.

Xia, Y. N., Wang, H. P., & Huang, Y. (2006). A stochastic model for workflow QoS evaluation *Science Progress, 14*(3-4), 251–265.

Yang, X. (2011). QoS-oriented service computing: Bring SOA into cloud environment. In Liu, X., & Li, Y. (Eds.), *Advanced design approaches to emerging software systems: Principles, methodology and tools* (pp. 274–296). Hershey, PA: ISI Global. doi:10.4018/978-1-60960-735-7.ch013

Yang, X., Nasser, B., Surrige, M., et al. (2012). A business-oriented cloud federation model for real time applications. Future Generation Computer Systems. Retrieved June 1, 2012, from http://www.sciencedirect.com/science/article/pii/S0167739X12000386

Zeng, L. Z., Benatallah, B., & Ngu, A. H. H. (2004). QoS-aware middleware for web services composition. *IEEE Transactions on Software Engineering, 30*(5), 311–327. doi:10.1109/TSE.2004.11

Zheng, Z. B., & Lyu, M. R. (2008). WS-DREAM: a distributed reliability assessment mechanism for Web services. In 2008 IEEE International Conference on Dependable Systems and Networks with FTCS and DCC(DSN) (pp. 392-397). Piscataway, NJ: IEEE Press.

Zheng, Z. B., & Lyu, M. R. (2009). A QoS-aware fault tolerant middleware for dependable service composition. In P. Carvalho, J. Craveiro, M. Kaaniche, et al., (Eds.), 2009 IEEE/IFIP International Conference on Dependable Systems and Networks (DSN) (pp. 239-248). Piscataway, NJ: IEEE Press.

Zheng, Z. B., & Lyu, M. R. (2010). Collaborative reliability prediction for service-oriented systems. In 2010 32nd International Conference on Software Engineering (pp. 35-44). New York, NY: ACM Press.

ADDITIONAL READING

Canfora, G., Penta, M. D., Esposito, R., et al. (2005). QoS-aware replanning of composite web services. In Proceedings, 2005 IEEE International Conference on Services Computing, Vol. 1 and 2 (pp.121-129). Los Alamitos, CA: IEEE Computer Society Press.

Chan, P. W., Lyu, M. R., & Malek, M. (2007). Reliable web services: Methodology, experiment and modeling. In L. J. Zhang, T. J. Watson, K. P. Birman, et al., (Ed.), Proceedings IEEE International Conference on Web Services (pp. 679-686). Los Alamitos, CA: IEEE Computer Society Press.

Chern, M. S. (1992). On the computational complexity of reliability redundancy allocation in a series system. *Operations Research Letters, 11*(5), 309–315. doi:10.1016/0167-6377(92)90008-Q

Coit, D., Taboada, H., & Baheranwala, F. (2007). Practical solutions for multi-objective optimization: An application to system reliability design problems. *Reliability Engineering & System Safety, 92*(3), 314–322. doi:10.1016/j.ress.2006.04.014

Coit, D. W. (2001). Cold-standby redundancy optimization for nonrepairable systems. *IIE Transactions, 33*(6), 471–478. doi:10.1080/07408170108936846

Eleni, A., & Haralarnbos, S. (2007). A simulated annealing algorithm for prioritized multiobjective optimization-implementation in an adaptive model predictive control configuration. IEEE Transaction on Systems, Man and Cybernetics. *Part B-Cybernetics, 37*(4), 902–915. doi:10.1109/TSMCB.2007.896015

Gokhale, S. S. (2007). Architecture-based software reliability analysis: overview and limitations. *IEEE Transactions on Dependable and Secure Computing, 4*(1), 32–40. doi:10.1109/TDSC.2007.4

Gokhale, S. S., & Trivedi, K. S. (2002). Reliability prediction and sensitivity analysis based on software architecture. In Proceedings 13th International Symposium on Software Reliability Engineering (pp. 64-75). Los Alamitos, CA: IEEE Computer Society Press.

Goseva-Popstojanova, K., & Grnarov, A. (1993). Dependability modeling and evaluation of recovery block systems. In Proceedings of 4th IEEE International Symposium on Software Reliability Engineering (pp.112-120). Los Alamitos, CA: IEEE Computer Society Press.

Halima, B. R., Fki, E., & Drira, K. (2010). A Large-scale monitoring and measurement campaign for web services-based applications. *Concurrency and Computation, 22*(10), 1172–1177. doi:10.1002/cpe.1576

Huang, C. Y., & Lyu, M. R. (2005). Optimal testing resource allocation, and sensitivity analysis in software development. *IEEE Transactions on Reliability, 54*(4), 592–603. doi:10.1109/TR.2005.858099

Hwang, S. Y., Wang, H., & Tang, J. (2007). A probabilistic approach to modeling and estimating the QoS of web-services-based workflows. *Information Sciences, 177*(23), 5484–5503. doi:10.1016/j.ins.2007.07.011

Krasnogor, N., & Smith, J. (2005). A tutorial for competent memetic algorithms: Model, taxonomy, and design issues. *IEEE Transactions on Evolutionary Computation, 9*(5), 474–488. doi:10.1109/TEVC.2005.850260

Kuo, W., & Wan, R. (2007). Recent advances in optimal reliability allocation. IEEE Transaction on Systems, Man, and Cybernetics-Part A. *Systems and Humans, 37*(2), 141–156.

Lee, C., Yun, Y., & Gen, M. (2002). Reliability optimization design using hybrid nn-ga with fuzzy logic controller. IEICE Transactions on Fundamentals of Electronics, Communications and Computer Science. *E (Norwalk, Conn.), 85A*(2), 432–447.

Levitin, G. (2006). Reliability and performance analysis of hardware-software systems with fault-tolerant software components. *Reliability Engineering & System Safety, 91*(5), 570–579. doi:10.1016/j.ress.2005.04.004

Li, Z., Liao, H., & Coit, D. (2009). A two-stage approach for multi-objective decision making with applications to system reliability optimization. *Reliability Engineering & System Safety, 94*(10), 1585–1592. doi:10.1016/j.ress.2009.02.022

Liang, Y., & Smith, A. (2004). An ant colony optimization algorithm for the redundancy allocation problem. *IEEE Transactions on Reliability, 53*(3), 417–423. doi:10.1109/TR.2004.832816

Liao, T. W. (2010). Two hybrid differential evolution algorithms for engineering design optimization. *Applied Soft Computing, 10*(4), 1188–1199. doi:10.1016/j.asoc.2010.05.007

Lin, F., & Kuo, W. (2002). Reliability importance and invariant optimal allocation. *Journal of Heuristics, 8*(2), 155–172. doi:10.1023/A:1017908523107

Lo, J. H., Huang, C. Y., Kuo, S. Y., et al. (2003). Sensitivity analysis of software reliability for component-based software applications. In Proceedings 27th Annual International Computer Software and Applications Conference (pp. 500-505). Los Alamitos, CA: IEEE Computer Society Press.

Lyu, M. R. (2007). Software reliability engineering: A roadmap. In Briand, L. C., & Wolf, A. L. (Eds.), *Future of software engineering* (pp. 153–170). Los Alamitos, CA: IEEE Computer Society Press. doi:10.1109/FOSE.2007.24

Moscato, P. (1989). *On evolution, search, optimization, genetic algorithms and martial arts: Towards memetic algorithm.* Pasadena, CA: CalTech.

Pietrantuono, R., Russo, S., & Trivedi, K. S. (2010). Software reliability and testing time allocation: An architecture-based approach. *IEEE Transactions on Software Engineering, 36*(3), 323–337. doi:10.1109/TSE.2010.6

Sato, N., & Trivedi, K. S. (2007). Accurate and efficient stochastic reliability analysis of composite services using their compact Markov reward model representations. In L. J. Zhang, W. VanderAalst, & P. C. K. Hung (Eds.), Proceedings, 2007 IEEE International Conference on Services Computing (pp. 114-121). Los Alamitos, CA: IEEE Computer Society Press.

Sharma, V. S., & Trivedi, K. S. (2007). Quantifying software performance, reliability and security: An architecture-based approach. *Journal of Systems and Software, 80*(4), 493–509. doi:10.1016/j.jss.2006.07.021

Stroulia, E., & Wang, Y. Q. (2005). Structural and semantic matching for assessing web-service similarity. *International Journal of Cooperative Information Systems, 14*(4), 407–437. doi:10.1142/S0218843005001213

Tang, M., & Ai, L. (2010). A hybrid genetic algorithm for the optimal constrained web service selection problem in web service composition. In *2010 IEEE Congress on Evolutionary Computation* (pp. 8). Piscataway, NJ: IEEE Press.

Teng, X. L., & Pham, H. (2002). A software-reliability growth model for N-version programming systems. *IEEE Transactions on Reliability*, *51*(3), 311–321. doi:10.1109/TR.2002.801853

Tran, V. X., Tsuji, H., & Masuda, R. (2009). A new QoS ontology and its QoS-based ranking algorithm for web services. *Simulation Modelling Practice and Theory*, *17*(8), 1378–1398. doi:10.1016/j.simpat.2009.06.010

Wang, Z., Tang, K., & Yao, X. (2010). Multi-objective approaches to optimal testing resource allocation in modular software systems. *IEEE Transactions on Reliability*, *59*(3), 563–575. doi:10.1109/TR.2010.2057310

Xia, Y., Zhu, Q., & Huang, Y. (2009). A novel reduction approach to analyzing QoS of workflow processes. *Concurrency and Computation*, *21*(2), 205–223. doi:10.1002/cpe.1339

Yang, X., Bruin, R., & Dove, M. (2010). Developing an end-to-end scientific workflow: A case study of using a reliable, lightweight, and comprehensive workflow platform in e-science. *IEEE Computational Science & Engineering*, *99*, 1.

Yang, X., Wang, L., & von Laszewski, G. (2009). Recent research advances in e-science. *Cluster Computing*, *12*(4), 353–356. doi:10.1007/s10586-009-0104-0

Yin, Y., Zhang, B., Zhang, X. Z., et al. (2009). A self-healing composite web service model. In *2009 IEEE Asia-Pacific Services Computing Conference (APSCC 2009)* (pp. 277-282). New York, NY: IEEE Press.

Yu, T., Zhang, Y., & Lin, K.J. (2007). Efficient algorithms for web services selection with end-to-end QoS constraints. *ACM Transactoin on the Web*, *1*(1).

Zitzler, E., & Thiele, L. (2000). Comparison of multiobjective evolutionary algorithms: Empirical results. *Evolutionary Computation*, *8*(2), 173–195. doi:10.1162/106365600568202

KEY TERMS AND DEFINITIONS

Dynamic Programming: A method for solving complex problems by breaking them down into simpler sub-problems.

Genetic Algorithm: A search heuristic that mimics the process of natural evolution, used to generate useful solutions to optimization problems.

Multi-Objective Optimization: Simultaneously optimizing two or more conflicting objectives subject to certain constraints.

Reliability: The ability of system to perform and maintain its required functions under any routine circumstances.

Sensitivity Analysis: The study of how the variation (uncertainty) in the output of a statistical model can be attributed to different variations in the inputs of the model.

Service Composition: Composed web services according to certain structures to fulfill certain business requirements.

Service-Oriented Architecture: An approach to organizing software in the form of independent, interoperable services that can be composed and recomposed dynamically.

Service Pool: A set of redundant services with similar functionalities and QoS values.

Chapter 16
Internet–Based Virtual Computing Infrastructure for Cloud Computing

James Hardy
University of Derby, UK

Cui Lei
Beihang University, China

Lu Liu
University of Derby, UK

Jianxin Li
Beihang University, China

ABSTRACT

Virtualisation is massively important in computing and continues to develop. This chapter discusses and evaluates the virtualisation technologies and in particular, a state-of-art system called iVIC (the Internet-based Virtual Computing) developed by Beihang University, China as it provides an all-in-one example of many of the major headline Cloud Computing titles of SaaS, IaaS, and HaaS. The chapter considers several virtualization packages which are either commercial, community, or experimental, before focusing on iVIC, a virtual machine cloning system that may be beneficial in a learning or office environment. The chapter introduces a test environment which is used to assess the performance of the iVIC process and the virtual machines created. Power requirements of virtual, as opposed to physical machines, are compared and evaluated. The chapter closes with conclusions regarding virtualisation and iVIC.

1. INTRODUCTION

Virtualisation has been used for many years; however its importance has increased significantly in recent times. The underlying reasons why virtualisation is undertaken have also diversified. It is commonplace for cost reduction, increased power efficiency and operational flexibility to be cited as the prime drivers but, whilst these points are clearly very important, testing, repeatability and massive parallelism should not be overlooked as potential motivators.

In this chapter, a state-of-art virtualisation system - iVIC (the Internet-based Virtual Comput-

DOI: 10.4018/978-1-4666-2854-0.ch016

ing) will be focused as it provides an all-in-one example of many of the major headline Cloud Computing titles of SaaS, IaaS, HaaS. Two or more iVIC hosts can be linked over a network and will provide some degree of VM load balancing; alternatively a single iVIC host can be used as a complete "Cloud in a box". The system creates new fully networked "user level" virtual machines as a cluster, as opposed to single entities, and is "on request" rather than "on demand". Each virtual machine in a powered on cluster is individually accessible over VNC, can be powered on or off and can be executing any compatible software at the request of the user. The entire cluster can be granted or denied access to the physical network which does not affect VNC to the virtual machines or the networking between machines located on separate hosts.

The main objective of this chapter is to discuss virtualisation and a specific virtualisation cloning platform known as iVIC. Particular emphasis is placed on underpinning technologies and system functions.

A comparison of several virtualisation packages is included and intended to show that there is no single method to create a virtual machine, no single business ethic or financial motivator and no guarantee of continued growth and success without significant exposure and general acceptance.

The next section of this chapter considers the background and objectives of virtualisation and also introduces some of the terminology used. Several virtualisation packages are discussed in general terms in following section, including the objective and target use of the packages. Two sections focus on the iVIC system, presenting by example the guide to the experimental setup and the results obtained in testing. Conclusions and future considerations are given in the final sections. There are two appendices containing a sample xml file and potential modifications to guest machines to overcome a networking issue.

2. VIRTUALISATION

2.1 Virtualisation History

Virtualisation has been in use for several decades. Some of the earliest references that have been obtained are dated from 1964 (Varian, 1997) and formed part of the operating system of IBM CP-40 for the S/360 mainframe.

Many of the reasons and principles of the early IBM "pseudo machines" such as separation of user environments and OS backwards compatibility are still of particular importance in today. As an example, Microsoft provides backward compatibility by including "XP Mode" with Windows 7 to "reduce possible operational downtime by extending the life of existing software" (Microsoft, 2011). XP Mode is a virtual machine "appliance" with an XP operating system.

The concept of operating system backwards compatibility can be expanded beyond purely software and into the realms of hardware. Hardware emulation allows software intended for a specific hardware platform to function on completely different hardware. Early examples are "games console emulators", where computers such as the Z80 based Sinclair ZX range from the very early 1980s were emulated on 6502 based Acorn and consequently Mac, DOS and several Windows variants (Scherrer, 2011). Although there is an apparently eternal interest in "retrospective gaming", the original motivators for these emulators were purely commercial from user community: to extend the life of game software purchased for a system that very quickly became obsolete.

Emulation can also be used to reduce development time and cross-system expertise. Many programs intended for Windows can be executed directly on Linux systems using "compatibility layer" technologies such as Wine (WineHQ, 2011). If wine is available, any ".exe" programs started in a Linux environment first invoke Wine.

The benefit to the software producer is that they do not need to write two sets of code, or employ two separate programmers. The result is reduced costs in production and maintenance, faster time to market and a significantly wider marketplace. The terms "emulation" and "virtualisation" are frequently used interchangeably, and any difference between the two is marginal. If there is a distinction, then it is that the host hardware is emulated whilst the guest is virtualised.

2.2 Virtualisation Objectives

There are numerous reasons why virtualisation is undertaken. Possibly the most commonly reported are reducing costs, increasing efficiency, operational flexibility and improved desktop security (Li, Jia & Liu, 2012). Each of these headline items is expanded in other research papers and marketing literature, for example to describe more fully where the cost savings can be realised. This type of virtualisation is generally single-machine-at-a-time virtualisation.

Less common are a smaller class of cloning virtualisation systems. The most pronounced feature of this class is the intention to generate multiple identical copies of an original virtual machine at a particular state to achieve one or more specific objectives. The majority of this chapter will discuss this class of virtualisation and its relevance to teaching, learning and research.

2.3 Key Terms and Definitions

The following terms and definitions are commonly used in this subject area. The choice of not including these in alphabetical order is deliberate and should imply the level of use and importance in the context of this chapter.

Guest is another name for the virtual machine. Emulation of the host hardware generally sets the restriction on a guest VM capability.

The host is the system that the guest is executed on. This is normally a physical system, however it is possible to use multi-layer virtualisation and the host may actually be a guest on some lower level system.

Hosted system virtualisation is where the virtualisation layer is installed as an application on an existing operating system. For this reason it is sometimes known as application virtualisation.

Hypervisor systems are often referred to as bare metal virtualisations. The virtualisation layer is installed directly on to clean x86-based hardware in place of a traditional operating system. This is a highly efficient method of virtualisation and is normally used for server consolidation.

Fully virtualised systems have the capability to emulate all essential physical hardware to the extent that the same unmodified operating system can be used on either a physical or virtual machine (Abels, Dhawan, & Chandrasekaran, 2005), making the transition from physical to virtual (p2v) and virtual to physical (v2p) relatively simple. It should be clear that this does not mean that absolutely *all* hardware is emulated and that this may lead to limitations in the capability of a p2v converted system. Fully virtualised systems are frequently referred to as being "virtualisation unaware".

Paravirtualised systems do not fully emulate all necessary hardware, instead the guest OS is modified to interact with standard hardware represented by the virtualisation layer. Major benefits are that the virtualisation layer can be simplified and that the responsiveness of the VM may improve due to the reduction in software based emulation (Abels, Dhawan, & Chandrasekaran, 2005) (Barham, et al., 2003). The negative aspect is that the modified OS cannot be used in a physical machine; it is not possible to directly convert from physical to virtual and vice versa. A guest system using paravirtualised hardware is sometimes referred to as "virtualisation aware".

Hardware virtualisation technology (VT) refers to "extensions to the x86 hardware architecture to improve virtualisation capability" and is a requirement for some virtualisation systems. Two major versions exist, AMD-V on AMD processors (AMD) and VT-x on Intel processors (Intel).

HVM or Hardware Virtual Machine is specific to Xen systems and refers to a fully virtualised system reliant on hardware VT such as AMD-V or VT-x.

Dom0, DomU. Again specific to Xen, these are "domains" or virtual hardware that guest OS run on. Dom0 is the highest level, and can control the hardware in the system; DomU is the "unprivileged" or user domain and has little control over the physical system. There can be multiple DomU in a system.

Ring 0, Ring 1, Ring 2, Ring 3. This refers to a concept that software privileges can and should be restricted according to the type of application that is running. For a traditional physical machine, software operating at Ring 0 is known as Kernel Mode and has the highest privilege; this is normally the operating system. Software in Ring 3 has the lowest privilege and is usually application software. Rings 1 and 2 are either unused or used for device drivers. For hypervisor based systems, the hypervisor is usually Ring 0, the Guest OS is Ring 1 and the Guest applications are Ring 3. (Abels, Dhawan, & Chandrasekaran, 2005) (Schroeder & Saltzer, 1971). The "rings" concept is frequently associated with computing security and there are some excellent descriptions in this context in section 5.4 of "Security in Computing" (Pfleeger & Pfleeger, 2007).

3. VIRTUALISATION SOFTWARE

Research was undertaken on the versions of Microsoft Hyper-V, VMware workstation, VMware vSphere, KVM, Xen, Qemu, Emotive, iVIC and SnowFlock that were generally available when the chapter was being written. A summary of the research is presented in this chapter. There are numerous other packages that are available; the ones presented here are a very small sample.

3.1 Classification

The products discussed have been classified to be in three groups, namely commercial, community and experimental. This is as a convenience for the purposes of this chapter only. The following summary explanation clarifies the intended meaning of the different groups. There is no "scale of importance" intended or implied by any comments in this section, but it should give some foresight about the software producers motivation and an understanding why some products develop while others do not. It may also suggest a level of expectation regarding the ease of installation or operation of the product.

3.1.1 Commercial

Product development is usually suitably financially and physically resourced, has specific documented objectives and will have a formal development plan with timescales. Success is ultimately measured by the profit that they generated (Bittman, Dawson, & Weiss, 2010). Subsequent product development and release is managed according to sales trends and prevailing market conditions. Documentation for these products is normally professionally produced and contains very good user level detail. There are often support and troubleshooting guides and it is common for the product producers to provide free one-to-one email support during installation and deployment. Documentation that ensures easy installation and use are significant goals for commercial organisations, especially in the era of attempting to convert "fully functional free trial software" into revenue generating fully licenced sales. The documentation is generally kept up to date and is frequently translated to multiple languages.

3.1.2 Community

Products are frequently open source, freely distributed and originally developed to satisfy a specific need using voluntary resource over an undefined continuous development period. Their success is generally measured by a consensus of opinion on the products technical capability. These products can become "commercial" or be developed within an otherwise commercial environment if an enterprise believes they may offer competitive advantage for themselves or their competitors. Of interest is that very few of the well-known "open source" virtualisation products are truly independent (Bittman, Dawson, & Weiss, 2010). Documentation is usually more informal and is updated by "communities". The documentation can quickly become out-dated and the community support information always lags behind the product release. The size of the community support can indicate the popularity of the product, but it can also suggest the number of problems that are being experienced by people attempting to use the product. Use of this software is going to be based upon the level of effort required to achieve a personal goal, something that cannot be easily predicted or measured.

3.1.3 Experimental

Products devised, designed and implemented mainly as college or university projects. The ultimate success of these projects is usually measured by the grade obtained for technical innovation and presentation. Experimental products may become, or form the basis of, community or commercial products at a later stage. Documentation of experimental products is normally technically based and limited to the minimum to achieve a working prototype or proof of concept. The documentation may not be generally publicly available and is unlikely to be updated in line with development. There is rarely any support community or troubleshooting guide and it is likely that the original designer or author will have moved on from the project or even the institution where the product was designed.

For this chapter Microsoft and VMware products are classed as commercial. Some of their products are distributed without cost, but the overall motivation of the supplier is profitability.

KVM, Xen and Qemu are essentially open source and generally available. They are classed as community products due to the method of distribution and support.

Emotive, iVIC and SnowFlock are classed as experimental.

3.2 Virtualisation Platforms

3.2.1 VMware Workstation

VMware Inc. was founded in 1998 and had revenues of US$ 2.9 billion in 2010. VMware have multiple virtualisation platforms aimed at satisfying many market sectors and are considered by many to be the best and most popular virtualisation provider (Bittman, Weiss, Margevicius, & Dawson, 2011). Of primary interest for this chapter are VMware Workstation and vSphere as they are highly relevant but intended for distinctly differing purposes.

Workstation is a virtualisation platform for individual virtual machines. As one of the oldest product ranges in the VMware portfolio, it has had many "major" and "minor" version upgrades since its original release. Version 8 was the current release at the end of 2011. Workstation is totally proprietary and runs as an application on a specific OS. There are versions available for most popular OS including many Windows and Linux releases. Workstation is intended for use in test, development, deployment and sandboxing of dissimilar applications. Installing Workstation is very simple; the different versions for Windows and Linux mean that users can install the version which they are most familiar with, possibly creating virtual machines based on the alternative operating systems.

3.2.2 VMware vSphere

vSphere is a hypervisor product. It replaces concept of an application running on an OS with the concept that the OS is actually the application and that many such applications can be installed under a single hypervisor. Communication between virtual servers created under a hypervisor normally uses IP stacks and virtual switch networks. vSphere is frequently referred to as either platform independent or "bare metal" install due to it not being installed on top of an existing OS.

Marketing for vSphere is heavily targeted towards private virtual Cloud Computing. The product is also marketed as offering many "green computing" benefits due mainly to server consolidation. Installing servers as applications has the advantage that numerous virtualised servers can be installed on the same hardware and so the number of physical servers and hence rack space, direct power consumption, noise and cooling requirements are all reduced. VMware claim that the number of servers can be reduced by factors of 10:1 or more and consequently overall energy requirements are reported to be reduced by as much as 80% (Taneja Group, 2009).

Installation is relatively easy using the documentation from the vSphere support pages., and there are also very simple "getting started" guides available on the internet (Natarajan, 2010). A second product, vSphere client is required to create and manage the virtual machines; this is installed in a separate network connected device. vSphere is totally proprietary to VMware, a commercial company, however there are 60 day trial and restricted capability free versions available on the vSphere website.

3.2.3 Microsoft HyperV Server

Microsoft were relatively late to market with the HyperV server and as a result are not leaders in the sector (Bittman, Weiss, Margevicius, & Dawson,

2011), however commercial awareness, and possibly the decision to allow free use of HyperV 2008, has allowed them to make significant advances in the marketplace (Bittman, Dawson, & Weiss, 2010) (Bittman, Weiss, Margevicius, & Dawson, 2011). The HyperV server is managed from a licenced (and hence not free) Windows Server 2008 or Windows 7 Professional system (Windows 7 Home versions cannot be used to manage the server). The server itself is very easy to install and there is a wealth of documentation available through the TechNet service. HyperV server is a Microsoft alternative to VMware vSphere and aimed at server consolidation. Similar and familiar Cloud Computing, power saving, green computing marketing descriptions are used throughout the documentation.

3.2.4 KVM

KVM or "Kernel-based Virtual Machine" is an open source virtualisation product for Linux platforms. It was originally released in 2007 and the kernel component has been included in mainstream Linux kernels since version 2.6.20. Although KVM is open source, Qumranet (the group that led development since its inception) were acquired by Red Hat in 2008 (Bittman, Weiss, Margevicius, & Dawson, 2011). The product still continues to be developed in the spirit of open source under the banner of "a Red Hat Emerging Technology Project".

KVM relies on the hardware virtualisation provided by VT-x or AMD-V and on Qemu to provide processor emulation. As a result, changes in Qemu are sometimes necessary to update KVM functions. KVM is in turn used as the basis for many other virtualisation packages.

KVM can be used as a command line method to create and use virtual machines or it can be called by graphical virtualisation packages such as virt-manager.

3.2.5 Xen

Xen is another open source product that is owned by a commercial organisation, this time Citrix. Xen is a hypervisor product and very different to the other open-source products mentioned in this chapter because of this. Xen is implemented at the kernel level and therefore cannot be installed as an add-on to an existing system. It also uses terminology such as Dom0 and DomU, which can be daunting when first encountered, especially to those who have experience of other virtualisation products. Xen support in some versions of Linux has been controversial, Dom0 kernels were not supported between Ubuntu 8.10 and 11.04. Xen was also removed from Red Hat Enterprise Linux 6 in favour of KVM. This may have been a political move (Red Hat own KVM, their competitor, Citrix, own Xen) (Marshall, 2010) but there are also statements that Xen was removed due to the increasing cost and complexity of maintaining it (Jackson, 2010).

Several other virtualisation packages are either built on or based upon Xen.

3.2.6 Qemu

Qemu is an open source emulator and virtualiser application. The difference between these terms is clearly important to the authors. Some sources state that Qemu is a processor emulator but in practice Qemu can be used as a command line virtual machine manager which also provides much of emulated hardware for itself and other platforms such as KVM. Terminology and use of Qemu is very similar to KVM, although command line switches may be different between the two.

3.2.7 Emotive

Emotive Cloud was created at the Universitat Politècnica de Catalunya, Spain by Dr. Íñigo Goiri with subsequent development by Barcelona Supercomputing Centre.

Emotive is an acronym for "Elastic Management Of Tasks In Virtualized Environments" and was primarily intended as a VM manager and scheduler, its modular design has meant that it has been extended to be used as a Cloud provider and can utilise the resources of external provision such as Amazon EC2.

There is a good explanation of the product including installation and use on the Emotive Cloud website (Barcelona Supercomputing Center, 2010). Emotive was created under Debian and uses Xen as its virtualisation package. There is a software download available from SourceForge (SourceForge, 2011) however installation may not be as straight forward as the documentation suggests.

3.2.8 SnowFlock

SnowFlock was created as PhD research by H. Andrés Lagar-Cavilla at the University of Toronto, Canada. It is based on Xen capable Fedora 8 and uses forking to generate multiple copies of an active VM on other participating physical devices. The objective is take an active multi-thread process running in a single VM and provide it with "on demand" resources to reduce completion time. SnowFlock uses multicast networking to simultaneously provide all other machines on the network with the opportunity to participate. According to the descriptive document (Lagar-Cavilla, et al., 2009), the time taken to create the clones is practically independent of the number of clones created. The document has data showing that 32 virtual machines are created in under one second (typically 600-800 milliseconds).

The SnowFlock packages were still available for be download during late 2011 (University of Toronto, 2009). SnowFlock unfortunately suffers from the same problem as many of the experimental software packages in that it is based on versions of Linux and Python that are no longer supported, in this case Fedora 8 and Python2.5. Having stated this, using the SnowFlock Manual (University of Toronto, 2008) and the correct base operating system, SnowFlock has been installed and tested with only minor changes.

3.2.9 iVIC

iVIC was devised in Beihang University and has been developed over several years. It uses KVM for virtualisation, MySQL for a database, Python as a programming language, Ruby on Rails to create a web application and Apache as its web server.

The system has many functions and capabilities; its primary intention, according to the portals own home page, is to create flexible virtual computing environments.

Although iVIC is installed as a portal application on a Debian operating system, the multiple-guest intention and inbuilt virtual networking means that functionally it has many similarities to a full hypervisor (Hardy, Liu & Antonopoulos, 2012). The authors describe it as a portal system meaning that the operations and created VM are not usually displayed on the server system; they are accessed by web browser or VNC viewer.

3.3 Summary

A comparison and summary of the packages described is provided in table 1. The use and application columns suggest the normal purpose of the packages described; it is not intended to state or imply any limitation of the package. For example, a Windows XP client can be created as a test vehicle on a hypervisor system but this is not as simple as using a hosted system, it requires dedicated physical hardware and does not make best use of the hypervisor capabilities.

4. EVALUATION OF THE INTERNET-BASED VIRTUAL COMPUTING (IVIC) SYSTEM

The iVIC (internet based Virtual Computing) system was conceived and created at Beihang University, China. Since its inception, there have been version updates to support newer operating systems, address functional and security issues and incorporate additional features. iVIC provides a means to store, graphically index and distribute Virtual Machines cloned from an original VM. Clone production and deployment is very fast in comparison to original VM creation and to most

Table 1. Package comparison

Package	method	Type	Use	Application
VMware workstation	application	Commercial	individual "user systems"	test / development
VMware vSphere	hypervisor	Commercial	multiple server systems	cost reduction, green computing
Microsoft HyperV	hypervisor	Commercial	multiple server systems	cost reduction, green computing
KVM	application	Community	individual "user systems"	test / development
Xen	hypervisor	Community	multiple server systems	test / development
Qemu	application	Community	individual "user systems"	test / development
Emotive	application	experimental	individual "user systems"	Cloud development
SnowFlock	application	experimental	clone single system	massive parallelism
iVIC	application	experimental	clone user systems	end user / education

methods of manual copying. The iVIC system has many uses including producing machines with an identical power on starting point, creating a single network of similar devices for test and experimentation and creation of virtual networks of dissimilar devices. These attributes make iVIC highly suited to the creation of environments that benefit from situation or periodic initialisation. Examples of this could be teaching and testing environments, where students are guaranteed to receive identical starting points or virtual office spaces where it could ensure that user personnel do not accidentally, or intentionally, create long term security problems.

There are many reasons for this chapter to focus on the iVIC system rather than any other Virtual Machine Manager. Primarily, the system is believed to be unique in being able to create a specified number of individually usable, identical, privately networked virtual machines within minutes. Given suitable hardware, iVIC should be capable of creating an entire virtual classroom or office of 30 machines in around 6 minutes. Other significant benefits of the system are derived from the virtual machines being identical clones of a single source machine. One point being that as they are identical at creation time and are executing on the same host hardware, they can be an ideal vehicle for direct real-time comparison of application software packages created by competing suppliers, for example the efficiency of commercial and freeware simulation packages. With similar reasoning, it is also possible to conduct experiments to compare the changes made by a virus or malware infection.

4.1 Experimental Environment

Practical use of iVIC relies on knowing the capability boundaries or proving that the boundaries exceed the normal use criteria.

Basic requirements for the system are

- Ability to create a useful number of VMs,

- Creation of VMs within a practical timeframe,
- Ability to successfully bring the created VMs to a usable state,
- The usable state to be achieved in a reasonable timescale,
- VMs to be capable of undertaking realistic levels of work,
- System power requirements must be acceptable.

To assess these requirements, the capability of iVIC to create and start a number of virtual machine clones has been tested based on available RAM and hard drive space.

4.1.1. Host System

The system used for the testing was built around a 2.83 GHz Intel Q9550 quad core processor with a variable amount of 667 MHz DDR2 RAM and single 500Gbyte SATA2 disk drive. The installed iVIC system was "revision 2.0+r8577+20110614" and the base operating system was Debian 5.0.8.

There are statistic and measurement tools within iVIC but in the interests of impartiality these were not used. Some of the measurements and statistics that were gathered for this chapter rely on the Debian sysstat package (Debianhelp) which was installed as an additional package.

4.1.2. Guest System

The virtual machine being used was Windows XP Home, service pack 2 configured as a single cpu system with 512Mbyte RAM and a 4Gbyte hard drive. The VM had been pre-installed with all drivers to eliminate the need for user interaction with any of the clones during start up. To further increase the workload on iVIC, start-up tests were completed with the guest drive having a "dirty" flag set, i.e. needing to perform an NTFS disk check. XP was chosen for use in testing due to it being allocated physical space for the entire virtual RAM during VM start-up and not releasing the memory until shutdown. Although this would normally be an undesirable feature, it ensures consistent VM memory use in the host throughout the testing.

4.2 Evaluation of Clone Deployment Overhead

The ability of iVIC to allow deletion, modification and recreation of VM clusters is particularly useful in a teaching environment where incremental changes can be made to a system to ensure consistent progression points. Similarly, the capability for an entire office system to be stopped and recreated in the event of a virus attack or network intrusion could prove to be particularly appealing to system owners. To be of practical use in these types of situation, the VM clones must be able to be created and recreated in a reasonable timeframe.

As a precursor, simple copy tests showed that the 4Gbyte guest virtual disk file took an average of 2 minutes +/- 2 seconds to copy within the same directory.

Figure 1 shows the time taken to create (or, as used in iVIC, "deploy") numbers of virtual machine clones for various amounts of physical RAM. The timing was undertaken manually, starting when the "confirm" button was selected and finished when the red status marker appeared on the vcluster page. It is clear that, for the numbers of clones being considered, the deployment speed is totally independent of amount of RAM installed. This result is not unexpected; the cloning process is mainly a copying process and as such will be most dependent on disk access and write speed. The result that may be unexpected is the actual time taken to create the clones, approximately 15 seconds per clone for the same 4Gbyte guest disk, a significant reduction on the expected 2 minutes per clone for a raw copy. The major reason for this is the conversion to qcow2 reducing the disk size to less than 100 Mbytes.

4.3 Evaluation of Start-up Overhead

The second requirement for a practical system is that the clone machines must power up to a useable state within a reasonable period of time. Timing for the start-up measurement began from selecting the "start cluster" icon. Timing finished when the "mu" vm completed its networking and the "keep windows up to date" shield was shown. This is clearly a fairly arbitrary point but did provide a consistent timing marker for comparison.

The "mu" vm refers to the name that iVIC allocates to the headnode clone. Again the choice is fairly arbitrary, the worknodes are named cu1, cu2 and so on; any of these could have been used if they had actually been created. Only mu and cu1 are created for a 2 vm cluster; mu, cu1, cu2 and cu3 for a 4 vm cluster and so on.

Figure 2 shows the start-up times for numbers of clones against varying amounts of RAM. The original VM was cloned at a stage when it required a disk check to be performed, this extended the start-up times beyond normal operating condition but the comparative times are still valid.

From the collected data shown in the graphs, the overall shape and knee points can be seen to generally coincide with physical memory availability. The start-up times show little variation whilst the total amount of RAM allocated to the VM cluster is significantly less than the available physical RAM. Techniques such as memory page swapping will automatically be used by the host machine when sum of the total cluster RAM plus the RAM required by the host server exceeds the amount of physical RAM installed in the host. Paging significantly decreases memory access speed and therefore increases the time taken to complete the task.

As an example, consider a cluster where each VM is allocated 512M RAM, six VMs therefore require 3G physical RAM. From the graph, there is little difference in start-up time when either 4G or 6G of RAM is installed in the host as there is at least 1G of RAM available to the host operating system. However, when the number of VMs is increased to eight, 4G of RAM is required by the VM cluster alone. Whilst this has no effect on the 6G system, the 4G system begins to use page swapping to provide enough RAM for the VMs and the operating system. This accounts for the non-linear response point on the graph. As the number of clones in the cluster is increased more paging is required, memory access time increases and so the time taken for the cluster to arrive at a stable usable point is much longer.

Also of significant interest from the graph is that Debian 5 and iVIC did not crash when excessively over-subscribed. Physical observation during this period did show that iVIC was unavailable for long periods and that Debian was very slow to respond. A negative aspect to this robust approach is that iVIC could not be shutdown in a controlled manner during this period. Crashing the server meant that the MySQL database and some directories had to be manually cleared.

4.4 Evaluation of Impact of Multiple VMC

The capabilities of an iVIC server can be extended by adding and configuring additional vStores. In this configuration two network connected iVIC servers are created, one acts as the portal and vStore, the other is configured only as a vStore. Both servers have quad core processors and 6G RAM, and creates a system which has the combined RAM and number of processor cores of the two hosts. When VMs are created and started, they will essentially load balance across the two (or more) servers. It is unlikely that the automatic allocation will be numerically even across the available vStores; allocation can, however, be manually controlled. Allocation is determined at deployment rather than start-up, the clones will always start from the vStore that they were originally allocated to.

Figure 3 shows the effect of adding a second vStore machine. To prevent uneven loading of the servers, VM deployment was manually configured across the vStores.

The results are a similar form to the single vStore results. Start-up times begin to increase significantly after 20 VMs which is where the combined level of VM RAM and operating system RAM exceeds the physical RAM for each server. Note that each server has its own OS memory overhead, six iVIC servers each with 2G RAM would have less memory available to be used by VMs than two servers with 6G.

Figure 1. Clone deployment times with varying amounts of host RAM

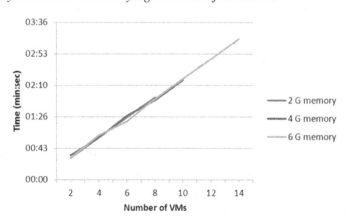

Figure 2. Start up times for numbers of clones with varying amounts of host RAM

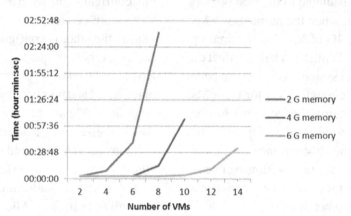

Figure 3. Startup and deployment times, two networked vStores, 12G Ram, 8 CPU

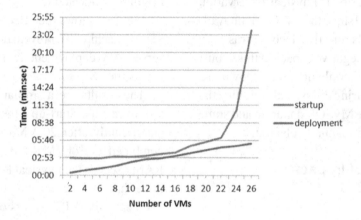

4.5 Evaluation of Impact on Power Consumption for Green Computing

One of the most appealing factors of virtualisation is the reduction in cost that can be realised (Liu, Masfary & Antonopoulos, 2012)(Li, Li & Wo, et al., 2012). The initial cost is reduced by minimising the amount of hardware purchased and a consequent rack space saving. More significant however may be the on-going cost in service. It is an obvious statement that virtual servers do not have individual power supplies, cooling fans, system boards or processors which, in a physical server, consume power and radiate heat.

To examine the input power requirements for iVIC, a digital wattmeter was connected to the power supply for the two servers, the screen and

a kvm switch. The measurements obtained are shown in the Table 2.

The table shows that a significant cost is attributable to powering on the monitor alone. It also shows that the power requirements for ten unloaded physical machines without monitors would exceed 800 watts, which is four times the power, and hence cost, of the two physical machines hosting ten virtual machines.

Powering the ten VMs to a usable desktop state contributed only approximately 23 watts to the power usage. As an attempt to increase the power use, the processor utilisation was increased using Prime95 (Mersenne Research Inc, 2011). The stress test utilised 100% of the virtual CPU in each of the VMs and, whilst this increased the power utilisation by 25%, it clearly showed that

Table 2. Power consumption during use

System Condition	power (watt/hrs)
System on standby, monitor in power saving	31
Desktop and laptop started	204
Desktop and laptop started, monitor in off	167
Logged in to iVIC	167
During deployment of 10 VM to 2 vStores	175
10 VMs started but idle	190
10 VMs started, 1 running stress test	198
10 VMs started, 2 running stress test	212
10 VMs started, 5 running stress test	219
10 VMs started, 10 running stress test	246

ten fully loaded VMs on two physical devices still consume less power than four unloaded physical devices.

4.6 Evaluation of VM Computational Performance

The final consideration is that the system must be capable of undertaking a realistic level of work. The benchmarking facility of Prime95 was used to generate a load and record the performance of individual VMs.

For the test, ten VMs were deployed across the two physical machines and two VMs from the same physical host were benchmarked. Using VMs from the same host ensured that the load on the host processor was consistent. As explained earlier, mu and cu7 are simply the iVIC generated names for the VMs. Comparison tests were undertaken where no other VMs were loaded and then with all the VMs fully loaded.

Figure 4 shows the minimum and average times to complete the benchmark test with only the test VMs loaded. The performance figures obtained are similar to the recorded figures for a physical Intel Celeron D at 3.2GHz on the Prime95 website (Mersenne Inc, 2011).

Figure 5 shows the comparison data recorded with all ten VMs running the benchmark process

simultaneously. The non-linearity of the plots is thought to be the result of the testing not being synchronised across the VMs. The final data points will have been recorded as some of the VMs complete the task and the overall loading begins to fall.

CONCLUSION

Virtualisation is massively important in computing and continues to develop. There is no single reason for the existence all of the numerous virtualisation packages and no one package satisfies all needs. Careful consideration must be given to making the most informed choice of package based on a clear understanding of the problem that needs to be solved.

In this chapter, we set up a series of experiments to systematically evaluate the performance and power consumption of iVIC system. According to the experiment results, we conclude that the amount of physical RAM has little or no impact on clone deployment times. Deployment is mainly a file copying process and will be affected by the size of the original VM, format of the image file and speed of the system drive. Moreover, The iVIC system could be very beneficial in a teaching / learning environment especially as it develops. The ability to run numerous virtual machines from within a portal application rather than as individual VMs locally installed significantly reduces administration time.

The networking component of iVIC is extremely useful in a classroom environment. Choices can be made over whether VMs have access to the physical network, including the Internet, or not. This choice does not affect whether the VMs are accessible over the network (and including over the Internet) or whether they have IP connectivity to the other members of the cluster.

Many of iVICs functions depend upon very specific naming in a free format text field, for example the operating system entry of the VM definition xml file. Creation, management and

Figure 4. VM response time when running alone

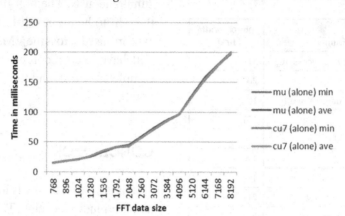

Figure 5. VM response time with all VMs running

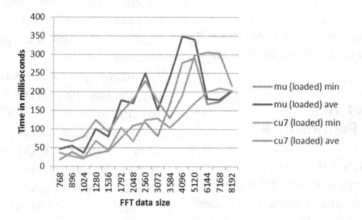

modification of the virtual machines could be simplified to make the system easier to use. A "point and click" method with drop-down menus for creating the initial xml files would be advantageous as would a single click method to shut down and undeploy a cluster and then open the original VM for editing.

FUTURE WORK

The iVIC system continues to be developed in Beihang. Some of the testing that has been undertaken will be repeated with the new version.

A practical classroom environment will be deployed and tested. The authors have already demonstrated the response of the system across an internet connection and performed some testing during separate experiments. This will be further expanded to include geographically remote host vStore environments.

Power consumption is a very significant aspect in Cloud Computing, reducing power requirements will reduce environmental aspects and cost of ownership. Work is going to be directed towards developing tests and methods of measuring the overall impact of iVIC and other systems.

FURTHER READING

The iVIC project is hosted at http://www.ivic.org.cn/ivic/. The public site does not always make all of the latest developments available but does have some interesting links and documents.

Further reading topics in the general field of virtualisation appear to increase in number almost every day. The rate of change and the absolute volume of information available mean that developments are rarely formally printed but are available at the websites of the major contributors such as VMWare, Microsoft, Xen and KVM. This list is not intended as definitive, it provides only a few possible starting points.

Most styles of Cloud Computing use virtualisation as a foundation component. Significant amounts of information and understanding can be derived from Cloud providers.

ACKNOWLEDGMENT

The work reported in this chapter has been supported by the RLTF HECloud Programme (Ref: RLTFD005), Visiting Scholar foundation of *Key Laboratory* of *Dependable Service* Computing in Cyber Physical Society (CPS-DSC 2012FWJJ01), National Natural Science Foundation of China Program, under contact No. 61272074 and China 973 Fundamental R&D Program (No. 2011CB302600).

REFERENCES

Abels, T., Dhawan, P., & Chandrasekaran, B. (2005, August). *An overview of xen virtualization*. Retrieved August 15, 2011, from http://www.dell.com/downloads/global/power/ps3q05-20050191-Abels.pdf

AMD. (n.d.). *AMD virtualization (AMD-V™) technology*. Retrieved July 12, 2011, from http://sites.amd.com/us/business/it-solutions/virtualization/Pages/amd-v.aspx

Barcelona Supercomputing Center. (2010, January). *EMOTIVE cloud Barcelona*. Retrieved September 12, 2011, from http://autonomic.ac.upc.edu/emotive/

Barham, P., Dragovic, B., Fraser, K., Hand, S., Harris, T., Ho, A., et al. (2003, October 19). *Xen and the art of virtualization*. SOSP'03. Bolton Landing, NY: ACM.

Bittman, T. J., Dawson, P., & Weiss, G. J. (2010, May 26). *Magic quadrant for x86 server virtualisation infrastructure*. Retrieved September 6, 2011, from http://www.vmware.com/files/pdf/cloud/Gartner-VMware-Magic-Quadrant.pdf

Bittman, T. J., Weiss, G. J., Margevicius, M. A., & Dawson, P. (2011, June 30). *Magic quadrant for x86 server virtualization infrastructure*. Retrieved September 4, 2011, from http://www.gartner.com/technology/media-products/reprints/microsoft/vol2/article8a/article8a.html

Debianhelp. (n.d.). *Monitoring debian system resources*. Retrieved September 2, 2011, from http://www.debianhelp.co.uk/resources.htm

EMOTIVECloud. (2011). *Quick user's guide*. Retrieved September 10, 2011, from http://autonomic.ac.upc.edu/emotive/?page_id=503

Hardy, J., Liu, L., Antonopoulos, N., Liu, W., Cui, L., & Li, J. (2012, April 11-13). Assessment and Evaluation of Internet-based Virtual Computing Infrastructure. *Proceedings of 15th IEEE ISORC 2012*, Shenzhen, China, (pp. 39-46).

Intel. (n.d.). *Intel® virtualization technology list*. Retrieved July 12, 2011, from http://ark.intel.com/VTList.aspx

Jackson, J. (2010, April 21). *Red Hat drops xen from RHEL*. Retrieved September 10, 2011, from http://www.pcworld.com/businesscenter/article/194663/red_hat_drops_xen_from_rhel.html

Lagar-Cavilla, H. A., Whitney, J. A., Scannell, A., Patchin, P., Rumble, S. M., de Lara, E., et al. (2009, April 1-3). *SnowFlock: Rapid virtual machine cloning for cloud computing*. EuroSys'09. Nuremberg, Germany: ACM.

Li, J., Jia, Y., Liu, L., & Wo, T. (2012). *Cyber-LiveApp: A secure sharing and migration approach for live virtual desktop applications in a cloud environment. Future Generation Computer Systems*. Elsevier Science.

Li, J., Li, B., Wo, T., Hu, C., Huai, J., Liu, L., & Lam, K. P. (2012, February). CyberGuarder: A virtualization security assurance architecture for green cloud computing. *Future Generation Computer Systems, 28*(2), 379–390. doi:10.1016/j.future.2011.04.012

Liu, L., Masfary, O., & Antonopoulos, N. (2012, May). Energy performance assessment of virtualization technologies using small environmental monitoring sensors. *Sensors (Basel, Switzerland), 12*(5), 6610–6628. doi:10.3390/s120506610

Marshall, D. (2010, May 3). *Red Hat drops Xen in favor of KVM in RHEL 6*. Retrieved September 8, 2011, from http://www.infoworld.com/d/virtualization/red-hat-drops-xen-in-favor-kvm-in-rhel-6-498

Mersenne Inc. (2011). *PrimeNet CPU benchmarks*. Retrieved September 19, 2011, from http://www.mersenne.org/report_benchmarks/

Mersenne Research Inc. (2011, March 4). *Great internet Mersenne prime search*. Retrieved September 18, 2011, from http://www.mersenne.org/freesoft/

Microsoft. (2011). *Do I need Windows XP mode?* Retrieved August 10, 2011, from http://www.microsoft.com/windows/virtual-pc/download.aspx

Natarajan, R. (2010, July 12). *VMware: How to create virtual machine and install guest OS using vSphere client*. Retrieved September 6, 2011, from http://www.thegeekstuff.com/2010/07/vmware-create-virtual-machine/

Pfleeger, C. P., & Pfleeger, S. L. (2007). *Security in computing* (4th ed.). Boston, MA: Pearson Education Inc.

Redhat. (n.d.). *Manage virtual machines*. Retrieved September 23, 2011, from http://virt-manager.org/index.html

Scherrer, T. (2011, July 16). *Emulators for Z80 and Z80 based products*. Retrieved August 12, 2011, from http://www.z80.info/z80emu.htm

Schroeder, M. D., & Saltzer, J. H. (1971, October 18). A hardware architecture for implementing protection rings. *Proceedings of the Third ACM Symposium on Operating Systems Principles*. Palo Alto, California: ACM.

SourceForge. (2011, August 5). *EMOTIVECloud*. Retrieved September 10, 2011, from http://sourceforge.net/projects/emotivecloud/

Taneja Group. (2009, September). *Evaluating the ESX 4 hypervisor and VM density advantage*. Retrieved September 6, 2011, from http://www.vmware.com/files/pdf/vmware-evaluating-hypervisor-density.pdf

University of Toronto. (2008). *Snowflock 0.2c release documentation*. Retrieved August 10, 2011, from http://compbio.cs.toronto.edu/snowflock/releases/0.2/SnowFlock_Manual.html

University of Toronto. (2009). *SnowFlock: Swift VM cloning for cloud computing*. Retrieved August 8, 2011, from http://sysweb.cs.toronto.edu/snowflock?type=Downloads

Varian, M. (1997, August). *VM and the VM community: Past, present, and future*. Retrieved August 10, 2011, from http://web.me.com/melinda.varian/Site/Melinda_Varians_Home_Page_files/25paper.pdf

WineHQ. (2011, August 19). Retrieved from http://www.winehq.org/

APPENDIX 1: SAMPLE XP XML DEFINITION FILE

Code 2. Sample template file

```
<?xml version="1.0" ?>
<vTemplate uuid="48b80d40-e99b-8397-b842-27dfe98bc964">
<Name>
 xp-pro
 </Name>
 <Description>
 A development environment
 </Description>
 <Capabilities>
 <vNode/>
 </Capabilities>
 <OS>
 <Type>
 windows
 </Type>
 <Distribution>
 Windows-xp
 </Distribution>
 <Release>
 xp
 </Release>
 <Kernel>
 generic
 </Kernel>
 <Packages>
 base-files
 </Packages>
 </OS>
 <Repository>
 local
 </Repository>
 <DeployInfo>
 <PreferedSettings>
 <vCPU>
  1
 </vCPU>
 <Mem>
  512M
```

continued on following page

387

Code 2. Continued

```
</Mem>
<DiskSize>
 20G
</DiskSize>
</PreferedSettings>
<Method>
nfsmount
</Method>
<URL>
  nfs://192.168.0.15/var/lib/ivic/vstore/nfsbase/xp-pro.img
</URL>
<COWDir>
  nfs://192.168.0.15/var/lib/ivic/vstore/nfscow
</COWDir>
</DeployInfo>
</vTemplate>
```

APPENDIX 2: NETWORK MODIFICATIONS – XP CLONES

The first file is created in the folder "C:\Documents and Settings\All Users\Start Menu\Programs\Startup" and is named start-net.bat, the content is given in Code 3.

Code 3: XP start-net.bat

```
@echo off
if not exist C:/networkconfig.bat goto notavm
call "cmd /c start c:\remove.bat"
C:/networkconfig.bat
:notavm
exit
```

This file checks for the presence of the "networkconfig.bat" file created by iVIC. If it is not present then this is not an iVIC clone and the file exits. If the file is present, then this is an iVIC clone and "remove.bat" should run concurrently with "networkconfig.bat". The second file is located in c:\ and named "remove.bat". It contains the commands shown in Code 4.

Code 4: xp remove.bat

```
@echo off
ping -n 1 127.0.0.1 > "C:\documents and settings\all users\start menu\pro-
grams\startup\ start-net.bat"
del "C:\documents and settings\all users\start menu\programs\startup\ start-
net.bat"
exit
```

This file sends one ping packet back to the loopback address of the VM and directs the output to the "start-net.bat" file. This introduces a 1 second delay to ensure that focus has passed from the "start-net.bat" file to the "networkconfig.bat" before the "start-net.bat" file is deleted, which prevents it from re-configuring the network on subsequent starts.

The "networkconfig.bat" file changes the name of the VM to a unique name and manually sets the IP address.

Compilation of References

Aaron, W. (2007). Computing in the clouds. *netWorker*, *4*, 16–25.

Abels, T., Dhawan, P., & Chandrasekaran, B. (2005, August). *An overview of xen virtualization.* Retrieved August 15, 2011, from http://www.dell.com/downloads/global/power/ps3q05-20050191-Abels.pdf

Adamov, A., & Erguvan, M. (2009). The truth about Cloud computing as new paradigm in IT. In The 3rd International Conference on Application of Information and Communication Technologies – AICT2009, Azerbaijan-Baku, (pp.1-3)

Adams, K., & Agesen, O. (2006). A comparison of software and hardware techniques for x86 virtualization. Proceedings of the 12th International Conference on Architectural Support for Programming Languages and Operating Systems (pp. 2-13). doi:10.1145/1168857.1168860

Aggarwal, G., et al. (2005). Two can keep a secret: a distributed architecture for secure database services. In Proceedings of the Conference on Innovative Data Systems Research 2005.

Agrawal, N., Bolosky, W. J., Douceur, J. R., & Lorch, J. R. (2007). A five-year study of file-system metadata. In *5th USENIX Conference on File and Storage Technologies* (pp. 31-45). Berkeley, CA: USENIX Association.

Ahmed, K. E. U., & Alexandrov, V. (2011). *Identity and access management in cloud computing* (pp. 115–133). Cloud Computing for Enterprise Architectures. doi:10.1007/978-1-4471-2236-4_6

Ahn, G. J., & Sekar, P. (2011). Ontology-based risk evaluation in user-centric identity management. In K. Hagimoto, H. Ueda, & A. Jamalipour (Eds.), IEEE International Conference on Communications (ICC) (pp. 1-5). Kypto, Japan: IEEE Press.

Ahn, G. J., Hu, H., & Jin, J. (2009). Security-enhanced OSGi Service Environments. *IEEE Transactions on Systems, Man and Cybernetics. Part C, Applications and Reviews*, *39*(5), 562–571. doi:10.1109/TSMCC.2009.2020437

Al-Aqrabi, H., Liu, L., Hill, R., Antonopoulos, N., & Liu, W. (2012). Taking the business intelligence to the clouds. *Proceedings of 3th IEEE International Symposium on Dependable Service-Oriented and Cloud Computing* (DSOC2012), (p. 1). Liverpool, UK: IEEE Computer Society Press.

Al-Aqrabi, H., Liu, L., Xu, J., Hill, R., Antonopoulos, N., & Zhan, Y. (2012). Investigation of IT security and compliance challenges in security-as-a service for cloud computing. *Proceedings of 15th IEEE International Symposium on Object/Component/Service-Oriented Real-Time Distributed Computing Workshops* (ISORC2012), (p. 3). Shenzhen, China: IEEE Computer Society Press.

Albrecht, C. C., Dean, D. L., & Hansen, J. V. (2005). Marketplace and technology standards for B2B e-commerce: Progress, challenges, and the state of the art. *Information & Management*, *42*, 865–875. doi:10.1016/j.im.2004.09.003

Alexander, L., Markus, K., Jens, N., Stefan, T., & Thomas, S. (2009). What's inside the Cloud? An architectural map of the Cloud landscape. Proceedings of the 2009 ICSE Workshop on Software Engineering Challenges of Cloud Computing, (pp. 23-31).

Al-Fares, M., Loukissas, A., & Vahdat, A. (2008). A scalable, commodity data center network architecture. Proceedings of the ACM SIGCOMM conference on Data communication, USA, (pp. 63-74). doi: 10.1145/1402958.1402967

Allen, S. (2008). Update from Amazon regarding Friday's S3 downtime. Retrieved February 3, 2008, from http://www.centernetworks.com/amazon-s3-downtime-update

Al-Masri, E., & Mahmoud, Q. H. (2007). QoS-based discovery and ranking of Web services. Paper presented at the 16th International Conference on Computer Communications and Networks (ICCCN), Honolulu, Hawaii, USA.

Alok, S. (1992). Client-server computing. *Communications of the ACM, 35*(7), 77–98. doi:10.1145/129902.129908

Alonso-Calvo, R., Crespo, J., Garc'ia-Remesal, M., Anguita, A., & Maojo, V. (2010). On distributing load in Cloud Computing: A real application for very-large image datasets. *Procedia Computer Science, 1*(1), 2663–2671. doi:10.1016/j.procs.2010.04.300

Amazon (2011). Amazon elastic compute cloud. Retrieved from http://aws.amazon.com/ec2

Amazon S3. (2009). Amazon S3: Simple storage service. Retrieved March 10, 2010, from http://www.amazon.com/s3/

Amazon. (2009). Amazon elastic compute cloud (EC2). Retrieved March 10, 2010, from http://www.amazon.com/ec2/

Amazon. (2012). Amazon web services. Retrieved June 1, 2012, from http://aws.amazon.com/

Amburst, M., Fox, A., Griffith, R., Joseph, A. D., Katz, R. H., & Konwinski, A. … Zaharia, M. (2009). *Above the clouds: A Berkeley view of cloud computing*, (p. 2). (Technical Report No. UCB/EECS-2009-28). Electrical Engineering and Computer Sciences, University of California at Berkeley. Retrieved January 24, 2012, from http://www.eecs.berkeley.edu/Pubs/TechRpts/2009/EECS-2009-28.pdf

Amburst, M., Fox, A., Griffith, R., Joseph, A. D., Katz, R., & Konwinski, A. (2010). A view of cloud computing. *Communications of the ACM, 53*(4), 50–58. doi:10.1145/1721654.1721672

AMD. (n.d.). *AMD virtualization (AMD-V™) technology*. Retrieved July 12, 2011, from http://sites.amd.com/us/business/it-solutions/virtualization/Pages/amd-v.aspx

Anderson, T., Peterson, L., Shenker, S., & Turner, J. (2005). Overcoming the Internet impasse through virtualization. *Computer, 38*(4), 34–41. doi:10.1109/MC.2005.136

Anthes, G. (2010). Security in the cloud. *Communications of the ACM, 53*(11), 16–18. doi:10.1145/1839676.1839683

Apache Hadoop. (2012). Welcome to Apache Hadoop. Retrieved January 12, 2012, from http://hadoop.apache.org/

Aparicio, M. IV. (2009). *Making memories: Applying neuron-inspired associative memories to national, business, and consumer intelligence*. Cary, NC: Saffron Technology, Inc.

Ardagna, D., & Pernici, B. (2007). Adaptive service composition in flexible processes. *IEEE Transactions on Software Engineering, 33*(6), 369–384. doi:10.1109/TSE.2007.1011

Ardissono, L., Console, L., Goy, A., Petrone, G., Picardi, C., Segnan, M., & Dupré, D. T. (2005, May). Towards self-diagnosing Web services. Paper presented at the meeting of the International Workshop on Self-Managed Systems and Services (SELFMAN), Nice, France.

Armando, A., Carbone, R., Compagna, L., Cuellar, J., & Tobarra, L. (2008). Formal analysis of SAML 2.0 web browser single sign-on: breaking the SAML-based single sign-on for google apps.

Armbrust, M., Fox, A., Griffith, R., Joseph, A. D., Katz, R., & Konwinski, A. … Zaharia, M. (2009). Above the clouds: A Berkeley view of cloud computing. Berkeley, CA: University of California Berkeley. doi:10.1.1.150.628

Asprey, D. (2012, January 06). The cloud ate my homework. Retrieved from http://Cloudsecurity.trendmicro.com/the-Cloud-ate-my-homework/

Atallah, M., Frikken, K., & Blanton, M. (2005). Dynamic and efficient key management for access hierarchies. In Proceedings of Computer and Communication Security.

Atallah, M. J., Blanton, M., Fazio, N., & Frikken, K. B. (2009). *Dynamic and efficient key management for access hierarchies* (pp. 1–43). ACM TISSEC.

Aulbach, S., Grust, T., Jacobs, D., Kemper, A., & Rittinger, J. (2008). Multi-tenant databases for software as a service: Schema mapping techniques. *Proceedings of the 2008 SIGMOD International Conference on Management of Data*, (pp. 1195-1206).

Avizienis, A., Laprie, J., & Landwehr, C. (2004). Basic concepts and taxonomy of dependable and secure computing. *IEEE Transactions on Dependable and Secure Computing, 1*(1), 11–33. doi:10.1109/TDSC.2004.2

Avram, A. (2011). Gartner's predictions for the next 5 years. Retrieved January 15, 2012, from http://www.infoq.com/news/2011/12/Gartner-Predictions-Next-5-Years

AWS Case Study: Washington Post. (n.d.). Retrieved from http://aws.amazon.com/solutions/case-studies/washington-post/

Aymerich, F., Fenu, G., & Surcis, S. (2009). A real time financial system based on grid and cloud computing. 2009 ACM symposium on Applied Computing, (pp. 1219 – 1220). Honolulu, Hawaii, USA.

Azure, M. (2011). Deploying and updating Windows Azure applications. Retrieved from https://www.windowsazure.com/en-us/develop/net/fundamentals/deploying-applications#benefits

Badger, L., Bohn, R., Chu, S., Hogan, M., Liu, F., & Kaufmann, V. ... Leaf, D. (2011). *U.S. government cloud computing technology roadmap – Volume II,* (pp. 10-15). (Special Publication 500-293, NIST). U.S. Department of Commerce.

Bailey, J. P., & Bakos, Y. (1997). An exploratory study of the emerging role of electronic intermediaries. *International Journal of Electronic Commerce, 1*(3), 7–20.

Bain, S. A., Merchant, F., Minns, B., & Thomas, J. (2010, March). Building a dynamic infrastructure with IBM power systems: A closer look at private cloud TCO. Retrieved December 22, 2011, from http://public.dhe.ibm.com/common/ssi/ecm/en/pow03043usen/POW03043USEN.PDF

Baran, D. (2008). Cloud computing basics. Retrieved November 10, 2008, from http://www.webguild.org/2008/07/cloud-computing-basics.php

Baranovski, A., Bharathi, S., Bresnahan, J., Chervenak, A., Foster, I., Fraser, D., et al. (2007). Enabling distributed petascale science. Journal of Physics: Conference Series, 78.

Barcelona Supercomputing Center. (2010, January). *EMOTIVE cloud Barcelona.* Retrieved September 12, 2011, from http://autonomic.ac.upc.edu/emotive/

Barham, P., Dragovic, B., Fraser, K., Hand, S., Harris, T., & Ho, A. ... Warfield, A. (2003). Xen and the art of virtualization. Proceedings of the Nineteenth ACM Symposium on Operating Systems Principles, USA, (pp. 164-177). doi: 10.1145/945445.945462

Barros, A., & Oberle, D. (Eds.). (2012). Handbook of service description. Springer. Retrieved from http://www.springer.com/computer/database management & information retrieval/book/978-1-4614-1863-4

Baude, F., Filali, I., Huet, F., Legrand, V., Mathias, E., Merle, P., et al. (2010). ESB federation for large scale SOA. In Proceedings of the 2010 ACM Symposium on Applied Computing (pp. 2459-2466).

Behrend, T. S., Wiebe, E. N., London, J. E., & Johnson, E. C. (2011). Cloud computing adoption and usage in community colleges. *Behaviour & Information Technology, 30*(2), 231–240. doi:10.1080/0144929X.2010.489118

Bertino, E., Paci, F., & Ferrini, R. (2009). Privacy-preserving digital identity management for cloud computing. *IEEE Computer Society Data Engineering Bulletin, 1*(32), 1–4.

Bertsekas, D. P. (1996). *Constrained optimization and lagrange multiplier methods.* Belmont, CA: Athena Scientific.

Bhaskar, P. Rimal, Eunmi, C., & Ian, L. (2009). A taxonomy and survey of cloud computing systems. In Fifth International Joint Conference on INC, IMS and IDC, (pp. 44-51).

Bhatti, R., Joshi, J. B. D., Bertino, E., & Ghafoor, A. (2003). Access control in dynamic XML-based web-services with X-RBAC. In L. J. Zhang (Ed.), First International Conference in Web Services (pp. 243-249). Las Vegas, USA.

Bhatti, R., Joshi, J. B. D., Bertino, E., & Ghafoor, A. (2005). X-GTRBAC: An XML-based policy specification framework and architecture for enterprise-wide access control. [TISSEC]. *ACM Transactions on Information and System Security, 8*(2), 187–227. doi:10.1145/1065545.1065547

Bianco, P., Kotermanski, R., & Merson, P. (2007). *Evaluating a service oriented architecture*. Software Engineering Institute, Carnegie Mellon University. Tech Report ESC-TR-2007-015.

Bila, N., Lara, E., Josi, K., Lagar-Cavilla, H., Hiltunen, M., & Satyanarayanan, M. (2012). Jettison: Efficient idle desktop consolidation with partial VM migration. Proceedings of the 7th ACM European Conference on Computer Systems (EuroSys '12), (pp. 1-14). Retrieved from http://lagarcavilla.com/publications/BilaEurosys12.pdf

Bin, W., Yuan, H. H., Xi, L. X., & Min, X. J. (2009). Open identity management framework for SaaS ecosystem.

Birget, J., Zou, X., Noubir, G., & Ramamurthy, B. (2002). Hierarchy-based access control in distributed environments. In Proceedings of IEEE International Conference on Communications.

Bisong, A., & Rahman, S. M. (2011). An overview of the security concerns in enterprise cloud computing. *International Journal of Network Security and its Applications, 3*(1), 30-45.

Bittman, T. J., Dawson, P., & Weiss, G. J. (2010, May 26). *Magic quadrant for x86 server virtualisation infrastructure*. Retrieved September 6, 2011, from http://www.vmware.com/files/pdf/cloud/Gartner-VMware-Magic-Quadrant.pdf

Bittman, T. J., Weiss, G. J., Margevicius, M. A., & Dawson, P. (2011, June 30). *Magic quadrant for x86 server virtualization infrastructure*. Retrieved September 4, 2011, from http://www.gartner.com/technology/media-products/reprints/microsoft/vol2/article8a/article8a.html

Blaze, M., Kannan, S., Lee, I., Sokolsky, O., Smith, J. M., Keromytis, A. D., & Lee, W. (2009). Dynamic trust management. *IEEE Computer, 42*(2), 44–51. doi:10.1109/MC.2009.51

Bloom, B. H. (1970). Space/time trade-offs in hash coding with allowable errors. *Communications of the ACM, 13*(7), 422–426. doi:10.1145/362686.362692

Blunk, L., Vollbrecht, J., & Aboba, B. (2002). The one time password (OTP) and generic token card authentication protocols. (IETF Internet Draft, draft-ietf-eap-otp-00.txt).

Bobroff, N., Kochut, A., & Beaty, K. (2007). Dynamic placement of virtual machines for managing SLA violations. International Symposium on Integrated Network Management, Munich, (pp. 119-128). doi: 10.1109/INM.2007.374776

Böhmer, M., Daniluk, D., Schmidt, M., & Gsell, H. (2012). Business object model for realization of individual business processes in the logistics domain. In Clausen, U. (Ed.), *Efficiency and logistics*. Berlin, Germany: Springer. doi:10.1007/978-3-642-32838-1_25

BOINC Project. (n.d.). Retrieved January 2012, from http://boinc.berkeley.edu/

Bolze, R., & Deelman, E. (2011). Exploiting the cloud of computing environments: An application's perspective. In S. A. Ahson & M. Ilyas (Eds.), *Cloud computing and software services: Theory and techniques* (pp. 173-196). CRC Press, Taylor and Francis Group.

Borthakur, D., et al. (2011, June) Apache Hadoop goes realtime at Facebook. SIGMOD '11: Proceedings of the 2011 International Conference on Management of Dat (pp. 1071–1080). doi: 10.1145/1989323.1989438

Breeding, M. (2009, November). The advance of computing from the ground to the cloud. *Computers in Libraries*.

Breiter, G., & Behrendt, M. (2009). Life cycle and characteristics of services in the world of cloud computing. *IBM Journal of Research and Development, 53*(4), 1–8. doi:10.1147/JRD.2009.5429057

Brian de. H. (2008). Cloud computing - The jargon is back! Cloud Computing Journal, online. Retrieved from http://cloudcomputing.sys-con.com/node/613070

Broberg, J., Venugopal, S., & Buyya, S. (2008). Market-oriented grids and utility computing: The state-of-the-art and future directions. *Journal of Grid Computing, 6*(3), 255–276. doi:10.1007/s10723-007-9095-3

Bruening, P. J., & Treacy, B. C. (2009). Cloud computing: Privacy, security challenges. Privacy & Security Law Report, the Bureau of National Affairs, Inc.

Burd, S. D., Seazzu, A. F., & Conway, C. (2009). Virtual computing laboratories: A case study with comparisons to physical computing laboratories. Journal of Information Technology Education: Innovations in Practice, 8.

Busacca, P. G., Marseguerra, M., & Zio, E. (2001). Multi-objective optimization by genetic algorithms: Application to safety systems. *Reliability Engineering & System Safety*, 72(1), 59–74. doi:10.1016/S0951-8320(00)00109-5

Butt, N. F., Chowdhury, M., & Boutaba, R. (2010). Topology-awareness and reoptimization mechanism for virtual network embedding. *Lecture Notes in Computer Science*, 27–39. doi:10.1007/978-3-642-12963-6_3

Buyya, R. R., & Calheiros, R. (2010). InterCloud: Utility-oriented federation of cloud computing environments for scaling of application services. 10th International Conference on Algorithms and Architectures for Parallel Processing (ICA3PP 2010), (pp. 13–31). Busan, Korea.

Buyya, R., Abramson, D., & Venugopal, S. (2005). The grid economy. Proceedings of the IEEE, 93(3), 698_714.

Buyya, R., Yeo, C. S., Venugopal, S., Broberg, J., & Brandic, I. (2008). Market-oriented cloud computing: Vision, hype, and reality for delivering computing as the 5th utility. Paper presented at the 2009 9th IEEE/ACM International Symposium on Cluster Computing and the Grid, Shanghai, China. doi:10.1016/j.future.2008.12.001

Buyya, R., Yeo, C. S., Venugopal, S., Broberg, J., & Brandic, I. (2009). Cloud computing and emerging IT platforms: Vision, hype, and reality for delivering computing as the 5th utility. *Future Generation Computer Systems, 2009*. doi:doi:10.1016/j.future.2008.12.001

Cappos, J., Beschastnikh, I., Krishnamurthy, A., & Anderson, T. (2009). Seattle: A platform for educational cloud computing. 40th ACM technical Symposium on Computer Science Education (SIGCSE09), (pp. 111–115). Chattanooga, USA.

Carr, N. G. (2003, May). IT doesn't matter. In Harvard Business Review. Retrieved from http://hbr.org/2003/05/it-doesnt-matter/ar/1

Carroll, M., Merwe, A., & Kotze, P. (2011). Secure cloud computing: Benefits, risks and controls. *Information Security South Africa Conference*, (pp. 1-9).

Carvalho, M. (2011). SECaaS–Security as a service. *ISSA Journal*, 20-24.

Catteddu, D., & Hogben, G. (2009). Cloud computing: Benefits, risks and recommendations for information security. European Network and Information Security Agency (ENISA) Report. Retrieved August 10, 2011, from http://www.enisa.europa.eu/act/rm/files/deliverables/Cloud-computing-risk-assessment/at_download/fullReport

Catteddu, D., & Hogben, G. (2009). *Cloud computing security risk assessment. European Network and Information Security Agency*. ENISA.

Cavoukian, A. (2008). *Privacy in the clouds: Privacy and digital identity - Implications for the Internet*. Information and Privacy Commissioner of Ontario.

Celesti, A., Tusa, F., Villari, M., & Puliafito, A. (2010). How to enhance cloud architectures to enable cross-federation. Proceedings of the IEEE third International Conference on Cloud Computing (CLOUD), (pp. 337-345).

CenterBeam. (2012). CenterBeam 365+ enterprise-class cloud solution. Retrieved January 12, 2012, from http://www.centerbeam.com/managed-it-services/CenterBeam365/

Ceselli, E. D., di Vimercati, S. D. C., Jajodia, S., Paraboschi, S., & Samarati, P. (2005). *Modeling and assessing inference exposure in encrypted databases* (pp. 119–152). ACM TISSEC. doi:10.1145/1053283.1053289

Chakraborty, S., & Ray, I. (2006). TrustBAC: Integrating trust relationships into the RBAC model for access control in open systems. In I. Ray (Ed.), 11th ACM Symposium on Access Control Models and Technologies (SACMAT06) (pp. 49-58). Tahoe City, UT: ACM Press.

Chang, M., He, J., & Castro-Leon, E. (2006). Service-orientation in the computing infrastructure. Proceedings of the 2nd IEEE International Symposium on Service-Oriented System Engineering (SOSE'06) (pp. 27-33). doi:10.1109/SOSE.2006.35

Chang, F., Dean, J., Ghemawat, S., Hsieh, W. C., Wallach, D. A., & Burrows, M. (2008). Bigtable: A distributed storage system for structured data. *ACM Transactions on Computer Systems, 26*(2), 1–26. doi:10.1145/1365815.1365816

Chao, Y., Bingyao, C., Jiaying, D., & Wei, G. (2010). The research and implementation of UTM. *IET International Communication Conference on Wireless Mobile and Computing,* (pp. 389-392).

Chase, J. S., Anderson, D. C., Thakar, P. N., Vahdat, A. M., & Doyle, R. P. (2001). Managing energy and server resources in hosting centers. Proceedings of the Eighteenth ACM Symposium on Operating Systems Principles, (pp. 103-116). doi: 10.1145/502034.502045

Chauhan, M. A., & Ali Babar, M. (2011). Migrating service-oriented system to cloud computing: An experience report. *CLOUD '11 Proceedings of the 2011 IEEE 4th International Conference on Cloud Computing*, (pp. 404-411). 4-9 July 2011, Washington, DC, USA.

Chen, F., Li, S., & Yang, H. (2005). Feature analysis for service-oriented reengineering. *12th IEEE Asia-Pacific Software Engineering Conference*, (pp. 201-208). 15-17 December 2005, Taipei, Taiwan.

Chen, G., He, W., Liu, J., Nath, S., Rigas, L., Xiao, L., & Zhao, F. (2008). Energy-aware server provisioning and load dispatching for connection-intensive internet services. Proceedings of the 5th USENIX Symposium on Networked Systems Design and Implementation, (pp. 337-350).

Chen, X., Liu, X., Huang, Z., & Sun, H. (2010, July). RegionKNN: A scalable hybrid collaborative filtering algorithm for personalized Web service recommendation. Paper presented at the International Conference on Web Services (ICWS), Miami, Florida, USA.

Chen, Y., Paxson, V., & Katz, R. H. (2010). What's new about cloud computing security? Technical Report No. UCB/EECS-2010-5, EECS Department, University of California at Berkeley. Retrieved August 10, 2011, from http://www.eecs.berkeley.edu/Pubs/TechRpts/2010/EECS-2010-5.html

Cheng, B. H. C., Sawyer, P., Bencomo, N., & Whittle, J. (2009). A goal-based modeling approach to develop requirements of an adaptive system with environmental uncertainty. *Lecture Notes in Computer Science, 5795,* 468–483. doi:10.1007/978-3-642-04425-0_36

Chorafas, D. N. (2011). *Cloud computing strategies* (pp. 65–70). London, UK: CRC Press, Taylor & Francis Group.

Chouhan, P. K. (2006). Automatic deployment for application service provider environments. Doctoral Dissertation.

Chowdhury, N., & Boutaba, R. (2010). A survey of network virtualization. *Computer Networks, 54*(5), 862–876. doi:10.1016/j.comnet.2009.10.017

Chung, S. S., & Ozsoyoglu, G. (2005). Processing aggregate queries over encrypted relational databases. Technical Report, Case Western Reserve University. Retrieved from http://art.case.edu/anti-tamper.pdf

Chung, S., Byang, J., & Davalos, S. (2007). Service-oriented software reengineering: SOSR. *HICSS '07 Proceedings of the 40th Annual Hawaii International Conference on System Sciences*, (pp. 170). 3-6 January 2007, Waikoloa, Big Island, Hawaii, USA.

Clark, C., Fraser, K., Hand, S., Hansen, J. G., & Jul, E. Limpach, C., … Warfield., A. (2005). Live migration of virtual machines. Proceedings of the 2nd Conference on Symposium on Networked Systems Design & Implementation, Vol. 2, (pp. 273-286).

Cloud Security Alliance. (2009). Security guidance for critical areas of focus in cloud computing v2.1. http://www.cloudsecurityalliance.org

Cloud Security Alliance. (2011). Security guidance for critical areas of focus in cloud computing V3.0. Retrieved December 10, 2011, from https://cloudsecurityalliance.org/guidance/csaguide.v3.0.pdf

Cloud Standards Coordination. (n.d.). Retrieved January 2012, from http://www.Cloudbook.net/directories/Cloud-groups/Cloud-standards-coordination

CloudRooms virtual classrooms. (n.d.). Retrieved July 2012, from http://www.redtray.co.uk/cloudrooms/

Cohen, W. W., Schapire, R. E., & Singer, Y. (1999). Learning to order things. *Journal of Artificial Intelligence Research, 5,* 243–270.

Computing, C. Delivering Internet-based information and technology services in real time. (n.d.). Retrieved March 20, 2011, from https://www.ibm.com/developerworks/university/Cloud/

Cook, K. (2009). Current wideband MILSATCOM infrastructure and the future of bandwidth availability. Paper presented to the 2009 IEEE Annual Conference, Big Sky, MT. doi: 10.1109/AERO.2009.4839401

Cormode, G., Srivastava, D., Yu, T., & Zhang, Q. (2008). Anonymizing bipartite graph data using safe groupings. In Proceedings of the 34th International Conference on Very Large Data Bases (VLDB 2008).

Cornish, E. (2004). *Futuring: The exploitation of the future*. Bethesda, MD: World Future Society.

Corrin, A. (2011, June 9). Navy needs a way to handle UAV, sensor data. Defense Systems. Retrieved December 29, 2011, from http://defensesystems.com/articles/2011/06/09/naval-it-day-afcea-tcped-intelligence-data-challenge.aspx

Coughlin, T. M. (2009). Virtualization of consumer storage. Paper presented to the 2010 IEEE 14th International Symposium on Consumer Electronics, Braunschweig, Germany. doi: 10.1109/ISCE.2010.5523736

Crampton, J. (2010). XACML and role-based access control. Retrieved from http://dimacs.rutgers.edu/Workshops/Commerce/slides/crampton.pdf

Credit Based Scheduler. (2007). Retrieved from http://wiki.xensource.com/xenwiki/CreditScheduler

Cukier, K. (2010, February 25). Data, data everywhere. *The Economist*. Retrieved January 10, 2012, from http://www.economist.com/specialreports/displaystory.cfm?story_id=15557443

Dai, Y., Yang, L., & Zhang, B. (2009). QoS-driven self-healing web service composition based on performance prediction. *Journal of Computer Science and Technology*, *24*(2), 250–261. doi:10.1007/s11390-009-9221-8

Damiani, E., di Vimercati, S. D. C., Foresti, S., Jajodia, S., Paraboschi, S., & Samarati, P. (2005). Key management for multi-user encrypted databases. In Proceedings of the ACM Workshop on Storage Security and Survivability, (pp. 74-83).

Damiani, E., et al. (2007). An experimental evaluation of multi-key strategies for data outsourcing. In Proceedings of the 22nd IFIP TC-11 International Information Security Conference.

Damiani, E., De Capitani di Vimercati, S., Foresti, S., Jajodia, S., Paraboschi, S., & Samarati, P. (2007). Selective data encryption in outsourced dynamic environments. *Electronic Notes in Theoretical Computer Science*. doi:10.1016/j.entcs.2006.11.003

Daniel, F., Koschmider, A., Nestler, T., Roy, M., & Namoun, A. (2010). Toward process mashups: Key ingredients and open research challenges. In Proceedings of the 3rd and 4th International Workshop on Web APIs and Services Mashups.

Daniel, N., Rich, W., Chris, G., Graziano, O., Sunil, S., Lamia, Y., & Dmitrii, Z. (2009). Eucalyptus: An open-source Cloud computing infrastructure. Journal of Physics: Conference Series, 180.

Dannen, C., & White, C. (2011). *Beginning iOS apps with Facebook and Twitter APIs* (pp. 9–14). Apress. doi:10.1007/978-1-4302-3543-9_2

Dashboard, I. T. (n.d.). Retrieved January 2012, from http://www.Cloudbook.net/directories/gov-Clouds/gov-program.php?id=100006

Data.gov. (n.d.). Retrieved January 2012, from http://www.Cloudbook.net/directories/gov-Clouds/gov-program.php?id=100005

Dean, J., & Ghemawat, S. (2008). MapReduce: Simplified data processing on large clusters. *Communications of the ACM*, *51*(1), 107–113. doi:10.1145/1327452.1327492

Debianhelp. (n.d.). *Monitoring debian system resources*. Retrieved September 2, 2011, from http://www.debian-help.co.uk/resources.htm

Deb, K., Pratap, A., & Agarwal, S. (2002). A fast and elitist multiobjective genetic algorithm: NSGA-II. *IEEE Transactions on Evolutionary Computation*, *6*(2), 182–197. doi:10.1109/4235.996017

Defense Information Systems Agency (DISA). (n.d.). Retrieved January 1, 2012, from http://www.Cloudbook.net/directories/gov-Clouds/disa-defense-information-systems-agency

Defense Information Systems Agency. (2009). DISA offers cloud computing with RACE. Retrieved October 15, 2010, from http://www.disa.mil/news/pressreleases/2009/race_100509.html

Defense Information Systems Agency. (2009). Rapid access computing environment (RACE). Retrieved October 15, 2010, from http://www.disa.mil/race/

Dejan, M. (2008). Cloud computing: Interview with Russ Daniels and Franco Travostino. *IEEE Internet Computing*, *5*, 7–9.

Delic, K. (2005, December 7-13). On dependability of corporate grids. ACM Ubiquity, 6(45).

Delic, K., & Walke, M. (2008). Emergence of the academic computing clouds. ACM Ubiquity Magazine, 9(31).

Derrick, K., Bahman, J., Paul, M., Franck, C., & David, P. A. (2009). Cost-benefit analysis of Cloud Computing versus desktop grids. Proceedings of the 2009 IEEE International Symposium on Parallel&Distributed Processing, (pp. 1-12).

Devanbu, P., Gertz, M., Martel, C., & Stubblebine, S. G. (2000). Authentic third-party data publication. In 14th IFIP Working Conference in Database Security.

di Vimercati, S. D. C., Foresti, S., Jajodia, S., Paraboschi, S., & Samarati, P. (2007). A data outsourcing architecture combining cryptography and access control. In Proceedings of the ACM Workshop on Computer Security Architecture, (pp. 63-69).

di Vimercati, S. D. C., Foresti, S., Jajodia, S., Paraboschi, S., & Samarati, P. (2007). Over-encryption: Management of access control evolution on outsourced data. In Proceedings of VLDB'07.

Dignan, L. (2008, November). Amazon launches Cloud-Front; Content delivery network margins go kaboom. Between the Lines. ZDNet.

Dillon, T., Wu, C., & Chang, E. (2010). Cloud computing: Issues and challenges. In 2010 24th IEEE International Conference on Advanced Information Networking and Applications (AINA). DOI: 10.1109/AINA.2010.187

DuraSpcace. (n.d.). Retrieved January 2012, from http://www.duraspace.org

EGEE-II Members. (2008). An EGEE comparative study: Grids and clouds - Evolution or revolution. Technical report, Enabling Grids for E-sciencE Project. Electronic version. Retrieved from https://edms.cern.ch/document/925013/

Ekanayake, J. Qiu, X. Gunarathne, T, Beason, S., & Fox, G. (2011). High-performance parallel computing with cloud and cloud technologies. In S. A. Ahson & M. Ilyas (Eds.), *Cloud computing and software services: Theory and techniques*, (pp. 276-307). CRC Press, Taylor and Francis Group.

EMOTIVECloud. (2011). *Quick user's guide.* Retrieved September 10, 2011, from http://autonomic.ac.upc.edu/emotive/?page_id=503

Erkoç, M. F., & Kert, S. B. (2011). Cloud computing for distributed university campus: A prototype suggestion. International Conference of the Future Education, Florence, Italy. Folding@Home. (n.d.). Retrieved January 2012, from http://folding.stanford.edu/

Estievenart, F., Francois, A., Henrard, J., & Hainaut, J. (2003). A tool-supported method to extract data and schema from web sites. *5th IEEE International Workshop on Web Site Evolution*, (pp. 3-11). 22 September 2003, Amsterdam, Netherlands.

Findthebest. (2011). Retrieved December 10, 2011, from http://cloud-computing.findthebest.com

Foster, I., Zhao, Y., Raicu, I., & Lu, S. (2008). Cloud computing and grid computing 360-degree compared. Proceedings of the IEEE Grid Computing Environments Workshop, (pp. 1-10).

Foster, I. T. (2005). Globus toolkit version 4: Software for service-oriented systems. In Jin, H., Reed, D. A., & Jiang, W. (Eds.), *NPC* (*Vol. 3779*, pp. 2–13). Lecture Notes in Computer ScienceSpringer.

Foster, I., & Kesselman, C. (2004). *The Grid 2: Blueprint for a new computing infrastructure.* San Francisco, CA: Morgan Kaufmann.

Foster, I., Kesselman, C., Nick, J., & Tuecke, S. (2002). *The physiology of the grid: An open grid services architecture for distributed systems integration.* Globus Projet.

Foster, I., Kesselman, C., & Tuecke, S. (2001). The anatomy of the grid: Enabling scalable virtual organizations. *International Journal of High Performance Computing Applications*, *15*(3), 200–222. doi:10.1177/109434200101500302

Fraunhofer, I. M. L. (2010). Market study cloud computing for logistics. Retrieved from http://www.ccl.fraunhofer.de/presse-medien/publikationenICS

Fu, X., Zou, P., Shang, Z., & Jiang, Y. (2008). Fault diagnosis for Web service composition based on Bayesian network. *Journal of Computer Applications*, *28*(5), 1095–1097. doi:10.3724/SP.J.1087.2008.01095

Galen, G., & Eric, K. (2008). What Cloud computing really means. InfoWorld. Retrieved from http://www.infoworld.com/article/08/04/07/15FE-cloud-computing-reality_1.html

Gambosi, G., Postiglione, A., & Talamo, M. (2000). Algorithms for the relaxed online bin-packing model. *SIAM Journal on Computing*, 5(30), 1532–1551. doi:10.1137/S0097539799180408

Ganek, A. G., & Corbi, T. A. (2003). The dawning of the autonomic computing era. *IBM Systems Journal*, 42(1), 5–18. doi:10.1147/sj.421.0005

Garey, M. R., & Johnson, D. S. (1985). A 71/60 theorem for bin packing. *Journal of Complexity*, 1(1), 65–106. doi:10.1016/0885-064X(85)90022-6

Gartner Group. (2008). Gartner's hype cycle report, 2008. Technical report, Gartner Group. Available at http://www.gartner.com/

Gartner. (2010). Gartner identifies the top 10 strategic technologies for 2011. Retrieved January 18, 2012, from http://www.gartner.com/it/page.jsp?id=1454221

gCube. (2012). *gCube framework*. Retrieved January 10, 2012, from http://www.gcube-system.org/

Geiger, H. (2010). Government drops warrantless email search case, highlighting need for reform. Center for Democracy and Technology. Retrieved May 22, 2012, from https://www.cdt.org/blogs/harley-geiger/government-drops-warrantless-email-search-case-highlighting-need-reform

Ghemawat, S., Gobioff, H., & Leung, S. (2003). The Google file system. Proceedings of the Nineteenth ACM Symposium on Operating Systems Principles, (pp. 29-43). doi: 10.1145/945445.945450

Gokhale, S. S., & Trivedi, K. S. (2006). Analytical models for architecture-based software reliability prediction: a unification framework. *IEEE Transactions on Reliability*, 55(4), 578–590. doi:10.1109/TR.2006.884587

Goldberg, D. (1992). Using collaborative filtering to weave an information tapestry. *Communications of the ACM*, 35(12), 61–70. doi:10.1145/138859.138867

Golden, B. (2009). How cloud computing can transform business. Retrieved August 15, 2011, from http://blogs.hbr.org/cs/2010/06/business_agility_how_Cloud_com.html

Goodrich, M. T., Papamanthou, C., Tamassia, R., & Triandopoulos, N. (2008). Athos: Efficient authentication of outsourced file systems. In Proceedings of the International Conference on Information Security (pp. 80-96).

Google App Engine. (2008). Retrieved from https://developers.google.com/appengine/

Google. (2008). Web-based reference implementation of SAML-based SSO for Google Apps. Retrieved Novmeber 10, 2011, from http://code.google.com/apis/apps/sso/saml_reference_implmentation_web.html

Google. (2012). Google maps API web services. Retrieved June 1, 2012, from https://developers.google.com/maps/documentation/webservices/

Google. _app engine. (2010). Retrieved from http://appengine.google.com

Göser, K., Jurisch, M., Acker, H., Kreher, U., Lauer, M., Rinderle-Ma, S., et al. (2007). Next-generation process management with ADEPT2. In Proceedings of the BPM 2007 Demonstration Program, CEUR-WS.org Workshop Proceedings, Vol. 272, Brisbane, Australia, Sept. 2007 (pp. 3-6).

Gowrigolla, B., Sivaji, S., & Masillamani, M. R. (2010). Design and auditing of cloud computing security. *5th International Conference on Information and Automation for Sustainability*, (pp. 292-297).

Goyal, V., Pandey, O., Sahai, A., & Waters, B. (2006). Attribute -based encryption for fine-grained access control of encrypted data. In Proceedings of Conference on Computer and Communications Security.

Greenberg, A., Hamilton, J. R., Jain, N., Kandula, S., Kim, C., & Lahiri, P. … Sengupta, S. (2009). VL2: A scalable and flexible data center network. Proceedings of the ACM SIGCOMM Conference on Data Communication, (pp. 51-62). doi: 10.1145/1592568.1592576

Greenstein, S. M., & Wade, J. B. (1998). The product life cycle in the commercial mainframe computer market, 1968-1982. *The Rand Journal of Economics*, 29(4), 772–789. doi:10.2307/2556093

Grosclaude, I. (2004). Model-based monitoring of component-based software systems. Paper presented at the International Workshop on Principles of Diagnosis, Carcassonne, France.

Groß, T. (2003). Security analysis of the SAML single sign-on browser/artifact profile.

Grossman, R., & Gu, Y. (2008). Data mining using high performance data clouds: Experimental studies using sector and sphere. 14th ACM SIGKDD International Conference on Knowledge Discovery and Data Mining (KDD 08), (pp. 920 – 927). Las Vegas.

Gruschka, N., & Jensen, M. (2010). Attack surfaces: A taxonomy for attacks on cloud services. 3rd IEEE International Conference on Cloud Computing (CLOUD), (pp. 276-279).

GSA. (2012). FedRamp: Federal risk and authorization management program. U.S. General Services Administration. Retrieved May 23, 2012, from http://www.gsa.gov/portal/category/102371

Gsell, H., & Nagel, R. (2012, June). Application integration in the logistics mall. Paper presented at the SDPS 2012 - 17th International Conference on Transformative Science, Engineering, and Business Innovation, Berlin, Germany.

Gu, Y., & Grossman R. (2009). Sector and sphere: The design and implementation of a high performance data cloud. *Theme Issue of the Philosophical Transactions of the Royal Society A: Crossing Boundaries: Computational Science, E-Science and Global E-Infrastructure, 367*(1897), 2429-2445.

Gul, I., Rehman, A. U., & Islam, M. H. (2011). Cloud computing security auditing. *International Conference on Next Generation Information Technology* (pp. 143-148).

Gulati, A., Merchant, A., Uysal, M., Padala, P., & Varman, P. (2009). Efficient and adaptive proportional share I/O scheduling. *ACM SIGMETRICS Performance Evaluation Review, 37*(2), 79–80. doi:10.1145/1639562.1639595

Hacigumus, H., Iyer, B., & Mehrotra, S. (2002). Providing database as a service. In Proceedings of 18th International Conference on Data Engineering.

Hacigumus, H., Iyer, B., Mehrotra, S., & Li, C. (2002). Executing SQL over encrypted data in the database-service-provider model. In Proceedings of the ACM Special Interest Group on Management of Data (SIGMOD).

Hadoop. (2011). *Welcome to Hadoop™ distributed file system!* Retrieved December 10, 2012, from http://hadoop.apache.org/hdfs/

Hamilton, D. (2008). Cloud computing seen as next wave for technology investors. Financial Post. Retrieved from http://www.financialpost.com/money/story.html?id=562877

Han, S., & Xing, J. (2011). Ensuring data storage security through a novel third party auditor scheme in Cloud Computing. IEEE International Conference on Cloud Computing and Intelligence Systems, (pp. 264-268).

Hand, E. (2007). Head in the clouds. *Nature, 449*, 963. doi:10.1038/449963a

Hansen, S. M., Skriver, J., & Nielson, H. R. (2005). Using static analysis to validate the SAML single sign-on protocol.

Hardy, J., Liu, L., Antonopoulos, N., Liu, W., Cui, L., & Li, J. (2012, April 11-13). Assessment and Evaluation of Internet-based Virtual Computing Infrastructure. *Proceedings of 15th IEEE ISORC 2012,* Shenzhen, China, (pp. 39-46).

Harney, H., Colgrove, A., & McDaniel, P. D. (2001). Principles of policy in secure groups. In Proceedings of NDSS01.

Hayes, B. (2008). Cloud computing. *Communications of the ACM, 51*(7), 9–11. doi:10.1145/1364782.1364786

Hazelhurst, S. (2008). Scientific computing using virtual high-performance computing: A case study using the Amazon Elastic Computing Cloud. Annual Research Conference of the South African Institute of Computer Scientists and Information Technologists on IT research in developing countries (SAICSIT 08), (pp. 94 – 103). Wilderness, South Africa.

He, P., Wu, K. W., Xie, Q., et al. (2011, August). Near-optimal configuration of service pool size in service composition. Paper presented at the 6th International ICST Conference on Communications and Networking in China (CHINACOM 2011), Harbin, China.

Henderson, T., & Allen, B. (2010). Cloud storage goes first class. Network World, August, 25-28.

He, P., Wen, J. H., & Ren, H. J. (2012). Multi-objective service monitoring rate optimization using memetic algorithm. *Journal of Software*, 7(5). doi:10.4304/jsw.7.5.990-997

Hill, Z., & Humphrey, M. (2009). A quantitative analysis of high performance computing with Amazon's EC2 infrastructure: The death of the local cluster? Proceedings of the 10th IEEE/ACM International Conference on Grid Computing (pp. 26-33).

Hines, M., & Gopalan, K. (2009). Post-copy based live virtual machine migration using adaptive pre-paging and dynamic self-ballooning. Proceedings of the 2009 ACM SIGPLAN/SIGOPS International Conference on Virtual Execution Environments (VEE '09), (pp. 51-60). doi: 10.1145/1508293.1508301

Holby, H., & Trienekens, J. (2010). Challenges in business systems integration. *Computers in Industry*, 61(9), 808–812. doi:10.1016/j.compind.2010.07.006

Holtkamp, B., Steinbuß, S., Gsell, H., Löffeler, T., & Springer, U. (2010). Towards a logistics cloud. In Proceedings of the Sixth International Conference on Semantics Knowledge and Grid, SKG 2010, Ningbo, China.

Houidi, I., Louati, W., Zeghlache, D., Papadimitriou, P., & Mathy, L. (2010). *Adaptive virtual network provisioning* (pp. 41–48). IEEE SIGCOMM.

Howard, J., Kazar, M., Menees, S., Nichols, D., Satyanarayanan, M., Sidebotham, R., & West, M. (1988). Scale and performance in a distributed file system. *ACM Transactions on Computer Systems*, 6(1), 51–81. doi:10.1145/35037.35059

Hu, H., Ahn, G. J., & Kulkarni, K. (2011). Ontology-based policy anomaly management for autonomic computing. In C. Pu & J. Caverlee (Eds.), 7th International Conference on Collaborative Computing: Networking, Applications and Worksharing (CollaborateCom2011), Orlando, FL, USA. Berlin, Germany: Springer.

Huang, S., Sheoran, S., & Keskara, H. (2005). Computer-assisted supply chain configuration based on supply chain operations reference (SCOR) model. DOI: http://dx.doi.org/10.1016/j.cie.2005.01.001

Huang, W., Gao, Q., Liu, J., & Panda, D. (2009). High performance of virtual machine migration with RDMA over modern interconnects. Proceedings of the 2007 IEEE International Conference on Cluster Computing, (pp. 11-20). doi: 10.1109/CLUSTR.2007.4629212

Huang, Y., Taylor, I., Walker, D., & Davies, R. (2003). Wrapping legacy codes for grid-based applications. *17th International Parallel and Distributed Processing Symposium*, (pp. 139-145). 24-26 April 2003, Nice, France.

Huang, A. F. M., Lan, C. W., & Yang, S. J. H. (2009). An optimal QoS-based web service selection scheme. *Information Sciences*, 179(19), 3309–3322. doi:10.1016/j.ins.2009.05.018

Huang, G., Zhou, L., & Liu, X. Z. (2006). Performance aware service pool in dependable service oriented architecture. *Journal of Computer Science and Technology*, 21(4), 565–573. doi:10.1007/s11390-006-0565-z

Huang, Y. J., Yuan, C. C., Chen, M. K., Lin, W. C., & Teng, H. C. (2010). Hardware implementation of RFID mutual authentication protocol. *IEEE Transactions on Industrial Electronics*, 57(5), 1573–1582. doi:10.1109/TIE.2009.2037098

Huan, S., Sheoran, S., & Wang, G. (2004). A review and analysis of supply chain operations reference (SCOR) model. *Supply Chain Management: An International Journal*, 9(1), 23–29. doi:10.1108/13598540410517557

Hubbard, D., Sutton, M., Deeba, A., Dancer, A., Shea, B., Balding, C., et al. (2010, December 2011). Top threats to cloud computing V1.0. Retrieved December 19, 2011, from https://cloudsecurityalliance.org/topthreats/csathreats.v1.0.pdf

Huber, N., Quast, M. V., Hauck, M., & Kounev, S. (2011). Evaluating and modeling virtualization performance overhead for cloud environments. *Proceedings of the 1ˢᵗ International Conference on Cloud Computing*.

Hughes, J., & Maler, E. (2005). Security assertion markup language (SAML) V2.0: Technical overview. (OASIS SSTC Working Draft sstc-saml-tech-overview-2.0-draft-08). Retrieved December 5, 2011, from http://www.oasis-open.org/committees/download.php/20824/sstc-saml-tech-overview-2%200-draft-11-diff.pdf

IBM/Google Academic Cloud Computing Initiative (ACCI). (n.d.). Retrieved January 2, 2012, from http://www.Cloudbook.net/directories/research-Clouds/ibm-google-academic-Cloud-computing-initiative

IDC. (2011). *Worldwide enterprise storage systems 2011–2015 forecast: "Emerging" once again is a keyword in the storage market*. IDC #228255, May 2011.

Ideas International. (2011, February). Private clouds float with IBM systems and software. Retrieved December 28, 2011, from http://public.dhe.ibm.com/common/ssi/ecm/en/xbl03006usen/XBL03006USEN.PDF

IEEE Standard 802.16 Working Group. (2004). IEEE standard for local and metropolitan area networks part 16: Air interface for fixed broadband wireless access systems (revision of IEEE standard 802.16-2001).

Il Kon, K., Pervez, Z., Khattak, A. M., & Sungyoung, L. (2010, 19-23 July 2010). Chord based identity management for e-healthcare cloud applications. Paper presented at the 2010 10th IEEE/IPSJ International Symposium on Applications and the Internet (SAINT).

Intel, I. T. Center. (2011, September). Planning guide; Cloud security. Retrieved December 15, 2011, from http://www.intel.com/content/www/us/en/Cloud-computing/Cloud-computing-security-planning-guide.html

Intel. (n.d.). *Intel® virtualization technology list*. Retrieved July 12, 2011, from http://ark.intel.com/VTList.aspx

Internet2. (2011). Shibboleth Project. Retrieved November 10, 2011, from http://shibboleth.internet2.edu/

iRODS. (2012). *iRODS: Data grids, digital libraries, persistent archives, and real-time data systems*. Retrieved January 10, 2012, from http://www.irods.org

Iscan, H., Flake, S., Tacken, J., Ley, M., & Schmülling, C. (2012, June). Service design studio (SDS) – The execution environment of the service design studio. Paper presented at the SDPS 2012 - 17th International Conference on Transformative Science, Engineering, and Business Innovation, Berlin, Germany.

Jackson, J. (2010, April 21). *Red Hat drops xen from RHEL*. Retrieved September 10, 2011, from http://www.pcworld.com/businesscenter/article/194663/red_hat_drops_xen_from_rhel.html

Jacobellis v. Ohio. (1964). Retrieved October 10, 2010, from http://caselaw.lp.findlaw.com/cgi-bin/getcase.pl?navby=case&court=us&vol=378&invol=184#197

Jaeger, T., & Schiffman, J. (2010). Outlook: Cloudy with a chance of security challenges and improvements. *Security & Privacy*, 8(1), 77–80. doi:10.1109/MSP.2010.45

Jaeger, T., & Schiffman, J. (2011). Outlook: Cloudy with a chance of security challenges and improvements. *Security & Privacy*, 8(1), 77–80. doi:10.1109/MSP.2010.45

Jajodia, S., Samarati, P., Sapino, M., & Subrahmanian, V. (2001). Flexible support for multiple access control policies. [TODS]. *ACM Transactions on Database Systems*, 214–260. doi:10.1145/383891.383894

Jansen, W., & Grance, T. (2011). *Guidelines on security and privacy in public cloud computing*, (pp. 4-60). Special Publication 800-144. National Institute of Standards and Technology (NIST), U.S. Department of Commerce.

Jeffrey, K., & Neidecker-Lutz, B. (Eds.). (2010). The future of cloud computing – Opportunities for european cloud computing beyond 2010. Expert Group Report, European Commission, DG INFSO.

Jensen, M., Schwenk, J., Gruschka, N., & Iacono, L. L. (2009). On technical security issues in cloud computing. 2nd IEEE International Conference on Cloud Computing (Cloud 2009), (pp. 109-116). Bangalore, India.

Jeremy, G. (2008). Twenty one experts define Cloud computing. Virtualization. Retrieved from http://virtualization.sys-con.com/node/612375

Jia, Y., & Zheng, S. (2012). *Software evolution based on service-oriented requirement in internet ware*. 4th International Conference on Computer Research and Development, 21-22 April 2012, Kunming, China.

Jiang, X., & Xu, D. (2003). SODA: A service-on-demand architecture for application service hosting utility platforms. Proceedings of the 12th IEEE International Symposium on High Performance Distributed Computing (pp. 174-183).

Jiang, Y., & Stroulia, E. (2004). Towards reengineering web sites to web-services providers. *8th European Conference on Software Maintenance and Reengineering*, (pp. 296-305). 24-26 March 2004, Tampere, Finland.

Jin, H., Deng, L., Wu, S., Shi, X., & Pan, X. (2009). Live virtual machine migration with adaptive, memory compression. Proceedings of the 2009 IEEE International Conference on Cluster Computing, (pp. 11-20). doi: 10.1109/CLUSTR.2009.5289170

Jin, R., Sun, H., Liu, X., & Li, X. (2010). SOArTester: An automatic composite service testing system based on test case reduction. *Chinese Journal of Electronics*, *38*(2A), 65–70.

Joshi, J. B. D., Bertino, E., Latif, U., & Ghafoor, A. (2005). A generalized temporal role-based access control model. *IEEE Transactions on Knowledge and Data Engineering*, *17*(1), 4–23. doi:10.1109/TKDE.2005.1

Joshi, J. B. D., Bhatti, R., & Bertino, E., & Ghafoor. (2004). Access control language for multi domain environments. *IEEE Internet Computing*, *8*(6), 40–50. doi:10.1109/MIC.2004.53

Juang, W. S., Chen, S. T., & Liaw, H. T. (2008). Robust and efficient password-authenticated key agreement using smart cards. *IEEE Transactions on Industrial Electronics*, *55*(6), 2551–2556. doi:10.1109/TIE.2008.921677

Junosphere. (n.d.). Retrieved July 2012, from https://www.juniper.net/as/en/products-services/software/junos-platform/junosphere/

Kai, H. (2008). Massively distributed systems: From grids and p2p to clouds. In The 3rd International Conference on Grid and Pervasive Computing - GPC-Workshops.

Kaiqi, X., & Harry, P. (2009). *Service performance and analysis in cloud computing* (pp. 693–700). Congress on Services.

Kandukuri, B. R., Paturi, R., & Rakshit, A. (2009). Cloud security issues. In 6th IEEE International Conference on Services Computing (SCC'09), (pp. 517-520). Bangalore, India.

Kao, I. L., & Milman, I. M. (2001). *Method and system for single sign on using configuration directives with respect to target types*. Google Patents.

Karlapudi, H., & Martin, J. (2004). Web application performance prediction. In Proceedings of the IASTED International Conference on Communication and Computer Networks, (pp. 281- 286).

Karve, A., Kimbrel, T., Pacifici, G., Spreitzer, M., Steinder, M., Sviridenko, M., & Tantawi, A. (2006). Dynamic placement for clustered web applications. Proceedings of the 15th International Conference on World Wide Web, (pp. 595-604). doi: 10.1145/1135777.1135865

Katzan, H. Jr. (2010). On the privacy of cloud computing. *International Journal of Management and Information Systems*, *14*(2), 5–12.

Keahey, K., Foster, I., Freeman, T., & Zhang, X. (2005). Virtual workspaces: Achieving quality of service and quality of life in the grid. *Science Progress*, *13*(4), 265–275.

Kemal, A. D., & Martin, A. W. (2008). *Emergence of the academic computing clouds*. ACM Ubiquity.

Kendall, M. G. (1938). A new measure of rank correlation. *Oxford Journals*, *30*(1/2), 81–93.

Khajeh-Hosseini, A., Greenwood, D., & Sommerville, I. (2010). Cloud migration: A case study of migrating an enterprise IT system to IaaS. *IEEE 3rd International Conference on Cloud Computing*, (pp. 450-457). 5-10 July 2010, Miami, USA.

Khalid, A. (2009). Cloud computing: Applying issues in small business. 2010 International Conference on Signal Acquisition and Processing (pp. 278-281). doi:10.1109/ICSAP.2010.78

Kher, V., & Kim, Y. (2005). Securing distributed storage: Challenges, techniques, and systems. In Proceedings of the ACM Workshop on Storage Security and Survivability, (pp. 9-25).

Kho, N. (2009, March). Content in the cloud. EContent Magazine.

Kim, K. H., Beloglazov, A., & Buyya, R. (2009). Power-aware provisioning of Cloud resources for real-time services. In Proceedings of the 7th international Workshop on Middleware for Grids, Clouds and E-Science, (pp. 1-6). New York, NY: ACM.

Kim, M., Joshi, J. B. D., & Kim, M. (2008). Access control for cooperation systems based on group situation. In E. Bertino & J. B. D. Joshi (Ed.), 4th International Conference on Collaborative Computing: Networking, Applications and Worksharing (CollaborateCom2008) (pp. 11-23). Berlin, Germany: Springer.

Kim, W. (2009). Cloud computing: Today and tomorrow. *Journal of Object Technology*, *8*(1), 65–72. doi:10.5381/jot.2009.8.1.c4

Ko, M., Ahn, G. J., & Shehab, M. (2009). Privacy enhanced user-centric identity management. In G. Fettweis (Ed.), IEEE International Conference on Communications (pp. 1-5). Dresden, Germany: IEEE Press.

Kodali, N. B., Farkas, C., & Wijesekera, D. (2004). Specifying multimedia access control using RDF. Journal of Computer Systems, Science and Engineering, 19(3).

Konstan, J. A., Miller, B. N., Maltz, D., Herlocker, J. L., Gordon, L. R., & Riedl, J. (1997). GroupLens: Applying collaborative filtering to usenet news. *Communications of the ACM*, *40*(3), 77–87. doi:10.1145/245108.245126

Kosmosfs. (2011). *Kosmos distributed filesystem*. Retrieved December 10, 2012, from http://code.google.com/p/kosmosfs/

Kossman, D. (2000). The state of the art in distributed query processing. *ACM Computing Surveys*, *32*(4), 422–469. doi:10.1145/371578.371598

Kouzes, R. T., Anderson, G. A., Elbert, S. T., & Gracio, D. K. (2009). The changing paradigm of data-intensive computing. *IEEE Computer*, *42*(1), 26–34. doi:10.1109/MC.2009.26

Kplan, R. S., & Norton, D. P. (1996, January-February). Using the balanced scorecard as a strategic management system. *Harvard Business Review*, 3–13.

Lagar-Cavilla, H., Whitney, J., Scannell, A., Patchin, P., Rumble, S., Lara, E., et al. (2009). SnowFlock: Rapid virtual machine cloning for cloud computing. Proceedings of the 4th ACM European Conference on Computer Systems (EuroSys '09), (pp. 1-12). doi: 10.1145/1519065.1519067

La, H. J., & Kim, S. D. (2009). In Jaatun, M. G., Zhao, G., & Rong, C. (Eds.), *A systematic process for developing high quality SaaS cloud services* (Vol. 5931, pp. 3–8). Lecture Notes in Computer ScienceBerlin, Germany: Springer-Verlag. doi:10.1007/978-3-642-10665-1_25

Lamont, J. (2010, January). SaaS: Integration in the clouds. KM World.

Leach, P. J., Mealling, M., & Salz, R. (2005). A universally unique identifier (UUID) urn namespace. Retrieved 15 December, 2011, from http://tools.ietf.org/html/rfc4122

Lee, Y., & Chen, K. (2010). Is server consolidation beneficial to MMORPG? A case study of World of Warcraft. Proceedings of the IEEE 3rd International Conference on Cloud Computing, (pp. 435 - 442).

Legislatures, S. (2010). Governments work in the clouds. *Journal of State Legislatures*, *36*(4), 10.

Lenk, A., Klems, M., Nimis, J., Tai, S., & Sandholm, T. (2009). What's inside the cloud? An architectural map of the cloud landscape. Proceedings of the ICSE Cloud '09 Workshop (pp. 23-31).

Lentz, R. F. (2009). *Statement by Mr. Robert F. Lentz Deputy Assistant Secretary of Defense, for Cyber, Identify, and Information Assurance before the U.S. House of Representatives Armed Services Committee Subcommittee on Terrorism, Unconventional Threats, & Capabilities*. Washington, DC: United States House of Representative.

Leong, L. (2011). Amazon outage and the auto-immune vulnerabilities of resiliency. Gartner. Retrieved from http://blogs.gartner.com/lydia_leong/2011/04/21/amazon-outage-and-the-auto-immune-vulnerabilities-of-resiliency/.

Li, G., Muthusamy, V., & Jacobsen, H. A. (2010). A distributed service-oriented architecture for business process execution. ACM Transactions on the Web, 4(1).

Li, J., Li, N., & Winsborough, W. H. (2005). Automated trust negotiation using cryptographic credentials. In Proceedings of Conference on Computer and Communications Security (CCS).

Li, M., Yu, S., Cao, N., & Lou, W. (2011). Authorized private keyword search over encrypted data in Cloud computing. Technical report. Retrieved from http://ece.wpi.edu/mingli/

Liberty Alliance Framework. (2007). Liberty Alliance Project. Retrieved December 10, 2011, from http://www.cs.helsinki.fi/u/chande/courses/cs/MWS/reports/reviews/15_1.pdf

Li, J., Jia, Y., Liu, L., & Wo, T. (2012). CyberLiveApp: A secure sharing and migration approach for live virtual desktop applications in a Cloud environment. [FGCS]. *Future Generation Computer Systems*, (August): 2011. doi:doi:10.1016/j.future.2011.08.00

Li, J., Li, B., Wo, T., Hu, C., Huai, J., Liu, L., & Lam, K. P. (2012, February). CyberGuarder: A virtualization security assurance architecture for green cloud computing. *Future Generation Computer Systems*, 28(2), 379–390. doi:10.1016/j.future.2011.04.012

Li, J., & Yang, H. (2006). Reengineering websites into stateful resources for grid service oriented evolution. *International Journal of Multiagent and Grid Systems*, 2(2), 89–100.

Li, J., Zhang, Z., & Yang, H. (2005). A grid oriented approach to reusing legacy code in ICENI framework. *International Journal of Automation and Computing*, 3(1), 47–55. doi:10.1007/s11633-006-0047-3

Linden, G., Smith, B., & York, J. (2003). Amazon.com recommendations: Item-to-item collaborative filtering. *IEEE Internet Computing*, 7(1), 263–266. doi:10.1109/MIC.2003.1167344

Lischka, J., & Karl, H. (2009). A virtual network mapping algorithm based on subgraph isomorphism detection. ACM Workshop on Virtualized Infrastrastructure Systems and Architectures, (pp. 81-88).

Litoiu, M., & Litoiu, M. (2010). *Optimizing resources in cloud, a SOA governance view. Proceedings of Governance of Technology, Information and Policies: Addressing the Challenges of Worldwide Interconnectivity, 7 December 2010* (pp. 73–74). Austin, Texas: ACM.

Liu, H., & Wee, S. (2009). Web server farm in the cloud: Performance evaluation and dynamic architecture. 1st International Conference on Cloud Computing (CloudCom 09), (pp. 369–380). Beijing, China.

Liu, L., Russell, D., Webster, D., et al. (2009). Delivering sustainable capability on evolutionary service-oriented architecture. In Proceedings of the 12th IEEE International Symposium on Object/Component/Service-Oriented Real-Time Distributed Computing (pp.12-19). Los Alamitos, CA: IEEE Computer Society Press.

Liu, L., Webster, D., Xu, J., et al. (2010). Enabling dynamic workflow for disaster monitoring and relief through service-oriented sensor networks. In 2010 5th International ICST Conference on Communications and Networking in China (pp.7). Piscataway, NJ: IEEE Press.

Liu, N., & Yang, Q. (2008). Eigenrank: A ranking-oriented approach to collaborative filtering. Paper presented at the 31st Annual International ACM SIGIR Conference on Research and Development in Information Retrieval (SIGIR), Singapore.

Liu, X., Qiao, C., & Wang, T. (2009). Robust application specific and agile private (ASAP) networks withstanding multi-layer failures. Optical Fiber Conference (OFC), (pp. 1-3).

Liu, Y., Ngu, A., & Zeng, L. (2004). Qos computation and policing in dynamic Web service selection. Paper presented at the 13th International World Wide Web conference on Alternate track papers & posters, New York, USA.

Liu, L., Antonopoulos, N., Xu, J., Webster, D., & Wu, K. (2011). Distributed service integration for disaster monitoring sensor systems. *IET Communications*, 5(12), 1777–1784. doi:10.1049/iet-com.2010.0630

Liu, L., Masfary, O., & Antonopoulos, N. (2012, May). Energy performance assessment of virtualization technologies using small environmental monitoring sensors. *Sensors (Basel, Switzerland)*, 12(5), 6610–6628. doi:10.3390/s120506610

Liu, L., Xu, J., Antonopoulos, N., Li, J., & Wu, K. (2012). Adaptive service discovery on service-oriented and spontaneous sensor systems. *Journal of Adhoc & Sensor Wireless Networks*, 14(1-2), 107–132.

Li, X., Qiu, W., Zheng, D., Chen, K., & Li, J. (2010). Anonymity enhancement on robust and efficient password-authenticated key agreement using smart cards. *IEEE Transactions on Industrial Electronics*, 57(2), 793–800. doi:10.1109/TIE.2009.2028351

LoadStorm. (2008-2011). Load Storm- Load testing tool. Retrieved October 10, 2011, from http://loadstorm.com/load-testing-tools

Love, R. (2004). Kernel korner: I/O schedulers. Linux Journal. Retrieved from http://www.linuxjournal.com/article/6931

Lu, J., & Wang, J. (2005). Performance modeling and analysis of Web Switch. In Proceedings of the 31st Annual International Conference on Computer Measurement (CMG05), Orlando, FL, Dec 2005.

Luand, J., & Turner, J. (2006). Efficient mapping of virtual networks onto a shared substrate. Washington University Tech. Report, WUCSE 2006-35.

Luis, M. V., Luis, R. M., Juan, C., & Maik, L. (2009). A break in the clouds: towards a cloud definition. ACM SIGCOMM Computer Communication Review, 39(1).

Luo, J., Li, Y., & Pershing, J. A. (2009). A methodology for analyzing availability weak points in SOA deployment frameworks. *IEEE Transactions on Network and Service Management, 6*(1), 31–44. doi:10.1109/TNSM.2009.090303

MacDonald, N. (2010). *Securing the next-generation virtualized data center*, (pp. 2-50). (Gartner Report no. G00173434).

Magellan. (n.d.). Retrieved January 3, 2012, from http://www.Cloudbook.net/directories/research-Clouds/research-project.php?id=100047

Magenheimer, D. (2008, April). Add self-ballooning to balloon driver [Electronic mailing list message]. Retrieved from http://old-list-archives.xen.org/archives/html/xen-devel/2008-04/msg00567.html

Magenheimer, D. (2009). Transcendent memory and Linux. Retrieved from http://oss.oracle.com/projects/tmem/dist/documentation/papers/tmemLS09.pdf

Managed Solution. (2012). Managed Solution. Retrieved December 28, 2011, from http://www.managedsolution.com/index.html

Marshall, D. (2010, May 3). *Red Hat drops Xen in favor of KVM in RHEL 6*. Retrieved September 8, 2011, from http://www.infoworld.com/d/virtualization/red-hat-drops-xen-in-favor-kvm-in-rhel-6-498

Martin, J., & Nilsson, A. (2002). On service level agreements for IP networks. In Proceedings of the IEEE INFOCOM.

Mauro, C., Sunyaev, A., Leimeister, J. M., Schweiger, A., & Krcmar, H. (2008). A proposed solution for managing doctor's smart cards in hospitals using a single sign-on central architecture.

McDonald, M. P. (2009). Leading times of transition: The 2010 CIO agenda. Retrieved July 13, 2010, from http://blogs.gartner.com/mark_mcdonald/2010/01/19/leading-in-times-of-transition-the-2010-cio-agenda/

McGregor, C., & Kumaran, S. (2002). Business processing monitoring using web services in B2B E-commerce. Proceedings of the International Parallel and Distributed Processing Symposium.

McKusick, M. K., & Quinlan, S. (2009). GFS: Evolution on fast-forward. *ACM Queue; Tomorrow's Computing Today, 7*(7), 10. doi:10.1145/1594204.1594206

McNett, M., Gupta, D., Vahdat, A., & Voelker, G. M. (2007). Usher: an extensible framework for managing clusters of virtual machines. Proceedings of the 21st Conference on Large Installation System Administration Conference, (pp. 1-15).

Mei, R. D., Meeuwissen, H. B., & Phillipson, F. (2006). User perceived quality-of-service for voice-over-IP in a heterogeneous multi-domain network environment. In Proceedings of ICWS.

Meisner, D., Gold, B. T., & Wenisch, T. F. (2009). PowerNap: Eliminating server idle power. Proceedings of the 14th International Conference on Architectural Support for Programming Languages and Operating Systems, (pp. 205-216). doi: 10.1145/1508244.1508269

Mell, P., & Grance, T. (2009). The NIST definition of cloud computing. Working Paper, National Institute of Standards and Technology. Retrieved from http://csrc.nist.gov/publications/drafts/800-145/Draft-SP-800-145_cloud-definition.pdf

Mell, P., & Grance, T. (2011). *The NIST definition of cloud computing. Special Publication 800-145*. National Institute of Standards and Technology.

Melucci, M. (2007). On rank correlation in information retrieval evaluation. SIGIR Forum, 41(1), 18–33.

Meng, F. C., Zhan, D. C., & Xu, X. F. (2005). Business component identification of enterprise information system: A hierarchical clustering method. *Proceedings of the IEEE International Conference on e-Business Engineering*, (pp. 473-480). 18-21 October 2005, Beijing, China.

Menzel, M., & Ranjan, R. (2011). CloudGenius: Automated decision support for migrating multi-component enterprise applications to clouds. Technical Report, Retrieved January 6, 2012 from http://arxiv.org/abs/1112.3880v1.

Mersenne Inc. (2011). *PrimeNet CPU benchmarks*. Retrieved September 19, 2011, from http://www.mersenne.org/report_benchmarks/

Mersenne Research Inc. (2011, March 4). *Great internet Mersenne prime search*. Retrieved September 18, 2011, from http://www.mersenne.org/freesoft/

Michael, A., Armando, F., Rean, G., Anthony, D. J., Randy, K., & Andy, K. ... Matei, Z. (2009). Above the clouds: A Berkeley view of cloud computing. UC Berkeley Reliable Adaptive Distributed Systems Laboratory. Retrieved from http://www.eecs.berkeley.edu/Pubs/TechRpts/2009/EECS-2009-28.pdf

Microsoft Azure. (2010). Retrieved March 12, 2010 from http://www.microsoft.com/azure/

Microsoft. (2009). Azure services platform. Retrieved March 10, 2009, from http://www.microsoft.com/azure

Microsoft. (2011). *Do I need Windows XP mode?* Retrieved August 10, 2011, from http://www.microsoft.com/windows/virtual-pc/download.aspx

Microsoft. (2012). Microsoft Office 365. Retrieved January 10, 2012, from http://www.microsoft.com/en-us/office365/what-is-office365.aspx#fbid=ruAfelsNEjx

Microsoft. (2012). Windows Azure. Retrieved January 10, 2012, from http://www.windowsazure.com/en-us/pricing/free-trial/?WT.mc_id= MSCOM_EN_US_SEARCH_EDITORSCHOICE_123LMUS014358

Mietzner, R., & Leymann, F. (2008). *Towards provisioning the cloud: On the usage of multi-granularity flows and services to realize a unified provisioning infrastructure for SaaS applications* (pp. 1–8). IEEE Computer Society Congress on Services. doi:10.1109/SERVICES-1.2008.36

Migeon, J. Y. (2008). The MIT Kerberos administrator's how-to guide. Kerveros Constortium. Retrieved November 30, 2011, from http://docs.huihoo.com/kerberos/adminkerberos.pdf

Mikkilineni, R., & Morana, G. (2010). Is the network-centric computing paradigm for multicore, the next big thing? MSDN. (2011). How to: Sign XML documents with digital signatures. Retrieved December 5, 2011, from http://msdn.microsoft.com/en-us/library/ms229745.aspx

Miklau, G., & Suciu, D. (2003). Controlling access to published data using cryptography. In Proceedings of the 29th VLDB Conference.

Miller, B. N., Albert, L., Lam, S. K., Konstan, J. A., & Riedl, J. (2003). Movielens unplugged: Experiences with an occasionally connected recommender system. Paper presented at the 8th International Conference on Intelligent User Interfaces, Miami, Florida, USA.

Miller, M. (2009). *Cloud computing: Web based applications that change the way you work and collaborate online* (pp. 24-30). Que Publishing, Pearson.

Miller, R. (2008). Microsoft: PUE of 1.22 for data center containers. Retrieved from http://www.datacenterknowledge.com/archives/2008/10/20/microsoft-pue-of-122-for-data-center-containers/

Ministry of Internal Affairs and Communications Japan (MIC). (n.d.). Retrieved January 4, 2012, from http://www.Cloudbook.net/directories/gov-Clouds/ministry-of-internal-affairs-and-communications-japan--mic

Moreira, J., Midkiff, S., Gupta, M., Atrigas, P., Wu, P., & Almasi, G. (2001). The NINJA project: Making java work for high performance computing. *Communications of the ACM*, *44*(10), 102–109. doi:10.1145/383845.383867

Morgan Stanley Research. (2009). The mobile internet report: Ramping faster than desktop internet, the mobile internet will be bigger than most people think. Retrieved from http://www.morganstanley.com/institutional/techresearch/pdfs/mobile_internet_report.pdf

Morgan Stanley. (2008) Technology trends. Retrieved Feb 10, 2008 from http://www.morganstanley.com/institutional/techresearch/pdfs/TechTrends062008.pdf

Mosharaf, N. M., Rahman, M. R., & Boutaba, R. (2009). Virtual network embedding with coordinated node and link embedding. IEEE International Conference on Computer Communication (INFOCOM), (pp. 783-791).

Motahari-Nezhad, H. R., Stephenson, B., & Singhal, S. (2009). *Outsourcing business to cloud computing services: Opportunities and challenges*. IEEE Special Issue on Cloud Computing.

Mukherjee, B. (2006). *Optical WDM networks*. New York, NY: Springer.

Mukhin, V., & Volokyata, A. (2011). Security risk analysis for cloud computing systems. *The 6th IEEE International Conference on Intelligent Data Acquisition and Advanced Computing Systems: Technology and Applications*, September 15-17 2011, Prague, Czech Republic, (pp. 737-742).

Mullender, S., & Tanenbaum, A. (1984). Immediate files. *Software, Practice & Experience*, *14*(4), 365–368. doi:10.1002/spe.4380140407

Mummigatti, V. (2010). The emerging confluence of BPM and cloud computing. White Paper, Virtusa Corporation. Retrieved from http://www.virtusa.com/practices/bpm

Murthy, S., & Banerjee, S. (2009). Region-based connectivity - A new paradigm for design of fault-tolerant networks. IEEE Conference on High Performance Switching and Routing (HPSR), (pp. 1-7).

Mykletun, E., Narasimha, M., & Tsudik, G. (2004). Authentication and integrity in outsourced database. In Proceedings of the 11th NDSS04.

Narasimha, M., & Tsudik, G. (2006). Authentication of outsourced databases using signature aggregation and chaining. Proceedings of the 11th International Conference on Database Systems for Advanced Applications.

NASA. (n.d.). Retrieved January 5, 2012, from http://www.Cloudbook.net/directories/gov-Clouds/nasa-national-aeronautics-and-space-administration

Natarajan, R. (2010, July 12). *VMware: How to create virtual machine and install guest OS using vSphere client*. Retrieved September 6, 2011, from http://www.thegeekstuff.com/2010/07/vmware-create-virtual-machine/

National Vulnerability Database. (2009). Vulnerability summary for CVE-2009-3733. Retrieved November 13, 2010, from http://web.nvd.nist.gov/view/vuln/detail?vulnId=CVE-2009-3733

Nebhuth, R. (2009). Daenet's. NET community: Signing a document. Retrieved December 27, 2011, from http://developers.de/blogs/rolf_nebhuth/archive/2009/05/13/signing-xml-documents.aspx

NEOTYS. (2005-2012). Neo Load. Retrieved October 10, 2011, from http://www.neotys.com/

Neustar-Webmetrics. (2012). Webmetrics. Retrieved October 20, 2011, from http://www.webmetrics.com/

Nicholas, K. (2009). Microsoft's cloud Azure service suffers outage. Retrieved from http://www.eweekeurope.co.uk/news/microsofts-cloud-azure-service-suffers-outage-396

Niyato, D. (2011). Optimization-based virtual machine manager for private cloud computing. *IEEE Third International Conference on Cloud Computing Technology and Science*, (pp. 99-106).

OCLC WorldShare. (n.d.). Retrieved January 2012, from http://www.oclc.org

OMG. (n.d.). BPMN. Retrieved December 31, 2011, from http://www.omg.org/spec/BPMN/2.0/

O'Neill, M. (2009, April 29). Connecting to the cloud, part 1: Leverage the cloud in applications. Retrieved January 5, 2012, from http://www.ibm.com/developerworks/library/x-Cloudpt1/

Open Applications Group. (2011). OAGIS release 9.5. Retrieved from http://www.oagi.org

Open-Demand-System. (2000-2011). OpenLoad - Load testing software. Retrieved October 5, 2011, from http://www.opendemand.com/openload/

OpenNebula. (2010). Project. http://www.opennebula.org/.

Ortega, M., Rui, Y., Chakrabarti, K., Mehrotra, S., & Huang, T. S. (1997). Supporting similarity queries in MARS. Paper presented at the ACM International Multimedia Conference Exhibition, Seattle, USA.

Owens, D. (2010). Securing elasticity in the cloud. *Communications of the ACM, 53*(6), 46–51. doi:10.1145/1743546.1743565

Padala, P., Hou, K., Shin, K. G., Zhu, X., Uysal, M., Wang, Z., et al. (2009). Automated control of multiple virtualized resources. Proceedings of the 4th ACM European Conference on Computer Systems, (pp. 13-26). doi: 10.1145/1519065.1519068

Padala, P., Shin, K. G., Zhu, X., Uysal, M., Wang, Z., & Singhal, S. … Salem, K. (2007). Adaptive control of virtualized resources in utility computing environments. Proceedings of the 2nd ACM SIGOPS/EuroSys European Conference on Computer Systems, (pp. 289-302). doi: 10.1145/1272996.1273026

Pan, Z., Dong, Y., Chen, Y., Zhang, L., & Zhang, Z. (2012).CompSC: Live migration with pass-through devices. Proceedings of the 2012 ACM SIGPLAN/SIGOPS International Conference on Virtual Execution Environments, (pp. 1-12).

Papazoglou, M. P., Traverso, P., Dustdar, S., & Leymann, F. (2007). Service-oriented computing: State of the art and research challenges. *IEEE Computer, 40*(11), 38–45. doi:10.1109/MC.2007.400

Paul, F. (2008). The cloud is the computer. IEEE Spectrum Online. Retrieved from http://www.spectrum.ieee.org/aug08/6490

Pearson, S. (2009). *Taking account of privacy when designing cloud computing services*, (pp. 2-10). Produced by HP laboratories for IEEE.

Pearson, S., & Charlesworth, A. (2009). *Accountability as a way forward for privacy protection in the cloud. Proceedings of CloudCom 2009, December 2009* (pp. 3–15). Beijing: Springer.

Peng, J., Zhang, X., Lei, Z., Zhang, B., Zhang, W., & Li, Q. (2009). Comparison of several cloud computing platforms. Proceedings of the Second International Symposium on Information Science and Engineering (pp. 23-27). doi: 10.1109/ISISE.2009.94

Peterson, L., Shenker, S., & Turner, J. (2005). Overcoming the Internet impasse through virtualization. *Computer, 38*(4), 34–41. doi:10.1109/MC.2005.136

Petrusha, R. (2011). MSDN: GUID structure. Retrieved December 5, 2011, from http://msdn.microsoft.com/en-us/library/cey1zx63.aspx

Pfleeger, C. P., & Pfleeger, S. L. (2007). *Security in computing* (4th ed.). Boston, MA: Pearson Education Inc.

Phelps, J. R., & Dawson, P. (2007). *Demystifying server virtualization taxonomy and terminology*, (pp. 1-9). Report ID Number: G00148373. Gartner Research.

Pioro, M., & Medhi, D. (2004). *Routing, flow, and capacity design in communication and computer networks*. San Fransisco, CA: Elsevier.

Pirooz, S. (2011). Cloud security: The best defense is a good offense. Retrieved January 12, 2012, from http://www.centerbeam.com/business-advantages-of-outsourcing-IT/Cloud-security/key-considerations-when-moving-to-the-Cloud/

Polze, A., & Tröger, P. (2011). Trends and challenges in operating systems—From parallel computing to cloud computing. *Concurrency and Computation.* doi:doi:10.1002/cpe

Public Works and Government Services Canada (PWGSC). (n.d.). Retrieved January 6, 2012, from http://www.Cloudbook.net/directories/gov-Clouds/public-works-and-government-services-canada--pwgsc

Qian, L., Luo, Z., Du, Y., & Guo, L. (2009). In Jaatun, M. G., Zhao, G., & Rong, C. (Eds.), *Cloud computing: An overview (Vol. 5931*, pp. 626–631). Lecture Notes in Computer ScienceBerlin, Germany: Springer-Verlag. doi:10.1007/978-3-642-10665-1_63

Ragouzis, N., Hughes, J., Philpott, R., Maler, E., Madsen, P., & Scavo, T. (2008). Security assertion markup language (saml) v2. 0 technical overview. *Committee Draft, 2*, 25.

Rahmani, H., & Abolhassani, H. (2008). Composite Web service failure recovery considering user non-functional preferences. In Next Generation Web Services Practices, (pp. 39-45).

Rahman, M. R., Aib, I., & Boutaba, R. (2010). Survivable virtual network embedding. *Lecture Notes in Computer Science*, 40–52. doi:10.1007/978-3-642-12963-6_4

Rajkumar, B., Chee, S. Y., Srikumar, V., James, B., & Ivona, B. (2009). Cloud computing and emerging IT platforms: Vision, hype, and reality for delivering computing as the 5th utility. *Future Generation Computer Systems*, *25*(6), 599–616. doi:10.1016/j.future.2008.12.001

Ramgovind, S., Eloff, M. M., & Smith, E. (2010). *The management of security in cloud computing* (pp. 1–7). IEEE Information Security for South Africa. doi:10.1109/ISSA.2010.5588290

Ranganathan, V. (2010). Privacy issues with cloud applications. *iS Channel, 5*(1), 16-20. London School of Economics and Political Science.

Rangan, K. (2008). *The cloud wars: $100+ billion at stake. Tech. rep.* Merrill Lynch.

Rankl, W., & Effing, W. (2010). *Smart card handbook* (4th ed.). Wiley. doi:10.1002/9780470660911

Rash, W. (2010, February). Cloud-based storage done right. eWeek.com.

Redhat. (n.d.). *Manage virtual machines*. Retrieved September 23, 2011, from http://virt-manager.org/index.html

Ren, Y. X., Gu, Q., Qi, J. X., et al. (2009). Reliability prediction of web service composition based on DTMC. In Proceedings of the 3rd International Conference on Secure Software Integration and Reliability Improvement (pp. 369-375). Piscataway, NJ: IEEE Press.

Renesse, R., & Schneider, F. B. (2004). Chain replication for supporting high throughput and availability. In *6th Symposium on Operation Systems Design and Implementation* (pp. 91-104). Berkeley, CA: USENIX Association.

Riteau, P., Morin, C., & Priol, T. (2010). Shrinker: Efficient wide-area live virtual machine migration using distributed content-based addressing. Research Report:RR-7198, IN-RIA. Retrieved from http://hal.inria.fr/docs/00/45/47/27/PDF/RR-7198.pdf

Robert, S. P., & Daniel, L. R. (2000). Econometrics models and economic forecasts. McGraw-Hill/Irwin. Retrieved December 31, 2011, from http://www.servicexchange.cn

Robert, F. (2009). Digital libraries: The systems analysis perspective: library in the clouds. OCLC Systems & Services. *International Digital Library Perspectives*, *25*(3), 156–161.

Rochwerger, B., Breitgand, D., Levy, E., Galis, A., Nagin, K., & Llorente, I. M. (2009). The reservoir model and architecture for open federated cloud computing. *IBM Journal of Research and Development*, *53*(4), 535–545. doi:10.1147/JRD.2009.5429058

Roy, B. (2008). Cloud computing: When computers really rule. Tech News World. Retrieved from http://www.technewsworld.com/story/63954.html

Ruan, K., Carthy, J., Kechadi, T., & Crosbie, M. (2011). *Cloud forensics: An overview,* (pp. 1-16). Centre for Cybercrime Investigation, University College Dublin.

Ruiter, J., & Warnier, M. (2011). Privacy regulations for cloud computing: Compliance and implementation in theory and practice. In Gutwirth, S., Poullet, Y., De Hert, P., & Leenes, R. (Eds.), *Computers, privacy and data protection: An element of choice* (1st ed., pp. 355–389). Springer. doi:10.1007/978-94-007-0641-5_17

Russell, L. W., Morgan, S. P., & Chron, E. G. (2003). Clockwork: A new movement in autonomic systems. *IBM Systems Journal*, *42*(1), 77–84. doi:10.1147/sj.421.0077

Sabahi, F. (2011). Virtualization-level security in cloud computing. *IEEE Computer Society 3rd International Conference on Communication Software and Networks,* (pp. 250-255).

Saeed, K., & Nammous, M. K. (2007). A speech-and-speaker identification system: Feature extraction, description, and classification of speech-signal image. *IEEE Transactions on Industrial Electronics*, *54*(2), 887–897. doi:10.1109/TIE.2007.891647

Saffron Technology. (2005). Saffron Technology: Technical white paper. Morrisville, NC: Author.

Sahlin, J. (2011). Workshop: Cloud architectures for government. Paper presented at the NDIA Cloud Computing Symposium, San Diego, CA. Retrieved December 22, 2011, from http://www.ndia-sd.org/attachments/article/76/Sahlin_Cloud%20for%20Government %20Workshop.final.pdf

Sahlin, J., Sarkani, S., & Mazzuchi, T. (2011). Enterprise consolidation for DoD using AdvancedTCA. Proceedings of the 7th Annual AdvancedTCA Summit & Exposition. Retrieved January 12, 2012, from http://www.advancedtcasummit.com/English/ Collaterals/Proceedings/2011/20111101_S2-101_Sahlin.pdf

Sahlin, J., Sarkani, S., & Mazzuchi, T. (2012). Optimizing QoS in distributed systems/cloud computing architectures. *International Journal of Computers and Applications*, *42*(18), 14–20. doi:10.5120/5791-8097

Salesforce. (2008). Salesforce.com for Google App engine: Connecting the clouds. Retrieved from http://developer.force.com/appengine

Salesforce. (2009). Salesforce customer relationships management (CRM) system. Retrieved from http://www.salesforce.com/

SalesForce.com. (2011). SalesForce.com and the environment: Reducing carbon emissions in the cloud. Retrieved October 25, 2011, from http://www.sfdcstatic.com/assets/pdf/misc/WP_WSP_Salesforce_Environment.pdf

Samarati, P., & De Capitani di Vimercati, S. (2010). Data protection in outsourcing scenarios: Issues and directions. In Proceedings of the 5th ACM Symposium on Information, Computer and Communications Security (ASIACCS '10) (pp. 1-14). New York, NY: ACM.

Sandhu, R. S., Coyne, E. J., Feinstein, H. L., & Youman, C. E. (1996). Role-based access control models. *Computer*, *29*(2), 38–47. doi:10.1109/2.485845

SAP AG. (2011). Internet of services. Retrieved from http://www.internet-of-services.com

Sarwar, B., Karypis, G., Konstan, J., & Riedl, J. (2007). Item-based collaborative filtering recommendation algorithms. Paper presented at the 10th International Conference on World Wide Web (WWW), Beijing, China.

Sasaki, M., & Gen, M. (2003). A method of fuzzy multi-objective nonlinear programming with GUB structure by hybrid genetic algorithm. *International Journal of Smart Engineering System Design*, *5*(4), 281–288. doi:10.1080/10255810390245591

Sasikala, S., & Prema, S. (2010). Massive centralized cloud computing (MCCC) exploration in higher education. *Advances in Computational Sciences and Technology*, *3*(2), 111–118.

Satyanarayanan, M. (1981). A study of file sizes and functional lifetimes. *ACM SIGOPS Operating Systems Review*, *15*(5), 96–108. doi:10.1145/1067627.806597

Saugatuck Technologies. (2008). Understanding the cloud taxonomy. Retrieved from http://www.slideshare.net/Rinky25/understanding-the-cloud-taxonomy

Saugatuck Technology Inc. (2008). *Meeting the challenges of cloud solutions billing: Outsourcing to a cloud services hub*. IP Applications.

Scherrer, T. (2011, July 16). *Emulators for Z80 and Z80 based products*. Retrieved August 12, 2011, from http://www.z80.info/z80emu.htm

Schneider, B., & White, S. S. (2004). *Service quality: Research perspectives*. Thousand Oaks, CA: Sage Publications.

Schroeder, M. D., & Saltzer, J. H. (1971, October 18). A hardware architecture for implementing protection rings. *Proceedings of the Third ACM Symposium on Operating Systems Principles*. Palo Alto, California: ACM.

Sedayao, J. (2008). Implementing and operating an internet scale distributed application using service oriented architecture principles and Cloud Computing infrastructure. 10th International Conference on Information Integration and Web-based Applications & Services (iiWAS 08), (pp. 417–421). Linz. SETI@Home. (n.d.). Retrieved January 2012, from http://setiathome.berkeley.edu/

Seelam, S. R., & Teller, P. J. (2007). Virtual I/O scheduler: A scheduler of schedulers for performance virtualization. Proceedings of the 3rd International Conference on Virtual Execution Environments, (pp. 105-115). doi:10.1145/1254810.1254826

Seltsikas, P., & Currie, W. (2002). Evaluating the application service provider (ASP) business model: The challenge of integration. Paper presented at the 35th Hawaii International Conference on System Sciences, Big Island, HI.

Seventh Framework Programme. (n.d.). Retrieved January 2012, from http://www.Cloudbook.net/directories/gov-Clouds/seventh-framework-programme

Shao, L., Zhang, J., Wei, Y., Zhao, J., Xie, B., & Mei, H. (2007, July). Personalized QoS prediction for Web services via collaborative filtering. Paper presented at the International Conference on Web Services (ICWS), Beijing, China.

Sharma, R., & Sood, M. (2011). *Cloud SaaS and model driven architecture* (pp. 16–23). New Delhi, India: RG Education Society, IETE.

Shen, Z., & Tong, Q. (2010). The security of cloud computing system enabled by trusted computing technology. *IEEE 2nd International Conference on Signal Processing Systems*, (pp. 11-15).

Shepler, S., Callaghan, B., Robinson, D., Thurlow, R., Beame, C., Eisler, M., & Noveck, D. (2003). *Network file system (NFS) version 4 protocol*. RFC 3530, Apr. 2003. Retrieved January 10, 2012, from http://datatracker.ietf.org/doc/rfc3530/

Sheu, P. C.-Y., Wang, S., Wang, Q., Hao, K., & Paul, R. (2009). Semantic computing, cloud computing, and semantic search engine. Proceedings of the 2009 IEEE International Conference on Semantic Computing (pp. 654-657). doi: 10.1109/ICSC.2009.51

Shieh, A., Kandula, S., Greenberg, A., Kim, C., & Saha, B. (2011). Sharing the data center network. Proceedings of the 8th USENIX Conference on Networked Systems Design and Implementation, (pp. 1-14). Retrieved from http://www.usenix.org/events/nsdi11/tech/full_papers/Shieh.pdf

Shin, D., & Ahn, G. J. (2005). Role-based privilege and trust management. Computer Systems Science & Engineering Journal, 20(6).

Siegele, L. (2008). Let it rise: A special report on corporate IT. The Economist.

Siegle, D. (2010). Cloud computing: A free technology option to promote collaborative learning. *Gifted Child Today, 33*(4), 41–45.

Sienknecht, T. F., Friedrich, R. J., Martinka, J. J., & Friedenbach, P. M. (1994). The implications of distributed data in a commercial environment on the design of hierarchical storage management. *Performance Evaluation, 20*(1-3), 3–25. doi:10.1016/0166-5316(94)90003-5

Silver, B. (2009). BPM and cloud computing. BPMS Watch, Industry Trend Reports. Retrieved from http://www.brsilver.com/bpm-and-cloud-computing-white-paper

Silvestre, J. (1987). Economies and diseconomies of scale. The New Palgrave: A Dictionary of Economics, Vol. 2, (pp. 80–84).

Singh, A., Korupolu, M., & Mohapatra, D. (2008). Server-storage virtualization: integration and load balancing in data centers. Proceedings of the 2008 ACM/IEEE conference on Supercomputing, USA, 1-12.

Sledziewski, K., Bordbar, B., & Anane, R. (2009). A DSL-based approach toward software development and deployment on cloud. Proceedings of the 2010 24th IEEE International Conference on Advanced Information Networking and Applications (pp. 414-421). doi: 10.1109/AINA.2010.81

Smith, M. A., & Kumar, R. L. (2004). A theory of application service provider (ASP) use from a client perspective. *Information & Management, 4*, 977–1002. doi:10.1016/j.im.2003.08.019

Sneed, H., & Sneed, S. (2003). Creating web services from legacy host programs. *5th IEEE International Workshop on Web Site Evolution*, (pp. 59-69). 22 September 2003, Amsterdam, Netherlands.

Soltesz, S., Potzl, H., Fiuczynski, M. E., Bavier, A., & Peterson, L. (2007). Container-based operating system virtualization: A scalable, high performance alternative to hypervisors. Paper presented at EuroSys' 07, Lisboa, Portugal. doi:10.1.1.88.8563

Sotomayor, B., Montero, R. S., Llorente, I. M., & Foster, I. (2009). Virtual infrastructure management in private and hybrid clouds. *IEEE Internet Computing, 13*(5), 14–22. doi:10.1109/MIC.2009.119

Soumya, B., Indrajit, M., & Mahanti, P. K. (2009). Cloud computing initiative using modified ant colony framework. World Academy of Science. *Engineering and Technology, 56*, 221.

SourceForge. (2011, August 5). *EMOTIVECloud*. Retrieved September 10, 2011, from http://sourceforge.net/projects/emotivecloud/

SRB. (2012). *The DICE storage resource broker*. Retrieved January 10, 2012, from http://www.sdsc.edu/srb/index.php

Sreenath, R. M., & Singh, M. P. (2003). Agent-based service selection. *Journal of Web Semantics*, *1*(3), 261–279. doi:10.1016/j.websem.2003.11.006

Standard Performance Evaluation Corporation. (2011). The SPEC organization. Retrieved from http://www.spec.org/spec/

Stemmer, M., Holtkamp, B., & Königsmann, T. (2011). Cloud-orienterte Service-Marktplätze (Cloud-oriented service marketplaces). White Paper, Fraunhofer ISST. Retrieved from http://www.isst.fraunhofer.de/Images/Fraunhofer-ISST_CSMP-Whitepaper_www_tcm81-98065.pdf

Stephen, S. (2008). Google App Engine suffers outages. Retrieved from http://news.cnet.com/8301-10784_3-9971025-7.html

Stoneburner, G., Gouguen, A., & Feringa, A. (2002). *Risk management guide for information technology systems*, (pp. 3-55). Special Publication 800-30, National Institute of Standards and Technology (NIST), U.S. Department of Commerce.

Strong, P. (2005, July/August). Enterprise grid computing. ACM Queue Magazine.

Stroulia, E., Thomson, J., & Situ, G. (2000). Constructing xml-speaking wrappers for web applications: Towards an interoperating web. *7th Working Conference on Reverse Engineering*, (pp. 59-68). 23-25 November 2000, Brisbane, Australia.

Stuer, G., Vanmechelena, K., & Broeckhovea, J. (2007). A commodity market algorithm for pricing substitutable grid resources. *Future Generation Computer Systems*, *23*(5), 688–701. doi:10.1016/j.future.2006.11.004

Subramanyan, R., Wong, E., & Yang, H. I. (Eds.). (2010). 34th Annual IEEE Computer Software and Applications Conference Workshops (COMPSACW 2010) (pp. 393-398), Seoul, South Korea: IEEE Press.

Supply Chain Council. (2011). Supply chain operations reference (SCOR) model, version 10. Retrieved from http://supply-chain.org/scor

Tagg, G. (2000, 2011, December 15). Implementing a Kerberos single sign-on infrastructure. Information Security Bulletin, Tagg Consulting Ltd [pdf-dokumentti] Marraskuu. Retrieved December 15, 2011, from https://koala.cs.pub.ro/redmine/attachments/download/151/10.1.1.105.9399.pdf

Taghavi Zargar, S., Takabi, H., & Joshi, J. B. D. (2011). DCDIDP: A distributed, collaborative, and data-driven intrusion detection and prevention framework for cloud computing environments. In C. Pu & J. Caverlee (Eds.), 7th International Conference on Collaborative Computing: Networking, Applications and Worksharing (Collaborate-Com2011), Orlando, FL, USA. Berlin, Germany: Springer.

Takabi, H., & Joshi, J. B. D. (2010). StateMiner: An efficient similarity-based approach for optimal mining of role hierarchy. In B. Carminati (Ed.), 15th ACM Symposium on Access Control Models and Technologies (pp. 55-64). Pittsburgh, PA: ACM Press.

Takabi, H., & Joshi, J. B. D. (2012). Policy management as a service: An approach to manage policy heterogeneity in cloud computing environment. In R. H. Sprague (Ed.), 45th Hawaii International Conference on System Sciences (HICSS). IEEE Press.

Takabi, H., Joshi, J. B. D., & Ahn, G. J. (2010). SecureCloud: Towards a comprehensive security framework for cloud computing environments. Cited in S. I. Ahamed, D. H. Bae, S. Cha, C. K. Chang, H. Takabi, J. B. D. Joshi, & G. J. Ahn (Eds.), Security and privacy challenges in cloud computing environments. IEEE Security and Privacy, 8(6), 24-31.

Takabi, H., Kim, M., Joshi, J. B. D., & Spring, M. B. (2009). An architecture for specification and enforcement of temporal access control constraints using OWL. In E. Damiani, S. Proctor, & A. Singal (Ed.), 2009 ACM Workshop on Secure Web Services (pp. 21-28). Chicago, IL: ACM Press.

Takabi, H., & Joshi, J. B. D. (2012). Semantic based policy management for cloud computing environments. *International Journal of Cloud Computing*, *1*(2), 119–144. doi:10.1504/IJCC.2012.046717

Takabi, H., Joshi, J. B. D., & Ahn, G. (2010). Security and privacy challenges in cloud computing environments. *IEEE Security and Privacy*, *8*(6), 24–31. doi:10.1109/MSP.2010.186

Taneja Group. (2009, September). *Evaluating the ESX 4 hypervisor and VM density advantage*. Retrieved September 6, 2011, from http://www.vmware.com/files/pdf/vmware-evaluating-hypervisor-density.pdf

Tang, C., Steinder, M., Spreitzer, M., & Pacifici, G. (2007). A scalable application placement controller for enterprise data centers. Proceedings of the 16th International Conference on World Wide Web, (pp. 331-340). doi: 10.1145/1242572.1242618

Tao, Z., & Long, J. (2011). The research and application of network teaching platform based on cloud computing. *International Journal of Information and Education Technology*, *1*(3).

Teo, L., & Ahn, G. J. (2007). Managing heterogeneous network environments using an extensible policy framework. In R. Deng & P. Samarati (Eds.), 2nd ACM Symposium on Information, Computer and Communications Security (pp. 362-364). Singapore: ACM Press.

Theseus. (2011). TEXO – Infrastructure for Web-based services. Retrieved from http://theseus-programm.de/en/914.php

Tian, X., Wang, X., & Zhou, A. (2009). DSP re-encryption: A flexible mechanism for access control enforcement management in DaaS. 2nd IEEE International Conference on Cloud Computing (Cloud 2009), (pp. 25-32). Bangalore, India.

Tip, F. (1995). A survey of program slicing techniques. *Journal of Programming Languages*, *3*(3), 121–189.

Tiwari, P. B., & Joshi, S. R. (2009). Single sign-on with one time password. Paper presented at the First IEEE Asian Himalayas International Conference on Internet, 2009.

Tonella, P., Ricca, F., Pianta, E., & Girardi, C. (2003). Using keyword extraction for web site clustering. *5th IEEE International Workshop on Web Site Evolution*, (pp. 41-48). 22 September 2003, Amsterdam, Netherlands.

Toolkit, G. (n.d.). Retrieved January 2012, from http://www.globus.org/toolkit/

Trivedi, K. S. (2001). *Probability and statistics with reliability, queuing and computer science applications*. New York, NY: John Wiley & Sons.

Tung, W. L., & Quek, C. (2010). eFSM - A novel online neural-fuzzy semantic memory model. *IEEE Transactions on Neural Networks*, *21*(1), 136–157. doi:10.1109/TNN.2009.2035116

Turnitin. (n.d.). Retrieved July 2012, from http://www.turnitin.com/

Tusa, F., Celesti, A., & Mikkilineni, R. (2011). AAA in a cloud-based virtual DIME network architecture (DNA).

U.S. General Services Administration (GSA). (n.d.). Retrieved January 2012, from http://www.gsa.gov

Ueno, H., & Hasegawa, S. (2009). Vintage: Hitachi's virtualization technology. Paper presented at the 4th International Conference on Grid and Pervasive Computing, Geneva.

UN/CEFACT. (2009). Core components technical specification, Version 3.0. Retrieved from www.unece.org/cefact/codesfortrade/CCTS/CCTS-Version3.pdf

Unal, E., & Yates, D. (2010). Enterprise fraud management using cloud computing: A cost-benefit analysis framework. 18th European Conference on Information Systems (ECIS), Pretoria, South Africa.

United States Government Accountability Office. (2010). *GAO report to congressional requesters: Information security federal guidance needed to address control issues with implementing cloud computing*. Washington, DC: U.S. GAO.

United States Navy. (2011, February 25). Information dominance, agile acquisition and intelligence integration: Q&A with Terry Simpson, PEO C4I's Principal Deputy for Intelligence. Retrieved December 30, 2011, from http://www.public.navy.mil/spawar/Press/Documents/Publications/2.23.11_TerrySimpson.pdf

University of Toronto. (2008). *Snowflock 0.2c release documentation*. Retrieved August 10, 2011, from http://compbio.cs.toronto.edu/snowflock/releases/0.2/SnowFlock_Manual.html

University of Toronto. (2009). *SnowFlock: Swift VM cloning for cloud computing*. Retrieved August 8, 2011, from http://sysweb.cs.toronto.edu/snowflock?type=Downloads

Upadhyay, M., & Marti, R. (2001). Single sign-on using Kerberos in Java. Sun Microsystems, Inc. Retrieved December 10, 2011, from http://ftp.ssw.uni-linz.ac.at/Services/Docs/JDK1.6.0/technotes/guides/security/jgss/single-signon.html

Van, L. B., Gemmel, P., & Van, D. R. (Eds.). (2003). Services management: An integrated approach. Financial Times. Harlow, UK: Prentice Hall.

Varia, J. (2008). Amazon white paper on Cloud architectures. Retrieved from http://aws.typepad.com/aws/2008/07/white-paper-on.html

Varian, M. (1997, August). *VM and the VM community: Past, present, and future*. Retrieved August 10, 2011, from http://web.me.com/melinda.varian/Site/Melinda_Varians_Home_Page_files/25paper.pdf

Vecchiola, C., Chu, X., & Buyya, R. (2008). Aneka: A software platform for. NET based cloud computing. *High Performance Computing Workshop 2008*, (pp. 267-295). 30 June-4 July 2008, Cetraro, Italy.

Verma, M. (2004). XML security: Control information access with XACML. Retrieved from http://www.ibm.com/developerworks/xml/library/x-xacml/

Vijayan, J. (2012). LAPD drops Google Apps plan. Computerworld. Retrieved from http://www.computerworld.com/s/article/9223227/LAPD_Drops_Google_Apps_Plan.

VMware, Inc. (2011). VMware and your cloud. Retrieved from http://www.vmware.com/files/pdf/cloud/VMware-and-Cloud-Computing-BR-EN.pdf

Vogels, W. (2008). A head in the clouds—The power of infrastructure as a service. In First Workshop on Cloud Computing and in Applications (CCA '08).

W3C. (2005). Unified service description language incubator group. Retrieved from http://www.w3.org/2005/Incubator/usdl

Waldspurger, C. A. (2002). Memory resource management in VMware ESX server. Proceedings of the 5th Symposium on Operating Systems Design and implementation, (pp. 181-194). doi: 10.1145/844128.844146

Walker, E., Brisken, W., & Romney, J. (2010). To lease or not to lease from storage clouds. *Computer*, *43*, 44–50. doi:10.1109/MC.2010.115

Wan, Z. (2011). A network virtualization approach in many-core processor based cloud computing environment. *Third International Conference on Computational Intelligence, Communication Systems and Networks*, (pp. 304-307).

Wang, C., Wang, Q., Ren, K., & Lou, W. (2009). Ensuring data storage security in cloud computing. Paper presented to the 2009 17th International Workshop on Quality of Service, Charleston, SC. doi: 10.1109/IWQoS.2009.5201385

Wang, G., Wang, C., & Chen, A. (2005). Service level management using qos monitoring, diagnostics and adaptation for networked enterprise systems. Paper presented at the 9th International Enterprise Computing Conference, Washington DC, USA.

Wang, L. J., Bai, X. Y., Zhou, L. Z., et al. (2009). A hierarchical reliability model of service-based software system. In I. Ahamed, E. Bertino, C. K. Chang, et al., (Eds.), 2009 33rd Annual IEEE International Computer Software and Applications Conference (COMPSAC 2009) (pp. 199-208). Piscataway, NJ: IEEE Press.

Wang, L., & von Laszewski, G. (2008). Scientific cloud computing: Early definition and experience. Proceedings of the 10th IEEE International Conference on High Performance Computing (pp. 825-830). doi:10.1109/HPCC.2008.38

Wang, L., Tao, J., Kunze, M., & Rattu, D. (2008). The Cumulus Project: Build a scientific cloud for a data center. Paper presented at Cloud Computing and its Applications, Chicago, IL. http://cca08.org/papers/Paper29-Lizhe-Wang.pdf

Wang, Y., Que, X., Yu, W., Godenberg, D., & Sehgal, D. (2011, November). Hadoop acceleration through network levitated merge. Proceedings of the 2011 International Conference for High Performance Computing, Networking, Storage and Analysis (SC) (pp. 1–10). E-ISBN: 978-1-4503-0771-0

Wang, Q., Wang, C., Ren, K., Lou, W., & Li, J. (2011). Enabling public auditability and data dynamics for storage security in cloud computing. *IEEE Transactions on Parallel and Distributed Systems*, *22*(5), 847–859. doi:10.1109/TPDS.2010.183

WAPT. (2003). Web application testing (WAPT). Retrieved from http://www.loadtestingtool.com/

Watson, P., Lord, P., Gibson, F., Periorellis, P., & Pitsili, G. (2008). Cloud computing for e-science with CARMEN. 2nd Iberian Grid Infrastructure Conference, (pp. 3-14). Portugal.

WebXML. (2012). WeatherWebService. Retrieved June 1, 2012, from http://www.webxml.com.cn/webservices/weatherwebservice.asmx

Weinhardt, C., Anandasivam, A., Blau, B., & Stößer, J. (2009). Business models in the service world. IT Pro, March/April, 36-41

Weiser, M. (1984). Program slicing. *IEEE Transactions on Software Engineering*, *10*(4), 352–357. doi:10.1109/TSE.1984.5010248

Wen, F., & Xiang, L. (2011). The study on data security in cloud computing based on virtualization. *International Symposium on IT in Medicine and Education* (pp. 257-261).

Wen, J. H., Jiang, Z., & Tu, L. Y. (2009). Task-oriented web service discovery algorithm using semantic similarity for adaptive service composition. *Journal of Southeast University*, *25*(4), 468–472.

Wiese, L. (2010). Horizontal fragmentation for data outsourcing with formula-based confidentiality constraints. In Proceedings of the 5th International Conference on Advances in Information and Computer Security (IWSEC'10). (pp. 101-116). Berlin, Germany: Springer-Verlag.

WineHQ. (2011, August 19). Retrieved from http://www.winehq.org/

Wood, T., Shenoy, P., Venkataramani, A., & Yousif, M. (2007). Black-box and gray-box strategies for virtual machine migration. Proceedings of 4th USENIX Symposium on Networked Systems Design and Implementation, (pp. 229-242). Retrieved from http://www.usenix.org/events/nsdi07/tech/full_papers/wood/wood_html/

Wu, G., Wei, J., Ye, C., Zhong, H., & Huang, T. (2010, July). Detecting data inconsistency failure of composite Web services through parametric stateful aspect. Paper presented at the International Conference on Web Services (ICWS), Miami, Florida, USA.

Wu, J., Ping, L., Ge, X., Wang, Y., & Fu, J. (2009). Cloud storage as the infrastructure of cloud computing. Proceedings of the 2010 International Conference on Intelligent Computing and Cognitive Informatics (pp. 380-383). doi:10.1109/ICICCI.2010.119

Wu, R., Ahn, G. J., & Hu, H. (2012). Towards HIPAA-compliant healthcare systems in cloud computing. 2nd ACM SIGHIT International Health Informatics Symposium (IHI 2012), Miami, Florida, USA. ACM Press.

Xiao, Z., Song, W., & Chen, Q. (2011). Dynamic resource allocation using virtual machines for cloud computing environment (unpublished paper). Peking University.

Xiao, Z., Song, W., Chen, Q., & Luo, H. (2010). Gone with the cloud: Adaptive resource virtualization for Amazon EC2-like environment (unpublished paper). Peking University.

Xia, Y. N., Wang, H. P., & Huang, Y. (2006). A stochastic model for workflow QoS evaluation. *Science Progress*, *14*(3-4), 251–265.

XML Encryption Syntax and Processing. (2002). W3C rec. Retrieved from http://www.w3.org/TR/xmlenc-core/

Xu, H., & Li, B. (2011). Egalitarian stable matching for VM migration in cloud computing. IEEE Conference on Computer Communications Workshops, Shanghai, (pp. 631-636).

Xu, D., Xiong, Y., Qiao, C., & Li, G. (2003). Trap avoidance and protection schemes in networks with shared risk links groups. *Journal of Lightwave Technology, 21*(11), 2683–2693. doi:10.1109/JLT.2003.819545

Yang, H., & Ward, M. (2003). *Successful evolution of software systems.* Boston, MA: Artech House.

Yang, X., Bruin, R., & Dove, M. et al. (2010) A service-oriented framework for running quantum mechanical simulation for material properties over Grids. IEEE Transactions on System, Man, and Cybernetic, Part C: Application and Reviews, 40(4).

Yang, X. (2011). QoS-oriented service computing: Bring SOA into cloud environment. In Liu, X., & Li, Y. (Eds.), *Advanced design approaches to emerging software systems: Principles, methodology and tools.* Hershey, PA: IGI Global. doi:10.4018/978-1-60960-735-7.ch013

Yang, X., Bruin, R., & Dove, M. (2010). Developing an end-to-end scientific workflow: A case study of using a reliable, lightweight, and comprehensive workflow platform in e-science. *IEEE Computational Science & Engineering, 99*, 1.

Yang, X., Dove, M., & Bruin, R. (2012). (in press). An e-science data infrastructure for simulations within grid computing environment: Methods, approaches, and practices. *Concurrency and Computation.* doi:10.1002/cpe.2849

Yang, X., Nasser, B., Surrige, M., & Middleton, S. (2012, March 10). A business-oriented cloud federation model for real time applications. *Future Generation Computer Systems.* doi:10.1016/j.future.2012.02.005

Yang, X., Wang, L., & von Laszewski, G. (2009). Recent research advances in e-science. *Cluster Computing Journal Special Issue, 12*(4), 353–356. doi:10.1007/s10586-009-0104-0

Yilmaz, E., Aslam, J. A., & Robertson, S. (2008). A new rank correlation coefficient for information retrieval. Paper presented at the 31st Annual International ACM SIGIR Conference on Research and Development in Information Retrieval (SIGIR), Singapore.

Yin, P.-Y., Glover, F., Laguna, M., & Zhu, J.-X. (2011, April-June). A complementary cyber swarm algorithm. *International Journal of Swarm Intelligence Research, 2*(2), 22–41. doi:10.4018/jsir.2011040102

Younge, A. J., Laszewski, G. V., Wang, L., Lopez-Alarcon, S., & Carithers, W. (2010). Efficient resource management for cloud computing environments. *Proceedings of the International Conference on Green Computing,* (p. 5).

Yu, H., Anand, V., Qiao, C., & Sun, G. (2011). Cost efficient design of survivable virtual infrastructure to recover from facility node failures. IEEE International Conference on Communications (ICC), (pp. 1-6).

Yu, H., Anand, V., Qiao, C., Di, H., & Wang, J. (2010). On the survivable virtual infrastructure mapping problem. IEEE International Conference on Computer Communication Networks (ICCCN), (pp. 199-204).

Yu, H., Qiao, C., Anand, V., Liu, X., Di, H., & Sun, G. (2010). Survivable infrastructure mapping in a federate computing and networking system under single regional failures. IEEE Global Communications Conference (GLOBECOM), (pp. 1-6).

Yu, S., Wang, C., Ren, K., & Lou, W. (2010). Achieving secure, scalable, and fine-grained data access control in Cloud computing. In Proceedings of IEEE International Conference on Computer Communications 2010 (pp. 15-19).

Yu, M., Yi, Y., Rexford, J., & Chiang, M. (2008). *Rethinking virtual network embedding: Substrate support for path splitting and migration* (pp. 17–29). ACM SIGCOMM Computer Communication Review.

Yuping, Z., & Xinghui, W. (2010). Research and realization of multi-level encryption method for database. 2010 2nd International Conference on Advanced Computer Control (ICACC), Vol. 3, (pp. 1-4, 27-29).

Zaharia, M., Konwinski, A., Joseph, A. D., Katz, R., & Stoica, I. (2011). Improving MapReduce performance in heterogeneous environments. Proceedings of the 8th USENIX Conference on Operating Systems Design and Implementation.

Zeng, L. Z., Benatallah, B., & Ngu, A. H. H. (2004). QoS-aware middleware for web services composition. *IEEE Transactions on Software Engineering, 30*(5), 311–327. doi:10.1109/TSE.2004.11

Zhang, L.-J., & Zhou, Q. (2009). CCOA: Cloud computing open architecture. In IEEE Conference on Web Services ICWS 2009 (pp. 607-616).

Zhang, S., Zhang, S., Chen, X., & Huo, X. (2009). Cloud computing research and development trend. Proceedings of the 2010 IEEE 2nd International Conference on Future Networks (pp. 93-97). doi: 10.1109/ICFN.2010.58

Zhang, X., Huo, Z., Ma, J., & Meng, D. (2010). Exploiting data deduplication to accelerate live virtual machine migration. Proceedings of the 2010 IEEE International Conference on Cluster Computing, (pp. 11-20). doi: 10.1109/CLUSTER.2010.17

Zhang, J. (2005). Trustworthy Web services: Actions for now. *IEEE IT Professional*, *7*(1), 32–36. doi:10.1109/MITP.2005.1407802

Zhang, L., Zhang, J., & Cai, H. (2007). *Service computing*. Beijing, China: Springer and Tsinghua University Press.

Zhang, Y., & Joshi, J. B. D. (2009). Access control and trust management for emerging multidomain environments. In Upadhyaya, S., & Rao, R. O. (Eds.), *Annals of emerging research in information assurance, security and privacy services*. Emerald Group Publishing Limited.

Zheng, S., Yang, H., Liu, L., & Wang, J. (2011). *Software evolution in setting internetware*. The 3rd Asia-Pacific Symposium on Internetware. 1-2 December 2011, Nanning, Guangxi, China.

Zheng, S., Yang, H., Ma, Z., & Liu, L. (2011). Understanding software reengineering requirements for cloud computing. *19th IEEE International Requirements Engineering Conference*. 29 August- 2 September 2011, Trento, Italy.

Zheng, Z. B., & Lyu, M. R. (2008). WS-DREAM: a distributed reliability assessment mechanism for Web services. In 2008 IEEE International Conference on Dependable Systems and Networks with FTCS and DCC(DSN) (pp. 392-397). Piscataway, NJ: IEEE Press.

Zheng, Z. B., & Lyu, M. R. (2009). A QoS-aware fault tolerant middleware for dependable service composition. In P. Carvalho, J. Craveiro, M. Kaaniche, et al., (Eds.), 2009 IEEE/IFIP International Conference on Dependable Systems and Networks (DSN) (pp. 239-248). Piscataway, NJ: IEEE Press.

Zheng, Z. B., & Lyu, M. R. (2010). Collaborative reliability prediction for service-oriented systems. In 2010 32nd International Conference on Software Engineering (pp. 35-44). New York, NY: ACM Press.

Zheng, Z., Ma, H., Lyu, M. R., & King, I. (2009, July). WSRec: A collaborative filtering based Web service recommendation system. Paper presented at the International Conference on Web Services (ICWS), Los Angeles, CA, USA.

Zhu, J., Jiang, Z., & Xiao, Z. (2011). Twinkle: A fast resource provisioning mechanism for internet services. 2011 Proceedings INFOCOM, Shanghai, (pp. 802-810).

Zhu, Y., & Ammar, M. (2006). Algorithms for assigning substrate network resources to virtual network components. IEEE International Conference on Computer Communications (INFOCOM), (pp. 1-12).

Zhu, Y., Ahn, G. J., Hu, H., Yau, S. S., An, H. G., & Chen, S. (2012). Dynamic audit services for outsourced storages in clouds. IEEE Transactions on Services Computing, 1-15.

Zhu, Z., Li, J., Zhao, Y., & Li, Z. (2011). SCENETester: A testing framework supporting fault diagnosing for web service composition. The 2nd International Workshop on Dependable Service-Oriented and Cloud Computing (DOSC 2011) in conjunction with 2011 IEEE 11th International Conference on Computer and Information Technology (CIT), Paphos, Cyprus, (pp. 109-114).

Zhu, Y., Hu, H., Ahn, G. J., Yu, M., & Chen, S. (2012). Cooperative provable data possession for integrity verification in multi-cloud storage. *IEEE Transactions on Parallel and Distributed Systems*, *99*, 1–14.

About the Contributors

Xiaoyu Yang (Kevin X. Yang) is a Senior Member of Wolfson College, University of Cambridge, UK, and a Research Fellow in Reading e-Science Center, University of Reading, UK. He completed his post-doctoral research in the University of Cambridge in 2008. He earned an MSc degree in IT (2001) and a PhD degree in Systems Engineering (2006) from "Faculty of Computing Science and Engineering" at the De Montfort University, UK. He was previously a Research Associate in the Department of Earth Sciences and affiliated Software Engineer in Cambridge e-Science Centre at the University of Cambridge. He joined School of Electronics and Computer Sciences, University of Southampton, UK as a Research Engineer after his post-doctoral research at Cambridge. Dr. Yang has participated or undertaken many EU framework projects and UK government funded research projects, and has a number of publications in referred journals. His technical interests include Systems Engineering, e-Science, Grid/Cloud computing, SOA, distributed system, and product lifecycle information management.

Lu Liu is a Reader in the School of Computing and Mathematics, University of Derby, UK. He joined the University of Derby as Senior Lecturer in 2010. Before joining University of Derby, he was Lecturer in School of Engineering and Information Sciences at Middlesex University. Prior to his academic career, he was Research Fellow in the School of Computing at the University of Leeds, working on NECTISE Project which was an UK EPSRC/BAE Systems funded research project involving ten UK Universities and CoLaB Project which was funded by UK EPSRC and China 863 Program. He received a Ph.D degree (funded by UK DIF DTC) from the University of Surrey and M.Sc. degree from Brunel University (UK). His research interests are in areas of service-oriented computing, software engineering, Grid computing, and peer-to-peer computing. Dr Liu has over 70 scientific publications in reputable journals, academic books, and international conferences.

* * *

Khandakar Ahmed received his B.Sc. (Engg.) degree in Computer Science and Engineering (CSE) from Shahjalal University of Science & Technology, Sylhet, Bangladesh in 2006 and the M.Sc. in Erasmus Mundus Networking and e-Business Centered Computing (EMNeBCC) in 2011 under the joint consortia of University of Reading, UK; Aristotle University of Thessaloniki, Greece, and Universidad Carlos III de Madrid, Spain. Currently, he is doing research in the school of Electrical and Computer Engineering. He is currently also a Lecturer in the Department of Computer Science and Engineering (CSE) of Shahjalal University of Science and Technology, Sylhet, Bangladesh. His research interest includes distributed computer systems with an emphasis on in-network data centric storage of wireless sensor network, peer-to-peer and content delivery network, and Cloud computing. He is a member of the IEEE and reviewer of the Elsevier's *Journal of Parallel and Distributed Computing*. His research works have been published in conferences, journals, and peer-reviewed book chapters.

Gail-Joon Ahn is an Associate Professor and the Director of the Security Engineering for Future Computing (SEFCOM) Laboratory in the School of Computing, Informatics, and Decision Systems Engineering at Arizona State University. His research interests include information and systems security, vulnerability and risk management, access control, and security architecture for distributed systems. Ahn has a PhD in Information Technology from George Mason University. He is a recipient of the US Department of Energy Career Award and the Educator of the Year Award from the Federal Information Systems Security Educators Association (FISSEA). Ahn is a senior member of IEEE and the ACM.

Hussain Al-Aqrabi is an Associate Lecturer in School of Computing and Mathematics, University of Derby. He is also currently a PhD candidate student working on his PhD within the Distributed and Intelligent Systems Research Group. Hussain received his M.Sc. degree in Computer Networks from University of Derby (UK). In addition to his university education, he holds Microsoft Systems Engineer (MSCE), Microsoft Certified Technology Specialist (MCTS), Microsoft Certified Solutions Associate (MCSA) certifications on Windows Server 2008, and he also holds Cisco Certified Network Associate (CCNA) certifications on Routing and Switching. Hussain has several published conference papers. His research interests are in areas of service-oriented computing, Cloud computing, grid computing, and network security.

Vishal Anand is an Associate Professor at The College at Brockport, SUNY. He received his B.S. degree in Computer Science and Engineering from the University of Madras, Madras (Chennai), India in 1996, and the M.S. and Ph.D. degrees in Computer Science and Engineering from the University at Buffalo, SUNY in 1999 and 2003. He has worked as a research scientist at Bell Labs, Lucent technologies and Telcordia Technologies (ex-Bellcore), where he investigated issues relating to traffic routing and survivability in optical networks. He is the co-inventor of a patent that cost-effectively improves the speed of traffic in the Internet backbone and is the recipient of the "Rising Star" and the "Promising Inventor Award" award from the Research Foundation of The State University of New York (SUNY), and the recipient of the "Visionary Innovator" award from the University of Buffalo (SUNY). His research interests are in the area of wired and wireless computer communication networks and protocols including optical networking, and cloud and grid computing.

Feng Chen was awarded his BSc, Mphil and PhD at Nankai University, Dalian University of Technology and De Montfort University in 1991, 1994 and 2007. He has been working in the area of Distributed Computing and Software Reengineering, which is focusing on the formal analysis of software systems with the long-term aim of building a coherent set of conceptual frameworks and methods for the development and reengineering of software systems, with an emphasis on narrowing the gap between theoreticians and practitioners by promoting and developing tools to assist the reengineering of such systems. As research outputs, Dr. Chen has published 30 research papers in the area of software reengineering and distributed computing.

Mark A. Gregory (M'82–SM'06) became a Member (M) of IEEE in 1982, and a Senior Member (SM) in 2006. Mark A Gregory was born in Melbourne, Australia and received a PhD and a Master of Engineering from RMIT University, Melbourne, Australia in 2008 and 1992, respectively, and a Bachelor of Engineering (Electrical) from University of New South Wales, Sydney, Australia in 1984. He is a Senior Lecturer in the School of Electrical and Computer Engineering, RMIT University, Melbourne, Australia. Research interests include fiber optic network design and operation, wireless networks, Cloud computing, security, and technical risk. Dr. Gregory is a Fellow of the Institute of Engineers Australia, a reviewer for journal papers for the IEEE Technical Societies, and an Associate Editor of the Australasian Journal of Engineering Education.

James Hardy is an Associate Lecturer in the School of Computing and Mathematics at the University of Derby. He gained a Bachelor's Degree in Electronic Engineering from Nottingham University and a Masters Degree in Computer Networks from The University of Derby. Long-term computing interests include practical networking, simulation, emulation, and virtualisation. Current research interests include green computing, trustworthy systems, and IaaS Clouds.

Pan He received the B.S. and M.S. degrees in Software Engineering from the School of Software Engineering, Chongqing University, China, in 2006 and 2008; she is currently working toward the PhD degree at the College of Computer Science, Chongqing University. She has worked in the field of multilevel redundancy allocation and monitoring resources allocation oriented at reliability optimization deign in distributed systems. She as joined several research projects including a Major Program of the National Natural Science Foundation of China (Behavior monitoring and reliable evolution of large-scale distributed software systems). She has published nine papers. Her research interests include services computing and service reliability engineering.

Jinpeng Huai is a Professor and President of Beihang University. Prof Huai is Academician of Chinese Academy of Science. He serves on the Steering Committee for Advanced Computing Technology Subject, the National High-Tech Program (863) as Chief Scientist. He is a member of the Consulting Committee of the Central Government Information Office, and Chairman of the Expert Committee in both the National e-Government Engineering Taskforce and the National e-Government Standard office. Prof. Huai and his colleagues are leading the key projects in e-Science of the National Science Foundation of China (NSFC) and Sino-UK. He has authored over 100 papers. His research interests include middleware, cloud computing, trustworthiness, and security.

Xiaomeng Huang holds a PhD degree in Computer Science and Technology from Tsinghua University and is now an Associate Professor with Center for Earth System Science (CESS), Institute for Global Change Studies, Tsinghua University, Beijing, China. Before joining CESS, he was with Department of Computer Science and Technology of the same university. Dr. Huang is especially interested in large-scale distributed system, computer networks and so on. His research work has appeared in *Journal of Parallel and Distributed Computing* (JPDC), *IEEE Transactions on Wireless Communications, Computer Networks,* IEEE International Conference on Distributed Computing Systems (ICDCS), IEEE International Conference on Network Protocols (ICNP), etc.

Ali R. Hurson is Professor and Chair of the Computer Science Department at the Missouri University of Science and Technology (S&T). Before joining S&T, he was a Professor of Computer Science and Engineering at the Pennsylvania State University for 24 years. He received the B.S. degree in Physics from the University of Tehran; and the M.S. and Ph.D. degrees in Computer Science, from the University of Iowa and the University of Central Florida, respectively. His research for the past 30 years has been supported by NSF, DARPA, DOE, ONR, the Air Force, Oak Ridge National Laboratory, IBM, NCR Corp., General Electric, and Lockheed Martin. He has published over 290 technical papers and book chapters in areas including object-oriented databases, multidatabases, global information processing, applications of mobile agent technology, computer architecture and cache memory, parallel and distributed processing, dataflow architectures, pervasive and mobile computing, ad hoc networks, and reconfigurable sensor networks.

Altaf Hussain received his B.Sc. (Engg.) degree in Computer Science and Engineering (CSE) from Shahjalal University of Science & Technology, Sylhet, Bangladesh in 2008. After graduation, he worked as a Software Engineer developing distributed service based applications providing citizen services. Altaf started his M. Sc. in Computer Science in St. Francis Xavier University, Antigonish, Canada in 2011. His research interest includes Cloud computing, Semantic Web, Semantic Web services and discovery, and distributed computing. His research works have been published in international conferences.

Adrian Jackson is a Technical Architect at EPCC where he has worked for the past 11 years. He received an MSc in High Performance Computing from EPCC in 2002, following the award of a first class Bachelor's of Science in Computer Science from The University of Edinburgh.

Jinlei Jiang is an Associate Professor with Department of Computer Science and Technology, Tsinghua University, Beijing, China. He received a PhD degree in Computer Science and Technology from the same university in 2004 with an honor of excellent dissertation. From May 2007 to April 2008, he visited Institut fuer Informatik, Technische Universitaet Muenchen, Germany as a Humboldt scholar. Dr. Jiang's research work has appeared in *Expert Systems with Applications, Journal of Computer Science and Technology, IEEE International Conference on Web Services* (ICWS), ACM Symposium on Applied Computing (SAC), and so on. His research interests mainly focus on grid and cloud computing, computer-supported cooperative work, and workflow management.

James B.D. Joshi is an Associate Professor and the Director of the Laboratory for Education and Research on Security Assured Information Systems (LERSAIS) in the School of Information Sciences at the University of Pittsburgh. His research interests include role-based access control, trust management, and secure interoperability. Joshi has a PhD in Computer Engineering from Purdue University. He is a member of IEEE and the ACM.

N Krishnadas is pursuing his PhD at Indian Institute of Management, Kozhikode. His research area is Information and Systems and he is conducting his research on Green IT. He decided to pursue his management research career to leverage upon his expertise in Computer Science Engineering (B.Tech). He has successful internship experiences with Microsoft and Honeywell. He has published research papers in international journals and has presented papers in reputed international conferences. He has won many awards in various management/engineering events including the Indian Innovator and International PhD Student competition award (Australia). He is currently the SAS Student Ambassador and has presented his research in Las Vegas at the SAS Global Forum 2011. He has special interest in field of e-governance, and he has made significant contributions in this field. He aspired to become a green IT expert and contribute to information systems and environmental sustainability.

Cui Lei is currently a PhD candidate at Advanced Computer Technology (ACT) lab in the School of Computer Science and Engineering, Beihang University; he received his Bachelor's degree in Computer Science in Dalian University of Technology. His current research interests include fault tolerance, virtualization, and large-scale distributed system. In ACT lab, he joined system works and research works funded by China 863 and 973 Program.

Jianxin Li is an Associate Professor of Beihang University, and he received his Ph.D. degree in Computer Software and Theory in Beihang University in 2008. His research interests include cloud computing, virtualization, and trust management. He is an editorial board member of *Journal of Cloud Computing*, and a member of IEEE, and ACM. He has published over 30 papers including Elsevier *Information Sciences, Journal of Peer-to-Peer Networking and Applications*, HASE 2008, SRDS 2007, eScience 2006 etc. He also is a program committee member of international conference IEEE Cloud 2009 -2011, IEEE SCC 2008/2010 SNPD 2010 etc. He has participated several international cooperation projects such as CoLab with Leeds University, EU EchoGrid project, Hongkong RGC, and NSFC project, etc.

Jianzhi Li received his PhD in Software Engineering from De Montfort University, Leicester, UK in 2007. His general research interests include software evolution, Web-based systems, and mobile software. Dr. Jianzhi Li has published a number of research papers in refereed journals and international conferences. Dr. Li has served as IPC member for many international conferences since 2007.

Xudong Liu is a Professor and Dean of the School of Computer Science and Engineering, Beihang University, Beijing, China. He serves on the deputy director of W3C China Office, technical team leader of standardized application supporting of national e-government. Has have leaded several China 863 key projects and e-government projects, and leaded a team for the development of the Web service product line in China Trustie project. He has published more over 30 papers including ICWS, SCC, etc., and more than 20 patents. His research interests include software middleware technology, software development methods and tools, large-scale information technology projects, and application of research and teaching.

Linlin Meng got her B.S. degree in Computer Science from Beijing University of Posts and Technologies in 2009 and M.S. degree in School of Computer Science and Engineering from Beihang University in 2012. Her research interests included service computing, quality of Web service, planetary-scale testing of Web service, Web service ranking, and recommendation. Based on the study, Meng published two papers in the international conference and owns two domestic patents in China.

R. Radhakrishna Pillai is currently a Professor in the Information Technology and Systems Area. He has been with IIM Kozhikode since January 2002. He graduated in Electronics and Communication Engineering from the University of Kerala (TKM College of Engg., Kollam) in 1987 with the University Gold Medal. After receiving the M.E. degree in Electrical Communications Engineering in 1989 followed by the Ph.D degree in 1993 (both from the Indian Institute of Science, Bangalore), he worked with the R&D Department of Tata Elxsi (India) Ltd., Bangalore, from 1993-95. Subsequently, he was carrying out R&D activities at the Institute of Systems Science (National University of Singapore) and at the

Kent Ridge Digital Labs, Singapore (currently known as the Institute for Infocomm Research), during 1995-2001. During the above period, he was also involved in managing international collaborative R&D projects on communication networks with multinational organizations like Ericsson and Siemens. His research interests are in information and communication technologies and their impact on the society, and the role of technology and spirituality in management.

John P. Sahlin is a Ph.D. candidate in Systems Engineering at the George Washington University. He is currently supporting SPAWAR Tactical Networks Program Office (PMW 160) as the Chief Engineer for Shipbuilding and Conversion, Navy/Other Customer Funded (SCN/OCF) Afloat Integration in San Diego, California. He has over seventeen years of Systems Engineering and Program Management expertise in both federal government and Managed Service Provider (MSP) commercial markets, where he designed and implemented a variety of cloud computing architectures. He is responsible for designing the future capabilities roadmap for the CANES Program of Record (PoR), as well as establishing paths for migrating contractor-furnished shipboard networks such as DDG 1000, LCS, and LPD 17 to Navy PoR solutions. His current research focuses on the application of cloud computing architectures to distributed environments with intermittent connectivity to the cloud enterprise, such as small military units, online gaming, and mobile computing.

Maria Salama received B.Sc. in Computer Science and Post-Graduate Diploma in Management Information Systems from Sadat Academy for Management Science, Cairo, Egypt in 2001 and 2003 respectively. She received M.Sc. in Computer Science from Arab Academy for Sciences and Technology in 2011. She is now assistant lecturer in the British University in Egypt. Prior to joining the BUE, she had a solid experience in the industry, stepping from Web development to project leading. Her research interests are in software and Web engineering, Web services, and Cloud Computing.

Sahra Sedigh is an Associate Professor of Electrical and Computer Engineering and Computer Science and a Research Investigator with the Intelligent Systems Center at the Missouri University of Science & Technology. She received the B.S. degree from Sharif University of Technology and the M.S. and Ph.D. degrees from Purdue University, all in electrical engineering. Her current research centers on development and modeling of dependable networks and systems, with focus on critical infrastructure. Her projects include research on dependability of the electric power grid, large-scale water distribution networks, and transportation infrastructures, including an instrumented bridge testbed funded by the US and Missouri Departments of Transportation. She was selected as one of 49 participants in the National Academy of Engineering's First Frontiers of Engineering Education Symposium in Nov. 2009. She was a Purdue Research Foundation Fellow from 1996 to 2000, and is a member of HKN, IEEE, and ACM.

Ahmed Shawish received the B.Sc. and M.Sc. degree from Ain Shams University, Cairo, Egypt in 1997 and 2002, all in Computer Sciences. In 2009, he got his Ph.D. degree from Tohoku University, Japan. He is currently Assistant Professor in the Scientific Computing department, faculty of Computer & Information Science, Ain Shams University, Egypt. His research covers supporting VoIP applications over wired and wireless networks. Currently, he is focusing his research on the Cloud Computing areas.

Weijia Song received his Master's degree from Beijing Instituted of Technology in March 2004. Since then, he has been working at Computer Center of Peking University for eight years. He is experienced in building IaaS Cloud services and network application development. He is currently a PhD student at Peking University. His research interests include resource scheduling for cloud computing environment and virtualization.

Sebastian Steinbuß is scientist at the Fraunhofer Institute for Software and Systems Engineering ISST in Dortmund (Germany). He is the project manager of the project Service Design Studio, which is part of the Leading-Edge Cluster EffizienzCluster LogistikRuhr and deputy project manager of the project Service Engineering Framework of the Logistics Mall. The key aspects of his scientific work are the Unified Service Description Language USDL, Cloud Computing, Web services, and Service Oriented Architectures, which will lead to the Internet of services and the Internet of things. He is working with modern portal technologies based upon Liferay or WebSphere and likes working with the Google Web Toolkit and the Google App Engine. He also likes HTML 5 and especially the canvas element. He has published several conference papers, and he speaks on conferences like the CloudConf in Munich, Germany.

Hassan Takabi is a PhD student in the School of Information Sciences and a member of the Laboratory of Education and Research on Security Assured Information Systems (LERSAIS) at the University of Pittsburgh. His research interests include access control models; trust management; privacy and Web security; usable privacy and security; and security, privacy, and trust issues in cloud computing environments. Takabi has an MS in Information Technology from Sharif University of Technology, Iran. He is student member of IEEE and the ACM.

Norbert Weißenberg is scientist at the Fraunhofer Institute for Software and Systems Engineering ISST in Dortmund (Germany). He received his diploma in Computer Science from the University of Dortmund in 1985. From 1985 to 1992, he was a research assistant at the Information Science Department of the University of Dortmund where he worked on different projects concerning the development of a system modeling and evaluation tool. Since 1992, he is a researcher at Fraunhofer ISST Dortmund. He has been involved in many projects on topics like ontologies, semantic service description, information logistics, information management, and process modeling and has published several papers on these topics. Currently he works in the Logistics Mall project on the topics business objects and process modeling and execution.

Michèle Weiland joined EPCC in 2006 after completing a PhD in Music and Artificial Intelligence at the University of Edinburgh. Michèle's expertise lies in high-performance computing benchmarking and performance optimisation, as well as novel programming models. She led the benchmarking team in the EU-funded DEISA project for three years, focussing on quantifying the performance of scientific application codes on supercomputers across Europe. Her current role as both a project manager and leader of technical work concentrates on optimising applications for future-generation multi-core architectures. Michèle is also actively involved in EPCC's MSc in HPC programme, teaching parallel programming, and supervising dissertations.

Steven White works at the Missouri State Highway Patrol in the position of Information Security Officer. In this position, he serves as the information and computer security point of contact for the Criminal Justice Agencies in State of Missouri. He has worked in the Information Technology area for the past seventeen years. He earned the B.S. degree in Electrical Engineering and the M.S. degree in Information Science and Technology from the University of Missouri – Rolla. He is currently pursuing a Ph.D. in Computer Engineering from the Missouri University of Science and Technology. His areas of research include cyber security, security in cloud computing, and cyber-physical security.

Yongwei Wu is a full Professor with Department of Computer Science and Technology, Tsinghua University, Beijing, China. He received a PhD degree in Applied Mathematics from the Chinese Academy of Sciences in 2002. He has published more than 40 research papers in refereed international journals or conferences such as *IEEE Transaction on Parallel and Distributed Systems* (TPDS), *Journal of Network and Computer Applications* (JNCA), *Concurrency and Computation: Practice and Experience* (CCP&E), *Future Generation Computer Systems* (FGCS), and IEEE/ACM International Conference on Grid Computing. He has been on the program, steering, or organization committees of quite some international conferences such as ICPP, Grid Middleware, CCGrid, etc. Dr. Wu's research interests mainly focus on grid and cloud computing, distributed processing, and parallel computing.

Zhen Xiao received his PhD degree from Cornell University in January 2001. After that, he worked as a senior technical staff member at AT&T Labs—New Jersey and then a research staff member at IBM T. J. Watson Research Center. Currently he is a Professor in the Department of Computer Science at Peking University. His research interests include cloud computing, virtualization, and various distributed systems issues. He is a senior member of the IEEE.

Qi Xie is currently a Ph.D. candidate in the College of Computer Science, Chongqing University, China. She received her M.Eng. degree in College of Computer Science from the Chongqing University, China, in 2008. She has worked in the field of Quality of service-aware Web services prediction and recommendation based on collaborative filtering in the step of service selection in order to recommend and select optimal Web services for services users. She joined several research projects including a Major Program of the National Natural Science Foundation of China (Behavior monitoring and reliable evolution of large-scale distributed software systems). She has published six papers. Her research interests include services computing and service reliability engineering.

Guangwen Yang is a full Professor with Department of Computer Science and Technology, Tsinghua University, Beijing, China, where he directs the Institute of High Performance Computing. Currently, he serves on the expert committee of China Cloud Initiative of The Ministry of Science and Technology. Once, he served on the expert committee of high performance computer and grid computing environment sponsored by the National High-Tech R&D (863) Program of China. Prof. Yang received a PhD degree in Computer Architecture from Harbin Institute of Technology in 1996. His research interests are mainly on parallel computing, grid computing, distributed systems, and machine learning.

Hongji Yang is a Professor working for both the Software Technology Research Laboratory (STRL) and the Institute of Creative Technologies (IOCT) at De Montfort University. His research interests include Software Engineering, Creative Computing and Internet Computing. He has published five books and over 300 refereed papers. He is a Golden Core Member of IEEE Computer Society. He has been an organising member for many international conferences, including acting as a Programme Co-Chair for IEEE International Conference on Software Maintenance (ICSM'99) and the Programme Chair for IEEE Computer Software and Application Conference (COMPSAC'02). He is currently serving as the Editor-in-Chief for *International Journal of Creative Computing* (IJCC).

Shang Zheng received his Bsc and Master at Northeast Normal University and Jilin University in China. Now he is studying for PhD at the Software Technology Research Laboratory, De Montfort University, England. His research areas include software evolution and Cloud computing, which aim at constructing a series of architecture framework and effective methods for integrating legacy software resources into Cloud computing environment and support the development of software evolution. Up to now, he has published a number of research papers in international conferences.

Zekun Zhu earned his B.S. degree in Mathematic Science from North China University of Technology in 2009, and a Master's degree in Computer Science in Beihang University in 2012. During his graduate study, he researched in the field of Web service, workflow, BPMN, and automatic test. In May 2011, he published a paper in the DSOC workshop of the "The 11th IEEE International Conference on Computer and Information Technology." He has developed an automatic tool called WSTester for SCENCE platform in China HGJ project.

Index